Introduction to Political Psychology

D0882379

This comprehensive, user-friendly textbook on political psychology explores the psychological origins of political behavior. The authors introduce readers to a broad range of theories, concepts, and case studies of political activity. The book also examines patterns of political behavior in such areas as leadership, group behavior, voting, race, nationalism, terrorism, and war. It explores some of the most horrific things people do to each other, as well as how to prevent and resolve conflict—and how to recover from it.

This volume contains numerous features to enhance understanding, including text boxes highlighting current and historical events to help students make connections between the world around them and the concepts they are learning. Different research methodologies used in the discipline are employed, such as experimentation and content analysis. This third edition of the book has two new chapters on media and social movements. This accessible and engaging textbook is suitable as a primary text for upper-level courses in political psychology, political behavior, and related fields, including policymaking.

Martha L. Cottam (Ph.D., UCLA) is a Professor of Political Science at Washington State University. She specializes in political psychology, international politics, and intercommunal conflict. She has published books and articles on US foreign policy, decision making, nationalism, and Latin American politics.

Elena Mastors (Ph.D., Washington State University) is Vice President and Dean of Applied Research at the American Public University System. Prior to that, she was an Associate Professor at the Naval War College and held senior intelligence and policy positions in the Department of Defense. She has published books, articles, and papers on the political psychology of conflict and armed groups.

Thomas Preston (Ph.D., Ohio State University) is a Professor of Political Science at Washington State University. He specializes in political psychology, leadership analysis, and international politics. He.has written books and articles on presidential leadership, weapons of mass destruction, and American foreign policy.

Beth Dietz (Ph.D., University of Pittsburgh) is a Professor of Psychology at Miami University, where she teaches a variety of courses in psychology. Her research interests include social identity theory, computer-mediated communication, and the scholarship of teaching and learning. She also has interests in online teaching and using technology to enhance student learning.

Introduction to Political Psychology

3rd Edition

Martha L. Cottam
Elena Mastors
Thomas Preston
Beth Dietz

Routledge
Taylor & Francis Group

NEW YORK AND LONDON

Third edition published 2016
by Routledge
711 Third Avenue, New York, NY 10017

Simultaneously published in the UK
by Routledge
2 Park Square, Milton Park, Abingdon, Oxon OX14 4RN

*Routledge is an imprint of the Taylor & Francis Group, an informa
business*

First edition published by Psychology Press 2004
Second edition published by Psychology Press 2010

Library of Congress Cataloging-in-Publication Data
Cottam, Martha L.
  Introduction to political psychology / Martha L. Cottam,
Elena Mastors, Thomas Preston, Beth Dietz.— 3rd Edition.
    pages cm
Includes bibliographical references and index.
  1. Political psychology. I. Title.
  JA74.5.C68 2016
  320.01´9—dc23
  2014048185

ISBN: 978-1-84872-671-0 (hbk)
ISBN: 978-1-84872-672-7 (pbk)
ISBN: 978-1-315-67193-2 (ebk)

Typeset in Warnock Pro
by Apex CoVantage, LLC

Printed and bound in the United States of America by Sheridan Books, Inc.
(a Sheridan Group Company).

CONTENTS

PREFACE

When colleagues from other disciplines ask us what we specialize in, they are often puzzled when we say political psychology. "What's that?" or "I didn't know there was such a thing" are frequently heard comments. That is primarily a result of the fact that political psychology is not a traditional field in the social sciences. First, it is interdisciplinary, using psychology to explain political behavior. The field is so interdisciplinary that calling it "political psychology" is misleading because it includes scholars from political science and psychology, but also from sociology, public administration, criminal justice, anthropology, and many other areas. Second, unlike many fields in the social sciences, political psychology uses multiple methodologies, from experiments to surveys to qualitative case studies and beyond. And, if our colleagues from other disciplines have not heard of political psychology, they will soon, because it is exploding. It is a burgeoning field because it is inherently interesting and because it is enormously important. Understanding the psychological causes of political behavior is crucial if we are to affect patterns of behavior that are harmful to humanity and to promote patterns of behavior that are beneficial to humanity. Political psychology is an important domain of academic research; students find it fascinating and often troubling as they are exposed to some of the most shocking examples of political violence, and policy makers would undoubtedly benefit greatly from a better understanding of political psychology.

As the field of political psychology has grown, so has the need for a comprehensive textbook that pulls many strands of research in political psychology together. This book is a result of the authors' frustration produced by teaching courses in political psychology without such a book. Rather than having students purchase a textbook on psychology (of which they will read only a portion) and a number of books describing political behavior (without a psychological explanation of that behavior), we decided to produce a book that presents the psychology used in *political* psychology, and explains types of political behavior with political psychological concepts in a single book. We introduce readers to a broad range of theories of political psychology and sketch many cases of political activity to illustrate the behavior. Readers do not need a background in psychology or political science to understand the material in this book. However, knowing that an introduction will stimulate a desire for more, we also include suggested reading in the details of the cases. Such readings are rich, nuanced studies of each of the political behaviors we introduce readers to in this book.

Once we embarked upon this project, we quickly discovered that the field of political psychology is much broader than those of us who teach and do research in the area may realize. It ranges from voting behavior to nuclear deterrence, from the politics of race to the politics of genocide. In the pages that follow, many of the patterns of behavior researched by political psychologists are presented, including leadership, group behavior, voting, media effects, race, ethnicity, nationalism, political extremism, social movements, genocide, and war and deterrence. Because political psychology is so broad, many of those who teach the courses tend to stick to the portion of political psychology we are familiar with. Consequently, another goal of this book is to educate educators by making it easier to get a background in areas of political psychology they are unfamiliar with. Specialists in voting behavior, for example, may not know much about genocide, but both topics are covered here, and using this book as a primer will enable those who teach political psychology to expand the content of their courses. Students, in turn, will learn the interconnectedness of many patterns of behavior that at first glance seem quite distinct. They will learn, for example, that the same John or Jane Doe who exercises his or her political rights in a democracy could, under the right circumstances, support an authoritarian dictatorship that forbids political competition and tortures its opponents. Relatedly, we include examples of political behavior from around the world, so students will see that these patterns of behavior are universal, not restricted to people who live in one particular culture or in one type of political system.

In this book, many of the major topics of political psychology are covered. The book begins with an introductory chapter that discusses what political psychology is and presents some of its history as well as methodological issues. The introduction also presents a representation of the "Political Being," a drawing of the generic political person, depicting the minds and hearts of people in a political environment. It places components of our thinking and feeling—personality, social identity, values, attitudes, emotion, and cognitive processes—in layers of the mind, with personality at its core, social identity and values in the next layers, and attitudes, cognitive processes, and emotions closest to the surface. The Political Being is also depicted in his or her political environment, with in-groups and out-groups representing the importance of group psychology as well as perceptions of political opponents.

Chapters 2, 3, and 4 introduce the reader to the central psychological theories used in political psychology and some of the most prominent frameworks used in the field as well. In this third edition of the book, findings from evolutionary psychology and neuroscience are added into each of the first four chapters. Many of these theories and frameworks reappear in the following chapters' discussion of patterns of behavior in various contexts. In addition, other frameworks not presented in the preliminary theory chapters are introduced where appropriate. Chapter 2 discusses personality-based theories and frameworks. Chapter 3 involves cognitive processes, attitudes, identities, and emotions, and Chapter 4 presents group psychology in politics. After Chapter 4, the book turns to patterns of behavior in politics. Chapter 5 looks at leadership—specifically, presidential leadership in domestic and international politics. Chapter 6 looks at political psychology and the political behavior of the average citizen in the USA, with some comparison with Great Britain. The chapter examines arguments concerning the structure and function of attitudes, how people process information, and how they decide for whom to vote. The effect of the media on voters' attitudes toward politics and politicians, as well as the media's roles in campaigns, is the topic of Chapter 7.

Chapters 8–12 draw upon psychological findings in studies of social identity, cognitive processes, group dynamics, and emotions in explorations of race, ethnic conflict, nationalism, social movements, and terrorism. Chapter 8 looks at race in the USA, Europe, Brazil, and South Africa. Chapter 9 examines ethnic relations and conflict in several cases across the globe, including Nigeria, Bosnia, Guatemala, and Iraq, and concludes with a discussion of genocide and the cases of the Holocaust, Rwanda, and Darfur. Chapter 10 presents an examination of the effects of nationalism on the behavior of citizens and leaders in both domestic and international politics. The cases used to illustrate the effect of nationalism on domestic politics include the conflicts in Northern Ireland, Yugoslavia, Kosovo, Cyprus, Chechnya, the Kurds in Turkey, and German unification. The effects of nationalism on foreign policy behavior are illustrated in this chapter with the cases of World War II, the American war on drugs, and the dispute between Ukraine and Russia. Chapter 11 explores the political psychology of social movements and includes the cases of the American Civil Rights Movement, the Tea Party, Occupy Wall Street, and the Arab Spring. Terrorism is the topic of Chapter 12, which concentrates on the political psychological causes of terrorism, recruitment and motivational patterns among terrorists, and state-sponsored repression and torture. Finally, Chapter 13 examines the political psychology of nuclear deterrence and conventional warfare, while Chapter 14 concludes with a look at possible approaches to conflict prevention and/or resolution.

Throughout the book, a number of learning tools are provided. These include a list of key terms and a glossary; concluding chapter lists of theories, concepts, and cases introduced in the chapter; text boxes with interesting related topics for class discussion; and tables and illustrative figures that summarize text discussion.

Like previous editions, the third edition of *Introduction to Political Psychology* is designed for upper division undergraduate and graduate courses on political psychology, but it has other uses. We introduce readers to many different methods of research; hence, it is useful to scholars outside of the classroom. The book also contains material that should be of interest to those in the policy-making community. It presents academic findings in a user-friendly way, and policy makers may be quite surprised to discover the extent to which perceptions, personality, and group dynamics affect the policy-making arena. In a challenge to the commonly held assumptions that self-interest drives behavior, this book shows over and over again, in one context after another, how psychological factors affect our behavior and that of others in ways we rarely recognize at the time the behaviors take place.

In many respects this is a disturbing book, for it describes some of the saddest events in human history and some of the most horrific things people do to each other for political purposes. But the book also presents many discoveries about how to prevent conflict, how to resolve conflict, and how to recover from it. We hope that after reading this book the reader will understand the enormous complexity of human behavior and realize the importance of understanding and using political psychology to improve the human condition.

ACKNOWLEDGMENTS

We have benefited from the comments, insights, and ideas of a number of colleagues and students. The third edition has two new chapters, and we are grateful to Travis Ridout for his vetting of the new chapter on the media. Others who deserve our thanks include Bruno Baltodano, Isabel Beck, Alyssa Deffenbaugh, Bob Hanes, Martin Garcia, Peg Hermann, Rick Herrmann, Joe Huseby, Bob Jackson, Faith Lutze, Otto Marenin, Craig Parks, Claudia Reye-Quilodran, Ann Rumble, Hayden Smith, Craig Whiteside, and Michael Young. We also are grateful to our editor, Paul Dukes, for his help and his patience.

About the Authors

Martha L. Cottam is a professor of political science in the School of Politics, Philosophy, and Public Affairs at Washington State University. She specializes in political psychology, international politics, and intercommunal conflict. She has published books and articles on U.S. foreign policy, decision making, nationalism, and Latin American politics. She received her Ph.D. from UCLA.

Elena Mastors is currently vice president and dean of applied research at the American Public University System. Previous to her work with APUS, she was an associate professor in the National Decision Making Department of the Naval War College, and also held various senior intelligence and policy positions in the Office of Undersecretary of Defense for Intelligence and the Defense Intelligence Agency. She has published numerous books, articles, and papers on the subject of the political psychology of conflict and armed groups. She received her Ph.D. from Washington State University.

Thomas Preston is a professor of political science in the School of Politics, Philosophy, and Public Affairs at Washington State University. He specializes in political psychology, leadership analysis, and international politics. He has written numerous books and articles on presidential leadership, weapons of mass destruction, and American foreign policy. He received his Ph.D. from The Ohio State University.

Beth Dietz is professor of psychology at Miami University. Her research interests include social identity theory, computer-mediated communication, and the scholarship of teaching and learning. She teaches a variety of courses in psychology, including introductory psychology, social psychology, research design and analysis, and a graduate teaching practicum. She has strong interests in teaching online and using technology to enhance student learning. She received her Ph.D. in social psychology from the University of Pittsburgh.

Chapter 1

POLITICAL PSYCHOLOGY

Introduction and Overview

WHY STUDY POLITICAL PSYCHOLOGY?

Why do people behave the way they do in politics? What causes conflicts such as those in Bosnia, Rwanda, or Northern Ireland? Is racism inevitable? Why do Presidents make the decisions they do? Why did 9/11 happen? These and many other questions about politics are of great concern to all of us, whether we are directly affected or are only eyewitnesses through the news. So much of political behavior seems to defy explanation and seems incomprehensible when looked at with hindsight: people start wars that are, in the end, thought of as pointless and futile, such as World War I or the war in Vietnam; civil wars erupt among people who have lived together harmoniously for years, but then commit hideous acts of barbaric violence against one another, as in the former Yugoslavia, Liberia, or Sierra Leone; groups commit acts of terrorism that kill numerous innocent civilians each year; and a scandal-plagued president cannot resist tempting fate by engaging in an extra-marital affair when he knows full well the extent of the scrutiny of those looking for more scandals. Unless one understands the thoughts and feelings of the people who make the decisions to commit those acts, one cannot fully understand why those things occurred. But an exploration of the psychology—the personalities, thought processes, emotions, and motivations—of people involved in political activity provides a unique and necessary basis for understanding that activity.

This is a book about the psychology of political behavior. In the chapters that follow, we will explore many psychological patterns that influence how individuals act in politics. At the outset, we challenge the traditional notion that people act in politics in a rational pursuit of self-interest. This argument concerning rationality is based on a set of assumptions that is common in political science, but which ignores the many studies done by psychologists. Many people assume that psychology is common sense because they believe that behavior is rational and predictable. But decades of research by psychologists reveal that behavior is anything but common sense. Although psychologists recognize that much of human behavior is not always rational, human beings, as social perceivers, often operate on the belief that behavior (their own and others') is quite rational. The motivation to expect behavior to be rational is based on two fundamental needs. First, people have a need to make sense of—to *understand*—their world. Second, people have a need to *predict* the likely consequences of their own and others' behavior. To the extent that behavior is perceived as rational, these two needs become easier to fulfill.

A more accurate picture of human beings as political actors is one that acknowledges that people are driven or motivated to act in accordance with personality characteristics, values, beliefs, and attachments to groups. People are imperfect information processors, struggling mightily to understand the complex world in which they live. People employ logical, but often faulty, perceptions of others when deciding how to act, and they often are unaware of the causes of their own behavior. People often do things that are seemingly contrary to their own interests, values, and beliefs. Nevertheless, by understanding the complexities of political psychology, we can explain behavior that often seems irrational. A few illustrations help us to bring this point home. These are examples of behavior that is not at all uncommon.

A common argument is that people vote in accordance with self-interest; therefore, people in higher income brackets will vote for the Republican Party and those in lower income brackets will vote for the Democratic Party. However, the authors of this book vote for the same candidates and party, despite the fact that their incomes and personal circumstances are quite different. Is one rational and the others not, or do we share certain values and beliefs that we put above economic self-interest? Another assumption is that people are fully aware of their beliefs and attitudes and that they act in accordance with them, behaving in such a way as to maximize values. But as the following example illustrates, we often act in ways that violate our beliefs and values:

> A friend of ours was sitting on a bench in a crowded shopping mall when he heard running footsteps behind him. Turning, he saw two black men being pursued by a white security guard. The first runner was past him in a flash, but he leapt up in time to tackle the second runner, overpowering him. From the ground, the panting black man angrily announced that he was the store owner. Meanwhile, the thief escaped. Our friend, who is white and devotes his life to helping the oppressed, was mortified.
>
> (Fiske & Taylor, 1991, p. 245)

Here the power of social stereotypes lay unknowingly deep inside the mind of the friend, despite his outward, and no doubt deeply held, values opposed to such stereotyping. This is an example of the power of what psychologists call social categorization, a process wherein we nonconsciously categorize others into groups. On the surface, the act of categorizing people into groups appears logical and rational. The danger, however, lies in the consequences of categorizing people into groups on the basis of characteristics that they might not possess. (The process of social categorization is one that we will devote a great deal of attention to in this book.) In the example above, little harm was done, but the same process can occur at society-wide levels and it can produce acts of terrific violence. Racial discrimination, ethnic cleansing in Bosnia, and genocide in Rwanda are all, in part, outcomes of stereotyping. They are political actions that cannot be understood through conventional political science explanations, yet they are some of the most important and damaging forms of behavior in human societies.

Consider the following account:

> The army was determined to stamp out the grass roots support for the guerillas. A company of one hundred soldiers from Santa Cruz del Quiché moved into Nebaj the next day and installed a detachment of military police. Within days, leading citizens of the towns began to disappear. Later their bodies were found mutilated and strung up on posts in the town square.
>
> (Perera, 1993, p. 71)

Now, consider this example:

> Juliette's family, who were well-off Tutsis, stayed inside their house that first night. The next night, Thursday, when the militia came searching for them, they ran and hid in a banana plantation. On Friday they ran to the school where her uncle . . . was an administrator. Two days later the family decided to go to the place where the Belgian United Nations soldiers were and seek protection from them. But 11 Belgian soldiers had been lined up against a wall and shot the day before, so all the other Belgian soldiers had left. Juliette's family then went to a sports stadium where a lot of other people were sheltering. But here the Interahamwe [militia men] caught up with them and ordered them to another place, an open field where thousands of others had also been rounded up. The Interahamwe told all the people who were Hutus to go; then they told all the others to sit down and they threw grenades at them. When Juliette became conscious the next morning, she found her mother and brothers dead. Her father was also dead and his body had been hacked to pieces.
>
> (Bone, 1999, p. 1)

These two stories depict real-life examples of two politically motivated atrocities committed during war that cannot be explained unless the psychology of the perpetrators is understood. What objective self-interest is served by using a machete to chop up a human being? Why not just quickly kill and be done with it if his or her death serves one's interests? These are true stories; the first is from Guatemala during the 1980s and the second from Rwanda roughly ten years later. These are two very different places, and these acts occurred at different times, yet these two countries have encountered similar experiences in terms of brutal acts of violence waged by one group against another. And people in many other countries have similar stories to tell. Political psychology helps explain political behavior along the continuum from everyday political behavior, such as voting, to the most extraordinary kinds of behavior, such as mass terror and violence.

WHAT IS POLITICAL PSYCHOLOGY?

Understanding the psychological underpinnings of these behaviors gives us a different, and arguably a much more complex, understanding of political behavior. Traditional explanations of political behavior often fail to adequately explain some of the most important political decisions and actions people take. Political psychology has emerged as an important field in both political science and psychology that enables us to explain many aspects of political behavior—whether it be seemingly pathological actions, such as those described above, or normal decision-making practices, which sometimes work optimally and other times fail. Both psychologists and political scientists have become interested in expanding their knowledge of issues and problems of common interest, such as foreign and domestic policy decision making by elites, terrorism, conflicts ranging from ethnic violence to wars and genocide, the minds of people who are racists, and more peaceful behaviors such as voting, among many other problems and issues traditionally of concern in political science. For example, if we understand the limitations of the abilities of policy makers to recognize the significance of specific pieces of information, then we can institute organizational changes that will help improve our abilities to process information adequately. Likewise, if we can understand the deeper personality elements of the most important of our political leaders, we can comprehend which situations they will handle well and which situations will require more assistance and advice from others. And, if we understand what motivates terrorists to act, we can find ways in which to try to address those motivations and thus counter terrorism.

One goal of political psychology is to establish general laws of behavior that can help explain and predict events that occur in a number of different situations. The approach that political psychologists use to understand and predict behavior is the **scientific method**. This approach relies on four cyclical steps that a researcher repeatedly executes as he or she tries to understand and predict behavior. The first step involves *making observations*. This step involves making systematic and unsystematic observations of behavior and events. From these observations, a researcher begins to form hunches about the likely factors, or **variables** (see box) that affect the behavior under observation. Step two involves *formulating tentative explanations, or a hypothesis*. During this stage, a researcher makes predictions about the nature of the relationship between variables. Step three involves making *further observations and experimenting* (see box). During this stage of the scientific method, observations are made to test the validity of the hypothesis. In step four, *refining and retesting explanations*, researchers reformulate their hypothesis on the basis of the observations made in step three. This might involve exploring the limits of the phenomenon, exploring causes of relationships, or expanding on the relationships discovered. Clearly, the scientific method requires a great deal of time making careful observations.

Variables

A *variable* is what we call something that is thought to influence, or be influenced by, something else. One seeks to identify variables in the first stage of the scientific method. Variables can vary in degree or differentiation. One question of interest in social sciences is the question of how variance in one variable explains change in something else. When variables are measured, the researcher wants ideally to have a measurement instrument that is *reliable*, that is, one that will produce the same results when used by another researcher. In addition, the measurement should have *validity*, that is, it should provide an accurate measurement of what it claims to measure.

Essentially, political psychology represents the merging of two disciplines, psychology and political science, although other disciplines have contributed to the literature and growth of the field as well. Political psychology can be described as a marriage of sorts that fosters a very fruitful dialogue. Political psychology involves explaining what people do, by adapting psychological concepts so that they are useful and relevant to politics, then applying them to the analysis of a political problem or issue. For example, psychologists have been helpful to political scientists who study negative political advertising. Psychologists have done studies whose outcomes provide evidence to suggest that negative political advertisements are often ineffective, because the sponsor of the negative ad is evaluated negatively by same-party voters. Psychologists have brought to political science fresh perspectives on how to make sense of politics, thus expanding our knowledge of the political world. Political scientists bring to the field their knowledge and understanding of politics. For example, psychologists often study the decision-making process employed by groups. Some of the ideas that psychologists have used to guide their theories about how groups make decisions come from real-life group decisions made by political groups (e.g., Bay of Pigs, the decision to enter the Vietnam War). Each must be well versed in the other field, and together they are able to expand the scope of study in both political science and psychology. As a result, political psychology makes a very important contribution to our understanding of politics and expands the breadth of that understanding.

Experiments

The three characteristics that define experimental research are the **manipulation** of an independent variable, **control** over extraneous variables, and random assignment of participants to conditions. An **independent variable** is the variable whose values are set and chosen by the experimenter. If an experimenter wanted to examine the effects of room temperature on mood, then room temperature is the independent variable. The experimenter can randomly assign participants to a room that

(Continued)

(*Continued*)

is 70 degrees or a room that is 90 degrees and then observe their moods. Manipulation of the independent variable involves exposing participants to various levels of it and observing its effects on another variable, the dependent variable. In an experiment, the dependent variable is the variable whose values are predicted to change as a function of the independent variable. For example, mood is predicted to change as a function of varying temperatures in a room, with a temperature of 90 predicted to cause a more negative mood than a temperature of 70. Another characteristic of an experiment is control over extraneous variables. **Extraneous variables** are variables that may affect the behavior that a researcher is studying but that he or she has no interest in at the moment. If some of the participants have just learned that they have won the lottery before showing up for the study, then their mood in response to room temperature may be different than if they had not just learned that. The variable "winning the lottery" is an extraneous variable. Because of the manner in which experiments are designed, they allow a researcher to have a great deal of control over extraneous variables.

Merging the two fields is not an easy enterprise. For example, one cannot use many of the experimental techniques in psychology to study politics, yet experiments are vital to psychologists' research and confidence in their findings. Because experiments in psychology are conducted under carefully controlled conditions, they allow psychologists to make inferences about relationships they suspect exist. Such insights are not possible with other research methodologies, especially those used by political scientists. The patterns of behavior observed in the laboratory, therefore, are not likely to be observed in such pristine quality in the real world, where many extraneous factors cannot be filtered out as influences on behavior. If, for example, a psychologist wants to study group behavior, he or she can design an experiment in which all other factors (such as competing group loyalties, personality characteristics, gender, or ethnicity) can be made irrelevant to the study. In the real world of politics, these things cannot be extracted from behavior. The simple point is that we cannot expect to see an exact parallel between what the psychologist sees and explains, and what we will see and explain in political behavior. Instead, we must take psychological concepts or explanations of behavior and ask ourselves, how are these things likely to be manifest in the real world of politics? This is one of the most difficult aspects of the development of the field of political psychology.

Some simple examples may clarify this problem. If psychologists tell us that personality traits influence behavior, political psychologists must figure out what personality traits are important in politics. Are there certain political personality traits? If so, what are they and why are they politically important? Political psychologists argue that there are indeed certain political personality traits that are important in influencing political behavior, such as how a person deals with conflict, how complex the person's thought processes are (that is, their **cognitive complexity**), and so on. If psychologists tell us that under certain conditions attitudes affect behavior, and we wish to know how this applies to deciding how to vote, then the political question becomes: which attitudes about politics, under what circumstances, affect how we vote? In the United States, attitudes about candidates, issues, parties, and groups affect how people vote. Those attitudes vary in importance in determining the vote under differing circumstances. These are examples of the steps that must be taken in applying psychology to the explanation of political behavior. The consequence is that psychology benefits political science because political scientists use psychological theories to understand political behavior. But political science also benefits psychology because tests of psychological theories in political settings can help psychologists refine their theories.

Despite these difficulties, political psychology is a rapidly growing field. Psychology has been used to explain political behavior for many years, but there has been an explosion in its application to politics since the early 1970s. The field began in the 1920s with studies of personality and politics, and in particular with psychoanalytic studies of political leaders. As time and psychology's understanding of personality progressed, political psychologists began looking at personal characteristics, such as motivation and traits in their analyses of political leaders. While the psychoanalytic studies tended to use psychobiographies—that is, life stories of a person for data—later studies relied upon new social scientific techniques such as questionnaires, interviews, experiments, and simulations for their research. This research is examined in depth in Chapters 2 and 5 in this book.

A second wave in the development of political psychology came in the 1940s and 1950s with increased interest in the systematic study of public opinion and voting behavior in the United States. Beginning in 1952, researchers at the University of Michigan began collecting survey data on public opinion and voting preferences. In 1960, with the publication of *The American Voter*, by Campbell, Converse, Miller, and Stokes, the tradition of using political psychology to study public attitudes toward politics took off. This book presented a number of centrally important findings about the nature of political attitudes in the United States. It sparked debate and fueled important, and often differing, models of attitudes and behavior in the United States. In the years that followed, political psychology has been used in analyses of political socialization, the role of the media in affecting political attitudes, racial politics in the United States, and a number of other aspects of American political behavior. Analyses of public attitudes and political behavior have been done in many other countries in addition to the United States. Chapters 3, 6, and 7 entertain research in these areas of political psychology.

The application of political psychology and the development of political psychological frameworks for the analysis of behavior in international affairs was the third wave, and it came a bit later, beginning in the 1960s with studies of Soviet-American perceptions of each other and studies of the conflict in Vietnam (Kelman, 1965; White, 1968). By the 1970s and continuing until today, concepts of political psychology have been applied to our understanding of nuclear deterrence; past wars, such as World Wars I and II; decision making in crises; nationalism; ethnic conflict; terrorism; and a wide variety of additional topics in international politics. This book explores many of these topics in Chapters 5 and 7–12.

A fourth arena in which political psychology has been used to explain behavior is what Sears (1993) refers to as "death and horror." This too is a growing body of literature and it covers the study of terrorism, ethnic cleansing, genocide, and other patterns of behavior that involve extraordinary levels of politically motivated violence. We review this literature in Chapters 9 and 12.

More recently, both evolutionary psychology and neuroscience have been used to explain such political psychology concepts as voting behavior, in-group bias, and party affiliation, for example. Briefly, **evolutionary psychology** suggests that we cannot fully understand human behavior without understanding its biological origins. More specifically, understanding how particular traits, behaviors, and abilities evolved over time allows for a richer and more comprehensive understanding of human behavior today (Bridgeman, 2003; Barkow, Cosmides, & Tooby, 1992). You are likely familiar with the roots of the evolutionary approach—Darwin's ideas about natural selection, for example. We will explore the evolutionary approach in Chapters 3, 4, and 9.

You've also likely heard a lot about **cognitive neuroscience** lately. This term refers to a field of study that focuses on how the function and structure of the brain and nervous system explain thoughts, feelings, and actions (e.g., Gazzaniga, Ivry, & Mangun, 2014). It is probably safe to claim that neuroscience is one of the hottest areas of inquiry within psychology. In part, this emphasis can be attributed to the advanced techniques (such as functional MRIs and EEGs) that we now have available to study the brain. It seems that the more we unlock techniques for studying the brain, the more able we are to use that knowledge to understand humans. Political behavior is no exception. In Chapters 2, 3, and 6, we will explore neuroscience perspectives on personality, social identity, and voting behavior.

Thus, there are many realms of political behavior amenable to a psychological analysis and we will explore quite a few of them in this book. There are so many ways of exploring political behavior that the number of concepts can become confusing. In part, this is because different concepts have emerged in psychology over time as that field has grown. The growth of a field, be it political science, psychology, or political psychology, is always haphazard. Concepts often appear under a new name that seem strikingly similar to old concepts. Discoveries are made in one area that were made long before in another area. The lack of cross-fertilization has meant that scholars looking at one aspect of behavior are often unaware of what those looking at another aspect of behavior are doing, and therefore they reinvent the wheel over and over again. One of the tasks of this book is to draw connections between ideas that have emerged in different realms of the study of political behavior in order to lessen the confusion that arises from so many similar ideas, concepts, and arguments with so many different names.

Another outcome of the haphazard development of political psychology is that related but slightly different concepts have become popular as explanatory tools for different kinds of political behavior. Attitudes, beliefs, schemas, images, and many other concepts appear in the literature but are rarely discussed in terms of how they overlap and still differ. We will undertake some clarification in this regard, but for the moment let us present our own general picture of how and why people think and act politically, based on the work that has been generated by political psychologists over the years. To put it most simply, people are driven to act by internal factors such as personality, attitudes, and self-identity; they evaluate their environment and others through cognitive processes that produce images of others; and they decide how to act when these factors are combined. In politics, people often act as part of a group, and their behavior as part of a group can be very different from their behavior when they are alone. Therefore, the political psychology of groups is an essential part of political psychology as a field. As the book proceeds, each of these factors is developed. By the end, the picture in Figure 1.1 will have been described and explained in detail; this is the generic political being in his or her political universe.

THE POLITICAL BEING

At the core of our Political Being is **personality**. Personality is a central psychological factor influencing political behavior. As we shall see in Chapter 2, personality is unique to the individual, although certain personality traits appear in many people. Many people, for example, have traits in common, such as a particular degrees of complexity in their thinking processes and desires for power and achievement, but the combination of those traits differs, and therefore each individual is unique. Consequently, we place personality in the center of the Political Being's brain. It affects other aspects of the thought process and is itself affected by life experiences, but personalities tend to be very stable in terms of amenability to change, and they influence our behavior and behavioral predispositions on an on-going constant basis. Moreover, personality affects behavior nonconsciously in that people rarely sit down and consider the impact of their personalities on their political preferences. It drives behavioral predispositions without our having to give conscious consideration to the source of those preferences. Personality is, in that sense, a core component of the engine of political thinking and feeling. Much of the discussion of personality in political psychology concerns the personality traits of political leaders and the impact of particular combinations of those traits on their leadership styles. Consequently, much of our discussion of personality in Chapter 2 is focused on the leadership dimension, and we have devoted a full chapter (Chapter 5) to leadership.

Next we have **values** and **identity**. These concepts involve deeply held beliefs about what is right and wrong (values) and a deeply held sense of who a person is (identity). Values often include a strong emotional component. We often feel very strongly about some of our beliefs and goals for ourselves, those we care about, and political principles. For example, a person may have a strongly held value that violence is wrong, which translates into a political predisposition to oppose war, refuse military service, and go to prison if necessary to defend that value. That person's identity involves personal self-descriptions that are usually tied to and emerge from close and enduring personal relationships. For our person with a strong value opposing violence, identity may include, for example, a strong attachment to a religion and religious affiliation. Being religious would be an important part of his or her identity and he or she would strongly value the religious group that is part of his or her identity. Values, emotions, and identities are also deeply held and fairly permanent aspects of one's psychology, and hence we place them deep in the mind of our Political Being. They are discussed

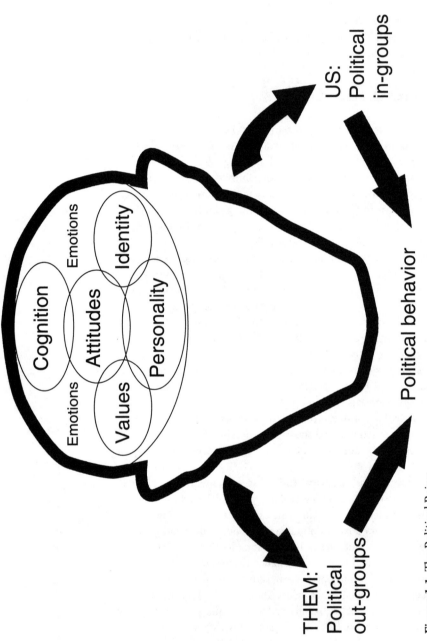

Figure 1.1 The Political Being

further in Chapter 3. Political values, emotions, and identity are also important concepts in our case studies of voting, race and ethnic conflicts, and nationalism—Chapters 6, 8, 9, and 10, respectively.

Next, our political being has **attitudes**. As we will see in Chapter 3, scholars define *attitudes* in different ways. Generally, they can be thought of as units of thought composed of some cognitive component (that is, knowledge) and an emotional response to it (like, dislike, etc.). For example, a person with an attitude on funding for public education may think it is a good thing, know how much his or her state spends on public education, and feel strongly that this particular level of spending is too low. Many important political attitudes are acquired through socialization, as we shall see in Chapter 6. In the diagram of the Political Being, they are placed toward the top of the mind because they are accessible to thinkers (who can be asked what they think and feel about an issue and can articulate an answer) and because they are subject to change based on new information, changes in feeling, or persuasion. Attitudes are the focus of attention in political psychology when it comes to voting decisions, political socialization, the impact of the media on how and what people think, and important political notions such as tolerance, all of which we will explore in Chapter 6. Studies of voting behavior are central areas of study in political psychology in general, and Chapter 6 provides an introduction to the topic with a look at public opinion and voting in the United States and a brief comparison with Great Britain. Voting is, of course, a central component of democratic politics, so it is a logical focus of political psychology.

We have left **emotions** floating in the mind of the Political Being in Figure 1.1. Politics can be an extremely emotion-evoking arena of life. Emotions affect all aspects and are affected by all aspects of the Political Being's mind. Values, identities, and attitudes are emotional, have emotional components, and emotions interact with the next portion of the Political Being's mind, cognition. Emotion permeates politics and the mind of the Political Being: hence, they are left to freely move about in our picture of the mind of the Political Being. We discuss emotion in every topical chapter in this book.

The final component of the mind of the Political Being is **cognitive processes**. Cognitive processes are the channels through which the mind and the environment first interact. They involve receiving and interpreting information from the outside. They are the mind's computer in that they facilitate the individual's ability to process information, interpret his or her environment, and decide how to act towards it. Cognitive processes help us understand an environment that is too complex for any individual to interpret. The cognitive system in our brains helps us organize that environment into understandable and recognizable units and to filter information so that we do not have to consciously assess the utility of every piece of information available to us in the environment. Take this following example. You are students in an institution of higher education. You know that the environment is divided into, among other social groups, professors and students. You know, without thinking, who is a professor and who is a student. You know what you are supposed to do as a student (study, go to lectures and take notes, take tests, write papers) and you know what your professors are supposed to do (give lectures, grade assignments, hold office hours, etc.). If a student walked up to the podium in your classroom and began to lecture, you would think it very odd, disregard the lecture, and not take notes. If the professor, on the other hand, takes over the podium, and says exactly the same thing that the student says, you would pay attention to it and you would take notes. These are cognitive processes in operation. They help people understand the environments they live in without paying close attention. They help us process information. We tend to accept information that is consistent with our preexisting ideas, beliefs, attitudes, and assumptions about the environment in which we live. Cognitive processes and organization are presented in Chapter 3.

At this point, we move from the internal components of the mind and look at the Political Being in a broader social and political environment. Political psychology involves not only the individual but also the individual's interaction with their political environment. On one side, we have those important social units, or **groups**, that are politically relevant to the Political Being and to which the Political Being is strongly attached. They constitute *us* in his or her mind, and are assessed in terms of studies of **social identity**. Social identity derives from membership in social groups such as nationality, gender, age, race, ethnicity, occupation, and other kinds of group membership. Groups are depicted in our picture of the Political Being generally in terms of in-groups (those groups people belong to) and out-groups (those they do not belong to). The creation of social categories can produce many important behavioral predispositions, including stereotyping, discrimination, and ethnocentrism. Our social identities, much like our values and attitudes, can strongly motivate behavior. We discuss social identity and groups in Chapters 3 and 4 and then provide a number of illustrations of their impact on behavior in the chapters that follow.

People belong to many different groups, and we are interested in the role played by attachment to politically relevant groups. Groups themselves have particular dynamics that influence people's behavior and this is the subject of Chapter 4, in which group psychology is introduced in and of itself and in the context of distinctly political groups. Groups demand loyalty, compliance, and obedience, and those psychological factors can override even strongly held values. Take, for example, perpetrators of genocide in the Holocaust who explained their behavior in terms of obedience to the norms of the group (e.g., "I did it because I was ordered to do so"). But social identity goes beyond group dynamics. People are influenced by groups, but they are also personally driven to support groups to which they are strongly attached. They make sacrifices that are sometimes extraordinary for the sake of the group. Illustrations of that behavior, as well as social identity factors, are found in Chapter 8 (race), Chapter 9 (ethnic conflict and genocide), Chapter 10 (nationalism), Chapter 11 (social movements), and Chapter 12 (terrorism). As we shall see, group dynamics can make people do things they would never consider doing on their own.

These topics were chosen for in-depth analyses for a number of reasons. Racial discrimination and conflict is a central aspect of American history and current politics, but it also marks the political systems in other countries. Ethnic conflict has many similarities with racial conflict and its prevalence in the post–Cold War world, as well as our failure to prevent it from causing hundreds of thousands of deaths, makes it an important issue for a book on political psychology to consider. The same can be said for nationalism, which cost millions of deaths in World War II and reappeared with ferocity after the Cold War. Terrorism is also of central importance in domestic and international politics, and not just because of the 9/11 attacks. It is a global concern. And, sadly, mass killings for political reasons continue, with genocide going on today in Darfur.

The other component of the environment that the Political Being interacts with is *them*, those groups to which that being does not belong, but must interact with in politics. People organize the political environment just as they do the social environment, and we will look at how people do so. There are a variety of perspectives on this, one of which, Image Theory, argues that people look at the world around them and organize it in terms of important political actors, such as enemies and allies (and many other categories, as we will see in Chapter 3). Some of those actors threaten the deeply held values and/or groups with which the Political Being strongly identifies. The enemy is such an actor. Others, such as allies, provide opportunities to achieve desired goals, things that are important to the individual Political Being and to the groups he or she identifies with. In Chapter 13, we examine the ultimate conflict with the other: war and efforts to deter it, a matter of importance to everyone in the nuclear era.

All of these psychological elements interact and all of the patterns of behavior we examine as illustrations are important. Of course, not all of them are functioning all the time. One's attitudes toward political candidates do not affect political preferences every day, but they do during elections. Nationalism is not important in affecting behavior until the nation is either threatened or an opportunity for its advancement appears. Moreover, at any point in time one of these factors may be more important than others. Personality can become overwhelmingly important when a President is dealing with a major crisis. Perceptions that another country is an enemy may be important during that crisis as well. The President's social identity with his ethnic group may not play a role during that crisis, but it may be important when he is pressing for a particular piece of legislation.

Our conceptualization of political psychology sees the political mind as composed of layers or levels. Different layers take on a more or less important role in different kinds of behavior or at different points in the political action process. Consequently, the chapters that follow focus on central psychological causes of different types of political behavior. When it comes to small group behavior and intricate decisions made by the members of that group, we look specifically at the personality of leaders and small group dynamics. When it comes to nationalism-based conflicts, we look at social identity, perceptions or images of other groups, and cognitive processes.

The organization of this book blends concepts and patterns in political psychology and political behavior with detailed illustrations of those concepts and patterns. Chapters 2, 3, and 4 introduce central concepts in political psychology with examples from psychology and politics for illustration. Then Chapters 5 through 13 examine some forms of political behavior, using the concepts introduced in Chapters 2 through 4, where appropriate, to explain those behaviors. Chapter 14 explores various conflict resolution and reconciliation strategies applicable to the cases in the previous chapters. We encourage you to try to amplify upon our explanations as you read the descriptions of the types of political behavior in each chapter. Chapter 5 focuses on political personality traits and leaders. Chapter 6 focuses on the political psychology of the average citizen in the voting booth and in his or her efforts to learn about and respond to political information. Chapter 7 takes a more detailed look at the role of the media in politics, and its influence on information processing by citizens generally and by voters during campaigns in particular. Chapter 8 moves us from the individual level to individuals and groups in an examination of racial politics. Chapter 9 explores similar patterns in ethnic conflicts and in cases of genocide. Chapter 10 looks at individual and group political psychology and behavior in the context of nationalism and its impact on domestic politics and foreign policy behavior. Chapter 11 is an overview of the political psychology of social movements, with case studies of the American Civil Rights Movement, the Tea Party, Occupy Wall Street, and the Arab Spring. Chapter 12 also focuses on individuals and groups in a look at terrorists and state terror. Chapter 13 explores individual and group decision making in international politics, specifically in international security and efforts to prevent war. Finally, in Chapter 14 we conclude with a look at possible approaches to conflict prevention and/or resolution. Each chapter includes a glossary of important terms and suggestions for further reading.

CONCLUSION

We began this introductory chapter with examples of political behavior that are both disturbing and difficult to explain. Let us conclude the chapter on a more personal note. The psychological causes of political behavior are interesting to study. However, for the individuals who live the realities that the following chapters describe, political behavior is not an academic exercise, but a life-shaping and altering experience. At the heart of political psychology is the question of whether by understanding why people behave as they do in politics we can prevent the worst of human behavior and promote the best. In the pages that follow, we present the work of many political psychologists who believe that this is an achievable goal, and a reasonable one to pursue; without an understanding of political psychology, it is an impossible one.

Suggestions for Further Reading

Kressel, N. (Ed.). (1993). *Political psychology: Classic and contemporary readings*. New York: Paragon House.

Monroe, K. R. (Ed.). (2002). *Political psychology*. Mahwah, NJ: Lawrence Erlbaum Associates.

Chapter 2

PERSONALITY AND POLITICS

As we mentioned in the previous chapter, personality is a central concept in psychology. For this reason, personality is placed at the bottom of the Political Being's brain, representing its roots and, therefore, the most fundamental element. Personality not only affects how people think and behave in the political arena; it is also affected by the life experiences of individuals. In this chapter, we consider some central questions about personality addressed in political psychology, including questions such as: How does personality affect political behavior? How deep must we go in understanding the development of a person's personality in order to understand his or her political inclinations (to the unconscious or more surface, conscious traits and motivations)? What personality characteristics are most politically relevant? Are people completely unique, or do they share personality traits in various combinations, making individuals more or less similar in their political behavior? How should we study personality when we can't very well put a political figure on the couch and ask him or her questions?

The study of personality and politics is the oldest tradition in political psychology (Lasswell, 1930/1960, 1948a; Adorno et al., 1950; Leites, 1951). Personality as a concept has been used to evaluate a wide variety of political behaviors, from the psychology of political leaders to psychopathologies of people who have committed politically motivated atrocities (such as Hitler and the Holocaust) to the average citizen and the role personality factors play in attitudes toward race and ethnicity, interest in politics, and willingness to obey authority. However, most studies employing personality-based frameworks focus on the impact of the characteristics of leaders on major decisions and policy-making issues such as leader-adviser relations. In fact, the studies of political personality and political leadership have developed conjointly in political psychology. As a result, it is problematic to seek to separate political personality from political leadership research in any textbook on political psychology.

In this chapter, we will discuss some of the broader theoretical arguments about personality and its effect on political behavior. We will begin with some of the central questions about the role of personality in political behavior. Then we will turn to the study of personality in psychology and look at some of the major scholars and approaches to personality from the psychological perspective. Next we will present an overview of some of the ways in which personality in politics, and particularly personality factors relevant to political leadership, have been studied. The portion of the Political Being emphasized in this chapter is, of course, the personality circle. But you will see also the links between personality and cognition, as well as the impact of personality on interactions with people in the political environment—shown as *US* and *THEM* in the Political Being diagram in Figure 1.1.

Despite the central role personality plays in psychology, political science, and political psychology, coming to an acceptable definition of *personality* is problematic, with research in psychology and political science tending to focus (and define) the concept quite differently. As Robert Ewen (1998, p. 3) points out, within the discipline of psychology "there is no one universally accepted definition of 'personality,'" nor is there any one recognized "theory of personality." Greenstein (1969, pp. 3–4) observed that the psychologist's usage of the term *personality* is comprehensive, subsumes all important psychic regularities, and refers to an inferred entity rather than to a directly observable phenomenon. In other words, personality refers to a construct that is introduced to account for the regularities in an individual's behavior as he or she responds to diverse stimuli (Hermann, Preston, & Young, 1996). Or, as Ewen notes, personality in the psychological literature refers to "*important* and *relatively stable* aspects of a person's behavior that account for consistent patterns of behavior," aspects of which "may be observable or unobservable, and conscious or unconscious" (1998, pp. 3–4). Gordon DiRenzo offers a related definition: personality is "one's acquired, relatively enduring, yet dynamic, unique, system of predispositions to psychological and social behavior" (1974, p. 16). At the same time, however, there is tremendous disagreement within the field between social psychologists and personality theorists regarding exactly what should be incorporated into such a comprehensive definition. Personality theorists would include cognition, affect, motivation, identification, and processes of ego-defense in their conceptions of personality; social psychologists usually seek to limit personality to a residual category that does not include emotion, cognition, or motivation (see Greenstein, 1969; George & George, 1998). There are many different theories of personality in psychology. Schultz (1981), for example, reviewed twenty personality theories organized into nine categories: psychoanalytic, neopsychoanalytic, interpersonal, trait, developmental, humanistic, cognitive, behavioristic, and limited domain.

In the political psychology literature, in contrast, analysts typically do not worry about arriving at a specific, comprehensive definition of personality. Instead, the focus is upon how particular aspects of personality translate into political behavior. Indeed, the study of personality in political psychology is best characterized as the study of individual differences. Rather than seek the whole, researchers selectively focus upon any number of individual aspects of a person's makeup (i.e., cognition, motivation, affect, ego, attitudes, etc.) to explain behavior. Obviously, this is a much narrower, more restrictive view of personality than that taken by most psychologists (especially the personality theorists). As a result, it is in our view unproductive to attempt to provide a commonly agreed-upon definition of personality for this textbook—there isn't one (Maddi, 1996; Ewen, 1998; Magnavita, 2002).

Further, we clearly cannot explore all theories of personality in this chapter. Instead, since our focus is upon political psychology, not psychology, we will limit ourselves to those theories most commonly used in political psychology: psychoanalytic, trait, and motivation. Furthermore, we will address research in this field that centers upon various kinds of individual differences to explain leadership, leadership style, and political behavior.

WHEN DO PERSONALITIES MATTER IN POLITICS?

Of course, just because personalities may sometimes matter with regards to policy outcomes, it would be a mistake to argue that they *always* matter. In fact, during the 1930s and 1940s, Kurt Lewin argued that to understand behavior, it is necessary to understand both a person's personality and the context in which the behavior is observed. Lewin (1935) emphasized that the interaction between the person and the situation was most important to understanding behavior. Similarly, Mischel (1973) focused attention on the degree to which situational factors govern behavior. In the early 1970s, Mischel (1973) reviewed research on the importance of personality in predicting behavior across a variety of situations. He found that people behave far less consistently across situations than had previously been thought. Instead, it appears that the situation exerts powerful effects on behavior. Indeed, it is generally accepted among scholars who work in the fields of personality or leadership that *context* (or situation) matters more (Greenstein, 1969; George, 1980; Hermann, 1987; Preston & 't Hart, 1999; Hermann, 2000; Preston, 2001). It is the situational context that provides the stage upon which the person will interact with his or her environment, providing both opportunities for action and constraints upon it. For example, in his classic book, *Personality and Politics*, Fred Greenstein (1969) observed that while personality is often unimportant in terms of either political behavior or policy outcomes, the likelihood of personal impact: (1) increases to the degree that the environment admits of restructuring; (2) varies with the political actor's location in the environment; and (3) varies with the personal strengths and weaknesses of the actor (1969, p. 42). In other words, when individuals have the personal power resources due to their position in the political system (i.e., as president, prime minister, general, mayor, etc.) and the situation allows them to exert this power to influence the policy process, what these people are like (i.e., strengths/weaknesses, personality, experience) will have an impact on policy. For Abraham Lincoln, this situation allowed him to educate his cabinet on the importance of the individual leader when, after a particularly contentious vote, he observed: "Gentlemen, the vote is 11 to 1 and the 1 has it." For Saddam Hussein, it meant that Iraq invaded Kuwait. On the other hand, in contrast to foreign policy, where there is more freedom of action, American presidents are well acquainted with their far weaker influence upon domestic policy, where Congress, the courts, interest groups, and many other actors play substantial roles in determining policy outcomes (see Neustadt, 1960/1990; Cronin, 1980; Light, 1982; Burke, 1992).

THEORIES AND APPROACHES TO STUDYING PERSONALITY

There are many different approaches or theories regarding personality, only some of which have been used in the study of personalities of political actors. Among the most important are psychoanalytic, trait-based theories, and motive-based theories. More recently, the genetic approach to personality, as it applies to political psychology, has gained enough traction to warrant mention. We will explain that approach as well. As was mentioned above, many of the frameworks in political psychology go beyond a single theoretical orientation. Below, we review some personality theories from psychology and then explore their use in political psychology. With each theoretical approach, we discuss some of the research methods typically used to study political actors.

Psychoanalytic Approaches

One of the oldest traditions in personality in psychology are **psychoanalytic or psychodynamic theories**. Psychoanalytic theories highlight the role of the **unconscious** in human behavior and the motives and drives that underlie behavior. The father of psychoanalytic theory is Sigmund Freud (1932, 1950, 1962). Freud introduced the idea that the mind is like an iceberg. Only a small part of the iceberg is visible floating above the water. Around ninety percent is under water and unobservable. Similarly, people are conscious of only a small part of the mind. The majority of the mind's operation is like the portion of the iceberg under water. It is unconscious. Freud viewed the personality as an energy system driven by aggressive and sexual drives. People are motivated to satisfy those drives, a force Freud called the **pleasure principle**. Behavior is a product of these drives and the unconscious efforts by individuals to suppress and channel the desire to act out in search of satisfaction. Living in society, from Freud's perspective, requires people to deny the pleasure principle. The consequence, in Freud's view, is pathologies such as anxiety, obsessions, and defense mechanisms.

Freud argued that the structure of personality is based upon three elements. The **id**, which is inherited, includes instincts and responses to bodily functions (e.g., hunger). The id follows the pleasure principle. The **ego** is the part of the personality that moderates between the id and its desire for pleasure and the realities of the social world. The ego, therefore, follows the **reality principle**. According to the reality principle, the demands of the id will be blocked or channeled in accordance with reality, but also in accordance with the final element of the personality, the **superego**. This is the moral arm or conscience of the personality (Hall & Lindzey, 1970). Thus, if you interact with an individual whom you do not like at all, the id may inspire you to lash out angrily at that person, but the ego keeps you from doing it because it is socially inappropriate, and the superego tells you to be kind to all people and forgive them for their obnoxious behavior. When the ego is threatened, people feel anxiety. The anxiety can be realistic, or it may be neurotic. **Neurotic anxiety** is a person's fear of being punished for doing something the id wants to do. Another type of anxiety is moral anxiety, which occurs when there is a conflict between the id and the super-ego. **Defense mechanisms** are also used to defend the ego. Defense mechanisms are unconscious techniques used to distort reality and prevent people from feeling anxiety. They include **repression**, wherein someone involuntarily eliminates an unpleasant memory. **Projection** is another defense mechanism, and it involves attributing one's own objectionable impulses to another person, projecting them onto another. **Rationalization** is a third defense mechanism. When people rationalize, they reinterpret their own objectionable behavior to make it seem less objectionable. A fourth defense mechanism is **denial**, wherein people may deny reality (e.g., denying the country is going to war despite the mobilization of troops) or they may deny an impulse (e.g., proclaiming that they are not angry when they really are).

Freud's ideas were evident in the theories of many psychologists who succeeded him. Eric Fromm (1941, 1955, 1964), for example, explored the interactions between people and society and argued that change in human society produced freedom from certain restraints such as serfdom and slavery, but in the process people experienced an increase in alienation and insecurity. To ameliorate this, they could pursue the positive freedom of a humanistic society in which people treat one another with respect and love, or they could renounce freedom and accept totalitarian and authoritarian political and social systems. Eric Erikson (1950, 1958, 1969) was also a depth psychologist trained as a Freudian who made many contributions to psychoanalysis. He too maintained an interest in politics and political leaders. Erikson is most well-known for his work on individual stages of personality development and identity. He maintained that the ego continues to grow after childhood and that society has an impact on personality. Among his important works are studies of Mahatma Gandhi (Erickson, 1969) and Martin Luther (Erickson, 1958).

Psychoanalysts employed a number of techniques that served the roles of data collection, broadly defined, and therapy. Freud and other psychoanalysts believed that much of the unconscious is repressed to avoid painful recollections, and one important component of therapy was to try to bring those repressed ideas and memories to the conscious level. One Freudian approach to therapy is known as free association. This involves having the patient lay on a couch, thinking of things in the past (free association), and saying everything that comes to mind. A second therapeutic technique was dream analysis. Freud believed that dreams are symbolic representations of thoughts—desires, fears, things that happened. Freud's research was based upon notes taken after therapeutic sessions with patients took place.

Psychobiographies: Clearly the couch and dream analysis are not options in political psychological research that uses psychoanalytical theories. Access problems, particularly to political leaders, prevent direct person-to-person psychoanalysis. Therefore, many scholars who adopt a psychoanalytic approach to the analysis of political figures use the psychobiographical method. Psychobiographies involve an examination of the life history of an individual. It is important to note that not all psychobiographies are psychoanalytic.[1] Some of these psychobiographies focus upon Freudian analysis or notions of ego-defense (e.g., Glad, 1980; Link & Glad, 1994; Hargrove, 1988; Renshon, 1996), whereas others concentrate upon specific kinds of personality disorders, ranging from narcissism to paranoid personality disorders (e.g., Volkan, 1980; Post, 1991; Birt, 1993; Volkan et al., 1999). Usually, psychobiographies take the form of quite detailed, in-depth case studies of individual leaders tracing their personal, social, and political development from early childhood onwards through young adulthood. Since it is assumed that leaders' personalities or political styles are shaped by their early childhood socialization experiences, psychobiographies generally seek to identify consistent patterns of behavior across time that can be explained using psychoanalytic analysis (see Schultz, 2005; Renshon, 2012).[2]

One of the most important examples of high quality psychobiography is the study of Woodrow Wilson written by Alexander and Juliette George. In their classic book *Woodrow Wilson and Colonel House* (1964), Alexander and Juliette George use a psychoanalytic approach to explain Wilson's highly moralistic, rigid and uncompromising political style while in the White House. They argue that it was a result of a childhood in a strict Calvinist household, where morality and distinctions between good and evil were emphasized above all else, and where Wilson's minister father constantly belittled and severely punished him for any perceived transgressions. As a result, Wilson developed a rigid, driven political personality in which he sought to accomplish great moral deeds to compensate for his own feelings of low self-esteem. Given his difficult relationship with his stern, disciplinarian father, Wilson bridled at authority figures and internalized their criticism as personally directed at him. Not only did he see the world in absolute terms, Wilson felt that compromise on moral issues was immoral. The Georges argue that these very patterns, developed throughout his childhood and young adult life, followed him into the White House. Indeed, Wilson's efforts to create the League of Nations took on the form of a great moral crusade. His conflict with Senate Majority Leader Henry Cabot Lodge (who ultimately defeated Wilson's efforts to bring the United States into the organization) took the form of a renewed conflict with another rigid, authoritarian figure: his father. The Georges see Wilson's political personality and his inability to compromise (not only on what he saw as a moral issue, but also in his conflict with Lodge) as the ultimate reason for his political defeat over the League of Nations.

As mentioned, another focus of psychoanalytical studies of personality and politics has been on psychopathology, or psychological disorders. The examination of political leaders' behavior as a possible product of psychopathologies began with Harold Lasswell's *Psychopathology and Politics* (1930/1960), wherein he maintained that the behavior of some people in political roles is affected by their psychopathologies. Lasswell attributed modern understanding of psychopathology to Freud's innovative ideas. Many political figures have also been analyzed based upon the identification of psychopathologies. For example, McCrae and Costa (1997) examined **neuroticism**, a personality disorder they argue is characterized in individuals by anxiety, self-consciousness, vulnerability, hostility, depression, and impulsiveness. In his study of **narcissism**, Volkan (1980) argues that narcissistic people seek leadership roles in a relentless search for power and use others in their climb to power. Further, such individuals often seem charismatic and rise to power in times of crisis when followers are searching for strong leaders who will improve things. Birt's (1993) analysis of Joseph

Stalin found that descriptions of his personality fit the pattern associated with **paranoia**. Paranoid personalities are quite complex. Birt argues that they function along two continua, aggression and narcissism. Aggression can be manifested at one extreme as a victim and at the other as an aggressor. Narcissism ranges from feelings of inferiority to superiority. Paranoid people swing from one end of each continua to the other. Birt argues that Stalin's paranoia not only affected the international policies of the Soviet Union, but Stalin's career as well. Stalin, he argues, "is the classical example of a paranoid individual whose paranoia helped him rise to the top of a highly centralized political structure and, once there, turn the bureaucratic institutions of the Soviet Union into extensions of his inner personality disorders" (1993, p. 611). Birt's analysis of one time period in Soviet foreign policy, the blitzkrieg attack by Germany during the Second World War, demonstrates that before the attack Stalin was in an aggressor/superior phase and did not believe Hitler would attack. After the attack, Stalin "assumed the position of victim/superior. He deserved better from Hitler. He was slighted. Insecurity set in. To Stalin, he, not the Soviet Union, was under attack" (1993, p. 619). As time progressed, he moved into the aggressor/inferior and then the victim/inferior modes; he then climbed out of his depression back to the aggressor/superior mode, where he was ready for action. The rest of the war was fought with Stalin in that mode.

Political psychologists seeking to examine personality disorders in leaders will usually employ the widely accepted American Psychiatric Association's diagnostic criteria to guide and structure their analysis of leader personality and behavior.

Freud and psychoanalysis in general have received numerous criticisms. Indeed, the criticisms of Freud have been so extensive, Hall and Lindzey argue that "no other psychological theory has been subjected to such searching and often bitter criticism than has psychoanalysis. Freud and his theory have been attacked, reviled, ridiculed, and slandered" (1970, p. 68). Among the more legitimate criticisms are those that point to the empirical problems arising from the fact that Freud's research was not controlled, and it relied upon his recollections of therapy sessions with patients, which he recorded after the fact. He presented his findings as personal conclusions, without the original data, and those conclusions may have been subject to biases as a result of the fact that he relied on his own recollection of discussions. His method for reaching conclusions was not revealed, and there was "no systematic presentation, either quantitative or qualitative, of his empirical findings" (Hall & Lindzey, 1970, p. 69). A second criticism often made of Freud's theory and psychoanalysis in general is that it is not amenable to empirical testing. This is partly because much of Freud's theory about personality is based upon unobservable abstract ideas and partly because there are so many theoretically possible behaviors that are manifestations of psychoanalytic issues a person may have. For example, recall the study of Stalin's paranoia. If diametrically opposite patterns of behavior can result from the same psychoanalytic condition, it is difficult to develop testable and therefore falsifiable hypotheses. Because of these criticisms and discussion of different perspectives on how important the unconscious is, a number of additional personality theories have emerged in psychology, to which we now turn.

Traits, Motives, and Individual Differences

There is a wealth of personality theories and research that looks at individual characteristics (or traits), motivations, and cognitive style variables and how these shape styles of decision making, interpersonal interaction, information processing, and management in office.

Trait Theories: If you were asked to describe your mother you might say she is smart, funny, loving, tidy, and humble. These are personality traits, which we all use to characterize other people and ourselves. **Traits** are personality characteristics that are stable over time and in different situations (Pervin & John, 1997). Traits produce predispositions to think, feel, or act in a particular pattern toward people, events, and situations. Trait theorists also regard traits to be hierarchically organized. Trait theories in psychology began with the work of Gordon Allport (1937, 1961, 1968). Allport disagreed with Freud's contention that personality dynamics are governed by the unconscious. He also believed that childhood experiences are less important in the adult's personality than Freud maintained. Allport regarded personality traits to be central in determining how people respond to their environments. He distinguished among cardinal traits, central traits, and secondary traits. *Cardinal traits* are critically important and dominate a person's life. An example would be authoritarianism, which is discussed below. Allport believed that these are rare and that most people have few cardinal traits, or none at all. A second type of trait is the *central trait*, which affects people regularly, but not in every situation. An example would be honesty. Finally, there are *secondary traits*, which are least important and most irregular in affecting behavior. Allport also emphasized the importance of understanding motivation as a driving force in human behavior. For Allport, motivation was not hidden in the unconscious or derived from childhood experience, but consciously considered through cognitive processes.

Another trait theorist whose work has influenced political psychology is Hans Eysenck (1975, 1979). He identified three personality trait dimensions: introversion-extroversion, neuroticism, and psychoticism. The *introvert-extrovert trait* refers to how outgoing a person is, the *neuroticism trait* to how emotionally stable a person is, and the *psychoticism trait* refers to how isolated and insensitive to others a person is. Eysenk used questionnaires to gather data on personality traits and employed a statistical technique called *factor analysis* to identify which traits cluster together. Other important early trait theorists include Raymond Cattell (1964, 1965; Cattell & Child, 1975) and David McClelland (1975), both of whom wrote extensively about motivation, a trait factor we consider below.

In recent years, psychologists have sought to develop a taxonomy of personality traits that constitute the basic units of personality. Using several different research techniques, including factor analyses of trait terms commonly used in everyday language and the analysis of trait questionnaires, they developed five central personality traits. The **Big Five** personality dimensions or traits have received considerable attention in the last two decades (Costa & McCrae, 1992; Hofstede & McCrae, 2004; Rubenzer & Faschingbauer, 2004; Dietrich et al., 2012). These traits are neuroticism, extraversion, agreeableness, openness to experience, and conscientiousness.

Each trait is arranged on a continuum. For example, those high in neuroticism are characterized as people who worry and are nervous and insecure, whereas those low in neuroticism are calm, secure, and unemotional. People who are high in extraversion are sociable, optimistic, fun loving, and affectionate, while those low in extroversion are quiet, reserved, and aloof. A person high in openness is curious, creative, and has many interests, while one low in openness is conventional and has narrow interests. People high in agreeableness are trusting, good natured, helpful, and soft-hearted, while a person low in agreeableness tends to be cynical, rude, irritable, and uncooperative. Finally, a person high in conscientiousness is organized, hardworking and reliable, while a person low in conscientiousness is aimless, unreliable, negligent, and hedonistic (Pervin & John, 1997).

The Big Five traits are viewed as superordinate and universal (Marsella et al., 2000), though some Big Five researchers have found some gender and cultural differences in these traits in studies across several countries (Costa et al., 2001). Indeed, Eagly and Carli (2007) found women scored higher than men on the warmth and positive emotion aspects of extraversion, but lower on the assertiveness aspect of extraversion. Other studies have looked at a variety of behavioral patterns associated with the Big Five personality traits. Olson and Evans (1999) have examined the relationship between the "big five" personality dimensions or traits and social comparisons. The authors used a new technique (the Rochester Social Comparison Record [RSCR]) wherein experimental subjects keep a diary recording their social comparisons, measuring to whom they compare themselves. The researchers also examined how people feel about those comparisons. They found that people high in Neuroticism felt more positive when they compared themselves "downward," that is, to others of less stature or status. People high in extraversion compared downward more than people low in extraversion, in part because they had stable positive moods. In addition, the authors argue "along with their greater tendency to experience positive affect, extraverts also might compare downward because of their tendency to be dominant, masterful, and assertive, attributes that are reflected in studies showing them to have a high degree of leadership ability" (1999, p. 1506). We shall see this illustrated later in this chapter and in Chapter 5, where we consider leadership in detail. People low in agreeableness tended to see themselves as superior to others and therefore compared downward more than those high in agreeableness. Finally, people high in openness compared themselves to superior groups more than those low in openness and tended not to experience a diminution of positive affect in the process. Still, Judge et al. (2002) found leadership effectiveness and emergence was significantly related to the traits of extraversion, conscientiousness, and openness to experience, with agreeableness also being related to leader effectiveness. For U.S. presidents, Gallagher and Allen (2014) found those high in excitement seeking were more likely to use force to carry out their foreign policy objectives than their opposites, while openness to action led to greater variation in their decision making. This builds upon previous work that has found leader risk propensities in decision making correlated to four Big Five measures—excitement seeking, openness to action, deliberation, and altruism (Kowert & Hermann, 1997; Rubenzer & Faschingbauer, 2004; Nicholson et al., 2005). There is also a body of literature on personality trait affect that explores the question of whether traits have particular affects associated with them. Schimmack, Oishi, Diener, and Suh (2000) argue that extroversion includes pleasant affects and neuroticism has unpleasant affects.

The traits used in political psychology are related to traits described in the psychological literature, but they are presented in their political manifestation. Openness to experience, for example, appears as cognitive complexity, interest in politics, integrative complexity, and other traits that are named and described in political form. Traits commonly used in political psychology and their measurement are discussed later in our section on profiling leader characteristics. But again, recent personality research in psychology emphasizes that some people vary in their trait expression over time, situations, or contexts more than do others (Fleeson, 2004; Kernis, 2003; Roberts & Donahue, 1994), so it remains important to view traits as not simply static or driven purely by situational factors (Mischel, 1968), but as more nuanced and dynamic—often variable across individuals and shaped by various contexts (Hermann, 1999a; La Guardia & Ryan, 2007; Marcus, 2013).

Somewhat similar to the Big Five is the application of the Myers-Briggs Type Indicator (MBTI) personality assessment measure to the study of political personality. The MBTI assumes that individual personality reveals itself in the form of specific preferences for certain kinds of environments, tasks, and cognitive patterns (Lyons, 1997, p. 793). Compared with the Big Five personality traits, the MBTI scales mirror similar factors, with the exception of neuroticism, which is not included in the MBTI system. As illustrated in Figure 2.1, the MBTI is composed of four scales of preferences that allow, across the various possible combinations, a total of 16 potential MBTI personality types (Lyons, 1997, p. 794).

For example, applying these measures to former President Bill Clinton's life prior to his arrival in the White House, Michael Lyons (1997, p. 801)

Introversion	**vs.**	**Extroversion**
(Introspective, Reserved, Seeking Solitude)	(Expressiveness and Gregariousness)	
Sensing	**vs.**	**Intuition**
(Favoring Literal, Empirical Perception)	(Favoring Abstract, Figurative Perception)	
Thinking	**vs.**	**Feeling**
(Favoring Objective, Detached, Logical Decision Making)	(Favoring Subjective, Value- or Emotion-Based Decision Making)	
Judging	**vs.**	**Perceiving**
(Seeking Resolution and Order)	(Curious, Spontaneous, Tolerant of Disorder)	

Figure 2.1 MBTI Personality Types

Note: From Lyons, M. (1997). Presidential character revisited. *Political Psychology, 18,* 794.

argues that Clinton falls squarely into the Extroversion, Intuitiveness, Feeling, and Perceiving categories (an ENFP type) of the MBTI. Given the predictions of the MBTI for the ENFP personality type, Lyons suggests that Clinton would be expected to seek close attachments to other people; be very adept at establishing such attachments; seek out "people to people work" professionally; be optimistic, warmly enthusiastic, high spirited, and charismatic; be brilliantly perceptive about other people, draw followers, and be an excellent politician; appear insincere sometimes because of a tendency to adapt to other people in the way he presents his objective; be innovative, yet undisciplined, disorganized, and indecisive; hate rules and find it difficult to work within the constraints of institutions; thrive on constant change and begin more projects than he can reasonably complete; find difficulty relaxing and commonly work himself into exhaustion; have his energies divided between competing interests and personal relationships; be ingenious and adaptable in a way that allows him to often improvise success; exhibit a highly empathetic world view, yet focus on data that confirms his biases, leading to a propensity to make poor choices and make serious mistakes of judgment (Lyons, 1997, p. 802).

Though the Myers-Brigg typology and test have been widely popular for decades as a means of assessing job candidates in business and advising people on careers, they are not without their problems—especially from a scientific point of view (Pittenger, 1993; Paul, 2004; McCrae & Costa, 2006; Grant, 2013). Numerous studies have suggested that there is little empirical support for the view that the MBTI actually measures truly dichotomous preferences or qualitatively distinct types, though four of the MBTI indices were shown to measure aspects of four of the five major Big Five dimensions (McCrae & Costa, 2006). In fact, Gardner and Martinko (1996) found few consistent relationships between MBTI type and managerial effectiveness; others have found a fifty percent chance of test takers finding themselves in an entirely different category only five weeks later upon retaking the exam (Krznaric, 2013). So while the use of the MBTI remains highly popular because of familiarity and marketing, many scholars argue it merely picks up on Big Five factors, lacks empirical support for some of its dimensions (the thinking-feeling dichotomy in particular), and does not merit the continued reliance of business upon it for assessment purposes (Paul, 2004; Grant, 2013).

Motive Theories

Some researchers look at the motives of individuals. There are many motive theories in psychology and many definitions of the term. In a study done over forty years ago, in 1961, for example, Madsen considered the works of *twenty* different motive theorists. Interest in motivation has come and gone and come around again in personality theory in psychology. **Motives** are those aspects of personality concerned with goals and goal-directed actions. Motives "energize, direct, and select behavior" (Emmons, 1997, p. 486). The motives that have received the most attention and are regarded as the Big Three in both psychology and political psychology are the **need for power** (i.e., concern for impact and prestige), **need for affiliation-intimacy** (i.e., concern for close relations with others), and **need for achievement** (i.e., concern with excellence and task accomplishment) (Winter, 1973; McClelland, 1975; Winter & Stewart, 1977; McClelland & Boyatzis, 1982; Winter, 1987; Winter & Carlson, 1988; Winter, Hermann, Weintraub, & Walker, 1991). For example, Winter and Stewart (1977) argued that those high in power and low in affiliation make better presidents. Those high in power also require a far greater degree of personal control over the policy process and the actions of subordinates than do low power personalities. In terms of interpersonal relationships, people high in the need for power exhibit more controlling, domineering behavior towards subordinates than low power people (Winter, 1973, 1987; McClelland, 1985). Motivation and leadership have received attention in Winter's (1987) study of the appeal of American presidents. He argued that a leader's popular appeal (measured by electoral success) is a function of the fit between his motives and those of society.

In psychology, a method for assessing motives used by clinical psychologists is the Thematic Apperception Test, or TAT. This method involves giving participants a picture, having them write imaginative stories about it, and then doing a content analysis of the stories. The stories reveal underlying personality characteristics. This method has been criticized as unreliable; regardless of its reliability, it is not available for the assessment of political leaders, so techniques for measuring motives from a distance have been developed using **content analysis** of texts, in particular the inaugural speeches of American presidents.[3]

What Is Content Analysis?

Content analysis is a research method used frequently by political psychologists using a wide variety of analytical approaches, including those discussed in this chapter and Chapter 3. Because in political psychology we often lack direct access to policy makers, we look at their statements and infer from those statements some aspects of their political psychological make-up. This is content analysis. To conduct a systematic content analysis, a researcher must 1) decide what materials he or she will use in the study (e.g., only statements written by the official you are examining, public statements written by others, interviews, etc.) and 2) how the material will be analyzed (or coded)—that is, how inferences will be drawn and recorded.

Genetic Theories

When thinking about genetic influences on personality, there are two related areas that we can explore. The first area is evolutionary psychology, which we mentioned in the first chapter. As applied to personality, evolutionary psychologists take the position that certain traits or patterns of behavior persisted and strengthened because they possessed high survival value. In other words, certain patterns of behavior helped a species to survive because they were adaptive. Evolutionary psychologists have studied such behavioral patterns as aggression (e.g., Lorenz, 1966), altruism (e.g., Dawkins, 1976), and self-esteem (e.g., Leary, 1999). For example, the altruism is said to have survival value because we are more likely to help out members of our own species, thereby ensuring the survival of that species.

Related to evolutionary psychology is **behavioral genetics**, which explains how individual traits and patterns of behavior get passed down from parents to children, as well as how those traits are shared between siblings. It basically asks the question of whether or not there is a family resemblance with regard to personality. In this section of the chapter, we will focus more on behavioral genetics because there is research to suggest a genetic component to personality.

First, to understand the research on behavioral genetics in political psychology, it might be helpful to review the basic aim of behavioral genetic research. You may recall from a biology or genetics class that a phenotype refers to the observable traits that a person possesses, while a genotype refers to the underlying genetic structure. Of course, the picture is quite a bit more complicated than that, as evidenced by the Human Genome Project, which mapped about 25,000 genes. For our purposes, it is important to understand that behavioral genetics concerns itself with the degree of variation in a phenotype that is attributable to the genotype. One way to answer that question is to engage in research on twins. Here again, it is wise to recall some information from your biology classes—monozygotic twins come from one egg, while dizygotic twins come from two eggs. Therefore, monozygotic twins are genetically identical.

Why is it important that monozygotic twins are identical? As you can imagine, there are many factors that can influence our personality. Some of these, such as motives and the unconscious, have been discussed already. But there may be other influences on our personality, such as social situations or the environment. Behavioral geneticists do not discount or ignore those influences, but instead, try to measure how much of our personality is attributable to genes and how much is attributable to environmental factors. This is where studies of twins are highly valuable. If a trait or a behavioral pattern is influenced by genes, then the trait or behavioral scores of monozygotic twins should be more highly correlated than they are for dizygotic twins or siblings. And of course, close relatives should have more highly correlated scores on traits or behavioral patterns than more distant relatives. So, how highly correlated are the traits of monozygotic twins? It turns out to be about .60 for monozygotic and .40 for dizygotic (Borkenau et al., 2001), suggesting that genes matter. Also, it appears that growing up in the same household does not lead to similar personalities. Adoptive siblings raised in the same household have a correlation of about .05 on personality traits (Funder, 2010).

There is increasing evidence for a genetic component to political behavior (Funk, 2013). More of this will be explored in later chapters, but for now, we will focus on the role of genetics in personality as it relates to political behavior. Specifically, there is evidence to suggest that many of our political beliefs have a strong genetic component. In a large-scale study of about 8,000 twins, Funk et al., (2013) studied a number of political traits and was able to measure the variability in those traits that were likely due to genetics and as well as to the environment. With regard to political attitudes, they found that such attitudes as political ideology and egalitarianism had strong genetic components, with about 58% of the variability in political ideology and 50% of the variability in egalitarianism attributable to genes.

You might recall the prior section on The Big Five personality traits. There is strong evidence to suggest that many of those traits are heritable. Funk et al. (2013) found that one of the reasons that we are the way we are is because of genetics. For example, consider the trait of extroversion. Funk et al. found that about 70% of the variability of that trait is due to genetic factors. And the other four traits in The Big Five were also shown to have high heritability scores, with agreeableness at 38%, conscientiousness at 42%, neuroticism at 42%, and openness at 43%. One trait that Funk et al. studied that is of particular importance in political psychology is authoritarianism. The twins in the study were asked such questions as, "Our country needs a powerful leader, in order to destroy the radical and immoral currents prevailing in society today," and "Our country needs free thinkers, who will have the courage to stand up against traditional ways, even if this upsets many people." Their results showed that about 48% of the variability in responses to these questions was attributable to genes.

SOME FRAMEWORKS FROM POLITICAL PSYCHOLOGY

In the sections that follow, we introduce readers to political psychological frameworks that employ various combinations of personality psychology discussed above. As mentioned at the outset of this chapter, the use of personality theories by political psychology has been eclectic. The frameworks presented below have drawn liberally from a variety of psychological theories. Most importantly, they have tried to adapt those theories and concepts to political contexts. Hence, for example, personality traits and motivations discussed in psychology may be directly used in political analyses, or they may be presented in a political manifestation. The need for power is directly applicable to politics. Ethnocentrism has been determined to be an important *politically relevant trait*, but is not considered to be a central personality trait in the personality literature.

The Authoritarian Personality

Although research into the authoritarian personality has a long history, interest in exploring authoritarian personality characteristics increased as a result of World War II and the Nazi regime in Germany. The rabid anti-Semitism of that regime along with its extreme right wing, fascist political principles lead researchers to explore the question of whether this political authoritarianism could be traced to a personality syndrome. The post–World War II study of an authoritarian personality type began with the work of T. Adorno, E. Frenkel-Brunswik, D. Levinson, and R. Sanford. *The Authoritarian Personality* (1950) was based on psychoanalytic arguments. Authoritarian personalities were, they argued, the product of authoritarian patterns of childhood upbringing and a resultant weak ego. The parents of authoritarians were insensitive to the difficulties children experience as they try to learn how to control id-derived impulses relating to sexual desires, bodily functions, and aggression. Instead of helping their children develop, these parents were demanding, controlling, and used severe disciplinary techniques. The parents were also described as being determined to raise their children to be highly conventional. As a result, the children did not develop effective ways of controlling their sexual and aggressive impulses, yet they feared those impulses. They developed iron-tight defensive techniques that would prevent them from having to confront those impulses. They regarded their parents, and subsequent authority in their lives, with a mixture of resentment and dependence. Adorno et al. saw the authoritarian personality as composed of several central personality traits, including conventionalism (rigid adherence to conventional values); submission to authority figures; authoritarian aggression (that is, aggressive impulses towards those who are not conventional); anti-intraception (that is, rejection of tenderness, imagination, subjectivity); superstition and stereotype (fatalistic belief in mystical determinants of the future and rigid thinking); high value placed on power and toughness; destructiveness and cynicism; projectivity (that is, the projection outward of unacceptable impulses); and an excessive concern with the sexual activity of others. Given the era in which the study was done, there was a natural interest in the extent to which authoritarian personalities would be susceptible to fascism of the Nazi Germany variety—anti-democratic and right wing in political ideology, anti-Semitic, ethnocentric, and hostile toward racial and other minorities.

The Authoritarian Personality study was done using a wide variety of research tools including questionnaires (with factual questions, opinion-attitude scales, and open answer questions) and clinical measures (interviews and TAT). The authors developed scales to measure several elements of authoritarian political attitudes. Scales combine several items from a questionnaire on the same topic, enabling the researcher to get a broader range of scores for a single person. This increases the reliability of the score. The fascism, or F scale, was developed to test for a person's propensity toward fascism. The other scales were the anti-Semitism (A-S) scale; the ethnocentrism (E) scale, which included Negro (N), minority (M), and patriotism (P) subscales; and the Politico-Economic Conservatism (PEC) scale. Each scale was designed to assess different elements of political authoritarianism. Adorno et al. argued that their empirical evidence demonstrated that this syndrome was closely associated with anti-Semitism, ethnocentrism, and, in turn, with political conservatism. But criticisms quickly emerged on conceptual and methodological grounds. One of the more important criticisms was presented by Edward Shils (1954) who noted that communists, who also held authoritarian political values, scored low in the Adorno et al. measurement scale, the F scale. Therefore, he argued, they apparently tested only for right wing authoritarianism and not left wing authoritarianism and therefore their F scale was not a true measure of authoritarianism. Other criticisms noted that Adorno and his colleagues did not control for education and income, and that the F scale question wording *provoked* a tendency to agree (acquiesce), thereby producing false positives (Bass, 1955; Gage, Leavitt, & Stone, 1957; Jackson & Messick, 1957). In short, much of the criticism was methodological and revolved around the question of whether the F scale actually tapped true authoritarianism and whether it actually established a relationship between those nine authoritarian personality traits and fascistic political principles.

More recently, additional criticisms have been made about the work of Adorno and his colleagues. For example, John Levi Martin (2001) argues that there is a fundamental flaw in the theoretical construct in that it is assumed that those high in authoritarianism have certain syndromes, and those low do not. Instead, he argues the whole issue should be approached as a question, and the difference between low and high should be studied as a continuum. What, for example, are those in the middle like? Second, Martin notes that the Adorno group was willing to distort or dismiss data that showed nonauthoritarian tendencies among the highs and authoritarian tendencies among the lows. This reached its acme in a differential interpretation strategy by which anything good said by a High (but not a Low) was evidence of the suppression of its opposite, and anything bad said by a Low (but not by a High) was taken as evidence of a healthy acceptance of one's shortcomings (Martin, 2001, p. 10).

The Authoritarian Personality debate, and renewed interest in the personality syndrome, was revitalized by the work of Robert Altemeyer (1981, 1988, 1996). Altemeyer's approach is trait based rather than psychoanalytic. He uses three of the nine personality traits identified by Adorno et al.: authoritarian submission, authoritarian aggression, and conventionalism. These he regards as central attitudinal clusters—orientations to respond in the same general way toward certain classes of stimuli (Altemeyer, 1996, p. 6) in right wing authoritarianism. Altemeyer did not include the more psychoanalytical traits because he was not convinced by the original psychoanalytic argument, noting that there was little inter-item consistency among the F scale questions that attempted to trace those traits. Instead, he conceptualized right wing authoritarianism psychologically rather than politically (that is, one ideology versus another). Psychologically, **right wing authoritarianism** is submission to perceived authorities, particularly those in the establishment or established system of governance (1996, p. 10). That system could be a repressive right wing system, as in Apartheid South Africa, or a communist system as in the People's Republic of China, or a democratic system as in the United States. Hence, right wing authoritarianism can occur in any political system. Altemeyer has developed a Right Wing Authoritarianism Scale (RWA) too. The scale includes statements with which the respondent must agree or disagree such as "life imprisonment is justified for certain crimes" and "women should have to promise to obey their husbands when they get married" (1996, p. 13).

In Altemeyer's view, right wing authoritarianism is a product of social learning, a combination of personality predispositions, and life events. Altemeyer argues that those high in right wing authoritarianism have greater difficultly than low scorers in engaging in critical thinking. They are more likely to agree with a statement of a fact without examining it critically (1996, p. 95). This is a consequence of having truths dictated to them by those in authority and being prohibited from challenging that authority. Therefore, when a scapegoat is selected upon whom a country's problems are placed, people high in right wing authoritarianism are more likely to uncritically believe that the scapegoat is responsible. It follows, then, that a second pattern of thinking among those high in right wing authoritarianism is the acceptance of contradictory ideas and an ability to compartmentalize them, thereby ignoring the contradictions. Any idea that comes from an authority figure is accepted as correct, even if it is in direct contradiction to another idea. Third, Altemeyer argues that those high in right wing authoritarianism see the world as a very dangerous place. Their parents taught them this, and the resulting fear drives a lot of their aggression; this makes them vulnerable to precisely the kind of overstated, emotional, and dangerous assertions a demagogue would make (1996, pp. 100–101). Fourth, high authoritarians are much more careful in looking for evidence to disprove ideas they are predisposed to reject than to disprove ideas they are predisposed to accept. Finally, Altemeyer argues that high authoritarians are particularly susceptible to the fundamental attribution error, wherein people attribute the behavior of others to internal dispositions and their own behavior to external forces (discussed more in Chapter 3).

Further research into the authoritarian personality is ongoing. Lambert, Burroughs and Nguyen (1999) used Altemeyer's right wing authoritarianism scale to examine the relationship between authoritarianism, belief in a just world, and perceptions of risk. They found that high authoritarians perceived risk to be lower if people believed in a just world (i.e., that good things come to good people). Low authoritarians did not have the same perception. In Chapter 8 we discuss some research regarding race-related attitudes and right wing authoritarianism. Tam, Leung and Chiu (2008) found that when people high in authoritarianism are more "mindful" or attentive to information, they become more punitive in their reactions to criminal behavior, contrary to the general assumption that individuals become less punitive when more attentive to information. The opposite was the case for authoritarians.

While Altemeyer argues that several political attitudes, such as anti-Semitism and hostility toward foreigners, correlate with his three central authoritarian attitude clusters, others such as Raden (1999) argue that the clustering of such attitudes is influenced by political and social change. Raden found that anti-Semitism was decreasingly likely to correlate with authoritarian personality characteristics as the twentieth century progressed. Martin (2001) has weighed in on Altemeyer's work as well, arguing that although he avoids the methodological problems of the Adorno et al. F scale, Altemeyer still failed to see authoritarianism as a continuum and does not compare the behavior of lows and highs, sticking to the examination of the behavior of highs. Furthermore, Altemeyer does not adequately explain why conventionalism is a manifestation of authoritarianism, and he uses evidence of differences in degree (that is, some lows agreeing with highs and some highs agreeing with lows in some question items) as evidence of a clear cut, mutually distinct, typological difference.

As was mentioned at the beginning of this chapter, studies of personality and leadership in political psychology are rather eclectic in that they draw not only from psychological personality concepts but other areas as well. As a result, scholars have built some frameworks that are used to analyze political leaders (but many could be used to examine the average citizen too). Below we provide an overview of some of those frameworks with some examples of their applications to political leaders. Political leaders are discussed in much greater depth in Chapter 5.

Leader Analysis Frameworks

There is an extensive literature in political psychology on the leadership or management styles of political leaders using many different frameworks.

Below we introduce several frameworks used to study political leaders, the presidential character framework developed by James David Barber, several trait assessment approaches, and the Operational Code. There also is no common, agreed-upon empirical approach to the study of political leaders in political psychology. Instead, there has developed a broad, methodologically diverse, interdisciplinary literature on the topic that has been tolerant of hybrid research approaches that borrow individual concepts or variables from a variety of sources. As a result, variables that psychologists would be quick to describe as personality-based (whether Freudian concepts, authoritarian measures, personal traits like need for power, self-confidence, distrust of others, etc.) are routinely combined with clearly nonpersonality-based variables (like an individual's first political success, their socialization experiences, their prior policy experience, or operational code belief systems) in the same analysis. Since the literature in political psychology addressing the impact of personal variables upon political leader behavior developed over a long process of selective borrowing by political scientists from a broad range of psychological literatures (on personality, cognition, groups, etc.), it is practically impossible to draw crisp, clear delineations between personality and political leadership in political psychology. Like the problem often facing surgeons in separating infants born conjoined, these two research traditions in political psychology share too many common elements to easily separate into two distinct bodies. This reality will become more apparent as many of the approaches to the study of personality and politics as well as political leadership are viewed in this chapter. There are some personality-based studies that are applied to both leaders and the average person, such as authoritarian personality studies. Below we will provide an overview of several theories and frameworks that focus on individual characteristics and their impact on political behavior.

Trait-Based Studies

Presidential Character

James David Barber's well-known book, *The Presidential Character* (1972), employs psychobiography to explain the personalities, styles, and character of modern presidents. Avoiding the psychoanalytic focus upon Freudian concepts (the id, ego, and superego), Barber's psychobiographies seek patterns in the early lives or political careers of leaders that create, through a process of socialization, the subsequent patterns of personality, style, and leadership one sees in office. Moreover, Barber argues that personality should not be studied as a set of idiosyncratic traits unique to individual presidents, where some presidents have a trait that others do not. Instead, he argues that personality is a "matter of tendencies," in which traits like aggressiveness, detachment, or compliancy are possessed by all presidents, but in differing amounts and combinations (1972, p. 7). As a result, the components of presidential personality (*character*, *world view*, and *style*) are patterned, fitting together in a "dynamic package understandable in psychological terms" (p. 6). *Style* reflects the habitual way a president performs his three political roles (rhetoric, personal relations, and homework), whereas *world view* consists of the leader's primary politically relevant beliefs regarding such things as social causality, human nature, and the central moral conflicts of the time (pp. 7–8). Lastly, *character* is seen as the way in which a president orients himself towards life and his own merits (i.e., his sense of self-esteem and the criteria by which he judges himself, such as by achievement or affection, p. 8). In order to put these pieces together, Barber employs a psychobiographical approach to trace the sociological development within presidents of the three patterns comprising personality (character, world view, and style) from their early lives on through to their critically important *first independent political successes*. It is that first political success that sets the pattern that follows, giving the leader a template for successful action and positive feedback that they emulate and seek to copy throughout their subsequent careers.

Perhaps one of the most famous typologies in political science, Barber's seeks to capture how *presidential character*, or "the basic stance a man takes toward his Presidential experience," finds itself reflected in two basic dimensions: (1) the energy and effort he puts into the job (*active or passive*); and (2) the personal satisfaction he derives from his presidential duties (*positive or negative*) (Barber, 1972, p. 6). The resulting typology is presented in Table 2.1, along with Barber's examples of American presidents who fit within each of the cells.

Applied to both Bill Clinton and George W. Bush, Barber's (1972) typology leads to a very generalized prediction of behavior and style in office. In Clinton's case, it is clear that he fits into the *active-positive* category of Barber's typology. Indeed, few presidents in American history have been so actively engaged personally in the details of policy making on a day to day basis, or enjoyed their presidential duties and responsibilities as much as Bill Clinton did in office (Preston, 2001). Barber's predictions for this type of personality are that such individuals want to achieve results and direct

Table 2.1 Barber Typology of Presidential Character

Energy Put Into the Job	*Personal Satisfaction With Presidential Duties*	
	Positive	*Negative*
Active	Derives great personal satisfaction and is highly engaged (examples: Jefferson, Roosevelt, Truman, Kennedy, Ford, Carter, Bush, Clinton)	Derives little personal satisfaction yet is highly engaged (examples: Adams, Wilson, Hoover, Johnson, Nixon)
Passive	Enjoys great personal satisfaction from the job, but puts little energy into it (examples: Madison, Taft, Harding, Reagan, G. W. Bush)	Derives little personal satisfaction and puts little energy into it (examples: Washington, Coolidge, Eisenhower)

much of their energy towards achievement, tend to be self-respecting and happy, are open to new ideas, are flexible and able to learn from mistakes, and tend to show great capacity for growth in office. While one might quibble with some of the predictions that seem to have problems in light of Clinton's White House behaviors regarding interns and the ability to learn from mistakes, the general predictions regarding his emphasis upon results and achievement, his generally happy demeanor, and his widely reported openness to new ideas and policy flexibility are strongly supported by his record in office. Similarly, Barack Obama would also be seen as *active-positive*, and despite obstructionism by Congressional Republicans throughout his two terms in office, he remains engaged, open to new ideas, flexible regarding policy, and focused upon results and achievement while enjoying being president.

In contrast, George W. Bush would likely be classified as a *passive-positive* according to Barber's typology. The early evidence of Bush's style in office supports this designation. He is an individual who tends to be less personally engaged or involved in the formulation and making of policy, preferring instead to delegate these tasks to subordinates, but who nevertheless greatly enjoys being president (Milbank, 2001; Kahn, 2000; Dowd, 2001). In terms of predicted behaviors arising from this style type, Barber describes passive-positives as primarily being after affirmation, support or love from their followers, while at the same time showing a tendency for policy drift, especially during times of crisis, in which you would expect to see confusion, delay, and impulsiveness on their parts. There certainly have been numerous examples of confusion, delay, and impulsiveness with regards to Bush's policies in the Middle East (especially with regards to the Israeli-Palestinian conflict and towards Iraq), in his reactions towards U.S. participation in many international treaties (ABM and Kyoto being only the most notable), and in his enunciation of an "axis of evil." Moreover, the Iraq War and U.S. actions in Afghanistan were, throughout Bush's presidency, characterized by considerable policy drift and inconsistencies (Preston, 2011).

Obviously, the typology is exceedingly general in nature, examines only two possible dimensions relating to presidential style, and has an intensely subjective element. Clearly, one could take issue with either the accuracy or usefulness of the Barber model, especially given that it basically places Franklin Roosevelt, Harry Truman, John Kennedy, Gerald Ford, Jimmy Carter, George Bush Sr., Clinton, and Obama all in the active-positive category, while Ronald Reagan, Warren Harding, and William Taft join George W. Bush as passive-positives. Given such minimal differentiation among such varied presidents, it was apparent to many leadership analysts that a more involved, nuanced approach was required if political psychological techniques were to provide a more nuanced portrait of leaders (Winter et al., 1991; Hermann & Preston, 1994, 1998; Preston, 2001). Indeed, while Barber's later book achieved the most notoriety, many see his book *The Lawmakers* (1965), which explored the motivations for Connecticut legislators running for office in the first place (i.e., making laws, doing their public service, etc.) and how these shaped their legislative behaviors and styles once in office, as being a superior approach to looking at leaders than his later typology. In fact, similar relationships between motivation for leadership and political behavior have also been found in a study of Middle Eastern revolutionaries (Winter, 2011).

Looking at other traits, Etheredge (1978), in a study of twentieth-century U.S. presidents and foreign policy advisers, noted the importance of traits such as dominance, interpersonal trust, self-esteem, and introversion-extroversion in shaping policy maker views and policy preferences. American leaders scoring high on measures of dominance tended to favor using force to settle disputes with the Soviet Union over the use of arbitration or disarmament. Moreover, leaders scoring high on introversion tended to oppose cooperation, while extroverted ones generally supported cooperation and negotiation with the Soviets. These results built upon earlier studies reported by Etheredge of over two hundred male U.S. foreign service officers, military officers, and domestic affairs specialists, where those who scored high on traits of dominance and competitiveness were more likely to advocate the use of force and to see the Soviet Union as threatening, while those high on interpersonal trust and self-esteem tended to hold a more benign view of the Soviets and to oppose the use of force (Winter, 2003). Other significant work in applying traits to political leaders has been done by Weintraub (1981, 1986, 1989), in his studies of U.S. presidential press conference responses, and by M. Hermann (1984, 1987, 1988) in her studies of the foreign policy orientations of world leaders.

Leaders' Characteristics: Motives and Traits

A wealth of research also exists surrounding the impact that various individual characteristics of leaders have upon their styles of decision making, interpersonal interactions, information processing, or management behaviors in office (cf., Stogdill & Bass, 1981; Hermann, 1980a, 1980b, 1983, 1984, 1987; Vertzberger, 1990; Winter et al., 1991; Hermann & Preston, 1994, 1998; Preston & 't Hart, 1999; Mitchell, 2005; Preston, 2001, 2011). In Chapter 5, ample illustrations of leader characteristics and decision-making patterns will be presented. Table 2.2 provides basic descriptions of several of the most important leader characteristics, along with the measurement techniques discussed.[4]

A few brief illustrations of several of these individual characteristics (power, complexity, expertise) should provide the reader with a clearer understanding of how these measures tend to be thought of in the literature.

The need for power (or dominance) is a personality characteristic which has been extensively studied and linked to specific types of behavior and interactional styles with others (Browning & Jacob, 1964; Winter, 1973, 1987; Winter & Stewart, 1977; Hermann, 1987; McClelland, 1975; House, 1990). Specifically, one would expect leaders with progressively higher psychological needs for power to be increasingly dominant and assertive in their leadership styles in office and to assert greater control over subordinates and policy decisions. For example, Fodor and Smith (1982, pp. 178–185) found that leaders high in need for power were more associated with the suppression of open decision making and discussion within groups than were low power leaders. Similarly, a number of studies have found high power leaders requiring a far greater degree of personal control than do low power leaders over the policy process and the actions of subordinates (Winter,

Table 2.2 Descriptions of Selected Individual Characteristics

Need for Power	Concern with establishing, maintaining, or restoring one's power (i.e., one's impact, control, or influence over others).
Locus of Control	View of the world in which an individual does or does not perceive some degree of control over situations he/she is involved in and whether government can influence what happens in or to the nation.
Ethnocentrism	View of the world in which one's own nation holds center stage; strong emotional ties to one's own nation; emphasis on national honor and identity.
Need for Affiliation	Concern with establishing, maintaining, or restoring warm and friendly relationships with other persons or groups.
Cognitive Complexity	Ability to differentiate the environment: Degree of differentiation person shows in describing or discussing other people, places, policies, ideas, or things.
Distrust of Others	General feeling of doubt, uneasiness, and misgiving about others; inclination to suspect and doubt others' motives and actions.
Self-Confidence	Person's sense of self-importance or image of his/her ability to cope with the environment.
Task-Interpersonal Emphasis	Relative emphasis in interactions with others on getting the task done versus focusing on feelings and needs of others.

1973, 1987; Etheredge, 1978). In terms of interpersonal relationships, studies have also found that leaders high in the need for power exhibit more controlling, domineering behavior towards subordinates than low power leaders (Browning & Jacob, 1964; Winter & Stewart, 1977; Fodor & Farrow, 1979; McClelland, 1985).

The cognitive complexity of decision makers is another individual characteristic that has long been argued to have a significant impact upon the nature of decision making, style of leadership, assessment of risk, and character of general information processing within decision groups (Driver, 1977; Stewart, Hermann, & Hermann, 1989; Tetlock, 1985; Wallace & Suedfeld, 1988; Hermann, 1980b, 1987; Vertzberger, 1990; Preston, 2001). For example, Vertzberger (1990, p. 134), among others, has noted that as the cognitive complexity of individual decision makers increases, they become more capable of dealing with complex decision environments and information that demand new or subtle distinctions. When making decisions, complex individuals tend to have greater cognitive need for information, are more attentive to incoming information, prefer systematic over heuristic processing, and deal with any overload of information better than their less complex counterparts (Schroder, Driver, & Streufert, 1967; Nydegger,

1975). In terms of interactions with advisers and the acceptance of critical feedback, several studies have shown that complex individuals are far more interested in receiving negative feedback from others—and are more likely to incorporate it into their own decision making—than are those who are less complex (Nydegger, 1975; Ziller et al., 1977). Indeed, Vertzberger (1990, p. 173) and Glad (1983, p. 38) have both noted that low complexity individuals tend to show symptoms of dogmatism, view and judge issues in black-and-white terms, ignore information threatening their existing closed belief systems, and have limited ability to adjust their beliefs to new information.

Complexity has also been linked to how attentive or sensitive leaders are to information from (or to nuances from within) their surrounding political or policy environments (Hermann, 1984; Preston, 1997, 2001). In fact, Hermann (1984, pp. 54–64) notes that the more sensitive the individual is to information from the decision environment, the more receptive the leader is to information regarding the views of colleagues or constituents, the views of outside actors, and the value of alternative viewpoints and discrepant information. In contrast, leaders with a low sensitivity to contextual information will be less receptive to information from the outside environment, will operate from a previously established and strongly held set of beliefs, will selectively perceive and process incoming information in order to support or bolster this prior framework, and will be unreceptive or close-minded towards alternative viewpoints and discrepant information. This is closely correlated with the degree to which individuals are *high versus low self-monitors*—i.e., those focusing upon and taking cues from their external environment when interacting with others as opposed to those who ignore such cues in order to "be who they are" (Snyder, 1987; Gangestad & Snyder, 2000; Day et al., 2002). Self-monitoring involves having one's antennae up to pick up on and be responsive to social situations, and it has been found to be related to being high in complexity (Preston, 2001, 2011).

In contrast, the **integrative complexity** literature differs slightly from the cognitive complexity literature discussed above in that it focuses upon both *differentiation* (which involves evaluatively distinct dimensions of a problem taken into account by decision makers) and *integration* (which involves the connections made by decision makers among differentiated characteristics), whereas the general complexity literature focuses principally upon differentiation alone (Tetlock, 1983). For example, according to Tetlock and Tyler (1996), integrative complexity presupposes a dialectical point-counterpoint style of thinking in which the speaker recognizes the legitimacy of contradictory points of view and then integrates those evaluatively differentiated cognitions into a higher-order synthesis. The concept of cognitive complexity, by contrast, requires merely that one have many distinct ideas or thoughts on a subject, not that those cognitions be in tension with each other or be organized into higher-order schemata or knowledge structures. For example, one could be cognitively complex by generating lots of reasons why one is right and one's adversaries are wrong, but still be integratively simple (p. 166).

In terms of impact on leaders, Suedfeld and Rank (1976) observed that successful revolutionary leaders needed the low complexity associated with single-mindedness to be successful, but those with this characteristic later found it difficult to govern after their successful revolutions since governing requires more "graduated, flexible, and integrated" views of the world (Suedfeld & Rank, 1976, p. 169). Indeed, it was only the revolutionary leaders who later showed a significant increase in their integrative complexity who found success in governing.

Finally, the **prior policy experience or expertise** of leaders has a significant impact upon presidential style, the nature of advisory group interactions, and how forcefully leaders assert their own positions on policy issues (cf., Barber, 1972; George, 1980; Hermann, 1986; House, 1990). Past experience provides leaders with a sense of what actions will be effective or ineffective in specific policy situations, as well as, which cues from the environment should be attended to and which are irrelevant (Hermann, 1986, p. 178). It influences how much learning must be accomplished on the job, the inventory of behaviors (standard operating procedures) possessed, and how confident the leader will be in interactions with experts. Leaders with a high degree of prior policy experience are more likely to insist upon personal involvement or control over policy making than are those low in prior policy experience, who will tend to be more dependent upon the views of expert advisers. Indeed, experienced leaders who have expertise in a policy area are far less likely to rely upon the views of advisers or utilize simplistic stereotypes or analogies to understand policy situations. Such leaders are more interested in gathering detailed information from the policy environment, and they employ a more deliberate decision process than their less experienced counterparts. Similarly, leaders lacking experience or expertise find themselves far more dependent upon expert advisers and more likely to utilize simplistic stereotypes and analogies when making decisions (see Khong, 1992; Levy, 1994; Preston, 2001). Knowing whether a leader is approaching foreign or domestic policy as a relative expert or novice provides insight into predicting how damaging such reliance upon analogy might be to a particular leader's information-management and information-processing styles. This individual characteristic is similar to George's (1980) *sense of efficacy*.

A major pioneer of modern leadership studies, Margaret G. Hermann (1983, 1984, 1986, 1999a, 2001) has led the way forward through her development of a rigorous leader assessment-at-a-distance technique and a huge body of path-breaking research that has explored many facets of how leaders shape and affect foreign policy. Not only has her **Leader Trait Assessment (LTA)** content-analytic technique become the most widely utilized and empirically rich of the existing approaches to leadership analysis, Hermann's work spawned the original development of the computer-based, expert system, Profiler-Plus, developed by Social Science Automation, a company co-founded by Hermann and Michael Young. Profiler-Plus' ability to code millions of words of text systematically with ease, create massive data bases of world leaders, and run comparisons across leaders, their characteristics, and a wide-range of other leadership dimensions has led to Hermann's work resulting not only a large academic literature, but to being widely used throughout the U.S. government by the practitioner community.

The LTA approach uses the spontaneous interview responses of leaders to code for seven specific individual characteristics: need for power, conceptual complexity, task versus interpersonal focus, self-confidence, locus of control, distrust of others, and ethnocentrism (Hermann 1999b). All available materials from interviews, press conference Q&A's across every issue area and across time are coded by Profiler-Plus, generating overall scores for each leader broken down by characteristic, audience, topic, and time period. This system not only has 100% intercoder reliability and removes the subjectivity so often associated with profiling techniques coded by hand, it also allows for the comparison of leader scores against a norming population of over 250 other world leaders. These comparisons can also be made within groups of leaders within a country or across a given region.

Moreover, there has been a great deal of empirical research that has actually provided support for the behavioral correlates that are linked by Hermann's approach to given leader scores. For example, Preston (2001) and Dyson and Preston (2006) profiled modern U.S. Presidents and British Prime Ministers respectively, and then compared the theoretical expectations for given LTA scores (given the psychological literatures) with the leaders' actual behavior across foreign policy cases using archival materials (i.e., their need for personal involvement/control, need for information, structuring/use of advisory systems, etc.). Similarly, in her study of sub-Saharan African leaders, Hermann (1987) found that unlike the styles of Western political leaders, who generally tend to emphasize task completion in office, her profiled African leaders emphasized constituent morale over task accomplishment. At the same time, however, Hermann's study also found substantial variability across the individual characteristics scores of these African leaders, meaning there was no single style type for sub-Saharan African leaders and illustrating the need to study each in depth and in context in order to predict their foreign policy behavior. Interestingly, across this broad leadership literature, Hermann and Preston (1994, p. 81) note that there are five main types of leadership variables that appear to be routinely identified as having an impact upon the style of leaders and their subsequent structuring and use of advisory systems: 1) leader involvement in the policy-making process; 2) leader willingness to tolerate conflict; 3) leader's motivation or reason for leading; 4) leader's preferred strategies for managing information; and 5) leader's preferred strategies for resolving conflict. Across Hermann and her colleagues' work, these variables have increasingly been the focus of their research.

Other studies applying Hermann's LTA approach have looked at U.N. Secretaries General (Kille, 2006), Iranian leaders (Taysi & Preston, 2001), European prime ministers (Karrbo & Hermann, 1998), sub-Saharan African leaders (Hermann, 1987), President Assad of Syria (Hermann, 1988); Soviet leaders (Winter et al., 1991), Irish nationalist leaders (Mastors, 2000), Indian prime ministers (Mitchell, 2007), Saddam Hussein and Bill Clinton (Hermann, 2006); the impact of leader characteristics upon bureaucratic and group dynamics (Stewart et al., 1989; Preston & 't Hart, 1999), leader selection and socialization dynamics (Hermann, 1979), democratic peace theory (Hermann & Kegley, 1995), use of analogy in decision making (Dyson & Preston, 2006), and leader management of crisis contexts (Preston, 2008; Boin et al., 2010). Across all of these studies, the differences in leader characteristics and styles have been shown to have substantial foreign policy impacts. Thus, while there are many fine assessment-at-a-distance techniques available (i.e., Winter's motive assessment, Suedfeld's integrative complexity, George and Walker's operational code, etc.), LTA is still the most rigorous and well-tested of current profiling techniques (due to its decades long track record of research, meticulous empirical work validating its links to actual behavior, and the sophisticated nature of its automation into the Profiler-Plus expert system).

Operational Code

A final approach to studying characteristics of political leaders to be presented in this chapter are studies of *operational codes*, a concept originally introduced by Leites (1951, 1953) in his study of the ideology and belief structures of the Soviet Bolsheviks. His work was later modified and stripped of its psychoanalytic elements by Alexander George (1969), who reconceptualized the operational code (as illustrated in Table 2.3) to represent the answers to ten questions centering around a leader's *philosophical beliefs* (what the nature of the political universe is) and *instrumental beliefs* (what are believed to be the best strategies and tactics for achieving goals). Operational codes are constructs representing the overall belief systems of leaders about the world (i.e., how it works, what it is like, what kinds of actions are most likely to be successful, etc.) (George, 1969, 1979; Holsti, 1977; Walker, 1983; Walker, Schafer, & Young, 1998; Malici & Malici, 2005; Walker & Schafer, 2007). Why is the discussion of the operational code in a chapter on personality and not in the next chapter where beliefs are discussed? The explanation is simply that the operational code is unique to the personality of the person under examination and, more importantly, because the operational code links **motivation** (a personality factor) with beliefs. Scholars who use the framework argue that the beliefs it depicts are motivating forces as well as information processing filters.

Table 2.3 Operational Code: Philosophical and Instrumental Beliefs of Leaders

Philosophical Beliefs	Instrumental Beliefs
The fundamental nature of politics and political conflict, and the image of the opponent;	The best approach for selecting goals for political action;
The general prospects for achieving one's fundamental political values;	How such goals and objectives can be pursued most effectively;
The extent to which political outcomes are predictable;	The best approach to calculation, control, and acceptance of the risks of political action;
The extent to which political leaders can influence historical developments and control outcomes;	The matter of "timing" of action;
The role of chance.	The utility and role of different means for advancing one's interests.

Note: From George, A. L. (1979). The causal nexus between cognitive beliefs and decision making behavior. In L. Falkowski (Ed.), *Psychological models in international politics* (p. 100). Boulder, CO: Westview.

As George (1979, p. 99) observed, operational code beliefs, unlike attitudes, represent central beliefs which "are concerned with fundamental, unchanging issues of politics and political action." By understanding the operational codes of leaders, scholars employing this technique argue that a better understanding of their likely decision-making styles and political behavior is gained. Operational codes are constructed either quantitatively or qualitatively through an examination of decision makers' speeches, interviews, writings, and other verbal or written materials. This technique has a long history of use in political science and been used to examine a wide range of political leaders. Moreover, an automated coding scheme for the operational code, *Verbs in Context* (or VICS), employing the Profiler-Plus computer program, has resulted in a dramatic increase in the use of operational code to assess the world. Though at times lacking the qualitative richness of traditional Georgian op-code case study analysis, the VICs op-codes substitute quantitative rigor and the ability to code massive amounts of material across leaders with relative ease. Included within this operational code literature are studies of a wide range of political leaders, including John Foster Dulles (Holsti, 1970; Stuart & Starr, 1981), John F. Kennedy (Stuart & Starr, 1981; Marfleet, 2000), Henry Kissinger (Walker, 1977; Stuart & Starr, 1981), Woodrow Wilson (Walker, 1995), Jimmy Carter (Walker et al., 1998), U.S. Presidents and Secretaries of State (Walker & Falkowski, 1984), Vladimir Putin (Dyson, 2001), and a large cross-section of world leaders (Shafer & Walker, 2006).

For example, in the case of President Vladimir Putin of Russia, an operational code analysis conducted by Stephen Dyson (2001, pp. 334–339) suggests that with regard to the five basic questions surrounding *philosophical beliefs*, Putin would: (1) view political life as harmonious to the extent that it was governed and regulated by laws, rules, and norms; (2) believe that one can be optimistic about making progress towards one's goals as long as the rule of law is enforced, but that anarchy and corruption will reign in its absence; (3) believe that the political future is predictable to the extent that one can rely upon the existence of enforced rules and norms; (4) believe that it is possible to achieve very little direct control over history, but that one's own environment and circumstances can be affected by engaging in an incremental, step-by-step approach; and (5) view chance as something to be avoided as much as possible through good organization and organizational planning. In terms of his five basic *instrumental beliefs*, Putin is argued to believe that: (1) the goals and objectives set for political action should be both achievable and measurable; (2) the best strategy for pursuing goals is to engage in an incremental, backward-mapping approach, planned step-by-step to stay within the norms of expected behavior; (3) political risk can be controlled by keeping a low political profile on his part while working behind-the-scenes; (4) the best timing of political action is one that preempts major difficulties, but does not occur so early as to cause difficulties itself; and (5) the prime tools of political interest advancement are incremental backward-mapping and flexibility on the leader's part (Dyson, 2001, pp. 339–343). Thus, Putin's op code suggest a leader who is incremental by nature, who judges the acceptability of actions by their chances of success, who sees adherence to norms as essential, and who views those who step outside of such norms as requiring reciprocal or violent treatment (Dyson, 2001, p. 343).

The value of such op codes in predicting the likely pattern of leader behavior given the answers to these basic philosophical and instrumental questions is potentially quite high and of great value to policy makers. For example, in summarizing the findings of the Putin op code, Dyson (2001) makes a number of potentially important observations regarding the predictability of certain patterns of behavior on the Russian leader's part:

> Putin's central belief in the harmony of political life when governed by rules and norms suggests a reciprocal, *quid pro quo* approach. Putin is unlikely to be impressed by unexpectedly bold or unconventional initiatives. His belief in the necessity of selecting goals which are both achievable and measurable, along with his personal propensity to "backward-map" a "step-by-step" approach towards an objective, suggests that agreements of an incremental design appeal to him . . . Putin's Operational Code suggests he will, chameleon-like, imitate his environment. One could not expect Putin to act in a norm-bound manner when those with which he is engaged do not. Putin is unlikely to "stick to the rules" in the face of deviation by another . . . instead, departure from agreed norms of behavior will in all probability entail a decisive break—an "all bets are off" attitude from Putin . . . [his] beliefs about political life . . . disposes him to prefer to retain a certain flexibility and freedom to maneuver. A recommendation would therefore be to design agreements and the like with clearly set out rules and schedules, but many "points of exit" for either side . . . [He] is unlikely to want to be tied to great statements of intent. Platitudes and vagaries can be expected from him, he will attempt to maintain a low profile until a clear "success" compels him to take political credit . . . Overall, the policymaker can feel confident that carefully constructed initiatives will not be dismissed out of hand, and that Putin is unlikely to make rash, impulsive or emotional gestures . . . However, the policymaker can feel warned that Putin will reciprocate "bad" as well as "good" behavior, and that a break down in co-operation will likely be quite bitter and long-lived.
>
> (p. 344)

CONCLUSION

This chapter has reviewed some of the major theoretical approaches to the study of personality in psychology, but only those that have been used in political psychology. There are many additional psychological theories of personality that have not been mentioned in this chapter. In addition, the chapter presented a review of some of the frameworks in political psychology that have been used to analyze personality and leadership in politics. In this chapter we have said little about the average person, as opposed to political leaders, because most of the personality-based studies in political psychology are of political leaders. Analyses of the political psychology of the average person are important and will be explored in Chapter 6 in this book. However, the concepts and theories used are those to be found in the next chapter, where we look at cognition and attitudes.

Topics, Theories/Explanations, and Concepts in Chapter 2

Topics	Theories/ Explanations and Frameworks	Concepts
Personality Greenstein's (1969) three factors determining whether personality is important or not	Individual Differences Psychoanalytic approaches	Context Id, ego, superego
	Disorders	Narcissism Neuroticism
Psychobiographies		
Traits	Big Five Personality Traits	Neuroticism, extraversion, agreeableness, openness to experience, conscientiousness
Motivations		Power, affiliation, achievement
Behavioral genetics Authoritarian personality		
Leadership Frameworks	Barber's (1972) typology of presidential character	Active/negative; passive/positive
	Operational code	Philosophical/ Instrumental beliefs
	Hermann's Leader Assessment at a Distance	
	Leader Traits	Need for power, locus of control, ethnocentrism, need for affiliation, conceptual complexity, distrust, self confidence

Key Terms

achievement motive
affiliation-intimacy motive
agreeableness
authoritarian personality
behavioral genetics
Big Five
cognitive complexity
conscientiousness

neurotic anxiety
neuroticism
openness
operational codes
paranoia
pleasure principle
power motive
projection

defense mechanisms	psychoanalytic or
denial	psychodynamic theories
ego	rationalization
ethnocentrism	reality principle
extroversion	repression
id	right wing
locus of control	authoritarianism
motives	superego
need for achievement	task-interpersonal emphasis
need for affiliation-intimacy	traits
need for power	unconscious

Suggestions for Further Reading

Altemeyer, B. (1996). *The authoritarian specter*. Cambridge, MA: Harvard University Press.

American Psychiatric Association. (2000). *Diagnostic and statistical manual of mental disorders: DSM-IV-TR*. Washington, DC: Author.

Ewen, R. (1998). *An introduction to theories of personality* (5th ed.). Mahwah, NJ: Lawrence Erlbaum Associates.

Feldman, O., & Valenty, L. (Eds.). (2001). *Profiling political leaders: Cross-cultural studies of personality and behavior*. Westport, CT: Praeger.

George, A. L., & George, J. L. (1964). *Woodrow Wilson and Colonel House: A personality study*. New York: Dover.

George, A. L., & George, J. L. (1998). *Presidential personality and performance*. Boulder, CO: Westview Press.

Greenstein, F. I. (1969). *Personality and politics: Problems of evidence, inference, and conceptualization*. Chicago, IL: Markham.

Maddi, S. R. (1996). *Personality theories: A comparative analysis* (6th ed.). Washington: Brooks/Cole.

Magnavita, J. (2002). *Theories of personality: Contemporary approaches to the science of personality*. New York: John Wiley and Sons.

Post, J. M. (Ed.). (2003). *The psychological assessment of political leaders*. Ann Arbor: University of Michigan Press.

Robins, R. S., & Post, J. (1997). *Political paranoia: The psychopolitics of hatred*. New Haven, CT: Yale University Press.

Smith, C., Atkinson, J., McClelland, D., & Veroff, J. (Eds.). (1992). *Motivation and personality: Handbook of thematic content analysis*. Cambridge: Cambridge University Press.

Notes

1. For a critique of psychobiographical method and a discussion of challenges faced by researchers who employ this methodology, see George and George (1998) and Greenstein (1969).
2. Other well-known studies of political leaders relying upon psychobiography with some elements of psychoanalytic analysis include those exploring the personalities of former U.S. Secretary of Defense James Forrestal (Rogow, 1963); Vladimir Lenin, Leon Trotsky, and Mahatma

Gandhi (Wolfenstein, 1971); John F. Kennedy (Mongar, 1974); former U.S. Secretary of State Henry Kissinger (Isaak, 1975); Richard Nixon (Brodie, 1981); Jimmy Carter (Glad, 1980; Hargrove, 1988); Ronald Reagan (Glad, 1989); Iraqi President Saddam Hussein (Post, 1991, 1993a); Josef Stalin (Birt, 1993); and Bill Clinton (Renshon, 1996). Some of these psychobiographies focus upon Freudian notions of ego-defense (e.g., Glad, 1980; Link & Glad, 1994; Hargrove, 1988; Renshon, 1996), whereas others concentrate upon specific kinds of personality disorders in these leaders, ranging from narcissism to paranoid personality disorders (e.g., Volkan, 1980; Post, 1991, 1993b; Birt, 1993).

3. Examples of leader studies using Winter's motive scoring technique (which looks at power, achievement and affiliation) includes: Richard Nixon (Winter & Carlson, 1988), U.S. Presidents (Winter, 1987); African political leaders (Winter, 1980), and Mikhail Gorbachev (Winter, Hermann, Weintraub, & Walker, 1991). For a more detailed discussion of motives and various coding techniques surrounding them, see Smith, Atkinson, McClelland, and Veroff's (1992) volume, *Motivation and Personality: Handbook of Thematic Content Analysis*, published by Cambridge University Press.

4. Among the political psychology or psychological studies that have focused upon either the traits themselves or how they relate to leaders have been ones examining personal needs for power (Winter, 1973, 1987; McClelland, 1975; Etheredge, 1978; Hermann, 1984, 1987; House, 1990), personal needs for affiliation (Browning & Jacob, 1964; Winter & Stewart, 1977; McClelland & Boyatzis, 1982; Winter, 1987), conceptual complexity (Suedfeld & Rank, 1976; Suedfeld & Tetlock, 1977; Driver, 1977; Tetlock, 1985; Hermann, 1984, 1987), locus of control (Rotter, 1966; Davis & Phares, 1967; Hermann, 1984, 1987), achievement or task/interpersonal emphasis (Bales, 1951; Bass, 1981; Byars, 1972, 1973; Winter & Stewart, 1977; Rowe & Mason, 1987; Hermann, 1987; Nutt, 1990), ethnocentrism (Levin & Campbell, 1972; Glad, 1983), and self-confidence (Hermann, 1987; House, 1990; Winter et al., 1991). For a more detailed discussion of these traits, see M.G. Hermann (1999) and Smith, Atkinson, McClelland, and Veroff (1992).

Chapter 3

COGNITION, SOCIAL IDENTITY, EMOTIONS, AND ATTITUDES IN POLITICAL PSYCHOLOGY

This chapter explores how individuals make sense of others and themselves in the context of political issues, choices, and conflict. How do people understand the political world? How do they interpret information and make decisions? How organized are their thoughts? How do emotions affect thoughts and actions in politics? This chapter reflects the thinking and feeling portions of the Political Being's mind: cognition, emotion, social identity, and attitudes and beliefs. We examine a number of ideas about how people process political information, the psychological techniques and mechanisms used to understand others and the environment in which they live, the importance of the groups to which people belong, and how people regard those groups they do not belong to. In addition, we explore the importance of emotion in politics, as well as in political attitudes. A number of concepts are introduced, including cognition, cognitive categories and schemas, social identity, images, affect and emotion, and attitudes. These concepts are tied to different kinds of political behavior in this chapter and are detailed in the chapters that follow.

Once again, the depiction of the Political Being in this chapter highlights the concepts that are covered here, and does so in a way that layers them. Attitudes and cognitive processes are at the top of consciousness: these are things we are well aware of, and they are important in information processing and everyday decision making. Values and social identities are deeper. We have to think harder to figure out how they affect our behavior. Emotions saturate the mind and influence the entire process of deciding how to act politically. In addition, more detail is provided on the *us* and *them* portions of the Political Being's environment.

We proceed with building blocks. First, we examine the thinking part of the Political Being. We begin with the topic of information processing and the limits people have in their abilities to process information. In doing so, we introduce two theoretical areas that provide insights into the patterns and causes of patterns in human information processing: attribution theory and consistency theories. Next, we turn to the question of how people make sense of the world they live in, through a process called cognitive categorization. In examining cognitive categorization, we discuss how people organize and simplify the complex social and political world in which they live, and we introduce the related notion of a stereotype. Next, we proceed to social identity theory, which provides us with information concerning how people see the groups that they belong to and those that they do not belong to—in-groups and out-groups. After that, we introduce a model of categories of other political actors—the political equivalent of out-groups—called image theory.

From here, we turn to the emotional part of the Political Being and look at emotions in politics. This is a relatively new area of political psychological research, but it is very important, because of the power of emotions in politically motivated violence and other patterns of behavior. After discussing emotions, we discuss attitudes, which combine emotion and thinking about politics. Our goal for this chapter is to introduce a wide range of central political psychological concepts regarding thinking and feeling about politics and the behavioral predispositions that result. These concepts are used throughout the rest of the book, as we look at different kinds of political behavior.

Let us begin with some puzzles. First, people need to understand the world around them, and particularly the people in that world so that they can understand and know what to expect. Perceivers need to explain and predict the behavior of others. In order to do this, they need to process incoming information from their environments and evaluate it. People like to think that they are good at processing information. We assume that we recognize and evaluate important information and that we store it in memory quite accurately. This is not always correct. Consider the following example.

In the criminal justice system, eyewitness testimony is commonly accepted as both notoriously inaccurate and also as having a strong impact on juries. As Loftus (1979) explains:

> Before a witness can recall a complex incident, the incident must be accurately perceived at the outset; it must be stored in memory. Before it can be stored, it must be within a witness's perceptual range, which means that it must be loud enough and close enough so that the ordinary senses pick it up. If visual details are to be perceived, the situation must be reasonably well illuminated. Before some information can be recalled, a witness must have paid attention to it. But even though an event is bright enough, loud enough, and close enough, and even though attention is being paid, we can still find significant errors in a witness's recollection of the event, and it is common for two witnesses to the same event to recall it very differently.
>
> (p. 22)

Second, people tend to see what they expect to see. They fit incoming information into the ideas or beliefs they already hold to be true, and they typically do not recognize that they do this. Discrepant information is often not noticed or rejected as incorrect. This is known as the *misinformation effect*, which occurs when someone incorporates misinformation into their memory of the event after receiving misleading information about it (Loftus, 1979, 2001). Consider some examples from the battlefields of World War II:

Common also are cases of outright refusal to believe reports that contradict a firm belief. . . . When Hermann Göring was informed that an Allied fighter has been shot down over Aachen, thus proving that the Allies had produced a long-range fighter that could protect bombers over Germany, he told the pilot who had commanded the German planes in the engagement: "I'm an experienced fighter pilot myself. I know what is possible. But I know what isn't too. . . . I officially assert that American fighter planes did not reach Aachen. . . . I herewith give you an official order that they weren't there." Similarly, when the secretary of the navy was told of the Japanese attack on Pearl Harbor, he said, "My God, this can't be true. This [message] must mean the Philippines." It is not without significance that the common reaction is not that the report is incorrect, but that it must be incorrect.

(Jervis, 1976, pp. 144–145)

These examples illustrate several important topics that we begin with in this chapter. The eyewitness testimony example shows important instances in which people do not process or remember information very well. People are sometimes imperfect information processors, and of course this will affect their processing, evaluation, and retention of political information, just like any other kind of information. Second, people do not process information on a tabula rasa. They have certain psychological mechanisms that facilitate the processing of information.

In psychology, the concept of cognition is central to understanding how people process information and understand the world around them. Cognition is "a collective term for the psychological processes involved in the acquisition, organization, and the use of knowledge" (Bullock & Stallybrass, 1977, p. 109). The knowledge is organized in our minds in a cognitive system. For example, our knowledge of birds might be organized as follows: birds have wings, feathers, and beaks; they use the wings to fly; they eat insects or seeds and are eaten by people. The terms *beliefs* or *attitudes* are often used to describe these components of the cognitive system. **Beliefs** are associations people create between an object and its attributes (Eagly & Chaiken, 1998). We believe that birds have wings and that Democrats are liberal. **Cognitive processes** refers to what happens in the mind while people move from observation of a stimulus to a response to that stimulus. Cognitive processes include everything from perception, memory, attention, and problem solving to information processing, language, thinking, and imagery. Let us turn first to cognitive processes involved with the acquisition of information from the environment and its evaluation.

INFORMATION PROCESSING

People are bombarded with vast amounts of information all the time. They cannot attend to all of it, and the mind has developed techniques for deciding what information is important and relevant and what information can be ignored. Several theories in psychology address patterns of information processing and provide explanations for different propensities in attending to and interpreting information. One theoretical perspective in psychology that focuses on how people judge and evaluate others is **attribution theory**. One of the earliest attribution theorists was Heider (1958), along with Jones and Davis (1965), Kelley (1967), and Weiner (1986). Attribution theorists also have a number of insights into information processing. They argue that people process information as though they are "naïve scientists," that is, they search for cause in the behavior of others, just as scientists search for the cause of a disease. However, people often do not properly employ the scientific method, and they tend to make a number of errors in this quest for the cause of others' behavior. Attribution theorists argue that individuals use **heuristics**, which are mental shortcuts, in processing information about others. Among the most important heuristics is the **availability heuristic**, wherein people predict the likelihood of something based on the ease with which they can think of instances or examples of it (Tversky & Kahneman, 1982)—for example, estimating the distribution of As in a political science class based on how many people you can think of who got As in the class last year.

Imaginability is another aspect of the availability heuristic. Imaginability is the tendency to retrieve information that is plausible without any regard for actual probabilities. As a result, individuals construct a series of possible behaviors based on their ability to imagine their occurrence. More specifically,

> Imaginability plays an important role in the evaluation of probabilities in real life situations. The risk involved in an adventurous expedition, for example, is evaluated by imagining contingencies with which the expedition is not equipped to cope. If many such difficulties are vividly portrayed, the expedition can be made to appear exceedingly dangerous, although the ease with which disasters are imagined need not reflect their likelihood. Conversely, the risk involved in an undertaking may be grossly underestimated if some possible dangers are either difficult to conceive of, or simply do not come to mind.
>
> (Tversky & Kahneman, 1982, pp. 12–13)

Biases can also occur due to the availability of instances. Thus, "when the size of a class is judged by the availability of its instances, a class whose instances are easily retrieved will appear more numerous than a class of equal frequency whose instances are less retrievable" (Tversky & Kahneman, 1982, p. 11).

> This bias is demonstrated by an experiment that used lists of male and female personalities. Individuals were asked whether a list of well-known personalities contained more men than women and they responded positively if the men were better known than the women were (and vice versa).
>
> (Tversky & Kahneman, 1982, p. 11)

This happened even though there were equal numbers of men and women. Increased familiarity made the male names more available, resulting in the bias. Salience is also influential. If you have just finished watching a news program about a local house fire, you will believe your chances of your own house catching fire will be greater.

The **representativeness heuristic** is another common example. This is a probability judgment. A person may, for example, evaluate the characteristics of another person and estimate the likelihood that that person belongs to a particular occupation (Fiske & Taylor, 1991). For example, medical professionals are commonly seen with stethoscopes. If you see someone with a stethoscope, you will assume that it is probable that that person is a medical professional.

Another consequence of the representative heuristic is misrepresentations of chance. A manifestation of this is the gambler's fallacy. This is illustrated by the game of roulette where after a long run of one color—say, black—red is believed to now be due. Thus, "chance is commonly viewed as a self-correcting process in which a deviation in one direction induces a deviation in the opposite direction to restore the equilibrium" (Tversky & Kahneman, 1982, p. 7). If you have ever been gambling, even if you only play the slots, you probably have experience with the gambler's fallacy: You don't leave the machine while losing because losing has to be followed by winning. Finally, another outcome of the representative heuristic is the "law of small numbers"; that is, individuals believe that small samples randomly drawn from a population are representative of the populations from which they are drawn (Tversky & Kahneman, 1982). For example, you meet an international student from a particular country and view him as representative of a larger population. The danger of holding on to such perceptions is that they can skew our perception, beliefs, and attitudes.

Anchoring and adjustment involve how individuals make estimates. Specifically, it refers to when individuals make estimates by starting from an initial value that is adjusted to yield the final answer. "The initial value, or starting point, may be suggested by the formulation of the problem, or it may be the result of partial computation. In either case, adjustments are typically insufficient. Different starting points yield different estimates, which are biased toward the initial values" (Tversky & Kahneman, 1982, p. 14).

In interpreting and evaluating information regarding the cause of behavior of other people, one of the most important aspects of perceptions of causality is whether it is attributed to internal states (personality) or to external forces (situation). People are more likely to attribute others' behavior to their general dispositions (personality traits or attitudes) than to the situation they are in. This is known as the **fundamental attribution error** (Ross, 1977). A study by Jones and Harris (1967) provides a clear illustration of the fundamental attribution error. Participants in that study were asked to read essays about a controversial topic—Cuba under the rule of Fidel Castro. Participants were either told that the essay writer had freely chosen to take a pro-Castro or anti-Castro position or that the essay writer had been assigned a particular essay position. Even when the essay writer was assigned the position, participants overestimated the role of internal dispositions (the writer's true position on Castro) and underestimated the role of the situation (lack of choice about which position to take), when asked to explain the position taken in the essay.

The fundamental attribution error is the most recognized, but we have others as well. For example, the **positivity effect** is the tendency to attribute positive behaviors to dispositional factors and negative behaviors to situational factors with individuals we like (Plous, 1993). When dealing with individuals we dislike, we tend to do the opposite; that is, attribute behavior to dispositional rather than situational factors (Plous, 1993). This is the **negativity effect**. There are numerous other biases identified in the literature. For example, the **self-serving bias** is when individuals are more likely to take responsibility for successes than failures (Plous, 1993). The **egocentric bias** is the tendency of individuals to accept more responsibility for joint outcomes than others attribute to them (Plous, 1993). The **confirmation bias** is seen when individuals tend to favor information that confirms already-existing beliefs. The **hindsight bias** is commonly described as "I knew it all along." Another bias is referred to as **childish games**. This occurs when individuals communicate something to another person that is familiar and meaningful to them, but not to the person communicated with (Pronin, Puccio, & Ross, 2002).

Another set of theories that contributes to our understanding of information processing comes under the general category of consistency theories. One of the earliest consistency theories was Heider's (1946, 1958) balance theory, which posits that people try to keep the components of the cognitive system in balance. He described **balance** as "a harmonious state, one in which the entities comprising the situation and the feelings about them fit together without stress" (Heider, 1958, p. 180). In other words, people want to see their environment, the people in it, and their feelings about it as a coherent, consistent picture. For example, if you consider yourself a responsible and serious student, you would not neglect your studies and go out partying with your friends the night before an exam. If you did, the cognitive system representing your knowledge about yourself would be out of balance, and you would try to change it. Partying, rather than studying the night before an exam, is not consistent with your self-perception that you are a serious student. A friend of one of the authors presents another example. She is a lifelong liberal Democrat from an eastern city, who advised a politician on his state's education policy. That politician was a Republican. She liked him, found him charming, and was proud that his policies improved education in his state. She would like to vote for him, and she is appalled at herself. How can she, a lifelong liberal Democrat, consider voting for a conservative Republican? That behavior would not be balanced, because it is inconsistent with her political beliefs. To achieve balance, she would either have to vote Democratic, change her ideology and join the Republican Party, or consider this single Republican vote an anomaly.

A related type of consistency pattern is described in dissonance theory, which addresses the inconsistencies between people's attitudes and behaviors (Festinger, 1957). **Dissonance** refers to an aversive state that results when our behavior is inconsistent with our attitudes. Dissonance creates psychological tension, which people feel motivated to avoid through selective attention to information. Once dissonance is experienced, people are motivated to relieve it. For example, suppose you ate a big piece of chocolate cake while you were on a diet. There are at least three ways that people can reduce dissonance: people can change their behavior (in this case that is not possible, because you already ate the cake); people can engage in cognitive strategies, such as trivialization (e.g., "It's not really that bad if I ate a big piece of chocolate cake") or distortions of information (e.g., "Chocolate cake has lots of nutritional value"); or people can change their attitude (e.g.,

"I really don't need to be dieting anyway"). Typically, people reduce dissonance by changing their attitude.

People can live with inconsistency and imbalance, but they would prefer
not to. When inconsistency is extreme, it can be psychologically painful,
for example, as when your significant other and best friend cannot abide
one another. Individuals can avoid inconsistency through information processing, and they can reestablish consistency in their cognitive system by
changing whatever is easiest to change. If our friend's attachment to the
Democratic Party is weaker than her liking for the Republican politician,
she will change parties. If not, she will either vote Democratic or consider
the situation an anomaly (incidentally, she voted for the Democrat, which
is an illustration of the power of political socialization, which we discuss in
Chapter 6).

Vertzberger notes that the drive for consistency occurs on three levels:
within attitudes between affect and cognition (thinking and feeling the
same way); across attitudes; and throughout what he calls the "cognitive
entirety" (1990, p. 137)—that is, attitudes, beliefs, and values. The drive for
consistency affects information processing in a number of ways. First, it
produces selective perception, which includes "selective exposure (seeking
consistent information not already present), selective attention (looking at
consistent information once it is there), and selective interpretation (trans-
lating ambiguous information to be consistent)" (Fiske & Taylor, 1991,
p. 469). Inconsistent information can be ignored, or it can be distorted so
that it appears consistent with attitudes or cognitive categories. Inconsistent behaviors can be compartmentalized so that people refuse to recognize
their own actions as serious. The process of balancing and avoiding inconsistency can also lead to **bolstering**, which involves selective exposure to
information, as people search for information supporting their decisions
and avoid information that would be critical of them. Bolstering also occurs
when people denigrate the alternative not chosen and amplify the attractive
aspects of the decisions they did make. Bolstering occurred in the Kennedy administration, before the Bay of Pigs invasion, when decision makers
convinced themselves that American involvement would remain secret by
avoiding arguments to the contrary. This incident is discussed (in Chapter 4) in the context of groupthink, a group decision making error involving
faulty information processing. President Johnson's decision in 1965 to use
air power in Vietnam shows evidence of bolstering, as well, in his belief that
the air campaign would not have to last long and that the war would end
quickly (George, 1980).

The drive for consistency in information processing has a number of
important political consequences. Accepting only information that conforms with expectations can lead people to miss important information, for
example, about a candidate's stand on a political issue, if that position is
inconsistent with their party's or with the candidate's other issue positions.
Interpreting information so that it conforms to expectations, rather than
to some other possibility, can lead to spiraling conflicts between countries
or political groups. Distorting information in a search for consistency can
produce a failure to recognize the need for value trade-offs in politics. The
avoidance of value trade-offs occurs when people mistakenly believe that
a policy that "contributes to one value . . . also contributes to several other

values, even though there is no reason why the world should be constructed in such a neat and helpful manner" (Jervis, 1976, p. 128). An example comes from the Vietnam War:

> Officials who favored bombing North Vietnam felt that this would: (1) decrease American casualties, (2) drastically increase the cost of the war to the North; (3) increase the chance of the North's entering negotiations, without increasing the danger of Soviet or Chinese intervention. Those who opposed bombing disagreed on all points.
>
> (Jervis, 1976, p. 134)

These patterns are tendencies, not absolutes. They occur often, but not always. People may be aware of, but ignore, inconsistent information, if it is unimportant to them. They may be forced by situational conditions to attend and respond to inconsistent information.

CATEGORIZATION

So far, we have noted that people organize and simplify their environment; they process information about that environment, based on the way they understand it; and they search for causes in the behavior of others. People keep the knowledge that is most useful about an environment, then use it to filter subsequent information. We expect the environment to be consistent and that what we know about it will be repeated. We accept as true information that conforms to our preexisting knowledge and reject as untrue, or irrelevant, information that does not conform. Consequently, the cognitive system helps us filter incoming information. If, for example, your cognitive system of politicians includes the belief that all politicians are dishonest, if you have evidence both confirming and disconfirming that politician Smith has taken a bribe, then you will believe the confirming evidence. But cognitive systems are more than a set of bits of knowledge. They are organized in order to enable people to move through their worlds without thinking too much and yet manage their environments effectively. Cognitive systems help people understand their world. Knowledge about the environment that people live in is organized, simplified, and used to make sense of complex social and physical realities. If we did not organize and simplify the environment, then we would not be able to process all the information available to us and could never make decisions. The world is too complex for our brains to handle. As Allport wrote in 1954:

> The human mind must think with the aid of categories. . . . Once formed, categories are the basis for normal prejudgment. We cannot possibly avoid this process. Orderly living depends upon it. . . . What this means is that our experience in life tends to form itself into clusters . . . and while we may call on the right cluster at the wrong time, or the wrong cluster at the right time, still the process in question dominates our entire mental life. A million events befall us every day. We cannot handle so many events. If we think of them at all, we type

them. . . . Bertrand Russell . . . has summed up the matter in a phrase, "a mind perpetually open will be a mind perpetually vacant."

(pp. 19–20)

People form and use cognitive categories that aid them in their need to process information efficiently. There is no set recipe by which categories are formed. Categories, the attributes or characteristics associated with them, and the beliefs about them, are formed through experience. Rosch (1978) argue that there are two principles involved in category formation. First, categories must provide the perceiver with a large amount of information with as little mental effort as possible. People need categories that enable them to discern and understand the world around them, but that also allow them to reduce small and irrelevant differences among people and objects. Second, people need categories that are suited to their own social and physical realities. If you live in a high crime, heavily populated urban area, you will need different social categories to understand and deal with people than if you live in a rural area with almost no crime and few people.

One way of looking at this is to think of the way that people organize and simplify their environment as creating a mental model of the environment that emphasizes only the most important points. People form categories of the most important elements of the environment. For example, in the natural world, we think of categories such as dogs, cats, horses, and birds. As we said before, the category of birds is filled with important information about what a bird is and how it behaves. The same is true of the categories of dog, cat, and so on. Of course, some birds are not good fits with the common characteristics associated with birds. Penguins do not fly, but they swim and have scrawny wings that they use like flippers. They do not fit the bird category very well in our minds. The same is true of the human world. We categorize people into groups, such as racial groups (Caucasian, Black, Oriental), ethnic groups (Latino or Hispanic, Italian-American), nationality groups (American, German, Chinese), and religious groups (Christian, Muslim, Jewish). This is to say, we organize the social world in terms of social categories. We all make assumptions about other people, ourselves, and the situations we are in. Sometimes we are very wrong, but often our expectations are functional. The first step in perceiving another person is to classify the person or situation as fitting a familiar category. Once you recognize someone as filling a particular role (e.g., a police officer or a professor) on the basis of particular attributes (uniform, gun, billy club; glasses, briefcase, lecture notes), then you can apply your knowledge about the role to guide the subsequent interaction with that person.

Once a person or situation is classified into a category, people apply organized generic knowledge, in the form of a category or **schema**, to process information about the person or situation and to make decisions about it or them. The terms *cognitive category* and *schema* are often used interchangeably. Psychologists define schema as "a cognitive structure that represents knowledge about a concept or type of stimulus, including its attributes and the relations among those attributes" (Fiske & Taylor, 1991, p. 8).

Stereotypes are a particular type of social cognitive category. The psychological roots of stereotypes, the reasons for their occurrence, and the impact they have on the behavior of those using them and those viewed through them, have been widely studied in psychology and political science (see Fiske, 1998, for a review). Stereotypes are beliefs about the attributes of people in particular groups or social categories, and should be a very familiar concept. Everyone has stereotypes or at least knows about stereotypes of others. Consider, for example, the well-known stereotype of Jewish people, called the anti-Semitic stereotype, which is based on an assumption that a particular group is an overachieving minority, superior in wealth and talent. It is also assumed that they are able to construct complex conspiracies that will increase their material wealth and influence. Finally, they are seen as standoffish, cliquish, and considering themselves to be superior to everyone else (Hunter, 1991). Other people who have been seen through the same stereotype are the Indians and Pakistanis in East Africa, the overseas Chinese in Southeast Asia, the Armenians in the Middle East, and the Ibos in Nigeria. Other stereotypes familiar to most readers denigrate people who are considered inferior. Most Americans are familiar with American racism, which is a result of holding negative stereotypes of African Americans, for example. Stereotypes are not limited to personality trait descriptions (e.g., "Germans are conscientious and hardworking") but can include any personal attribute—physical, affective, visual, or behavioral—that can be seen as characteristic of that group (e.g., "Germans are fair, tall, and rigid"). Stereotyping, as in all social categorization, is a mental short-cut that enables people to know quite a bit about a person or group of persons, whether that knowledge is accurate or not. It occurs quickly and without conscious thought (Fiske, 1998). We discuss social stereotypes in more detail in Chapters 8, 9, and 10.

Discrimination is not an inevitable consequence of stereotyping. Recent research (e.g., Devine & Elliot, 1995) suggests that, even though people possess knowledge of stereotypes, they are not necessarily prejudiced. Only those high in prejudice tend to accept stereotypes about a group of people. A person can have knowledge of stereotypes and not discriminate. For the moment, let us leave it that stereotypes are social categories, and that, when people are evaluated through a stereotype, they often suffer from discrimination. They are assumed to have the characteristics of a stereotype, whether they do or not. Those who hold the stereotype and behave toward that group in a discriminatory fashion are said to be prejudiced.

Once information about a person is noticed, it is classified nominally in terms of what it is about or which category or attitude it is relevant for. If you notice a person who is tall, blond, blue-eyed, and speaks with an accent, you may classify that person in the category "German." The availability heuristic is important in this stage, because information is more likely to be classified in categories that are readily accessible. Hence, you may be more likely to use the German social category if you are in a town with a high percentage of German immigrants. Once this judgment has been made, the information is evaluated in terms of its fit in to the category. If, for example, you walk into a classroom and the professor looks like he is 15 years old, is wearing shorts, a ripped t-shirt, and no shoes, that information about him is not typical of what you expect to see when interacting with a professor. It affects how you regard this particular person in his role as professor: you may think he is not very qualified, because he looks young and dresses like a teenager.

Moreover, when this kind of social judgment is made, it is also influenced by **assimilation** and **contrast** effects. The prototypical example of a social category serves as an anchor or central reference point for incoming information. Information is compared to that anchor and, when it is different from expectations, the contrast effect makes it seem more so. For example, most people would expect a priest to be honest. Learning that a priest has done something objectively moderately dishonest will be interpreted as extremely dishonest, in the context of having been done by someone from whom complete honesty is expected. The assimilation effect produces the opposite perception. Information similar to that which is expected can be perceived as even more similar than it objectively is (Eiser & Stroebe, 1972; Herr, 1986; Manis, Nelson, & Shedler, 1988). The category in which a person, group, or country is placed has yet another effect on information and information processing. Missing information can be supplied by the category or image itself. If you do not know if a person has a particular characteristic, because you do not have the information, then you can guess, based on the social category in which the person is placed (Taylor & Crocker, 1981).

We also categorize the political world. Some scholars argue that we organize the international environment in terms of types of states, such as the enemy or the ally. These cognitive categories are called images, and images function very much like stereotypes. **Image theory** is a political psychological approach that draws connections between policymakers' images of other countries and their resulting behavior (Blanton, 1996; Cottam, 1986, 1994; Cottam, 1977; Herrmann, 1985a, 1985b, 1988, 1991; Herrmann, Voss, Schooler, & Ciarrochi, 1997; Holsti, 1962; Schafer, 1997; Shimko, 1991). **Images** contain information about a country's capabilities, culture, intentions, kinds of decision-making groups (lots of people involved in decision making or only a few), and perceptions of threat or opportunity. Capabilities include economic characteristics, military strength, domestic political stability, and effective policy making and implementation. Cultural attributes consist of judgments of cultural sophistication. When assessing a country, decision makers judge whether its capabilities and culture are equal, inferior, or superior to their own country. Another appraisal is whether the country or group has threatening or defensive (good) intentions or presents an opportunity to achieve an important goal. Lessons of history that policymakers associate with a particular type of state are also included in each image. In other words, leaders use historical incidents to explain a conflict and to make predictions about the outcome of a conflict.

Policymakers also draw upon a variety of policy options, which are measures that they see as appropriate in dealing with a country. Some policy options include military threat, economic sanctions or incentives, and diplomatic protests. The model also proposes that certain tactics are relevant to each image. For example, when decision makers hold the so-called colonial or client image of another country, they consider that country and its people to be inferior in terms of culture and capabilities. They also assume that the people are incompetent and childlike and are ruled by a small elite, who are generally not a threat and who are often corrupt. This image produces behavioral tendencies that are coercive and noncompromising (you do not negotiate with children; you tell them what to do). When an enemy image is held, that country is seen as equal in capability and culture, and threatening in intentions. The enemy is ruled by a small elite, but one that can cleverly strategize policies that will attempt to hurt the perceiver's country. The tactics used in responding to such a state are global in focus, competitive, and noncompromising, because you cannot trust such a country to keep its word.

The ally is perceived as equal in terms of its capability and culture, but also as very similar to your own group in values. The intentions of an ally are believed to be good. Barbarians are superior in capability and inferior in culture. They are also aggressive in intentions, which makes them very frightening. An imperialist country is perceived to be superior in culture and capability, but its intentions can be either harmful or benevolent. Either way, imperialists are a dominating people, and resisting them would be very difficult. The rogue is inferior in capability and culture, but is also very harmful in intentions. This is the bad seed, the irresponsible child, who, it is believed, can and should be punished until it reforms its ways. Last, there is the image of the degenerate. A degenerate may be powerful and culturally advanced, but also undisciplined and lacking the will to follow through on expressed goals and plans of action.

The ways that policymakers make distinctions among these types of images are a matter of their perceptions of the country's capabilities, culture, threat, response alternatives, and event scripts. The images are summarized in Table 3.1.

Although this particular example demonstrates images of other countries used by policymakers in foreign affairs, images are used to organize and guide responses to people's action in any political domain. In fact, Jackson (2001) has gathered impressive data concerning the images used by police officers of the communities in their districts and the patterns of response to crime associated with those images. We return to the discussion of images later, after introducing some additional psychological concepts. Chapters 8, 9, and 10 also contain many examples of how images affect political behavior.

SOCIAL IDENTITY

We classify others into groups, and we classify ourselves into groups, as well. Groups we belong to are called in-groups, and those we do not belong to are out-groups. Conflict among political groups is, of course, a central issue in political psychology. Group conflict and behavior are examined in detail in Chapter 4. Here, we want to consider groups as social categories and as part of the general cognitive organization of the social and political world. Much of the work on the social psychology of intergroup relations has focused on intergroup conflict and discrimination. The seminal research using this approach can be found in Tajfel's (1970) work on intergroup conflict, in which the author speculated that something about group membership alone might stimulate conflict with other relevant groups. He postulated that individuals are likely to act in a discriminatory manner whenever they are in a situation in which intergroup categorization is made salient and relevant.

In other words, whenever individuals find themselves in a situation in which there exists clear evidence of an "us" and a "them," they are likely to

Table 3.1 Images of Cultures

Images	Capability	Culture	Intentions	Decision makers	Threat or opportunity
Enemy	Equal	Equal	Harmful	Small elite	Threat
Barbarian	Superior	Inferior	Harmful	Small elite	Threat
Imperialist	Superior	Superior	Exploitive	A few groups	Threat
Colonial	Inferior	Inferior	Benign	Small elite	Opportunity
Degenerate	Superior or equal	Weak-willed	Harmful	Confused, differentiated	Opportunity
Rogue	Inferior	Inferior	Harmful	Small elite	Threat
Ally	Equal	Equal	Good	Many groups	Threat/opportunity

discriminate against the out-group (them) and in favor of the in-group (us). To test this idea, Tajfel (1970) designed a series of experiments based on the minimal group paradigm, in which individuals are arbitrarily assigned to one of two groups. In one typical experiment, assignment to a group was based on whether individuals tended to overestimate or underestimate a series of dots presented on a screen. Individuals participating in the experiment were then assigned to either the overestimator or underestimator group, presumably on the basis of their estimating tendencies. In reality, this assignment was purely arbitrary; the tendency to over- or underestimate was in no way related to accuracy. This arbitrary assignment procedure proved to be important and necessary, for several reasons. First, it ensured that there was no personal reason for one group to discriminate against the other group. An individual presumably had nothing to gain personally by discriminating against the other group. Second, the procedure ensured that there was no existing hostility between the groups. Prior to categorization, individuals never thought of themselves as being a member of a group that tends to underestimate, or that other individuals are members of a group that overestimate, for example. Further, there was no chance for the groups to interact with one another, thus eliminating any possibility that group members would come to like the in-group or dislike the out-group. Third, such a procedure ensured that individuals had no conflicts of interest. There was nothing inherently valuable about being a member of a group that under- or overestimates.

Following this categorization procedure, individuals were asked to assign rewards and penalties, by allocating small amounts of money to two anonymous group members (see Brewer, 1979; Insko & Schopler, 1987; Turner, 1978, for a review of allocation matrices). To eliminate self-interest as a possible influence, individuals were told that they should not allocate any money to themselves. The results of this experiment showed that, even in this minimal group, the allocation decisions, concerning both an in-group and out-group member, led to in-group favoritism and out-group discrimination. Individuals gave more money to members of their own group than to members of the other group. Thus, even though these individuals were assigned to a group on the basis of unimportant and seemingly meaningless criteria, they still acted in a discriminatory or competitive manner. Providing an explanation for this effect is what led to Tajfel and Turner's (1979, 1986) social identity theory.

According to Tajfel (1978), social identity is "that part of an individual's self-concept which derives from his [her] knowledge of his [her] membership in a social group (groups) together with the value and emotional significance attached to that membership" (p. 63). Tajfel and Turner (1979) summarized this theory with three theoretical principles. First, group members strive to achieve or maintain a sense of positive social identity. Second, group members base this social identity on favorable comparisons that can be made between in-group and relevant out-group members. The social categories or groups of which individuals are members provide individuals with a social identity by enabling them to compare their in-group with relevant out-groups. These comparisons are said to contribute to individuals' self-esteem, because they allow individuals to define the members of their group as being better than other groups. In other words, in an attempt to gain a positive sense of self, individuals compare their group with other groups, to create a favorable distinction between the groups. Third, group members will attempt to leave their group or join a more positively distinct group when their social identity is not satisfactory to them.

Tajfel and Turner (1979) imply that intergroup discrimination is a result of a motivation to evaluate one's own group more positively than a relevant out-group. By comparing one's in-group to a relevant out-group, individuals attempt to differentiate their group from other groups so that their social identity will be enhanced. In addition to the necessary precondition of social categorization into in-group and out-group, Tajfel and Turner (1979) maintained that there are at least three additional variables that should influence intergroup differentiation. First, members of a group must have internalized their group membership as an aspect of their self-concept. In other words, they must clearly perceive themselves as a member of the in-group and be likely to describe themselves as a group member, if asked a question such as: Who are you? Second, the social situation must allow for intergroup comparisons. Group members must be able to make evaluative group comparisons, in order to perceive their in-group as positively distinct from the out-group. Third, the out-group must be perceived as a relevant comparison group. Members of an in-group do not compare their group to any available out-group. Instead, factors such as similarity, proximity, and situational salience determine whether an out-group is considered a valid and reliable comparison group (see Campbell, 1958).

Tajfel (1978) and Tajfel and Turner (1979) also discuss three ways in which individuals might react to threatened or actual negative social identity. Social mobility is the enhancement of positive social identity by advancement to a group of higher status. If an individual's social identity is threatened or is perceived as being negative, the individual will attempt to dissociate him- or herself from the in-group by joining a group that is higher in status. A second reaction to threatened or negative social identity is social creativity, which includes three strategies: (1) comparing the in-group to the out-group on a different dimension; (2) reevaluating the comparison dimension, so that previously negative dimensions are perceived as positive; and (3) comparing one's in-group to a different or lower status out-group. Finally, social competition is another reaction to a threatened or negative social identity. In-group members might directly compete with the out-group to attain positive distinctiveness or positive social identity, or at least with the intention of attaining a positive social identity.

In a review of research that has examined strategies of identity enhancement, van Knippenberg and Ellemers (1990) concluded that the permeability of group boundaries appears to play a key role in determining which strategy is used to enhance social identity. For example, when it is relatively easy for a group member to move to a higher status group, that member is more likely to move to the new group than when it is more difficult to change group memberships.

Much of the research on social identity has tested the original in-group bias effect, that is, whether individuals tend to favor their own group over a relevant out-group, and has shown this to be true (see Brewer, 1979). The arbitrary assignment of individuals to groups has been repeatedly demonstrated to result in preferential reward allocations to in-group members (e.g., Billig & Tajfel, 1973; Tajfel & Billig, 1974), heightened in-group attractiveness (e.g., Rabbie & Wilkins, 1971), perceptions of in-group similarity and homogeneity (e.g., Allen & Wilder, 1979; Linville & Jones, 1980), and assignment of positive traits to in-group members (e.g., Howard & Rothbart, 1980). Thus, when individuals are categorized into two distinct groups, there is a tendency for individuals to favor their own group over another relevant group, presumably to enhance their social identity. However, some research has sought to identify ways in which in-groups and out-groups may cooperate with one another or extinguish the tendency to compete.

To add to the body of knowledge on social identity, in particular categorization (Hogg & McGarty, 1990), other research by Turner and colleagues (Turner, 1985, Turner et al., 1987) focused on the role of the social self-concept—that is, "the concept of self based on comparison with other people and relevant to social interaction" (Turner, 1985; Turner et al., 1987, p. 42). *Self-categorization theory* explains these processes and argues that when the self and others are categorized into in-groups and out-groups, the self and other become prototypical group members. The process whereby the self cognitively integrates into the group is known as *depersonalization*. As Hogg (2004) elaborates,

> The core idea is that we categorize ourselves just as we categorize others, and thus we depersonalize ourselves . . . Prototype-based depersonalization of the self is the process that makes group behavior possible. It transforms self-conception so that we conceive of ourselves prototypically (prototypes define and evaluate the attributes of group membership), and our behavior assimilates or conforms to the relevant ingroup prototype in terms of attitudes, feelings, and actions. Self-conception in terms of an ingroup prototype is a representation and evaluation of the self in collective terms—a representation of self in term of qualities shared with others.
>
> (p. 208)

As he further explains, a collective self represents the social identities obtained through belonging to groups. Self-categorization results in uncertainty reduction, whereby the prototype defines things such as beliefs, attitudes, and so forth (Hogg, 2000).

More recent research has focused on the role of evolution in in-group bias. You may recall from previous chapters that, according to evolutionary psychologists, behavior that has persisted over time is the sort of behavior that allows us to survive as a species. If one group in a population thrives, then the genes of those in that group survive. So, what does this have to do with how groups interact with one another? There is evidence suggesting that our tendency to favor our own groups over others may be motivated by a desire to insure the continuation of our group, which offers, among other things, survival and reproductive benefits (e.g., McDonald, Navarrete, & Van Vugt, 2012). In other words, it is adaptive for humans, and other species as well, to display in-group favoritism.

Evolutionary psychologists have looked more closely at ethnocentrism, which is the belief that our own ethnic group is superior to all others. The preference for our own ethnic group is so widespread that it seems that all ethnic groups and cultures exhibit this preference (e.g., Mullen, Brown, & Smith, 1992). But, exactly what evolutionary factors can explain why this is or how ethnocentrism is displayed is still uncertain (Sidanius & Kurzba, 2013). For example, we know that group norms dictate that members of a group behave in roughly the same manner (Boyd & Richerson, 1985), which is basically what conformity is. And the greater the extent to which all members of the group conform to the group norms, the more likely those behaviors, and the group, are to survive. But of course, some groups have stronger norms than others, and some members of a group are more likely than others to adhere to the norms. Environmental factors might also play a role. According to Sidanius and Kurzba (2013), the strength of ethnocentrism might be related to such factors as the economic uncertainty, population density, and the tendencies of political elites.

There are instances in which people accept a group's inferior situation, if they believe that their position is just and legitimate. These kinds of patterns were evident historically in the submission to and eventual rejection of colonial domination. People in territories that were conquered by such colonial powers as Britain, France, Germany, and others often accepted that domination. They perceived the colonial powers through the imperialist image and thus saw them as superior in culture and capability. Resisting that domination would have brought severe punishment, and they often accepted domination as just and legitimate. But, over time, independence movements grew, and political activists in the colonies argued that their subservience to the colonial power was unfair, unjust, and illegitimate. Once that change in perception occurred, they began to compare their situations with that of the colonial power and decided that the colonial country was rich and they were poor, and that difference was unacceptable, particularly because the colonial power took the resources of the colonies and used them to enrich itself. The result was a willingness by the subjugated colonized people to risk everything, even their lives, for independence. They did so when they believed independence was a real possibility. In other words, they compared themselves to the other group (the colonial power), found the comparison to be unacceptably negative, sought and found an alternative, and engaged in social competition (rebellion) to achieve it.

AFFECT AND EMOTION

Our discussion so far has centered on cognition and politics. But the discussion of social identity leads easily to another important element in political psychology: emotion. People have emotional responses to political issues, actors, and events, and also to political principles and ideals that they value. When social categories and stereotypes are discussed, there is a tendency for the emphasis to be placed on cognitive processes and properties, such as beliefs, assumptions, and knowledge about different kinds of people, groups, or countries. But clearly cognitive phenomena, such as stereotypes, information processing, and making political decisions, such as for whom to vote, involve affect and emotion, too. Analysts tend to focus on cognition versus affect, depending upon what they are studying and the relative importance of each in affecting how people think. Affect and emotions are difficult to study because of considerable disagreement about what they are and how to measure them, and, in political science, it is often argued that rational decision making must be unemotional. Nevertheless, it is crucial that political psychology make advances in understanding the impact of affect and emotions on behavior. Not only is emotion, in the form of prejudice, more closely associated with behavior than the cognitive component (Fiske, 1998), but we cannot understand mass violence, including genocide, without understanding the role of emotions. Moreover, emotion can play a positive role in decision making (e.g., Baumeister, Vohs, & Tice, 2006). One study found, for example, that suppressing emotions impairs memory (Richards & Gross, 1999). Thus, not only is emotion important, but trying to be unemotional can actually impede important elements in decision making.

Various scholars have defined affect and emotion differently. Fiske and Taylor (1991) define affect as "a generic term for a whole range of preferences, evaluations, moods, and emotions" (p. 410). Neuman, Marcus, Crigler, and MacKuen (2007) define affects as "the evolved cognitive and physiological response to the detection of personal significance" (p. 9). Affect can be positive or negative, that is, evaluations or preferences that are either pleasant or unpleasant. Ottati and Wyer (1993), on the other hand, have a more narrow definition and consider affect to be a physiological state that is experienced as either pleasant or unpleasant, positive or negative. Fiske and Taylor (1991) regard emotion as a "complex assortment of affects, beyond merely good feelings or bad to include delight, serenity, anger, sadness, fear and more" (p. 411), but Ottati and Wyer (1993) define emotions as affective states that are more precisely labeled, such as anger, hatred, fear, love, and respect.

How affect and cognition are interrelated is an issue of debate. As we already noted, cognition is "a collective term for both the psychological processes involved in the acquisition, organization, and the use of knowledge" (Bullock & Stallybrass, 1977, p. 109). Some have argued that affect follows cognition. In other words, a person makes a cognitive appraisal, then affect is evoked. The alternative picture is that people feel first, and this then evokes cognition (Marcus, Neuman, & MacKuen, 2000; Zajonc, 1980a). Marcus, Neuman, and MacKuen (2000) also emphasize the role of emotion in information processing. They argue that there is a dual role played by emotion. In one, emotion forms a dispositional system that affects our responses to normal, familiar situations. In the second, emotion performs a surveillance role, alerting us to novel and possibly threatening situations. Information processing in the former is below the conscious level, while in the latter it is in the forefront of consciousness. Stephan and Stephan (1993) present a network model of affect and cognition, in which they maintain that cognition and affect are a set of interconnected parallel systems. In other words, people have a cognitive system (a system of thoughts, ideas, knowledge) and an affective system (a system of feelings and various emotions). They are separate systems in the mind, linked by various cognitive and affective nodes. The links can vary in strength.

Is it important to have a better understanding of the relationship between affect and cognition? We suggest that it is. As we see in Chapter 6, the relationship between affect and cognition in influencing political tolerance in American is an important area of research. Another important area of inquiry is the role of cognition and emotion in politically motivated violence, and we examine many cases of such violence in Chapters 8–13. When does emotion take over in the process of committing acts of violence? Are some conflicts dominated by cognitive factors and others dominated by affect? An interesting study by a clinical psychologist, Beck (1999), compares domestic violence with group-to-group violence and to international violence. He emphasizes the cognitive side of violent actions, in the sense that he explores what people are thinking before they attack someone—their spouse or children—and he notes that it is difficult to get people to recognize what they are thinking before they lash out in violence: they really do not think they are thinking anything in particular, but, when really pressed, they recognize self-demeaning thoughts and hurt feelings that precede the violence. On the flip side, there is the question of what happens to the thought process when emotions are essentially turned off, if they are, when people commit atrocities over a long period of time. We see cases of this in Chapter 9, when we look at people who commit torture and genocide.

Affect and emotions clearly influence information processing, decision making, and some predispositions for behavior. Isen (1993), in a review of studies of positive affect, notes that positive affect and emotions promote improvements in problem solving, negotiating, and decision making. Positive affect seems to expand peoples' abilities to see interrelationships and connections among cognitive items. On the other hand, when compared to neutral affect, positive and negative affect, but particularly positive affect, reduce peoples' ability to perceive variability in other groups (Park & Banaji, 2000; Stroessner & Mackie, 1993). Cassino and Lodge (2007) note that positive affect is associated with a greater use of heuristics in information processing, while negative affect results in deeper information processing strategies.

Predispositions for behavior resulting from particular emotions have also been studied. Anger, for example, has been found to be associated with moving against, or lashing out at, the perceived source of the anger (Izard, 1977). Contempt, on the other hand, is described by Izard (1977) as cold and distant, leading to depersonalization and dehumanization of others: "It is because of these characteristics that contempt can motivate murder and mass destruction of people" (p. 340). Anxiety leads to intensified attention to the environment and heightened perceptions of threat (Cassino & Lodge, 2007).

Emotions and the behaviors they influence are intricately related to goals at stake in a situation. Political goals naturally vary over time, given particular political contexts and values. Even so, people generally assume that out-groups hinder in-group goals, and therefore the out-group is automatically associated with negative emotions. Out-groups, by definition, are assumed to be different and thus have different goals.

Emotions also vary in intensity, which can increase in response to certain psychological properties, as well as to the nature and impact of events. One of those event characteristics is simply how real the event seems to the person experiencing the emotion (Ortony, Clore, & Collins, 1988). Second, the closer the emotion-producing situation is in time, that is, its proximity, the greater the intensity of the emotion. Third, unexpected events or actions increase intensity. Fourth, physical arousal and the flow of adrenaline increase the emotional intensity. Fifth, in terms of psychological properties, leaving aside individual differences, the salience of social identity groups will increase emotion intensity. The stronger the sense of belonging to a group, the more important belonging is to members' self-esteem, the more salient will be group membership, and the more intense will be emotions generated by that membership. Emotional reactions to events affecting the group may not be observed often, even when one identifies strongly with that group. As long as things are normal, there may be little emotion. However, intense relationships produce the potential for strong emotions, when that relationship, and normal forms of behavior in the context of that relationship, are interrupted (Berscheid, 1987). Thus, one can expect politically motivated emotions to be intense when important political identity groups face threats or unusual opportunities. The intensity of the emotion may come as a great surprise to outside observers, if it has not been witnessed before.

The intensity of affect and emotion is also determined by perceptions of the other group. Out-groups are reacted to more negatively and with greater intensity than are in-groups. Also, extreme stereotyping corresponds with more extreme affect. Groups perceived to be threatening (e.g., out-groups) are seen as more homogeneous and extreme as threat perceptions increase (Corneille, Yzerbyt, Rogier, & Buidin, 2001). Conversely, more complex cognitive processes are associated with more moderate reactions (Linville, 1982). Thus, because a group member perceives their group more complexly than the out-group, evaluations of the in-group are typically less extreme than evaluations of an out-group. However, research (Marques, Abrams, Paez, & Hogg, 2001) shows that, when an in-group member engages in positive behavior or is described in positive terms, they are evaluated more favorably than an out-group member who engages in the same behavior or is described in the same positive terms. But, when an in-group member engages in negative behavior or is described in unfavorable terms, that person is evaluated more unfavorably than an out-group member who engages in similar behavior or is described in unfavorable terms. This has been termed the *black sheep effect* (Marques, Yeerbyt, & Leyens, 1988). Group members might derogate a "bad" in-group member, so that they can distance themselves from that member, thus restoring their sense of positive social identity. The purpose of that study was to test the hypothesis that strength of group identification is related to strength of derogation of an errant in-group member.

Generally, we would expect positive emotions to be associated with in-groups and negative emotions with out-groups. This is an important principle to keep in mind when looking at emotion and political behavior. Social psychologists have examined the emotions associated with social groups that are lower or higher in power and status, under varying circumstances, which help with another important pattern regarding emotion and politics (Smith, 1993; Duckitt, 1994). Those studies can be complex, because emotions can be bundled together. Prejudice, the affective partner of a cognitive stereotype, is a good example of this. "Hot prejudices" are composed of these emotions: disgust, resentment, hostility, and anger. Let us turn to a number of politically relevant emotions first, and then consider how they may cluster with different political groups.

The list of negative emotions is long, and one in particular, anger, is an emotion often found in political behavior. Anger is a negative emotion, wherein blame for undesirable behavior, and resulting undesirable events, is directed at another person or group. It occurs when goals are thwarted and attention is focused on the source of the obstacle to the goal (Stein, Trabasso, & Liwag, 1993). Anger produces a desire to regain control, remove the obstruction, and, if necessary, attack the source of injury (Frijda, 1986; Izard, 1977; Lazarus, 1991). Whether a person acts on anger depends on the situation, norms and values, and the characteristics of the offending party. Anger can also be triggered by particular schema. When a person has experienced intense emotion, such as anger, in a previous situation, the schema of that situation can trigger anger when a similar situation is identified. If, for example, a person witnessed an act of cruelty and was angered by it, the same emotion can be triggered by similar situations, or even by thinking about acts of cruelty in general.

Other emotions are closely related to anger and are also politically important, including frustration, resentment, contempt, and disgust. Disgust involves being repulsed by the actions or characteristics of others. It can be quite severe and lead people to fear that the very social order is being contaminated. The behavior that disgust can produce includes the possibility of wanting to destroy the offending group. On the other hand, because the level of interest and degree of distress when one is disgusted is lower than when one is angry, disgust does not produce as much aggression as anger. Contempt, on the other hand, involves feeling superior to another group and can lead to domination and dehumanization of others (Frijda, 1986). Dehumanization, in turn, leads to extremely violent behavior, even genocide (Izard, 1977; Kressel, 1996). The less human another person or group appears, the easier it is to kill them en masse.

Guilt, shame, sympathy, pity, envy, and jealousy can also affect political behavior. Guilt occurs when people do something they consider morally unacceptable and want to atone or make amends to those they have hurt (Lazarus, 1991; Swim & Miller, 1999). Shame, on the other hand, occurs when a person does something that violates how they see themselves. When feeling shame, people tend to avoid others who have observed whatever they did to produce the shame. Humiliation is another strong emotion; it produces a desire for revenge (Gilligan, 1997; Weingarten, 2004; Lindner, 2006).

Fear and anxiety, two other emotions important in politics, both occur when danger is perceived, but they differ, in that fear is associated with a clear and certain threat, and anxiety is associated with uncertainty about the threat. Typically, when people experience fear, they want to avoid or escape the threat. When they experience anxiety, however, they do not really know what to do or how to respond, and they tend to worry about what to do and how to do it (Lazarus, 1991; Marcus, Neuman, & MacKuen, 2000; Mac-Kuen, Marcus, Neuman, & Keele, 2007).

There are positive emotions that are also important in politics, such as pride in the achievements of one's group or country or happiness, when an opportunity to achieve an important goal occurs. As mentioned earlier, positive emotions tend to make people more flexible and more creative in problem solving. They are able to see more nuances and have more complex evaluations of other people, when feeling positive emotions. Clearly, these emotions, such as pride in your country, or joy and happiness when the country does well in things like economic development and growth or in international athletic competitions, are associated with politics.

As alluded to earlier, there are a few psychological studies of emotions that are associated with groups of varying degrees of power, in different contexts. Duckitt (1994), for example, looked at emotion and behavior patterns associated with groups considered malicious superior, oppressive, inferior, threatening, and powerful. He found punitiveness, intropunitive abasement, extrapunitive hostility, hostility, derogation, and superficial tolerance associated with each, respectively. Smith (1993) also examined perceptions of different groups (strong or weak, compared to the perceiver's group and the emotions associated with it), in a study of emotions and stereotyping. Smith found that minorities with low power felt fear regarding high-power or majority groups; members of high-status groups felt disgust in regard to low status groups; contempt was felt by any group toward any out-group; anger was felt by members of high-power or majority groups when low-power or minorities made demands or threats; and jealousy emerged among low-status groups toward high-status groups.

Mackie, Devos, and Smith (2000) also examined an important issue regarding the experience of negative emotions resulting from interactions with an out-group. They argue that either fight (e.g., anger) or flight (e.g., fear) emotions are possible, depending upon appraisals of the out-group by, and in relation to, the in-group. Marcus et al. (2000) examined emotion in the American electoral context, in an interesting study that drew upon current studies in neurosciences, among other fields; they argued that there are "two systems associated with the brain's limbic region, the disposition and the surveillance systems" (p. 9). From the dispositional system come the emotions of satisfaction and enthusiasm or frustration and depression. The surveillance system determines feelings of relaxation and calm or anxiety and unease, depending upon political conditions. Both cause people to be more or less attentive to the political arena and their evaluation of candidates and participation in politics. In a look at emotions and images of other states, Cottam and Cottam (2001) argued that certain emotions are closely associated with particular images. Some of these images can be translated to domestic contexts, as well. Following is a review of the images and emotions associated with them. These patterns are beginning to receive empirical verification from experimental studies (Alexander, Brewer, & Herrmann, 1999). The images and strategic patterns discussed next are summarized in Figure 3.1.

Image of Other Political Actor		Threat/ Opportunity		Strategic Preference
Enemy image	→	Threat high	→	Containment
Barbarian image	→	Threat high	→	Search for allies, augment power
Imperial image	→	Threat high	→	Submit/revolt when possible
Rogue image	→	Threat moderate/low	→	Crush
Degenerate image	→	Opportunity high/ moderate	→	Challenge, take risks
Colonial image	→	Opportunity high	→	Control, exploit
Ally image	→	Threat/Opportunity (will help in either context)	→	Negotiate agreements, common strategy

Figure 3.1 Political Images and Strategic Preferences

The Diabolical Enemy

The image of an enemy is associated with intensely perceived threat and very intense affect and emotions. The enemy is perceived as relatively equal in capability and culture. In its most extreme form, the diabolical enemy is seen as irrevocably aggressive in motivation, monolithic in decisional structure, and highly rational in decision making (to the point of being able to generate and orchestrate multiple complex conspiracies). Citizens who do not share this image, or who merely have a more complex view of the enemy, are often accused of being, at best, dupes of the enemy and possibly even traitors. This is unfortunate, particularly because the ability to view the threatener in more complex terms makes it possible to identify a broader range of policy options, some of which might stave off a crisis or at least allow for a more complex strategic response.

Some of the emotions associated with the enemy include anger, frustration, envy, jealousy, fear, distrust, and possibly grudging respect. An enemy's successes are considered unfair, and when bad things happen and goals are not met, the enemy is blamed. People tend to be both antagonistic and reactant in responding to an enemy. People compete with the enemy and try to prevent the enemy from gaining anything. The approach to conflict makes sense in light of the cognitive properties of the image. The enemy is as powerful and capable as one's own country, so there is an even chance of losing if the approach to the conflict is entirely zero sum. Thus the enemy image makes a strong, aggressive defense the logical choice. If such a defense should eliminate the threatener altogether, so much the better.

However, a strategy of containment may be the only recognized alternative in most political contexts, simply because the odds of defeating an enemy are 50–50, at best. Containing your enemy, preventing them from becoming more powerful or achieving its desired goals, may be all you can do.

The consequences of stereotypical enemy image can be tragic, when the motivations of the country considered to be an enemy are really misunderstood, that is, when the people and leaders are essentially acting toward that country based upon a stereotype of an enemy. It can produce a self-fulfilling prophecy. The people and leaders of enemy countries will see themselves as having been aggressed against and will develop an enemy image (or mirror image) because each sees the other as an enemy and will adopt the same tough strategy. The result could be an unnecessary and disastrous security dilemma that would be extremely difficult to overcome. **Security dilemmas** are situations in which the efforts made by one state to defend itself are simultaneously seen as threatening to its opponents, even if those actions were not intended to be threatening. They easily lead to **spiral conflicts** in which each side matches and one-ups the actions taken by the other side. This can produce arms races and other types of aggression that result from misunderstanding each other's motives. The enemy stereotype is virtually nonfalsifiable. It can explain any response, including appeasement, on the part of the enemy. In Chapters 9 and 10, a number of cases are presented in which this image is evident. Spiral conflicts and the security dilemma are discussed in more depth in Chapter 13.

The Barbarian

The barbarian image appears when an intense threat is perceived as emanating from a political entity viewed as superior in terms of capability, but as inferior culturally. Historical examples of this image can be found in the ancient Greek depiction of the Germanic tribes to the north. The image of the barbarian is of an aggressive people who are monolithic in decisional structure, cunning, and willing to resort to unspeakable brutality, including genocide, and who are determined to take full advantage of their superiority. Emotions commonly associated with this image are disgust more than contempt (because the barbarian is considered greater in capability, even though culturally inferior), anger, and fear. The latter is a product of the superior capability of the barbarian. People who do not share this image will be accused of cowardice and treason.

Because of both cognitive and emotional properties, this image does not lead to an aggressive defense posture. Fear produced by capability asymmetries will make people prefer to avoid direct conflict. A more reasonable primary course of action for dealing with a barbarian is a search for allies who can be persuaded of the probability that a failure to deal with this threat will affect, seriously and adversely, their own national interests. In social identity theoretical terms, perceivers would probably like to engage in direct competition with this hated and disgusting opponent, in the most violent form of eliminating the threat altogether, but they cannot, because they are too weak. Instead, they must build coalitions to overcome their weakness and improve their ability to at least contain the barbarian.

There are some examples of this image in recent international and domestic political conflicts. International cases include Israeli perceptions of the Arab world. Although the Arab states are not superior in military capability to Israel, their large populations and resource advantages lead to an Israeli expectation that they have the potential for becoming superior. Despite perceived cultural inferiority, the probabilities are seen as high that superiority in conventional arms is not only attainable but unavoidable. A second example occurred in the disintegration of Yugoslavia (explored in detail in Chapter 9), in which the Croatians believed themselves to be culturally superior to the Serbs, but much weaker in capability (Cottam & Cottam, 2001). In both cases, allies were sought: Israel looked to the United States and Europe, and the Croatians looked to Slovenia and other European states for support in their efforts to achieve independence from Yugoslavia.

The Imperial Image

This image occurs when the people of a polity perceive threat from another polity viewed as superior in terms of both capability and culture. That is a situation that was fairly commonplace during the height of colonialism in the nineteenth century. The imperial stereotype now is viewed primarily in a neocolonial variation, reflecting the disappearance of formal colonialism. People view the imperial power as motivated by the desire to exploit the resources of the colonized people. The decisional structure of the imperial power is viewed as less monolithic than in the enemy and barbarian images, because an anti-imperialism element is frequently perceived to be present in the imperial power. People assume that decisions are made in a subtle and discrete manner in the imperial power, in the form of an elaborate web of institutions and individuals. People also believe that, even though their own country has its own institutions and leader, the imperial power is pulling the strings, often at a very detailed level. The imperial power is viewed as having the capacity to orchestrate developments of extraordinary complexity and to do so with great subtlety. The style is often described as operating through a hidden hand, which is what gives the imperial power superiority in capability. People who collaborate with the imperial power are viewed by those resisting it as profiting hugely from the relationship and are judged as having betrayed their nation. But the reality is that, historically, many people in colonial and neocolonial countries did collaborate with the imperial powers. From a social identity standpoint, this makes sense if collaborators made comparisons not between themselves and the imperial power, but between themselves and other groups in the colony dominated by the imperial power. They may have seen imperial control as just and legitimate, and thereby accepted their own inferior status, if they saw their own circumstances improved in comparison to other groups because of the imperial power's presence. Therefore, the image is sometimes associated with strong perceptions of injustice and illegitimacy, but not by everyone.

The complex of emotions associated with this image is affected by perceptions of whether or not the relationship is a just or legitimate one. When the colonial–imperial relationship is seen as legitimate or just, emotions associated with the image include fear of the imperial power. The behavioral tendencies that result involve self-protection and avoiding conflict with the fear-inducing agent (Duckitt, 1994). In addition, when the relationship is considered just and legitimate, respect is likely by the subordinate people for the imperial group, as is benevolent paternalistic affection by the imperial group for the subordinate group (Duckitt, 1994). The behavioral preferences would be simply to maintain the relationship as it is currently conducted, with the imperial group making major decisions and allowing symbolic concessions to the colonial subject group.

Emotions and action preferences are different on both sides, when the relationship and interaction is considered unjust by the weaker, subordinate group. The extremity of mutual stereotyping increases in such situations, and the people in the subordinate position start to make demands for greater equality. They may feel jealousy, anger, and shame that they are in the inferior position (Smith, 1993). These perceptions and emotions can push people toward antagonistic and hostile actions toward the superior group, including rebellion, even though they are well aware of the potential consequences. However, actions as risky as outright rebellion tend to occur only when social mobility and creativity options are not available and when real alternatives are perceived to exist. For example, after World War II, the European colonial powers were so weak that the prospect of actually achieving independence looked good enough to leaders of independence movements to push hard for the end of colonialism. This image is also important in a case study presented in Chapter 10 of U.S.–Mexico relations in the war on drugs.

The Rogue Image

The rogue image is relatively new. During the Cold War, leaders of the West held an image of a dependent of the enemy, in which a country was viewed as inferior in capability and culture, but controlled and supported by the enemy. That image disappeared with the end of the Cold War and the demise of the Soviet Union. Nevertheless, former allies of the Soviet Union, along with some other countries (such as North Korea, Cuba, Iraq, Libya, Serbia, and Iran), were seen as both inferior and threatening. American policymakers often refer to these as rogue states. For example, Anthony Lake (1994), when national security adviser, wrote:

> Our policy must face the reality of recalcitrant and outlaw states that not only choose to remain outside the family [of nations] but also assault its basic values. There are few "backlash" states: Cuba, North Korea, Iran, Iraq and Libya. For now they lack the resources of a superpower, which would enable them to seriously threaten the democratic order being created around them. Nevertheless, their behavior is often aggressive and defiant. . . . These backlash states have some common characteristics. Ruled by cliques that control power through coercion . . . these nations exhibit a chronic inability to engage

constructively with the outside world, and they do not function effectively in alliances.... Finally, they share a siege mentality. Accordingly, they are embarked on ambitious and costly military programs.

(pp. 45–46)

Look at the words Lake used. There are references to a family (bad children), the weakness of these states, the incompatibility of their values with those of the rest of the family of nations, their aggressive behavior, decisions made by a small elite, and the impossibility of dealing with them rationally and constructively. Responses to this type of state are driven by a sense of superiority. They are bad children who must be taught a lesson, and that lesson is taught with force. One does not negotiate with bad children; one punishes them. There are many examples. American reaction to Saddam Hussein's resistance to weapons inspection was to attack with the full force of America's military might. President Bush repeatedly stated that there would be no negotiations with Saddam Hussein and that he had to do what he was told to do or be punished. When Slobodan Milošević resisted points in the Rambouillet accords that would have given North Atlantic Treaty Organization (NATO) forces the right to wander unimpeded throughout Yugoslavia, negotiations ceased and Yugoslavia was bombed. When Manuel Noriega thumbed his nose at U.S. efforts to promote free elections, Panama was bombed. Often, one individual is assumed to be responsible for the behavior of the rogue state (e.g., eliminate Noriega, Saddam, or Milošević, and the problem will be solved overnight).

The Degenerate Image

The degenerate image is one associated with the perception of an opportunity to achieve a goal at the expense of a country that is seen as relatively equal or even greater in capability and culture. Even though a country seen as a degenerate may be more powerful than the perceiver's country, it is also seen as uncertain and confused in motivation and is characterized by a highly differentiated leadership that lacks a clear sense of direction and that is incapable of constructing an effective strategy. They are believed to be unable to muster the will and determination to make effective use of their power instruments or to mobilize effective public support. Fellow citizens who do not share this image are seen as wimps. As in the case of the enemy stereotype, disconfirming evidence is likely to be interpreted as confirming, and the image is extremely difficult to falsify.

The emotions associated with the image are disgust, contempt, scorn, and anger, all of which may ultimately turn to hatred. This combination leads to a desire to eliminate the offensive group and can lead to a dangerous underestimation of an adversary's abilities (Izard, 1977). Contempt and disgust combine with anger and scorn, and this can lead to dehumanization and to genocidal violence. Because the motivations of a country seen as a degenerate are assumed to be harmful, the drive to eliminate the problem is likely to be strong. Leaders of Germany and Japan before World War II made statements about and committed acts toward Great Britain, the United States, and France that indicated their degenerate image of those countries. A more recent example of this stereotypical view was Saddam Hussein of Iraq, in his confrontation with the United States and its allies in 1990. Saddam Hussein apparently believed to the end that the United States and its allies would not have the will to engage him on the issue of the invasion of Kuwait. More typical was the operating worldview of Hitler, Mussolini, and the Japanese military. They at least did possess formidable war capabilities, and all saw a reality that made plausible the achievement of their aggressive ends.

The Colonial Image

A second stereotypical image associated with perception of opportunity is the colonial image, which is the flip side of the imperial image. It occurs when an opportunity is identified to gain control over another polity or group perceived as significantly inferior in capability and culture. The people are perceived as childlike and inferior, and the political elite are typically perceived to fall into one of two groups: one group is seen as behaving moderately and responsibly, as is indicated by its willingness to collaborate with the imperial power; the other group, in contrast, is seen as behaving in an agitating and irresponsible manner, opposing the imperial purpose, sometimes to the point of allying with and serving the interests of enemies of the imperial power. The moderate, responsible section is motivated to support what is perceived as the civilizing mission of the imperial power. The agitating group is seen as monolithic in decisional structure and cunningly destructive, as it tries to mobilize the most alert elements in a mostly apolitical and passive populace. The imperial power capability advantage rests on the perceived immaturity of the colonial population, as manifest in an inability effectively to recruit, organize, and lead a military force and to make effective use of advanced weaponry. Those citizens of the imperial power who do not share this essentially contemptuous view will be regarded as having "gone native" and lost perspective.

Members of the imperial power polity tend to regard the colonial populace with disgust and contempt, but also with pity. Behaviors associated with the image and its emotional baggage include wanting to avoid contamination from contact with the inferior, or moving forcefully against them to punish bad behavior. This was the Cold War pattern in U.S. foreign policy. Countries in this image, who moved in political directions that U.S. policymakers did not approve of, were punished, sometimes through the overthrow of their governments. Examples include the overthrow of the governments in Iran (1953), Guatemala (1954), and Chile (1973). The fear was that they would become infected with socialism and that it would spread to other countries, and they were simply not going to be allowed to do this. In less dangerous contexts, such as disagreements regarding economic matters, there is little a colonial country can do to seriously threaten the imperial power, and policy preferences are for nonviolent repression in the form of economic sanctions, isolation, refusal to give trade preferences, and so on. The actions and demands of the colonial country are still considered illegitimate and inconsistent with the goals of the perceiver, and responsibility for the conflict is attributed to the colonial country.

We describe this image in terms of international politics, but the dynamic repeats itself in any domestic political context in which one group considers itself vastly superior to, and therefore rightfully in control of, another group. White resistance to the civil rights movement in the United States in the 1960s South is an example. African American political leaders were also divided into "moderate" and the "irresponsible" classifications. This image is also evident in the case study of U.S.–Mexico interaction in Chapter 10.

ATTITUDES

The discussion of images and their emotional components tells us something about the interaction of cognition and emotion. There has also been a great deal of research on the cognitive and emotional elements in the individual attitudes that make up a cognitive system. The concept is defined and thought of in different ways by different psychologists. A standard definition of **attitudes** is that they are an enduring system of positive or negative beliefs (the cognitive component), **affective** feelings and emotions, and action tendencies regarding **attitude objects**, that is, the entity being evaluated. Stone and Schaffner (1988), for example, regard attitudes as "an organized set of beliefs, persisting over time, which is useful in explaining the individual response to tendencies" (p. 63). Eagly and Chaiken (1998) define attitudes as "a psychological tendency that is expressed by evaluating a particular entity with some degree of favor or disfavor" (p. 269). Duckitt (1994) reviews two different ways in which attitudes have been conceptualized in psychology. In one, they are seen to be composed of cognitive, affective, and behavioral components. However, there were many criticisms of this conceptualization of attitudes, because there was little in the way of specifics as to how these three components interacted and whether they were always consistent with each other. We saw earlier, in our discussion of balance and consistency, that affect and cognition are not always consistent, and most people know from personal experience that attitudes and behavior are often inconsistent.

One of the most important controversies in attitude research has concerned the behavioral component in the original conceptualization of attitudes. Originally, it was simply assumed that a person's attitudes determine his behavior. A person who favors a certain politician is likely to vote for him. A person who smokes marijuana is likely to support bills legalizing marijuana. A person who is racially prejudiced is unlikely to send their child to a school where African Americans and Hispanic Americans, or whoever the person does not like, are in the majority. In 1934, however, a major study was done, which found interesting results and which challenged the notion that there is a direct connection between attitudes and behavior. This study was conducted by La Pierre, who was a Caucasian professor. He toured the United States with a Chinese couple during a period when there was a great deal of prejudice against Asian people in this country. They stopped at 66 hotels and 184 restaurants. Only once were they turned away by a hotel and never by a restaurant. Later, a letter was sent to the same hotels and restaurants, asking whether they would accept Chinese customers. Ninety-two percent of those who responded (128) said that they would not. The study showed that people do not always behave in accordance with their attitudes. Later studies raised similar concerns (Deutscher, 1973; Katz & Stotland, 1959; Kuntner, Wilkins, & Yarrow, 1952; Minard, 1952). This, of course, led to the question of when and under what circumstances attitudes and behavior are likely to coincide.

Attitudes that are strong, clear, and consistent over time, and that are directly and specifically relevant to the behavior under examination, are more likely to be associated with attitude–behavior consistency (Fazio & Williams, 1986; Fishbein & Ajzen, 1980; Krosnick, 1989). Inconsistencies can come from weak or ambivalent affect. In addition, the affective and cognitive components of an attitude may be in some conflict, which also reduces the changes of attitude–behavior consistency. For example, some men and women may think intellectually gender-based discrimination is wrong, but they are emotionally upset when men and women do not conform to gender-related roles. Also, if one is going to study the relationship between attitudes and behaviors, one needs to look at behaviors that are directly related to attitudes in order to get an accurate picture of the relationship. For example, several studies tried to examine the relationship between religious attitudes and religious behavior, by asking subjects whether they believe in God or consider themselves religious, then noting whether they attended church. Usually, there was only a weak relationship between the two. The problem is that going to church is not directly related to belief in God or even to being religious. Many people who believe in God do not go to church. Other people go to church for social reasons, more than because they believe in God. In addition, it may be important to look at a series of a person's actions over time, to get an accurate picture of the relationship between attitudes and behavior (Epstein, 1979; Fiske & Taylor, 1991). This eliminates interference from situational conditions that interfere in the attitude–behavior relationship.

This brings us to situational pressures, which can also affect the relationship between attitudes and behavior. Whenever a person engages in overt behavior, they can be influenced both by their attitudes and by the situation they are in. When situational pressures are very strong, attitudes are not likely to be as strong a determinant of behavior as when situational pressures are relatively weak. Situational pressure can include social norms (a person may be a bigot, but know that others will think poorly of him if he acts that way) or contextual effects, which heighten the salience of or perspective on, a certain attitude (Bentler & Speckart, 1981; Fishbein & Ajzen, 1975; La Pierre, 1934). Individual differences are also important in explaining inconsistencies between what people think and how they behave. Some people are high self-monitors, meaning that they are very attentive to social norms and the impression they make in social situations. They are less likely to act consistently on the basis of their attitudes and instead act as they think the situation demands (Perloff, 1993; Snyder, 1987).

Given these issues, other perspectives on attitudes have been offered. Fishbein and Ajzen (1980) offer a unidimensional approach to attitudes, wherein they regard attitudes solely as affect. They separate the cognitive and behavioral components and argue that these should be observed and measured separately. As Duckitt (1994) explains,

> This approach does not expect a strong relationship between an atti-
> tude to an object and specific behaviors to that object. To predict
> a specific act, both the attitude to that act and act-specific social
> norms need to be considered as well. On the other hand, a general-
> ized attitude toward an object should predict the overall tendency to
> behave in a generally favorable or unfavorable way toward that object,
> as aggregating over a variety of different situations and acts should
> largely average out normative and situational influences.
>
> (p. 13)

Judd and Krosnick (1989) take a similar approach and define an attitude as "an evaluation of an attitude object that is stored in memory" (p. 100). Others have limited attitudes to affect and beliefs alone (Levin & Levin, 1982).

No agreement exists on a universally accepted understanding of what an attitude is and how its component parts relate to each other, but the attitude concept has been widely used in studies of voting behavior, persuasion, and media effects on political behavior, as seen in Chapter 6. Unlike the image and stereotype concepts, the attitude concept can more easily separate cognition and affect, and for that reason it can be very useful in studying voting behavior, particularly in a country such as the United States, where people have political attitudes that often are based upon little, and often inaccurate, cognition. An attitude can be driven mostly by affect, but as our discussion of images and stereotypes shows, there is considerable knowledge, although often inaccurate, embodied in them. Alternatively, an attitude may be primarily cognitive in content, that is, based solely on beliefs without affect (Eagly & Chaiken, 1998).

Attitude studies have been conducted on many issues, one of which is, as mentioned, the relationship between cognition and affect, particularly when they are not consistent (i.e., what you think about an object and how you feel about it are different). Marcus et al. (2000) examine the role affect plays in the behavior of American citizens in elections and regarding important issues. They argue that emotions help people monitor and take surveillance of politics. Their study includes survey results demonstrating the importance of enthusiasm and anxiety in electoral preferences for the presidency in the 1980s. For example, enthusiasm for Reagan and lack of anxiety about the country's circumstances, they argue, contributed strongly to Reagan's reelection in 1984. They also explain the lack of everyday interest in politics in America by noting that the average citizen uses emotions to act as an alarm: when the citizen starts to feel anxiety, they then turn to the news and find out more about what is going on. The emotional system is a watch-dog that operates nonconsciously. We discuss this research in more detail in Chapter 6.

Another broad issue concerns the consistency among, and structure of, attitudes, for example, whether Republicans are consistently conservative and Democrats are consistently liberal on all political issues, and how those attitudes are linked together. Attitudes can be bipolar, wherein people recognize and understand both sides of an issue, or they can be unipolar, in which case people see only their preferred position. Eagly and Chiaken (1998) cite a number of studies that suggest that attitudes on controversial issues are likely to be bipolar (e.g., Pratkanis, 1989; Sherif, Sherif, & Nebergall, 1965).

In addition, there is a large body of literature on the complexity of beliefs, which we introduce in Chapter 2 and explore in detail in Chapter 5, where political leaders are discussed. Many studies concerning how political attitudes are formed, and how they change, are examined in Chapter 6.

CONCLUSION

This chapter has introduced readers to many different concepts in cognitive and social psychology, and it has briefly introduced their application to political psychology. We began with basic patterns in information processing, then turned to an overview of the cognitive system. To this, we added the importance of the groups to which people belong (in-groups) and their reactions to groups to which they do not belong (out-groups). We presented a model of out-groups (image theory), which depicts out-groups in international politics, but which can be used in domestic political arenas as well. In subsequent chapters, where we examine race, ethnicity, nationalism, and political extremists, we explore some of the groups in politics to which people have powerful attachments, as well as patterns of behavior toward out-groups. We looked at emotion in politics, and readers may find that, although emotions have not been systematically examined in the patterns of political behavior we discuss in succeeding chapters, they are deeply important. Indeed, readers may find themselves having powerful emotional reactions to some of the cases presented in the chapters that follow. Finally, we presented the concept of attitudes, to which we return when we look at public opinion and voting in Chapter 6. Thus far, in Chapters 2 and 3, we have explored the content of the Political Being's mind. In the next chapter, we turn to the Political Being and the outside world, with a look at groups and group behavior.

Topics, Theories/Explanations, and Concepts in Chapter 3

Topics	Theories	Concepts
Information Processing	Attribution theory	Heuristics: availability, representativeness, fundamental attribution error
	Balance theory	Need for consistency
	Dissonance theory	Selective exposure, attention, interpretation; avoidance of value trade-offs; bolstering
Cognition and cognitive systems	Categorization; social identity	Cognitive categories; schemas; stereotypes; in-groups and out-groups
	Image theory	Enemy, barbarian, imperial, rogue, degenerate, colonial
Emotions		
Attitudes		

Key Terms

affect	dissonance
ally image	emotion
anchoring and adjustment	enemy image
assimilation effect	fundamental attribution
attitudes	error
attribution theory	heuristic
availability heuristic	hindsight bias
avoidance of value	image theory
balance	imperialist image
barbarian image	in-group
beliefs	out-group
bolstering	processes
childish games	representativeness
cognition	rogue image
cognitive	schema
colonial image	security
confirmation bias	social identity
contrast effect	stereotypes
degenerate image	trade-offs
dilemmas	

Suggestions for Further Reading

Alexander, M.G., Brewer, M.B., & Herrmann, R.K. (1999). Images and affect: A functional analysis of out-group stereotypes. *Journal of Personality and Social Psychology, 77,* 78–93.

Cottam, M. (1994). *Images and intervention.* Pittsburgh, PA: University of Pittsburgh Press.

Cottam, M., & Cottam, R. (2001). *Nationalism and politics: The political behavior of nation states.* Boulder, CO: Lynne Rienner.

Eagly, A.H., & Chaiken, S. (1998). Attitude structure and function. In D.T. Gilbert, S.T. Fiske, & G. Lindzey (Eds.), *The handbook of social psychology* (4th ed.). New York: McGraw-Hill.

Fiske, S., & Taylor, S.E. (1991). *Social cognition.* New York: McGraw-Hill.

Frijda, N. (1986). *The emotions.* Cambridge: Cambridge University Press.

Mackie, D., & Hamilton, D. (Eds.). (1993). *Affect, cognition and stereotyping: Interactive processes in group perception.* New York: Academic Press.

Marcus, G., Neuman, W.R., & MacKuen, M. (2000). *Affective intelligence and political judgment.* Chicago, IL: University of Chicago Press.

Neuman, R. Marcus, G., Crigler, A., & MacKuen, M. (Eds.). (2007). *The affect effect.* Chicago, IL: Chicago University Press.

Tajfel, H. (1982). *Human groups and social categories.* Cambridge: Cambridge University Press.

Westen, D. (2007). *The political brain: The role of emotion in deciding the fate of the nation.* New York: Public Affairs.

Chapter 4

THE POLITICAL PSYCHOLOGY OF GROUPS

This chapter looks at Political Beings in their environment, that is, in the presence of, and as a member of, groups. Groups have a prominent role in politics. Small groups are often given the responsibility of making important political decisions, creating political policies, and generally conducting political business. Larger groups, such as the Senate, also hold a special place in politics and are responsible for larger-scale decisions and tasks, such as passing legislation. Finally, large groups, such as states and countries, carry with them their own dynamics, especially regarding how they view each other and how they get along. Because so much political behavior is performed by groups, it behooves us to learn more about the basic processes that govern groups. Although groups are comprised of individuals, group behavior cannot be understood by studying individual behavior. Obviously, understanding groups involves an understanding of the individuals who compose a group, but there are dynamics of groups that cannot be observed from examining individuals alone. Many observers (e.g., Durkheim, 1938/1966; LeBon, 1895/1960) note that individuals often behave quite differently when they are together compared to when they are alone. Consequently, although the workings of the Political Being's mind are still operative, we are interested in the impact of the sociopolitical environment on behavior in this chapter.

The study of groups in social psychology has a short history, with some of the first studies being conducted just before World War II (e.g., Lewin, Lippitt, & White, 1939; Newcomb, 1943; Sherif, 1936; Whyte, 1943). Nonetheless, a vast amount of information is available about group behavior, and most of it can be applied to the study of groups in political settings. In this chapter, we review a variety of information about groups. The first half of the chapter focuses on the structural characteristics of groups, such as composition, formation, and development. The second half of the chapter focuses on the unique behaviors that take place in groups or because of groups, including influence, performance, decision making, and intergroup conflict.

THE NATURE OF GROUPS

Definition of a Group

Imagine all of the different types of collectives that exist in political settings. People work together to solve problems, set political policies and agendas, serve constituents, make legal decisions, run political campaigns, and make decisions about world problems. Do all of these collectives constitute groups? Groups researchers have been unable to answer that question. There is little consensus in the field about what characteristics of a collective make a group. Although most social psychologists would agree that a group is a collection of people who are perceived to belong together and are dependent on one another, there are other ways to conceptualize groups. For example, Moreland (1987) discusses "groupiness" or social integration as a quality that every collection of individuals possesses to some degree. As the level of social integration increases, people start to think and act more like a group than a collection of individuals. Other social psychologists (Dasgupta, Banji, & Abelson, 1999; Lickel et al., 2000) maintain the importance of the perception, named **entiativity**, that refers to the extent to which a collection of people is perceived as a coherent entity. Some groups, such as people in line at a bank, are perceived as being low in entiativity. Other groups, such as members of a family or members of a professional sports team, are perceived as being high in entiativity.

Types of Groups

When thinking about groups, it is sometimes useful to consider the various types of groups that exist. Several groups researchers have provided typologies of groups. For example, Prentice, Miller, and Lightdale (1994) investigated **common-bond** and **common-identity** groups. Common-bond groups, such as social groups, are based mostly on the attachments between group members. In common-bond groups, the attachments to the group are based on such things as member similarity, likability of fellow group members, and familiarity with group members. Common-identity groups, on the other hand, are based primarily on attachments to the group identity. Examples of common-identity groups include music groups, sports teams, and performing groups. Individuals in common-identity groups are far more attached to the group identity than they are to individual members of the group.

Deaux, Reid, Mizrahi, and Ethier (1995) provide another perspective on types of groups. In research focusing on the dimensions of social identity, they identified five types of social identities: personal relationships (e.g., friend, husband), vocations/avocations (e.g., student, gardener), political affiliation (e.g., Democrat, Republican), stigmatized groups (e.g., alcoholic, unemployed person), and ethnic/religious groups (e.g., Catholic, Hispanic).

A more recent typology of groups is provided by Lickel et al. (2000). In their study, participants were asked to rate a variety of groups on such dimensions as perceived entiativity, interaction, common goals, similarity, permeability, duration, size, and importance. The results of their investigation showed that groups could be divided into three types. One type, intimacy groups, consisted of small groups with frequent interactions, high similarity, and importance to their members. Examples of intimacy groups include families, friends, and fraternities. A second type, task groups, consists of groups that are fairly small in size, but with high interaction, similarity, and importance. Task groups are groups such as members of a jury, labor unions, and student study groups. The third type of group, social categories, consist of large groups that are usually low in interaction, importance, and similarity of group members. These groups include women, Blacks, and Jews, for example.

Why is it important to consider types of groups? One reason may be the different functions that groups serve or the types of needs they fulfill. For example, a recent study (Johnson et al., 2005) showed that intimacy groups tended to fulfill needs for affiliation, task groups tended to fulfill the need for achievement, and social category groups were associated with needs for identity. Understanding the relationship between group types and individual needs can be useful for knowing what types of groups to look for to satisfy various social needs. In addition, knowing what types of groups fulfill what needs might help to explain dissatisfaction with a group. For example, if a person has a strong need for affiliation but is not getting that need satisfied in their study group, then it is likely because study groups usually do not help to fulfill a need for affiliation.

Group Composition

Groups come in all shapes and sizes, and political groups are no exception. Groups can differ in size, composition, and type. Concerning group size, research suggests that naturally occurring groups are typically small, containing just two or three persons (Desportes & Lemaine, 1988). People may prefer smaller groups because they are confused by large groups (James, 1951) or because they cannot easily control what happens to them in larger groups (Lawler, 1992). Research has examined some interesting effects of group size. For example, as the size of the group increases, group members participate less (Patterson & Schaeffer, 1977), display less commitment to the group (Widmeyer, Brawley, & Carron, 1990), and show higher levels of tardiness, absenteeism, and turnover (Durand, 1985; Spink & Carron, 1992). Other group dynamics are also affected by group size. In larger groups, there tends to be more conflict (O'Dell, 1968), less cooperation (Brewer & Kramer, 1986), and less conformity to group norms (Olson & Caddell, 1994). Finally, group performance can also be affected by the size of a group. In large groups, coordination is more difficult (Diehl & Stroebe, 1987; Latane, Williams, & Harkins, 1979), leading to decrements in performance, and it is easier to social loaf and free ride, which can have harmful effects on the performance of a group (Karau & Williams, 1993). In the chapters that follow, we examine large groups, such as ethnic, national, and racial groups, as well as small groups involved in political decision making and small groups involved in political violence.

Groups can also differ in terms of their composition. The characteristics of individual group members, such as sex, race, ethnicity, and physical attractiveness, can be very important to the functioning of the group.

Recently, however, attention has focused on the diversity within a group (Levine & Moreland, 1998). Research examining the effects of diversity on communication suggests that diversity can be harmful. As the degree of diversity increases, group members tend to communicate with each other less and in more formal ways (Zenger & Lawrence, 1989). When group members communicate less often, interpersonal conflicts become more likely (Maznevski, 1994). Diversity, however, can also be beneficial to group performance (McLeod & Lobel, 1992). Diversity allows a group to be more flexible, foster innovation, and improve the quantity and quality of relationships outside of the group.

Groups can also be distinguished by their type. In a recent study (Lickel et al., 2000), participants were asked to categorize a large number of groups. Their sorting resulted in four categories of groups: first, some groups, such as families and romantic relationships, were categorized as *intimacy groups*; second, *task-oriented groups* consisted of groups such as committees and work groups; third, groups such as women and Americans were categorized as *social categories*; and, finally, *weak social relationships or associations* included such groups as those who enjoy a certain type of music or those who live in the same neighborhood. Political groups certainly fall into the task-oriented type, whether they are government working groups, juries, political interest groups such as Greenpeace or Human Rights Watch, or committees and subcommittees in Congress. Political groups can also be social categories, such as ethnic groups, racial groups, or women, all with particular political issues of concern.

Group Structure

Another important characteristic of a group is its structure. Every group has a structure, and it tends to develop quickly and change slowly in most groups (Levine & Moreland, 1998). Apparently, group members need to know what the structure of a group is and are reluctant to alter it once it is set. For example, understanding the structure of a group, and how aspects of a group's structure can influence conflict and performance, is important. Aspects of group structure include status, roles, norms, and cohesion.

Status in a group refers to how power is distributed among its members. Indicators of high status include nonverbal behavior, such as standing more erect, maintaining eye contact, and being more physically intrusive (Leffler, Gillespie, & Conaty, 1982), as well as verbal behavior, such as speaking more, interrupting more, and being more likely to be spoken to (Skovertz, 1988). The manner in which people acquire or are assigned status can be explained by two theories: expectation states theory (Berger, Rosenholtz, & Zelditch, 1980) suggests that the expectations of a person, based on their personal characteristics, contribute to group members' sense of the sorts of accomplishments a person can achieve; ethological theories (Mazur, 1985) maintain that a group member acquires status when other group members assess the person's strength by evaluating their demeanor and appearance. However status is acquired, it is generally slow to change. Because high status is associated with rewards, those high in status are reluctant to give it up. And, because those high in status are usually evaluated more favorably than those low in status, other group members are reluctant to remove status (Messe, Kerr, & Sattler, 1992).

The various roles that group members hold constitute another important component of group structure. **Roles** are expectations about how a person ought to behave. Little is known about how roles in groups develop (Levine & Moreland, 1998), except that task roles emerge before socioemotional ones. Regardless of how roles develop, it is clear that well-played roles can be beneficial to a group (Barley & Bechky, 1994; Bastien & Hostager, 1998). Much of the research on roles in groups focuses on the conflicts they create. Some role conflicts occur as a result of *role assignment*, which refers to the decisions that are made about who plays what role. Other conflicts center on *role ambiguity* (uncertainty about how to behave in a role) or *role strain* (lacking knowledge or ability to fulfill the role).

The norms of a group can be an important aspect of group structure. **Norms** refer to expectations about how all group members should behave. Like roles, the formation of norms in a group can be difficult to identify. Some argue that a group's initial behavior can be transformed into norms (Feldman, 1984). Others argue that norms can arise from the expectations for behavior that people bring with them when they join a group (Bettenhausen & Murnighan, 1991). Regardless of how norms are formed, there is strong pressure to maintain them. Group members can impose strong sanctions on members who violate the standards of behavior, and for good reason. Research suggests that adherence to norms improves the performance of a group (Seashore, 1954). For example, in groups that have norms of productivity or success, group members become more motivated to engage in behaviors or tasks that ensure the success of the group. On the other hand, adherence to norms can sometimes impede the performance of a group. If a norm of laziness develops, for example, then group members might work less hard to achieve their goals.

Cohesion refers to the factors that cause a group member to remain in the group (Festinger, 1950). The importance of cohesion to a group's well-being cannot be underestimated. It exerts powerful effects on a group's longevity. As such, understanding how cohesion in a group develops is important. There are several factors that affect the development of group cohesion. First, the more time group members spend together, the more cohesive they become (Griffith & Greenlees, 1993). Second, the more group members like each other, the more cohesive the group is (Lott & Lott, 1965). Third, groups that are more rewarding to their members are more cohesive (Ruder & Gill, 1982). Fourth, external threats to a group can increase the group's cohesiveness (Dion, 1979). Fifth, groups are more cohesive when leaders encourage feelings of warmth among group members. Most studies on the effects of cohesion on well-being and performance find a positive relationship. For example, members of cohesive groups are more likely to participate in group activities and to remain in the group (Brawley, Carron, & Widmeyer, 1988), and, in a meta-analysis on the effects of cohesion on performance, Mullen and Copper (1994) found that cohesive groups tend to perform better.

There are many studies of political decision-making groups, particularly American presidents and their close advisers, that show differences among those groups in status, roles, norms, and cohesion. These studies are reviewed extensively in Chapter 5. Here, let us simply take a couple of examples. President John F. Kennedy preferred an advisory group that was collegial. Although he was at the top in terms of status, the various advisers in his group were seen as colleagues. The group was formed at the outset of the administration, and each member had his own domain of expertise, which provided him with a particular role. In terms of norms, conflicting viewpoints were encouraged, and all sides were taken into account in searching for solutions to problems. President Nixon was very different. His advisory group structure was hierarchical, with him on top. Again, each adviser had a role to play, but conflict and brainstorming were not encouraged. The emphasis in problem solving was on technical rather than political considerations. In the Clinton administration, role assignments were ambiguous, which led to many delays and much turmoil in policy making.

Group Formation

If you think about all of the groups you are a member of, do you know how or why each of those groups formed? What were the circumstances surrounding the formation of each of your groups? Some of the answers may be easier than others. For example, the animal shelter you volunteer at formed because there was a need to care for stray dogs and cats, and the group of people you spend free time with formed because the members liked one another. But how did the church you attend get started? Why did the Tuesday night intramural softball team that you play on come to be? Groups researchers have yet to develop a comprehensive theory to explain how and why groups form, but there are two perspectives that offer promise. The *functional perspective* suggests that groups form because they serve a useful function or fulfill a need for their individual members (Mackie & Goethals, 1987). For example, your animal shelter formed to fulfill the need created by so many homeless dogs and cats. The *interpersonal attraction perspective* suggests that groups form because its members like one another and seek to spend time together. Thus, the group of friends you spend time with formed because you all liked one another and wanted to spend time together.

Functional Perspective

According to the functional perspective, groups satisfy many needs, including survival, psychological, informational, interpersonal, and collective. Groups can be functional, in that they can fulfill many of our *survival* needs, including feeding, defense, nurturance, and reproduction (Bertram, 1978; Harvey & Greene, 1981; Scott, 1981). Many of these needs were stronger during earlier periods in history, but we still rely on groups to fulfill many of these functions today. For example, we rely heavily on our military forces to defend our country. We depend on farmers to provide some of our food. And, to the extent that we have a need to defend our country, for example, we might decide to join one of our country's armed forces. From an evolutionary psychology perspective, membership in groups can help groups to fulfill their evolutionary goals of survival, for most of the reasons expressed above.

Political Action Groups and the Internet

The Internet seems to affect everything, even group formation patterns. Consider, for example, a political action group called MoveOn. Two Silicon Valley entrepreneurs, Joan Blades and Wes Boyd, organized MoveOn in 1998, when they reached a level of frustration with the effort to impeach President Clinton. Then, after 9/11, Eli Pariser started an online petition for peace. They joined forces and formed the MoveOn. org political action committee, creating an international association of over 2 million online activists.

This is an example of a cybergroup formed to achieve functional goals of affecting politics through interest group activity. Will the opportunity to form and join cybergroups affect group psychology? Will it affect group influence in politics? (To learn about MoveOn, naturally, you should visit their Web site, www.moveon.org.)

Groups can also satisfy a host of psychological needs, some of which we introduced in Chapter 2. For example, joining a group can satisfy the need for affiliation. Those with a high need for affiliation join groups more often, communicate with others frequently, and seek social approval (McClelland, 1985). Groups can also satisfy the need for power. People with a high need for power want to control others (Winter, 1973). This need can often be accomplished by joining a group. Schutz's **Fundamental Interpersonal Relations Orientation (FIRO)** can also explain how joining a group can fulfill psychological needs (Schutz, 1958). According to this perspective, joining a group can satisfy three basic needs: *inclusion* (the desire to be part of a group), *control* (the need to organize an aspect of the group), and *affection* (the desire to establish positive relations with others). Joining a group offers individuals a way to fulfill these needs.

Another category of needs that can often be served well by groups is informational needs. Festinger (1950, 1954) argued that people join groups to provide standards with which to compare their own beliefs, opinions, and attitudes. People often have a need to determine if their own viewpoints are correct or accurate. One way to make such determinations is to seek similar people with whom to compare our views. This perspective suggests that people join groups to better understand social reality.

Groups can also meet people's interpersonal needs. Many groups can provide social support, giving emotional sustenance, advice, and valuable feedback. Social support can be a valuable function of groups. Groups can protect us from the harmful effects of stress (Barrera, 1986). The social support of groups can also protect us from being lonely. Research indicates that people who were members of many groups reported less loneliness (Rubenstein & Shaver, 1980). College students who eat dinner with others and spend time with their friends also report being less lonely (Russell, Peplau, & Cutrona, 1980).

Finally, groups can fulfill important collective needs. Sometimes, groups can be more productive and efficient than individuals working alone. Groups often form because individuals believe that pooling the efforts of multiple people will lead to better outcomes than if individuals simply work alone. Some of the collective goals sought by groups include engaging in the performing arts, enriching the leisure time of their members, changing the opinions of persons outside the group, and making routine individual tasks more tolerable (Zander, 1985).

Interpersonal Attraction Perspective

Sometimes, groups form because individuals discover that they like each other and want to spend more time together. There are many factors that influence our liking of another. First, we tend to be attracted to those who are most similar to us in attitudes, beliefs, socioeconomic status, physical appearance, and so on (Newcomb, 1960). This suggests that we prefer to form or join groups with people who are most similar to us. Second, we tend to form relationships with those who are physically closer to us (Festinger, Schachter, & Back, 1950). Thus, we tend to make friends with those who live next door, those we sit next to in class, and those with whom we work closely. We are likely, then, to form or join groups with people who are physically close. Third, we like people who like us (Newcomb, 1979). We are thus more likely to form or join groups with people who are fond of us. Fourth, we are attracted to people who are physically attractive. With the exception of those who are extremely attractive, physically attractive people are more accepted than those less physically attractive.

In summary, people join groups for a variety of reasons. One reason that people join and form groups is to satisfy a number of important needs, including survival, psychological, informational, interpersonal, and collective needs. We are more likely to join groups that can effectively satisfy our needs. Another reason that people join groups is to spend more time with people they like. Such situations, especially when reciprocal, can be very rewarding.

Group Development

Think again about the groups you belong to. Have they remained the same over time, or have they changed somehow? Most likely, groups that you are a member of have changed somewhat over time, but how? *Group development* refers to the stages of growth and change that occur in a group, from its formation to its dissolution (Forsyth, 1990). Of course, there is disagreement among groups researchers about the number and types of stages, but most models include the following basic stages: forming, storming, norming, performing, and adjourning (Tuckman, 1965; Tuckman & Jensen, 1977).

The first stage refers to the point during which the collection of individuals is **forming**. This stage is also referred to as the orientation stage, because prospective members are orienting themselves to the group. During this stage, individuals are getting to know one another. The stage is often characterized as one with a fair amount of tension—prospective group members are on guard, reluctant to share much information or to discuss their personal views. Also, as you can imagine, group norms have not yet formed, making this a difficult period of development. In fact, the tension can be so high that those who believe they lack the skills necessary to effectively handle such a situation try to avoid group membership (Cook, 1977; Leary, 1983). Over time, tensions lessen and group members begin to exchange more information. Also, feelings of interdependence—one of the defining features of a group—increase during this stage. In Chapters 10 and 12, we look at a number of groups of political extremists, such as the Nazi SS and terrorists. In such cases, careful attention is given to this stage to ensure that only people with particular characteristics are included.

The second stage of group development, **storming**, is characterized as one of conflict. Many types of conflict exist. Some conflicts occur when a person's position or action is misinterpreted (Deutsch, 1973). Other conflicts arise when a group member's behavior is deemed to be distracting, such as when a group member consistently arrives 15 minutes late for meetings. Other types of conflicts can escalate, such as when minor disagreements turn into major points of contention. Although conflicts, especially those that escalate, can disrupt the group, they can serve as important catalysts for group development. Conflicts can serve to promote group unity, interdependence and stability, and cohesion (Bennis & Shepard, 1956; Coser, 1956; Deutsch, 1969).

Norming, the third stage of group development, is a phase in which conflict is replaced with cohesion and feelings of unity. When groups become more cohesive, they have a heightened sense of unity. The relationships among members become stronger, as do individual members' sense of belonging. The degree of group members' identification is heightened during this period. Another characteristic of groups in this stage of development is stability. There is a low turnover of members, a low absentee rate, and a high rate of involvement.

Urban Street Gangs as Groups

Urban street gangs in the United States, and elsewhere, provide illustrations of the power of group demands for loyalty, conformity, and obedience. In the book *Monster: The Autobiography of an L.A. Gang Member* (1993), Sanyika Shakur, a.k.a. Monster Kody, describes those group dynamics: 1. Belonging to the group enhances self-esteem, and cohesive groups demand strong loyalty: "Actually, I wasn't fully aware of the gang's strong gravitational pull. I knew, for instance, that the total lawlessness was alluring, and that the sense of importance, self-worth, and raw power was exciting, stimulating, and intoxicating beyond any other high on this planet. But still I could not explain what had happened to pull me in so far that *nothing* outside of my set mattered" (p. 70). 2. Loyalty and solidarity are described in passages such as this: "I went to trial [for murder] three months later. The gang turnout was surprising. Along with my family, at least fifteen of my homeboys came. All were in full gear (gear as in gang clothes, colors and hats—actually uniforms)" (p. 23). 3. He describes the norms of his gang as "You are your brother's keeper"; when war is declared, all members are expected to fight; reject family and other agents, like the schools and teachers and police, to associate with the gang; respect and honor others according to their status; protect the gang turf; and retaliate against all perceived offenses. 4. Shakur also outlines what the gang values, including trouble (fighting, drinking, drugs, and sex), toughness, smartness (respect for streetwise savvy), and fatalism (they did not believe they would grow old).

During this stage of development, group members also report a high degree of satisfaction with the group. They enjoy the group more, note increases in self-esteem and security, and have lower levels of anxiety. Finally, the internal dynamics of the group begin to intensify. There is greater acceptance of the group's goals by group members, a low tolerance for disagreement, and increased pressures to conform.

The fourth stage of group development is characterized by **performing**. Performance usually only occurs when groups mature and have successfully gone through the previous stages of development (Forsyth, 1990). In a study of neighborhood action groups (Zurcher, 1969), only 1 of 12 groups reached the performing stage. All others were stuck in the conflict or cohesion stages.

A group's decision to dissolve (**adjourning**) can either be planned or spontaneous. A planned dissolution occurs when the group accomplishes its intended goals or exhausts its time and resources. Examples of groups with planned dissolutions include a jury that has reached a verdict, a softball team playing its last game of the season, or a class that dissolves because the semester has come to an end. Spontaneous dissolutions occur when unanticipated problems arise that prevent the group from continuing. Examples of groups with unplanned dissolutions include those that have repeatedly failed or those that fail to satisfy their members' needs.

INFLUENCE IN GROUPS

Groups can exert a great deal of influence over their members. When people are in groups, there is a strong tendency to adhere to the groups' norms. When group members act in accord with group norms, they are conforming. **Conformity** refers to the tendency to change one's beliefs or behaviors so that they are consistent with the standards set by the group. Americans tend to be ambivalent about the notion of conformity. On the one hand, to conform is to be "spineless" and "wishy-washy"; because Americans tend to value individualism, being labeled a conformist can be a negative label. On the other hand, conformity is valued because it leads to harmony and peace. Imagine a world in which no one conformed. In this section, we examine some of the early studies on norm formation and conformity. We also explore the reasons that people conform, as well as when people conform.

One of the earliest studies of conformity was conducted by Sherif (1936), who was interested in how group norms form. To understand norm formation, he made use of the *autokinetic effect*, which refers to a perceptual illusion that occurs when a single point of light in a darkened room appears to be moving. In Sherif's experiments, he asked participants to stare at the point of light and estimate how far it moved. In reality, the light does not move at all, so there is no correct answer on this task. In his first experiment, Sherif asked individual participants to estimate, over a series of trials, how far the light moved. The pattern of responses was nearly identical for all participants: initially, their estimates were quite variable, but over time, they settled on a single estimate, such as 3 inches, for example. In the next experiment, Sherif asked pairs of participants to estimate, over a series of trials, how far the light moved. Again, the pattern of responses for each pair was nearly the same—variability in their initial estimates, then convergence on how far the light moved. These experiments were important in showing how norms form. Eventually, individual or pairs of participants formed a standard for how far the light moved. In Sherif's third experiment, he sought to determine if people could be persuaded to conform to the judgment of another person. Participants in this experiment made judgments in groups of two. In reality, only one of the persons was a real participant; the other was a confederate of the researcher. The confederate was asked to make estimates either lower or higher than the real participant. Over time, the participant began to make estimates that were close to the estimates of the confederate, suggesting that participants were conforming to the standards set by the confederate. These experiments were important in demonstrating that, in ambiguous situations, where there is no correct answer, people tend to conform to a norm. Another researcher, Asch (1955), wondered if participants would be as likely to conform when the situation was not so ambiguous, that is, when there was a correct answer on a judgment task. To answer this query, Asch asked five participants to take part in a perceptual judgment task. The participants were shown a series of three lines, varying in length. Their task was to determine which of the three lines matched a target line. The task was designed to be unambiguous: there was clearly a correct answer. Each participant, in turn, was asked to indicate, aloud, his answer to the experimenter. In reality, the first four participants were confederates of the experimenter. The person sitting in the fifth position was the real participant. On half of the trials, the four confederates were instructed to give the (clearly) wrong answer. The question was: would the fifth (real) participant also give the wrong answer? The results showed that 75% of the participants went along with the group and gave the wrong answer at least once. Apparently, the pressure to conform was so strong that, even on this unambiguous task with a clearly correct answer, participants were willing to give an answer that they knew was wrong.

Both of these experiments are important in showing that people conform. But why do they? Research suggests that people conform for two reasons: to be liked and to be correct (Cialdini & Trost, 1998). In Sherif's (1936) study, people conformed because they wanted to be correct. One way to be correct is to gather as much information as possible before acting or making a decision. For example, one of the authors was recently in London and had to take a train to the airport. Not knowing where or how to buy a train ticket or where to board the train, she spent time observing what other people were doing. In doing so, she gathered enough information so that she was able to successfully purchase a train ticket and board the correct train. Whenever we use other people's actions or opinions to define reality, we conform because of **informational social influence**.

Conformity on the basis of informational social influence occurs whenever we are uncertain about the correct or appropriate action. In the Sherif (1936) studies, for example, the task was novel and ambiguous. Under these circumstances, the best course of action is to gather information from other participants, to arrive at the best answer. If we have a great deal of confidence in our knowledge or ability to make the right decision, then there is little reason to rely on others for information. Research suggests that, when our motivation to be correct is high, we tend to conform more when we are uncertain about the correct answer than when we are certain (Baron, Vandello, & Brunsman, 1996).

In Asch's study (1955), people may have conformed not because they wanted to be correct but instead because they wanted to be liked; this is called **normative social influence**. Sometimes, as in the Asch line study, people give a clearly wrong answer in order to be liked and accepted by the group. In these situations, the group has a powerful, if unspoken, influence over group members' behavior. In an interesting twist on normative social influence, two social psychologists have investigated "jeer pressure," or the tendency to conform in order to avoid rejection from peers (Janes & Olson, 2000). When we observe another person being rejected by the group, there is a tendency to conform even more strongly to the standards set by the group, presumably to avoid similar rejection from group members.

Situational Conformity

If you think about your own behavior, there probably have been times when you conformed or felt the pressure to conform more than others. Some aspects of a situation lead to more pressure to conform than do others. These factors include the size of the group, group unanimity, commitment to the group, and individuation and deindividuation.

Intuitively, one would predict that the pressure to conform is greater as the size of the group increases. Early research (Asch, 1956) suggested that, as group size increased, so did conformity, but only to a point. Once the size of the group reached about three members, conformity seemed to level off. But more recent research (Bond & Smith, 1996) suggests that conformity increases up to a group size of eight members. So, it seems that the larger the group, the greater is our tendency to conform. Group unanimity is also important. Imagine being in the Asch line study—in which all of the group members give the (clearly) wrong answer. Now, it is your turn to give your answer. What do you do? Asch's results suggest that you would give the wrong answer at least once. But now imagine that just one other member of the group gives the correct answer, one that disagrees with the other group members. Now, what answer would you give? Research (Asch, 1955; Morris & Miller, 1975) suggests that conformity drops if there is even just one dissenter in the group.

Groups whose members are highly committed to the group are more likely to conform to the group than members with less commitment (Forsyth, 1990). Obviously, group members who are highly committed to the group want to be liked and accepted by other group members. One way to ensure being liked and accepted is to go along with the group.

One individual difference variable that predicts the tendency to conform or not is **individuation**. Individuation refers to the desire to be distinguishable from others in some aspect (Maslach, Stapp, & Santee, 1985; Whitney, Sagrestano, & Maslach, 1994). Some people have a greater desire than others to differentiate themselves. Those high in the desire for individuation are less likely to conform than those low in individuation. Conversely, **deindividuation** can increase conformity. When this occurs, people attribute their behavior to being part of the group's behavior, and there is a diffusion of responsibility. People feel less responsible for their actions when those actions take place in a group context than they would if they committed those acts alone.

The Tulsa Race Riot, May 31–June 1, 1921

Mobs and riots are one of the most frightening and destructive instances of group behavior, resulting, in part, from situational conformity factors. One example of mob behavior with racist motivations occurred in Tulsa, Oklahoma, in 1921. At that time, Tulsa was home to the most prosperous African American community in the United States, called Greenwood. About 10,000 people lived in this 34-block neighborhood. It was separated from the White community by railroad tracks. Tensions between the Black and White communities increased in May, 1921, when a Black man was accused of assaulting a White woman. Fighting ensued, and on May 31 a White mob pushed the Blacks across the railroad track and proceeded to burn down Greenwood. It soon became evident that the Whites would settle for nothing less than the complete destruction of the Black community and every vestige of Black prosperity. They spread gasoline inside homes and businesses and set them on fire. Blacks fled; some were shot down while they ran, and some burned to death in the buildings. The Whites arrested any Blacks they caught but didn't kill. Before they burned, they looted and stole personal property. It still is not known if the mob acted spontaneously, or if it was organized by the KKK, the police, or another entity. For the full story, read Tim Madigan's book, *The Burning* (2001).

Power

Implicit in our discussion of influence in groups is power. *Power* is the capacity to influence other people (French & Raven, 1959). In groups, power can be advantageous. Powerful group members can resolve group conflicts more efficiently than those with less power (Levine & Moreland, 1998), and powerful members are better-liked and are deferred to more than less powerful group members (Shaw, 1981). Of course, the possession of power can also serve as a disadvantage: those with power are granted the responsibility to be effective leaders (Hollander, 1985), exercising power can be stressful (Fodor, 1985), and exercising power can lead to faulty perceptions of oneself and others (Kipnis, 1984). In this section, we examine the bases of power, as well as the reactions of group members to the exercise of power.

One of the most influential typologies of power is French and Raven's (1959; Raven, 1965) **critical bases of power**. The typology assumes that a group member's ability to exert power over another group member or the entire group can be derived from one or more of the following kinds of power: reward, coercive, legitimate, referent, and expert. **Reward power** is defined as the ability to control the distribution of positive and negative reinforcers. In groups, many rewards are to be had: praise for good performance, money for work completed, and trophies for winning championships. Group members who can control the distribution of those rewards are granted the most power. For example, teachers can exert power over students to study hard, because they control the distribution of good grades. Of course, the group member who controls the distribution of rewards is only powerful if the rewards are valued by the group member, the group member depends on the power holder for the reward, and the power holder's promises are sincere (Forsyth, 1990). When a power holder is the only one in the group who can distribute rewards, their position as a power holder becomes more secure. **Coercive power** refers to the capacity to punish those who do not comply with requests or demands. For example, if one country threatens another with attacks or boycotts, then the country is using coercive power. Teachers can use coercive power to get students to work harder by assigning extra work. Research suggests that, given the choice of using reward or coercive power, most will choose reward (Molm, 1987, 1988). Those with **legitimate power** have a right, by virtue of their position, to require compliance. For example, when a military officer orders troops into battle, that officer is exerting legitimate power. With legitimate power, the power holder has the right to exercise power, and the target has a duty to obey the power holder. An interesting characteristic of legitimate power is that the power holder is typically chosen to occupy the position of power, granting them the support of the majority.

When we identify with someone because they are similar to us or because we want to be like that person, the person then possesses **referent power**. When a child imitates an older sister because the child wants to be like her, this is an example of referent power. Of course, advertisers make use of referent power, when, for example, they encourage young people to purchase cigarettes by implying that they will look like the attractive models in the advertisements. Special knowledge, skill, or ability that one possesses can serve as a basis for **expert power**. Physicians, for example, are often afforded a great deal of power, because of the knowledge and ability they possess. Of course, expert power can only be exerted if the target of power is aware of the power holder's special knowledge or talent (Foschi, Warriner, & Hart, 1985).

Reactions to the Use of Power

One of the goals of power exertion is to affect change. When one country threatens to attack another country, if that country does not comply with certain demands, there is an expectation that the target country will change. Of course, other changes may occur in the target country as a result of the use of power tactics, including compliance, attraction, conflict, rebellion, motivation, and self-blame (Forsyth, 1990). **Compliance** occurs when a powerful member of the group asks a less powerful member of the group to do something, and the member does what is asked. This response is consistent with the *complementarity hypothesis* (Carson, 1969; Gifford & O'Connor, 1987; Kiesler, 1983): when one person acts in a powerful manner, the other person becomes submissive. Such a response also ensures that the power holder will retain their power. Of course, the complying group member need not change their attitudes or behaviors permanently. In fact, although a group member agrees to the demands or requests of the power holder, this does not necessarily correspond to a permanent change in behavior or attitude (Kelman, 1958, 1961). Only when the target of power internalizes the power holder's views does a permanent change in behavior or belief occur. Note that compliance is different than conformity, although both types of social influence can result in a change in behavior. Compliance involves behavior motivated by a particular request; conformity involves behavior motivated by a need to be liked or a need to be correct.

Attraction is also affected by having power. A potential consequence of having power is not being liked by targets of power. In general, we tend not to like those who use power in direct and irrational ways (Forsyth, 1990). This is not to suggest that we dislike all powerful people. Research indicates that the targets of power tend to like those who influence them via discussion, persuasion, or expertise, more than those who influence them via manipulation, evasion, or threat (Falbo, 1977). Regarding the bases of power discussed earlier, research shows that managers who use referent power are liked the most, and those who use coercive power are liked the least (Shaw & Condelli, 1986).

Another consequence of the use of power in a group is **conflict** and tension (Forsyth, 1990). Some types of power use engender more conflict than others. For example, group members often respond to coercive power with anger and hostility (Johnson & Ewens, 1971), except in situations when the group is successful (Michener & Lawler, 1975), they have a trusted leader (Friedland, 1976), or the use of coercive power is normative for the group (Michener & Burt, 1975). One problem with responses that involve anger and conflict is that the functioning of the group may be compromised (Forsyth, 1990). One group member's anger can be fueled by another group member's anger, which can result in an escalation of anger and hostility. Research suggests that, if a group member abuses power, a typical response is **rebellion** on the part of other group members (Lawler & Thompson, 1978). Abuses of power can also lead to *reactance*, a feeling that one's freedom has been limited or taken away (Brehm, 1976). When group members believe that their freedom (of choice, for example) has been removed, they respond by becoming defiant and refusing to go along with the leader (Worchel & Brehm, 1971).

Motivation can also be influenced when power is exercised in a group. Often, group members are motivated intrinsically, that is, they enjoy being productive and doing good work, because they are personally satisfied by it. But, if a leader uses reward or coercive power, which often involves the use of extrinsic rewards (e.g., money, promises), it can lead group members to become less motivated to work hard and do a good job.

In some circumstances, a leader might be so abusive that they cause group members to suffer tremendously. If group members believe that the world is just, then they are likely to think that they got what they deserve (Lerner & Miller, 1978). That is, they might come to believe that they deserve to suffer and will engage in self-blame. A belief such as this allows suffering group members to make sense of their plight.

Group leaders can exercise their power in a number of ways. They have at their disposal several bases of power, some of which are more conducive to certain situations than others. If group leaders have a choice about which bases of power to use, it behooves them to carefully consider the consequences of the use of that base of power. As we have seen, the use of power can engender many reactions, some of which can be good for the functioning and well-being of the group, but others of which can be detrimental to the group.

Minority Influence

A final topic of interest for the study of social influence in groups is minority influence. Sometimes, in groups, there are lone dissenters or a small faction of the group that refuses to go along with the group. Of interest to social psychologists is how successful minorities are in exerting influence on the group. Research suggests that minorities successfully influence majorities under specific circumstances (Kaarbo, 1998; Kaarbo & Beasley, 1998; Moscovici, 1985). First, for minorities to be successful in exerting influence on majorities, they must be consistent in their opposition (Wood, Lundgren, Ouellette, Busceme, & Blackstone, 1994). Members of a consistent minority are perceived as being more honest and competent (Bassili & Provencal, 1988). If they are inconsistent or appear divided in any way, then their influence is greatly diminished. Second, minorities are more successful if they are able to refute the majority's arguments successfully (Clark, 1990). Third, minorities are more successful if the issue is not of great personal relevance to members of the majority (Trost, Maass, & Kendrick, 1992). Finally, minorities are likely to be successful when they are similar to the majority groups in most respects, except for the disagreement at hand (Volpato, Maass, Mucchi-Faina, & Vitti, 1990). For example, if a member of the Republican Party was trying to convince other Republicans to change their views on homeland security, that member would be more successful than if the would-be persuader was a Democrat. In this case, the Republican dissenter is more similar (in terms of party membership) to the majority than is the Democrat.

Successful minorities may be able to change the position of the majority, which, in the political realm, may amount to a policy change. Short of affecting policy as a whole, they may be able to have an indirect effect through pressuring the majority to move in a particular direction, or affecting the information received by the majority. Finally, studies show that minorities can improve the quality of a group's decision making (Nemeth, 1986). Given the inter-agency nature of many government decision-making units, which makes the presence of minorities a frequent occurrence, understanding the role of minorities can help us understand both change in policy and shifts in policy. Kaarbo and Gruenfeld (1998) point to a number of examples: change in Japan's foreign aid policy, from one that emphasized Japan's self-interest to one that reflected humanitarian interest, was the result of a small minority in the foreign ministry, which was pitted against the large and powerful ministries of finance and international trade. Soviet policy toward Czechoslovakia, in 1968, was changed by the prointerventionist minority, who, through manipulation of information and the decision-making process, moved themselves from the minority to the majority.

GROUP PERFORMANCE

One of the primary functions of a group is to perform a task, and one of the unique characteristics of a group is that its tasks are typically performed in the presence of others. For some groups, tasks are performed in the presence of other people, such as in a factory. For other groups, tasks require that group members depend on one another to successfully complete the task, such as in an assembly line. In this section, we examine research suggesting that sometimes the presence of other people enhances performance (social facilitation) and that, at other times, it hinders performance (inhibition).

Groups are often assumed to accomplish more than individuals and to perform better than individuals. Yet, research suggests that groups do not always perform better than individuals. We examine the various productivity losses in groups, including coordination and motivation losses. Finally, we explore some of the techniques used to help groups function more effectively.

Social Facilitation and Inhibition

Have you ever noticed that, when you run a 5K race, for example, your time is always better than when you time yourself during training? Why is it that the speech you gave in your communications class was better than when you practiced it at home by yourself? In some situations, we appear to perform better in the presence of other people than when alone, which is an effect known as *social facilitation*. One of the first experiments ever conducted in social psychology was designed to examine the effects of the presence of others on an individual's performance. Norman Triplett (1898) tested the hypothesis that people perform better in the presence of others than when alone. In his study, he had children play a game alone or with one other person. His results confirmed his hypothesis: when paired with another person, individual performance is better than when performing alone. This and subsequent research suggests that, if given a choice between working alone or in the presence of other people, we would be better off performing a task in the presence of others.

Now imagine another situation. You are playing on a basketball team. Your coach spends hours helping you learn to shoot a left-handed layup, which is not an easy shot for a right-handed person. When by yourself, you can shoot 20 left-handed layups easily. But what happens when you are playing a game in front of a cheering audience? Evidence suggests that you would miss the layup. This effect, known as *social inhibition*, occurs when the presence of others inhibits performance. According to research in this area, we would be better off working alone than in the presence of others.

These two effects—facilitation and inhibition—seem contradictory. One suggests that working in groups can enhance performance, but the other suggests that it can inhibit it. Zajonc (1965) reconciled these two seemingly contradictory findings, by suggesting that the presence of others enhances performance on well-learned or simple tasks, but inhibits performance on difficult or novel tasks. The presence of other people enhances the tendency to display the *dominant* (well-learned) response and inhibits the tendency to suppress the *nondominant* response. Because running is a fairly simple task, the presence of others during a race should enhance performance. But shooting a left-handed layup when you are right handed is a difficult task, so the presence of a cheering crowd or other teammates should hurt performance because our tendency is to shoot the ball with our right hand. A comprehensive review of research in this area basically confirms Zajonc's perspective (Bond & Titus, 1983). The presence of others improves the quantity of performance on simple tasks and decreases the quality and quantity of performance on difficult tasks.

Zajonc's (1965) perspective explains when facilitation and inhibition occur, but why do these effects occur? What is it about the social situation that causes improvement in performance on simple tasks, but decreases performance on difficult tasks? Researchers in the area have developed three explanations: arousal, evaluation apprehension, and distraction. Zajonc (1965, 1980b) argued that the mere presence of others increases the arousal level of the performer. When individuals are in a heightened state of arousal, the tendency to display a dominant response is increased. If the dominant response (shooting the ball with your right hand) is the correct one, then social facilitation occurs. If the dominant response is not the correct one, then social inhibition occurs. Cottrell (1972) agrees that the presence of others causes arousal, but he argues that the source of arousal is evaluation apprehension, or the anxiety created by the fear that one is being evaluated. In a study to test this idea (Cottrell, Wack, Sekerak, & Rittle, 1968), participants were asked to work on a task alone, in the presence of others who were also working on the task, or in the presence of others who were blindfolded (and thus could not see what participants were doing). The results showed that social facilitation occurred only when the others present could see the participant perform the task. When the possibility of evaluation was removed (in the blindfolded participants' condition), social facilitation did not occur. Finally, according to the distraction explanation, the presence of others is potentially distracting. When one is distracted, paying attention to the task at hand can be difficult. Such distractions create conflict as to whether to pay attention to the audience or to the task. When one is distracted, more effort is required to focus attention on the task, thereby improving performance on simple or well-learned tasks. When tasks are difficult, even the increase in effort is not enough to improve performance and usually leads to impaired performance (Baron, 1989; Groff, Baron, & Moore, 1983).

Productivity Losses

As mentioned previously, there is a belief that groups will be more productive than individuals. More than likely, you have been in a group that seems not to have lived up to its fullest potential. Clearly, groups are not always as productive as they should be. According to Steiner (1972), there are two reasons for process losses in groups. One reason is that the responses of individual group members are not combined in a way that enhances group productivity. Decrements in performance caused by poor coordination are known as *coordination losses*. In an operating room, for example, coordination losses occur if the surgeon is not handed the correct surgical instruments. Another reason for productivity losses is known as *motivation losses*. These occur when individual group members fail to exert their maximum effort on a task. The operating room team will not perform at its maximum level if one of the team members does not complete his or her assignment effectively. Although both coordination and motivation losses in groups are interesting, most attention has been paid to motivation losses. One such motivation loss that has received a great deal of attention is social loafing.

Social loafing refers to the tendency of group members to work less hard when in a group than when working alone. One of the earliest studies of social loafing was conducted by Ringelmann (1913), who found that people exerted less effort when pulling a rope or pushing a cart if they worked in a group than if they worked alone. In another interesting study (Latane et al., 1979), groups of six participants were asked to wear a blindfold, sit in a semi-circle, and listen (via headphones) to the noise of people shouting. Participants were asked to shout as loud as they could, while listening to the noise through their headphones. On some trials, participants believed that they were shouting alone or with one other person. On other trials, they believed that everyone was shouting. When participants thought they were shouting with one other person, they shouted 82% as intensely as when they thought they were alone. When they thought everyone was shouting, they shouted 75% as intensely.

Because social loafing can lead to severe performance decrements in groups, efforts have been made to reduce or eliminate it. First, social loafing can be reduced if each group member's contributions are clearly identifiable (Hardy & Latane, 1986; Kerr & Bruun, 1981). When the possibility of being evaluated is evident, group members appear to give maximum effort (Harkins, 1987). Second, if group members find the work to be interesting and involving, then they are less likely to loaf (Brickner, Harkins, & Ostrom, 1986; Harkins & Petty, 1982; Zaccaro, 1984). Third, if group members take personal responsibility for the group's outcome, then they are less likely to loaf (Kerr & Bruun, 1983). Group members need to believe that their individual efforts will have an impact on the group's outcome.

Improving Productivity

In addition to efforts to reduce social loafing in groups, researchers have developed techniques to help groups function more effectively and avoid production losses of any kind. One such technique is *team development*, which includes a variety of techniques, such as sensitivity training, problem identification, and role analysis (Dyer, 1987). Techniques such as these are designed to improve both the task and interpersonal skills of group members. A similar technique involves the use of *quality circles* (Marks, Mirvis, Hackett, & Grady, 1986). If group members engage in regular meetings to discuss problems with productivity and ways to solve the problems, then productivity losses can often be reduced. Another technique involves the use of *autonomous work groups* (Pearson, 1992). This technique involves the use of self-managed work teams who can control how tasks are performed.

Many of these techniques require that groups change how they function. There are also techniques that focus on individual group members. For example, in *participative goal setting*, individual group members are responsible for setting the group's productivity goals (Pearson, 1987; Pritchard, Jones, Roth, Stuebing, & Ekeberg, 1988). Another technique, *task design*, involves changing the attributes of the task to make it more attractive to group members (Hackman & Lawler, 1971). Both of these techniques involve changing group members' perceptions of the task, rather than the task itself.

GROUP DECISION MAKING

The discussion of group productivity attests to the fact that groups are frequently called upon to perform a variety of activities. An important activity that groups, especially political ones, are often asked to do is to make decisions. Political groups are often responsible for making decisions with large-scale consequences, such as whether to send troops to a region in conflict or to escalate an existing conflict. As in productivity tasks, groups are often assumed to make better decisions than individuals. Groups can pool all of the best resources that individual group members can offer. In this section, we examine the group decision-making process, including how decisions are made, the stages of group decision making, and how individual resources are pooled; then we examine research on the effectiveness of individual versus group decisions. We also look at research suggesting that groups often make bad decisions, and, finally, we explore some tactics to improve the decisions made by groups.

The Decision-Making Process

Imagine that a group of people, such as a jury, have been assembled to make an important decision. A jury spends time listening to testimony and the presentation of evidence. When all of the evidence has been presented, the jury meets to discuss their verdict. At the end of their deliberations, which can last from a couple of minutes to weeks and months, they reach a final, typically unanimous, decision. From the perspective of an observer, the jury appears to leave the courtroom and magically return with a verdict. But what happened between the time the jury left the courtroom to deliberate and when they returned with a verdict? How did this group of people reach a decision about what should happen to the defendant? The group decision-making process has been studied extensively, and several models exist that can help us understand how groups arrive at a decision.

Three-Stage Model of Group Decision Making

According to Bales and Strodtbeck (1951), groups proceed through three stages, before eventually arriving at a decision. In the *orientation* stage, group members spend time defining the problem and planning their strategy for solving the problem. Research (Hackman & Morris, 1975) suggests that most groups spend little time in this phase, assuming that planning is a waste of their time, but that groups who spend a fair amount of time in the orientation phase are more successful than groups that do not (Hackman, Brousseau, & Weiss, 1976; Hirokawa, 1980). In the *discussion* stage, group members spend their time gathering information, identifying and evaluating alternatives. The amount of time groups spend in this stage is also related to the quality of the group's decisions (Harper & Askling, 1980; Laughlin, 1988). However, groups do not often make full use of this stage (Janis & Mann, 1977; Stasser & Titus, 1987). In addition, the use of information by groups at this stage is problematic, in that new information brought forth by one member of the group, but unknown to other members, is not fully considered in discussion. In fact, groups tend to "omit unshared information from discussions while focusing on information that all members already know" (Wittenbaum & Stasser, 1996, p. 5). In the *decision-making* stage, groups choose a solution. How groups combine the individual preferences to reach a group decision can be explained by understanding the group's social-decision scheme.

Social-Decision Schemes

Social-decision schemes refer to the process by which groups combine the preferences of all the members of the group to arrive at a single group decision (Stasser, Kerr, & Davis, 1989). If groups use the *majority-wins rule*, then they combine individual preferences by opting for whatever position is supported by the greatest number of group members. For example, if 10 of 12 jury members believe they should deliver a "guilty" verdict, then the group's final decision will be "Guilty." In the *truth-wins rule*, group members tend to be persuaded by the truth of a particular position. This rule tends to be adopted when group members are discussing facts rather than opinions. Another decision scheme that groups use is the *first-shift rule*, by which groups tend to adopt the decision that is consistent with the first shift in group members' opinions.

Describing social-decision schemes from a research perspective may leave you with a sense that the process occurs without pressures or emotions, but pressures, such as conformity pressures, occur during this process, and they can be extreme. A book describing jury deliberations in a murder case, written by the foreman of the jury, describes the pressure put upon the only person reluctant to vote "Not guilty":

> Without pausing, I took the cards out of my pocket and passed them around. . . . There was silence as the cards started to come back, each folded in half. I counted them. Nine. We waited, and two more came in. Eleven. We waited. Still eleven. At this point there was no confusion about who still held a card. Adelle [the holdout] sat at the corner of the table to my left. . . . She was looking fixedly away, up, behind her, out the window. No one spoke. . . . One sensed everyone in the room concentrating on the blank card in rapt meditation. Adelle breathed audibly, wrote something rapidly on the card, closed it on itself, and pushed it into the middle of the table. I placed it, consciously and more or less conspicuously, at the bottom of the pile. I wanted the

full dismay of the room to land on her if she had voted for a conviction. Then I began to open the cards and read them: not guilty, not guilty. . . . And the last one: Not guilty.

(Burnett, 2001, p. 166)

Emotions and Decisions

As you can imagine, people and groups make decisions for a variety of reasons ranging from the mundane (e.g., choosing the background on a print advertisement) to the serious (e.g., deciding whether or not to engage in a terrorist activity). As such, some decisions are made with weak emotion; others with quite strong emotions. One question that is useful to ponder is what effect emotions have on decision making. The answer to this question is more complicated than it may appear on the surface. Research (Leith & Baumeister, 1996) on the effects of emotion on risky decisions shows that when people are angry, embarrassed, or upset, they tend to make risky decisions, presumably in an attempt to gain a positive outcome, thereby offsetting or neutralizing the negative emotion. Why do people experiencing negative emotions make riskier decisions? The answer is that when people are angry or embarrassed or upset, their ability to cognitively process rational information is diminished. They appear to be less able to think things through and consider all of the possible outcomes (Leith & Baumeister, 1996).

So, does this mean that people should not make decisions when they are feeling emotional? Not necessarily. Baumeister, Vohs, & Tice (2006) suggest that sometimes being emotional can lead to good decisions and sometimes to bad decisions. What matters is the type and nature of the emotion. Some emotions are anticipatory in nature; that is, they are emotions that people expect to feel once the decision has been made. Consider a decision such as deciding whether or not to break up with your significant other. How you expect to feel once the break-up has been enacted will influence your decision to initiate the break-up or not. Baumeister, Vohs, & Tice (2006) found that anticipated emotion can have beneficial effects on decision making because people are likely to base their decision on trying to achieve the best emotional outcome, such as feeling better or feeling good. On the other hand, one's current (as opposed to anticipated) emotional state can lead to poor decisions because people want to make a decision that will improve their mood or affect, thus causing them to engage in risky decisions. Current emotional states, if they are negative, motivate people to make decisions that will make them feel better right now. Such a strategy often causes people to make irrational and bad decisions.

Groups and Political Decision-Making Units

Political decisions are made in response to a perceived problem, and they tend to occur sequentially, that is, frequently a set of decisions is made, one after another, without pausing to evaluate the effect of each decision along the way. Decisions are also made by different actors, agencies, and coalitions. The type of group making authoritative decisions can have an impact on the policies that result. Hermann (2001) has proposed a model of foreign policy decision making by groups, which can also be used in domestic political contexts. She argues that there are three types of decision-making groups, or units. The **predominant leader** group has "a single individual who has the ability to stifle all opposition and dissent as well as the power to make a decision alone, if necessary" (p. 56). The **single group** is a decision unit that includes "a set of individuals, all of whom are members of a single body, who collectively select a course of action in consultation with each other" (p. 57). This can be an ad hoc group set up to respond to a crisis, such as the Office of Homeland Security established by President Bush after the attack of September 11, 2001, or a standing bureaucracy (which Homeland Security eventually became) or interagency committee. Finally, a **coalition of autonomous actors** is a decision unit that is composed of multiple groups that can act independently. U.S. trade policy, for example, is affected by a wide variety of domestic and international interest groups, multilateral organizations, government bureaucracies, and so forth. Each can act independently, and each has some impact at different times on decisions and policies.

Hermann maintains that each kind of decision-making unit has different decision processes and different behavioral patterns. The first two kinds of decision units can be analyzed with political psychological concepts. In the *predominant leader unit*, the most important factors affecting how the group behaves and makes decisions are the personality characteristics of the leader, which are discussed in Chapter 2. The *single group pattern* is determined by group psychology, particularly the techniques used by the group to handle disagreements and conflict in the group. There are three alternatives: groupthink (discussed in more detail later), wherein groups attempt to minimize disagreement by promoting conformity; bureaucratic politics, wherein group members acknowledge that disagreements will occur and attempt "to resolve the conflict through debate and compromise" (Hermann, 2001, p. 65); and finally, the implementation of a social-decision scheme, discussed earlier.

Individual vs. Group Decision Making

Evidence indicates that groups are not necessarily better decision makers than individuals (Hill, 1982). According to Hastie (1986), whether groups make better decisions than individuals often depends on the characteristics of the task. On numerical estimation tasks, for example, group judgments tend to be a little better than the average individual judgment, but on problem-solving tasks, such as logic problems, group solutions tend to be much better than average individual judgments, but worse than the best individual judgment. One of the keys to determining the superiority of group or individual judgments, according to Hastie (1986), is whether the task involves a demonstrably correct solution. When there is, groups tend to perform better than individuals. Some recent research indicates that groups make better decisions than individuals when they have been working together for a long time and the task is important to the group members (Michaelsen, Watson, & Black, 1989; Watson, Michaelsen, & Sharp, 1991).

Individual solutions have also been compared to group solutions in *brainstorming* tasks, which require participants to generate as many different suggestions as they can. Intuition suggests that groups would perform better than individuals on brainstorming tasks (more people should produce more ideas), but research suggests that individuals often produce more and better ideas when working alone than when working in brainstorming groups (Mullen, Johnson, & Salas, 1991; Taylor, Berry, & Block, 1958). Several explanations have been offered for the failure of groups to perform as well as individuals on brainstorming tasks. First, when one group member is speaking, another is prevented from speaking at the same time, which often causes other group members to forget what they were going to say (Brown & Paulus, 1996). This situation might lead to a loss of ideas. Second, group members may have evaluation anxiety and fear that their ideas will be ridiculed by other group members (Camacho & Paulus, 1995). As a consequence, they might be reluctant to share new ideas.

Consistent with the idea that groups often perform worse than do individuals on problem-solving or brainstorming tasks is the notion that groups often make worse decisions than individuals. In fact, many group decisions in political history (e.g., Bay of Pigs, Vietnam War) suggest that groups often make bad decisions with serious consequences. Researchers have identified several faulty decision-making processes to describe some of the bad decisions that groups make, including groupthink, new group syndrome, bureaucratic politics, group polarization, and the escalation of commitment.

Groupthink

Groupthink refers to an irrational style of thinking that causes group members to make poor decisions (Janis, 1972). Janis maintained that many major political decisions, such as the Bay of Pigs invasion, the United States' failure to defend against the attack on Pearl Harbor, the Vietnam War, and Watergate, provide evidence for groupthink. According to Janis (1982), there are a number of observable features of these groups that provide evidence for the existence of groupthink. First, in all of these decision-making groups, group members felt a strong pressure to *conform* to the group. There were strong sanctions for disagreeing with other group members or criticizing their opinions. Second, *self-censorship* was present in most of the groups. Although many group members may have disagreed with the decisions that were being made, they felt pressured to not express these disagreements openly. Third, *mindguards* in the group prevented group members from learning of new information that might disrupt the flow of the group's proceedings. Fourth, there was an *apparent unanimity* of opinion. All of the group members seemed to agree with one another. Fifth, *illusions of invulnerability* allowed group members to feel confident in their decisions. Most group members believed that their judgments could not be wrong. Sixth, *illusions of morality* prevented group members from ever questioning the morality of their decisions. They believed that because they were a member of an elite decision-making group, all of their decisions were moral and justified. Seventh, group members had a *biased perception of the other group.* In the Bay of Pigs decision, a decision by the Kennedy administration to sponsor a group seeking to overthrow Fidel Castro in Cuba in 1961, members of the President's advisory committee believed Castro to be a weak and evil leader. Derogatory comments about Castro were frequently voiced during meetings. Finally, many of the decisions made by these groups represented *defective decision-making strategies.* Decisions made in groupthink situations are often described as fiascos, blunders, and debacles.

In addition to specifying the characteristics of the group and the group decision-making process that indicates evidence for groupthink, Janis (1972) also specified the causes of groupthink. One cause is *cohesiveness.* When groups are very cohesive, as was the case in the Bay of Pigs advisory committee, disagreements are typically held to a minimum, creating the perfect conditions for faulty decision making. Another cause of groupthink is *isolation.* When groups, such as the president's advisory committee, are discussing top-secret issues, they do so in isolation, which prevents outsiders from entering the group to review the group's deliberations. Another cause of groupthink is the presence of a *directive leader,* who has control over the discussion and can prevent any disagreements from being voiced. Finally, *stress* can also create symptoms of groupthink.

In the only book-length study of the groupthink phenomenon, 't Hart (1990/1994) expanded upon Janis's concept by noting that, in addition to groupthink being a product of high in-group cohesion under stress, it may also emerge as the result of anticipatory compliance by group members seeking to reach decisions that they believe will meet the views or desires of powerful leaders or peers. Further, 't Hart (1990/1994) notes that the situational conditions in which groupthink becomes most likely include situations of threat and stress (the context emphasized originally by Janis) and situations perceived by group members as major opportunities requiring rapid and major commitment to a pet project or policy to achieve major success (Fuller & Aldag, 1997).

Groupthink has received mixed support (Levine & Moreland, 1998). Some studies support parts of the groupthink model. For example, one study (Tetlock, Peterson, McGuire, Chang, & Feld, 1992) analyzed records of 12 different political decisions and found that it was possible to distinguish between groups whose decisions were indicative of groupthink and those that reflected good decision making. But the research was not especially successful in locating evidence for all of the factors thought to cause groupthink. Other work (Aldag & Fuller, 1993; Fuller & Aldag, 1997) suggests that research has failed to provide convincing support for the existence of groupthink and that the model itself has become an unnecessary constraint upon researchers seeking to adequately examine the true dynamics of group decision making under the conditions explored by Janis. Indeed, Fuller and Aldag suggest, along with many current scholars of political group dynamics (see 't Hart, Stern, & Sundelius, 1997), that, rather than proceed with further studies utilizing the outdated groupthink model, scholars should unpack the various component parts from the model and embrace a wider range of new research and literature on group function and dynamics that better reflects the behavior of actual political decision groups.

New Group Syndrome

Another analysis of conformity problems in group decision making is called *new group syndrome*, which is part of a recent collection of articles seeking to move beyond groupthink ('t Hart et al., 1997). Stern (1997; see also Stern & Sundelius, 1994) uses social psychological findings regarding the life cycle of groups in a reexamination of the Bay of Pigs disaster, one of Janis's groupthink cases. Group cohesion, norms, status hierarchy, and strength of group identity all change as the group ages. With good performance, cohesion increases. With time, the status hierarchies and role responsibilities become clear and routine. Norms and accepted decision rules are internalized. When groups are new, Stern (1997) argues, members bring with them extragroup baggage, in the form of values, beliefs, and past experiences that affect the decision making in the new group. In addition, leaders are particularly important in the early stages of a group's life, and that is particularly the case when the leader is the president of the United States. At this stage, leaders can establish roles, norms, and group decision-making processes that lead to effective and critical policy option deliberation, rather than to group conformity. Some leaders do this early on, but others do not, and this leads to new group syndrome. When a leader does not establish norms and decision-making patterns, "there is a serious risk that group interaction will spontaneously evolve in a fashion leading to excessive degrees of conformity or conflict (an abrupt shift into the storming stage)" (Stern, 1997, p. 163). In this early forming stage, the group members are uncertain about how they should behave, are anxious to do a good job, and, therefore, are very vulnerable to conformity pressures, if group leaders do not encourage the opposite by establishing roles, norms, and decision-making procedures. This is new group syndrome. As an explanation of excessive group conformity, it differs from groupthink, in that it is not dependent upon situation pressures such as extreme stress. The phenomenon can occur in any group, in any context.

The Bay of Pigs fiasco shows evidence of new group syndrome. Kennedy had been in office for only four months, the plan itself came from the previous administration, Kennedy was under pressure to do something about Castro, and the advisory group he used in making the decision was informal and interagency in nature. Kennedy had campaigned against the Republicans, in part, on the platform that they had been lackadaisical in confronting communism, and he swept away the previous administration's policy-making system. Stern (1997) describes the group culture in the decision-making group as follows:

> A number of analysts have suggested that a norm of "boldness" associated with the "New Frontier" mentality permeated the proceedings. Another important norm appears to have been "rally to the President" when his "project" came under the criticism of outsiders. . . . Another apparent norm that proved dysfunctional was "deference to experts." Finally, an emergent norm of deference to the leader is noticeable, a norm of which the president himself appears to have been unaware. . . . Kennedy, having little previous management experience, reportedly had a relatively simplistic view of small group and organizational management. He placed a premium on talent, believing that

this quality was the key to achieving policy and political success. In other words, he believed that it was enough to assemble a number of talented people, throw them in a room together, and wait for good things to happen.

(pp. 174, 177)

What he got instead was failure. The Cuban exiles, sponsored by the United States to invade Cuba and overthrow Castro, landed in a swamp, the Bay of Pigs, and were quickly captured by the Cuban military. The popular uprising against Castro, which they counted on in their plan to overthrow Castro, never happened.

Bureaucratic Politics

Another set of group-related decision-making problems that plague political decisions comes under the rubric of bureaucratic politics. Although political systems differ widely, many political decisions are affected by the interactions of groups based in governmental bureaucracies. Those groups have differing perspectives and interests; they see issues and problems differently, and they compete for policy dominance and resources. At the same time, these groups have to interact in a variety of policy contexts and need to work together. Consequently, their interactions are often characterized as "pulling and hauling," that is, bargaining, coalition formation, compromise, competition, and the selective use and sharing of information to enhance the position of the group or faction in question. The result is policy decision making based upon organizational and group interests, rather than on an objective assessment of the policy issue. The often-quoted phrase, "Where you stand depends on where you sit," reflects this pattern.

Early studies of bureaucratic politics focused primarily on the standard operating procedures and conflicts among bureaucratic groups, both of which can negatively affect decision making. The seminal study by Allison (1971), on the Cuban missile crisis of 1962, illustrated the impact of bureaucratic struggles in one of the most dangerous episodes of American foreign policy, which nearly led to nuclear war. Rather than keeping a focus on the national interest, the bureaucracies fought continuously for control of the policy. In August 1962, there were increasing concerns in the Central Intelligence Agency (CIA) that the Soviet Union was placing, or would place, offensive nuclear missiles in Cuba. During the next month, these concerns spread, and the question of whether to send U-2 spy planes to take pictures of Cuba, in search of missile sites, was discussed. This was considered to be a risky enterprise because of the diplomatic fallout should a U-2 be shot down. Bickering between the Air Force and CIA, over which agency would get to fly the U-2s over Cuba, caused a 10-day delay in spotting the missiles. Those 10 days were crucial for the installation and arming of the missiles and made the conflict that followed, between the United States and USSR, much more dangerous.

More recent studies of bureaucratic politics have focused more precisely on the group nature of decision making in bureaucracies (Preston & 't Hart, 1999; Stern & Sundelius, 1997; Vertzberger, 1990). This has enabled analyses of the whole range of decision-making patterns that can emerge from group

Optimal Process				
Bureaucratic Consensus-Making				**Bureaucratic Confrontation**
Bureaupolitical oversimplification	←	(1) Reality testing Bureaupolitical deliberation	→	Bureaupolitical distortion
Bureaupolitical isolation	←	(2) Acceptability Bureaupolitical compromise formation	→	Bureaupolitical paralysis
Bureaupolitical haste	←	(3) Efficiency Bureaupolitical economy	→	Bureaupolitical waste

Figure 4.1 Bureaucratic Politics: The Normative Dimensions

interaction in bureaucracies, a range that spans from consensus seeking, the most extreme form of which is groupthink, to extreme intergroup conflict verging on bureaucratic warfare. Consensus and cohesion occurs within groups, particularly when pressured by intense intergroup conflict. Hence, bureaucracies can be the locale of a long continuum of group-produced behaviors (see Figure 4.1).

For example, Preston and 't Hart (1999) have argued that the actual degree to which bureaucratic politics pervades the policy-making process is variable, and that it is important to see bureaucratic politics as a continuum in which such dynamics will have varying degrees of impact (both positive and negative) upon the quality of the decision-making process. They employ three criteria developed by George (1980) for evaluating the quality of decision making on that continuum. The three criteria are *reality testing* (Does information get to the central decision makers and are multiple options considered?), *acceptability* (Are relevant players involved in the decision-making group and are they listened to?), and *efficiency* (What are the costs of the decision-making process?). Preston and 't Hart (1999) argue that, at the consensus end of the spectrum, one sees the decision-making pathologies of bureaupolitical *oversimplification*, when reality testing is poor; *isolationism*, when acceptability is poor; and *hasty decision making*, when efficiency is poor. On the extreme conflict end of the scale, one sees bureaupolitical *distortion*, when reality testing is poor; *paralysis*, when acceptability is poor; and *waste*, when efficiency is poor.

Manipulation

Manipulation occurs when a group member, often a leader, rigs decision making, and may get a group to "accept a commitment which would have been rejected out of hand had the full implications and full extent of the project been revealed from the start" (Stern & Sundelius, 1997, p. 131).

Manipulators use at least three strategies: they affect the group's structure, so that their allies dominate decision making; they manipulate the procedures the group follows, by setting the agenda and framing issues in a particular way; and they manipulate their personal relationships with group members, both formally and informally, to put themselves in a favorable position to influence the decision's outcome (Hoyt & Garrison, 1997).

Group Polarization

Groups researchers have long been interested in whether groups make riskier decisions than individuals. Janis's (1972) groupthink model suggests that groups take risky courses of action that cannot be justified. Research on the *risky shift* phenomenon suggests that the decisions made by groups are often riskier than those made by individuals (Stoner, 1961; Wallach, Kogan, & Bem, 1962). But there also exists evidence suggesting that groups sometimes make more cautious decisions than individuals (Wallach et al., 1962), and some evidence suggests that groups make both more risky *and* more cautious decisions (Doise, 1969).

Groups make both very risky and very cautious decisions, compared to individuals. When in a group, there is a tendency to make extreme decisions. Whether the decision is extremely risky or extremely cautious depends on what position dominated at the outset of the discussion. **Group polarization** refers to the tendency for individuals' opinions to become more extreme after discussion than before discussion (Myers & Lamm, 1976). For example, if group member A's pregroup-discussion opinion tended to be moderately cautious, then their postgroup-discussion opinion would probably be extremely cautious. Likewise, if group member B's pregroup-discussion opinion was moderately risky, it will become even more risky after group discussion. Although there is a tendency to assume that extreme decisions, in either direction, are bad decisions, such is not the case. Extremely risky or cautious decisions can have positive or negative outcomes.

A number of explanations have been offered to account for polarization effects. One explanation is based on the *persuasive arguments perspective*, which assumes people are likely to be exposed to persuasive arguments that favor their initial position (Burnstein & Vinokur, 1977). Although group discussions are likely to contain some arguments for and against an individual's initial position, there is a tendency to sample information that is consistent with our own point of view. Such biased information sampling is likely to shift a group member's opinion further in the direction of their initial position. Additionally, a group member is likely to share their initial position with the rest of the group. The mere expression and restatement of ideas may increase the shift toward a more extreme view (Brauer, Judd, & Gliner, 1995). Those members committed to a more risk-prone decision may be more committed, more vocal, and hence more influential in persuading others. However, as Vertzberger notes (1997), when more cautious members are more committed, they can sway the group toward that pole.

Another explanation for group polarization is based on *social comparison* processes. According to this perspective, group members often compare themselves to others, in order to gain approval for their views. Comparisons with other group members might lead to the realization that others have similar opinions and still others have more extreme opinions. Motivated by a need to be viewed positively by other group members, individuals may shift their opinions to a more extreme position (Brown, 1974; Myers, 1978). Social comparison processes can be so strong that polarization can be produced by merely knowing of others' positions, in the absence of exposure to supporting arguments (Isenberg, 1986).

A third explanation for group polarization is based on *social identity* processes (Hogg, Turner, & Davidson, 1990; Mackie, 1986). According to this perspective, group discussion causes individual group members to focus on the group, which can often lead to pressures toward conformity. Rather than perceiving the average opinion of the group, individual group members often perceive the group's opinion to be more extreme. Pressures to conform lead individuals to adopt a position that is more extreme than their initial position.

Escalation of Commitment

In making political decisions, people sometimes decide on a course of action that proves detrimental to the achievement of their goals. Both individuals and groups can become overly committed to these failing endeavors. Situations such as these have been referred to as escalation situations (Staw & Ross, 1989), or situations in which some course of action has led to losses, but in which there is a possibility of achieving better outcomes by investing further time, money, or effort (Brockner, 1992; Staw & Ross, 1987, 1989). Thus, there is still a glimmer of hope that, by investing additional resources, the project will become successful. Three characteristics define escalation situations (Staw & Ross, 1987). First, escalation situations involve some loss or cost. Second, there must be a lapse in time from the initial decision: escalation situations do not refer to one-shot decisions; instead, they refer to a series of decisions made over time. Third, withdrawal from the situation is not obvious or easy. Countless examples of these escalation situations exist at both the individual and group levels (Ross & Staw, 1986). Individual-level examples include a person deciding whether to invest more money in a broken car or in a declining stock.

Decision making during the war in Vietnam illustrates the impact of commitment. In his memoir, former Secretary of Defense Robert McNamara reviews the debates within the policy advisory circles of the Johnson administration. The administration, under the influence of the *domino theory* prominent during the Cold War, believed that, if South Vietnam were overtaken by the communist government of North Vietnam, regimes all over Asia would become communist as well, like dominoes falling. Yet the government of the South was corrupt and illegitimate, and the determination of the North, as well as of the Viet Cong (the guerrillas operating in the South) was clear. Important voices in the military warned that the administration's hopes in 1964—that the insurgency problem could be solved by bombing the North, thereby eliminating the need for U.S. ground troops—would not work. Bombing North Vietnam into oblivion would still not stop the Viet Cong's efforts to overthrow the government of South Vietnam. They also knew, from an intelligence report, that the chances of a stable South Vietnamese government emerging—one with popular support and that could pursue the war on its own terms—was very unlikely. As McNamara (1995) recalls:

> These two assessments should have led us to rethink our basic objective and the likelihood of ever achieving it. We did not do so, in large part because no one was willing to discuss getting out. . . . We . . . wished to do nothing that might lead to a break in the "commitment dike" as long as there appeared to be some alternative. . . . It is clear that disengagement was the course we should have chosen. We did not. Instead we continued to be preoccupied by the question of which military course to follow.
>
> (pp. 154, 164)

They decided to pursue a course that led to a quagmire from which they could not and would not extract themselves, a situation causing thousands of American and Vietnamese casualties, which would have been avoided by an earlier withdrawal of American military forces.

Project, psychological, social, and organizational factors could all affect escalation behavior. Project factors are the most obvious determinants of commitment to a failing course of action. The manner in which a failing project is structured seems to influence whether an individual or group withdraws from it or persists. One such factor is whether a setback is the result of permanent or temporary causes (Leatherwood & Conlon, 1987). Commitment is more likely to escalate when the setback results from a temporary cause. In the Vietnam case, the focus upon military options led the decision-making group to think that a change in military strategy would work and that their inability to win the war was a temporary result of incorrect military strategy, rather than the result of permanent irremediable political realities. Similarly, when future costs required for the project's success are expected to be small, commitment is more likely to escalate (Brockner, Rubin & Lang, 1981). Escalation of commitment can also depend on how often previous commitments have succeeded (Goltz, 1992; Hantula, 1992; McCain, 1986). When previous investments have been successful, people are more likely to escalate their commitment to a project, even when the project is currently failing. Commitment to a failing project is also more likely to escalate if the size of the initial investment is relatively large (Teger, 1980). Finally, escalation of commitment is stronger when the size of the payoff from continued investment is likely to be high (Rubin & Brockner, 1975).

There are also several psychological factors that can influence persistence in an escalation situation. Information-processing errors, for example, can be very important. Individuals often misinterpret or seek data in a manner that supports their beliefs (Frey, 1986), thus strengthening their commitment to a failing course of action (Bazerman, Beekun, & Schoorman, 1982; Caldwell & O'Reilly, 1982; Conlon & Parks, 1987). A related factor is the type of goal individuals set before initiating the project. If people do not set explicit goals about the maximum size of their investment (Kernan & Lord, 1989) or the extent of their commitment (Brockner, Shaw, & Rubin, 1979), then they are likely to escalate their commitment to a failing project. The pattern was also evident in Vietnam. The escalation of force was gradual and incremental, with no set limit on size or time at which point there would be an evaluation of the effort to determine if it had failed, and no upper limit was identified on how many U.S. troops would be committed.

Self-justification is another psychological factor that has been shown to influence commitment. Individuals often commit further resources to a losing course of action to justify previous behavior, such as advocating the project in the first place (Bazerman et al., 1982; Bazerman, Giuliano, & Appelman, 1984; Staw, 1976; Staw & Fox, 1977). Recent research suggests that conscientiousness can also impact whether individuals escalate their commitment. When individuals felt a sense of duty, they escalated less than did individuals who were motivated by an achievement obligation (Moon, 2001). Finally, groups whose members identify strongly with their group are more likely to escalate their commitment to a failing project than groups whose members identify weakly with a project (Dietz-Uhler, 1996).

Another set of factors that can influence the escalation of commitment is social in nature. One such factor is the need for external justification. Individuals or groups may persist in order to save face or avoid losing credibility with others (Brockner et al., 1981; Fox & Staw, 1979). Another factor that might influence persistence is external binding, which occurs when individuals or groups become strongly linked with their actions related to a project. For example, a project may become so associated with the primary decision maker (e.g., Reaganomics) that withdrawal is difficult or impossible (Staw & Ross, 1989). Research on the "hero effect" has found that, under some conditions, people who remain committed to a failing project are evaluated more favorably than people who withdraw (Staw & Ross, 1989).

Finally, structural or organizational factors can also influence commitment to a failing project. One such determinant of persistence is institutional inertia. Because change in an organization (especially a large organization) is often difficult, it may seem easier to persist in a losing course of action than to somehow mobilize the organization for change (Staw & Ross, 1989). Another organizational determinant of persistence is the operation of political forces. There may be strong political support for the continuation of a project, even though it is not economically feasible. Groups that are interdependent or politically aligned with a project may also demand support for it (Staw & Ross, 1989). Finally, cultural norms can also affect the likelihood of escalating commitment (Geiger, Robertson, & Irwin, 1998; Greer & Stephens, 2001).

Escalation of commitment to a failing project is a robust phenomenon. Escalations of commitment have been demonstrated in many laboratory and real-life situations, and many factors have been shown to account for the phenomenon in such situations; what is so intriguing is that the decisions appear to be so irrational. From a rational point of view, it often seems that the best choice in these situations is to withdraw and avoid greater losses. However, several researchers (Barton, Duchon, & Dunegan, 1989; Beeler, 1998; Beeler & Hunton, 1997; Bowen, 1987; Northcraft & Neale, 1986; Northcraft & Wolf, 1984) have noted that decisions to continue investment in a failing project are not necessarily irrational, at least from the perspective of the decision maker(s). For example, Northcraft and Wolf (1984), and Whyte (1986) have argued, from an information-processing perspective, that the manner in which decisions are framed determines whether individuals escalate their commitment to a failing project. If a decision is framed as a certain loss, then people tend to abandon the project. However, if a decision is framed as an attempt to recoup an investment, then people tend to escalate their commitment to the project. In escalation situations, decisions are often framed as an attempt to recoup an investment. Thus, to an outside observer, these decisions seem to be irrational, but, to the decision maker(s), they can seem quite rational, because of the way in which they have been framed.

Improving Group Decisions

Because the decisions made by groups have often been disappointing, efforts have been made to develop techniques to improve groups' decisions. One technique that has been suggested is to appoint a group member to serve as a devil's advocate (Hirt & Markman, 1995). The role of the devil's advocate is to disagree with and criticize whatever plan is being considered by the group. This technique can be effective because it encourages group members to think more carefully about the decisions they are contemplating. A related approach involves the use of authentic dissent, in which one or more members of the group actively disagree with the group's initial plans, without being assigned to this role (Nemeth, Connell, Rogers, & Brown, 2001). This technique can be effective, because it encourages the group to consider alternatives and often moves the group away from their initial preferences.

A technique that makes a great deal of sense in political decision making is **multiple advocacy** (George, 1980; George & Stern, 2002). In this process, manipulation is avoided by having the deliberation procedures managed by a neutral person, a custodian manager, while the advocates of different positions are allowed to fully develop their proposals and advocate the advantages. Mutual criticism by the advocates of various proposals should, in theory, flesh out the strengths and weaknesses of the different policy options. This is done for the benefit of the final decision maker, or chief executive (the president, prime minister, etc.), who listens, evaluates the options, and makes an informed decision. Many American presidents have tried to use this approach for improving decision making in their administrations. In fact, the National Security Council (NSC), and particularly the national security adviser, has evolved into the role of the custodian manager, since its foundation in 1947. As George (1980) describes it, the NSC has taken on a number of tasks in its role as custodian manager:

1. Balancing actor resources within the policymaking system
2. Strengthening weaker advocates
3. Bringing in new advisers to argue for unpopular options
4. Setting up new channels of information so that the president and other advisors are not dependent upon a single channel
5. Arranging for independent evaluation of decisional premises and options, when necessary
6. Monitoring the workings of the policy-making process to identify possibly dangerous malfunctions and institute appropriate corrective action. (pp. 195–196)

Nevertheless, establishing and consistently using a multiple advocacy system to improve group decision making is difficult, and many presidents fail to keep it alive. First, the custodian manager has to ensure that a wide range of views and proposals is heard and that the appropriate people are involved in the group deliberations. This is difficult to achieve, particularly given the fact that this role is typically held by someone from the administration and therefore a person with their own political perspective and career, subject to pressure from many different agencies and individuals ('t Hart, 1997). For similar reasons, it is difficult for the chief executive to use the system. Choosing the best option is often impossible, because of domestic or international political pressures and obstacles. Finally, some presidents, such as Ronald Reagan, do not want to hear the debate and discussion of multiple options.

CONFLICT IN GROUPS

When people are working together to achieve a goal, there will inevitably be some conflict, which occurs when group members believe their goals are not compatible (Pruitt & Rubin, 1986). Group members can conflict with another in many ways. For example, if group members have to compete for scarce resources, conflict can arise. Group members can also experience conflict when one group member tries to exert influence or gain prestige in the group (Levine & Moreland, 1998). In this section, we examine the various types of conflict that can exist in a group, particularly in situations in which group members are motivated to both compete and cooperate. A discussion of the causes of conflict in groups follows; we then briefly examine the formation of coalitions in groups. Finally, we examine strategies designed to reduce conflict in groups.

Types of Conflict: Social Dilemmas

Much of the research on conflict in groups examines mixed-motive situations—ones in which the motivation to compete is mixed with the motivation to cooperate. Perhaps the most famous mixed-motive game is the **prisoner's dilemma game** (Luce & Raiffa, 1957; see Figure 4.2). Research of this type is used to determine how tendencies to cooperate and compete can lead to various outcomes for groups. In this game, participants cannot communicate with one another, yet the outcome of the game for each person is contingent on what the other person decides. The game is set up so that (1) if both players cooperate, they receive a moderately favorable outcome; (2) if one cooperates and the other competes, the cooperator receives an unfavorable outcome and the competitor receives a favorable outcome; and (3) if both players compete, they receive a moderately unfavorable outcome. In this situation, the dilemma is whether to compete or cooperate. The situation is rigged so that both players benefit equally if they cooperate, but there is a tendency to not trust the other player, so many people compete (Pruitt & Kimmell, 1977). More recently, research on mixed-motive interactions has used an N-person social dilemma—that is, a social dilemma with more than two people (Levine & Moreland, 1998). In these dilemmas, several outcomes are possible. First, a player always benefits more from a non-cooperative than cooperative choice. Second, a noncooperative choice is harmful to others in the group. Third, the amount of harm to others, as a result of a noncooperative choice, is larger than the profit received as a result of any choice.

There are several types of social dilemmas (Messick & Brewer, 1983). In a **collective trap**, behaviors that reward an individual group member can be harmful to the rest of the group, especially if engaged in by enough group members. For example, during a water shortage, individuals who use too much water harm everyone else by prolonging the shortage. The best strategy for the collective is if each individual takes a little. In **collective fences**, the entire group is harmed if behaviors that are costly to individuals are avoided by enough people. For example, if each person does not donate money to medical research, then everyone will be worse off. The best strategy is for everyone to give a little. In either situation, people are tempted to "free ride," or enjoy the group's resources without penalty. Research using collective traps and collective fences can tell us much about human tendencies to be selfish or prosocial, as well as how a person's value orientation (e.g., cooperative or competitive) can influence their behavior in social dilemmas.

Figure 4.2 The prisoner's dilemma. In this classic game, two prisoners, A and B, accused of a crime, have the options of confessing or not confessing. If they maintain their alliance and neither confesses, both get short sentences. If each of them confesses, they each get a heavy sentence. But if one confesses and the other does not, the prisoner who confessed is rewarded with freedom, while the one who did not confess gets a severely heavy sentence. The dilemma for each prisoner is that, if he trusts the other not to confess, his best option is to rat out his partner in crime.

Causes of Conflict

Conflicts, such as social dilemmas, typically arise when group members have competing goals or see their goals as being incompatible. There are many factors that can contribute to the origination of conflict, as well as to its escalation. In the previous chapter, the concept of **attributions** was introduced. They play a role in group conflict, as well as in individual perceptions. *Attributions* refer to the explanations generated for the causes of our own and others' behavior. Imagine playing a prisoner's dilemma game in which you realize that the best strategy is for you to cooperate, but your partner seems to always make the competitive choice. Why? You may generate many reasons why your partner makes the competitive choice: perhaps he does not understand the game; perhaps he was told by the experimenter to make consistently competitive choices; maybe he is just an evil person. Attributing the cause of another's behavior to dispositional, rather than situational, factors is the **fundamental attribution error** (Ross, 1977). If, during conflict, we blame another group member, conflict is likely to escalate, rather than to be resolved (Forsyth, 1990). Thus, if you blame your partner's personality for the competitive choices they make, then you are likely to also make competitive choices. People also have a tendency to perceive their own views as correct and objective, but to perceive others' views to be biased (Keltner & Robinson, 1997; Robinson, Keltner, Ward, & Ross, 1995). A consequence of this bias in perception is that we are likely to exaggerate the difference in perspective between ourselves and another group member, which is likely to serve as fuel for conflict.

Second, when in potential conflict situations, communicating effectively can be difficult. Sometimes, group members criticize one another harshly. If you have ever been on the receiving end of harsh criticism, then you realize that it can be unpleasant and uncomfortable. Such discomfort can often instigate revenge, which only serves to escalate the conflict (Cropanzano, 1993). If group members do not communicate reasonably and effectively, then conflict will likely occur and may even be escalated. One particularly destructive variant of faulty communication is *nay-saying*, a pattern in which group discussions are crippled and paralyzed by negativism and bickering over everything, down to the smallest details of a decision (Stern & Sundelius, 1997). Whenever conflict becomes stronger, so do anxiety and tension (Blascovich, Nash, & Ginsburg, 1978; van Egeren, 1979). According to the arousal/aggression hypothesis (Berkowitz, 1989), group members become frustrated when they are unable to attain their goals. Frustration can lead to aggression, which is often displayed by lashing out at other group members. If group members are aggressive, then conflict will occur and probably escalate.

Third, and more recent, are theories and research about the gendered nature of group conflict. Much of this thinking is based on principles of evolutionary psychology, which we have discussed in prior chapters. The primary idea of the gendered nature of group conflict is that the experience and reasons for group conflict differ for males and females, and they do so because of different reproductive motivations for males and females. One of the hypotheses derived from this perspective is referred to as the "outgroup male target hypothesis" (Sidanius & Kurzba, 2013). According to this hypothesis, in-group bias is more prominent for males than females. In other words, discrimination against out-group males is more pervasive and severe than discrimination against out-group females. For example, archival evidence shows that Black males are more than six times more likely to be imprisoned than White males, while the disparity in imprisonment rates for Black and White females is about half of that rate (McDonald, Navarrete, & Sidanius, 2011). This and other evidence (see Sidanius & Kurzba, 2013, for a review) suggests that there are much larger gaps in discrimination against male out-groups than against female out-groups.

Of course, this disparity in out-group discrimination against males and females begs the question, "Why?" The answer lies in evolutionary psychology. Male aggression against out-group males appears to be motivated by aggressive tendencies and the desire to gather resources and status in order to present as ideal mates. The picture for females, however, is quite a bit different. Female motivation to discriminate against the out-group is primarily rooted in fear of sexual coercion and assault. In an interesting study that led to this conclusion, it was found that females displayed more bias against out-group males when their risk of conceiving was at its highest level (Navarrete et al., 2009).

These ideas are consistent with the male warrior hypothesis, according to which males form coalitions that allow them to plan and execute out-group aggression. McDonald et al. (2011) found that males have a stronger desire than females to control and dominate out-groups, while female out-group bias is primarily predicted from their self-assessed vulnerability to sexual coercion. There seems to be ample support for the male warrior hypothesis, including findings that: 1. Men discriminate against out-groups more than women, 2. Men prefer group-based hierarchies more than do women, 3. Males are more likely than females to defend their in-group, and 4. Males are more likely than females to engage in intergroup competition and aggression (McDonald, Navarrete, & Van Vugt, 2012). Consistent with the male warrior hypothesis, the rationale for this hypothesis lies in the idea that group conflict affords males the opportunity to attract reproductive mates, property, and status. But for females, group conflict is largely avoided because it increases the opportunity and risk of being sexually assaulted by out-group males (McDonald, Navarrete, & Van Vugt, 2012).

Finally, in the review of the research on escalation of commitment, we learned how group members can easily become committed to a course of action, even if it is a failing one. Group members can also become committed to their viewpoints, especially when they are under attack (Staw & Ross, 1987), for several reasons. First, we tend to seek information to confirm, rather than to refute, our beliefs (Petty & Cacioppo, 1986). Such action tends to make us even more committed to our beliefs. Second, in a public situation, there is often a desire to appear strong and as having conviction in our beliefs. Third, once an individual commits to a belief, they rationalize their choice by overestimating its favorableness and increasing their dedication to it (Batson, 1975). Fourth, attacks from other group members can create reactance (Brehm, 1976), which occurs whenever we sense a loss of freedom. The consequence is that we become even more committed to our belief or position.

Coalitions

Sometimes, conflicts exist between more than two group members. Sometimes, group members persuade other group members to join forces by forming a **coalition**, a small collection of group members who cooperate in order to achieve a mutually desired goal. Coalitions have a number of characteristics in common (Forsyth, 1990). First, they all typically involve group members who disagree on fundamental issues, but who decide to set aside those differences and focus on the problem at hand. Second, they form for the purpose of achieving certain goals. Third, coalitions tend to be temporary, and there is often little commitment on the part of the participants, except to the current goal. Fourth, coalitions typically form in mixed motive situations: group members who formerly competed with one another must cooperate to achieve the current goal. Fifth, coalitions are adversaries. The goal is to make sure, in the end, that they are better off and that another coalition is worse off.

There are a number of theories that have been put forth to explain when and why certain coalitions are likely to form. According to **minimum-resource**

theory (Gamson, 1961, 1964), group members form coalitions on the basis of equal input–equal output. That is, the most likely grouping of people is one that involves the fewest number of people with the fewest number of resources, yet that is most likely to win. The theory makes two assumptions: first, people in groups are primarily motivated by the need to maximize power and payoffs and believe that forming coalitions will satisfy this goal; second, members of coalitions believe that the distribution of power and rewards should be divided equally among the members of the coalition.

Another theory that explains when and why coalitions form is **minimum-power theory** (Shapley, 1953). According to this theory, coalition members expect payoffs that are directly proportional to their ability to turn a losing coalition into a winning one. This type of power is referred to as pivotal power (Miller, 1980). In this theory, power, not resources, is the most important determinant of coalition formation. The pivotal power of any group member is determined by the number of times that member could turn a winning coalition into a losing one by withdrawing from the coalition. Thus, coalitions form on the basis of the highest chances of winning with the lowest amount of pivotal power.

According to **bargaining theory** (Komorita & Nagao, 1983), coalitions form on the basis of considering expected payoffs, which are based on norms of equity and equality, and group members will appeal to whichever norm provides them with the largest payoff. This theory assumes that group members prefer to form coalitions with those who will not withdraw. It also assumes that the amount of payoff may change over time, to compensate for extra rewards given to coalition members who are being tempted to join another coalition.

In addition to these theories of coalition formation, research has identified other factors that influence the formation of coalitions, including the number and size of existing coalitions (Komorita & Miller, 1986; Kravitz, 1987), expectations of each group member in forming coalitions (Miller & Komorita, 1986), and the availability of other influence strategies that do not require the formation of coalitions (Komorita, Hamilton, & Kravitz, 1984).

CONCLUSION

This chapter reviewed some of the central findings from psychological research on groups and their behavior. We have also reviewed some of the key patterns of group behavior in politics, and we have discussed how and why groups form, how they make decisions, and what problems arise in group decision making. We examined intra- and intergroup conflict dynamics, as well as some techniques for conflict resolution. Several of the chapters that follow provide additional information and illustrations of group behavior. Chapter 5 provides examples of small-group dynamics in leadership management styles. Chapters 8, 9, and 10 provide examples of group behavior in cases of race, ethnic, and nationalist group conflicts. Chapters 9 and 12 look at the behavior of extremist groups, such as terrorist organizations, perpetrators of genocide, and others. They provide several illustrations of obedience to, and compliance with, group demands.

Topics, Theories/Explanations, and Concepts in Chapter 4

Topics	Theories/Explanations	Concepts
Definition of groups; central characteristics: size, composition, type		Entiativity
Group structure: status, roles, norms, cohesion; group formation	Expectation states theory; ethological theories; functional perspective; interpersonal attraction perspective	
Group development		Stages: forming, storming, norming, performing, adjourning
Influence in groups		Conformity
Conformity	Informational social influence; normative social influence	
Situational conformity	Group size; group unanimity; commitment to the group; individuation	
Power: reward, coercive, legitimate referent, expert; minority influence		
Reaction to power: compliance, attraction, conflict, rebellion, motivation, self-blame	Complementarity hypothesis	
Group performance; social facilitation and inhibition	Arousal; evaluation apprehension; distraction	
Productivity losses; group decision making	Social loafing; three stage model	
Groups and political decision making units		Predominant leader; single group; coalitions
Group decision making	Groupthink; new group syndrome; bureaucratic politics; manipulation; group polarization; escalation of commitment	

(*Continued*)

(Continued)

Topics, Theories/Explanations, and Concepts in Chapter 4

Topics	Theories/Explanations	Concepts
Improving group decisions; conflict in groups		Social dilemmas; collective traps; collective fences
Causes of conflict	Faulty attributions; faulty communications; biased perceptions; personality; commitment; arousal and aggression	
Coalitions	Minimum resource theory; minimum power theory; bargaining theory	

Key Terms

attributions

autokinetic effect

bargaining theory

coalition

coalition of autonomous
    actors

coercive power

cohesion

collective fences

collective trap

compliance

conformity

deindividuation

entiativity

escalation of commitment

expected payoffs

expert power

forming

Fundamental Interpersonal Relations
    Orientation (FIRO)

group

group development

group polarization

groupthink

individuation

informational social influence

legitimate power

minimum-power theory

minimum-resource theory

normative social influence

norming

norms

performing

predominant leader

prisoner's dilemma

rebellion

referent power

reward power

roles

social-decision schemes

social loafing

status

storming

third-party intervention

three-stage model of group
    decision making

Suggestions for Further Reading

Forsyth, D. R. (1990). *Group dynamics*. Pacific Grove, CA: Brooks/Cole.

George, A., & Stern, E. (2002). Harnessing conflict in foreign policy making: From devil's advocate to multiple advocacy. *Presidential Studies Quarterly, 32*, 484–508.

Janis, I. L. (1982). *Groupthink: Psychological studies of policy decisions and fiascoes* (2nd ed.). Boston, MA: Houghton Mifflin.

LeBon, G. (1960). *The crowd: A study of the popular mind*. New York: Viking. (Original work published 1895)

Levine, J. M., & Moreland, R. L. (1998). Small groups. In D. T. Gilbert, S. T. Fiske, & G. Lindzey (Eds.), *The handbook of social psychology* (4th ed., pp. 415–469). New York: McGraw-Hill.

Moscovici, S., & Doise, S. (1994). *Conflict and consensus: A general theory of collective decisions*. London: Sage.

Prentice, D., & Miller, D. (Eds.). (1999). *Cultural divides: Understanding and overcoming group conflict*. New York: Sage.

Preston, T., & 't Hart, P. (1999). Understanding and evaluating bureaucratic politics: The nexus between political leaders and advisory systems. *Political Psychology, 20*, 49–98.

't Hart, P. (1994). *Groupthink in government: A study of small groups and policy failure*. Baltimore, MD: Johns Hopkins University Press. (Original work published 1990)

't Hart, P., Stern, E. K., & Sundelius, B. (1997). *Beyond groupthink: Political group dynamics and foreign policy-making*. Ann Arbor: University of Michigan Press.

Chapter 5

THE STUDY OF POLITICAL LEADERS

The preceding chapters have developed a number of important concepts, theories, and analytical frameworks in political psychology. We can now turn to an examination of important topics in political psychology, and we begin with a look at leaders. In this chapter, aspects of personality, cognition, and small group behavior, all considered in depth in the previous chapters, will be brought together to explore political leaders' management and leadership styles. We begin with a consideration of types of leaders and then explore a number of analytical frameworks. The case of President George W. Bush will be used to illustrate the use of the concepts of leader analysis. The Political Being (see Figure 1.1) considered in this chapter is, of course, a leader. The elements of the Being of interest in this chapter are personality, cognition, emotion, and also the interaction with *us* (that is, political in-groups in the form of advisers).

We can begin with an illustration of the importance of the personality of political leaders. In recalling the Cuban Missile Crisis, Robert Kennedy remarked: "The fourteen people involved were very significant—bright, able, dedicated people, all of whom had the greatest affection for the U.S. . . . If six of them had been President of the U.S., I think that the world might have been blown up" (quoted in Steel, 1969, p. 22).

Robert Kennedy's chilling observation about the men within President John F. Kennedy's decision-making group (the Ex Comm, or Executive Committee of the National Security Council) during the Cuban Missile Crisis of 1962 dramatically illustrates the importance of personality and other individual leader characteristics in politics. What a leader is like, in terms of personality, background, beliefs, and style of leadership, can have a tremendous impact upon the policy-making process and its outcomes. In the case of Cuba, Kennedy's pragmatism, sensitivity to the needs of his adversaries, his openness to advice and feedback from his staff, and his own extensive, personal foreign policy expertise led to a willingness on his part to debate the pros and cons of the airstrike option (which he initially favored) and to consider arguments in favor of the less-confrontational blockade option to remove the Soviet missiles. Within the decision group itself, Kennedy's collegiality enabled advisers to express their unvarnished opinions during Ex Comm sessions and his desire for outside advice led to the inclusion within the group of several notable foreign policy experts from outside of his administration. More importantly, his willingness to consider the possible consequences of his policy actions and his sensitivity to the need for his opponent (Khrushchev) to have a face-saving way out of the crisis enabled Kennedy to successfully avoid war (Allison & Zelikow, 1999; Preston, 2001).

Would a different president have brought the same personal qualities or style of leadership to the situation? For Robert Kennedy, the answer was clearly no. Among the Ex Comm advisers, there were many who lacked Kennedy's pragmatism, favoring instead an aggressive, immediate response to resolve the crisis. Others lacked his empathy towards Khrushchev and his awareness of his opponent's domestic political position. Some clearly had less need for information when making decisions, less desire to search out alternative viewpoints on policy matters, and far lower tolerances for dissent or disagreement over policy than had Kennedy. Had any of these individuals been President instead of JFK, the outcome of the Cuban Missile Crisis might have been very different indeed.

In his classic book *Leadership* (1978), James MacGregor Burns describes two basic types of leadership: the transactional and transformational. According to Burns (1978: 18), "leadership over human beings is exercised when persons with certain motives and purposes mobilize, in competition or conflict with others, institutional, political, psychological, and other resources so as to arouse, engage, and satisfy the motives of followers." This definition is significant in that it distinguishes between relationships based upon "naked power" and those based upon "leadership." For Burns, true leadership involves a relationship between the leader and followers in which the leader taps the motives of followers in order to realize *mutually* held goals. This can take the form of either **transactional leadership**, where the leader approaches followers with an eye towards exchanging one valued thing for another (i.e., jobs for votes, subsidies for campaign contributions, etc.), or **transformational leadership**, in which leaders engage their followers in such a way that they raise each other to higher levels of motivation and morality. As Burns (1879: 20) describes it:

> Transforming leadership ultimately becomes *moral* in that it raises the level of human conduct and ethical aspiration of both leader and led, and thus it has a transforming effect on both. Perhaps the best modern example is Gandhi, who aroused and elevated the hopes and demands of millions of Indians and whose life and personality were enhanced in the process. Transcending leadership is dynamic leadership in the sense that the leaders throw themselves into a relationship with followers who will feel "elevated" by it and often become more active themselves, thereby creating new cadres of leaders.
>
> (p. 26)

On the other hand, the use of naked power is not leadership, but instead is based purely upon a coercive, one-sided relationship with followers built upon a leader's own power position or resources (Burns, 1978). No exchange of valued commodities takes place and the followers' motives are irrelevant to the leader. Instead, the leader employing naked power enters into neither a transactional or transformational relationship with followers, but merely forces them to comply with his or her own desires.

Later scholars such as Barbara Kellerman have expanded upon Burns' explicitly moral, normative definition of transformational leadership by including the notion that such leaders can also tap into their followers' needs for authority or for the "security of a firm and coercive program" (1984, p. 81). Thus, the transformation brought about by the leader can be *either* elevating (as Burns argues) or debasing. In particular, charismatic leaders often embody for followers, by virtue of their unusual personal qualities, the promise or hope of salvation (or deliverance from distress) and, as a result, take on a transformational role. This relationship—in which the leader evokes so strong an emotional response that his misdeeds and mistakes are ignored or trivialized—can lead to elevation or disaster. If the charismatic leader is transforming, he or she will, according to Burns, capitalize on the strength of his followers' devotion and engagement to "raise the level of human conduct and aspiration." But another kind of charismatic leader—a Hitler, a Jim Jones—will lead his still-willing followers to destruction. Yet whether we who are outside the group judge the charismatic leader to be benign or malignant, the main point here is that he apparently emerges in response to some deeply felt group need or wish.

Are Leaders Born or Made?

A substantial debate in leadership studies has revolved around the issue of whether leaders are born or are made. The **"great man" theory of leadership** suggests that people who become leaders are special—that they have personal qualities or characteristics that set them apart from nonleaders. According to this line of thinking, Abraham Lincoln and Winston Churchill were special and would have become great leaders even in the absence of the crises during which they emerged (the American Civil War and World War II, respectively). On the other hand, the **situational (or zeitgeist) theory of leadership** holds that it is the context that is special, not the person, and that the situation itself determines the type of leaders and leadership that will occur. For example, this theory suggests that in the absence of the outbreak of the World War II and Chamberlain's political humiliation by Adolf Hitler at Munich, Winston Churchill would have remained in the shadows and never risen to the rank of British Prime Minister. It was the particular nature of the times and the dire crisis facing Britain (i.e., the hardships of the blitz, Britain's isolation and lack of allies, and the danger of imminent invasion by Germany) that created the stage for the charismatic, strong, uncompromising Churchill to lead. Further, just as the war had created the proper situational context for Churchill's leadership, the end of the war resulted in a dramatically altered context and his defeat in the first postwar national elections in 1945. Thus, it was the convergence of a unique situation with an individual whose personal qualities matched up well with the requirements of that situation that led to the emergence of Churchill's leadership.

In fact, a useful distinction has been proposed in the leadership literature focusing upon the concept of *destructive leadership*, which is created by a "toxic triangle" of leader, followers, and environmental factors enabling it (Padilla et al., 2007). This focus disagrees with Burns' notion that Hitler was not a leader by acknowledging the role played by followers and the environment in creating a form of destructive leadership, which is leadership nonetheless (see Table 5.1 below).

The toxic triangle leading to destructive leadership described by Padilla et al. (2007) is composed of three points: 1) Destructive Leaders (possessing charisma, personalized power, narcissism, negative life themes, and an ideology of hate); 2) Susceptible Followers (composed of either conformers or colluders); and 3) Conducive Environments (where instability, perceived threats, cultural values, and lack of effective institutions or checks and balances provide a breeding ground for destructive leadership). Such destructive leaders may be narcissistic, dangerously charismatic, or simply have strong elements of psychopathy in their personalities, allowing them to be effective at rising to leadership positions and manipulating followers (Rosenthal & Pittinsky, 2006; Schouten & Silver, 2012). It is a form of leadership, albeit a destructive one.

Building upon and paralleling James MacGregor Burns' focus upon leadership and followership are a number of studies in political science, especially in the field of presidential studies, dealing explicitly with the leadership (or management) styles of presidents and how these impact their interactions with advisers (followers). Although the primary focus of most of this work still rests squarely upon the personal qualities and characteristics of the leaders themselves, usually taking the form of discussions of types of presidential style, implicit in all of these discussions is the importance of the leader-follower relationships as well. This was illustrated in Chapter 2 where we discussed the presidential character studies of Barber (1972).[1] Beginning with Richard Neustadt's seminal *Presidential Power* (1960/1990), which focused upon the personal rather than institutional presidency, and emphasized the importance of the *persuasive powers* of presidents, the U.S.

Table 5.1 Five Features of Destructive Leadership

1. Destructive leadership is seldom absolutely or entirely destructive; there are both good and bad results in most leadership situations.
2. The process of destructive leadership involves dominance, coercion, and manipulation rather than influence, persuasion, and commitment.
3. The process of destructive leadership has a selfish orientation; it is focused more on the leader's needs than the needs of the larger social group.
4. The effects of destructive leadership are outcomes that compromise the quality of life for constituents and detract from the organization's main purposes.
5. Destructive organizational outcomes are not exclusively the result of destructive leaders, but are also products of susceptible followers and conducive environments (Padilla et al., 2007, p. 179).

presidential literature began to focus much more intently upon the importance of leadership style. Indeed, this followed naturally given Neustadt's observation that due to the inherent limitations on their institutional powers, presidents are forced to rely upon their interpersonal skills and arts of persuasion to carry out their policies. Although this description of presidential power appeared at first glance to place individual presidents squarely into an institutional context that constrained most of their freedom of action, Neustadt's depiction of presidential power emphasized the fundamental importance of the *personal presidency* as well. Neustadt viewed the personal characteristics (or qualities) of presidents as critical to successful presidential leadership—and to the ability of presidents to obtain the kind of "personal influence of an effective sort on governmental action" which he defined as *presidential power*.[2] However, before they can *persuade*, presidents must formulate and develop their policies, gather and analyze immense amounts of information, adapt their strategies and policies to a rapidly changing political environment, and surround themselves with advisers and advisory systems capable of dealing with all of these difficult tasks effectively. Across all of these areas, the individual characteristics of presidents play a critical role.

For Neustadt, the personal qualities necessary for successful presidents were those traits found in "*experienced politicians of extraordinary temperament*,"—ones possessing political expertise, unpretentious self-confidence in their abilities, and who are at ease with their roles and enjoy the job.[3] Noting that the Presidency "is not a place for amateurs," Neustadt points to the importance of prior policy experience or expertise.[4] Further, Neustadt emphasized the need for presidents to be active information-gatherers and to seek out multiple sources and differing perspectives on policy problems. This involves leaders cultivating enhanced sensitivity to the policy environment through both "sensitivity to processes" (who does what and how in the political environment) and "sensitivity to substance" (the details and specifics of policy).[5] The clear message from Neustadt's work is that the personal qualities of leaders play a significant role in successful (or unsuccessful) presidential leadership—and that presidents who fail to effectively utilize their advisory systems, or who lack appropriate *sensitivity to the policy context*, are unlikely to develop the foundations of power necessary to persuade anyone.

Indeed, reflecting upon the centrality of this leader-follower relationship, Fred Greenstein observed, "Leadership in the modern presidency is not carried out by the president alone, but rather by presidents with their associates. It depends therefore on both the president's strengths and weaknesses and on the quality of the aides' support" (1988, p. 352). Yet, across this broad literature, Hermann and Preston (1994, p. 81) have argued that there are five main types of leadership variables that appear to be routinely identified as having an impact upon the style of leaders and their subsequent structuring and use of advisory systems: 1) leader involvement in the policy-making process; 2) leader willingness to tolerate conflict; 3) leader's motivation or reason for leading; 4) leader's preferred strategies for managing information; and 5) leader's preferred strategies for resolving conflict.

The focus upon types of leadership style, personality, or character in the political science literature can be traced back to Harold Lasswell, who first argued in his classic *Psychopathology and Politics* (1930/1960) that it is possible to classify leaders as particular types because, although leaders are different in fine details, important similarities can be seen across leaders that allow us to argue that two or more leaders are of the same type. For example, after Barber's (1972) active-passive/positive-negative typology of presidential character, perhaps the best known typology of presidential management style is Richard T. Johnson's (1974) classification scheme. Johnson argued that among modern-day presidents there were three management styles: the **formalistic**, **collegial**, and **competitive management styles** (see Table 5.2).

These management styles essentially establish group norms, an important part of group behavior presented in Chapter 4. The formalistic style

Table 5.2 General Characteristics of Johnson's (1974, pp. 3–7) Typology of Formalistic, Competitive, and Collegial Management Styles

Management Style	*Advisory System Characteristics*
Formalistic (examples: Truman, Eisenhower, Nixon administrations)	Emphasis upon strictly hierarchical, orderly decision structures. Formalized staff system funnels information to top where leader weighs options on their merit. Emphasis upon technical over political considerations (underplays politics). Analytical and dispassionate advisers selected. Stress upon finding best solution to problems instead of working out compromises among conflicting views. Discourages staff conflict; emphasis on order and analysis.
Competitive (example: Franklin Roosevelt administration)	Relatively unstructured information network with leader placed in arbiter position among competing advisers with overlapping areas of authority. Leader thrives on conflict and uses it to stay informed and exploit existing political environment. Seeks aggressive advisers with divergent opinions. Encourages staff conflict as means of generating creative ideas and opposing viewpoints. Emphasizes bargaining over analysis with tendency to settle upon short-term solutions.
Collegial (examples: Kennedy, Carter and G. H. W. Bush administrations)	Emphasizes teamwork, shared responsibility, and problem solving within group. Advisers seen as colleagues who work as cooperative group to fuse strongest elements of divergent views. Leader has strong interpersonal skills and will work collegially with advisers rather than dominate group by pushing one position. Discourages staff conflict, encourages conflicting viewpoints, takes into account all sides of issues to forge solutions that are substantive and politically acceptable.

(Harry S. Truman, Dwight Eisenhower, Richard Nixon) is designed to reduce the effects of human error through a well-designed management system that is hierarchical, nonconfrontational, focused on issues rather than personalities, and oriented toward generating options and making the best decision. The focus of this style is on preserving the president's time for the big decisions. In contrast, the collegial and competitive styles emphasize less hierarchical organization. The collegial style (John F. Kennedy, Jimmy Carter, Bill Clinton) focuses on working as a team, sharing responsibility, and consensus-building, with an interest in generating options, openness to information, and reaching a doable as well as best decision. Leaders organizing their advisers around the collegial style want to be involved in policymaking and are uncomfortable when they are not in the middle of things. On the other hand, the competitive style (Franklin Roosevelt) centers around confrontation, with the leader setting up an organization with overlapping areas of authority to maximize the availability of information and differing perspectives. The emphasis in competitive systems is upon debate and advocacy, with the leader playing the role of final arbiter.

Alexander George (1980) built on Johnson's work, abstracting out three stylistic variables that seemed to shape what presidential advisers do. The first, **cognitive style**, refers to the way the president gathers and processes information from his environment. Does the president come with a well-formulated vision or agenda that helps to shape how he perceives, interprets, and acts on information or is he interested in sounding out the situation and political context before defining a problem and seeking options? The way this question is answered suggests the types of advisers the president will have around him and the kinds of information the president will want in making a decision. In the first instance, the president seeks advisers and information that are supportive of his predispositions; in the second instance, he is interested in experts or representatives of his various constituencies who will provide him with insights into the political context and problem at any point in time. At issue in this second instance is what fits with the context: what is doable at this particular moment.

The second stylistic variable centers on a **sense of efficacy** or competence. Sense of efficacy for George relates to how the president's agenda is formed. The problems he feels most comfortable tackling and the areas he is most interested in are likely to dominate his agenda. If, like George Bush, the president feels more at ease with foreign than domestic policy, his presidency will probably favor foreign over domestic policy. If, like Ronald Reagan, he has an arena of problems that are of particular importance, such as building the military strength of the United States vis-à-vis the Soviet Union, these issues may dominate much of the time of his administration.

The third stylistic variable George calls **orientation toward political conflict**. How open is the president to face-to-face disagreements and confrontations among his advisers? The more open the president is to such debate and crossfire, the easier it is for him to forge an advisory system exhibiting the characteristics of Johnson's competitive model; the more uncomfortable such a milieu makes him, the more likely the president is to want an advisory system that either emphasizes teamwork (all of us work together) or formal rules (here are the gatekeepers who manage what gets to the president). George argues that this orientation tends to shape the president's dealings with his cabinet and the executive bureaucracy as well as the White House staff. It colors the way he wants his advisory system to run. Moreover, it helps to define the type of control the president will want over the policy-making process and how much loyalty he will demand from those around him. If conflict is to be minimized, the president will have to expend resources to keep it under control; one way to achieve such control is to choose advisers who are loyal to the president and have served him for some time. If conflict can be tolerated and, perhaps, even used, the president may see high turnover among his staff as egos are bruised or tempers flare. But advisers are more likely to be policy advocates and know what they want the president to do. Examples of presidents with low tolerances for political conflict include Richard Nixon and Lyndon Johnson. Indeed, Johnson's intolerance of dissent from advisers and desire for loyalty among advisers on policy lines adopted by the administration were defining characteristics of his Vietnam policy style (Preston & 't Hart, 1999; Preston, 2001, 2012). On the other hand, Franklin Roosevelt's skillful use of a competitive management style provides the prototypical example of the leader high in tolerance of political conflict (Johnson, 1974; George, 1980).

Other scholars particularly interested in the presidency (Campbell, 1986; Crabb & Mulcahy, 1986; Smith, 1988) have added to what Johnson and George have described. These writers have been interested in leadership style variables that are relational in form; that is, they focus on what the president does vis-à-vis his advisers and the bureaucracy. One such variable is the degree to which the president does business personally or through institutionalized routines. Is the president a hands-on person like Lyndon Johnson, who wanted to talk to commanders in Vietnam or the ambassador in the Dominican Republic about what was really going on, or is he more likely to want what comes up through the bureaucracy to be culled and organized before it gets to him for his reflection? Anyone can become an adviser to the first type of president: the gatekeepers at the end become the advisers for the second type of president.

Another relational variable concerns how proactive versus reactive the president's policy making is. Is the president interested in shaping policy and enlisting the aid of others in selling the policy, or is the president more responsive to what comes to him from others rather than searching out activities? The proactive president is more likely to want a loyal staff with similar predispositions who are sold on the president's program and ready to enlist support for it. Consider the staff that supported Reagan in seeking the release of American hostages in Lebanon by selling arms to Iran. The reactive president becomes more dependent on how others define and represent problems and the pressure they place on him to act. The issues that the more reactive president focuses on are a function of whom he has on his staff.

A third relational variable centers on distrust of the bureaucracy. How much does the president trust the executive branch bureaucracy to carry out his decisions and program? Those presidents like Nixon with an inherent distrust of what the bureaucracy will do to their policies often centralize authority so that it rests with those they can trust, or they bypass the bureaucracy altogether by bringing policy making into the White House and under their control. With more trust of the bureaucracy comes more interest in recommendations from those further down in the hierarchy and more interest in interagency commissions and task forces. Two scholars writing about political leadership in general (Hermann, 1987; Kotter & Lawrence,

1974) have stressed several further leadership styles that can influence how advisers are chosen. The first focuses on the leader's preferred strategies for resolving conflict. Which of the following strategies does the leader generally use to resolve conflict among advisers: leader preferences, unanimity/consensus, or majority rule? Each strategy suggests a difference in the advisory system. If the strategy focuses on insuring that the leader's preferences prevail, the leader is going to play a more forceful role in the proceedings than if the strategy involves building a consensus or engaging a coalition to make a majority. Consensus-building demands more of a facilitative role from the leader, while engaging in coalition formation suggests an emphasis on negotiation and bargaining with trade-offs and side payments. Moreover, the advisers the leader selects may differ with these strategies. If the leader generally wants his preferences to prevail, he will probably seek out advisers who have a similar philosophy, are loyal, and predisposed to please him. If consensus is the name of the game, the leader will seek out advisers who are, like himself, interested in facilitating the process of bringing different views together and more conciliative than confrontational. Advisers to leaders whose preferred strategy is coalition building probably need skills at ascertaining where constituents stand and persuading others to join with them (Preston, 2001, 2011).

Another leadership style variable centers upon the issue of **social identity** and, given that true leadership involves getting followers to actually follow, scholars like Haslam et al. (2011, p. xxii) suggest the need for an *identity leadership* approach in which leaders are: 1) seen as "one of us," or part of the in-group prototype; 2) seen as "doing it for us," or advancing in-group interests; 3) seen as actively "crafting a sense of us," by involvement as a skilled entrepreneur of identity in shaping a shared understanding of who the in-group is; and finally, 4) be seen to "make the group matter," taking in-group values and priorities and making them become reality. It is a view of leadership that is not necessarily the interaction between leaders and followers as individuals, but as group members (Haslam, 2001; Haslam & Platow, 2001; Haslam et al., 2011).

Also impacting leadership is the role played by individual beliefs and generational effects. Abelson (1986) warned that beliefs are like cherished possessions that leaders hold onto dearly before relinquishing, and which have significant implications for the types of political questions/environments likely to be salient to leaders and the goals and strategies subsequently adopted. These can take the form of operational code beliefs (discussed later in this chapter), various worldview beliefs about other countries (Rosati, 1987, 1990), or the relevance of historical lessons and analogies in framing current events or policy options (Neustadt & May, 1986; Khong, 1992; Hagan, 2001; Dyson & Preston, 2006). Common generational experiences among leaders, who share having lived through certain historical events/periods, the cultural norms and values of earlier times, etc., often lead to disconnects or radical differences between older and younger leadership cohorts in countries (Strategic Assessment Group, 2003; Jennings 2004). For example, generations of leaders who came of age during the Cold War in Eastern Europe will have very different perceptions of their relationship to the U.S. and Russia than will a younger generation of leaders in the coming years who did not live through that conflict. Similarly, the older generation of Iranian leadership and clergy who took part in the revolution against the

Shah in 1979 have a fundamentally different world view than the majority of the current Iranian population that is sixteen years old and younger, who were not even alive during that period—which would eventually be expected to impact policy (whether in terms of a new Green Revolution or a softening of the hard line of the original revolutionaries in Iran's foreign policy).

Indeed, prior experiences can have significant effects on leaders' behavior and how they perceive their environments and process information. For example, David Kay, the former UNSCOM weapons inspector whom President Bush sent to Iraq in 2004 to lead the hunt for WMDs, was chosen primarily because of his preexisting beliefs (which fit the narrative being pushed by the Administration at the time). But, while Kay's previous experiences in Iraq after the First Gulf War had led him to believe strongly, prior to going, that WMDs were being hidden, once he was on the ground, his expertise as a weapons inspector quickly led him to the conclusion that none existed. Here, the individual difference of prior expertise on the part of Kay allowed him to modify his preexisting views in the face of new evidence. In contrast, Vice President Cheney, with his own ideological beliefs and experiences from the First Gulf War (when WMDs were found), refused to accept the truth of this reporting, and CIA Director George Tenet literally told Kay that he didn't care what he said, he was always going to believe there were WMDs in Iraq (Preston, 2011)! This illustrates the difficulty of new information breaking through these strong beliefs, which in the case of Cheney and Tenet were truly cherished possessions, and the importance of expertise over ideology in allowing new, disconfirming information to be considered. Interestingly, during conversations with former Iraqi Foreign Minister Tariq Aziz, Kay was told that Saddam was so convinced, given his own past experiences of the United States bombing for a while and then going away (and of not being willing to occupy Iraq in 1991), that the initial invasion of March 2003 was not really perceived for what it really was, with the Iraqi leader even ordering his front line troops to not engage the Coalition forces because it was all a bluff (Preston, 2011).

Another interesting variable impacting leadership involves the physical and mental health of leaders, and how illness can influence their decision making, policies, and styles of interacting with others (Post & Robins, 1993; McDermott, 2008). For example, the Shah of Iran's efforts to modernize Iran (The White Revolution) in the 1970s was intended to be a slow process, but his diagnosis of terminal cancer led to him to push for change more rapidly—resulting in instability and ultimately the Iranian Revolution and his overthrow (Post & Robins, 1993). Advancing age in leaders can sometimes result in lower capacities to deal with chronic stress, the need for medications that can impact cognition, or hardening of the arteries that impairs intellect, judgment, and emotional stability (McDermott, 2008). Examples of impacts of health cited among scholars exploring this field of leadership include those of Hitler and Stalin's extreme paranoia (a mental health issue perhaps brought on by physical ailments) late in their rule, Franklin Roosevelt's hardening of the arteries during the last years of his life (impacting his WWII decision making), John Kennedy's Addison's disease and need for powerful pain killers to deal with his chronic back pain (impacting cognition), British Prime Minister Anthony Eden's bizarre behavior during the Suez Crisis in 1956 (possibly linked to amphetamine withdrawal), Ronald

Reagan's Alzheimer's disease during his second term (impacting his cognition, engagement, and memory), and Woodrow Wilson's strokes (and earlier hypertension) possibly influencing his ability to achieve ratification of U.S. entry into The League of Nations in the U.S. Senate—and later his very ability to govern at all (Weinstein, 1981; Post & Robins, 1993; Park, 1993; Link, 1996; George & George, 1998; McDermott, 2008). Clearly, the potential for leaders' personalities and styles being impacted by underlying physical or mental health issues, drugs, or simple aging is a significant factor to be taken into account when assessing leaders at a distance (for scholars or practitioners) since these often have significant real-world consequences.

The last leadership style variable centers on the **general operating goal** of the leader—what is driving the leader to accept a leadership position. Why is a person interested in running for president? The type of goal indicates whom the leader is likely to seek for advisers. Leaders interested in a particular cause seek advocates around them; those interested in support seek a cohesive group around them; those interested in power and influence seek implementers around them; those who want to accomplish some task or change some policy seek experts around them. Advisers are sought that complement the leaders' needs and facilitate the leaders doing what they perceive needs to be done.

Thinking more broadly regarding the leader-follower relationship, Hermann, Preston, and Young (1996) propose a typology of foreign policy leadership style types for world leaders based upon three dimensions: 1) their responsiveness to (or awareness of) constraints; 2) their openness to information; and 3) their motivational focus (i.e., task/problem accomplishment versus interpersonal/relationship emphasis). As Table 5.3 illustrates, the dimensions result in eight specific foreign policy styles: expansionistic, evangelistic, actively independent, directive, incremental, influential, opportunistic, and collegial.

Finally, another recent typology of leadership style proposed in the political psychology literature focuses upon two main dimensions: 1) the leader's need for control and involvement in the policy process; and 2) the leader's need for information and general sensitivity to context (Preston, 2001). Measuring the individual characteristics of past American presidents using M. G. Hermann's LTA technique, discussed in Chapter 2, Preston suggests that a leader's need for power and prior experience/policy expertise in a given policy domain will shape how much control or involvement a president will insist upon having in the policy making process. Indeed, as the psychological literature on the need for power suggests, individuals differ greatly in their desire for control over their environments, with some insisting upon a more active role than others (see Table 5.4).

In terms of the second dimension, Preston uses cognitive complexity and prior experience/policy expertise in the policy domain as indicators of a president's *general sensitivity to context* (i.e., general cognitive need for information, attentiveness and sensitivity to the characteristics of the surrounding policy environment and the views of others). As the literature on complexity and experience illustrates, individuals differ greatly in terms of their general awareness of, or sensitivity towards, their surrounding environments. Indeed, individuals vary radically even in their general cognitive need for information when making decisions: some prefer a broad

Table 5.3 Leadership Style as a Function of Responsiveness to Constraints, Openness to Information, and Motivation (Hermann, Preston, & Young, 1996)

Responsiveness to Constraints	Openness to Information	Motivation	
		Problem Focus	*Relationship Focus*
Challenges Constraints	**Closed to Information**	**Expansionistic** Focus of attention is on expanding leader's, government's, and state's span of control.	**Evangelistic** Focus of attention is on persuading others to join in one's mission; in mobilizing others around one's message.
Challenges Constraints	**Open to Information**	**Actively Independent** Focus of attention is on maintaining one's own and the government's maneuverability and independence in a world that is perceived to continually try to limit both.	**Directive** Focus of attention is on maintaining one's own and the government's status and acceptance by others by engaging in actions on the world stage that enhance the state's reputation.
Respects Constraints	**Closed to Information**	**Incremental** Focus of attention is on improving state's economy and/or security in incremental steps while avoiding the obstacles that will inevitably arise along the way.	**Influential** Focus of attention is on building cooperative relationships with other governments and states in order to play a leadership role; by working with others, one can gain more than is possible on one's own.
Respects Constraints	**Open to Information**	**Opportunistic** Focus of attention is on assessing what is possible in the current situation and context given what one wants to achieve and considering what important constituencies will allow.	**Collegial** Focus of attention is on reconciling differences and building consensus—on gaining prestige and status through empowering others and sharing accountability.

Table 5.4 Presidential Need for Control and Involvement in Policy Process

	Prior Policy Experience or Expertise in Policy Area (General Interest Level of Desire for Involvement in Policy)	
	High	Low
	Director	*Magistrate*
Need for Power High	Decision making centralized in inner circle; Preference for direct control and involvement throughout policy process; Advocate own policy views, frame issues, and set specific policy guidelines; Leader relies upon own policy judgments more than those of expert advisers.	Decision making centralized in inner circle; Preference for direct control over decisions but limited need for involvement throughout policy process; Sets general policy guidelines, but delegates policy formulation and implementation; Leader relies more upon views of expert advisers than own.
	Administrator	*Delegator*
Need for Power Low	Decision making less centralized and more collegial. Leader requires less direct control over policy process and subordinates; Enhanced roles of subordinates; Actively advocates own views, frames issues, and sets specific policy guidelines; Leader relies more upon own judgments than those of expert advisers.	Decision making less centralized and more collegial. Leader requires little/no direct control/ involvement in policy process; Enhanced roles of subordinates; Delegates policy formulation and implementation for subordinates; Tendency to rely upon (and adopt) views of expert advisers in final policy decision.

information search before reaching conclusions, whereas others prefer to rely more upon their own existing views and other simplifying heuristics. In Table 5.5, the leaders' cognitive complexity interacts with their prior substantive policy experience or expertise to produce an overall style regarding the need for information and sensitivity to external context.

Developed through empirical testing of its hypothesized relationships between leader characteristics and their foreign policy decision making and uses of advisory systems against the archival record in the presidential

Table 5.5 Sensitivity to Context (Including Policy Environment, Institutional Constraints, Views of Subordinates)

	Prior Policy Experience or Expertise in Policy Area	
	High	Low
Cognitive Complexity High	**Navigator** High general need for information & interest in foreign policy (FP). Active collector of information from policy environment. Greater sensitivity to constraints & enhanced search for information and advice from outside actors.	**Observer** High general need for information, but limited personal interest in FP. Interested in information on policy specifics, but heavily dependent on expert advice. Reduced sensitivity to constraints on policy & less awareness of (search for) information & advice from outside actors.
Cognitive Complexity Low	**Sentinel** High personal interest in FP, but low need for information. Greater sensitivity to constraints & advice from outside actors. Seeks to guide policy along path consistent with own personal principles, views, or past experience. Avoids broad search for policy information beyond that deemed relevant given past experience or existing personal views.	**Maverick** Low need for information & limited personal interest in FP. Avoids broad collection of general information—decisions driven by own idiosyncratic policy views & principles. Reduced sensitivity to constraints on policy & less awareness of (search for) information & advice from outside actors.

libraries, Preston's model produces a nuanced, composite style typology that is sensitive to differences in leaders across these two dimensions and across differing policy domains (see Table 5.6). In other words, this allows presidents to vary from one another in more than just the one simple dimension of their need for control and involvement in the policy process (as in the typologies of Barber, discussed in Chapter 2, and Johnson), but also in terms of their general sensitivity to policy information and context. In addition to providing greater variation in style types, the resulting typology provides

Table 5.6 Composite Leadership Style Types (Preston, 2001)

	Foreign Policy	*Domestic Policy*
Truman	Magistrate-Maverick	Director-Sentinel
Eisenhower	Director-Navigator	Magistrate-Observer
Kennedy	Director-Navigator	Magistrate-Observer
Johnson	Magistrate-Maverick	Director-Sentinel
Reagan	Director-Maverick	Sentinel-Maverick
G. H. W. Bush	Administrator-Navigator	Delegator-Observer
Clinton	Delegator-Observer	Administrator-Navigator
G. W. Bush	Delegator-Maverick	Delegator-Maverick
Obama	Administrator-Observer	Administrator-Navigator

greater analytical capability to study the impact of leadership styles across different policy domains by incorporating a more contingent notion of leadership style into the analysis of presidents. For example, a serious weakness of previous typologies has been their firm roots in either foreign policy or domestic policy, with presidential styles generally appearing to be incompatible between the two domains. Although personality traits (i.e., need for power and complexity) are stable in form over time within individuals, and should have the same impact upon presidential behavior regardless of policy domain (foreign or domestic), this is not the case for nonpersonality-based characteristics like prior policy experience or expertise (see, Winter, 1973; McCrae, 1993). In the typology presented above, leadership styles for presidents vary across the foreign and domestic policy domains based upon the leaders' degree of prior policy experience in the particular area. Table 5.6 compares the composite leadership style designations for a number of modern U.S. presidents across both foreign and domestic policy.

AN ILLUSTRATION OF APPLICATION OF POLITICAL PSYCHOLOGY APPROACHES TO LEADERS

In the final section of this chapter, an illustration will be provided of how a number of the political psychological approaches discussed so far can be applied to a political leader, George W. Bush. Obviously, examples of all of the techniques discussed would be impractical given space constraints in a textbook. While some illustrations were provided in Chapter 2, a lengthy examination of Bush's characteristics using two additional approaches will demonstrate the utility of leadership analysis for understanding the behavior of this president.

The Example of George W. Bush

Political psychology approaches to the study of political leaders can range from those which make fairly general, simple predictions of overall styles of behavior to those providing much more involved, detailed analyses. An example of the former would be Barber's (1972) typology focusing upon the two dimensions of active/passive (i.e., how much energy do presidents put into the job) and positive/negative (i.e., the personal satisfaction they derive from presidential duties), which we discussed in Chapter 2 with reference to Presidents Clinton, Bush, and Obama. Examples of more complex approaches would include more involved leader profiles using the LTA approach of Hermann (1999a), discussed in Chapter 2, or the style typology developed by Preston (2001).

Again using the example of Clinton, Hermann's (1999b) LTA technique, employing content analysis of leader interviews to produce profile scores along seven characteristics (i.e., need for power, locus of control, ethnocentrism, task-interpersonal focus, complexity, self-confidence, and distrust of others), suggests quite different style consequences for the two presidents. For example, in terms of Hermann, Preston, and Young's (1996; see also Keller, 2005) typology focusing upon whether leaders *challenge or respect constraints* and whether they are *open or closed to information*, Bill Clinton (based upon his measured, moderate profile scores on need for power and locus of control) is seen as generally accepting of (or respectful of) constraints, but under certain circumstances willing to challenge what appear to be inappropriate or unfounded limitations on his role (Hermann, 1999b, p. 3).[6] As Hermann (1999b, p. 3) notes, leaders with moderate scores like Clinton's will work within the parameters they perceive to structure their political environment (and) because of the limitations within which they perceive they have to work, building consensus and achieving compromise are important skills for a politician to have and to exercise. Clinton's high scores on complexity and self-confidence suggest he is open to information, will be more highly attuned to feedback from the political environment, and be much more active in monitoring his surroundings and gathering advice when making decisions. At the same time, however, such intensive monitoring of the environment for feedback and information before taking actions can lead outside observers to see their behavior as erratic and opportunistic (Hermann, 1999b, p. 3) In terms of the degree to which he is *motivated by the problem or the relationship*, Clinton's moderate score on task-interpersonal emphasis suggests that he has the ability to direct his attention to the problem when that is appropriate to the situation at hand or to building relationships when that seems more relevant, essentially shifting between these as called for by the context (Hermann, 1999b, p. 4). As Hermann explains regarding Clinton's style:

> Clinton's pattern of scores on the seven traits help us determine the kind of leadership style he will exhibit. By ascertaining that he is likely to (1) generally respect constraints in his political environment, (2) be open to, and search out, information in the situation, (3) be motivated by both solving the problem and keeping morale high, and (4) view politics as the art of the possible and mutually beneficial, we know from extensive research that Clinton will exhibit a collegial leadership style. His focus of attention is on reconciling differences and building consensus, on retaining power and authority through building relationships and taking advantage of opportunities to work with others toward specific ends. Clinton's leadership style predisposes him

toward the team-building approach to politics. Like the captain of a football or basketball team, the leader is dependent on others to work with him to make things happen. Such leaders see themselves at the center of the information-gathering process. With regard to the advisory process, working as a team means that advisers are empowered to participate in all aspects of policymaking but also to share in the accountability for what occurs. Members of the team are expected to be sensitive to and supportive of the beliefs and values of the leader.

(pp. 4–5)

Another approach that can be applied to Clinton and Bush is Preston's (2001) typology of leadership style, which also makes use of the LTA technique to obtain scores for a president's need for power and complexity, but adds a measure for prior policy experience or expertise. In the foreign policy arena, Clinton, who scores low in need for power and prior policy experience, but high in complexity, is classified as a *Delegator-Observer*. As a result, the typology would predict that while interested in policy matters, Clinton would require less direct personal control over the policy process, actively delegate policy formulation and implementation tasks to subordinates, and rely heavily upon the expertise or policy judgments of his senior specialist advisers when making decisions. On the other hand, his high complexity suggests that he has a high need for information when making decisions. This would lead him to seek out multiple policy perspectives from advisers, engage in extensive search in the policy environment for information and feedback, and exhibit a more tentative, less decisive decision style that avoids rigid, black-and-white reasoning while focusing upon the shades of gray in issues. Clinton would be expected to demonstrate a pragmatic approach to policy issues and not rigidly adhere to a given ideological or political position if feedback from the policy environment suggested a different context. Advisers would be drawn not only from those who share his views, but also from those who express varied and competing viewpoints.

In contrast, George W. Bush, who scores low in power, complexity, and prior policy experience, would fit the *Delegator-Maverick* style (the same style as Ronald Reagan). LTA profile scores for George W. Bush show him to be low in *cognitive complexity*, but high in *self-confidence* and *in-group bias* (nationalism). Further, in terms of his *prior foreign policy experience* and *degree of expertise* in that domain, Bush scores low on both counts. As a result, Bush's foreign policy style has been found in previous research to be one characterized by low sensitivity to the surrounding context, heavy dependence upon expert advisers (to whom most policy formulation/implementation tasks are delegated), a closed advisory system emphasizing limited search for information or divergent viewpoints, and the assembly of like-minded advisers into the White House inner circle (Preston & Hermann 2004; Preston 2008). Moreover, Bush's low complexity scores suggest that his own personal information processing style would be characterized by black-and-white, absolute categorizations of the surrounding policy environment, heavy use of stereotypes and analogies, a strongly ideological approach to policy and the framing of problems, and more uncritical adoption of preexisting images of other countries (Preston, 2001; Preston & Hermann, 2004; Dyson & Preston, 2006; Cottam & Preston, 2007). Further, such use of images by Bush would be expected to not only be uncritical of their fit to the existing policy environment (to which he is generally insensitive), but also be highly resistant to modification or reconsideration once adopted. Bush's high score on *in-group bias* (or nationalism) would be expected to further exacerbate this dynamic.

One consequence of Bush's extremely delegative nature is to enhance the potential for bureaucratic conflict over policy among subordinates (see, Preston & 't Hart, 1999; Preston, 2011). Bureaucratic in-fighting and conflicts over the shape of Bush's foreign policy have been quite visible, pitting Administration hard-liners like Defense Secretary Donald Rumsfeld and Vice President Cheney against the more moderate Secretary of State Colin Powell (see Sipress, 2002; Zakaria, 2002). For example, Powell's efforts to pursue mediation to break the deadlock between the Israelis and the Palestinians were repeatedly undercut and blocked by Bush's more influential hard-line advisers (Sipress, 2002; Preston, 2011). As a result of this in-fighting, Bush's foreign policy in the Middle East and elsewhere was inconsistent, and at times incoherent (Duffy, 2002; Sanger, 2002; Preston, 2011). Similar conflicts occurred between Powell, Rumsfeld, and Cheney over policy towards Iraq, North Korea, the United Nations, and over continued U.S. commitments to international agreements. Further, Bush's own personal dislike for conflict and controversy, as well as his own lack of substantive policy knowledge, made it difficult for him to end these adviser conflicts (Preston, 2011). Instead, Bush sought the comfort zone provided by those advisers (principally Rumsfeld and Cheney) who shared his own ideological beliefs and was usually more influenced by their advice. This often resulted in a rather closed information-gathering advice system, where the more hard-line inner circle excluded the participation of Powell or external actors who differed with them over policy.

Bush also has a tendency to see the world in stark, undifferentiated terms, a pattern that is complicated by his often-reported lack of attention to the details of policy (Mitchell, 2000; Bruni, 2002). For example, Bush's categorization of Iraq, Iran, and North Korea as an axis of evil served to simplify three quite distinct regions and policy situations into a more easily understood, black-and-white frame for policy making. After the events of 9/11, Bush's simple moral clarity about the world seemed to resonate with a changed political climate in America in which good and evil seemed easily delineated. Stating that "either you are with us or you are with the terrorists" and that bin Laden would be brought back "dead or alive," or that the new struggle was between good versus evil, civilization versus anarchy, that it was a "crusade" that America was now embarked upon—resonated with the American public, if not always with foreign publics (Buzbee, 2001; Duffy, 2002). And, as the Administration's manipulation of evidence and extremely selective ("cherry picking") search for information to justify the invasion of Iraq in 2003 (and its subsequent conduct of the war since then) has illustrated, Bush's advisory system strongly fits what his LTA scores would have predicted. Namely, it is best characterized as closed to information contradicting favored (often ideologically-derived) policy conclusions, preferring simplistic analogies and images of opponents, and rigidly adhering to failing policies despite overwhelming, contradictory evidence from the surrounding domestic and international policy environments—to which he is largely insensitive (see, Woodward, 2004; Bamford, 2005; Baker & Hamilton, 2006; Fallows, 2006; Alfonsi, 2006; Isikoff & Corn, 2006; Preston, 2011).

Moving beyond the above discussion, which merely lays out how some of the many different types of political psychological approaches might explain or predict a political leader's behavior, we will now take one specific example from the above, Preston's (2001) typology, and discuss in a more detailed fashion the empirical evidence supporting its predictions to illustrate the application of such approaches to the study of the personality and styles of leaders. At the same time, it should be emphasized that there are many available elaborations of the approaches discussed in this chapter in published research on political leaders that is worth examining in more depth than is allowed in any textbook chapter. For example, the psychoanalytic approach has previously been applied to Bill Clinton in works by Stanley Renshon (1996), the operational code to Clinton by Mark Schafer and Scott Crichlow (2000), and the Myers-Briggs Type Indicator (covering introversion vs. extroversion, sensing vs. intuition, thinking vs. feeling, and judging vs. perceiving scales) by Michael Lyons (1997, discussed in Chapter 2). All provide useful cuts on the different dimensions of personality or individual characteristics that make up Bill Clinton. Together, they provide scholars and students alike with a more nuanced, well-rounded portrait of a complex individual. None of the approaches alone provides all of the answers. Rather, the scholarship on personality and leadership across the political psychology literature provides us with multiple methods and approaches to the study individuals across many differing dimensions. Such approaches can be applied to political leaders across cultural and national boundaries, as well as be applied to nonleaders and individual citizens (see Hermann, 1984, 1987; Winter et al., 1991; Kaarbo & Hermann, 1998; Taysi & Preston, 2001). It is the research question you ask that should drive your selection of approach and what dimensions of personality, style, or leadership you focus upon. The purpose of this chapter is to lay out some of the options on this quite lengthy menu.

George W. Bush as a *Delegator-Maverick*: A Case Study

Based upon his LTA profile scores, George W. Bush would be expected to exhibit the *Delegator's* preferences for control and involvement in the policy process and the *Maverick's* needs for information and sensitivity to the contextual environment in his foreign policy decision making. Table 5.7 provides a summary of the composite *Delegator-Maverick* leadership style predicted for Bush in foreign affairs. In the following section, the predictions of the typology will be compared to the secondary literature on Bush, as well as interviews conducted with White House advisers from his administration.

In looking at the personal characteristics of George W. Bush, it is useful to note that like Ronald Reagan and Lyndon Johnson, Bush saw the world in absolute, black-and-white terms and had hardly any prior experience or exposure to foreign affairs before entering the White House. In this, Bush exhibits a *Maverick* style as far as his *sensitivity to context*. On the other hand, in terms of his *need for personal control and involvement in the*

Table 5.7 Expectations for the Composite Delegator-Maverick Leadership Style

Composite Style (The Delegator-Maverick)	Expectations: Leader Style and Use of Advisers
Dimensions of Leader Control and Involvement in Policy Process	Relegative presidential style in which leader requires limited direct personal control over the policy process;
	Preference for informal, less hierarchical advisory structures designed to enhance participation by subordinates;
	Leader actively delegates policy formulation and implementation tasks to subordinates and adopts (relies upon) the expertise and policy judgments of specialist advisers when making decisions;
	Inner circle decision rule: Advisory group outputs and leader policy preferences reflect the dominant views expressed by either expert advisers or the majority of group members.
Dimension of Leader Need for Information and General Sensitivity to Context	Leader has low need for information & advice, limited search for broad-ranging information, selective processing favoring information & advice consistent with existing beliefs, extreme dependence on subordinate advice.
	Leader is largely insensitive to external constraints on policy making (due to lack of information gathering and reliance on simplifying frames (such as ideology) to gap-fill. (*Challenger*)
	Advisers selected based on loyalty & ideological fit with leader and his/her beliefs over expertise/competence.
	Decisions driven by leader's own idiosyncratic policy views, ideology, and principles.
	Heavy use of simplifying heuristics like analogies, ideologies, & stereotypes to frame the decision environment, assess its feedback, and consider policy options.

policy process, Bush was far more interpersonally oriented (placing far more emphasis upon maintaining personal relationships) and was much lower in his personal need for involvement and control over policy making. As a result, Bush falls into the *Delegator* style category, thereby heightening the importance of key, influential advisers around him in policy making.

This becomes critically important as we consider the amalgam of Bush's quite hierarchical, centralized advisory structures that existed alongside his highly delegative style—a setup that at first glance would seem out of place. However, for leaders who require less personal, active engagement in policy and who lack their own personal policy experience, it is the *nature* of the delegation to subordinates that plays a major role in the shaping of the subsequent inner circle structures. For Bush, the trusted adviser to whom he delegated much of the transition-related organization and staffing of the White House was Dick Cheney, his eventual Vice President. Unlike Bush, Cheney's own personal style was very control-oriented and he developed probably the most powerful vice presidential staff organization in history to assert his control over policy. Indeed, Cheney falls into the *Director-Sentinel* style of leadership—one that emphasizes high control and engagement along with a moderate to low degree to sensitivity to context.

For the *Delegator-Maverick* Bush, the selection of a more hands-on, directive Vice President was quite complementary to his style, allowing him to focus more upon the personal side of the presidency he enjoyed (while Cheney focused more on the task side). As a result, Cheney (along with other subordinates like Defense Secretary Donald Rumsfeld) were allowed to play quite powerful policymaking roles in the administration, and given their loyalty and ideological fit with Bush, served to provide policy substance (or flesh) to the President's own, preexisting ideological views on policy. They would serve to frame (or explain) the policy environment for him, and largely formulate the types of policy choices the President would choose amongst during the decision process. And during the Iraq War policy making process (both pre- and post–March 2003), this would have the consequence of limiting dissenting policy views and isolating the White House within a closed advisory system housing an insular inner circle at the top (Preston, 2011). It would encourage subordinates, who had been delegated substantial freedom of action, to compete with one another for influence with the President and over policy (e.g., Cheney's office or Rumsfeld's Pentagon competing with Powell's State Department over Iraq policy, etc.). Given Bush's style and the inner circle advisers he selected, the policy making dynamics that would be seen within his Administration over Iraq (and in many other areas) were largely to be expected, and were quite consistent with what would have been predicted (Preston & Hermann, 2004; Preston, 2008). Let us now explore these style effects on the President's inner circle in more detail.

The Importance of Loyalty in the Bush Inner Circle

One quality that certainly played a major role in defining George W. Bush's interpersonal style in the White House (and how he would structure his inner circle) was the heavy emphasis that was placed upon loyalty—both in the expectation that staff would be unfailingly loyal to him, and his own belief that he should reward that loyalty with loyalty in return. It was a tendency the younger Bush shared with his father; it was a Bush family standard (Dowd & Friedman, 1990; Moens, 2004; Draper, 2007). It represented a kind of social contract for Bush, a two-way street of responsibilities between those he worked closely with and himself. And, as even the most ardent supporters of the administration acknowledge, within the President's inner circle, loyalty and absolute fidelity to White House policy were an unquestioned component (Moens, 2004; Burke, 2004).

Yet, while laudable on a personal level, the down-side of such an emphasis upon loyalty is that leaders tend (as a result) to surround themselves with political or policy doppelgängers who never provide healthy criticism or challenges to policy (or to the leader). The higher the degree to which loyalty is emphasized by leaders, the more likely they are to become insulated inside a phalanx of supporters and detached from a more healthy process, whereby negative (and potentially useful) feedback might reach the inner circle. In fact, it has been noted (see Preston, 2011) that many of the inner circle advisers surrounding Bush, even if they did influence the specifics of policy, did not markedly differ from the President's own predispositions (in terms of ideology, world view, etc.). What they generally tended to add was flesh to the skeleton, not create the skeleton itself—with Rove, for example, being described by Heclo (2003, p. 34) as providing experience and merely complementing Bush's own political mind. And among leaders who seek the warm cocoon of loyalty within their inner circles, one often also sees a lower comfort zone for any dissent that does occur. As Gellman (2008) observed:

> Bush generally hated it when advisers disagreed, demanding that they get their acts together. At decision time, according to Cheney aide Ron Christie, Bush wanted to hear that "your senior advisers believe X." . . . Bush valued not only consensus but finality. "Once he's made up his mind, controversy ceases, so getting to him at just the right time is extremely important."
>
> (p. 79)

Moreover, an emphasis upon loyalty also results in leaders often selecting subordinates for roles in their administrations based more upon that dimension than upon their competence, expertise, or prior experience dealing with a given issue or policy area. Unfortunately, this is often coupled with a slow response to making personnel changes, and an ineffective blame-avoidance response, when loyal, yet unqualified subordinates become political liabilities due to their ineffective or incompetent handling of policy problems. For Bush, this resulted in his hanging on to Secretary of Defense Donald Rumsfeld long after his mishandling of the Iraq war had become a major political liability in 2006, provoking even former senior military leaders to publicly criticize him. It also led Bush to stand firmly behind former FEMA Director Michael Brown during the hurricane Katrina response and, much to his detriment, express publicly the belief that "Brownie" had done "a heck of a job"—despite obvious evidence to the contrary (Preston, 2008). Indeed, as one exasperated senior administration official observed, "the president thinks cutting and running on his friends shows weakness," even though politically it would have been the smart move to make (Baker, 2007).

Unfortunately, equating "conformity with existing policy" with loyalty on the part of advisers has the effect of allowing advice that disagrees with the existing policy line, even if only in terms of means, to be dismissed by the broader group. In an echo of the Vietnam inner circle dynamics that occurred during the Johnson administration, different bureaucratic actors or advisers who disagreed with President Bush and his core inner circle's policy views on Iraq were not only dismissed, but viewed with hostility as opponents. As Assistant Secretary of State Richard Armitage noted, "Tenet, the CIA, and the State Department were the hated enemies of the White House. They hated us! Because sometimes the intelligence didn't comport with whatever the bullshit the White House wanted to come up with. Or we would raise issues. So we were both seen, for different reasons, as not being on the team" (Preston, 2011, p. 28). When it was observed that a lot of people would use the term cherry-picking of information to describe that kind of dynamic, Armitage replied:

> That's fair. Yeah. That's fair. See, I'm, by the way, I'm thrilled that they dropped us out of meetings! It speaks very well of us. For instance, on detainees and abuse, water-boarding. We were not even told there were meetings. Why? Because we raised objections.
>
> (Preston, 2011, p. 28)

The Need for Control and Involvement in the Policy Process

George W. Bush reveled in seeing himself as "The Decider" who made all the tough, final policy decisions, almost channeling his own inner Harry Truman to model his leadership image upon (Woodward, 2002). And it is certainly true that Bush often (though not always) made the final call on policy matters within his inner circle, much as Truman made the final decisions after staff brought him questions to be decided (Preston 1997, 2001). But such deciding does not necessarily require active presidential engagement in the policy making process preceding the decision point (where policy formulation and the fashioning of options take place), nor does it preclude a heavy reliance on the leader's part upon expert advisers to frame the policy environment and provide options to decide amongst. Certainly in the case of Truman, these earlier elements were delegated to subordinates (like Secretary of State Dean Acheson), who would fashion policy and lay out the option(s) for the President to decide upon—while still preserving his final yea or nay (Preston, 1997, 2001). This was similarly the case with Bush, who retained the final decision authority, but delegated much of the policy formulation tasks to his tight, inner circle of advisers. And as former White House press secretary Scott McClellan (2008, p. 154) observed, the President "liked to compartmentalize information within the White House. There were regular meetings between the President and the Vice President, or Andy Card or Karl Rove that were strictly private." Indeed, in terms of the tightness of Bush's inner circle, Thomas and Wolffe (2005, p. 33) remarked that he "may be the most isolated president in modern history, at least since the late-stage Richard Nixon." But unlike Nixon, who insisted on retaining a great deal of personal control over policy, Bush tended to delegate. And this would have a significant effect on policy making, as Colin Powell's former chief of staff, Lawrence Wilkerson, later observed during an interview:

> Now, here's the point where I think he really failed, in a major sense! Not only was he a President who *believed* in being aloof from the details, being the "great decision maker" as he himself has said. The guy who makes the big ones. And then leaves them alone for execution. Not only was that his nature. . . . he was also lazy in my view. Intellectually, and what I would call execution-wise. And he'd say, "My decision's made! It's sacrosanct!" A certain amount of hubris and arrogance associated with this too. "No one would *dare* not carry out my decision the way I have conceived that decision!" But he may not have even articulated the way he conceived of that decision. He just made the decision. You know? And then the bureaucracy went out and did what it damned well pleased, usually with its own pre-dispositions and its own biases, and so forth. And the President had no *attentiveness* to that execution.
>
> (Preston, 2011, p. 29)

And just as would sometimes happen during the Truman administration, where bureau-political competition between lower level subordinates would determine how policy decisions were implemented (see Preston, 1997), this would also happen with the delegative style of Bush. As Wilkerson observed:

> A great case in point was when the brouhaha occurred over who made the decision to disband the Iraqi Army down to the lowest private. Well, the President had made the decision just a week or two earlier that the Iraqi Army would not be disbanded any further than battalion—about six to nine hundred men—those units would be kept intact. The brigade commanders, the division commanders, and their staffs maybe will go away, but the battalions and their people would stay, and they would form a new Iraqi Army. That's the decision the President made! Well, a couple of weeks later, without telling anybody, Jerry Bremer issues an order disbanding the Iraqi Army down to the lowest private. No one *knew* who made that decision! And the President *himself*, as far as I know, has made the same statement! I listened to him one day in an interview, and I think what I heard him say was, "I don't know who changed that decision."
>
> (Preston, 2011, pp. 29–30)

Off-the-record descriptions of the President by many former White House officials, and other colleagues who knew him well, tends to provide more support for an explanation based on his general lack of interest in details and delegation to subordinates. Indeed, Armitage recalls a presidential style that was highly delegative and not focused on the details of policy:

> I'll give you a couple of examples . . . the President wanted to get out of the ABM Treaty. We wanted the Treaty of Moscow. Powell said, "I can get ya this. I can do this! Just keep the animals off my back basically." And the President, "okay." But there, he wasn't interested

in the details, he was interested in the result, and we got it. We get to war planning and what-not, the President would always say to the generals, whoever they were, "You get what you need? You have what you need?" And they'd say, "yes" or "I need this." Generally, they'd say, "yes sir!," because Mr. Rumsfeld had brow-beat them so much. But he wasn't interested in the, what's it gonna be used for, etc. Part of it, I think, was what he's read about Vietnam. That Vietnam was run from the President's desk and all that, and you let the generals fight the war. It's gotta be both. The President commits young men and women to battle and then he wants to be sure that he's fighting in the best possible way. And Mr. Bush, in my view, took a very, too much hands-off view. . . . he wasn't steeped in details.

(Preston, 2011, pp. 30–31)

The resulting combination of a President who saw loyalty as the first-and-foremost quality in advisers and wanted to be a decisive decider while tending to delegate substantially to subordinates is what characterized the Bush *need for control or involvement in the policy process*. While questioning whether Bush's national security adviser, Condi Rice, really did an adequate job of calibrating for the President's "headstrong style of leadership" or "appreciate the need to keep his beliefs in proper check," McClellan (2008) observes:

Overall, Bush's foreign policy advisers played right into his thinking, doing little to question it or to cause him to pause long enough to fully consider the consequences before moving forward. And once Bush set a course of action, it was rarely questioned. That is what Bush expected and made known to his top advisers. The strategy for carrying out a policy was open for debate, but there would be no hand-wringing, no second-guessing of the policy once it was decided and set in motion.

(p. 128)

But how do we reconcile the view of Bush as "The Decider" versus the image of him as a leader heavily influenced (or dominated) by the views of his inner circle advisers—two competing images around which much of the literature on his presidency revolves? Essentially, it could be argued that these debates between the two poles miss the fundamental point. Bush could be in charge of the final decisions and have similar world views to that of his inner circle advisers, yet still be dependent upon their judgment and expertise in formulating policy approaches and deciding upon courses of action. This is the difference between the caricature of a puppet (which no doubt was incorrect regarding Bush) and the more accurate depiction of a leader lacking experience in substantive policy areas who delegates to expert advisers and is dependent upon their guidance during the policy making process. In this, Bush was hardly dissimilar from Bill Clinton, Lyndon Johnson, or Harry Truman in the foreign policy realm—as a President who leaned heavily upon his inner circle foreign policy experts (Preston, 2001, 2011).

Indeed, George W. Bush entered the White House as, arguably, the least experienced or knowledgeable about foreign affairs of any modern American president! Not only had he not traveled abroad to any significant degree (lacking even a passport until only a few years prior to his presidential run), he possessed no real prior experience or knowledge of foreign policy matters. This lack of knowledge required a crash course under the tutelage of Condoleezza Rice during the campaign to try to avoid his obvious weakness in this area during the debates and in speaking with reporters on the trail. Soon, the campaign focused upon emphasizing the degree to which Bush would be surrounding himself with experienced policy experts if he were elected, men like his Vice President Dick Cheney, who had served in many capacities in Washington. Experienced advisers with names like Rice, Colin Powell, Donald Rumsfeld, and others were described as individuals likely to play key roles in the new administration—roles that would compensate for the public's concerns about Bush's own relative inexperience. As Lawrence Wilkerson, Powell's chief of staff, observed, this emphasis being placed upon surrounding Bush with experienced advisers was critical, because "it allowed everybody to believe that this Sarah Palin-like president—because, let's face it, that's what he was—was going to be protected by this national-security elite, tested in the cauldrons of fire" (Preston, 2011, p. 32).

And, as would be expected for an inexperienced leader, Bush tended to delegate substantial authority to subordinates and defer to his loyal, inner circle policy experts. During foreign policy meetings, Bush "often deferred to Cheney" on issues (Draper, 2007, p. 114), a pattern that he often repeated even in domestic affairs (where he also had limited substantive experience)—with former Treasury Secretary Paul O'Neill recalling that Bush "seemed to be limited in his knowledge of most domestic issues" (Suskind 2004, p. 88). Indeed, for O'Neill, the problem was that:

> This President's lack of inquisitiveness or pertinent experience—Jack Kennedy, at least, had spent a decade in Congress—meant he didn't know or really care about the position of the U.S. government. It wasn't just a matter of doing the opposite of whatever Clinton had done, which was a prevalent theme throughout the administration. This President was starting from scratch on most issues and relying on ideologues like Larry Lindsey, Karl Rove, and, he now feared, his old friend Dick. Not an honest broker in sight.
>
> (Suskind, 2004, p. 126)

And for O'Neill, it was clear that Bush often ceded significant authority over policy to others inside his administration and was clearly signing on to strong ideological positions that had not been fully thought through. But, of course, "that's the nature of ideology. Thinking it through is the last thing an ideologue wants to do" (Suskind, 2004, p. 127). As McClellan (2008, p. 85) would observe, because the President lacked "a deep background in foreign policy, Bush counted on a team of foreign policy heavyweights with diverse expertise to help him formulate policy based on his guiding principles, such as freedom, a strong military, and free trade." Unfortunately for a President who is less sensitive to context, having a team of heavyweights with diverse expertise only helps to compensate for a closed advisory-information gathering system if they also possess diverse viewpoints and perspectives. And this, the Bush inner circle lacked, with the exception of Colin Powell, who generally was ignored and whose influence was minimal when compared to the central core advisers like Cheney, Rumsfeld, and Rice (Preston, 2011).

Bush's Sensitivity to Context/Use of Information

The *Maverick* style of Bush, with his low sensitivity to context and limited, highly selective information search, is one that is pretty well documented and reinforced by interviews with many former advisers, staffers, and individuals who have briefed him (see Preston, 2011).[7] As would be expected for such a leadership style, the Bush inner circle was one in which diversity of view and wide information-search was severely constrained. Advisers within the inner circle tended to share very similar views (both politically and ideologically), and as typical within closed advisory systems, those with policy views or perspectives that challenged the prevailing ones within the core group were either ignored or never granted access. Where information search occurred, it often was highly selective, and sought out only material that supported existing policy or assisted in implementing or selling it politically. The *Maverick* style is also quite idiosyncratic, and certainly Iraq policy was driven from a basic foundation, an absolute view of the world, based within George W. Bush's own personal ideological beliefs. While it is true that Bush was extremely dependent upon his inner circle advisers to provide the details and substance to the formulation of policy, it is equally true that the basic directions which Iraq policy took were not divergent from the President's own personal views or beliefs. In this way, again, it is inaccurate to characterize him as a puppet of the neocons. Though they influenced his thinking and suggested paths to follow, these roads were not ones that Bush was disinclined to take. Moreover, typical of belief systems that are of the simple, black-and-white variety, leaders possessing them tend to be more decisive and confident in their own idiosyncratic policy choices, and see no need to search for lots of additional information or alternative viewpoints. After all, if you already see the world in terms of "you are either with us or against us," and you know what is right or wrong or true or false—the decisions are much more straightforward in your mind. And you don't need to gather information that challenges those absolutes. For the *Maverick* Bush, these elements played a central role in how the Iraq policy was developed and later implemented—and governed much of the inner circle dynamics governing the policy debate (Preston, 2011).

One of the characteristics normally associated with less sensitive leaders is their tendency to rely more upon their own idiosyncratic beliefs (whether these be ideological or religious) in judging situations, as opposed to gathering lots of varied information from multiple sources. Certainly, George W. Bush's general pattern fits perfectly into that description. As his former White House Press Secretary Scott McClellan (2008, p. 127) observed, "Bush has always been an instinctive leader more than an intellectual leader. He is not one to delve deeply into all the possible policy options—including sitting around engaging in extended debate about them—before making a choice. Rather, he chooses based on his gut and his most deeply held convictions. Such was the case with Iraq." Indeed, as Woodward (2002) remarked, during interviews the president spoke a dozen times about his "instincts" or his "instinctive" reactions, including his statement, "I'm not a textbook player, I'm a gut player." It's pretty clear that Bush's role as politician, President, and commander in chief is driven by a secular faith in his instincts—his natural and spontaneous conclusions and judgments. His instincts are almost his second religion.

(p. 342)

This style of gathering information and making decisions has the tendency to often short-circuit policy debate and reduce circumspection on the part of leaders. And, as Baker (2007) notes, this certainly appeared to be the case with how Bush interacted with his environment:

> To an extent, Bush walls himself off from criticism. He does read newspapers, contrary to public impression, but watches little television news and does not linger in the media echo chamber. "He does a very good job of keeping out the extreme things in his life. . . . He doesn't watch Leno and Letterman. He doesn't spend a lot of time exposing himself to that sort of stuff. He has a terrific knack of not looking through the rearview mirror." Rep. Jack Kingston (R-Ga.), who attended a legislative meeting with Bush last month, said his impervious nature works both ways. "The things that make him unpopular also help him deal with all the pressure . . . He's stubborn. He's loyal to his philosophy."

This insensitivity to context, and more black-and-white manner of viewing the world, also contributed to a tendency that many former Bush administration officials have noted during interviews, of a President who was relatively incurious (intellectually) about the details of policy beyond big picture or broad brush-stroke treatments of subjects. For example, former Treasury Secretary Paul O'Neill has remarked that whether it was in large or small meetings, Bush tended to be relatively unresponsive and behave differently than had previous presidents he had served under, and related this experience briefing Bush on a detailed memo he had written on the economy:

> There were a dozen questions that O'Neill had expected Bush to ask. He was ready with the answers . . . Bush didn't ask anything. He looked at O'Neill, not changing his expression, not letting on that he had any reactions—either positive or negative. . . . The President said nothing. No change in expression. Next subject. Certainly, each president's style is different. But O'Neill had a basis for comparison. Nixon, Ford, Bush 41, and Clinton, with whom he had visited four or five times during the nineties for long sessions on policy matters. In each case, he'd arrived prepared to mix it up, ready for engagement. You'd hash it out. That was what he was known for. It was the reason you got called to the office. You met with the President to answer questions. "I wondered, from the first, if the President didn't know the questions to ask," O'Neill recalled, "or did he know and just not want to know the answers? Or did his strategy somehow involve never showing what

he thought? But you can ask questions, gather information, and not necessarily show your hand. It was strange."

(Suskind, 2004, pp. 57–58)

But for those inner circle advisers who briefed Bush frequently, it was apparent that while the President would often engage more than O'Neill experienced, it still took the more limited form typical of leaders who don't look for the minutia. Richard Clarke (2004, p. 243) recalls that "Bush was informed by talking with a small set of senior advisers" rather than casting his net more widely for advice, and that "early on we were told that 'the President is not a big reader' and goes to bed at 10." As a result, the type of advice Bush sought from his inner circle, or those who briefed him, did not lend itself to broad information gathering or a focus upon the details of policy. For example, McClellan (2008, p. 128) recalled that Bush believed "it's important for his advisers to think about specific actions in terms of larger, strategic objectives—how they fit into the bigger picture of what the administration seeks to accomplish." As Clarke (2004) would later note regarding Bush:

> It was clear that the critique of him as a dumb, lazy rich kid were somewhat off the mark. When he focused, he asked the kind of questions that revealed a results-oriented mind, but he looked for the simple solution, the bumper sticker description of the problem. Once he had that, he could put energy behind a drive to achieve his goal. The problem was that many of the important issues, like terrorism, like Iraq, were laced with important subtlety and nuance. These issues needed analysis and Bush and his inner circle had no real interest in complicated analyses; on the issues that they cared about, they already knew the answers, it was received wisdom.
>
> (p. 243)

However, as one former White House official, who worked for Bush for over two years, observed, "With argument comes refinement, and there was none of that. . . . It's fine to say he's a big-picture leader and doesn't get bogged down in the details. But that's another way of saying he's lazy—not physically lazy, but intellectually lazy."[8] Indeed, Draper (2007, p. 416) noted that "most of all, Bush evinced an almost petulant heedlessness to the outside world." This detachment from the context and strategy of avoiding information would certainly not be one advocated by most business schools advising future CEOs. It is far more common for books on leadership in business to emphasize flexibility and the gathering of a variety of different kinds of information in order to make optimal decisions. Instead, according to several former White House officials, Bush generally preferred "short conversations—long on conclusion, short on reasoning," which often served to short-circuit the kinds of inner circle policy debates that would have fleshed out problems:

> In subtle ways, Bush does not encourage truth-telling or at least a full exploration of all that could go wrong. A former senior member of the Coalition Provisional Authority in Baghdad occasionally observed

Bush on videoconferences with his top advisers. "The president would ask the generals, 'Do you have what you need to complete the mission?' as opposed to saying, 'Tell me, General, what do you need to win?'—which would have opened up a whole new set of conversations," says this official, who did not want to be identified discussing high-level meetings. The official says that the way Bush phrased his questions, as well as his obvious lack of interest in long, detailed discussions, had a chilling effect. "It just prevented the discussion from heading in a direction that would open up a possibility that we need more troops."

(Thomas & Wolffe, 2005, p. 37)

Interestingly, a similar observation was made during an interview with Dr. David Kay, the former Chief UNSCOM inspector in Iraq, who briefed Bush several times on the search for Iraqi WMD:

I briefed him directly twice on what was going on in Iraq (I met other times) . . . And usually when you give a briefing you know where all the holes are in your own briefing. There's no briefing that doesn't have holes when you're dealing with something as complex as Iraq. And so you're prepared for the tough questions. Or you at least know that they're coming. In his case, he just expressed confidence. . . . and all he said afterwards was essentially, "What else can we do for you?" . . . Everyone whose dealing with a complex issue, and particularly if you go to the White House, everyone has their own agenda. Their own sets of issues. Things are *never* as good as you'd like the people to believe they are. And so, you expect . . . I expected greater curiosity and skepticism from the President. And I got a lot less than I'd gotten when I was doing my own graduate work, or certainly than I gave my own graduate students when they would come in with it. And it was just not at that level, it was just a lack of intellectual curiosity as much as anything else. The questions, even later on, tended to be questions that went to, sort of personality issues, not to the deep factors that might be involved.

(Preston, 2011, pp. 35–36)

Comparing Bush to Clinton, whom he also served under, Clarke (2004, pp. 243–244) observed that not only were there "innumerable differences between Clinton and Bush . . . the most telling . . . was how the two sought and processed information," with Bush wanting "to get to the bottom line and move on" while "Clinton sought to hold every issue before him like a Rubik's Cube, examining it from every angle to the point of total distraction for his staff." And in this comparison, one sees the difference between how the complex, highly sensitive to context Clinton sought out information (see Preston 2001) and the pattern typical of less sensitive leaders like Bush. As McClellan (2008) would later observe:

(Bush's) leadership style is based more on instinct than deep intellectual debate. His intellectual curiosity tends to be centered on knowing what he needs in order to effectively articulate, advocate, and defend his policies. Bush keenly recognizes the role of marketing and selling policy in today's governance, so such an approach is understandable to some degree. But his advisers needed to recognize how potentially harmful his instinctual leadership and limited intellectual curiosity can be when it comes to crucial decisions, and in the light of today's situation, it has become reasonable to question his judgment.

(pp. 145–146)

It should be emphasized again that this notion of *sensitivity to context* is completely unrelated to intelligence or IQ in leaders, and refers merely to how much they tend to differentiate in their environments and attend to information. Indeed, Harry Truman's less sensitive to context style was augmented by tremendous basic common sense and intelligence. Lyndon Johnson could be accused of being many things, but unintelligent would certainly not be among them. But like these former presidents, Bush shared with them a less sensitive, big-picture focus that was driven by a commitment to his own idiosyncratic policy beliefs (see Preston, 2001). As David Kay would later observe, during an interview recounting his experience briefing Bush on the ongoing problems impacting the search for WMDs in Iraq, his general style of information gathering was definitely not detail-oriented:

Certainly in my case, and what I observed, it was *very* broad-brush. It was like, ten thousand feet above the details. Now like I say, at one stage, I certainly appreciated this because I was trying to pick apart something that was very complex and I didn't know exactly what the shape of this elephant was either. . . . I remember coming back, I guess it was in October, and talking to him. And . . . things were *not* going well in Iraq on the security problem. And that was affecting how we carried out our activities of discovering. And he was concerned about *safety*, but he wasn't concerned about *what does that mean*? What are the broader implications? Why is it like that now issues? And I remember describing to him that one of the hurdles we had in trying to find weapons of mass destruction was the vast amount of looting that took place immediately after the war. And he didn't show any curiosity at all in the extent of the looting, why it might have taken place, all of that. I mean, issues that, just for me, were of great concern and understanding, and I didn't find, I didn't have someone across the table that seemed to be that interested in it.

(Preston, 2011, p. 37)

Indeed, as Armitage recalled about Bush, "he doesn't look around corners, in my view" (Preston, 2011, p. 37) And to some extent, as one senior official who played key roles in the 9/11 and WMD Commissions observed, this lack of interest in information (and divergent views) may be related to the lesson that George W. Bush took away from the electoral defeat of his father, the belief that this had occurred primarily because "he wasn't *enough* of a decider! He was *too* inclusive. He sought too many conflicting views" (Preston, 2011, p. 37). In fact, when Senator John McCain was asked by Brent Scowcroft if Bush had ever asked his opinion on policy, McCain admitted, "No, no, he hasn't. . . . As a matter of fact he's not intellectually curious. But one of the things he did say one time is he said, 'I don't want to be like my father. I want to be like Ronald Reagan'" (Woodward, 2006, pp. 407–408). And while Henry Kissinger liked Bush personally, he told colleagues that it was not clear to him that the President really knew how to run the government. One of the big problems, he felt, was that Bush did not have the people or a system of national security policy decision making that ensured careful examination of the downsides of major decisions" (Woodward, 2006, pp. 407–408).

Given the absolute views of the world that Bush possessed, there was almost a belief on the President's part that the policy clarity provided by his beliefs alone would allow his Iraq policies to succeed (and reduced his tolerance of information questioning that view). As a result, Bush had "little patience for briefings," often telling briefers to "speed it up, this isn't my first rodeo!" (Woodward, 2008, p. 408). Indeed, as Woodward (2008) reported from an interview with David Satterfield, who served as Senior Adviser on Iraq to Secretary of State Rice:

> If Bush believed something was right, he believed it would succeed. Its very rightness ensured ultimate success. Democracy and freedom were right. Therefore, they would win out. Bush . . . tolerated no doubt. His words and actions constantly reminded those around him that he was in charge. He was the decider.
>
> (p. 407)

In fact, Satterfield recalled that "it was difficult to brief him because he would interject his own narrative, questions or off-putting jokes," which meant "presentations and discussions rarely unfolded in a logical, comprehensive fashion" (Woodward 2008, p. 408). Moreover, Woodward (2008, p. 431) noted that for Bush, "his instincts are almost his second religion," and as a result, he "didn't want an open, full debate that aired possible concerns and considered alternatives. He was the 'gut player,' the 'calcium-in-the-backbone' leader who operated on the principle of 'no doubt.'" And this had implications for the types of advisers that Bush wanted around him, with the President noting to Woodward (2008, p. 431) that "I don't need people around me who are not steady . . . And if there's kind of a hand-wringing going on when times are tough, I don't like it." In fact, one former aide remarked that no matter how many people Bush consulted, he heeded only two or three (Baker, 2007). A similar concern was expressed by former national security adviser Brent Scowcroft, who worried that "the White House was taking the wrong advice and listening to a severely limited circle" of like-minded advisers on Iraq (Goldberg, 2005, p. 57). For Scowcroft, the influence of Vice President Dick Cheney on Bush was seen as particularly powerful:

> The real anomaly in the Administration is Cheney . . . I consider Cheney a good friend—I've known him for thirty years. But Dick Cheney, I don't know anymore . . . I don't think Dick Cheney is a neo-con, but allied to the core of neo-cons is that bunch who thought we made a mistake in the first Gulf War, that we should have finished the job.
>
> (Goldberg, 2005, p. 57)

Indeed, the influence on Bush's thinking by his inner circle advisers was far more complex than just the standard neocon influence that is often suggested to have played the key role. Undoubtedly it was important. But, not all of the key players within the inner circle were actually neoconservatives. Agreeing with Scowcroft's interpretation, Powell's former chief of staff Lawrence Wilkerson noted during a recent interview that he didn't even think Bush himself was really a neocon:

> I think there was an unholy alliance there between hyper-nationalists like Cheney and Rumsfeld, neo-cons like Feith, Bolton, Wolfowitz . . . although Paul's in a category all by himself. And Bush's tendency to be evangelical and to be a hyper-nationalist himself if rubbed the right way. I think that all came together in this unholy conglomeration of decision making that haunts us still. Although Condi has attenuated it a lot.
>
> (Preston, 2011, p. 38)

But the less complex lens through which Bush tended to view his environment combined the President's own, quite personal, idiosyncratic beliefs (including his evangelical views) with those of hyper-nationalists like Cheney and neoconservatives like Wolfowitz to greatly shape Iraq policy. During a White House meeting on the Middle East with scholars and theologians, participants saw these characteristics in play in shaping how Bush viewed the world. One noted that "Bush seemed smarter than he expected," but that the discussion about the Middle East took on a predictable, low complexity flavor with "much of the discussion focused on the nature of good and evil, a perennial theme for Bush, who casts the struggle against Islamic extremists in black-and-white terms" (Baker, 2007). Similarly, Michale Novak, a theologian who participated, later remarked that "it was clear that Bush weathers his difficulties because he sees himself as doing the Lord's work" (Baker, 2007). In observing that Bush tended to lack intellectual curiosity and view things in absolute terms, Wilkerson noted that "I don't think you can get at Bush and his decision making style, and some of the decisions he's made, without thinking about the evangelical aspect, without thinking about the spiritual aspect, in the sense that he gets advice from a 'higher authority'" (Preston, 2011, p. 39). But again, even those who worked for Bush quickly acknowledge that the President's views (and the influences upon them) were more complicated than simply his religious beliefs. As Wilkerson observed:

> The President did listen to a lot of voices. He had *pre-dispositions*, if you will, and those pre-dispositions if they were not fed by some of the voices—reinforced, confirmed by some of the voices—then the tendency was to quicker rather than later turn those voices away, or off, or not listen . . . if the advice being rendered didn't fit, more often than not, with pre-conceived notions, then that began to taper off in its importance and . . . his listening began to taper off too. Plus, the pre-conceived ideas were very hard to penetrate. Some have said, the most revealing remark about him was when he said he listened to a "higher father". And that had a lot to do with those pre-conceived notions. Someone, somewhere, in prayer at night on bended knee,

had told the President, or indicated to the President, or the President felt he perceived that this was the right way to go. And come Hell or high water, he was gonna go the right way. It's my firm view . . . strong view . . . buttressed by some experience up-close-and-personal, but more, my 35 years in the government and understanding how these things work bureaucratically. That oftentimes, the pre-disposition was influenced not by God, but by Dick Cheney. And the fact that Dick Cheney is the most unprecedentedly powerful Vice President we've ever had. Steeped in defense, and military-industrial complex, congressional issues. The President isn't. He's the gray eminence, if you will, the President isn't. He's the guy whose done foreign policy before, national security policy, the President hasn't. He's the guy that goes into the Oval Office after everyone else has left and gets the last bite at the apple. So, I think a lot of the President's pre-disposition was not necessarily, exclusively the Vice-President's influence, but if there was a single influence that *hardened*, and that might be a better word, rather than created that pre-disposition, it was the Vice President. The Secretary of State put it this way to me one time. "Bush has a lot of shoot-from-the-hip, cowboy hat, buck-skin inclinations. The Vice President knows how to bring those out." So, maybe the pre-disposition was there. For whatever reason. In a nascent form. The Vice President astutely recognized that and then used that "shoot-from-the-hip", that "you're with us or against us" type pre-disposition to reinforce a much wider perspective on an issue or a foreign policy. So it wasn't like the President didn't have any complicity in this. He was pre-disposed, perhaps, to listen to the piper.

(Preston, 2011, p. 39)

Even as the Iraq situation was spinning out of control in mid-2007, and Bush was forced to remain heavily focused on Iraq policy, he still refused to second-guess himself. As Irwin Stelzer, a senior fellow at the Hudson Institute who met privately with Bush in the White House during this time, noted, "You don't get any feeling of somebody crouching down in the bunker . . . this is either extraordinary self-confidence or out of touch with reality. I can't tell you which" (Baker, 2007). Similarly, Henry Kissinger noted that he found Bush "serene" and of the view that "he feels he's doing what he needs to do and he seems to me at peace with himself" (Baker, 2007). Yet this certainty shown by Bush also led to some strong criticisms of his decision making style:

A president must be able to get a clear-eyed, unbiased assessment of the war. The president must lead. For years, time and again, President Bush has displayed impatience, bravado and unsettling personal certainty about his decisions. The result has too often been impulsiveness and carelessness and, perhaps most troubling, a delayed reaction to realities and advice that run counter to his gut.

(Woodward, 2008, p. 433)

As one senior Administration official later observed, Bush clearly "is a very self-confident man, which in the view of many, including myself is both his greatest strength and his greatest weakness" when it comes to policy making (Preston, 2011, p. 40)! Not only did Bush like "to appear to be the Decider," the official noted, but his sense was that the President *"believes* himself to be the Decider" and that this was used "as a reference point" for him (Preston, 2011, p. 40).

Bush's Interpersonal Style

One of Bush's foremost strengths as a leader has always been his engaging, charming interpersonal style. It is a basic likability that both his friends and political opponents have acknowledged. Those who know Bush remark that he "finds being around people invigorating and uplifting" (McClellan, 2008, p. 40). Even during his days as a student back at Harvard, Draper (2007, p. 29) observed that the "young Bush's particular genius—the facility for wiping out in milliseconds the distance separating himself from total strangers"— was one that drew other boys to him through the use of his uncanny ability to generate instant familiarity through "remembering their names (or, if one's surname twisted the tongue, assigning a nickname), flinging arms around shoulders, acute eye contact, a gruff yet seductive whisper." Indeed, Draper (2007, p. 29) notes that "formality never suited him—he wasn't really a prince, just a senator's grandkid—so George W. swept it aside." Even in his critical memoir about his time as White House Communications Director, Scott McClellan (2008, p. xi) notes that Bush possesses a "disarming personality" and observes "that much of what the general public knows about Bush is true. He is a man of personal charm, wit, and enormous political skill." Yet as McClellan (2008) also suggests, this great skill could be a double-edged sword for the President:

> Bush likes familiarity and does not like change, especially in regard to key staff members he has come to trust and rely on. This had led to a close bond between Bush and a number of us senior staffers, particularly fellow Texans and people like Andy. His personal charm and approachable demeanor also make for an enjoyable working environment where people *want* to stick round—maybe longer than they should. It's a great personal strength of George W. Bush that he is able to inspire such loyalty. But for President Bush it is also a potential source of weakness. Bush's discomfort with change makes it difficult for him to step back from the bonds he develops and make clear-eyed decisions about what is best.
>
> (p. 242)

Similarly, Wilkerson also emphasized the *very* high emphasis placed by Bush upon personal relationships, characterized by his quickly "giving you a nick-name" followed by the "hail Fellow, well met!" and "all that good Texas stuff" (Preston, 2011, p. 41). Agreeing with this characterization, Armitage recalled Bush "was a big nick-namer, and everybody's got a nickname, I was Tiny for instance. And he likes that. I mean we used to joke, call it locker-room talk, but he's kind of that way. The dynamic of talking with the President, he wasn't intimidating in his manner or anything of that nature" (Preston, 2011, p. 41). And since advisers within Bush's inner circle were selected based upon their perceived loyalty and ideological fit, there tended to not be a lot of direct conflict among advisers during meetings with the President (although there was often a tremendous amount of bureaucratic conflict between various department heads outside of Bush's sight competing for policy influence). Avoiding head-on collisions was also accomplished by excluding outside players who might disagree with policy positions from having access to the inner circle, where their views might upset the group's harmony. For example, while former NSC adviser Brent Scowcroft was appointed chairman of the President's Foreign Intelligence Advisory Board in the first term, he was not consulted on plans for Iraq and (after he publicly criticized the policy) was not reappointed to the position at the end of 2004 (Goldberg, 2005, p. 58). Observing that the White House "ignores ideas that conflict with its aims," a colleague of Scowcroft noted that he was "not the only person to be frozen out," a clear reference to James Baker and other officials who had also expressed reservations about Iraq policy (Goldberg, 2005, p. 58).

Another consequence of avoiding head-on collisions and open conflict within inner circles (especially ones where loyalty is emphasized—and loyalty is usually seen as a two-way street)—is a reluctance to fire close subordinates. For Armitage, this element within the Bush style is in no place seen more clearly than in the handling of Defense Secretary Donald Rumsfeld and the degree to which the White House stuck with him long after he had become a political liability. According to Armitage:

> I think a leader, to be a great leader, you need three primary attributes. You gotta have a vision, which people can believe in. He had that. Whether you agree with it or not is different, he had the vision. So that part of leadership he got right. But a leader demands, in various ways, and each leader's different, is execution of that vision. And then, right alongside of execution he demands accountability. So, vision, execution, accountability. Mr. Bush had, first, vision. He didn't have any demand for execution, he didn't hold anyone accountable. I once described in a speech here, I was asked, not so long ago, what I thought of the firing of Mr. Rumsfeld. And I described it as a national tragedy! It came five and a half years too late! *(laughs)* So, you know, he didn't man the execution, didn't man the accountability.
>
> (Preston, 2011, p. 42)

The Case of Hurricane Katrina (2005)

From the standpoint of presidential crisis management, Hurricane Katrina in August 2005 posed stark challenges to an administration already losing credibility with the public over its handling of the war in Iraq, a leak inquiry, and its truthfulness regarding its use of intelligence surrounding WMDs. This *preexisting political context* meant the Administration could ill afford to appear unprepared, ineffectual, or purposefully misleading over Katrina—primarily because this would serve to immediately activate preexisting political frames in the public's mind that could all too readily link this event with other perceived policy failings. During the initial response to Katrina, the overly optimistic responses by Bush and White House spokesmen about the federal response and the situation on the ground in New Orleans were immediately refuted by media coverage of the situation and rescue workers on the scene (Stevenson, 2005; Thomas, 2005). This caused immense political damage to the President, who was seen by detractors as being either out of touch with events (at best) or downright duplicitous (at worst)—neither of which helped the Administration deflect blame. Past political decisions also increased Bush's vulnerability to blame. In the case of Katrina, Bush's own style of substantial delegation to subordinates, limited active involvement, and emphasis upon loyalty over expertise in appointments served to *preset* the roles of many of the policy actors prior to Katrina—actors whose performances would later be criticized as lacking (such as FEMA director Brown, Homeland Security Secretary Chertoff, etc.). Media investigations of the backgrounds of Bush political appointees afterwards further opened the Administration up to charges of cronyism and placing officials (like Brown) into positions for which they weren't qualified (Tumulty, Thompson, & Allen, 2005)—an especially damaging charge given the obvious importance (and failure) of the federal emergency managers during Katrina.

In the case of Katrina and its aftermath, those who had long worried about, and modeled, the impact of a major hurricane on New Orleans (and lobbied for the matter to be given higher priority), viewed the crisis as a long-standing vulnerability that had existed for many years. For the Bush administration, Katrina was generally argued to be an event that was difficult to fully anticipate ahead of time. Obviously, crises with long run-ups (providing ample warning or time to react had policy makers been more vigilant and competent) are much easier to assign blame to than are crises that could have legitimately arrived as a *bolt-from-the-blue* (Parker & Stern, 2005). For example, Bush's statement on 1 September that "no one could have foreseen the levees being breached" can be seen as an attempt to define the crisis one way, while a competing definition would note that Bush was told 56 hours before landfall by the National Weather Service and the National Hurricane Center that there was an "extremely high probability" New Orleans would be flooded (Hsu, 2006).

Leaders must also calculate the *contestability* of existing perceptual frames held by the public, the media, or the political system regarding their allotment of responsibility (or blame) for an event. As long as policy makers believe the final image (or perceptual frame) of the crisis and its aftermath remain contestable—or malleable enough to be shaped by either denial of responsibility, deflection of blame to others, or positive spin (showing themselves or their management of events in a positive light)—leaders will continue to adopt various tactics of blame avoidance to protect themselves (Boin et al., 2010). Obviously, less sensitive leaders (like Bush) who employ closed advisory systems gathering limited information from the surrounding political environment are far more likely to miscalculate such contestability than are more sensitive leaders (who closely monitor that environment). Further, given their general rigidity towards changing adopted policy positions, insensitive leaders tend to contest the public frame for as long as possible—often long past the point where political damage is avoidable. Indeed, the Bush administration, which made a hallmark of never admitting to policy mistakes or reverses publicly, followed this general pattern on Iraq,

WMDs, and Katrina—contesting frames long after public opinion on the topics shifted away from the image the White House continued to try to present.

Consistent with his delegative, less engaged style, Bush took lengthy vacations on his Crawford, Texas, ranch during the summers, leaving most policy tasks to trusted subordinates in Washington. Such delegation, especially given his closed advisory system and tight inner circle, makes it critical for trusted advisers to be on hand to adequately monitor the policy environment. Unfortunately, as Katrina formed, not only was Bush on vacation, but other senior members of the Administration were as well, with Vice President Cheney in Wyoming, Condoleezza Rice in Manhattan, White House chief of staff Andy Card in Maine, and both White House communications director Nicolle Devenish and senior media adviser Mark McKinnon in Greece (Cooper 2005, p. 51). This served to impede the flow of advice and information to the President, magnifying the seeming disconnect between Bush's actions/statements and developing events. It was fully 24 hours after Katrina hit (30 August) before senior aides finally decided Bush should cut his five-week vacation short to return to Washington, where he could meet top advisers the next day (Thomas, 2005, pp. 30–31).

That Bush remained on vacation (and didn't immediately return to Washington) during such a catastrophe was broadly criticized by the media, and the lack of strong presidential statements regarding the situation aggravated this public perception of detachment. While often boasting that he doesn't read newspapers or watch the media, in the case of Katrina, Bush did seem surprisingly uninformed throughout the crisis about events that were being covered live by most U.S. news networks. For example, observers noted that four days after Katrina, during a briefing for his father and Bill Clinton, Bush's own rosy perception of the progress being made in New Orleans "bore no resemblance to what was actually happening" (Allen, 2005, p. 44). Indeed, White House staffers, who had been watching the increasingly dire reports coming out of New Orleans, made up a DVD of the newscasts so Bush could watch them (and presumably catch up with events) as he flew over the Gulf Coast the morning of 31 August (Thomas, 2005, p. 32). Although photos taken of Bush aboard Air Force One, peering intently out of his window at the devastation below, were intended by the White House to show the President's engagement and concern, their impact on public opinion and how they were covered by the media (especially when coupled with the lack of significant federal assistance to the region and his perceived slowness to end his vacation) conveyed the entirely unintended image of detachment. Later that day, in a Rose Garden speech, Bush sought to demonstrate he was engaged, reciting statistics on the number of meals-ready-to-eat delivered, and of people rescued or in shelters (Sanger, 2005). But significant political damage had already occurred, as the photos aboard Air Force Once became the first visual image of the President's response to Katrina.

As days passed and the situation in New Orleans continued to deteriorate in the absence of effective relief efforts, the Administration faced a growing need to reverse the political damage being inflicted upon it due to the growing public perception that it was out of touch or incompetent. Competing with the President during this period, where he sought to show his engagement and an effective federal response, was the constant, largely negative, media coverage coming out of New Orleans. This coverage was uncomfortably juxtaposed against Bush's 1 September Oval Office statement expressing sympathy for the victims, his belief the federal government had "an important role to play," and his expressed desire "to make sure I fully understand the relief efforts" (Stevenson, 2005, p. A8). This response again fell short of what the public expected and was roundly criticized in the media. Bush argued in an ABC interview that same day that no one had expected the levees in New Orleans to be breached. However, the intensity and salience of the media images continued to overwhelm the White House explanations. On 2 September, Bush acknowledged on the South Lawn of the White House (as he left for his first, highly visible tour of the Gulf Coast and New Orleans) that the results of the federal relief efforts were not acceptable thus far—with the symbolism of his trip intended to convey a more engaged, active leadership role on his part for the efforts (Stevenson, 2005, p. A8).

Although his visits to Alabama, Mississippi, and Louisiana were timed to coincide with the arrival of relief supplies and National Guard troops in some of the areas, a series of well-publicized statements by Bush weakened these efforts. For example, during his visit to Mobile, Alabama, Bush touched only briefly on the hundreds of thousands of displaced people in the region, and instead focused upon wealthy Senator Trent Lott's intentions to rebuild his upscale home and his own desire to sit on Lott's porch when it was done (Stevenson, 2005, p. A8). This public identification with his wealthy friend's plight, which hardly compared to the situation facing poorer evacuees or those still stranded in New Orleans, was immensely damaging politically and widely criticized. Even more damaging politically was Bush's infamous public congratulations on camera to FEMA director Michael Brown ("You're doing a heck of a job Brownie!") during a meeting with government officials in Mississippi (Stevenson, 2005, p. A8)—while tens of thousands still remained stranded and without aid days after the storm. When *Time* magazine published its own investigation of cronyism in the Administration (Tumulty et al., 2005), it found numerous examples similar to Brown (where appointees had no relevant professional experience to qualify for their posts, beyond being Bush loyalists). Such charges and continued publicity about Brown (and Chertoff's) qualifications served to undercut White House efforts to avoid blame.

As this brief example of Katrina illustrates, leaders and their management styles play a critical role in shaping not only how they approach the task of crisis management, but also how vulnerable to blame they will be in the face of policy reversals. The personalities of leaders shape not only their strategies for dealing with blame, but also create (through the development of various types of advisory systems) decision making and management processes that either strengthen or greatly reduce their ability to cope with (and deflect blame arising) from crises. During Katrina, as expected for a less controlling, insensitive leader, Bush's lack of personal engagement and substantial delegation to subordinates, coupled with his lack of attention to the surrounding policy environment, greatly slowed his personal response to the crisis. Moreover, given the insular, closed nature of the White House advisory system, where information tended to flow in primarily from loyal insiders, it is hardly surprising that Bush's political response to the crises was often out of step with the views (and perceptions) of those outside of his inner circle. This led to the clear disconnect observed during the Katrina response between those events being widely covered by the media (and viewed by the public) and White House pronouncements on the subject. Given the normal policy rigidity associated with such styles, it was to be expected that Bush would be slow to either adapt his policy approach once it had been adopted or accept blame. This rigidity was particularly damaging given the immense emotive power of the imagery coming out of New Orleans, which easily overpowered the White House's clumsy attempts at positive spin. Bush's own leadership style ill-fitted to the nature of the crisis in which he found himself, serving to greatly exacerbate his administration's vulnerabilities to blame through appointment of loyalists rather than experts to critical positions and lack of focus on the details of policy problems or environment.

CONCLUSION

Obviously, this chapter serves as only a starting point for students interested in political psychological approaches to personality or leadership. However, this overview of a number of the more widely known psychological approaches used in research on political questions, as well as the case study application example above, should give the reader a sense of how these approaches tend to be employed. The leader personality and style variables discussed in this chapter also will have significant impacts upon the political behavior of the masses, which is discussed in Chapter 6.

Topics, Theories/Frameworks, and Cases Covered in Chapter 5

Topics	Theories/Frameworks	Cases
Burn's transactional and transformational types of leadership		
Leader management style	Johnson's (1974) formalistic, competitive, and collegial management styles	Clinton
		Bush
	George's (1980) cognitive style, sense of efficacy, tolerance of political conflict	
	Hermann et al.'s (1996) three leadership style dimensions: responsiveness to constraints, openness to information, and motivational focus	
	Preston's (2001) typology and three style dimensions: leader need for control, prior policy experience/expertise, and sensitivity to context	

Key Terms

cognitive style

collegial management style

competitive
   management style

formalistic management style

forming norms

orientation toward political
   conflict

sense of efficacy

storming

transactional leadership

transformational leadership

Suggestions for Further Reading

George, A. L. (1980). *Presidential decisionmaking in foreign policy: The effective use of information and advice*. Boulder, CO: Westview Press.

George, A. L., & George, J. L. (1998). *Presidential personality and performance*. Boulder, CO: Westview Press.

Greenstein, F. I. (1988). *Leadership in the modern presidency*. Cambridge, MA: Harvard University Press.

Hermann, M. G., Preston, T., Korany, B., & Shaw, T. M. (2001). Who leads matters: The effects of powerful individuals. *International Studies Review, 3*(2), 83–131.

Preston, T. (2001). *The president and his inner circle: Leadership style and the advisory process in foreign policy making*. New York: Columbia University Press.

Preston, T. & 't Hart, P. (1999). Understanding and evaluating bureaucratic politics: The nexus between political leaders and advisory systems. *Political Psychology, 20*, 49–98.

Preston, T. & Hermann, M. G. (2004). Presidential leadership style and the foreign policy advisory process. In E. Wittkopf & J. McCormick (Eds.), *The domestic sources of American foreign policy: Insights and evidence* (4th ed.). Lanham, MD: Rowman & Littlefield.

Notes

1. See also Johnson, 1974; George, 1980; Porter, 1980; Greenstein, 1982; Campbell, 1986; Crabb and Mulcahy, 1986; Pika, 1988; Hargrove, 1988; Jones, 1988; Burke and Greenstein, 1991; Haney, 1997; George and George, 1998; Preston, 1997, 2001; Greenstein, 2000.
2. Neustadt, 1960/1990, p. ix.
3. Ibid., pp. 207–208.
4. Ibid., pp. 152–153, 162.
5. Ibid., pp. 128–130.
6. Hermann, M. G. (1999b). *Leadership profile of Bill Clinton*. Columbus, OH: Social Science Automation, Inc.
7. Interviews with multiple senior Bush administration policymakers and staff who requested anonymity, as well as briefers from various government departments and agencies.
8. Allen, M., & Broder, D. S. (2004, August 30). Bush's leadership style: Decisive or simplistic? *Washington Post*, p. A1.

Chapter 6

THE POLITICAL PSYCHOLOGY OF MASS POLITICS

How Do People Decide for Whom to Vote?

How do Americans think and feel about politics? The political thoughts and feelings of the American public have been the subject of intense and prolific research since the 1950s. Political psychology asks questions such as: How sophisticated is the public about politics and democratic ideals? How much attention do Americans pay to political information? How do people process and use information (particularly during electoral campaigns)? How do Americans make decisions when deciding for whom to vote?

Another important question raised by political psychologists about American political beliefs concerns the issue of how tolerant Americans are of views contrary to their own. Needless to say, in a democracy this is an extremely important matter, because democratic ideals hinge upon the notion that even very unpopular views may be expressed without fear of reprisal or repression. This chapter looks at some of the findings and controversies in political psychology regarding the political attitudes of ordinary American citizens. The Political Being in this chapter is an average citizen. We focus primarily upon the attitudes and cognition component of the citizen's mind and the *us* part of the political environment: we are looking at the Political Being in the context of politics in the United States and also studies conducted about voting behavior in Great Britain and the United Kingdom. We will also touch upon the "political brain" and how genetics and biology play a role in political thinking and behavior.

We begin with some concepts and then turn to the classic study by the Michigan school of thought on the nature of American political attitudes and sophistication. We then consider some critics of the Michigan school's perspective. From that topic, we turn to studies of how people process information during campaigns and how their feelings affect for whom they decide to vote, and political tolerance in America. After that we compare American political attitudes with those in Great Britain/United Kingdom. To begin, let us review some of the central concepts analysts use to study public opinion.

BELIEFS, VALUES, IDEOLOGY, ATTITUDES, AND SCHEMAS

In Chapter 3, the term **beliefs** was defined as associations people create between an object and its attributes (Eagly & Chaiken, 1998). Another useful definition of beliefs is "cognitive components that make up our understanding of the way things are" (Glynn, Herbst, O'Keefe, & Shapiro, 1999, p. 104). When beliefs are clustered together, we call it a **belief system**. Most Americans, for example, have a belief system about democracy that includes such beliefs as "Free speech is a necessity," "The people have a right to decide who holds political power," and "All citizens should have the right to vote."

Values are closely related, but have an ideal component. Beliefs reflect what we think is true; values reflect what we wish to see come about, even if it is not currently true. Rokeach (1973) argued that there are two types of values, *terminal values*, which are goals, and *instrumental values*, which endorse the means to achieve those goals. For example, Americans want a safe society and want the police to maintain law and order. This is a terminal value—a concern for the well-being of the people. At the same time, Americans value civil liberties, defined in the constitution, and endorse only those behaviors by the police that enforce public safety and order through means that do not violate civil liberties. This is an example of instrumental values.

Values and beliefs are closely related, and when we refer to political values and belief systems, we call it an **ideology**, which is "a particularly elaborate, close-woven, and far-ranging structure" of attitudes and beliefs (Campbell, Converse, Miller, & Stokes, 1960/1964, p. 111). American political values and ideology are rooted in Lockean liberalism, that is, the philosophical ideas of John Locke, and, although attitudes about many issues changed over time, these values remain much the same, even after more than 200 years (McClosky & Zaller, 1984).

A central concept in the study of political psychology used in this chapter is **attitudes**, which we present in Chapter 3 as an enduring system of positive or negative beliefs, affective feelings and emotions, and subsequent action tendencies regarding an attitude object, that is, the entity being evaluated. Some of the controversies regarding this type of definition are discussed in Chapter 3, as well. In terms of research on the political psychology of Americans and their subsequent political behavior, some central questions regarding attitudes were: (1) Are attitudes consistent with one another? In other words, do people have consistently liberal or consistently conservative attitudes? (2) Are political attitudes consistently related to political behavior? For example, do people who consider themselves to be Republicans, and who hold Republican views on political issues, also vote for Republican Party candidates? (3) How do people use attitudes to process political information? (4) How do people acquire their political attitudes? (5) How sophisticated are political attitudes in a given population? Are they cognitively complex? (6) If people do have inconsistent attitudes, how do they balance the inconsistencies?

The attitude concept has a long tradition in the study of public opinion, but, more recently, the schema concept has been introduced. As we saw in Chapter 3, a **schema** is defined as a "cognitive structure that represents knowledge about a concept or type of stimulus, including its attributes and the relations among those attributes" (Fiske & Taylor, 1991, p. 8).[1]

POLITICAL SOPHISTICATION AND VOTING IN AMERICA

Beginning in the late 1940s, researchers armed with surveys set out to investigate the nature of American political attitudes. They were interested in the question of how sophisticated Americans were and in the internal consistency of their attitudes. The deeper question underlying this research concerned the quality of democracy in America. Presumably, a functioning democracy requires citizens to make informed decisions when they vote. This requires some degree of political sophistication, that is, knowledge about the political system they live in and the issues that are important. However, despite the importance attributed to political sophistication, there is considerable disagreement as to whether it should be considered knowledge about politics, or, more broadly, knowledge, attention, interest, and involvement in politics (McGraw, 2000).

The Michigan School

The groundbreaking study of American political sophistication, *The American Voter* (Campbell et al., 1960/1964), was discouraging for those who believe democracy must be founded on a citizenry interested in, and informed and thoughtful about, democratic principles and political issues of the day. Because *The American Voter* was based upon survey results from the Survey Research Center at the University of Michigan, its model of the American voter became known as the Michigan school, or Michigan model. Specifically, the researchers were interested in finding out whether people had consistently liberal or conservative values, whether those values were related to their party identification and loyalty and to their policy preferences, and how they determined for whom to vote.

The authors began with the assumption that Americans should have an integrated mental map of the political system:

> The individual voter sees the several elements of national politics as more than a collection of discrete, unrelated objects. After all, they are parts of one political system and are connected in the real world by a variety of relations that are visible in some degree to the electorate. A *candidate* is the nominee of his *party*; party and candidate are oriented to the same *issues* or *groups*, and so forth. Moreover, we may assume that the individual strives to give order and coherence to his image of these objects.
>
> (Campbell et al., 1960/1964, p. 27)

In other words, these are the cognitive categories utilized by Americans to simplify and organize American politics.

Campbell and colleagues then anticipated that American attitudes about candidates, issues, party, and group interests would be structured, that is, would be functionally related to each other and to an ideology. Ideally, people should know what liberal and conservative values are, what positions on important political issues are liberal and conservative positions, which party represents liberal and which party represents conservative principles, and which candidates stand for which issues. For example, a person who opposes big government (a conservative ideological attitude) should also feel an attachment to the Republican Party (the conservative party in the United States), vote for candidates espousing similar views, and belong to groups that benefit from minimal government. In addition, that person should favor other conservative positions on other issues, such as taxes, labor rights, federal versus state power, and so on. This type of person could justifiably be called an ideologue. A liberal ideologue would be equally consistent, with liberal attitudes regarding party (Democratic party), issues, and candidate preferences. An ideologue was considered a political sophisticate in the sense that such a person would presumably be politically aware, could understand and process political information consistently, and would make political choices suitable for their personal, group, and value-based interests.

What the authors of *The American Voter* (1964) reported, however, was that very few Americans fit the profile of an ideologue, that is, of a person who understood the differences between liberal and conservative principles and who could locate each party and the issues along liberal and conservative dimensions. They conducted surveys in which they asked people what they liked and disliked about the parties and candidates and coded the surveys in terms of the nature of the response. If the respondent expressed likes and dislikes in terms of ideological principles, that person was considered an ideologue. They classified people into one of several possible **levels of conceptualization**, on the basis of the primary attitudes used to express likes and dislikes about the parties and candidates. The levels of conceptualization are arranged in terms of degrees of sophistication. In fact, they found that only about 2.5% of their respondents fell into the ideologue level of conceptualization. The second level of conceptualization of respondents was called the "near-ideologues." These people claimed to know the differences between liberal and conservative principles, but were less confident about, and less able to articulate, those principles. About 9.5% of the sample fell into the near-ideologue level of conceptualization.

The next level of conceptualization, the "group benefits" level, was populated by people who saw political issues in terms of concrete benefits for their group, compared to those for other groups in society. At this level, "there is little comprehension of 'long-range plans for social betterment,' or of basic philosophies rooted in postures toward change or abstract conceptions of social and economic structure or causation" (Campbell et al., 1960/1964, p. 135). Forty-two percent of the respondents fell into this category. Level four was populated by "nature of the times" folks, who had no conception of ideology, no recognition of group interests, and who, when they did think of politics, thought simply in terms of whether times were good or bad for themselves and their families. Good times meant that the party of the president was good; bad times meant that the party of the president should be punished. The category also included people who identified a single isolated issue with a party (e.g., Social Security benefits and the Democratic party). Twenty-four percent of the respondents fell into this category.

The final level was "absence of issue content"—the booby prize level. These people, 22.5%, knew nothing about political issues and approached politics solely in terms of party membership (absent any understanding of the party's position on issues) or candidate appeals (looks, religion, or sincerity, rather than issue positions), when they had anything resembling a political opinion. Few of the people at this level of conceptualization bothered to vote.

What this study demonstrated was that Americans are not political philosophers and that a deep understanding of politics and democracy was not the foundation of their decisions on how to vote. Subsequent studies using similar survey tools (but with important changes in question wording, which positively affected respondents' ability to express knowledge of politics) found an improvement in knowledge after the 1950s. In particular, *The Changing American Voter* (1976), by Nie, Verba, and Petrocik, covered elections from 1952 through 1976, and found that, as politics became more exciting in the 1960s, levels of conceptualization improved in terms of the numbers in the highest levels (they identified 31% ideologues), as did levels of issue consistency (i.e., people tended to take consistently liberal or conservative positions on a number of issues). However, a significant number of people remained fairly ignorant about politics. Later works, such as *The Unchanging American Voter* (1989), by Smith, although critical of important components of *The American Voter* (particularly the levels of conceptualization idea, which Smith argues is not a valid measurement of how people actually think about politics), provide further data supporting the argument that American political attitudes do not revolve around sophisticated political ideologies and ideological thinking. The political attitudes of Americans do not have a cognitive component sophisticated enough to understand abstractions such as liberalism and conservatism. Table 6.1 shows trends in levels of conceptualization over time. From this table, the reader can easily see that there was an upsurge in ideologues during the "hot politics" years of the 1960s and early 1970s. But, by and large, the American public remains nonideological.

Just how little Americans know about politics is revealed in the findings of survey researchers. For example, for many years, pollsters asked people

Table 6.1 Levels of Conceptualization Over Time

Levels of conceptualization	*1956*	*1960*	*1964*	*1968*	*1972*	*1976*	*1980*	*1984*	*1988*
Ideologues	12%	19%	27%	26%	22%	21%	21%	19%	18%
Group benefit	42	31	27	24	27	26	31	26	36
Nature of the times	24	26	20	29	34	30	30	35	25
No issue content	22	23	26	21	17	24	19	19	21
N		1,740	1,741	1,431	1,319	1,372	2,870	1,612	2,257	2,040

Note: From Niemi, R. & Weisberg, H. (Eds.). (1993). *Controversies in voting behavior* (3rd ed., p. 89). Washington, DC: Congressional Quarterly.

after a national election which party won the most seats in the House of Representatives and which party has the most members in the House. In 1980, only 14% knew both (Smith, 1989). In 1986, 24% of Americans were either unable to recognize Vice President George Bush's name, or could not identify his office, even though he had been in the office of Vice President for six years (Zaller, 1992). In a 1966 national election study, only 1.9% of the public could name even half of the members of the Supreme Court, and not one of the 1,500 people surveyed could name all nine members of the Supreme Court (Zaller, 1992). In March 2000, after months of intense and often bitter competition, both Al Gore and George W. Bush secured enough delegates to get the nomination for the presidential candidacy from the Democratic and Republican parties, respectively. But only 66% of Americans could correctly name both candidates, and 20% could name neither (Gallup Poll, 2000). A Gallup poll taken in July 2001 found that only 11% of Americans claimed to follow the national missile defense issue closely, despite heavy news coverage of that controversial proposal by the Bush administration. Fifty-eight percent thought that the United States already had a missile defense system, and only 28% knew that the United States did not have a missile defense system. On a more humorous note, a 1998 study by the National Constitution Center found that only 41% of American teenagers can name the three branches of government, but 59% know the names of the Three Stooges; although only 2% know the name of the chief justice of the Supreme Court, we can all be comforted by the fact that 95% know the name of the actor who played the Fresh Prince of Bel Air on television (Will Smith) ("Teens Sharper," 1998).

The political attitudes that many Americans do have are not constrained or consistent, nor are they stable, that is, the same over time (Converse, 1964). In terms of constraint, this means that people do not have consistently liberal or conservative attitudes: they may be conservative on one issue and liberal on another. Without an underlying ideological guideline, such lack of constraint is not surprising, but the implication in terms of American political sophistication is controversial. In terms of stability, Converse (1964) noted that responses to attitude questions from some people remained very stable, but for others the responses changed in an apparently random pattern. He called this the **black and white model** of attitude change. We return to the issue of how Americans organize and process political information later, but let us turn now to the question of which attitudes affect how Americans vote, and how they changed.

The authors of *The American Voter*, and others included in the Michigan school, presented a model of political attitudes, and their relationship to each other, that depicted the causes of the vote. The model is called the **funnel of causality** (see Figure 6.1), and it distinguishes between long-term factors or attitudes that affect how Americans vote (which are attachment to a party, or **party identification**, and **group interests**) and short-term factors (currently important **issues** and **candidates'** personal characteristics). Party identification is an attitude by which a person considers him- or herself to be a Democrat or a Republican. Party identification is acquired through socialization and other life experiences and, the authors argued, tends to remain fairly stable, that is, it does not change over one's lifetime. Partisanship does vary in intensity, and the Michigan school scholars argued that those who were more strongly attached to a political party were more likely to be interested in and involved in politics. They were more likely to know more about politics and to vote. In the United States, the strength of attachment to the political parties diminished over the generations, since the height of party loyalty and attachment in the Great Depression, at which time the Democratic Party became the majority. Bartels (2000), however, presented data indicating that attachment to the parties reached its low point in 1996 and has since increased, but only for those who actually vote. Another

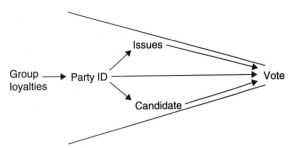

Figure 6.1 The Funnel of Causality

change since the Depression is that, as new generations entered the electorate, the Democratic Party's majority status changed. The Depression generation was strongly attracted to the Democratic Party, because of its perception that Franklin Roosevelt and his New Deal policies, designed to end the Depression, were beneficial to the workers, the young, and immigrants who recently acquired citizenship. As that generation passes on and new generations come of voting age without the same strong pull, the Democratic and Republican parties became about equal in voter identification, and over one third of voters (about 35% in the 1990s) consider themselves to be Independent, as well (although two thirds of the self-identified Independents lean toward one of the two parties). The Pew Research Center found in 2008 a decline from 2004 in the percentage identifying with the Republican Party. They found 36% identifying as Democrats, 27% Republican (down from 33% in 2004), and 37% Independent. However, among those Independents, 15% leaned Democratic, 10% Republican, and 12% indicated no leaning at all (Pew Research Center, 2008a).

Party identification strongly affects how people vote, particularly those who identify intensely with their party. When you consider how little Americans actually know about politics, the importance of party identification seems obvious. If people know little about the current issues, those who identify always have their party attachment to guide them in the voting booth. Party identification also affects how people view short-term forces, such as issues and candidates. It is used to screen information, and it colors the voter's interpretation of issues and candidates. But people do not always vote for candidates of their own party, nor do they always agree with their party's stance on particular issues. When people defect and vote for the other party's candidates, it is the result of short-term forces. For example, a moderate conservative who is a member of the Republican party, but who favors reproductive choice, might decide not to vote for George W. Bush, because he is opposed to abortion rights. Or, recall our friend from Chapter 3, who is a lifelong Democrat and a strong party loyalist, who briefly considered voting for George W. Bush, but ended up voting for Al Gore. Education policy was one of several important short-term forces for her (the others favoring Gore), and partisanship kept its strong pull.

The Michigan school developed a formula for analyzing the impact of partisanship, issues, and candidate characteristics in each election. Because partisanship is a long-term factor affecting the vote, they reasoned that an election in which people voted according to their party identification, and in which Independents split evenly between the two parties, could be considered a baseline, or an ideal typical election. They labeled such an election a **normal vote** (Converse, 1966). They could then look at different elections and determine the relative importance of partisanship, issues, and candidate characteristics. In the 1950s, 1960s, and 1970s, when the Democratic party was the majority party, a normal vote was 54% Democratic and 46% Republican. Thus, the 1952 and 1956 elections deviated from the normal vote, because Dwight Eisenhower, the Republican candidate for the presidency, won. His election was mostly the result of candidate appeal short-term forces (he was immensely popular), pro-Republican foreign policy attitudes, and a negative popular reaction to Democratic skills in managing government. The distribution of party identification changed in the last part of the twentieth century, so that Republican and Democratic identifiers were each roughly 33% and independents are the other 33%. As noted above, Republican identifiers are an even smaller percentage as of 2008.

The arguments that partisanship lasts a lifetime, even when one defects repeatedly and votes for the other party, and that it outweighs short-term factors when people decide how to vote, came under attack. Rational choice analysts, who are not political psychologists, argue that people vote on issues in terms of self-interest calculations and that partisanship itself is a collage of short- and long-term forces (e.g., Brody & Rothenberg, 1988; Fiorina, 1981; Franklin, 1992; Franklin & Jackson, 1983; Markus & Converse, 1979; Page & Jones, 1979). Political psychologists, on the other hand, studied candidate evaluations from a cognitive information-processing perspective, findings to which we turn a bit later. Miller and Shanks defended the Michigan model's emphasis on partisanship in 1996 in *The New American Voter*.

More recently, evidence suggests that the brain plays a role in partisanship and the strength of political affiliation. For example, recent studies have examined the heritability of party affiliation. It had been largely accepted that party affiliation is primarily environmental, with family members generally affiliating with the same political party. And it turns out that environment is still influential in determining party affiliation, but genetics are equally important. Funk, Smith, Alford, & Hibbing (2010) found that although environment played a strong role in predicting party identification, so did genetics. Dawes and Fowler (2009) found a genetic correlate (the DRD2 dopamine receptor) of party identification, suggesting that the tendency to affiliate with a particular political party is inherited. This dopamine receptor, by the way, plays a role in cognitive functioning and in social attachments (such as to a political party). Of course, this also explains why party affiliation seems to be environmental—we identify with the same party as our parents, and that affiliation may have environmental as well as genetic origins.

There also seems to be a genetic role in the strength of political affiliation. Settle et al. (2009) found that although environment explains why people are strongly attached to a political party, so do genetic factors. Similarly, Hatemi et al. (2009) found that very strong political ties was explained by a combination of genetic and environmental factors. All of this recent work on genetics and heritability is important as it suggests that environment alone cannot account for party affiliation or the strength of our partisan ties. To the extent that we can explain more of the variability in party affiliation and the strength of those ties, the better able we are to make predictions about political behavior.

The Maximalists

The Michigan model is not the final word on the sophistication of the American voter. Lane (1962, also Lane & Sears, 1964) and others had a more optimistic evaluation of the quality and quantity of political knowledge Americans had and sought. Some argued that, even if Americans do not have consistently liberal or conservative political attitudes, they may organize their attitudes, anyway, but in a way different than that expected by the Michigan school. Perhaps the biggest political psychological challenge to the Michigan model is the Maximalist school. These scholars maintain that the Michigan model is a minimalist picture of the American political worldview. They argue that, looked at differently, Americans are much more politically sophisticated than the Michigan model maintains.

Sniderman, Brody, and Tetlock (1991) traced the challenge to the minimalist picture of the American political thinker to the alternative picture painted in *The Changing American Voter* (Nie et al., 1976) and to an article by Stimson (1975). The former we already mentioned—they provided data indicating that, when politics gets more exciting, the public becomes more informed and sophisticated. Stimson, and later Neuman (1986), argued that the problem with the Michigan model is that it attempts to treat the public as one group, but, in reality, there is great variation across the public. Neuman (1986) maintained that there are three publics: (1) the political sophisticates (about 5%), who know a great deal about politics and who are very active; (2) the majority (about 75% of the public), who have advanced education and, in effect, have cognitive abilities, but who are not often strongly motivated to use them in the realm of politics; and (3) those who are truly apolitical (about 20% of the population), who will never be interested or involved and who lack the cognitive capabilities to be so, even if they wanted to.

The Maximalists challenged the Michigan model's basic premises about how people think about politics (the cognitive component), and they added the importance of affect into the process of thinking about politics (Sniderman et al., 1991). Their argument is that the Michigan school's assumption that people organize their political thoughts in a linear (liberal to conservative) manner diverts attention from how people actually think about politics. In their own words:

> Belief systems, we reasoned, acquired structure through reasoning about choices. To see the structure they possessed, it was necessary to identify how people managed choices—that is, the considerations that they took into account and the relative weights they placed on them. The standard approach in effect asked: To what extent is one idea element connected to another *on the assumption the connections are approximately the same for everyone.*
>
> From our perspective, idea elements could, and likely were, connected in a variety of ways depending upon both the characteristics of the problem that a person was trying to work through and the characteristics of the person trying to work it through. Political choices pose problems, and the object of political psychology accordingly is to give an account, not simply of how people recollect their preferred solution to a problem, but of how they figured it out in the first place.
>
> (Sniderman et al., 1991, pp. 3–4)

The authors posed a question: the minimalist model assumes that liberals and conservatives should have consistent positions on two issues, for example, government spending and pornography, but how does one get from one of those issues to the other (Sniderman et al., 1991)? Because they are not obviously related, one can connect them using only a higher order construct, that is, liberal or conservative ideology. Using ideology as a guideline, a person is expected to take either liberal or conservative positions on both issues, in order to be considered politically sophisticated by the minimalists. But why should we assume that this is the reasoning path people follow, and why grant this path the honor of being the hallmark of political sophistication? Why assume that such a deductive inference (i.e., using the higher order construct to connect the issues) is more likely to occur than a paired association (in this case, there is none, so why should one expect a related position on both issues)? According to Sniderman et al. (1991), the minimalist school

> asks us to suppose that the positions we take on issues, so far as we arrive at them through reasoning, are the product of logical entailment. This is an excessively cerebral account of political thinking, minimizing the role of affect, or feelings in political reasoning.
>
> (p. 7)

They maintain that, although not expert in political philosophies of liberalism and conservatism, people can process political information and decide where they stand on political issues, which we consider later. Sniderman and Tetlock (1986) argued that the minimalist view of belief system structure assumes that it is, and should be, organized in a straight line along a liberal–conservative continuum. They offered a different perspective that beliefs can also be seen as organized in a weblike structure, with pockets of beliefs consistently related to other pockets. They noted studies of Americans during the Cold War that demonstrated that people have internally coherent outlooks on topics, such as the rights of communists to speak freely, write, and work in mass media, universities, and even in defense plants. A person who granted communists one of those rights tended to grant them the others, too. Moreover, this pocket of beliefs would often be linked to other pockets. People who granted civil rights to one group of people did so not only because of their beliefs about civil liberties, but also because of their feelings toward other groups, beliefs about tolerance, and so forth. The authors further argued that depending on how cognitively complex a person is, there can be many such pockets or only a few. Cognitive complexity, in turn, depended on how adept the person is at abstract reasoning. From this perspective, they determined that at least one third of the mass public is cognitively complex and that another third is well-organized, at least in terms of the basic American values regarding democracy and capitalism.

Having reviewed some of the debate on the level of political sophistication in America, at least in terms of how much people know about politics, we turn to the question of whether it matters. Do people take issue positions and vote in accordance with their interests, despite variations in levels of information and knowledge? Delli Carpini, and Keeter (1996) argued that they do not, noting that those who were poorly informed did not connect their votes to their views on issues. Bartels (1996) agreed that there is an important difference in the voting patterns of informed and uninformed voters and that many uninformed voters would vote differently if they had full information. On the other hand, Lau and Redlawsk (1997; 2006) conducted experiments on voting and information. They defined "correct" voting as voting in accordance with the voters' own values. Subjects in the experiments were given limited information before voting and full information after voting, with the chance to change their vote. Only 30% chose to change their votes when given additional information.

Knowledge Structures

A related approach to reconceptualizing attitude complexity looks at **knowledge structures**. In a recent review of this literature, McGraw (2000) divided it into three categories: The first focuses on how people mentally organize information about political actors, a second body of research explores how those knowledge structures (e.g., stereotypes of the political parties) affect learning and decisions about political candidates, and a third body of literature examines how attitudes about issues are represented in the mind. Lavine (2002) divided the literature somewhat differently. He argued that one body of literature maintains that attitudes are affected by people's **memory**—what they recall about a candidate when they decide for whom to vote and what they think about issues. Another body of literature is one that examines **online** information processing, wherein people keep a running tally of information as they form attitudes on political issues.

The architecture of knowledge (or online) structures is a subject of debate. As mentioned earlier, Sniderman et al. (1991) believed that the architecture varies in complexity from individual to individual, but that it exists in weblike pockets of attitudes related to one another. Similarly, Judd and Krosnick (1989), along with McGraw and Steenbergen (1995), argued that people have **associative networks**, that is, knowledge structures embedded in long-term memory, which consist of nodes linked to one another, forming a network of associations. When nodes are linked together, thinking about one draws thoughts about the other(s). This is illustrated with a network of knowledge regarding a candidate, which becomes more complex as more is learned about the candidate. An associative network of a candidate would look like Figure 6.2.

As Judd and Krosnick (1989) explained, the linked nodes may be within a single category of political objects, or between different categories altogether:

> Thus, for instance, the policy of affirmative action may be linked to the policy of school integration. At the same time, the policy of affirmative action is also likely to be linked to more abstract value nodes, such as freedom or equality, as well as to object nodes representing political reference groups (e.g., Blacks) and candidates.
>
> (p. 109)

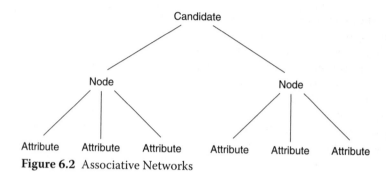

Figure 6.2 Associative Networks

Linked nodes imply that there is a positive or negative relationship between them (e.g., affirmative action is positively associated with equality and negatively associated with freedom). Nodes, and subsequently their links, also vary in strength, which affects the probability that the activation of one node will activate another, as well as the likelihood that the associated evaluations will be consistent (Judd & Krosnick, 1989). The stronger a node, the more likely it is to be linked to other relevant nodes in a consistent manner. The more nodes and the more links among them, the more consistent and complex a person's attitudes toward politics. One interesting aspect of this model is that is it entirely conceivable that a person may be quite sophisticated about politics in one domain, such as domestic politics, but not at all in another domain, such as foreign affairs. Indeed, in Chapter 5, we saw that this even occurs among people very sophisticated about politics, such as President Clinton. In addition, when people are more complex in their thinking, they look for and process more information when an attitude is important to them (Berent & Krosnick, 1995).

There is, however, considerable debate about whether Americans hold such precomputed opinions about issues (Lavine, 2002). Part of the reason for this debate about the political sophistication of Americans is that this research relies very heavily upon surveys. As Zaller (1992), explained, surveys are likely to pick up what is on the top of the respondent's head:

> Most people really aren't sure what their opinions are on most political matters, including even such completely personal matters as their level of interest in politics. They're not sure because there are few occasions, outside of a standard interview situation, in which they are called upon to formulate and express political opinions. So, when confronted by rapid-fire questions in a public opinion survey, they make up attitude reports as best they can as they go along. But because they are hurrying, they are heavily influenced by whatever ideas happen to be at the top of their minds.
>
> (p. 76)

Zaller took this point beyond surveys, however. He maintained that people are ambivalent on many political issues much of the time. Putting the public in the context of politics, in the midst of debate about an issue, enables one to see the complexity of the multiple attitudes involved. A person may, for example, support a woman's right to reproductive choice generally, but may be very ambivalent about late-term partial birth abortions. When politicians discuss complex issues, they frequently do so in terms of summary judgments, a conclusion that overrides underlying ambivalence. Survey questions ask respondents to do the same thing, and therefore, they pick up seeming instability in responses, because ambivalent attitudes can swing in different directions when a summary judgment is required. In Zaller's (1992) view, people do not have true attitudes, such as those expected by the Michigan school,

> but a series of partially independent and often inconsistent ones. Which of a person's attitudes is expressed at different times depends on which has been made most immediately salient by change and the details of questionnaire construction, especially the ordering and framing of questions.
>
> (p. 93)

The debate now turns to the question of how people actually process political information in America.

INFORMATION PROCESSING AND VOTING

A central question addressed by the knowledge structure inquiries concerns how those structures are used to process information and make political choices, such as how to evaluate a candidate and for whom to vote. Those who know a lot about politics, and are interested in it, process information differently than those who know little and are not interested in politics (Lodge & Hamill, 1986; Sniderman, Glaser, & Griffin, 1990). But even people who have a great deal of interest in, and knowledge about politics, will take information shortcuts. They rely upon **attitudes**, **schemas**, and **heuristics** to help process information and make decisions. Pratkanis (1989) reminds us that a schema (or category) consists

> of both *content* (information in the schema and its organization) and *procedure* (the usage of this information in knowing). The dual role of a schema . . . is similar to that of the heuristic as cue (an evaluation stored in memory) and strategy (the use of this cue in problem solving). A schema differs from a heuristic in its complexity. A heuristic is one simple rule, whereas a schema is an organization of many rules and pieces of data within a domain.
>
> (p. 89)

Associative network models argue that nodes and links with greater strength are more easily summoned for thinking and information processing than are those with weak links (Judd & Krosnick, 1989; McGraw & Steenbergen, 1995). Associative network studies drew upon schema research to develop ideas about information processing. The accessibility of political schemas influences how people think and what they are alert to. Those that are more frequently and most recently used are readily available for use again (Popkin, 1994; Ottati & Wyer, 1993). Schemas are used to filter information, providing people with a means for deciding which information is correct, irrelevant, or incorrect. Schemas or category-based knowledge, that is, pre-existing beliefs already present in a person's political mind, is also used as a source for substitute information, when current information about a political issue or candidate is missing.

How do people process political information? The steps through which people presumably proceed, upon receiving information, are as follows: information is received, and the appropriate node or schema is primed; the information is matched to the knowledge structure and appropriate nodes; the information is assessed and stored in memory; finally, that evaluation is retrieved from memory, when the individual is called upon to make a decision about a political action (how to vote, what to think about a policy, etc.) (Anderson, 1983; Brewer, 1988; Fiske & Pavelchak, 1986; Graber, 1984; Lodge & Stroh, 1995; Ottati & Wyer, 1990). In the process, feelings about candidates also emerge and are stored in memory (Rahn, Aldrich, Borgida, & Sullivan, 1990). Rather than placing feeling along a continuum from very negative to very positive, Lavine (2002) argued that people have stores or stockpiles of negative and positive feelings toward candidates, issues, and groups.

Of course, attention to information can be very selective (Iyengar, 1990; Ottati & Wyer, 1990). Some people are members of issue publics and are interested in particular issues. For example, the so-called soccer moms were intensely interested in education, child care, and health insurance issues, during the 1992 and 1996 elections. People can easily be more interested in one issue than another, and hence attentive to information about the issues they are interested in, but not to information about the issues they are not interested in. Delli Carpini and Keeter (1993, 1996) found that political elites have a remarkably large amount of information about politics and the political system. They pay very close attention to politics. For these people—political elites and issue publics—schemas related to political issues will be quite accessible. The more accessible a schema or node is, the more information related to it will be noticed by the perceiver. Accessibility varies, depending on how important an attitude is to the perceiver (Berent & Krosnick, 1995; Holtz & Miller, 1985; Huckfeldt, Levine, Morgan, & Sprague, 1999; Krosnick, 1988, 1989). Also, Lau (1995) maintained that people use those schemas or nodes that are primed, that is, are most readily accessible. In addition, as is discussed in more detail later, issue nodes can be made more accessible when the media focuses on a particular issue in depth (Iyengar, 1990).

People are selective in their attention to information, and studies have also questioned how well they actually remember information as campaigns progress. Lodge and Stroh (1995; see also Lodge, 1995; Lodge, McGraw, & Stroh, 1989) argue that, as information is acquired, it is used to enhance, or update, beliefs about a candidate or party, and the specific details of the information are forgotten. Likes and dislikes are influenced by the information, and are remembered, but a person may well be hard-pressed to explain what the liking or disliking is based upon. This **impression-based model** of information processing, memory, and evaluation of political candidates, stands in contrast to more traditional models, which maintain that people store in memory the evidence supporting their evaluations (see Dreben, Fiske, & Hastie, 1979; Hastie & Park, 1986; McGraw, Lodge, & Stroh, 1990; Srull & Ottati, 1995; Srull & Wyer, 1989). In another study looking at voters' use of information, Lodge, Steenbergen, and Brau (1995) also addressed the question of how much information voters remember from the campaign, when they go to vote. They argue that voters do forget lots of information, but that does not mean the information did not have an impact on their knowledge level when it was received. Voters keep a running tally or an online tally, from which information is used in forming an impression of the candidates. The specifics of the information may be forgotten, but the overall impression remains and is important in determining the vote.

A number of different heuristics, knowledge structures, and schema are important in processing political information (Lau, 1986; Ottati & Wyer, 1990; Rahn et al., 1990). There are many different heuristics serving as shortcuts in political information processing and judgments. Fiorina (1981) presents evidence of a retrospective voting heuristic, wherein voters make decisions about current candidates for office, based upon those candidates' performance in the past. The representativeness heuristic, presented in Chapter 3, also plays an important role in political judgments. Recall that the representativeness heuristic is a rule of thumb for deciding what kind of person someone is based on how closely that person fits a stereotype.

In deciding for whom to vote, according to Popkin (1994), "the most critical use of this heuristic involves projecting from a personal assessment of a candidate to an assessment of what kind of leader he[sic] was in previous offices or to what kind of president he[sic] will be in the future" (p. 74). People decide how well a candidate will perform in office based upon the goodness of fit between the candidate and the perceiver's stereotype of a good president or mayor or whatever office the person is running. Popkin went on to argue that this results in the generation of narratives about people, wherein specific traits serve as the foundation of a fuller picture of the individual under observation. This, in turn, results in **Gresham's law of political information,** which says that

> personal information can drive more relevant political information out of consideration. Thus there can be a perverse relationship between the amount of information voters are given about a candidate and the amount of information they actually use: a small amount of personal information can dominate a large amount of historical information about a past record.
>
> (Popkin, 1994, p. 79)

Another informational shortcut is the **drunkard's search,** named after the drunkard who loses his keys in the street and looks for them under the lamppost because the light is better there—not because that is where he lost the keys. This is analogous to when people reduce complicated issues and choices among candidates to simple comparisons—because it is easier. This occurs in comparisons of candidates for office, when people use one-dimensional searches, focusing on obvious single issues or candidate characteristics, rather than searching for the complexities of both candidates and issues (Popkin, 1994; Jervis, 1995).

Heuristics are one form of mental shortcuts, and schemas are another. Among the most important schemas for Americans are partisanship, issues, and candidate schemas. The role of each type of schema is difficult to separate, because they interact with one another. Ottati and Wyer (1990) illustrated this with the following possibilities:

> A voter may infer that a candidate endorses a given set of issue positions (e.g., favors bombing Libya or favors military intervention in Nicaragua) because he or she believes the candidate has certain personal traits (e.g., assertive) that combine to form the candidate's "image." Conversely, a voter may infer the candidate's personal traits from his or her stands on various issues. Analogously, a voter's perception of a candidate's personal characteristics or issue orientation may elicit emotional responses to the candidate. On the other hand, a voter's assessment of his or her own reactions to the candidate may lead the voter to infer that the candidate has certain personal characteristics or holds issue positions that are evaluatively consistent with these reactions.
>
> (p. 205)

The earliest studies of voting behavior demonstrated the importance of partisanship as a schema. *The American Voter* (Campbell et al., 1960/1964) described *partisanship* as an attitude used early on in information acquisition and that a candidate's party is the first consideration, with issue positions and a candidate's personal characteristics second. Party also affects people's impressions of candidates, so, from this perspective, it is the most important schema (Markus & Converse, 1979). For example, the schema or category "Democrat" has multiple pieces of information embodied in it. If a person is a Democrat, has the appropriate schema, and knows that candidate Smith is a Democrat, but has not bothered to get any information about where candidate Smith stands on issues, the association with the Democratic party will lead to assumptions that Smith agrees with the perceiver on important issues. A study by Lodge and Hamill (1986) showed some of the effects of partisan schema on information processing. When presented with statements by a fictitious congressional leader, people with party schemas were more able to correctly categorize statements as being Republican or Democrat than were people without party schemas. Those with schemas were better able to recall statements that were consistent with the party than those that were inconsistent. Schematics also "systematically distort the congressman's stance on the issue by imposing more schematic order on his policy positions than was actually present in the campaign message" (Lodge & Hamill, 1986, p. 518) indicating a bias in political information processing.

Candidate schemas or knowledge structures were studied extensively and are believed to be closely associated with how a particular candidate appeals to voters on particular issues (Funk, 1999; Graber, 1984; Jacobs &

Shapiro, 1994; Kaid & Chanslor, 1995; Kinder, 1986; Markus, 1982; Miller & Shanks, 1996; Rahn et al., 1990). Miller, Wattenberg, and Malanchuk (1986) examined whether there exists a presidential schema, or a prototype of the president. In other words, do individuals have a preexisting schema about the president that they use to evaluate a candidate? In their examination of elections from 1952 to 1985, those authors found that individuals do in fact hold a presidential schema, central to which is the notion of competence (past political experience, ability as statesman, comprehension of political issues, and intelligence), which they regard as a performance-related criterion. Other dimensions, such as integrity (i.e., trustworthiness, honesty, sincerity, just another politician) and reliability (i.e., dependable, strong, hardworking, decisive, aggressive), became more relevant after 1964. Miller et al. (1986) note that these expectations about the performance of presidents "appear to reflect in part the actions of past presidents and in part the agenda set by the media or by current candidates" (p. 535).

The importance of candidate schemas in information processing is further emphasized by Rahn et al. (1990), who maintain that, although different people rely differentially on schemas of parties, issues, candidates, or groups, almost all of the massive amount of information available to voters during an election can be used in evaluating candidates. Hence, candidate appraisals are particularly important. Moreover, they maintain that, in election after election, five characteristics of candidates are important in determining how much voters like or dislike a candidate: competence, integrity, reliability, charisma, and personal characteristics (Rahn et al., 1990). Funk (1999) found that candidates and campaigns vary in the underlying trait dimensions that emerge as important in evaluations of candidates. The substantive content of traits makes a difference. In her study, Funk found that the leadership characteristic significantly affected overall evaluations of George Bush and Michael Dukakis in 1988. In 1992, Bush was evaluated in terms of leadership and empathy characteristics. Ronald Reagan, in 1984, was evaluated in terms of empathy and integrity; Walter Mondale, his opponent, was evaluated in terms of leadership during that election. In 1992 and 1996, Bill Clinton was evaluated in terms of all three characteristics: leadership, empathy, and integrity.

Schemas and attitudes about issues compose a third important element in the American view of politics. An **issue** is a dispute about public policy. Popkin (1994) argued that issues are effective in waging a campaign for office only when voters see connections "(1) between the issue and the office; (2) between the issue and the candidate; and (3) between the issue and the benefits they care about" (p. 100). People are more likely to attend to issues about which information is easily acquired, that is, issues that are immediate in their lives and that are easy to understand. This presents a formidable task for candidates for office. If candidates wish to campaign on issues, they must make the potential voters aware of where they stand on issues, that their position will benefit the voter, and that once in office they will actually have the power to affect the promised change.

Consequently, how issues are **framed** by candidates for office makes a big difference in whether or not, and how, the public will consider the issues (Gamson, 1992; Nelson & Oxley, 1999; Popkin, 1994; Zaller, 1992). Issue frames are "alternative definitions, constructions, or depictions of a policy problem" (Nelson & Oxley, 1999, p. 1041). How issues are framed influences the way voters look at the issues, and it also affects how accessible the issue attitude is in the perceivers' minds. Studies have shown framing to be important in presidential politics, as well as in race-related politics in the United States, which is a topic covered in Chapter 8 (Kinder & Sanders, 1996; Mendelberg, 2001; Popkin, 1994). The studies done at Columbia University in 1948, for example, showed that the campaign changed the relative importance of international issues versus domestic issues in voters' minds. Thinking about the positions of the candidates on domestic issues, instead of on international issues, affected voter preference in that election, because they framed the candidates differently. Popkin (1994) summarized the findings regarding presidential politics and framing as follows:

> There is enough differentiation in people's images of presidents for formulation effects to matter; changing people's ideas about problems facing the president changes the way people think about presidents; and changing the ways people think about presidents affects their assessments of presidents as well as their votes.

(p. 84)

Candidates who engage in *frame alignment* (pointing out how their position on issues is consistent with voters' position) are likely to gain more support than candidates who do not.

Many of these information processing patterns are pulled together in Lau and Redlawsk's *How Voters Decide* (2006). The note four models of decision making commonly found in the political science literature: the Rational Choice model wherein it is assumed that people carefully evaluate all information and make a voter choice based on self-interest; an early socialization and cognitive consistency model, the Confirmatory Decision Making model, is essentially that of the *American Voter*, wherein people start with the identification of a candidate's party and then passively acquire short-term information; a Fast and Frugal Decision Making model in which people look for specific bits of information about matters of importance to them, and ignore everything else; and a bounded rationality model, the Semiautomatic Intuitive Decision Making model, in which people only get as much information as they need to make a voting decision and no more. Lau and Redlawsk then examined a variety of cognitive processes, which were discussed in Chapter 3, to devise propositions about the decision strategies and information processing patterns associated with each model.

Beginning with the notion that processing all information is simply beyond what people are capable of, Lau and Redlawsk argued that there are five heuristics voters are likely to use. **Affect referral heuristic** is a heuristic in which people vote for a candidate they are both familiar with and whom they regard highly. The **endorsement heuristic** refers to a shortcut wherein people select a candidate who has been endorsed by people the voter has confidence in. The **familiarity heuristic** comes into play when people are familiar with one candidate, but not the others, and they are at a minimum at least neutral toward that candidate. The **habit heuristic** is simply voting as the same way as last time. Finally, the **viability heuristic** is a selection of a candidate based on the likelihood that he or she will win (2006, p. 28).

The models presented in this book are considered to be broad decision strategies. Lau and Redlawsk classify decision strategies by "the extent to which they confront or avoid conflict" (2006, p. 30). When a voter experiences conflict between his or her preferences on one issue and a preference on another issue, they can use one of two decision strategies. The first is a **compensatory strategy,** which involves the careful assignment of positive or negative values to each position. The voter then engages in an assessment of the trade-offs involved and resolves the conflict with a choice. The second strategy is a **noncompensatory strategy,** which essentially avoids the conflict by not getting complete information.

The authors also argued that new techniques are needed to observe how people acquire information. Only by understanding how people acquire information can we understand the decision rules and heuristics they use to make a decision. The *content* of the information sought is the well-known items that were reviewed above: party affiliation, issues and the positions candidates take, candidate traits, group interests and so on. The *process*, Lau and Redlawsk maintained, is also central. It involves the depth of the search for information, the comparability of the search across alternatives, and the sequence of the search (2006, pp. 33–34). They add additional variables, which were introduced above as well, such as political sophistication, campaign dynamics, memory, and candidate evaluation, to develop their theory of voter decision making. Lau and Redlawsk's (2006) conclusions include the following assessments of decision strategies for each model:

> **Rational Choice** model: "the most cognitively difficult decision strategy, albeit one that promises a value maximizing outcome . . . more likely to be chosen when there are only two alternatives in the choice set, by experts in any particular domain, and when decision makers are primarily motivated to make good decisions" (p. 45). The consequences of these decision strategies are "more moderate, less polarized candidate evaluations, higher quality decisions when decision tasks are relatively easy, or when the strategy is employed by a relative expert" (p. 46).

> **Confirmatory Decision Making** model: "most likely to be chosen by strong political partisans . . . [D]ecision makers should be motivated to learn candidates' party affiliations as soon as possible. And particularly when they are exposed to information that might lead them to question their standing decision, they should be motivated to seek disproportionate information about their in-party candidate" (p. 45). The consequences of these decision strategies include "Polarized candidate evaluations; lower quality decisions" (p. 46).

> **Fast and Frugal Decision Making** model: "most likely when a decision is particularly difficult or when decision makers are working under severe time pressure" (p. 45). The consequences of these decision strategies include "[m]ore moderate, less polarized candidate evaluations; better quality decisions when decisions are—or are perceived to be—extremely difficult" (p. 46).

> **Semiautomatic Intuitive Decision Making** model: "Any factor that leads decision makers to be primarily motivated by desires to make an easy decision, particularly increasing task difficult" (p. 45)

leads to the use of this model. The consequences include "[p]olarized candidate evaluations, better quality decisions when decisions are (perceived to be) relatively difficult" (p. 46).

Lau and Redlawsk also introduce a method of assessing information processing that does not rely on surveys, as so much of the research in the study of public opinion does. Instead, Lau and Redlawsk use a dynamic processing methodology in which they create information boards that provide subjects with changing information about candidates during a hypothetical election. The information ebbs and flows, moving from information about the candidates to their issue positions, support base, and so on. The subjects react to the information as it comes in, which allows the researchers to gather data on their information processing as it occurs and changes.

We cannot discuss information processing and voting without mentioning the role of the brain in voting and voter turnout. In the book, *The Political Brain*, Westen (2007) highlights the role of the brain, based on brain scanning studies, in voting behavior. The origins of this research are the multitude of studies on brain activity and political ideology, with results showing that different areas of the brain are activated for those with liberal versus conservative beliefs. Clearly, the brain plays an important role in determining voting behavior.

With regard to actual voter turnout, Fowler et al. (2008), using a twin-study methodology, found that there is a genetic component to habitual voter turnout. More specifically, they found that more than half (53%) of the variance in voter turnout can be attributed to genetic factors. Similarly, Fowler and Dawes (2008) examined the relationship between MAOA (an enzyme that is sometimes called the "warrior gene") and 5HTT (sometimes referred to as a depression gene) genes on self-reported voter turnout. Their results found a small effect of MAOA on self-reported voter turnout. There was an effect of 5HTT on voter turnout, but only through an association with religious involvement. In fact, this result makes some sense, as political and activity and religious involvement both represent an interest in affiliating with a social group.

Most recently, French et al. (2014) examined voter participation rates in the United States, which have historically been low (40–60% voter turnout). They measured cortisol levels to determine if they could predict voting behavior. Cortisol is a hormone that is often referred to as the "stress hormone" or the "fight or flight" hormone because it plays an important role in our body's reaction to stress. Our body produces more cortisol when it is stressed or in fearful situations. Their results showed that lower cortisol levels (when measured late afternoon) were associated with increased voting activity in major elections. Interestingly, cortisol levels were not associated in any meaningful way with nonvoting political behavior.

Other research has examined particular parts of the brain to determine their role in voting behavior. One brain structure that has been implicated in this research is the amygdala, structure in the brain responsible for several cognitive processes, but also emotional responses such as anxiety. Rule et al. (2010) examined the role of the amygdala in voting behavior across cultures. The basis for their study involved the observation that American and Japanese voters agreed in their judgments of candidate's faces, but they chose to elect different candidates. Japanese voters selected candidates judged to be warm; American voters selected candidates they judged to be powerful. Rule et al. (2010) was interested in brain activity while making these voting choices. Making use of functional Magnetic Resonance Imaging (fMRI), their study emphasizes two important findings. First, activity in the amygdala was able to predict the preferred candidate of the potential voter. Moreover, this held true regardless of the potential voter's culture, or the culture of the candidate. Second, activity in the amygdala was more pronounced for out-group than for in-group candidates. This latter result, of course, has implications for a host of group behavior, but most specifically, for out-group bias that has been discussed previously in this text. As we will see below, emotions do indeed play a role in voting.

EMOTION AND VOTING

In Chapter 3, the importance of emotion in political behavior is discussed, and the work of Marcus et al. (2000) was introduced. In 1993, Marcus and MacKuen published a study that pointed to the importance of anxiety and enthusiasm in political learning and involvement. They argued that people do not simply respond to candidates positively or negatively (i.e., valence), but with specific emotions. Traditional notions of the effect of emotions on voting maintained that positive or negative feelings toward candidates directly influence how people vote. Marcus and MacKuen (1993), however, offered a more precise picture of how emotions affect political behavior during election time. Two emotions are central in responses to political events and candidates: fear (or anxiety) and enthusiasm. Enthusiasm affects the decision of for whom to vote; anxiety increases the search for information about candidates. When people do not experience anxiety, they tend to rely upon habit in determining how they will vote (e.g., party identification). Thus, anxiety has an important role in information processing, and it stimulates learning.

This argument is presented as a theory of affective intelligence in *Affective Intelligence and Political Judgment* (Marcus et al., 2000). Those authors examined interviews with people during the 1980, 1984, 1988, 1992, and 1996 presidential election campaigns, looking for trends in emotional responses to the candidates and voting decisions. They made assessments of voters' preferences, using the "standing choice" factors for these elections, that is, partisanship, issues, and the candidates' personal qualities. Then they added in an analysis of voters' enthusiasm and anxiety. For example, in the 1980 election, President Jimmy Carter began the campaign with public support and sympathy in the midst of the Iran hostage crisis and the Soviet invasion of Afghanistan. By October, however, the hostage rescue scheme had failed, the economy was in the doldrums, and public enthusiasm for Carter had waned. In addition, public anxiety regarding the competence of the administration grew, albeit modestly. Enthusiasm for Ronald Reagan, Carter's 1980 opponent, was modest, but the study shows an increase in anxiety regarding Reagan, after the Democrats launched a scare campaign in an effort to persuade voters that Reagan would be dangerous in foreign policy. In the 1984 campaign, enthusiasm for Reagan, by then a popular president, was high, and anxiety was not. The challenger, Walter Mondale, evoked neither enthusiasm nor anxiety. In 1988, when Vice President George Bush ran against Massachusetts Governor Michael Dukakis, the public's anxiety about Dukakis was increased by the famous Willie Horton ads (discussed in more detail in Chapter 8), which portrayed Dukakis as weak on crime. Overall, in their analyses of all five races from 1980 to 1996, Marcus et al. (2000) found that anxious voters were much less likely to rely upon partisanship in making a voting decision and much more likely to look for and attend to information about the candidates' personal qualities and issue positions. A caveat is that this anxiety must involve the voter's own candidate, the one they would ordinarily vote for, based upon partisanship. To be anxious about the other candidate is normal—one is always anxious about the candidate from the other party, nothing unusual about that—but doubts about the person one would ordinarily vote for produce anxiety.

Redlawsk, Civettini, and Lau (2007) tested some of the hypotheses generated by the Affective Intelligence theory using their dynamic processing method discussed above. They considered several hypotheses:

1. When voters agree with a candidate on an issue they will be enthusiastic about the candidate. When they disagree, they will be angry. When there is some distance, but not enough to make them angry, voters will experience anxiety.
2. New information that produces enthusiasm will not be processed more rapidly than neutral information. However, new information that prompts the surveillance system into action (discussed in Chapter 3) will produce anxiety (or anger) and will take longer to process.
3a. When the surveillance system is activated and anxiety is produced, voters will search for more information about the candidate who is associated with anxiety. Anger, on the other hand, produces aversion to more information.
3b. Anxiety about a candidate will result in greater accuracy in knowing where the candidate stands on issues. Anger and enthusiasm produce the opposite, less accuracy in assessing the candidate's issue positions.

These hypotheses were tested with respect to a preferred candidate and a rejected candidate. Their findings supported hypothesis 1. Hypothesis 2 was supported in terms of the effect of enthusiasm. However, they found that both anxiety and anger did increase processing time, but only for candidates the subjects preferred. Regarding hypotheses 3a and 3b, they found that "in a high-threat environment, anger and anxiety both show learning effects, and subjects are much better able to place their preferred candidate. In the low-threat environment, however, both affective responses lead to *less accurate* placement" (2007, p. 176). They conclude that:

> The weight of the evidence supports aspects of the affective intelligence thesis, albeit with important caveats. Anxiety, which is presumed to cause heightened attention and processing, only operates for preferred candidates and in an environment where there is substantial information that defies expectations. In a high-threat environment anxiety leads to more careful processing, more effort to learn about

the candidate who generates the anxiety, and better assessment of that candidate's position on the issue . . . But in a low threat environment, anxiety appears to do very little to increase either processing efforts or learning. Furthermore, regardless of threat environment, anxiety does not have any effects on processing information about rejected candidates . . . Anger, which ought to generate aversion, exhibits the expected effect, at least in low-threat environments. In such environments greater attention is paid to information that invokes anger, but then that anger is aimed at an initially liked candidate, aversion occurs as voters turn toward other candidates. The result is to incorrectly recall where such as candidate stands with regard to issues.

(2007, p. 177)

The Presidential Election of 2008

The election of 2008 in the United States, which resulted in the election of the first African American to the American Presidency, provided an opportunity to look at both cognitive and emotional elements in voting. Democrat Barack Obama won by 52% to Republican John McCain's 46%. Thousands of people raced through Grant Park in Chicago to get a view of Obama during his victory speech, and the tears of joy on so many faces showed the powerful emotions felt by Obama supporters. Many Americans, his supporters and opponents alike, felt great pride when America crossed that highest racial threshold and elected an African American to the country's highest office. Clearly short term factors were extremely important in determining Barack Obama's success. The economy was in crisis by October 2008, and the wars in Afghanistan and Iraq, the latter of which Obama opposed, were increasingly unpopular. The standing president, George W. Bush, was the least popular president ever, and despite John McCain's efforts, the McCain campaign was unable to break the public association of McCain with the Bush administration. (At the time of the election, 71% disapproved of President Bush and 48% thought McCain would continue along the same policy lines [Pew Research Center, 2008b]). The two candidates had strengths and weaknesses in terms of candidate characteristics. Obama had less experience, and he was African American, and McCain was seen as too old and somewhat volatile. Turnout was very high, at over 60%. As it turns out, Obama did well in many different demographic groups. Sixty-one percent of Obama's votes were cast by whites compared to 90% of McCain's, 23% of Obama's votes came from African American voters compared to 1% of McCain's, 11% of Obama's votes were from Hispanics compared to 6% of McCain's, and 30% of Obama's votes came from people under the age of 30, compared to 13% of McCain's (Curry, 2008). Forty-six percent of white women voted for Obama, more than the percent of white women who voted for either Al Gore in 2000 (42%) or John Kerry in 2004 (41%) (Barnes & Shear, 2008). The Republican Party was less able to attract Independent voters in this election than in the previous two. Clearly neither partisanship nor candidate characteristics won the election for Barack Obama; issues did.

The race issue was very interesting during the campaign and the election itself. The Obama campaign was determined that Obama would not be seen as a Black candidate. They wanted his campaign to transcend race. There were times in which race became a direct issue, such as the controversy that erupted after Obama's former minister, Reverend Jeremiah Wright, was shown on video denouncing the United States. Nevertheless, race did not play a large role in the voters' choice. There were significant concerns all along that race would be important and cast a negative impact on the Obama candidacy. A 2008 study of Democrats and Independents by researchers at Stanford University found that survey results indicated that racial prejudice could have an important role in the 2008 election. They found that over a third of white Democrats and Independents agreed with at least one negative characterization of Blacks and that their negative feelings could prevent them from voting for Obama (AOL News, September 20, 2008). This, among other developments, raised concerns about a repeat of the so-called **Bradley effect**. Los Angeles Mayor Tom Bradley ran for the governor's office in California in 1982. Despite his lead in the polls, he lost the election, and analysts believed this was a result of white voters lying about their willingness to vote for a Black candidate. This did not occur in the 2008 election. Polls showed Obama ahead of McCain by 51%–43% (NBC News-Wall Street Journal), 53%–42% (Gallup) and 51%–42% CBS News) (Curry, 2008). Those figures were pretty close to the actual vote. Years later, academic studies addressed the role of race in the election. For example, Schaffner (2011) examined the extent to which racial salience had a moderating influence on Whites' (and, in particular, racial conservatives') support for Obama. He found that when race was salient for White voters, they were less likely to vote for Obama, and maintained that the president-elect focused too much on Blacks.

Issues and emotions. The economy was the issue of greatest concern to Americans in the 2008 election. Sixty-three percent of the voters cited the economy as their greatest concern, and Obama was favored on that issue. Fifty-nine percent of those who said the economy was their greatest concern voted for Obama (Pew Research Center, 2008b). One third of the voters expressed concern about access to affordable health care, and among those voters 65% voted for Obama (Pew Research Center, 2008b). Those who said the war in Iraq was their top issue also voted for Obama over McCain by 59% to 39%. The one issue area in which McCain dominated was terrorism, and he got 86% of the votes from people who cited terrorism as their top issue (Pew Research Center, 2008b). However, only 9% of the electorate saw terrorism as the most important issue.

Early analyses showed how important the issues were in this election and the importance of emotion. Obama's supporters were more likely to express excitement and optimism at the prospect of his being elected than McCain's supporters by 56% to 28%. When asked if an Obama or McCain presidency "scared" them, 24% said Obama scared them and 28% said McCain scared them (Pew Research Center, 2008b).

The 2012 Election

In the 2012 election, exit polls indicated that "more than 90% of self-identified Democrats voted for Obama, with 45% of Independents doing so as well"

(Norpoth & Bednarczuk, 2013). Further, according to the Pew Research Center, Romney did not poll favorably throughout the campaign.

Just 47% of exit-poll respondents viewed him favorably, compared with 53% for Mr. Obama. Throughout the campaign, Mr. Romney's favorable ratings were among the lowest recorded for a presidential candidate in the modern era. A persistent problem was doubt about his empathy with the average voter. By 53% to 43%, exit-poll respondents said that Mr. Obama was more in touch than Mr. Romney with people like themselves.

(Kohut, November 2012, p. 1)

Election and survey results reported by the Roper Center (2012) revealed insights from the election. 59% of Whites voted for Romney and 93% of Blacks, 71% of Hispanics and 73% of Asians voted for Obama. Sixty percent (down from 66% in 1988) of those ages 18–28, and 45% of men and 53% of women voted for Obama. Fifty-four percent of voters making over $100,000 voted for Romney, while 60% of those making under $50,000 voted for Obama. The most important issue for Obama voters was health care while Romney voters cited defense and then the economy. In their analysis of the election, Norpoth and Bednarczuk (2013) argued that Obama had the incumbency advantage and was given the benefit of the doubt. This was demonstrated in exit polls where Obama was punished less than George Bush for the economy. While Romney was a strong Republican nominee, he could not "trump" the incumbent advantage.

POLITICAL SOCIALIZATION

How do people acquire their political attitudes in America? Research on political socialization began in the 1950s and looked at the ways in which "people acquire relatively enduring orientations toward politics in general and toward their own particular political systems" (Merelman, 1986, p. 279). The research reached its peak in the 1970s and suffered a decline, then a renewed interest in the 1990s (for earlier reviews, see Merelman, 1986; Niemi, 1973; Sears, 1975). Why did the field suffer a decline? As Niemi and Hepburn (1995) put it, "The field atrophied because it was based on exaggerated premises and because of misinterpreted and misunderstood research findings (and lack of findings)" (p. 7). Thus, there were several efforts to revitalize the field and offer new directions for research (see Merelman, 1986; Niemi & Hepburn 1995; Sigel, 1995). Let us begin with a brief look at the development of this body of literature, as seen through the eyes of the scholars themselves, and then discuss ways in which they suggest bringing it back to life.

The earliest socialization studies focused on children. Studies were conducted on their views of political authority figures (see, for example, Easton & Dennis, 1973) and on their acquisition of political attitudes. The first authority figures recognized by children, as they became aware of politics, were the president and the policeman (Easton & Dennis, 1973). As children mature, their cognitive abilities increase, and they can advance from thinking of government in personal, concrete terms (e.g., George Washington and the flag) to more abstract notions, such as institutions and lawmaking. Moreover, these studies found that children like government. Easton and Dennis (1973) suggested that children proceed through stages in political socialization: politicization (learning there is authority beyond family and school); personalization (becoming aware of authorities, through individuals such as police and the president); idealization (the belief that political authority is trustworthy and benevolent); and institutionalization (association with depersonalized objects, such as government) (Niemi, 1973). Concerning the acquisition of political attitudes, family was considered to be the most important agent of transmission (Jennings & Niemi, 1974; Maccoby, Matthews, & Morton, 1954); followed by schools (Hess & Torney, 1967); then peers, media, and events (Jennings & Niemi, 1974). Jennings and Niemi (1974), for example, found that parents transmit partisanship to their children, although the attachment tends to be weaker in the children.

The aforementioned studies shed considerable light on how children are socialized, but whether or not they continued to have those same attitudes into adulthood was also an important question. The early socialization studies examined children precisely because they thought that socialization was completed by age 18 years or so, and that the attitudes were retained through the life cycle. But, as Niemi and Hepburn (1995) explained:

> These studies were fascinating and often had amusing twists. The problem, however, was in trying to determine their long-term significance. Here, socialization research fell victim to two assumptions that are, at best, highly questionable. First, it was assumed that what was learned prior to adulthood remained unchanged later in life. This "primacy" principle was most explicit in political science with respect to partisanship. . . . Party identification was very nearly immutable both between generations and across lifetimes. Yet even as socialization work was getting up a full head of steam, the first cracks in this assumption were appearing, as the number of independents underwent a significant increase in the late 1960s.
>
> (p. 8)

The primacy principle, advanced by the claims in *The American Voter* (Campbell et al., 1960/1964), was subsequently challenged by many studies indicating that partisanship is not necessarily constant. Other elements, such as political trust, also changed over time. Niemi and Hepburn's (1995) conclusion is that attitudes and behavior do change over time and that what is learned early on may not be relevant later in life. Instead of the focus being on children, it should turn to individuals between the ages of 14 and 25 years. Why? "First, there is little dispute that youth is a time of extraordinary psychological and social change. Second, these are the years during which our society traditionally attempts to educate youth for citizen participation" (Niemi & Hepburn, 1995, p. 9). Those authors also offer several ways to "reestablish socialization as a viable and vibrant field of study" (pp. 13–14). First, eliminate what, for many purposes, is the artificial distinction between those aged under 18 and those 18 and over. Second, undertake a major new socialization study devoted specifically to the study of intergenerational and youthful change and development. Third, conduct more major youth studies and be more involved in new studies at the design stage. Fourth, pay more attention to high school and college courses and their probable effects on young people. Fifth, think more theoretically and write about all aspects of socialization. Sixth, conduct more comparative socialization work, especially if it is to contribute to our understanding of the significance of learning in early childhood.

In another assessment, Sigel (1995) pointed out that there are four problems with socialization research: lack of conceptual clarity, poor choice of subjects, insufficient attention to historical and cultural factors, and inappropriate methodology. As Sigel explains the first problem:

> What really do we understand by the term *political socialization*? As currently used in the literature, the term is applied to many different phenomena. Scholars not only disagree among themselves in their definitions of it, but at times operate with a variety of definitions or conceptualizations even in their own work, applying one definition at one time and another—not necessarily a compatible one—at another, and often doing so in the same research enterprise.
>
> (p. 17)

Reviewing the literature, Sigel found numerous definitions of political socialization, including learning (political knowledge and comprehension), the developmental sequence through which knowledge and comprehension are acquired, continuity over time of knowledge and attitudes, acquisition and internalization of society's norms and behaviors, and synonyms for civic or political education.

The second problem is the focus of the studies on young children. Like Niemi and Hepburn, Sigel (1995) asks whether these views carry over into later years. In addition, "virtually no literature exists that has actually studied and observed the manner by which 'agents' [those who do imprinting] do or do not make influence attempts" (p. 18). Finally, she questions the idea that young people are passive and gullible to outside influences. The author suggests taking a life-span approach to understanding why orientations are maintained, modified, or abandoned. In addition, more attention should be paid to the historical and cultural context in which the observations of attitudes are made. Finally, political scientists need to pay more attention to methodology. The reliance upon close-ended survey questionnaires was criticized as inappropriate for studying the process of attitude change along the life span. Sigel (1995) suggests other methods, such as field observations, collection of life histories, simulations, or direct observations.

Socialization studies are certainly interesting and important. They can help us understand the foundations of support for a political system. There is, as mentioned, a renewed interest in studying political socialization. In

September 1999, for example, a collection of articles on political socialization appeared in *Political Psychology*. The studies are cross-national, including studies in Germany, the Netherlands, Sweden, the United States, and the Arab–Israeli conflict. As Special Editor Richard Niemi points out, although these authors concentrated on different aspects of socialization research, they demonstrate the resurgence of the subject, and a new approach that is cognizant of the problems with previous research.

In addition to those studies, there is another, broader, approach to the study of political socialization, which is particularly evident in the works of Milburn and his colleagues (Milburn & Conrad, 1996; Milburn, Conrad, Sala, & Carberry, 1995). Drawing upon earlier works by Lasswell (1930/1960) and Merelman (1969), these scholars argued that much of the traditional political socialization literature focused too narrowly upon the transmission of political attitudes from parents to children. Instead, Milburn et al. (1995) took an approach to political socialization that employs cognitive and emotional elements in the development of political ideas, or lack thereof. A central thesis is that "childhood experiences can affect the way we view the world and the political perceptions and understanding we develop" (Milburn & Conrad, 1996, p. 3), but that that understanding includes not only what we think and feel, but what we refuse to think about, that is, the political realities that people cannot face, because they are too painful and threatening. They also argued that anger from childhood treatment by parents contributes to long-term political attitudes. That anger is displaced onto political issues, and people with particularly punitive upbringings tend to be attracted to conservative ideologies.

POLITICAL TOLERANCE

If asked, most Americans are likely to maintain that the United States is a country with a great deal of tolerance for minority viewpoints on political issues. After all, the Constitution provides assurances that majority rule will not result in the repression of the rights of minorities. Since 1937, researchers asked how much tolerance Americans have for politically deviant groups. At that time, the questions mainly revolved around tolerance for civil liberties for communists and their rights to free speech, to hold public office, to have public meetings, and so forth. The early studies found that most Americans favored restrictions on communists' rights in these areas. A major study conducted by Stouffer in 1955 found high levels of intolerance. For example, only 59% thought that a person who favors government ownership of all the railroads and big industries (an indicator of socialist ideas) should be allowed to speak in their community. Only 37% would allow a person to speak against religion. Only 27% would allow an admitted communist to speak. Community leaders were more tolerant than the average citizen, however: 84% would allow a socialist to speak, 64% an atheist, and 51% an admitted communist. Higher levels of education also correlated with greater tolerance. Stouffer argued that education teaches people not to stereotype or to rigidly categorize people into groups, and to respect differing points of view.

Studies show an increase in tolerance between 1954 and 1973, when another major study (Nunn, Crockett, & Williams, 1978), in an effort to replicate Stouffer's study, was conducted. Now 52% would permit an admitted communist to speak publicly, and 65% would let an atheist speak. However, Sullivan, Piereson, and Marcus (1979, 1982) suggest that, although tolerance toward communists, atheists, and socialists increased, it may only be a product of diminished perceptions of threat from these groups. People may have become less worried about these groups, and thus had less motivation to deny them their freedoms, but that does not necessarily mean that tolerance in a general sense had increased. Sullivan et al. argued that tolerance should only be said to exist when one is willing to tolerate those groups one dislikes. It is irrelevant in responses to groups one likes.

Sullivan et al. (1982) are essentially making the argument that tolerance, or lack thereof, is a political position driven primarily by emotion, rather than by cognition. One can only test levels of tolerance by looking at attitudes toward groups a person dislikes. Therefore, a person on the left end of the political spectrum who expresses a willingness to grant civil liberties to a communist is probably not expressing tolerance, because that person does not dislike communists in the first place. Ask that same person how they feel about granting civil liberties to a Nazi, and then you will see how tolerant they really are. Sullivan et al. (1982) are fairly pessimistic about levels of tolerance in the United States, because it was studied mostly in the context of attitudes toward leftist political groups, which, as noted above, are less threatening now, and therefore are less likely to evoke negative emotions. Therefore, increased willingness to grant those groups their civil liberties is meaningless as a reflection of growth in tolerance. Empirical studies supported this argument: Sullivan et al. (1982) let their respondents decide which groups they disliked, rather than presenting them with a group the researchers assumed they disliked—a technique they called a "content-controlled" measurement of tolerance. When looked at that way, they found that levels of tolerance had not increased since the 1950s. Another implication of this approach to the study of tolerance is that American ideals regarding basic civil liberties are much less important in producing tolerance than are emotional responses to groups people dislike.

Sniderman et al. (1991) disagree. They examined tolerance toward a different variety of groups, including

> people who are against all churches and religion; people who believe that blacks are genetically inferior; people who admit they are communists; people who advocate doing away with elections and letting the military run the country; and people who admit they are homosexual.
> (p. 123)

This assortment of groups was guaranteed to evoke dislike for at least one group by the various respondents. They found consistent responses toward the groups, meaning that, if people were tolerant toward one group, they were tolerant toward the others. Therefore, the implication is that, if people hold tolerance as a value, their attitudes toward all groups reflect that attitude, even if they personally dislike the group in question. Given that every respondent would dislike at least one group, the researchers maintained that people are responding on the basis of their principles regarding tolerance, rather than on the basis of which group they dislike or like.

The difference between these two assessments of tolerance is a reflection of different emphases: affect versus cognition. The relative role of thinking and feeling, when it comes to political tolerance in the United States, is an interesting and important topic. A study by Kuklinski, Riggle, Ottati, Schwartz, & Wyer (1991), for example, found that, although people initially endorse tolerance, that is, they respond in support of the value, the more they think about the group in question, the more intolerant they become, because the negative affect toward the group takes precedence over principle. The role of affect and cognition will continue to be debated and studied as time goes on. In the meantime, one clear trend is that the increase in tolerance, evident from the 1950s to the 1970s, slowed down, although public opinion polls in some areas, such as civil liberties for homosexuals, continue to show increases in tolerance. In 1977, for example, 56% of respondents to a Gallup poll supported equal rights, in terms of job opportunities for homosexuals, whereas, in 1999, 83% supported equal rights (Gallup, 1999).

VOTING BEHAVIOR IN BRITAIN

Needless to say, the United States is not the only country whose public's political behavior was studied. However, the approaches used to study voting behavior in other countries are generally American in origin, with a heavy reliance on survey data. Like the United States, party identification in Britain was studied extensively. During the 1950s and 1960s, people tended to align strongly with either the Conservative or Labour parties. Two widely accepted factors determined a person's party identification: parents' affiliation and class. People tended to identify with their parents' party; working-class folks belonged to the Labour party, and middle-and upper-class people overwhelmingly identified with the Conservative party. The association between class and partisanship in Britain was very strong. The central difference between Britain and the United States, in terms of party alignment, was the greater importance of class in partisan alignment in Britain than in the United States. Other factors, such as age, sex, religion, and region, had some influence in British party alignments, but much less so than did class and family (Butler & Stokes, 1974; Denver, 1994). As in the United States, British voters were affected by short-term factors, which caused them to defect and vote for the other party. Indeed, during the 1950s and 1960s, the Conservative party would never have won an election were it not for short-term factors that led the majority Labour party identifiers to defect and vote Tory.

What Is Social Class?

Although an important concept in social science, the term *social class* does not have a universally accepted definition. We generally think about class in terms of occupation, income, and lifestyle. Often, classes are divided into upper, middle, and working class. For purposes of measuring public opinion, classes are categorized as (A) high-level professional, managerial and administrative; (B) middle management, professional or administrative; (C1) supervisor, clerical, nonmanual; (C2) skilled manual labor; (D) semi-or unskilled manual; (E) occasionally employed or reliant upon government benefits (Denver, 1998). These are then grouped together as manual workers (C2, D, E) and nonmanual workers (A, B, C1). This is known as the Alford Index. In recent years, there was considerable debate as to whether or not a manual worker–nonmanual worker basis for distinguishing class is useful for postindustrial societies in which heavy industry is no longer dominant in the economy.

Beginning in 1970, Britain began to experience both partisan and class dealignment, which means that fewer people identify with the traditionally dominant Labour and Conservative parties, and those who do identify with a party do so with less strength of attachment. By 1997, less than 20% of the electorate in Britain identified strongly with either the Labour or Conservative parties, down from 38% in 1964 (Jones & Kavanagh, 1998). In part, partisan dealignment was a result of the pull from other parties, including the Liberal party and the nationalist parties in Scotland and Wales: the Scottish Nationalist party and Plaid Cymru, respectively. Other factors leading to dealignment were increases in levels of education, enabling more independent judgments by voters, rather than reliance upon the parties for issue positions; a decline in support for the more social welfare, pro-union principles of the Labour party; changes in campaigns, allowing for more direct and challenging reporting on candidates and issues; and general dissatisfaction with the performance of the two dominant parties when in office (Denver, 1994). Class dealignment also took place after 1970, meaning that people were less and less likely to vote for the party associated with their class. As Britain moved from a predominantly blue-collar to white-collar society and economy, class interests became more diverse. For example, the working class of pre–World War II days had divided into different subclasses, with vestiges of the old working class—those who work in factories, live in council houses (i.e., government funded housing), and so on—and a newer, more affluent working class with more skills, who work in light manufacturing and who own their own homes. As Norris (1997) puts it, "The nature of class inequalities has become more complex in postindustrial society" (p. 90). Other social identities, including region, ethnicity, and religion increased in importance and influence on the vote in Britain, as class identity fragmented (Bartle, 1998; Norris, 1997).

During the alignment era, British voters, like Americans, tended to be fairly ignorant of political issues. Butler and Stokes (1974) found that, when

British voters did express attitudes on issues, the attitudes changed frequently, indicating that they were not true attitudes, but randomly changing opinions. In a series of four interviews with the same respondents, only 43% were consistent in their positions on nationalization of industries, which was an important issue in Britain at the time. In addition, respondents' attitudes were not consistently related to other attitudes. For example, in principle, a person who is pro-private enterprise should oppose a growth in trade union power, but this was not often the case in Britain in the era of alignment. Most people used partisanship to make a voting decision, rather than attitudes toward issues.

After dealignment, however, British voters began to engage in issue voting. Studies of voting in Britain use the same standards of analysis as studies of American voting. A voting decision is considered to be based on an issue (issue voting), if the voter is aware of the issue, has a position on the issue, understands where the parties stand and how they differ from each other on the issue, and finally, votes for the party perceived to be closest to their own position on the issue (Butler & Stokes, 1974). A number of studies maintain that the majority of British voters were casting issue votes in the dealignment era (summarized in Denver, 1994). Issues such as taxes and government spending, unemployment, privatization of publicly owned industries, the European Union, racial conflict, and the status of Scotland and Northern Ireland, among others, influenced the vote in Britain in recent years.

The transformation of the Labour party in Britain, and its spectacular success in the 1997 election, is plausibly a reflection of the changes in the British voter. Starting in 1974, the Conservative party regularly beat the Labour party. In 1979, Margaret Thatcher became prime minister and stayed in office for 12 years. She was succeeded by another Conservative, John Major, and, even in the context of a struggling economy, Labour lost in 1992. This sparked a reform effort and the emergence of new leadership. According to the Labour Party director of communications, David Hill, the party came to be regarded as "too old fashioned, too tied to the past, too linked to minorities rather than majorities, and too associated with old images of the trades unions" (quoted in Seyd, 1998, p. 51). The public became mistrustful of Labour's stance on taxation, support for income redistribution, support for trade unions, and other traditional positions. Tony Blair, a relatively young man of 41, became the party's new leader in 1994. He set about devising some fundamental reforms of the party, referring to it as the New Labour party. Among those reforms was a revision of clause 4 in the party's charter, which changed the party's emphasis from supporting trade unions, first and foremost, to making trade unions only one among many important sectors, along with a thriving private sector, which the party promised to work for. This move was strongly supported by the party's members, and it is a reflection of change in class, society, and the economy in Britain. The Labour party was set to target the middle class and to address increases in issue voting. The Conservative party, on the other hand, had made a series of blunders since 1992, including economic failures, which destroyed its reputation for financial competence, and association with a number of scandals (Denver, 1998; King, 1998). The Labour party continued its electoral gains but Tony Blair resigned in 2007 having lost favor due to a variety of issues, such as the war in Iraq, the WMD fiasco, support for Israel, and the terrorist attack in London.

More recent studies such as Webb (2013) have identified two types of British voters: the dissatisfied democrat and the stealth democrat. While both types exhibit low trust in political elites, dissatisfied democrats are more politically interested and want to participate. In another study, Benoit and Benoit-Bryan (2013) analyzed the first-ever three live prime minister debates before the 2010 elections between Gordon Brown (Labour incumbent), David Cameron (Conservative) and Nick Clegg (Liberal Democrat). The authors looked at the use of claims, attacks and defenses, the topics of policy and character, and the target of attack. They found that candidates used claims most commonly, and Brown used them the most. Further, the discussion of issues trumped character. Brown and Cameron, the forerunners in the election, were the targets of most attacks, with Brown attacking less.

National identity is an issue in discussions of Great Britain and the United Kingdom. The drive for Scottish independence is carefully watched as it has implications for Wales, England, and even Northern Ireland. There exists a perception that Westminster Parliament and executive governance is an English dominated enterprise. Scotland, Wales, and Northern Ireland have devolved government responsible for local governance. The future members and configuration of Great Britain and the United Kingdom will greatly depend on perceptions of identity (Mycock & Hayton, 2014). Are they English, Scottish, Welsh, British, or some combination of both? In Northern Ireland, for example, the majority of Protestants identifies as British and is committed to the union with the United Kingdom. They are prepared to defend their identity and stake in the UK. More specifically, the 2011 census revealed that 48.36% of the population in Northern Ireland views itself as Protestant or brought up Protestant, 39.89% of the population identify as British only, while 6.17% identify as British and Northern Irish only. The Catholic community generally identifies as Irish, and many, but not all, with the Republic of Ireland. Thus, 45.14% of the population considers itself Catholic or brought up Catholic and 25.26% of the population identifies as Irish as a national identity only, while 1.06% Irish and Northern Irish only. Only 20.94% of the population identifies as Northern Irish only (Nolan, 2013).

CONCLUSION

This chapter examined public opinion and voting behavior in the United States and Britain. We began the chapter with a review of some of the concepts first presented in Chapter 3, such as attitudes, beliefs, and schemas, in addition to new concepts such as values and ideology, all of which are commonly used in the analysis of public opinion and voting behavior. The analysis of American voting behavior was more thorough, looking at the Michigan school versus the Maximalist views on a variety of topics: attitudes and political sophistication in the United States, ideology, information processing and voting behavior, emotions and voting, the election of 2008, and political tolerance. In the case of Great Britain, the British were noted to be traditionally much more reliant upon class as a basis for partisanship than are Americans. We also looked at issue trends in British elections and the reemergence of the Labour party under the auspices of New Labour.

One of the central issues underlying the study of voting behavior is the question of how those who participate in politics—the average voters—affect the quality of a democracy. Ideally, a democracy should run on the basis of decisions made by informed and thoughtful citizens. We believe that a careful study of the political psychology of voting behavior, particularly the roles of ideology and information-processing patterns, provides students with a better basis for coming to their own conclusions about the quality of democracy in America and elsewhere.

Topics, Theories/Explanations, and Cases Covered in Chapter 6

Topics	Theories/Explanations	Cases
Public opinion	Beliefs, belief systems	Political sophistication
	Values	in America
	Attitudes	
	Schema	
	Ideology	
Voting in America	Michigan school	Normal vote
	Levels of	Long-term and short-
	conceptualization	term forces
	Funnel of causality	
	Genetics and biology	
	Maximalists	Knowledge structures
Information processing	Cognitive patterns	Elections
and voting	Role of emotion	
Political socialization	Primacy principle	New studies
Political tolerance		
Voting in Great Britain	Class	

Key Terms

agenda setting

associative networks

belief system

black and white model

Bradley effect

drunkard's search

funnel of causality

Gresham's law of political
    information

ideologue

ideology

impression-based model of
    information processing

issue

issue frames

knowledge structures

levels of conceptualization

Maximalists

Michigan model

normal vote

party identification

priming

values

Suggestions for Further Reading

Ansolabehere, S., Behr, R., & Iyengar, S. (1993). *The media game*. New York: Macmillan.

Campbell, A., Converse, P., Miller, W., & Stokes, D. (1960/1964). *The American voter*. New York: Wiley.

Denver, D. (1994). *Elections and voting behaviour in Britain*. London: Harvester Wheatsheaf.

Glynn, C., Herbst, S., O'Keefe, G., & Shapiro, R. (1999). *Public opinion*. Boulder, CO: Westview.

Iyengar, S. (1991). *Is anyone responsible? How television frames political issues*. Chicago, IL: University of Chicago Press.

Iyengar, S., & McGuire, W. (Eds.). (1995). *Explorations in political psychology*. Durham, NC: Duke University Press.

Marcus, G., Neuman, W.R., & MacKuen, M. (2000). *Affective intelligence and political judgment*. Chicago, IL: University of Chicago Press.

Miller, W., & Shanks, M. (1996). *The new American voter*. Cambridge, MA: Harvard University Press.

Patterson, T. (1993). *Out of order*. New York: Knopf.

Popkin, S. (1994). *The reasoning voter: Communication and persuasion in presidential campaigns*. Chicago, IL: University of Chicago Press.

Smith, E. (1989). *The unchanging American voter*. Berkeley: University of California Press.

Note

1. There is some debate as to whether schemas and attitudes are the same thing. Kuklinski, Luskin, and Bolland (1991) maintain that they are the same concept; Conover and Feldman (1991) maintain that they are not. They argue:

> The central meaning of the attitude concept—the meaning common to all competing definitions—is fundamentally *affective* in nature. At its core, an attitude is a "person's evaluation of an object of thought" (Pratkanis & Greenwald, 1989, p. 247). The central meaning of the schema concept stands in sharp contrast. Though it, too, was defined in a variety of ways, at its core a schema is fundamentally a *cognitive* structure. . . . Traditionally, attitudes are linked to consistency theories while schemata are tied to information-processing theories. (p. 1366) Others claim that attitude theories always looked at attitudes as information-processing filters, hence they are cognitive in nature and the same as schemas (e.g., Eagly & Chaiken, 1998).
>
> Each argument has some validity, but, in our view, the debate is making a mountain out of a molehill. Neither concept needs to replace the other, and the different concepts were used mostly to examine different questions. Early research on public opinion found that American political attitudes are sorely lacking in cognitive content (i.e., Americans know little about politics), and hence

the concept of attitude did emphasize affect (as in art, people may not know much about politics, but they know what they like and dislike). Later researchers were curious about how people process political information. Newly developed theories about information processing, emphasizing cognitive properties, were used to explore information processing, using the concepts of schema and heuristics. (p. 1366)

Chapter 7

THE POLITICAL PSYCHOLOGY OF THE MEDIA IN POLITICS

Communication is central to human society, and therefore to politics. It involves the production and dissemination of political information. This occurs through the media as well as personal interactions. In this chapter, we will examine the role of the media in influencing political opinions in general, and the effects of the media during campaigns in influencing the vote in particular. First, we review several important points about communication between people in societies. Harold Lasswell (1948b) called attention to three central aspects of communication in a society. It provides surveillance of events that may affect a society, it correlates knowledge of those events among members of society, and it enables the transmission of norms and values among members of the society.

The communications media important in political communication are now very broad and include print, advertisement, broadcast, electronic, and social media, among others. It has become centrally important in political communication as technological advances made it cheap and easily disseminated. It was only in the mid-1800s that technological advances made newspapers available to the average person (Glynn, Herbst, O'Keefe, & Shapiro, 1999). Radios and movies were important sources of information during the 1930s and 1940s, and by the 1950s, televisions became an important source of political information (Glynn et al., 1999). Satellite technology in the 1980s expanded television news to real-time global news coverage. Then, of course, the Internet and social media, now familiar tools of communication, further expanded communication capabilities.

Despite these developments, people are still people, and their information processing limitations discussed in Chapter 3 remain. The use of heuristics, the fundamental attribution error, the positivity and negativity effects, the drive for balance, the desire to avoid cognitive dissonance, and the avoidance of value tradeoffs all affect the processing of information coming from the media. In addition, attitudes that people hold for a long period of time have a strong affective component, which automatically comes to mind. For example, a strong partisan Democrat is likely to react to information about Republicans with a preset negative emotion. People are also cognitively lazy. They want to be accurate and have reasonable ideas, but they also often lack the motivation to assess whether new information warrants a reconsideration of their attitudes. This pattern is reinforced because people tend to associate with other people who share their views, so exposure to contrary information or opinions is not part of everyday life (Valentino & Nardis, 2013). People are also often stubbornly unwilling to admit that perhaps they are factually wrong in regard to information they believe supports their attitudes.

This brings us to the controversial issue of selective exposure. Do people maintain their political attitudes by selectively exposing themselves to information that supports their preexisting attitudes? The evidence on this issue is mixed and complex. Looking at several studies showing contradictory patterns of selective exposure, Stroud and Muddiman (2013) argued that the studies show several important aspects of selective exposure:

> First, they tell us that selective exposure doesn't always occur. Different contexts can affect the extent to which selective exposure occurs. Interview situations may motivate different information selection patterns in comparison to political brochures. Strong arguments may motivate different selection patterns in comparison to weak arguments. Second . . . it appears that politics may inspire a greater degree of selective exposure in comparison to other topics . . . Why might politics inspire the selection of like-minded information? Politics can spark strong emotions and feelings of self-identity—just the sort of circumstances that may lead people to prefer information matching their beliefs.
>
> (pp. 7–8)

Therefore, it should not be surprising that Republicans tend to watch Fox News and Democrats watch CNN (Stroud & Muddiman, 2013). Given the information processing patterns discussed above and in Chapter 3, the desire to avoid dissonance, the use of heuristics, and cognitive laziness would all contribute to selective exposure. People do not want to experience the dissonance that contrary information would expose them to, and they are not strongly motivated to seek out massive amounts of information since they already limit their conscious use of information by using heuristics and other cognitive shortcuts. Selective exposure is not necessarily a bad thing. Some studies found that exposure to views and information contrary to their own views can have a boomerang effect, making people even more firm in their original beliefs (Stroud & Muddiman, 2013, p. 17).

Finally, information is not neutrally observed and evaluated. The influence informational items have is affected by the source, as the discussion of selective exposure would imply. Democrats are more likely to believe news from NPR, Republicans are more likely to believe Fox News. The credibility and likeability of the communicators themselves also influences the acceptability of one source over another (Valentino & Nardis, 2013). Thus, given all of these information processing factors, there are many questions and mysteries in the general issue area of how political information affects political opinions and behaviors of the average citizen.

What is the role of the media in influencing public opinion? There are different schools of thought. Thus, the study of the media is approached from different perspectives, often couched in terms of agenda setting, priming, framing, or attitude change and persuasion. We also focus on the research on social media and discuss the limited attention devoted to this important new area of research. In this chapter, we introduce the different perspectives and the research and empirical studies associated with each. As will be apparent, studies agree that the media are important, but they are often focused on different areas and variables. As a result, the literature is far from conclusive, and some of it overlaps from one category to another. Further, research is conducted in multiple disciplines, such as political science, psychology, and communications, and uses different methodologies. While many studies use the same terminology, the definitions can differ.

Before beginning our discussion of the media, we first address the prevailing assumption of media bias. The Media Research Center reports on survey research in the area of ideological research. Clearly, the public maintains the view that there is a **media bias**. A commonly held argument, particularly among conservatives, is that the media is biased in a liberal direction. In fact, in a Pew poll reported by the Center conducted in 2012, "67 percent of Americans see 'a great deal' or 'fair amount' of 'political bias' in the news media." Men (41%) were more likely than women (33%) to assert bias. Further, those who watch Fox News or listen to Fox Radio as their predominant source of campaign news were more likely to assert liberal bias in the news. But do academic studies bear this out? In a study of the 1992 election, Beck, Dalton, Greene, and Huckfeldt (2002) found no clear pattern of bias in volume of coverage. In fact, they argue that "where there was partisan favoritism in news reports and editorials, it was demonstrably small in most cases. A majority of those exposed to television received messages that were close to evenly balanced; similarly, biases in newspaper coverage were often slight" (p. 62). They also found that people who were highly partisan perceived a bias against their preferred candidate, even when none existed. While studies do not bear out partisan favoritism, media outlets exist that are known for their partisanship in agenda and editorial content. MSNBC blogs and Huffington Post are known for their liberal slant, while the Drudge Report and Fox News for their conservative one. In another study, media bias was also examined in a foreign context. Specifically, Goltz (2012) looked at Western reporting of the Armenian–Azerbaijani in western Azerbaijan called Karabakh between 1991–1994. The preponderance of media reports supported the Armenian side of the story. The author found that this was due to the Armenian propaganda machine's ability to spin stories and thus frame the conflict.

There are additional, structural types of media biases, which are different from the partisan/ideological bias accusations. The media can engage in **gatekeeping**, wherein the editors or program managers decide which stories will be told. This means that some stories are not reported. This can lead to a bias in favor of the status quo as new perspectives and issues are left unreported. Another type of bias is **coverage bias**, which refers to how much time or space is devoted to a particular story. Fewer lines in a newspaper article, and placement on page 12, will result in less attention to the story. Then there is **statement bias** wherein a member of the media inserts his or her own views in the reporting of a story (D'Alessio & Allen, 2000;

Denton & Kuypers, 2008). In addition, the news media is often accused of negative reporting, particularly by Presidents and presidential candidates. However, Groeling and Kernell (1998) found that negative coverage is a pattern in presidential elections, but that negative reporting coincides with increases in negative polls about the candidates.

AGENDA SETTING

Many analysts agree with Cohen (1963), who wrote, "The press may not be successful much of the time in telling people what to think, but it is stunningly successful in telling its readers what to think about" (p. 13). People are limited in how much time and attention they can or wish to devote to politics. They rely upon the media to tell them which issues need attention and in what form. This is referred to as **agenda setting**. Studies examined the amount of reporting issues received and find strong correlations between quantity of coverage and the importance attributed to issues by the public (McCombs & Shaw, 1972). Other studies looked at the order in which issues are covered by the press and regarded as important by the public and found that the press reporting comes first, followed by public perceptions of an issue's importance (Glynn et al., 1999). Miller (2007), however, argued that content is paid attention to if it invokes negative emotions. Kim and McCombs (2007) maintained that attributes in the news, whether positive or negative, affect views of gubernatorial and U.S. Senate candidates. Those attributes that received the most attention in the media had more impact on those who were heavy readers of newspapers.

PRIMING

Priming is another psychological concept. As Hobert and Tchernev (2013) noted, "Intricately connected to the process of salience transfer (from the media to the public) detailed in agenda setting theory is the subsequent process of political media priming effects." According to Dragojlovic (2011) "priming effects occur when the mention of a specific consideration in one context (the prime) increases the *accessibility* of that consideration, leading to an increase in the use of that trait later in later evaluations of a social target" (p. 991). Because political issues are many in number and extraordinarily complex, people need help in deciding which issues are important and which aspects of those issues need to be attended to. The news media deliver that guidance by priming; that is, pointing out to the public which elements of which issues are important—a context for understanding (Glynn et al., 1999; Iyengar & Kinder, 1987; Iyengar, Peters & Kinder, 1982). For example, when primed by the media on an issue such as rising gas prices, individuals judge President Obama on how well they think he kept rising prices at bay. How does this work? As Miller and Krosnick (1996) explained, when making day-to-day decisions, people tend to **satisfice**, that is, they make a decision that is adequate rather than optimally based upon full consideration of all relevant information. They also do this when making political judgments.

Using the example of how people rated presidential performance, those authors elaborated:

> To decide how well the president is doing his job, a person could evaluate how well he has been handling all issues on which he has been working. This would be a very tough task, however, because presidents typically address a great many issues in very short periods of time. In his first year in office, for example, President Clinton worked on a number of issues, including reform of the U.S. health care system, staffing of the U.S. military, abortion laws, reducing the deficit, appointments to his Cabinet, U.S. involvement in Somalia, the North American Free Trade Agreement, Supreme Court appointments, and more. A careful evaluator could have graded his handling of each of these issues and then averaged those grades together into an overall assessment. Most Americans, however, probably had neither the information nor the motivation to do such labor-intensive thinking. Instead, they probably satisficed his handling of just a few issues.
>
> (p. 260)

Again, the media plays an important role in the priming process because they determine which issues come to the forefront. Therefore, to use another of the authors' examples, if the media pays attention to the economy, and people think about this issue, then the economy will probably become a consideration when evaluating presidential performance. What is the specific impact of any media story? In other words, does one story about an issue prime another issue? Those authors believe that, in related issues, this may occur. In their view, if policies are viewed as related, coverage of one will prime the other. For example, affirmative action and school busing (the former priming the latter) are viewed as related because both could be seen as related to improving the lives of minorities. However, news coverage of affirmative action probably would not prime inflation.

The existence of priming is supported by several experimental studies (see Druckman, 2004; Iyengar, 1991; Iyengar & Kinder, 1987; Iyengar, Peters, & Kinder, 1982; Iyengar, Peters, Kinder, & Krosnick, 1984). Krosnick and Kinder (1990), for example, found that the decline in the popularity of President Reagan was a result of two elements: (1) the media's newfound fascination with covert aid to the Contras and (2) the public's opposition to intervention in Central America. In their look at priming and presidential evaluations through several case studies (President Bush and the Gulf War and the 1992 election, Ronald Reagan and Iran–Contra), Miller and Krosnick (1996) argued that what the media decides to cover does impact the standards by which people evaluate the president. Moreover, media coverage can affect the cognitive complexity of the public's evaluation of issues. Milburn and McGrail (1992) found that the effect of vivid images in news coverage was a reduction of recall of information among viewers, as well as a reduction in cognitive complexity in their discussions of the issues involved. Having noted the importance of the media in priming people to attend to particular issues, some caveats must necessarily be added. First, the impact of the media is, not surprisingly, strongest on those who have little independent interest in politics, who are weakly attached to a party, and who are less educated (Iyengar & Kinder, 1987). In addition, personal involvement with an issue affects its salience, and, therefore, people for whom an issue is personally salient will attend to that issue, regardless of the amount of media coverage. Iyengar and Kinder (1987), for example, found in their experiments that subjects who were unemployed attended to media stories about employment more than those who were employed during a period of low unemployment, but that even people who were employed attended to unemployment stories during periods of higher unemployment. They concluded that employment was of concern only to the unemployed during periods of low unemployment, but that everyone felt a stronger personal stake in employment issues during periods of higher unemployment.

Another way of examining priming is through nonexperimental studies. For example, using content analysis of media campaign coverage and exit polling of the U.S. Senate race in Minnesota in 2000, Druckman (2004) found the campaign primed those voters who were exposed and focused so that they based their decisions of the candidate in the issues and images prevalent in the campaign. In a more recent study, Dragojlovic (2011) examined priming, the Obama effect, and evaluations by Canadians of the United States. The "Obama effect" refers to President Barack Obama's popularity with foreign audiences. In particular, the study asked whether this affect was the result of his effective management of high-level diplomacy or foreign policy changes that in turn influenced foreign perceptions of the United States. After the 2008 election, there was an increase in the salience of his image in the Canadian media and in coverage of the United States beginning in 2007 regarding the election. Because of the increase in coverage, there was a high degree of awareness of U.S. policy and frequent exposure to coverage mentioning Obama. Priming resulted in a more positive opinion of the United States. Pardos-Prado, Lancee, and Sagarzazu (2014) found that apprehension over immigration fostered stronger identification with a center-right party owning the issue, and in particular when primed by the media. Focusing on a foreign context, Bilali and Vollhardt (2013) investigated the role of priming in the aftermath of genocide in Rwanda as it related to Radio La Benevolencija's fictional radio drama Musekeweya. The drama aims to thwart violence and instead promote reconciliation. The Rwandan participants in the study listened to an audio-delivered questionnaire that was either recorded in the voice of a main character from Musekeweya or from an unknown person. Those who were primed by the main character were less distrustful of the out-group and exemplified more historical perspective-taking and less competitive victimhood.

The literature also distinguishes between explicit and implicit psychological processes. Explicit processes are those that are accessible and are able to be self-reported while those that are implicit are "expressed in behavior, but are generally unavailable to consciousness, and so are not readily measured by surveys or questionnaires" (Weinberger & Westen, 2008). Studies focused on implicit processes often address subliminal stimulation (see for example, Dijksterhuis, Aarts, & Smith, 2005; Westen, 1998). For instance, in two experiments, Weinberger and Westen (2008) examined subliminal messages via the Web and the influence on evaluations of politicians. The second experiment examined whether subliminal presentations of one known political figure (President Clinton) could affect evaluations of another candidate (Governor Gray Davis). Negative evaluations as opposed to positive evaluations were easier to influence and that regardless of subliminal messaging, positive evaluations of Clinton resulted in positive evaluations of Davis. The same held true of low evaluations. However, the meaning of the findings was not conclusive. In the second study, they focused in on this ambiguity. Those that held strongly held attitudes with regard to party and ideology were less influenced by being showed a photograph of Clinton and with regard to views of Davis, as opposed to swing voters, who were highly influenced.

FRAMING

Another area of research is framing, which refers to when the media not only provides the content but also "how to understand and think about it" (Slothuus, 2008). Put another way, framing influences the understanding of the issue and also the evaluation of it. Another important aspect regarding issue framing, and what the media focuses on, concerns the presentation of an issue, or what is often referred to as spin. How an issue is reported on can make a difference. Most political issues have multiple elements, but the media may focus on only one or two.

There are different schools of thought on framing (Slothuus, 2008). Some such as Kinder and Nelson (2005) suggested that framing depends on the individual and attention to the issue. In other words, the preexisting views are made more accessible. This is referred to as the accessibility model (Slothuus, 2008). Another, the importance change model, proposed that frames make some considerations more important than others (Slothuus, 2008). For example, Nelson, Clawson and Oxley (1997) presented an example in a study of local television news outlets and a rally by the Ku Klux Klan in Ohio. Among their findings, media framing influenced the opinions of individuals toward the KKK. Specifically, if the media presented the story as having implications for free speech, individuals were more tolerant of the KKK. However, they had less tolerance for the KKK if the media framed the rally as one that may bring about a clash between two angry groups. Those elements then receive attention, and the resulting debate regarding moral and/or policy implications revolves around those elements, rather than others. Finally, those such as Zaller (1992) maintain that new issues are brought to the forefront and, therefore, can influence thinking. This is referred to as the content change model (Slothuus, 2008).

In a related argument, Patterson (1993) noted that journalists operate with different schemas than those used by voters, which in turn produces a particular pattern in framing issues and candidates during campaigns; in particular, he argued, journalists' dominant schema "is structured around the notion that politics is a strategic game" (p. 57), rather than competing ideas about issues, appropriate policies, and matters of principle. The public, on the other hand, functioned with a schema that views politics as an arena in which policies are discussed and in which leaders are selected who will attempt to implement particular policies. These game and governance schemas interact, and voters and journalists are cognizant of each other's perspective, but Patterson (1993) contended that because of the press game schema, the focus of the news buries and distorts the substance of the information conveyed to the public during a campaign.

Most of the literature on framing cites some or multiple perspectives in the literature either building on the schools of thought or presenting it as background in a literature review. The literature on framing is robust and is replete with different issues and approaches. Some studies are highlighted below.

Entman (1993) examined framing with an example from the Cold War. During that time, civil wars in other societies were discussed in the American media in terms of the implications for alliances with either the United States or the Soviet Union, rather than in terms of the domestic issues in those societies that led up to civil war. Bayulgen and Arbatli (2013) assessed U.S. newspaper reporting related to the 2008 Russia-Georgia war. The authors concluded that U.S. newspaper framing was anti-Russia. Further, with an increase in exposure to media reports finding fault with Russia there was an increased likelihood of blame being focused on Russia. In an other study, Woods (2011) applied framing to perceptions of threat regarding terrorism. The author exposed participants to articles and found that the term terrorism did not invoke a threat response, however, the threat was more pronounced when it specifically came from radical Islamist groups as opposed to homegrown terrorists and when nuclear versus other technology was mentioned. Another article by Gulati (2011) focused on coverage of human trafficking by the *New York Times* and *Washington Post* between the years 1980–2006. Interestingly, they found that the media coverage consisted mostly of official sources and that the framing, therefore, paralleled the same view. In turn, policymakers legitimized their views and alternative views were marginalized. The exception was investigative journalists that reported alternative views. In a study of the nightly news and framing the Iraq War, Coe (2013) maintained that the presentation of rationales regarding the war only had some impact on attitudes regarding U.S. military action. In another approach, Heim (2013) examined the 2008 Democratic Presidential nomination race prior to the Iowa caucus. The author analyzed blogs, major news sources, and candidate press releases. In the case of Hillary Clinton, the author found that journalists and her campaign had a "second-level intermedia agenda setting effect" (p. 511). Additionally, bloggers followed the lead from journalists and "were unable to seize control of the campaign narrative from other actors" (p. 511).

In his study, Slothuus (2008) investigated the role of frame mediation. Specifically, he looked at what individual-level factors moderated issue framing effects and what mediated issue framing effects. He found that "framing effects on opinion are mediated not only through a process of changing cognitive importance of a receiver's issue-relevant considerations" as indicated in the literature, "but also through a process of altering the content of issue-relevant considerations" (p. 2). This, he argued, was a "two-process model." In another study focused on the identity of the messenger, Schatz and Levine (2010) examined framing with regard to U.S. public diplomacy and Central Asia. They found that the identity of the messenger had an impact. Specifically, they discovered that a quote attributed to President George Bush invoked lower opinions of the United States, rather than the same quote attributed to an unnamed U.S. Ambassador, an ordinary American, or no one.

In other work on elite framing, Druckman and Holmes (2004) examined elite framing, specifically, President G. W. Bush's 2002 State of the Union address. Prior to the address, Bush was encountering a flailing economy but high approval ratings on his handling of security (86%). They found in their analysis that he framed the address in terms of terrorism/homeland security (49%) and only 10% on the economy. In another study, Druckman, Jacobs, and Ostermeier (2004) found that President Nixon would focus framing of domestic issues based on public support.

Recent work on framing looks at competitive frames. Typically, people are exposed to more than one frame regarding candidates or issues. When there are **competitive frames**, which is likely to win? Initially, it was argued that the frames would cancel each other out, and people would rely on their values when deciding what to think. Sniderman and Theriault (2004) found that when people were exposed to free speech frames and public safety frames in the context of a hate group demonstration, they chose the position consistent with their values. They argued that "competing frames make alternative positions equally accessible, which increases the likelihood that people will be able to identify and choose the side that is consistent with their ideological values" (Klar, Robison, & Druckman, 2013, p. 180). However, Druckman and Chong (2007) postulated that frames may differ in strength and that stronger frames will dominate when there are competitive frames. Strength is determined by the availability of the frame (that is, the perceiver's ability to see a connection between the frame and the issue); the accessibility of the frame (that is, "the frame must actually come to mind as a consideration when thinking about the topic"); and the applicability of the frame (that is, the "individual must view the consideration as compelling or persuasive for it to be considered strong") (Klar et al., 2013, p. 180).

Other authors extended research to foreign media, although this seems to be an area with a need for further scholarship. One such study by Rane and Ewart (2012) studied Australian television news and the tenth anniversary of September 11, 2001. The found that the news media had shifted from conflating terrorism with Muslims and Islam. Instead, the news focused on U.S.-Australian relations, reconciliation, and that the tenth anniversary coverage was presented with the frames of reconciliation. As the authors elaborated, "The dominant frame across the five free-to-air Australian television news broadcasts was commemoration through the memorials and ceremonies taking place both in the USA and Australia for which the central focus was the remembrance of the victims. Notably absent from the coverage was any reference to Islam or Muslims in terms of responsibility for the 9/11 attacks" (p. 320).

What about the role of emotions in framing? Gross (2008) argued that investigating the role of emotion had received limited attention in the literature and has since examined emotions in a specific context or issue (see for example, Gross & D'Ambrosio, 2004; Kinder & Sanders, 1990). Gross looked at the general rhetorical devices of episodic and thematic framing applicable to a range of issues where there are "ways of telling a story to make it more understandable, accessible and compelling to the audience" (p. 170). There are differences between the type of frames: episodic provides an example, case study, or event-oriented report on an issue and thematic takes an issue and puts it into a greater context. Building on the work of Iyengar (1991), Gross (2008) examined "how the use of episodic and thematic framing in a persuasive message affects emotional response and how these emotions might help us understand the link between these frames and policy views" in the case of mandatory minimum sentencing (p. 170). The author concluded that there were both cognitive and affective routes, and episodic framing influences the emotional response. The influence of the frame depended on the ability to bring about sympathy and pity and individuals use these emotions to form opinions. Frames can actually minimize attitudinal change in the case of individual as opposed to societal matters, yet they can also increase persuasion in the case of an individual if the story is persuasive enough to elicit "intense emotional reactions" (p. 184).

THE ATTITUDE CHANGE AND PERSUASION

If the media influences what people think about, does it also influence how they think, that is, their attitudes toward an issue or a political candidate? Many of the aforementioned studies take on the study of attitudes; however, it warrants further attention here due to the focus and attention this question receives and the multiple perspectives that exist on attitude change.

Related is the body of research examining the role of **persuasion** and attitude change of the media. Fishbein and Ajzen (1972) noted the lack of coherence in the early literature. Petty and Cacioppo (1986) also argued that while there were multiple studies conducted on the role of persuasion, "there was surprisingly little agreement concerning if, when, and how the traditional source, message, recipient and channel variables . . . affected attitude change" (p. 125). Thus, research then focused on organizing and framing the literature. In doing so, Petty and Cacioppo (1986) proposed the **Elaboration Likelihood Model (ELM)** that integrated the disparate approaches. The ELM focuses on cognition and rests upon the concept of the elaboration likelihood continuum. The continuum is "defined by how motivated and able people are to assess the merits of a person, issue or a position (i.e., the attitude object). The more motivated and able people are to assess the central merits of the attitude object, the more likely they are to effortfully scrutinize all available object-relevant information" (Petty & Wegener, 1998, pp. 327–328). The ELM purports there are two routes to attitude change through persuasion: a central route and peripheral route. The central route is when an individual has "careful and thoughtful consideration of the true merits of the information presented in support of an advocacy" (p. 125). In this route, the elaboration likelihood is high. People arrive at a decision through a reasoned and informed thought process. The peripheral route is different in that it results from an attractive cue without scrutiny. The higher a person goes along the elaboration continuum, the more central route processes are important. Conversely, the farther down one goes along the continuum, the less important central route processes become. The ELM shows that attitude change varies depending on the mental effort put into considering the attitude object. The attitudes that result through the peripheral route tend to be weaker than those formed through the central route (Petty & Wegener, 1998). Related research focused on mood and messaging. Taking these into account, Wegener and Petty (1994) offered the **Hedonic Contingency Model**, which offered distinctions between happy and sad moods. If an individual is in a sad mood, they pay little attention to information. The reverse is true for those in a happy mood. Wegener, Petty and Smith (1995) tested this proposition and found that when individuals had an expectation of happiness from a message, those in a happy mood paid more careful attention. Handley, Lassiter, Nickell and Herchenroeder (2004) maintained that mood is automatic and found support for their hypothesis by studying individuals who were brought into happy, sad, and neutral moods and asking them to rank their inclinations for future activities. Summarizing the dominant persuasion models in the literature, Petty and Wegener (1998) noted that

> These models placed greater focus on the moderation and media-
> tion of attitude change effects and explained how the same variable
> (e.g., source credibility, mood) could have different effects on attitude
> change in different situations, and how a given variable could produce
> the same persuasion outcome by different processes in different situ-
> ations. A key idea in these new frameworks was that some processes
> of attitude change required relatively high amounts of mental effort,
> whereas other processes of persuasion required relatively little mental
> effort.
>
> (p. 3)

Another related model of persuasion is the **Heuristic-Systematic Model (HSM)** (Chaiken, 1980; 1987; Chen & Chaiken, 1999). Systematic informa-tion processing focuses on the information provided in a comprehensive manner. This is essentially the same as the ELM's concept of the central route. Heuristic information processing involves the use of heuristics which are "easily processed judgment relevant cues . . . rather than individualistic or particularistic judgment-relevant information" (Chen & Chaiken, 1999, p. 76). As was noted in Chapter 3, people often use heuristics to reach judg-ments because they involve less cognitive effort than a careful assessment of information. The HSM takes this a step further through the *sufficiency principle*, which holds that people attempt to maintain a balance between their desire to expend as little cognitive effort as possible and their desire to be accurate in their judgments. If a person uses heuristics to evaluate a message, which are low-effort cognitive devices, but is not confident that they have made a judgment that is as correct or accurate as they would like, the person will engage in systematic information processing (Chen & Chai-ken, 1999). For example, take a person who is concerned about wildlife and is interested in the issue of whether the introduction of a wolf population in the Rockies would restore a natural balance among species or cause a new imbalance, particularly a decline in the size of the elk population, a favorite wolf meal. If a wildlife biologist informs that person that there is a decline in the elk population because of habitat loss, the person can use a heuristic to evaluate the message (wildlife biologists are experts; experts are usually correct). However, if the same person concerned with wildlife is informed by a hunter advocacy group that the decline in the elk population is because of wolves, and that wolves should therefore be killed off, the person would engage in systematic information processing because he or she would be concerned about establishing an accurate position on the issue. Another approach is illustrated by the **Receive-Accept-Sample (RAS)** model (Zaller, 1992). Zaller (1992) argued that individuals have competing opinions on issues. The view that prevails results from what is on one's mind at the time.

If attitude persuasion occurs, how long does it last? Research indicates that while persuasion causes attitude change, it is not on a long-term basis. Many studies were conducted that sought to find out under what conditions attitude change could be made less than fleeting (Hill, Lo, Vavreck, & Zaller, 2013). Research focused on multiple messages, source credibility, nature of the voice of the persuasive message and peer pressure (see, for example, Cook & Insko, 1968; Kelman & Hovland, 1953; Johnson & Watkins, 1971; Schopler, Gruder, Miller, & Rousseau, 1968). However, according to Hill et al. (2013), "Often these manipulations worked as expected to increase duration of change, but their strength and obtrusiveness underscore the difficulty of achieving lasting opinion change under ordinary circumstances" (p. 523). As the authors further explained:

> Laboratory studies show that persuasive communication tends to produce durable opinion change when subjects have been induced to engage in effortful processing. But most evidence also indicates that relatively few people habitually engage in effortful processing. Hence, we should expect that, under the uninvolving conditions of mass persuasion, some persuasive effects will be durable, but most will be short-lived. Field studies show rapid decay in the effects of mass communication but do not estimate the rate of decay or determine whether any long-term change occurs.
>
> (p. 527)

Therefore, the authors investigated the rate of decay and focused on advertising on broadcast television for candidates running for national and subnational office. They found that decay acts quickly because of memory-based processing. Alternatively, those who stored information in their long-term memory experienced a slower decay. They further found that "short-lived attitude change affects behavior in the period before it has decayed" (p. 541) and, interestingly, that decay effects occur at a more rapid pace in races other than the presidential one.

PERSUASION AND POLITICAL CAMPAIGNS

Early studies of the effects of the media in political campaigns in the 1940s and 1950s (Lazarsfeld, Berelson, & Gaudet, 1944; Berelson, Lazarsfeld, & McPhee, 1954) found that partisanship was so solid for so many people that the media's effect on their attitudes was much less than anticipated. Instead, people attended to information in the media that supported their preexisting preferences. Moreover, people who did not have candidate preferences early in the campaign tended to be influenced more by family and friends than by the media. Later studies, reflecting societal changes, such as the advent of television, the general weakening of partisanship, and the diminished importance of extended families and communities as important influences on political attitudes, argued that media had a stronger impact on the content and complexity of public attitudes (Milburn, 1991). People are influenced by opinions expressed by reporters, of which there are more now than in the past, by experts, and by popular presidents. Glynn et al. (1999) summarized the current perspective on media influence as follows:

> Most theories of media influence today generate from a view of audiences being largely active players in choosing what they hear, watch, or read, and responding accordingly. However, we cannot reject the notion that at times people are quite passive or reactive in attending to media—or in everyday conversations for that matter, simply letting words or images wash over them, leaving themselves more open to influence or manipulation. This juxtaposition of more active versus more passive possibilities for audience involvement with media has led many researchers to look at media effects on public opinion as a more *interactive* or *transactional* process. The nature of the relationship between audiences and media likely changes and shifts across different personal traits, moods, contexts, and situations.
>
> (p. 407)

In a democracy such as the United States, one of the most important times in which the media may influence public opinion is during campaigns. Candidates use the media as part of their campaign strategy to deliver their campaign message, and the media also report on the candidates, issues, and campaign as an independent observer. In addition, the media cover candidate debates. The media are also widely criticized for providing only lightweight coverage of issues during elections, focusing instead on poll standings of candidates, character issues, and campaign gaffes, rather than on core issues regarding policy positions and past performance in office (Ansolabehere, Behr, & Iyengar, 1993; Mayer, 1996; Sabato, 1991).

What about the effect of negative campaigning on attitudes? **Negative campaign ads** are ads in which one candidate criticizes another candidate by name (Ridout & Franz, 2011; Krupnikov & Easter, 2013). In a positive ad the candidate promotes him or herself. This does not mean that only negative ads are associated with negative emotions. Positive ads can provoke anger or fear. An example is Republican presidential candidate Mitt Romney's 2007 ads in which he promises to protect "freedom loving" Americans from terrorists attempting to build a worldwide "jihadist caliphate" (Ridout & Franz, 2011, p. 79). This is a scary prospect, but Romney does not mention his opponent Barack Obama, so it is considered a positive ad. Ads that criticize the opponent while praising the candidate are called contrast ads (Krupnikov & Easter, 2013). As far as the effects of negative ads, the results are mixed. Some have argued that negative campaigning decreases voter turnout. This may be because voters feel ineffective when they are exposed to negativity. Another possibility is that negative ads produce a negative response to the candidate being criticized, but also a boomerang of negativity toward the candidate who sponsored the negative ad to begin with (Krupnikov & Easter, 2013). Others demonstrated that negative ads can mobilize voters. Some possible explanations are that negative ads provide more useful information than positive ads, or that people are tuned in more to negative information than positive information, and therefore are able to evaluate candidates quickly and confidently when exposed to negative information (Krupnikov & Easter, 2013). Krupnikov (2011) argued that the timing of negative ads may explain the mixed results. When they occur early in the election before voters have decided on the candidate they prefer, negative ads may be informative and help them make a choice. When they occur after the voter has decided, they may simply be discouraging, causing the voter to decide not to vote.

In other studies, negative messages from the sources were shown to be effective, while in others they were not (Carraro & Castelli, 2010). Carraro and Castelli (2010) argued that mixed findings were due to a number of factors, including murky definitions of negative campaigns and differences in evaluated dimensions and level of measurement. Thus, in their three studies, the authors investigated the impact of negative campaigning on attitudes, taking into account these three dimensions. In Study 1 (but not 2), they found that "not all negative messages led to comparable effects" (p. 626). In particular voters were inclined to have more negative evaluations of a candidate when personal features (person-based evaluations) of the other candidate were attacked as opposed to ideology or political programs. The authors also found that in the evaluation of interpersonal qualities, negative person-based messages dampened evaluations and in particular if the member was part of the in-group. The messages had much less effect on evaluation of power and competence. They further found a discrepancy between explicit and implicit responses. As they explain, "indeed participants expressed overt disliking toward the politician who relied on negative evaluations, but they were nonetheless forced to follow him in the spontaneous conformity task. This measure likely captures the tendency to consider the candidate as a reliable and powerful individual who is focused on his goals and is actively engaged in pursuing them. As a consequence, participants were more likely to follow his advice" (p. 637). Participants in the study also felt less interpersonal closeness with candidates who used negative messages. Even so, conformity emerged. Finally, in Study 3, the researchers found that individuals follow competent as opposed to warm politicians.

SOCIAL MEDIA

In the media and political context literature, social media is not as heavily examined as other types of mainstream media. Because of its importance, the literature to date warrants a separate discussion. Social media broadens the exposure of the message and increases "the speed, with networks of friends and associates sharing the information instantly" (Papic & Noonan, 2011). With Facebook, individuals are able to make posts to their specific page that can then be seen immediately by those friends in their network and can also be searched publicly. With Twitter, individuals can convey short 140-character messages in the form of tweets. With YouTube, individuals are able to upload videos in the hopes that they may go viral, adding to their further dissemination. Unlike text messaging, social media can spread messages in a rapid manner as the message can be transferred to individuals outside of one's own social network. With this new means of media communication proliferating throughout the world, the news media has generated some momentum for phrases like "Twitter Revolution" and "Facebook Revolution" to convey the idea that social media has had a major impact on how we communicate. Research also demonstrates that both Facebook and Twitter are particularly important forms of media and news for younger generations (Enjolras, Steen-Johnsen, & Wollebæk, 2012).

How is social media being used in a political context? Social media is used in an organizing capacity for protests, as will be seen in the chapter on social movements. Not only do information cascades have an informational effect, they can also have a motivational effect in that social media publicize people's decisions to join a group or sign up for an event (Enjolras, Steen-Johnsen, & Wollebæk, 2012). Social media is also tool to rapidly spread protest information, getting individuals out of their houses and into the streets (Valenzuela, 2013). Tufekci and Wilson (2012) focused on the Tahrir Square protests and found that individuals received protest information from electronic media like Facebook, Twitter, and other Internet blogs, in addition to print media. Outside of protests, in a recent study, Groshek and Al-Rawi (2013) investigated the framing of social media with regard to the 2012 presidential election campaign. In particular, they examined social units from Facebook and Twitter to determine prevailing issues and themes. They found that on opposing Facebook pages and nonpartisan election Twitter feeds, the presidential candidates were not framed in an overly critical manner. These were similar to what is found in mainstream media. In their study of live tweets during the 2012 Republican Primary, Hawthorne, Houston and McKinney (2013) found that the views of elites spread faster than nonelites.

Social media is now widely used in political campaigns. Candidates now have their own websites (the first was Senator Dianne Feinstein's 1994 website) containing their issue positions, campaign schedules, biographies, and contact information (Edgerly, Bode, Kim, & Shah, 2013). The websites are also quite happy to take your donation. The early websites were basically electronic brochures and were not updated or very informational (Edgerly et al., 2013). As the political world became more familiar with the Internet, the websites changed and campaigns became more adept at using social media to influence voters. Campaigns use Facebook, YouTube, and Twitter. In the 2006 election, Facebook created the "Election Pulse 2006" feature, which candidates used to create profiles. It enabled voters to learn about different candidates, and it also let them know when their Facebook friends supported their candidate preference, too (Edgerly et al., 2013). In the years since 2006, candidates have developed Facebook pages that "allow campaigns the ability to post a variety of information (e.g., website links, YouTube videos, announcements, and photos)" (Edgerly et al., 2013, p. 83). However, Bronstein (2013) looked at the Facebook pages of candidates in the 2012 election three months before the election and found that candidates used emotional and motivational appeals; they revealed very little about their personal lives and did not address controversial issues. The candidates used Facebook to raise money and for mobilization. They encouraged affective allegiances between them and the posters. These political watchers commented and produced "likes" and they were influenced by the persuasion of the posts.

More generally, campaign practices have adapted to the digital age. They can now specifically target particular voters with information they think will be important for those potential voters. For example, on the day one of this book's authors was writing this particular section of the book, she received e-mails from the Democratic National Headquarters (three of them), Barack Obama, Rich Cowan (not sure who he is, but he knows me by my first name), Bill Foster (not sure who he is either), and Debbie Wasserman Schultz, all with information and requests for action the Democratic Party thinks she would want to receive. (Joe Biden's e-mail came yesterday.) This kind of communication helps voters feel that they can interact with political candidates. It also reflects the tendency to sustain engagement with potential voters rather than simply contact them close to Election Day (Edgerly et al., 2013, p. 86). The e-mails sent to this author come every day, from a variety of sources, all providing information about current issues, who in Congress is supporting or opposing what, what the President needs in terms of political support, asking for money, or reporting the results of recent polls so that the author recipient can gauge the pulse of the nation.

Clearly the study of how social media is used in the political context is receiving attention. The actual persuasion and attitude change from social media is an emerging area of interest with the potential for more studies.

CONCLUSION

This chapter covered a number of approaches to studying the media. The major approaches included agenda setting, priming, framing, and attitudes. We also addressed the limited literature on social media effects. The literature on the media continues to evolve, contributing to more clarity regarding its impact.

Topics, Theories/Explanations, and Cases Covered in Chapter 7

Topics	Theories/Explanations	Cases
Media	Agenda Setting	Multiple
	Priming	Multiple
	Framing	Multiple
	Attitudes and Persuasion	Multiple
	Social Media	Multiple

Key Terms

agenda setting

attitudes

competitive frames

framing

media bias

persuasion

priming

satisfice

Suggestions for Further Reading

Druckman, J.N. (2011). What's it all about? Framing in political science. In G. Keren (Ed.), *Perspectives on framing* (pp. 279–302). New York: Psychology Press.

Giles, D. (2010). *Psychology of the media*. London: Palgrave Macmillan.

Hobert, R.L., & Tchernev, J.M. (2013). Media influence as persuasion. In J.P. Dillar & L. Shen (Eds.), *The SAGE handbook of persuasion: Developments in theory and practice* (2nd ed., pp. 36–52). Thousand Oaks, CA: Sage.

van Dijck, J. (2013). *The culture of connectivity: A critical history of social media*. Oxford: Oxford University Press.

Wallace, P. (2006). *The psychology of the Internet*. Cambridge: Cambridge University Press.

Chapter 8

THE POLITICAL PSYCHOLOGY OF RACE

Racial prejudice and discrimination have been considered the "great American dilemma" (Myrdal, 1944) for decades. Yet on November 4, 2008, Americans elected the first African American to the office of the President of the United States of America, Barack Obama. Racism was responsible for one of the most repressive regimes in modern history—the apartheid government of South Africa—yet South Africa had its first Black president in 1994, Nelson Mandela. Understanding racial divisions and conflicts requires us to go beyond explanations that rely upon competition for resources as causes of these conflicts. From the political psychological perspective, we can understand the intransigence of group conflict as the result of the continual human drive to form in-groups and out-groups and to compare one's group with others. Political psychology also enables us to understand how racial (and ethnic) groups can live together harmoniously for years, then erupt in horrific internecine violence. Identities can be manipulated by leaders, and emotions can rise to extremes of hatred and fear, when people are convinced by leaders and by rumors that their group is threatened by others. Political psychology also turns our attention to the ways in which issues can be framed to produce particular anxieties in the minds of citizens. Stereotypes can be subtly or openly manipulated to produce stereotype-driven behaviors and attitudes.

Chapters 8 and 9 look at the underlying causes of political conflicts produced by racism and ethnocentrism. We begin with some concepts and definitions—some introduced in earlier chapters, others new—that enable us to have a common understanding of the perceptions and behaviors involved in race and ethnicity. These chapters explore most of the Political Being's personality, attitudes, cognition, emotions, and identities in relation to *us* (in-groups) and *them* (out-groups). In this chapter, we look at race and politics in the United States, Brazil, and South Africa. In the next, we examine cases of ethnic conflict, including Nigeria, Bosnia, and Guatemala, and we look at the most horrific form of inter-group violence, genocide.

Race and ethnicity are social constructs, not scientific distinctions. George Fredrickson (1999) noted:

> Throughout its history, the United States has been inhabited by a variety of interacting racial or ethnic groups. In addition to the obvious "color line" structuring relationships between dominant

Whites and lower-status Blacks, Indians and Asians, there have at times been important social distinctions among those of White or European ancestry. Today we think of the differences between white Anglo-Saxon Protestants and Irish, Italian, Polish, Jewish Americans as purely cultural or religious, but in earlier times, these groups were sometimes through of as "races" or "subraces"—people possessing innate or inborn characteristics and capabilities that affected their fitness for American citizenship.

It can therefore be misleading to make a sharp distinction between race and ethnicity when considering intergroup relations . . . Ethnicity is "racialized" whenever distinctive group characteristics, however defined or explained, are used as the basis for status of hierarchy of groups who are thought to differ in ancestry or descent.

(p. 23)

Having set forth this caution, we look at race in this chapter and ethnicity in Chapter 9 only as reflections of their social construction in real situations. In other words, when societies consider race to be race rather than ethnicity, so do we, in order to reflect the language used in these societies and the studies published about them.

This chapter is concerned with race because group differentiations, in terms of race, are so frequently associated with political inequalities. These patterns of political activity stem from stereotyping of, and prejudice toward, groups of different race (or ethnicity). What is **prejudice**? It is a commonly used term, but there are many definitions. Reviewing various interpretations of prejudice, Sniderman, Piazza, and Harvey (1998) note four components of prejudice that are generally agreed upon in the literature: a response to group members based on their membership in the group; a negative evaluative orientation toward a group and consequently and aversion to group members; an attribution of negative characteristics toward a group and its members that is incorrect; and, finally, consistency in the negative orientation toward the group and its members.

Prejudice is closely associated with a concept we introduced in Chapter 3: a **stereotype**, which we defined as "a set of beliefs about the personal attributes of a group of people" (Duckitt, 1994, p. 8). Stereotypes and prejudices that produce discriminatory behavior are filled with negative evaluations of the group and its members. Rothbart and Johns (1993) note that stereotypes have descriptive and evaluative components. The problem, they argue, "is that the evaluative component, which is a judgment that the observer makes about the group, is not perceived as a judgment *about* the group, but as an attribute *of* the group itself" (p. 40). This is called the **phenomenal absolutism error.** For example, a group that does not spend a great deal of money can be thought of as thrifty or stingy. Either characterization is an evaluation of a behavior, but that evaluation comes to be considered a characteristic of the group, not an evaluation or one of several possible evaluations of the behavior noticed. In a negative stereotype, a group whose members do not spend much money may be considered inherently stingy people. The use of prejudices and preexisting beliefs in evaluation of others also occurs in ambiguous situations, which is known as the **ultimate attribution error** (Pettigrew, 1979).

EXPLAINING RACISM AND ETHNOCENTRISM

Why do people stereotype others and engage in discriminatory behavior? One of the oldest explanations for prejudice and discrimination is **realistic conflict theory** (Bobo, 1983). According to this explanation, discrimination is a result of competition over scarce resources such as jobs, housing, and good schools. Thus, whenever such commodities are in short supply, the demand for them increases. Additionally, research suggests that as competition becomes more severe, those involved tend to view the other in increasingly negative terms (White, 1977). For example, members of groups tend to solidify boundaries that exist between them, derogate the other group, and believe that their own group is superior. One of the earliest investigations of realistic conflict theory was conducted by Sherif, Harvey, White, Hood, and Sherif (1961). That study involved dividing a group of 11-year-old boys, who were attending a summer camp, into two groups. For one week, the boys in each group lived together, ate together, played together, and generally engaged in enjoyable activities. Then, the boys in both groups were told that they would be engaging in a number of competitions, the winners of which would receive valuable prizes (e.g., trophies). Over the next two weeks, as the boys competed with another, tensions escalated. They taunted each other, attacked one another's cabins, overturned beds, and destroyed some of the others' personal belongings. In only two short weeks, the boys, who were friends before the study, came to behave in hostile ways toward one another, as a result of the competition.

In an attempt to restore the boys' friendships, Sherif and his colleagues (1961) created a series of *superordinate* goals—ones that both groups desired and that required the cooperation of both groups to achieve. When their water supply was severely reduced (as a consequence of being sabotaged by the researchers), for example, both groups of boys had to work together to restore it. Similarly, when the boys wanted to rent a movie, but could not afford it on their own, they pooled their money. The introduction of these superordinate goals worked to reduce the tensions created as a result of the competitions. Additionally, many of the boys, who were in different groups, were able to restore their friendships. This investigation is important in revealing how competition over scarce resources can quickly escalate into full-scale conflict.

A second explanation for prejudice and discrimination is **social learning theory**. According to this view, children learn negative attitudes and discriminatory behavior from their parents, teachers, family, friends, and others when they are rewarded for such behavior. Rewards can be in the form of praise, agreement, love, and so on. Children have a strong need to be accepted and loved by those who are important to them. One way to be accepted and loved is to adopt the same attitudes that valued others have toward certain groups. *Social norms* (rules governing appropriate and acceptable behavior) are also a powerful mechanism for learning prejudice. Most people choose to conform to their own group's norms. For example, a child might assume that if a member of their group does not like another group, then the child will also not like the other group. Recent research (Towles-Schwen & Fazio, 2001) suggests that individuals' attitudes toward particular racial groups are determined by the attitudes of their parents, as well as by their childhood experiences with members of minority groups. These with less prejudiced parents and more positive experiences with minority group members have more favorable racial attitudes. The media also plays a strong role in shaping our attitudes toward members of racial groups. When minority group members are portrayed (on television, in movies, in commercials) in stereotypical ways, media consumers tend to adopt stereotypical (prejudiced) attitudes.

Another explanation for the development of prejudice is **social identity theory,** first presented in Chapter 3. Social identity studies have found that prejudice and stereotyping among groups occurs even in the absence of conflicting goals. Competition can occur even when the stakes are only psychological, and among groups that are arbitrarily formed by experimenters with no real interaction or conflicting goals (**minimal group paradigm)** (Tajfel, 1982; see Brewer & Brown, 1998, for a thorough review). In Chapter 4, we note that social categorization and social identity are partially responsible for the initial process of group differentiation into in-groups and out-groups. With this process comes the accompanying perception of the superiority of the in-groups. In addition, psychologists have found that people remember negative behaviors of out-groups far better than positive behaviors and positive behaviors of the in-groups far better than negative behaviors (Rothbart & John, 1993; Fiske, 1998), but this kind of bias in favor of the in-group is not in and of itself stereotyping and prejudice. As Allport (1954) noted, many years ago, "not every overblown generalization is a prejudice" (p. 9). Such generalizations become prejudices when they are resistant to disconfirming information, that is, when information indicating that they are wrong is ignored, disbelieved, or rejected out of hand.

A core argument in social identity theory is that social categorization produces a basic motivation for intergroup social competition. Once social categories are formed, people strive for positive social identity, which in turn creates intergroup competition. This causes perceptual biases and discriminatory behavioral patterns as people strive to view their in-group in a positive light, compared to out-groups. This explanation helps us understand general ethnocentrism: it directs our attention to the role of social cues that make salient intergroup distinctions and to the importance of status differentials—that is, the need to see one's own group as superior to others. But does it explain why prejudice toward some groups is so deep, but almost nonexistent for others? Not really. To do this, we must add in factors relating to the social context, the perceived legitimacy of intergroup relations, and individual personality characteristics.

Motivation and personality **traits** have also been examined in efforts to explain the causes of racism and ethnocentrism. One additional explanation for racial and ethnic prejudice that should be considered is related to studies of personality, discussed in Chapter 2. As mentioned in that chapter, there was a revival in the study of the authoritarian personality. Studies by Altemeyer (1981, 1988, 1996) and others argue that three central characteristics of the authoritarian personality covary across cultures and are directly related to ethnocentrism and prejudice. Those characteristics are authoritarian submission (to authority), aggression (against nonconformist groups), and conventionalism (blind acceptance of social norms). Altemeyer (1996) argues that these characteristics are strongly linked to right-wing authoritarianism in particular, and his studies have found them to be highly correlated with ethnocentrism. People who earn high scores in measures of authoritarianism tend to be more prejudiced toward low status out-groups than are people whose authoritarianism scores are low (Altemeyer, 1996; Meloen, 1994). Those high-scoring individuals stereotype out-groups as inferior to their own groups. In general, despite ongoing debates about theory and methods, evidence indicates that individual differences account for degrees of racism, prejudice against out-groups (particularly those who are visible and low-status), likelihood of being ethnocentric, likelihood of being less cognitively complex, and being more likely to rely on stereotypes in ambiguous contexts (Perreault & Bourhis, 1999). Other personality traits have also been associated with ethnocentrism. Perreault and Bourhis (1999), for example, found that ethnocentrism and personal need for structure predicted both in-group identification and discriminatory behavior.

Social Dominance Scale

The social dominance orientation scale is based on responses to the following questions. Along a 7-point scale, respondents are asked to disagree or to agree.

1. Some groups of people are just more worthy than others.
2. In getting what your group wants, it is sometimes necessary to use force against other groups.
3. Superior groups should dominate inferior groups.
4. To get ahead in life, it is sometimes necessary to use force against other groups.
5. If certain groups of people stayed in their place, we would have fewer problems.
6. It is probably a good thing that certain groups are at the top and other groups are at the bottom.
7. Inferior groups should stay in their place.
8. Sometimes other groups must be kept in their place.
9. It would be good if all groups could be equal.
10. Group equality should be our ideal.
11. All groups should be given an equal chance in life.
12. We should do what we can to equalize conditions for different groups.
13. Increased social equality.
14. We would have fewer problems if we treated groups more equally.
15. We should strive to make incomes more equal.
16. No one group should dominate in society.

(Sidanius et al., 2000, pp. 234–235)

Another explanation that examines personality characteristics, but that is also group related, is **social dominance theory** (Pratto, Sidanius, Stallworth, & Malle, 1994; Sidanius, 1993; Sidanius & Pratto, 1993, 1999;

Sidanius, Singh, Hetts, & Federico, 2000). Social dominance theory presents a social dominance orientation measure that differentiates those who prefer social group relations to be equal or hierarchical, and the extent to which people want their in-group to dominate out-groups. Social dominance orientation personality dimensions concern the degree to which a person favors an unequal, hierarchical, dominance-oriented relationship among groups. The Social Dominance Scale can be seen in the feature box. Clearly, those high in social dominance orientation would strongly agree with questions 1–8 and disagree with 9–16. The scale has produced results similar to the right-wing authoritarian measurements by Altemeyer (1998), although those high in social dominance are unlike authoritarians in that religion is not particularly important to them, and they "do not claim to be benevolent" (p. 61), but right wing authoritarians do (Whitley, 1999).

Sidanius (1993) argues that despite its strengths, social identity theory cannot explain experimental findings that demonstrate out-group favoritism, and it cannot predict how and along what dimensions discrimination against out-groups will occur. He argues that social identity theory expects out-group discrimination, yet studies have found evidence of low-status groups admiring high-status out-groups.[1] How can one explain this? Social dominance theory seeks to explain these behaviors as a product of social status and a human predisposition to form social groups that are arranged in a social hierarchy. There are three broad hierarchies in societies: gender (males dominate females); age (adults rule); and a third category, which varies from society to society, but that consistently includes socially constructed groups identified as differentiated in terms of race, ethnicity, class, clan, or nationality. These studies are primarily concerned with "the specific mechanisms by which social hierarchies are established and maintained and the consequences these mechanisms have for the nature and distribution of social attitudes and the functioning of social institutions within social systems" (Sidanius, 1993, p. 198). Those mechanisms are ideologies and political values that ascribe legitimacy to the social hierarchy. The people who support and promote such ideologies (e.g., the Protestant work ethic and liberalism/conservatism) are, of course, those who are at the top of the group hierarchy. They are able to use their dominance to perpetuate ideas and institutions that maintain their dominance. People accept inferiority because they are socialized to do so, and those at the top of the hierarchy survive; governments use coercion, when necessary, to defeat challengers. In essence, the theory attempts to look at individual, group, and social-structural variables to explain racism. People in dominant groups are socialized, as individuals, to have a social dominance orientation. They belong to groups that are on the top of the hierarchy, the social and political system benefits them the most, and they use social and political structures to maintain the hierarchical relationships among groups (Sears, Hetts, Sidanius, & Bobo, 2000; see also Rabinowitz, 1999). The theory was also applied to groups in the United States and other countries (e.g., Levin & Sidanius, 1999).

The why question—why racism and ethnocentrism occur—must be followed by the who question—what explains who the particular targets are? This is particularly perplexing when one considers the artificiality of race. As we noted earlier, people tend to think of race as denoting biological differences among people, but in fact it is largely socially constructed. Why is it that race is so important as an identifying marker for discrimination and prejudice in the United States, particularly when it comes to African Americans as perceived by Euro-Americans? Why were Jews the scapegoats in Nazi Germany, the Armenians in Turkey, the Tutsis in Rwanda, and the Maya in Guatemala and other parts of Central America? What determines who gets picked on in a society? In addition, perceptions of those who are targets for harsh treatment vary. Some, like the Maya in Guatemala or African Americans in the United States, are perceived to be inferior and have been victims of chronic and systematic discrimination. Others, like the Armenians, Jews, and Tutsis, are identified as the culprits to blame for bad things happening to society and as having far more than their fair share of the power and wealth.

The social dominance perspective provided one explanation about which groups receive the worst treatment: there are three potential hierarchies, and society maintains the status differential through legitimizing myths, institutions, and force, if necessary. Likewise, realistic conflict theory cites competition for resources as a motivating factor producing prejudice. But does that hostility necessarily evolve into the view of the other group as inferior? For example, did the Nazis and Hutus perceive the Jews and Tutsis, respectively, as inferior, or was that perception preceded by a perception that they were in a superior position in society? If so, how and why does that perception occur?

Social identity theory provides some insights here. It maintains that **scapegoating** is a result of social causality assessments—finding an out-group to blame for bad things that happen to the in-group (Hogg & Abrams, 1988; Kecmanovic, 1996; Staub, 1989). It is sensible that out-groups identified as responsible for some problem the in-group is facing will have negative characteristics attributed to them. Whether the scapegoat begins in a superior position or not, they are ultimately described as inferior. Some analysts draw more from psychoanalytic concepts and argue that **projection**—that is, ascribing one's own unacceptable and repressed impulses or attributes to out-groups—explains why they are regarded as inferior. In particular, repressed anger is displaced on to the scapegoat, and that group is not only regarded with contempt, but reacted to with powerful emotions of anger, fear, and resentment (Milburn & Conrad, 1996). Experimental studies, such as those of Rogers and Prentice-Dunn (1981), demonstrate the importance of anger, for example, in studies that found that White subjects, when not angered, react with more hostility toward Whites than toward Blacks, but when White subjects were angered in the experiment, they reacted with more hostility toward Blacks than toward Whites.

The Political Psychology of Race

Our intention is to discuss the issue of race as portrayed in many academic studies on the United States that focus on this concept in particular. We also provide a discussion of the groups in the United States and Europe that focus on racial issues. Finally, we include some international examples and look at the cases of Brazil and South Africa.

RACE IN THE UNITED STATES, EUROPE, BRAZIL, AND SOUTH AFRICA

Race in the United States

American attitudes on race and race-related issues go right to the heart of democratic principles. Those attitudes have changed greatly since the 1950s, and in a positive direction, in terms of the democratic principles of equality.[2] Nevertheless, the socioeconomic reality of Black and White American living standards indicates continuity in the wide disparity of wealth and power. Changing attitudes have not produced socioeconomic equality between Blacks and Whites in the United States. For example, in 1968, 8.4% of White families with children lived in poverty and 34.6% of Black families with children lived in poverty. In 1998, the figures were 6.1% and 30.5%, respectively; an improvement, but still a great disparity in percentages of families living in poverty, when White and Black families are compared (Joint Center for Political and Economic Studies, 2001).

More African Americans attend college today than in the 1940s, and more graduate from high school. By 2006, 17% of African Americans over the age of 25 had completed college, up from 4% in 1970 (Pew Research Center, 2007, p. 11). On the other hand, Hoffman and Llagas (2007) made the following four points about Blacks and higher education:

1. In 1999–2000, the proportion of associate's degrees earned by Blacks was greater than the proportion of bachelor's degrees earned by Blacks.
2. Nearly one-quarter of all bachelor's degrees earned by Blacks in 1999 were earned at historically Black colleges and universities.
3. The proportion of Blacks completing college increased between 1975 and 2000; however, Blacks still remained less likely than Whites to earn degrees.
4. In 1999, Black instructional faculty in colleges and universities were more likely to be assistant professors and instructors than professors or associate professors.

More Blacks are employed in white-collar jobs today, up from 5% in 1940 to 32% in 1990 (Sears et al., 2000). Still, Hoffman and Llagas note that "fewer Black and Hispanic men and women than White men and women held managerial or professional positions in 2000." Furthermore, Blacks still make less money than Whites, even with equal levels of education. In 1997, for example, Black women with high school diplomas earn $926 for every $1,000 earned by a White female high school graduate. Black men with a high school education earn $723 for every $1,000 earned by a White male high school graduate. The figures for Black and White male college graduates are $767 for every $1,000, respectively (Shipler, 1997). Hoffman and Llagas (2007) note that in 2000, Blacks at all educational levels had higher unemployment rates than both Whites and Hispanics. In addition, progress in equalizing income actually reversed between 2000 and 2006, when African Americans' median income went from 65% of Whites' median income to 61% (Pew Research Center, 2007, p. 18). In 2006, the median household income for Whites was \$52,423; for Blacks, \$31,969; and for Hispanics, \$37,781 (Pew Research Center, 2007, p. 12).

Racial attitudes have also changed dramatically in the United States, but not enough to eradicate racism. For the most part, White Americans no longer regard African Americans as biologically inferior to Whites, as they did during slavery and the Jim Crow era that followed. As late as 1942, survey data indicated that more than half of Whites believed Blacks to be less intelligent than Whites and opposed integration of schools and public transportation (Schuman, Steeh, Bobo, & Krysan, 1997). By the end of the century, those attitudes had changed dramatically, with over 90% of Whites favoring school integration and willing to vote for a Black political candidate, and only around 10% believing that Blacks are inherently unequal to Whites (Schuman et al., 1997).

Race and the Obama Election

Did racial prejudice influence the election of Barack Obama to the Presidency? Generally, it did not. We saw in Chapter 6 that concerns about the Bradley effect were misplaced. Whites were truthful in saying they would vote for a Black candidate. But Whites did favor John McCain by 12%, while 95% of African Americans voted for Obama. Moreover, of the 7% of Whites who said race would affect their decision for whom to vote, two-thirds voted for McCain (Pew Research Center, 2008b).

Does this election of Barack Obama mean racism is a thing of the past in the United States? No. It signals tremendous progress, but this election alone cannot undo the socioeconomic impact of the racism of the past.

Studies have found that racist attitudes in the United States have diminished as education levels increased over the years. Those with more formal education are less likely to express racist attitudes. But their support for policies designed to address inequality between the races is another issue entirely, as we see later (Jackman, 1978; Carmines & Merriman, 1993; Schuman et al., 1997). A 2007 Pew Research Center study found that by 2007, 82% of Whites had a favorable (57%) or very favorable (25%) view of Blacks. On the other hand, 80% of Blacks had favorable (53%) or very favorable (27%) view of Whites (p. 50). Whites also tend to believe that Blacks and Whites share important values and this grew from 62% of Whites in 1986 to 72% in 2007 (Pew Research Center, 2007, p. 20).

Nevertheless, vestiges of the past remain. Peffley and Hurwitz (1998), for example, found that a plurality of Whites have a positive perception of Blacks, but a surprisingly high proportion still see Blacks as lazy (31%), not willing to succeed (22%), aggressive (50%), and undisciplined (60%). At the heart of all of this is affect—negative feelings toward Blacks by Whites. But these perceptions are not just confined to Whites. In their study of Latinos in Durham, North Carolina, McClain et al. (2006) examined their perceptions of Blacks. Durham, according to the authors, had a significant increase in its Latino population.

> We found that 58.9% of the Latino immigrants in our study reported feeling that few or almost no blacks are hardworking; approximately one-third (32.5%) of the Latino immigrants reported feeling that few or almost no blacks are easy to get along with; and slightly more than a majority (56.9%) of the Latino immigrant respondents reported feeling that few or almost no blacks could be trusted.
>
> (p. 578)

However, the reverse was not true; that is, Blacks viewed Latinos much more favorably than Latinos viewed Blacks.

> Almost three-fourths (71.9%) of blacks feel most or almost all Latinos are hardworking, two-fifths (42.8%) believe most or almost all Latinos are easy to get along with, and only one-third (32.6%) indicate almost no or few Latinos could be trusted.
>
> (p. 579)

In the study they also examined what groups, Asians, Blacks or Whites, Latinos believe they have the most in common with. They found that Latinos believe they have more in common with Whites (78.3%) and the least in common with Blacks (52.8%). Nearly forty-seven percent of Blacks felt they had the most in common with Latinos and 45.5% believed they had the most in common with Whites. While this is one study, clearly, with the influx of Hispanics into the United States and the changing composition of the United States (Whites are projected to be only 50.1% of the population by 2050 and Latinos close to 25%; see McClain et al., 2006), race relations and issues cannot be discussed as just a Black and White matter anymore and the examination of the complexity of race relations is a going to be a necessity for future studies.

Needless to say, the topic of race relations in America today is enormously complex. It can be understood best by breaking it down into component parts and central questions. First, what is the relationship between attitudes toward race and positions on central political issues? This is a confoundingly difficult question to answer.

In the past, how one stood on equal housing, busing, affirmative action, voting rights, equal access to public facilities, and so on, was determined by how one felt about African Americans. Sniderman and Piazza (1993) argue that today, a distinction must be made among policies directed at equal treatment (e.g., in housing, schools, etc.); policy areas that are explicitly racially conscious, such as affirmative action; and social welfare-related policies. They argue that only equal treatment and race-conscious policies are uniquely related to racial attitudes. Social welfare policies involve programs for the poor, regardless of race or ethnicity. A person's positions on the social welfare issues reflect attitudes toward the role of the government, its size, its influence on the lives of citizens, and its role as agent of social change, rather than simply on race.

More generally, Schuman et al. (1997) examined trends in White racial attitudes regarding principles of equal treatment, implementation of equal treatment, social distance, beliefs about inequality, and affirmative action. Looking at survey results for several decades (when possible), they found a number of interesting patterns. There was an increase in White acceptance of the principles of equal treatment, but less change when Whites were asked about policies that would implement those principles. For example, White support increased for implementation of open access to public accommodation and housing, but a gap remained between those supporting the principle and those supporting policy to implement the principle, and the percent supporting federal government efforts to integrate schools actually declined over time (Schuman et al., 1997). The social distance patterns were also mixed. Over the years, Whites expressed an increased willingness to send their children to schools with Black children in attendance, to the point that nearly 100% accepted integrated schools by the 1990s. But when they were asked about truly integrated schools, schools in which their children may be a minority (i.e. 51% of Black children), the picture changed. By 1996, 49% of White parents said they would not send their children to a school that was over 50% Black (Schuman et al., 1997). Looking at the issue from a different perspective, in 2007 only 23% of Whites believed it was more important to send their children to racially mixed schools than to neighborhood schools, whereas 65% preferred neighborhood schools. Blacks, in contrast, believed (56%) that it was more important to send children to mixed schools than neighborhood schools (33%) (Pew Research Center, 2007, p. 10). Acceptance of integrated neighborhoods showed a similar pattern, with 13% of Whites indicating that they would only live in an all-White neighborhood in 1994, compared to 28% in 1976, but with little change in those wanting to live in a mostly White neighborhood (Schuman et al., 1997).

In terms of beliefs about the causes of inequality, the percentage of Whites who believe that African American socioeconomic disadvantages are the product of slavery and discrimination declined since the mid-1960s. Whites today prefer explanations that divide the blame between Blacks themselves and historical social discrimination against Blacks (Schuman et al., 1997). Finally, regarding affirmative action programs that explicitly attempt to compensate Blacks for past discrimination in housing, jobs, and access to education, White support remained at or below one third (Schuman et.al., 1997). Sniderman and Piazza (1993) sum up the results of the various surveys with the following evaluation:

> With the exception only of citizens who are uncommonly well educated and uncommonly liberal, what is striking is the sheer pervasiveness throughout the contemporary American society of negative characterizations of Blacks—particularly the stereotype that most Blacks on welfare could get a job. Perceptions of Blacks as inferior were supposed to represent an archaic stock of beliefs that were in the process of dying out, and some indeed do appear to be fading out. But it completely misreads contemporary American culture to suppose that all negative characterizations of Blacks are dwindling away. On the contrary, images of Blacks as failing to make a genuine effort to

work hard and to deal responsibly with their obligations is a standard belief throughout most of American society.

(pp. 50–51)

Nevertheless, there is a deep disagreement among political psychologists in their answers to questions of how prevalent and how deep racial prejudice is in the United States today. One camp is led by Sniderman, Piazza, Tetlock, Kluegel and others. They propose a model, which they have not named, but which we call the **politics-is-complicated model** (also known as the **principled objection model**), wherein it is argued that White Americans vary in the degree to which they blame the inequalities between the races on structural factors (such as the historical legacy of slavery and the current system-wide discrimination), as opposed to individual factors (individual acts of prejudice and discrimination, rather than system-wide factors). The other camp, led by Kinder and Sears, maintains that what we have in America today is **symbolic racism** disguised as traditional American individualist values. Let's take a look at each argument in some detail.

Data do not provide clear-cut evidence about the degree of racism among White Americans. For example, Sniderman and Piazza (1993) report 81% of surveyed Whites agreeing that Blacks on welfare could find jobs; 43% agreed that Blacks need to try harder, 36% agreed that Blacks have a chip on their shoulder, but only 6% agreed that Blacks are born with less ability.

Are people who agree with a negative description of another group of people necessarily prejudiced toward that group? The politics-is-complicated camp's answer is no: "Apart only from the characterization of Blacks as inherently inferior to Whites, [the negative characterizations] cannot be entirely reduced to bigotry, for these characterizations capture real features of every day experience" (Sniderman & Piazza, 1993, p. 43). Moreover, they note that Blacks have an even harsher characterization of Blacks than Whites do: 59% of Blacks agree that Blacks are aggressive, compared to 52% of Whites; 39% of Blacks agree that Blacks are lazy, compared to 34% of Whites; and 40% of Blacks agree that Blacks are irresponsible, compared to 21% of Whites (p. 45).

There are racists in America today, but scholars in this school of thought maintain that true racists are people who express prejudicial attitudes toward Blacks and that they also systematically express anti-Semitic attitudes toward Jews and hostility toward other minorities. They accept stereotypes of Blacks as lazy, violent, and innately inferior to Whites, and of Jews as shady in business practices, arrogant, and concerned only with the well-being of other Jews, for example (Peffley & Hurwitz, 1998; Sniderman & Piazza, 1993). This indicates that such people are broadly ethnocentric, hold a number of social stereotypes, and are generally socially intolerant. Advocates of the politics-is-complicated model argue that values related to authoritarianism, such as obedience to authority and hostility toward those different from one's own group, are more strongly correlated with negative attitudes toward Blacks than with values of individualism (e.g., the symbolic racism model) (Peffley & Hurwitz, 1998; Sniderman & Piazza, 1993).

An additional problem is a lack of consistency between support for equality between the races and lack of support for policies to achieve that equality. The politics-is-complicated model maintains that the inconsistency is not racism, but is attributable to changes in American politics and attitudes about policies related to race, but also to other political attitudes. Attitudes toward race, they argue, do not always dominate political choice. For example, if two people (one liberal and one conservative) both express support for equality, but only the liberal supports spending by the federal government to help Blacks, is the conservative then inconsistent and a closet racist? From the politics-is-complicated perspective, the answer is no because a conservative would believe that federal spending per se should be opposed. The conservative would maintain that he supports racial equality, but that less government is more important and/or that government support for Blacks actually produces dependence on government, rather than giving a leg up. This point is extended to explain one of the paradoxes found among those with higher levels of education. The more educated White people are, the more likely they are to respond to political issues associated with race in terms of affect (liking or disliking Blacks) and cognition (understanding the broader political context and linking issues to ideological principles). The resulting cognitive complexity allows people to consider a variety of differentiated considerations in making a policy choice. Hence, more educated people are more likely to consider issues other than, or in addition to, race, when deciding on their issue positions. Therefore, the conservative described earlier will consider race, but several other principles and policy characteristics, along with race, will also affect their decision, thus diminishing race-related principles in the overall decision-making process (Sniderman et al., 1991).

The politics-is-complicated model maintains that, in America today, there are "multiple agendas in racial politics, distinguishing the equal treatment agenda from the social welfare and the race conscious agendas" (Sniderman, Crosby, & Howell, 2000, p. 257). Some of these agendas, while having race-related implications, are not dominated by race-based attitudes when policy choices are expressed. The politics of race changed since the 1950s and 1960s, when they centered around legally sanctioned racial inequality; that is, Jim Crow laws, which created and enforced racial segregation and discrimination in schools, public facilities, housing, employment, and voting rights. Today's issues are more complex and include government enforcement of school integration through busing, affirmative action, assistance to Blacks to improve their economic situation, and government guarantees of equal opportunity.

Sniderman and Piazza (1993) maintained that there are three issue agendas in the United States today: the social welfare agenda, the equal treatment agenda, and the race-conscious agenda. The social welfare agenda is broadly defined to include governmental assistance to the disadvantaged, regardless of their race. However, because Blacks generally are at lower socioeconomic levels than Whites, race can become an issue in approving or rejecting social welfare policies. Sniderman and Piazza (1993) argue that "Whites tend to base their position on social welfare assistance for Blacks to significant degree on judgments about effort and fairness" (p. 118). Whites are more likely to approve of social welfare policies if they believe Blacks have been the victims of prejudice and discrimination, regardless of the White person's level of education. Whites are more likely to oppose these policies if they believe that Blacks do not try hard enough, again, regardless of education.

Ideology influences judgments of social welfare policies as well, particularly among the more educated, who as noted, are more cognitively complex. Conservatives are more likely than liberals to believe Blacks do not try hard enough and less likely than liberals to believe that Blacks have been treated unfairly in the United States. Ideology plays a role for the more educated, but not for the less educated, in determining their support for social welfare policies. The implication here is that for the less educated, prejudice toward Blacks leads to the view that they have not been treated poorly and do not try hard enough, but for the more educated, ideology, rather than prejudice toward Blacks, produces opposition to welfare policies. Sniderman and Piazza (1993) explicitly note that the "more prejudiced a person is, the more likely he or she is to perceive Blacks to be failing to make a genuine effort to deal with their problems on their own" (p. 120), and that this attitude is a result of a general negative view of Blacks as lazy and irresponsible. They maintain that, in statistical analysis, there is little correlation between prejudices (which they continue to assess not only by anti-Black attitudes, but also by anti-Semitic attitudes) and ideology. This means that conservatism and prejudice can be statistically pulled apart and are not found to hang together. Hence, they maintain that ideology (liberalism and conservatism) plays a separate and distinct role in determining attitudes toward social welfare policies, not a general dislike of Blacks. This also affects White responses to the next issue agenda—equality (Sniderman & Hagen, 1985).

Looking at the equal treatment agenda, Sniderman and Piazza (1993) examine attitudes about antidiscrimination laws. Here they find that support or opposition for laws, such as fair housing, are only slightly related to the reasons Whites favor or oppose social welfare support by the federal government for Blacks. In the issue area of fair housing, prejudiced opposition stems from social distance factors; prejudiced Whites do not want to live close to Black people. Again, Sniderman and Piazza (1993) found that prejudice is low among those with higher levels of education. For those with higher education, opposition to fair housing laws stems from the belief that government power should not be used to enforce equality.

Finally, in their examination of the race-conscious agenda, Sniderman and Piazza (1993) examine attitudes toward affirmative action. There is generally strong White opposition to affirmative action, although the authors found about 40% willing to support set-asides (in which a certain portion of federal contracts are reserved for minorities). White opposition to affirmative action is profound, regardless of whether or not they like or dislike Blacks. In a study by Sniderman and Carmines (1997), 9 out of 10 prejudiced Whites opposed affirmative action, and 8 of 10 Whites who were neutral in their attitudes toward Blacks objected.

In short, this is the politics-is-complicated model. Different issue agendas related to attitudes toward race are also related to attitudes toward other principles in American politics. They are more complicated than race alone, and must be examined in terms of that complexity.

This school of thought is strongly opposed by the advocates of the symbolic or new racism model, led by Sears and Kinder (1971; Kinder & Sears, 1981) and a number of others who took the argument in different directions (e.g., Bobo & Smith, 1994; Gaertner & Dovidio, 1986; Kinder & Sanders, 1996; Mendelberg, 2001; Pettigrew & Meertens, 1995). Symbolic racism arguments maintain that a new form of racism replaced that of the old pre–civil rights era racism and that, rather than being rooted in self-interest or group competition, the new racism has its foundation in conservative political values and the Protestant ethic's moral values. There is substantial White resentment of Blacks today, a resentment embodied in and fueled by the campaigns and policies of Nixon and Reagan, along with other politicians (Kinder & Sanders, 1996). Kinder and Sanders (1996) ask the important question of whether racial resentment is associated with racial stereotyping, and, looking at the results of surveys, they found that racial resentment and stereotyping are closely related. However, the data indicate that modern White prejudice toward Blacks is not based on the old notions of biological inferiority, but on the belief that Blacks fail to try hard enough.

Symbolic racism advocates maintain that the lack of consistency between support for equality between the races and support for policies to achieve that equality is evidence of underlying ongoing racism in White America (see Figure 8.1). Negative views of Blacks are still socialized into White Americans, who are conditioned to respond negatively to particular symbols regarding race-related issues, such as school busing (Sears, 1993). In terms of content, this new racism embodies the beliefs that "discrimination no longer poses a major barrier to the advancement of Blacks, that Blacks should try harder to make it on their own, that they are demanding too much, and that they are too often given special treatment by government and other elites" (Sears et al., 2000, p. 17). More specifically, symbolic racism is composed of a conviction that Blacks are no longer treated unfairly; that they do not have traditional American values, such as the work ethic and obedience to authority; that, despite this, they continue to demand special treatment from the government; and that they get that special treatment undeservedly (Sears, Henry, & Kosterman, 2000). Sears et al. (2000) maintain that these attitudes and beliefs account more powerfully for the attitudes on policy issues just discussed than does ideology.

The dispute between the two models centers mostly around the relationship between conservative values, particularly those ranking individualism very high, and racism. The role of individualism is particularly important, because it emphasizes the importance of individuals "pulling themselves up by their boot straps" and not being reliant on government help to get ahead. Those who fail to do this are looked upon with disdain. Because

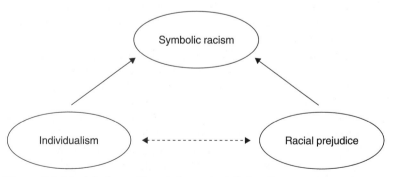

Figure 8.1 Model of constituent elements defining the new racism

many White Americans believe that Black Americans do not work hard enough, they regard Blacks with disdain; this is a new form of racism, based upon American values. Those values giving primacy to individualism are held most strongly by conservatives, whereas liberals tend to value equality (of opportunity, under the law, etc.) more highly; hence, the relationship between conservative values and the new racism. Thus, the symbolic racism school maintains that hostile feelings toward Blacks blend with conservative values to produce a new form of racism. The politics-is-complicated model claims that conservative values are independent of prejudice (as discussed previously).

Also of importance to the symbolic racism school is the use of race-related issues in electoral campaigns. In Chapter 7, we discussed the role played by **framing** and **priming** during campaigns in American politics. Those factors play a particularly important role in race-related issues during elections. The two dominant parties in the United States are deeply divided by the social cleavage of race. During the civil rights era, the Democratic Party moved left and the Republican Party moved right, in positions on issues related to government intervention on behalf of racial equality for Blacks. The Democratic party became the party to which most Blacks hold allegiance, and many southern Whites left the Democratic party (Kinder & Sanders, 1996; Mendelberg, 2001). Strategically, therefore, Democratic candidates will want to mobilize Black votes, without alienating White voters in the process. Democratic candidates are frequently accused of merely ignoring Black interests, assuming that Blacks have little choice other than to vote Democratic. Republican candidates will generally want to mobilize White voters who hold conservative views on race-related matters, without alienating more moderate Whites. Added to the strategic problems is the advent of the norm of racial egalitarianism. The overwhelming majority of White Americans do not openly endorse racist ideas or practices; they embrace the norm of racial equality. However, as we saw, racial resentment remains a real part of race relations in the United States.

Willie Horton and the Race Card

In the 1988 presidential race, Vice President George H. W. Bush squared off against Massachusetts Governor Michael Dukakis. In an effort to demonstrate that Bush was tougher on crime than Dukakis, a pro-Bush campaign organization, in collaboration with the Bush team, developed an ad showing the mug shot of Willie Horton, an African American convicted of murder in Massachusetts, who was allowed weekend furloughs from jail. During one of the furloughs, Horton ran away, ending up in Maryland, where he brutally beat a man and repeatedly raped a woman. Dukakis refused to revoke the furlough policy. The Bush team argued that this was evidence that Dukakis was soft on crime. However, many argued that the Willie Horton ad was an implicit effort to use the race card. Horton was shown on television with a big afro, scruffy beard, and scary scowl. He looked like a criminal and he was Black (Mendelberg, 2001).

These trends in White attitudes and emotions produce a strategic dilemma, particularly for Republicans running for office. Democrats need only keep quiet on race to keep their coalition of Black and White voters together. Republicans, however, must appeal to racial conservatives while not alienating moderate Whites, and they must do that without violating the social norm of racial equality. In other words, they cannot get caught "playing the race card" openly. Consequently, according to symbolic racism studies, they do it implicitly, through the use of code words, whereby implicit reference to race is made, and, by being implicit, it can be denied. References to issues like law and order, urban crime, local control of schools, voting blocs, and protection of property rights are all code words or phrases used to implicitly prime resentments against Blacks among those who believe that Blacks do not try hard enough and are lazy, violent, and take power away from Whites. This pattern was noted in Richard Nixon's campaign strategy in 1968, as well as in the Reagan campaigns in the 1980s (Kinder & Sanders, 1996; Mendelberg, 2001). Perhaps the most infamous and hotly debated example of the use of implicit campaign advertisements is the Willie Horton campaign during the 1988 Presidential elections. This ad was run by the George H. W. Bush campaign (see box).

This area of research is important for the symbolic racism argument because it digs through the layers of denial that these scholars believe cover latent racism in America (see also Milburn & Conrad, 1996). The denial is not difficult to understand, because it is a way of avoiding painful conflict between competing ideas and emotions. The psychological processes are familiar ones, as Mendelberg (2001) notes:

> The conflict between negative racial predisposition and the norm of race equality can generate ambivalence; in turn, ambivalence creates a greater susceptibility to messages. A racial appeal thus has the capacity to affect public opinion about matters related to race. It is most likely to do so by making racial predispositions—stereotypes, fears, and resentments—more accessible. Once primed by a message, these predispositions are given weight when white Americans make political decisions that carry racial associations . . . Racial priming can take place without the awareness of the individual, safeguarding the person's commitment to egalitarian conduct.
>
> (p. 112)

The disagreement between the politics-is-complicated and symbolic racism camps about race in America cannot be settled here. Much of it rests on disagreements regarding the meaning and appropriate measurement of individualism. The book *Racialized Politics: The Debate About Racism in America*, edited by Sears, Sidanius, and Bobo (2000), contains recent and informative discussions of both debates. Nevertheless, we can say there is a real conceptual disagreement here that can be unresolvable. The politics-is-complicated school clearly believes that people think in an additive way; that is, people hold a number of distinct ideas (about policy, government's role, and Blacks); they unconsciously weigh those cognitive properties when making decisions; and, based upon the priority they give them separately, they produce a policy position on race-related issues. They regard the cognitive process as complex and linear, moving from cognition to recognition of information regarding political realities and policy options among which the people must choose, to a choice. The symbolic racism camp takes more of a gestalt view of how people think, with ideas, values, information, and choice occurring in an ebb and flow, with complexity lying in their interaction and, most important, the idea that the mental system is a unique system that is different from the sum of its parts. The symbolic racism camp believes that the interaction of portions of the race-related mind should not be separated, because that gives an inaccurate and artificial picture of the nature of modern racism.

While these debates are ongoing, others are revisiting some of the claims and focusing on the measurement of certain concepts. For example, Federico and Sidanius (2002) set out to examine some measurement issues with regard to educational background and political sophistication. They first outline the debate, already examined above, and then explain,

> while much of this debate has taken the form of a basic agreement about the relative explanatory power of racial and race-neutral predispositions and the degree to which concern for formal equality has become evenly diffused throughout the political spectrum, an additional—and perhaps more interesting—disagreement about the effects of education on the relationship between these variables has also arisen. . . . Several researchers argued that education may attenuate the relationship between racial hostility and opposition to affirmative action, as well as the relationship between racism and various race-neutral predispositions. . . . Since poorly educated individuals lack the expertise necessary for the comprehension and use of abstract political concepts, their racial policy attitudes—and more broadly, their general political outlook—should be more heavily colored by prejudiced considerations. In contrast, the knowledge possessed by well-educated individuals should allow them to bring complex ideological principles to bear on their racial policy attitudes . . . Other analyses have offered less support for the hypothesis that education should attenuate the effects of racism and have instead suggested that education may simply allow individuals to better align their racial policy preferences—and broader political outlook—with a desire to protect the dominant position of the in-group.
>
> (pp. 147–8)

Federico and Sidanius conclude that this was not adequately tested by proponents and critics alike. The issue for them is the relationship between education and political sophistication; the latter does not necessarily mean the former. "While education may very well provide individuals with the cognitive sophistication necessary for an advanced understanding of politics . . ., it does not guarantee attention to and comprehension of political ideas, as suggested by the relatively low correlation between education and various measures of interest in policies, such as media exposure to political information" (p. 149). In their study of National Election Data from 1986–1992, the authors defined political sophistication as "actual political knowledge" and used this as a basis for their examination of "the relationships between affirmative action attitudes, prejudice, race-neutral political considerations, and beliefs about equality among white respondents with different political sophistication" (p. 169). The authors conclude that,

> Our results provide little or no support for the notion that a better understanding of abstract political ideas and the norms of American political culture would attenuate the significance of racist and antiegalitarian motives. First of all, beliefs about racial superiority and inferiority were more strongly associated with affirmative action attitudes among the sophisticated than they were among relatively unsophisticated whites. Furthermore, rather than being less strongly related to superiority beliefs among sophisticates, political conservatism was, in fact, more strongly related to racism among these individuals. Perhaps more interestingly, we found little support for the notion that opposition to affirmative action may be driven by egalitarianism, particularly among sophisticated respondents. Not only was egalitarianism negatively (rather than positively) related to affirmative action opposition, but the magnitude of this relationship actually increased with political sophistication. . . . Rather than being embedded in support for egalitarian values, opposition to affirmative action shows every appearance of being driven by antiegalitarian values, particularly among those who should best understand the principles of the American Creed.
>
> (p. 169)

The authors also found that political conservatives were less supportive of equality of opportunity, and it was particularly so among those considered knowledgeable.

In addition to measurement and conceptual issues, there is another reason that it is difficult to determine which of these two models is best, and that is the difficulty today in knowing racism when we see it. Richard Ford (2008), for example, takes a hard look at the issue of whether racism was involved in the terrible conditions faced by so many African Americans in the aftermath of hurricane Katrina in 2005. Critics noted that the French Quarter, the heart of tourism, and the White parts of New Orleans were spared. The worst damage was done to the poorest parts of the city, which were largely African American. Was the lack of effective response by the federal government a result of racism and, if so, who were the racist decision makers? Kanye West famously gave his answer to that question with the statement, "George Bush doesn't care about Black people" (quoted in Ford, 2008, p. 42). Many others criticized the press for racist coverage of the aftermath when Black people carrying supplies were "looting" while White people doing the same thing were "finding" necessities. But Ford makes a very interesting argument regarding this case in particular and a general problem in evaluating racism in America today. Too often, we see racism without racists. The social, economic, and racist conditions that produced both the poverty and the segregation in New Orleans were the product of racists who are long dead, yet the legacy still exists. It is a "type of racism—or, more precisely, racial injury *without* racists—[that] accounts for a large and growing share of racial injustice in our society" (Ford, 2008, p. 58).

Having reviewed some of the central scholarly arguments about race in America, let's return to a more anecdotal conclusion. Clearly, blatant racism remains in America, and clearly there was change in that over time, but it is very difficult for Black and White Americans to interact comfortably. We are, as Shipler (1997) puts it, a country of strangers. We illustrate this point with a few passages from Shipler's look at Black and White interaction, or lack thereof. Blacks and Whites each assume the other wants no interaction, and so none takes place. Shipler interviewed White college students, asking if they would talk to Blacks in the self-selected "Black section" of the college cafeteria:

> "It wouldn't be something you would do," explained a young White woman . . .
> "You aren't invited."
> Do you have to be invited to sit down with somebody in the lunchroom?
> "Well, no, but when you sit down with somebody at a table, you don't just sit down with people that you don't know. And if they don't invite you, you're not going to walk over."
> "It's like an attitude, I don't know," one woman said. "It's like they try to scare you. I don't know."
> Can you be precise? Why do they scare you?
> "I don't know, I feel like they're looking at me like I think that I'm better than them, even though I don't. But they just perceive that we all think that, so they try and, like, have this rule by fear, like the only way maybe to defend themselves is to scare you, I guess."
> So it's the look? body language?
> "Yeah, they would look at you "Why are you coming to sit with us?" Or sometimes they think that you're trying to be, like, diversified . . . so then they have the attitude "Oh, you're just coming over here because you want to meet us because we're Black." '
> Did that ever actually happen to you?
> "No." She giggled.
>
>   (pp. 27–28)

Here a White woman feels uncomfortable about interacting with Black people, because she is concerned, based on no actual evidence, that she would be snubbed for her willingness to do so. Her statement reflects fear of Blacks, fear of even trying to interact with them on an individual level, and some sense of an assumption that Blacks are responsible for their own segregation.

In a discussion of the cultural divide between Black and White Americans, Shipler (1997) notes that Blacks are not free to behave in accordance with Black culture when in a White world. They have to adapt; Whites do not. They have to learn to walk in two worlds; Whites do not. For example:

> Every morning, Consuella Lewis consciously transformed herself as she drove to her job as director of the Office of Black Studies at Claremont-McKenna College. About a block away from the . . . campus . . . she reached down to her radio, lowered the volume, and changed the music from throbbing rap to soothing classical . . . She

had no apologies, even for the change of radio stations. "You're riding around, you may see someone, it's a small community, so you so the switching thing," she explained.

(p. 71)

Or:

The differences come in explicit and subtle forms. Daphne LeCesne, an African-American psychologist . . . used culture to explain issues of time, status and organization that affect how she thought Black children learned. Her comparisons were heavily value laden. "African-American learners," she insisted "respond to a warm, interactive style, sensitivity to relational issues, and interact with you—accept interaction from you—on the basis of your personal attributes. The reason is, in a slave culture . . . you acquire strength and power by being verbally adroit. . . . Whereas there's tons of research that suggests that a European style is more dependent upon positional authority: your status, your role, the job you've been given . . . It's more European to be very time conscious and role-conscious."

"Suburban birthday parties are a wonderful example", she said. "a great suburban birthday party for White folks—I discovered the first party I went to—starts promptly at two, just like it says on the invitation. And if you run late, people will call you and say, 'You comin'?' Of course we're coming, 'Well, we're waiting.' You're waiting? You're holding up the party and waiting? OK, we'll be there. You go, it starts promptly, there are no parents in sight. Everyone drops off their kids, they leave. When you stay, they look at you like 'You have an anxiety problem or something? You know you can go shop.' Well, I don't leave my kids and go shop. 'Well OK, fine.' You need any help? They look affronted: 'You think I'm not organized here?' And at four, these people come back, and they take their kids. And of course, since you came late and your kids aren't used to this, they're like, 'Can we stay and play?'"

"A great African-American party . . . doesn't start on time. If you come on time you expect to cook, OK? And you're needed to help cook because this is an extended family event. You better have food enough for the adults, and you better have adult quality food. It's terrible—you got hotdogs here. Where's the chicken? Don't expect it to start on time and don't expect it to end abruptly."

(pp. 80–81)

Americans think that we have forged a common identity amongst groups. However, a recent study by Barlow, Taylor and Lambert (2000) shows that African American women perceived themselves to be Americans, but doubted that White Americans see them as American. This is a reflection of the lack of interaction, the extent to which there is still a large social distance between Whites and Blacks in the United States, and a sad illustration of the ongoing legacy of slavery.

The African American Perspective on Race and Politics

How do African Americans view the politics of race relations in the United States? African Americans are not a monolith. In terms of political ideologies, they, like White Americans, have differing perspectives. In some respects, there is a wider range of ideological systems in the African American community. Dawson (2001) argues that the ideologies found in the African American community include Black nationalism, Black feminism, Black Marxism, Black conservatism, and disillusioned Black liberalism, with the latter being the most common ideology. He argues that African American liberals tend to desire a stronger state than other American liberals, because it is needed to reinforce equality of opportunity and to prevent the exercise of power by white racists. Dawson also argues that for African American liberals the "advancement of the self, the liberation of the self, is a meaningless concept outside the context of one's community" (p. 255) and that therefore individualism is a less important concept for African Americans.

Several studies found that African American identity is very strong for Blacks in the United States (e.g., Dawson, 2001; Sniderman & Piazza, 2002). There is a firm conviction that, for example, what happens to the community affects individual members. That strong identity as a group added some complexity, however, in that 37% of African Americans in a recent study stated that African Americans no longer constitute a single race (Pew Research Center, 2007, p. 24). African Americans also strongly identify with the national community . . . However, unlike White American opinion referred to above, only 54% of Blacks in 2007 believed that White and Black Americans share important values (Pew Research Center, 2007, p. 20).

African Americans differ markedly from Whites in terms of perceptions of the extent to which racial discrimination occurs today. Comparing Black and White perceptions of discrimination against Blacks, 67% of Blacks believe they are faced with discrimination when looking for employment compared to 20% of Whites; 65% of Blacks believe they face discrimination when trying to find housing compared to 27% of Whites; 43% of Blacks believe they face discrimination when applying to college compared to 7% of Whites; and 50% of Blacks believe they face discrimination when dining out or shopping compared to 12% of Whites (Pew Research Center, 2007, p. 30). Clearly there is a big disparity in White and Black perceptions of the occurrence of discrimination against African Americans today. At the same time, when asked why some African Americans fail to get ahead in life, the majority (53%) of Black respondents in the same study attributed this to individual responsibility rather than discrimination. Whites (71%) also attributed this to the individual rather than systematic discrimination, as did Hispanics (59%) (Pew Research Center, 2007, p. 33).

In terms of some of the issues that are usually thought of as racial, Blacks tend to want more integration in housing than Whites do (62% compared to 40%), but they are basically equal in approving of school integration, with 96% of Whites and 95% of Blacks approving of it (Pew Research Center, 2007, p. 51). However, Blacks value going to integrated schools more than Whites do if a trade-off must be made between going to an integrated school versus going to a school in their community (56% vs. 23%) (p. 51). In terms of party identification, African Americans overwhelmingly identified with the Democratic Party, with 62%, as opposed to only 6% identifying with the Republican Party (p. 62). This is down slightly from the early 1990s by 2% (p. 51).

One of the most important developments for the country and for the African American populace is the 2007–2008 candidacy for the Democratic Presidential nomination of Barack Obama. In the Pew 2007 public opinion survey, Obama was viewed favorably by 89% of Blacks, but also by 65% of Whites, and 74% of Hispanics (p. 58). Obama's strong candidacy is a measure of changes in American racial attitudes, and the serious prospects for a successful run for the presidency by an African American are reflected in opinions on the question of whether his race would help, hurt, or have no effect on his prospects. Overall, 18% believed it would help him, 26% that it would hurt him, and 44% that is would make no difference (p. 60). African Americans were more pessimistic than whites, however, with 39% of Blacks, as opposed to 26% of Whites, believing his race would hurt him (p. 60).

The Hispanic Perspective on Race and Politics

The Hispanic community is the largest minority in the United States and also suffers from discrimination based upon racist stereotypes. The Hispanic population is about 46 million, or 15% of the U.S. population (Pew Research Center, 2007, p. i). It is diverse. The largest group is of Mexican origin, followed by Puerto Rican and Cuban origin, but Hispanics in the United States may have ancestral origins in any of the countries of Latin America. As we mentioned, race is socially constructed, and in the United States, Hispanics, or Latinos/Latinas, were traditionally thought of as a racial classification. Nevertheless, this is really an in-between racial group, in part because Hispanics are racially diverse, with various combinations of indigenous, African, and European ancestries. White negative stereotypes of Hispanic Americans have primarily concentrated on Mexican Americans, as they are the largest Hispanic group. Conflict with between Whites and Mexican Americans for resources and power occurred early on in the southwestern part of the United States. The White stereotype depicted Mexican Americans as lazy, violent, backward, poor, unskilled, and prone to committing crimes (Marger, 2003). On the positive side, they are also perceived as being religious and family-oriented. There have been conflicts between Anglos and other Hispanic groups, including resentment about the strong Cuban American presence and power in the Miami area.

As Marger (2003) notes, "because of their 'in-between' minority status, Latinos have not been subjected to the dogged prejudice and discrimination aimed at African Americans; but neither have they been dealt with as European immigrant groups were" (p. 337). Nevertheless, like African Americans they endure segregation in public facilities such as restaurants and schools (Mindiola, Flores Nieman, & Rodriguez, 2002) and their economic status is lower than that of Anglos. Of the Hispanic workforce, only 14% are white-collar professionals (National Society of Hispanic Professionals, 2008). The median income for Hispanic families in 2004 was $34,241, compared to non-Hispanic Whites' income of $48,977, and 22% of Hispanics lived below the poverty rate, compared to 8.6% of Whites in 2004 (U.S. Department of Commerce, 2005, p. 1).

Hispanic identity in terms of race has many interesting patterns, and provides an example of the extent to which race is socially constructed and not a biological fact. The U.S. federal government does not consider Hispanics to be a separate race. Consequently, when asked which race they belong to on the census report, they can select White, Black or African American, American Indian or Alaska Native, Native Hawaiian and other Pacific Islander, or Some Other Race (SOR). In the 2000 census, 48% of Hispanic identifiers considered themselves "White" and 42% checked "some other race" (Tafoya, 2004). Research found that those who identified themselves as White had higher levels of education and income, and felt more enfranchised than those who selected SOR (Tafoya, 2004, p. 1). Moreover, those who selected SOR were more likely to be foreign born. Forty-six percent of foreign-born Hispanics selected SOR, compared to 40% of native Hispanics. Not surprisingly, 85% of the native-born Hispanics who consider themselves White are registered to vote, compared to 67% of native-born Hispanics who consider themselves SOR (p. 2). The author of this research concludes that "The differences in characteristics and attitudes between those Hispanics who call themselves white and those who identify as some other race, suggests they experience racial identity as a measure of belonging: Feeling which seems to be a reflection of success and a sense of inclusion" (p. 3). It is not surprising, therefore, that 55% of the native-born Hispanics who consider themselves White identify first as Americans, while only 36% of the same population who consider themselves SOR do so (p. 18).

In terms of partisanship, 57% of Hispanics say they are Democrats or Democratic Party leaners (Taylor & Fry, 2007, p. 1). Only 23% identify with the Republican Party. During the early 2000s, Hispanic voters had moved farther toward the Republican Party, but this trend was reversed by late 2007. Hispanics have a number of values that can be appealed to, and were appealed to by President Bush, in 2004. These include anti-abortion and anti-gay rights, as well as support for small business (Hutchison, 2007). Hispanic registered voters tend to believe that the Democratic Party cares more for Hispanics (44%, although 41% say neither party cares), that the Democratic Party has a better approach to the issue of immigration, and they showed a marked preference for Hillary Clinton in the 2008 contest for the Democratic Party presidential nomination (Taylor & Fry, 2007).

Of the many political issues under debate in the 2008 presidential contest, Hispanics point to education, followed by health care, the economy and jobs, crime, immigration, and the war in Iraq, in that order, as important to them (Taylor & Fry, 2007, p. 10). The Hispanic community differs from the general population in the United States in favoring bilingual education and in terms of attitudes toward immigration. In the latter issue, majorities of Hispanics do not support open immigration, but they are more supportive of recent immigrants, and more supportive of amnesty for illegal immigrants (Sanchez, 2006). There is quite a bit of difference within the Hispanic community regarding immigration, depending upon their ancestral country of origin, whether they are native-born Americans or immigrants, and where they live (see Sanchez, 2006).

Immigration is an issue of growing importance to Hispanics. As mentioned, Hispanics do not favor open borders, but the immigration issue is also an indicator to many of vestiges of White prejudice. A 2008 poll conducted by the Pew Hispanic Institute found that close to 10% of Hispanics had been questioned by authorities about their residency status, 15% found it hard to get work because they are Hispanic, and 57% were concerned that they or someone they care about could be deported (Gaouette, 2008). The survey also found that 34% said that immigration was extremely important to them, and would affect their vote in the 2008 presidential race. The effect would benefit the Democratic Party, which about half of the respondents said was best on the immigration issue. Only 7% said the Republican Party was better on the issue (Gaouette, 2008).

Asian and Pacific Islander American Perspective on Race and Politics

Another minority racial group that experienced tremendous prejudice and discrimination at the hands of the White society is the Asian community. Beginning with the hostility toward Chinese immigrants in the 1840s, there was concern among Whites that Asians would take their jobs, and there have been very negative stereotypes of Asians.

Historically, discrimination against Asians began when Chinese immigrants, mostly men, came to the United States after the gold rush started. They continued to work in difficult circumstances as laborers building railroad lines and in other areas. They were restricted in terms of occupation and where they could live, resulting in the ghettos we still identify as Chinatowns in major American cities, and particularly in the western part of the United States. The Chinese immigration was received with such hostility that the Chinese Exclusion Act was passed in 1882, which prohibited immigration from China altogether. It was not repealed until 1943. After Chinese immigration stopped, immigration from Japan increased. They also engaged in labor occupations. The backlash against Japanese immigration produced the "Gentleman's Agreement" between the U.S. and Japan in 1908, as a result of which the only Japanese who could enter the United States were relatives of those already here and those who were not laborers in occupation. This was followed by the Oriental Exclusion Act of 1924, which prohibited all Japanese immigration.

Accompanying these actions were strong negative stereotypes of Asians as inherently inferior to white people, inscrutable, dirty, and unassimilable. As a "yellow peril," they were forbidden to become citizens, were relegated to the lowest status jobs, were restricted in their movements and residency, and were socially excluded, as well, making it impossible to learn English and American values (Kitano & Nakaoka, 2001; Marger, 2003). With the advent of Japanese power in the 1930s, the stereotype included an element of fear and suspicion.

These actions made it clear that Americans were hostile to immigration from Asia. But the most egregious act of prejudice and discrimination was the internment of Japanese Americans during World War II. People of Japanese ancestry—American citizens—all along the west coast were sent to camps with one suitcase of belongings. Many lost businesses and land. A total of 120,000 were interred until the last waning months of the war.

After World War II, federal legislation changed and Asians were permitted to become citizens. There was an influx of Asians from other countries in addition to Japan and China, including the Philippines, Korea, Vietnam, India, American Samoa, Guam, and many other places.[3] There still are vestiges of the earlier stereotype and more. On the one hand, there are positive attitudes about Asian Americans (more specifically Chinese Americans) evident in a 2001 survey (Marilla Communications Group, 2001). They are believed to have strong family values (90% agreed), are honest in business (77% agreed), are patriotic Americans (68% agreed), and highly value education (67% agreed) (p. 21). On the other hand, 23% of Americans dislike the idea of an Asian president, 25% dislike the idea of intermarriage between a family member and an Asian person, and 17% do not want to live with a large number of Asians in their neighborhoods (pp. 44–46). The modern stereotype of Asian Americans can be simultaneously that of the "pollutant, the coolie, the deviant, the yellow peril, and model minority, and the gook" (Lee, 1999, p. 8). There is a considerable amount of resentment of the successes of Asians as well. The study of attitudes toward Chinese Americans, for example, found that 34% of respondents thought they had too much influence in high tech, 32% thought they liked to be at the head of things, and 26% thought they were aggressive in the workplace (Marilla, 2001, p. 22). In summarizing, the study divided Americans into three categories in terms of attitudes toward Chinese Americans: 32% had positive stereotypes, 43% somewhat negative stereotypes, and 25% very negative stereotypes (p. 24).

The stereotypes lump very diverse people together, ignoring the significant cultural and socioeconomic differences among Asian groups in the United States. The diversity of the Asian American community can be seen in their identity patterns. Lien, Conway, and Wong (2004) conducted a study in which they sought to discover what percentages of Asian Americans identified as nonethnic (American), as ethnic American (e.g., Chinese American), as ethnic only (Chinese) or as panethnic (Asian). They found a big difference between groups. Japanese Americans were those most likely to identify simply as American (41%) while Chinese and Vietnamese Americans were least likely to do so (1%). Chinese and Vietnamese Americans were most likely (42% each) to identify as ethnic only (p. 42). Looking at other indicators of identity, they found that only 10% of their survey respondents believed that Asian groups in America are very similar culturally, but 41% thought they were somewhat similar (p. 47). The complexity of the identity patterns are summed up by the authors as follows:

> [E]thnic self-identification varies greatly by ethnic origin. Japanese Americans are most likely to identify only as "American"; Chinese, Korean, and Vietnamese are most likely to identify only as "ethnic." While both Filipinos and South Asians are most likely to identify as "ethnic American," South Asians have the highest percentage of "Asian American" identifiers. When other conditions are controlled, South Asians, compared to Chinese, are more likely to self-identify not only as "Asian American" but also with the two other American-based identities. This is not the case with respondents of other ethnicities, except that a person of Japanese or Filipino descent is also more likely to identify only as "American" than as ethnic.
>
> (2004, p. 66)

Table 8.1 Percentage Distribution of Political Orientation by Ethnic Origin

	All	*Chinese*	*Korean*	*Vietnamese*	*Japanese*	*Filipino*	*South Asian*
very liberal	8	4	4	12	9	8	18
somewhat liberal	28	26	29	10	25	32	43
middle of the road	32	42	28	47	37	18	16
somewhat conservative	18	11	27	5	20	29	14
very conservative	4	2	4	4	4	5	3
not sure	10	15	8	21	4	6	6

Source: Lien, P., Conway, M. M., & Wong, J. (2004). *The politics of Asian Americans: Diversity & community*. New York: Routledge, p. 75.

Politically, Asian Americans tend to be more liberal than conservative. The Lien, Conway, and Wong (2004) study found 8% surveyed considered themselves very liberal, 28% somewhat liberal, 32% middle of the road, 18% somewhat conservative, and 4% very conservative (p. 74). Moreover, higher income Asian Americans were more likely to consider themselves very or somewhat liberal; lower income Asian Americans had a larger percentage who considered themselves somewhat or very conservative (p. 74). Not surprisingly, this distribution blurs the distinctions among specific groups of Asian Americans. Table 8.1 shows the differences.

Radical White Racists and the Racial Divide

The residue of the racial divide is apparent in the dialogue of a cluster of White groups in the United States and Europe. They include a wide variety of groups loosely organized through a circuit of leaders and lieutenants (Ezekiel, 1996). These groups glorify violence and reinforce group members' loyalty through rituals associated with religion and mythology, as well as by uniforms, banners, hierarchy, and symbols such as the swastika. These groups are concerned about, and threatened by, social change, including influxes of immigrants, perceived special privileges given to minorities and women, changes in gender roles, race mixing and other trends (Ezekiel, 1996; Green, Abelson, & Garnett, 1999; Langer, 1990). The members of these groups have a sense of injustice, of being deprived of their rightful status in society, of being left behind. There is of course racism in their views. Whites, they believe, should have higher status than any other groups, including Blacks, Jews, Asians, Indians, and others. These other groups should not have special status; some of these groups suggest sending any non-White immigrant back home to their original countries, while others are content to form their own White homelands within countries. Among them, there is a distrust of government to be an advocate for Whites.

In looking at these groups, we found that there are too many groups to mention individually. However, since there is considerable overlap in their views, we chose to provide a more general discussion of some of their issue areas. That way, we provide a macro view of their beliefs. In addition, discussion boxes provide information about certain groups more specifically.

Southern Poverty Law Center Battles Racism

Morris Dees, a lawyer with the Southern Poverty Law Center, brought some high-level suits against the United Klans of America in 1991 and Aryan Nations in 2000. The case against the Klan involved a 1981 murder of a Black teenager. Dees won the suit against the United Klans and several of its members. The headquarters of the Klan was sold and the proceeds given to the mother of the victim.

The Klan was formed in 1866 by a group of Confederate soldiers in order to provide amusement. At first, the organization simply engaged in practical jokes, but soon it evolved into a group that would intimidate, harass, whip, and murder Blacks (Ridgeway, 1995). Several Klan groups still exist, but the organization was seriously weakened not only by the efforts of Dees, but also by the Federal Bureau of Investigation.

In the case of the Aryan Nations, Victoria Keenan and her son Jason were driving by the compound of the organization in North Idaho when their car backfired. The guards in the compound pursued them for two miles and shot at them. After their car went into a ditch, the guards assaulted them. Dees won $330,000 in compensatory damages and $6 million in punitive damages for the woman and her son against Saphire Inc., the corporate body of the Aryan Nations.

The Southern Poverty Law Center is an organization that carefully tracks these groups in the United States. It listed 884 active groups as of 2006 and classified them into the Klan, Neo-Nazi, Racist Skinhead, Christian Identity, Neo-Confederate, and Black Separatist groups. The estimates concerning membership size for these groups vary greatly. The Southern Poverty Law Center and Center for Democratic Renewal maintain that hard-core membership is about 23,000–25,000, with another 150,000 sympathizers and possibly half a million interested enough to read movement literature (Ezekiel, 1996). Others note the number of militias dropped dramatically since the Oklahoma City bombing, from 858 in 1996 to only 194 in 2000 ("McVeigh helped," 2001), because McVeigh's association with the militia movement discredited it. Abanes (1996) argues that there are possibly 5 to

12 million members. He characterizes these members as representing many groups. On the one hand is the "moderate" side—that is,

> Christians dissatisfied by the current state of American politics. Their primary concern is changing the government through political activism. More radical participants include both Christians and non-Christians who deny their U.S. citizenship, drive without licenses, and refuse to pay income taxes in an effort to live outside "the system." Interspersed among these two groups are the most dangerous and unpredictable "patriots"— Klansmen, neo-Nazis and Christian Identity believers. These persons are extremely difficult to detect among mainstream conservative Christians because they blend their white supremacist views with pseudo-Christian thought.
>
> (p. 2)

Given the breadth of the groups, there is not one single view or philosophy that can be used to describe all of the groups involved. However, there are a few elements that provide a basis for understanding their wide-ranging views. In his examination of these groups, Abanes (1996) argued there are four common elements: (1) an obsessive suspicion of the government; (2) belief in antigovernment conspiracy theories; (3) a deep-seated hatred of government officials; and (4) a feeling that the U.S. Constitution, for all intents and purposes, was discarded by Washington bureaucrats (p. 2). Abanes also adds that most patriots believe that the government is illegitimate. These groups hate government officials for what they see as excessive governmental regulation and restrictions, which intrude on their lives and violate their rights. However, Abanes further noted,

> to complicate matters, large segments of the patriot/militia movement are being driven by religious beliefs and/or racism, two powerful forces that historically have often led to episodes of violence. This raises another disturbing issue: the unholy alliance that has formed between racists and anti-Semites on the one hand, and some conservative Christians on the other. The common ground between these two groups is apocalypticism (e.g., a belief that at some divinely appointed time in the future, the world as we know it will end through a cataclysmic confrontation between the forces of good and evil, out of which will emerge the righteous kingdom of God).
>
> (p. 3)

The right-wing militias, patriots, and Christian Identity groups live their lives according to their interpretation of the Constitution and Bill of Rights. One of the most important elements in their interpretation of the Constitution lies in the Fourteenth Amendment. In the patriot movement's view, no one may change the constitution. Before the Fourteenth Amendment, everyone was a natural citizen of the state or republic in which they were born. The Fourteenth Amendment grants citizenship to former slaves and others who become citizens of the federal government and receive benefits from it. This, in the view of the patriots, is an inferior and secondary form of citizenship, entered into by Americans who were duped by the federal government and who unknowingly placed themselves under the authority of that government by entering into illegal contracts with it (e.g., birth certificates, driver's licenses, and social security numbers). These documents make one a federal citizen and revoke the superior state citizenship. This particular interpretation of the Fourteenth Amendment is the reason why many patriots refuse to pay federal taxes. Another example of patriot thinking was expressed on the American Patriot Network (2002) homepage, where they asked, "How dead are the Bill of Rights?" They proceeded to describe the ways in which the Bill of Rights has been unlawfully changed by the federal government via court cases or laws passed. For example, the Second Amendment was said to be 90% dead. The culprit they point to is the Crime Bill of 1994, which banned 19 types of semiautomatic rifles.

The National Alliance

William Pierce was the founder of the National Alliance, a neo-Nazi group based in the United States. The ideology of the National Alliance is National Socialism, which has its roots in German Nazism. Before forming the National Alliance, he was affiliated with the John Birch Society, the National Socialist White People's Party, and the National Youth Alliance. Pierce was not only the founder of the National Alliance, but a centerpiece in the group.

Pierce was best known for his 1978 book the *Turner Diaries*, which is widely read by white supremacist groups. The book is supposed to be the diary of Earl Turner, a member of a White Patriot group called the Order, which is part of a larger group called "Organization." In his "diary," Turner describes an escalation of the war in which Jews, Blacks, and other people of color are killed by beatings, hangings, guns, and knives. Pierce also wrote *Hunter*, published in 1984, which is about a killer whose goal is to cleanse the United States of its "sickness" by murdering interracial couples and assassinating Jews.

After Pierce's death in 2002, the National Alliance vowed to continue on his work. The group is now run by Eric Gliebe.

An integral part of these groups' identities is the belief that the federal government is not only untrustworthy, but conspiratorial. As George and Wilcox (1996) explain:

> The range of conspiracy theories may be almost encyclopedic, but they all have one thing in common: some kind of diabolical plot by the dark forces to do in the champions of righteousness and freedom. The details vary considerably, but they usually involve secrecy and deception, complicated scenarios by which the people are fooled, sometimes even by those claiming to oppose the plotters. All this ends with the control or enslavement of the masses by a self-appointed elite.
>
> (p. 266)

Evil, Filthy, Rotten Conspiracy

The following song, which was written by Carl Klang and published in the patriot newspaper, *The Idaho Observer*, in February 1998, encapsulates these beliefs and demonstrates the extent of conspiracy theories:

> Now have you seen them flying saucers
> Or some of them black helicopters
> Flyin' down low and over my back yard recently?
> Seen them foreign troops in ninja suits
> Leavin' imprints of their combat boots
> In the meadow down near the neighbor next to me?
> Heard they're buildin' concentration camps
> From the rate hike off our postage stamps
> To protect and defend their great democracy
> Though my vote in the last election
> Didn't quite match the same projection
> Made by those beautiful talking heads on my TV
> When I called them to complain—and asked them to explain
> They just said that it proves you're not in the groove
> Of the new majority
> Well just between you and me—can't you just feel the conspiracy?
> Can't you sense the hypocrisy as they call it democracy
> Well it's a threat to your sanity, not to mention your liberty
> And it's all an evil filthy rotten conspiracy.
> So as they redirect our mail
> And all our incoming phone calls
> To the Central Intelligence Agency
> We'll just hope and pray someday they'll see
> That you and me are not the enemy
> Nor do we believe in cult theology
> And as their police try to bust us
> We'll keep tryin' to find some justice
> Though it's hidden behind a wall of masonry
> We'll keep working out our Salvation
> With the feelin' and fear and tremblin'
> Hopin' and praying someday that truth might set us all free
> And just 'cause the media won't respond—don't mean there's noth-
>   in' going on
> And brother what'll ya do if there's somethin' to
> All the words inside this song?

More specifically, these theories range from a plot by the United Nations to establish a one-world government to federal cover-ups of UFOs. Many group members prepare for armed conflict by stockpiling weapons, ammunition, and food, among other things, which they believe they will need to survive. They believe that this is necessary because of the inevitable consolidation of the new world order. There are some small variations in the explanation of the true meaning of the new world order and who is behind it; however, it can be generalized as a wide conspiracy of different individuals, including international bankers, socialists, liberals, politicians, members of the military, and elites whose aim is to form a UN-centered, one-world government. Groups are readying themselves to defend American sovereignty.

An element of many of these groups is Christian Identity. An unusual reading of the Bible central to Christian Identity is the notion that the true descendants of the Israelites are White Europeans. They also believe that White people descended from Adam and Eve, but non-Whites, whom they deem "mud people," came from another form of creation. Christian Identity believers also argue that Jews are descendants of Satan (as a result of Eve mating with the serpent). The religious doctrine justifies, in their minds, their derogation of African Americans and their deep anti-Semitism (Bushart, Craig, & Bames, 1998). Not all right-wing extremist group members follow Christian Identity. However, racists and anti-Semites have found common ground with the Christian Identity movement because both believe that the end of the world will occur after a battle between good and evil. The difference lies in the former believing that a race war will occur after the destruction of the Jews (government is a pawn of the Jews), with Whites emerging victorious; the latter "view Washington politicians as evil conspirators laying the foundation for the soon-to-be revealed Antichrist, whose reign of terror will end only when Jesus Christ returns to earth in glory" (Abanes, 1996, p. 3). How is it that they share such beliefs? According to Abanes (1996):

> A preoccupation with the end-times is shared by Christians and White supremacists because many White supremacists emerged from mainstream Christian denominations. Unfortunately, these non-Christian defectors from the faith have borrowed heavily from their Christian roots, picking up those doctrines that are most appealing—especially beliefs associated with end-times—and blending them with racial prejudice.
>
> (p. 3)

The *National Vanguard* Magazine

In the May/June 2007 issue of the *National Vanguard*, the magazine of the National Alliance, leader Erich Gliebe (2007) discussed Jewish behavior:

> It is easy to list the things that Jews do: but it is less easy to offer a reasonable explanation of why they do the things they do. If one thinks about it logically, there is no immediate rational reason for Jews to behave the way they do. In America, for example, this country opened its doors to them, allowing them to flee persecution for their behavior from many European countries. They were allowed to settle, flourish, and gain positions of great influence here.
>
> And what do they do in return? Jews are active in almost every single movement that seeks to destroy the very same America that gave them sanctuary. From immigration issues through attempts to suppress freedom of speech, with anti-First amendment bills before Congress like the current "hate crimes" legislation, you name it: Jews are behind it.

European Groups and the American Connection

In their book, Kaplan and Weinberg (1998) provide an account of what they call the Euro-American right. Is there an international movement of groups and political parties such as the militias, patriots, neo-Nazis, and skinheads? The authors examine the relationship between groups in the United States and Europe. They argue that there are several conditions evident in both Europe and the United States that aided in the mobilization of this transatlantic movement. According to Kaplan and Weinberg (1998) "movements are sustained interactions between aggrieved social actors and allies, and opponents and public authorities" (p. 77). These factors include the rise in the number of immigrants seeking a better life in advanced industrial countries, the weakening of the family, a changing economic situation, and less confidence in democratic institutions. The authors also suggest that the recent emergence of radical-right groups represents a counterrevolution against new social movements, such as environmentalism, women's movements, and so on. The Euro-American right share a common subculture: "It consists of a shared set of myths, symbols, beliefs, and forms of artistic expression that set it apart on a transnational basis from other subcultures" (Kaplan & Weinburg, 1998, p. 18). They also have a common identity, which, for the most part, is White racial solidarity. However, cultural affinity, common historical experience, and belief in shared destiny can also form the basis of this identity.

Jared Taylor and the American Renaissance Group

Jared Taylor's views on race, as quoted in Swain and Nieli (2003, pp. 90–91): I think race relations are essentially unchanged for the last forty or fifty years. I think that the greatest set of problems having to do with race is simply inherent to multiracialism. There has never been a multiracial society on the face of the earth in which there was *not* racial friction, and in fact the most stable multiethnic or multiethnic societies that I can think of have been ones in which there was some kind of quite firm hierarchy of different groups, whether it be in the United States—if you're just speaking of blacks and whites, for example—or South Africa . . . Race of course isn't the only source of group conflict.

Probably language may be the most fertile source of conflict after that, but any kind of group identification, be it religion, language, race, culture, tribe, all of these things are sources of friction—far from being the kind of course of strength that we have been encouraged to take them to be. But as far as the United States is concerned, I think, well, there are many, many subsidiary aspects of this problem, but, as I say, the great source—the original problem, the original sin, if you will—is the attempt to try and construct a society of such disparate racial elements.

Connections have been made across Europe and the Atlantic with like-minded groups (Lee, 1997). In fact, much of the influence is from east to west. These connections may be personal, a result of movement entrepreneurs who want to spread the word in person or distribute materials abroad. Contact could also be through a cybercommunity. Kaplan and Weinberg (1998) conclude that the existence of such a movement is not an immediate threat to Western democracy. In other words, they are not a "single minded conspiratorial organization" (p. 77). Nevertheless, these connections do take place, and the conditions exist to keep the connections alive. For example, ties with the National Alliance extend beyond U.S. borders, notably Europe. The National Alliance has ties to groups such as the British National Party (BNP) and the National Democratic Party (NPD) in Germany, amongst others. C18 is a British neo-Nazi group said to be inspired by the work of William Pierce (Ryan, 2003), but his reach extends far beyond them. According to Ryan (2003), "he holds mythical status among white supremacists, running an international empire, which is particularly strong in northern Europe and Scandinavia" (p. 18).

The British National Party

The British National Party's (2007) views on immigration, from its Manifesto:

> On current demographic trends, we, the native British people, will be an ethnic minority in our own country within sixty years. To ensure that this does not happen, and that the British people retain their homeland and identity, we call for an immediate halt to all further immigration, the immediate deportation of criminal and illegal immigrants, and the introduction of a system of voluntary resettlement whereby those immigrants who are legally here will be afforded the opportunity to return to their lands of ethnic origin assisted by a generous financial incentives both for individuals and for the countries in question. We will abolish the 'positive discrimination' schemes that have made white Britons second class citizens. We will clamp down on the flood of "asylum seekers", all of whom are either bogus or can find refuge much nearer to their homes.

Leaders, Members, and Recruitment

There is little systematic analysis available of the leaders and members. However, what is clear is that the leaders are men, and most of the members are, as well. Women are expected to perform traditional roles in the group (Ezekiel, 1996; Ryan, 2003). One study by Ezekiel (1996) argues that the groups draw from lower income sectors of White society, although the Christian Patriots also draw from the middle class. One leader of the Michigan patriot movement, Robert Miles, put it bluntly: "We work with losers" (quoted in

Ezekiel, 1996, p. 30). In fact, the decline in the militia movement, for example, is attributed in part to Timothy McVeigh, but also to the improvement in the economy during the last part of the 1990s, the improved availability of jobs, and the end of the Clinton administration, despite the irony of that administration's oversight of economic growth and prosperity. According to one former Michigan militia member, "The militia grew because of fear, and without fear, the militia will recede. People [i.e., militia members] have the feeling George Bush is America's savior. They have cable TV, and the beer's cold" ("McVeigh helped," 2001).

That being said, some groups are attempting to widen the scope of their membership to appeal to more educated and wealthy individuals. Jared Taylor of the American Renaissance Group claims the group's magazine has readers that are educated and of "above average income."

> We did a reader survey some years ago. My recollection is that, oh, something on the order of about 75 percent of the readers or subscribers were men, they tended to be of an average age of about forty to forty-five, they are overwhelmingly college educated, and they have above average income. Also, they tend to be conservative in their political views, and my recollection is that about half of them pronounce themselves to be Christians. The other half expressed no particular religious orientation.
>
> (Swain & Nieli, 2003, p. 90)

Nick Griffin, leader of the British Nationalist Party (BNP) believes that his party can appeal more broadly to people. Ryan (2003) relates his impressions of the interview with Griffin several years ago, before he became the leader of the BNP.

> As I listen to Griffin's soft, smooth words, I reflect that, to your average member of the public, the BNP's supporter is still more likely this SiegHeiling skinhead than the small businessman or graduate Griffin tells me he's now so keen to attract. It is a difficult image problem.
>
> (p. 58)

Membership in these groups tends to fluctuate, but committed leaders recruit constantly.

One thing that is clear is that they are not all suffering from mental illness. Take the case of Timothy McVeigh, who admitted orchestrating the Oklahoma City bombing, and considered the deaths of 19 children "collateral damage." (Collateral damage is a term used by the U.S. military to describe civilian death during times of war.) After 25 hours of psychiatric evaluation, a psychiatrist "concluded that his patient was deeply depressed and singularly focused, but not insane" (Romano, 2001, p. A3). As the execution of Timothy McVeigh approached, the weekly magazine *Newsweek* published a special edition on evil, and the journalist writing the story was quickly disabused of any notion that people who commit either serial killings, mass genocide, or terrorist acts like those committed by McVeigh or Ted Kazinski, the Unabomber, are irrational or insane.

In addition to holding public forums and meetings, these groups used a variety of methods to gain new recruits and to disseminate information. There are magazines, newsletters, radio broadcasts, television appearances, and music CDs. For example, the National Alliance publishes a magazine (National Vanguard), has a newsletter (National Alliance Bulletin), radio addresses (American Dissident Voices) and has a variety of book and record businesses (Anti-defamation League, n.d.). Those affiliated or interested in Jared Taylor's American Renaissance group can read *American Renaissance Magazine*. As Taylor explains, "the purpose of *American Renaissance* is to discuss issues that are of interest to whites. After all, every other racial group in the country has groups and media organs that speak for them, and the purpose of *American Renaissance* is to speak for whites" (Swain & Nieli, 2003, p. 88).

Leaders such as Tom Metzger of the White Aryan Resistance are well versed in the importance of using music. There are White supremacist recording labels, such as Resistance Records, and numerous racist bands with names like Angry Aryans (with albums titled, for instance, *Racially Motivated Violence*), Blue Eyed Devils, and Beserkr (*Crush the Weak*). In his discussion of the British neo-Nazi group, Combat-18, Ryan (2003) pointed out that control over the music business is lucrative and has actually resulted in violence between members of this group. In his book he describes an internal struggle that took place in C18 between Will Browning and Charlie Sargent, resulting in the killing of one member, Chris Castle, who was one of Browning's men, by Charlie Sargent.

> The reality on the ground for Combat-18 was football violence and the far right music scene. When I first met Charlie, for example, he was holding a large bag of illegal white-power CDs, which he willingly displayed. These discs helped fund the group's activities. With the formation of ISD Records—the name taken from the late lead singer of skinhead band Skrewdriver, neo-nazi hero Ian Stuart Donaldson—C18 launched into the world of commerce. It was the first time a right-wing group had controlled such a large money-making venture. ISD produced scores of albums and made hundreds of thousands of pounds for the gang.
>
> (p. 74)

These profits, though, were one of the main causes of the feud within C18 and the murder of Chris Castle. Browning controlled the music business and differed with Charlie over how to spend the funds. During the autumn of 1996, the two men began to argue over spending and over the group's future direction. Sargent wanted to dominate the far-right scene as a territorial, tribal gang—an extension of a football hooligan firm, really—while Browning preferred to create a smaller, terrorist-style organization. This disagreement eventually resulted in Castle's murder and a series of Danish letter bombings, with each side accusing the other of working for the State and acting as police informants. The surviving C18 faction became committed to existing as a smaller, more hard-line group (pp. 28–29).

The Internet also serves as a way to disseminate information and of course to keep groups and members connected to each other. These groups can then also post their information to the Internet. Others such as *Stormfront* are dedicated to putting out the word from all groups. According to Swain and Nieli (2003) "*Stormfront* is really a web junction box that provides the web surfer with links to literally hundreds of other white racialist websites ranging from fairly mainstream European heritage organizations to the outer fringes of neo-Nazi and white militia groups. *Stormfront* reportedly receives many tens of thousands of visitors each month" (p. 153).

Race in Brazil

The United States is not the only country in the Western Hemisphere with a history of slavery. Indeed, Brazil had the largest slave population in the hemisphere. Despite myths to the contrary (e.g., Freyre, 1956; Tannenbaum, 1947), slavery in Brazil was brutal. Slave death rates were so high that reproduction rates were low, the average mining slave lived only 7–12 years, and 80% of slave children did not live long enough to reach adulthood (Marx, 1998; Mattoso, 1986). Slaves died from disease and harsh working conditions, and, because of the terrible conditions in which they lived, there were numerous slave revolts. Finally, in 1888 slavery was abolished, but the Black former slaves were left in dreadful conditions, "lacking any means to advance themselves or to compete, isolated in rural areas or in the newly emerging urban slums, or favelas" (Marx, 1998, p. 161).

Despite the legacy of slavery, Brazil prides itself on having a nonracist society. This is also a myth, one that has been increasingly decried by Brazil's Afro-Brazilian community. The myth arises from the fact that, after abolition of slavery, Brazil sought to avoid the kind of race-based conflicts that occurred in the United States. This was done through a conscious policy of miscegenation, encouraging the intermarriage of Black and White people in order to water down African heritage (in sharp contrast to the prohibition of race mixing in the United States after slavery).

There was certainly racial prejudice in Brazil, but inequality was socially, rather than politically, enforced. After slavery, for example, Whites were encouraged to immigrate from European countries and Africans were not allowed to, even though formal discrimination was prohibited by law. In addition, Brazilians appreciated and embraced many African cultural remnants in art, music, and dance, in particular. This, along with official encouragement of people to label themselves White, reduced Black racial group identity, and reduced the incentives of Blacks to mobilize politically. The average White income is twice that of Blacks'; Afro-Brazilians have a higher unemployment rate than Whites, and, when employed, they are in lower skilled and lower paying jobs; Afro-Brazilians have shorter life expectancies than Whites; and race is correlated with poorer physical health, as well (Hanchard, 1993; Marx, 1998).

Beginning in the late 1970s, in part as the result of the beginning of a gradual return to civilian government following 20 years of military rule, Brazil began to experience a newly mobilized Afro-Brazilian movement, particularly the *Movimento Negro Unificado*. Yet, many Afro-Brazilians, including Black politicians, are still reluctant to challenge the myth of Brazil's racial democracy. The great irony in Brazil is that, without systematic and institutional racial discrimination, group identity and mobilization were limited, despite the fact that race matters in Brazil, and Afro-Brazilians have a great deal to say about the de facto inequality in Brazilian society.

South Africa

In 1948, the system of apartheid, which divided people according to racial categories, was instituted in South Africa. According to Eades (1999), "Apartheid was a radical and extreme extension of a system of segregation originating with colonial conquest and gradually evolving into complex sometimes uncoordinated institutions in the late nineteenth and early twentieth centuries" (p. 4). Within the system of apartheid were four racial categories: the Whites, the Coloreds, the Indians, and the Africans. Beginning with the Whites, each category was considered inferior to the one preceding it. In other words, Whites were considered superior to Coloreds, Indians, and Africans; Coloreds were superior to Indians and Africans; and so forth.

The Whites were made up of British English speaking settlers and Dutch Afrikaner settlers. Even though they were considered part of the same White category, Afrikaners and English speakers were not a unified, homogenous group. There were considerable clashes between these two distinct ethnic groups, exhibited mostly during the Boer War (1899–1902), as both tried to assert their power in South Africa (Marx, 1998). But as Eades (1999) explains:

> As Afrikaners came to dominate state power in South Africa, their sense of identity and destiny increasingly became more racial than cultural. A study carried out among Afrikaners in 1977 illustrated this shift. Before 1948 most of the Afrikaners' focus was on distinguishing themselves from the English-speakers. After 1948, however, the focus changed to race as apartheid based itself on racial distinction and had to be made legitimate.
>
> (p. 35)

The Coloreds were a broad racial category that included slaves from Madagascar, Indonesia, and tropical Africa, as well as indigenous Khoisan people. They were Christians and Muslims, farm laborers and artisans, and had many cultural differences (Eades, 1999). The mostly Hindu Indians were descendants of workers who were brought to work on sugar plantations between 1860 and 1911. Another wave of Indian immigrants, who were mostly Muslim, came as British subjects beginning in the 1870s. Finally, the Africans were the largest category, making up 70% of the population of South Africa. This category encompassed many different tribes and clans and was not by any means a homogenous group.

In addition to classifying individuals, other legislation was passed that prohibited the mixing of races by marriage or sexual contact between them. The Bantu Authorities Act also established "homelands," which were essentially independent states that each African was assigned to. Thus, Africans became citizens of a homeland and not South Africa. Therefore, they had no natural political rights. In essence, the apartheid system determined the political, social, and economic status of an individual because being in a certain group afforded one a certain status. In this system, Whites benefited the most. Thus, Afrikaners, in particular, had a vested interest in maintaining such a system. They did this through brutal repression of the non-White population.

The dismantling of the system began in February 1990, when President F. W. deKlerk announced sweeping changes in the country. The constitution was rewritten and elections were held, bringing Nelson Mandela, an African, to the presidency. Why, after all those years, did this system of institutionalized racism finally end? There was significant pressure internationally upon the South African government to end apartheid. In addition, domestic pressure became more intense. Possibly, deKlerk and many other Afrikaners realized that they could not maintain such a system, given that the Black majority, in particular, would no longer accept their inferior status in society.

The end of apartheid is also understandable in the context of the political psychological theories set forth at the beginning of this chapter. White powerholders did not give up without a struggle. Perceptual change among Whites was gradual, and is attributable in part to a freer media, which showed the opposition as reasonable and organized, thereby pushing the "skeptical master race to the necessity of negotiations as equals" (Adam & Moodley, 1993, p. 230). Increased de facto integration in universities and churches also influenced a change in White values. But it was perhaps the strategy of inclusive national identity of the African National Congress (ANC), the umbrella opposition organization, that was crucial. By informing the South African Whites that they would be included as equals, not punished, in the post-apartheid South Africa, ANC reduced the threat to the White identity group. Whites came to understand that things would change, but that they would not face retribution. After apartheid ended, South Africa engaged in extensive efforts to heal the wounds. The truth and reconciliation process in South Africa lasted from 1996 to 1998. A more extensive discussion of the process can be found in Chapter 14.

The South African case is interesting, because it demonstrates a pattern anticipated by both realistic conflict theory and social identity theory and also by patterns of group formation discussed in Chapter 4. With regard to realistic conflict theory, the non-White groups competed with each other for resources (access to jobs, rights, etc.), until a superordinate goal—eliminating apartheid—united them. In terms of social identity, the South African case shows the malleability of race and ethnicity. The architects created a form of social categorization that would unite non-Whites. African ethnic groups ("tribes") had many conflicts among themselves and were divided from the Coloreds. However, apartheid gave them a common cause and enabled them to bridge their differences, thus changing ethnicity as a central political dividing point to race as a central factor in uniting these groups to oppose the apartheid regime (Marx, 1998).

Duckitt (1994) examined the political psychology of racism in South Africa and argues that getting to its roots is complicated when the system as a whole institutionalizes racism. It offers the opportunity to explore the role of conformity pressures in producing prejudice, as well as arguments that authoritarian personality characteristics are associated with prejudice toward out-groups. After reviewing a number of studies, Duckitt (1994) relates that studies of authoritarianism, using Altemeyer's right-wing Authoritarianism Scale, did find that authoritarianism is important in producing prejudice in South Africa. In addition, during the apartheid era in South Africa, there were differences in degrees of racism, with English-speaking Whites being less racist than Afrikaans-speaking Whites. As in the United States, education made a difference, with prejudice falling as years of education increased. However, conformity pressures did not emerge as an important factor in prejudice in South Africa. Instead, racially prejudiced attitudes were learned through socialization.

Finally, South Africa offers a laboratory for the study of perceptions by the previously oppressed of their former oppressors, once the power tables are turned. Duckitt and Mphuthing (1998) examined this question. Studies from the apartheid era show that Black Africans resented the power and privilege of Afrikaners more than that of English-speaking Whites. The supremacy of the Afrikaners was seen as illegitimate. Black Africans perceived themselves to be disadvantaged compared to Afrikaners, and were outraged about it. The Duckitt and Mphuthing study examined African attitudes toward Afrikaners, before and after the first democratic election in South Africa in May 1994. The two studies were done just four months apart. Before the election, which was won by Nelson Mandela and which ended the Afrikaner lock on political power, Africans saw themselves as less disadvantaged relative to Afrikaners. Duckitt and Mphuthing note that in a 4-month period, the socioeconomic disadvantages of the African communities did not change significantly. What did change was the power they held and their sense that the political system was legitimate and just. Under those circumstances, "inequality in post-transition South Africa could be viewed as less unfair and less equitable than it was before the election" (1998, p. 827).

CONCLUSION

In this chapter, a number of theories are used to look at different aspects of race. Although race in the United States has received the lion's share of study in political psychology, we did look at some cross-national examples in Brazil and South Africa. The theories used to examine different takes on race relations included realistic conflict theory, social identity theory, social learning theory, and social dominance theory. In our discussion of race, we entertained difficult arguments found in the literature about how much racism remains in the United States. As far as the literature on the United States is concerned, one camp argues that attitudes toward politics changed, in that race-related issues are not judged by many Whites in terms of racial attitudes, but in terms of other attitudes. Hence, for example, White Americans who favor racial integration may oppose school busing, not because they are closet racists, but because they do not want their children going to schools miles away from home. On the other side of the debate is the symbolic racism school, which maintains that racism is alive and well in America, but that people know it is considered inappropriate to be openly racist, so they hide their racist views behind traditional values such as Protestant ethic and individualism. They say they disapprove of politics designed to help Black Americans not because the beneficiaries are Black, but because no one, White or Black, should get a government handout. Although not explicitly argued, there is a strong relationship between symbolic racism arguments and the arguments made in social learning theory that people learn racial attitudes from their families and societies are rewarded for them. Racism in the United States and other countries is alive and well, as we also demonstrated with our discussion of the various White groups that exist and continue to perpetuate racist ideas.

Topics, Theories/Explanations, and Cases Covered in Chapter 8

Topics	Theories/Models	Cases
Race	Realistic conflict theory	United States
	Social learning theory	Brazil
	Social identity theory	South Africa
	Social dominance theory	
	Politics-is-complicated model	
	Symbolic racism model	

Key Terms

contact hypothesis

minimal group paradigm

phenomenal

   absolutism error

politics-is-complicated model

prejudice

projection

realistic conflict theory

social dominance theory

social learning theory

symbolic racism

ultimate attribution error

Suggestions for Further Reading

Duckitt, J. (1994). *The social psychology of prejudice*. New York: Praeger.

Fiske, S. (1998). Stereotyping, prejudice, and discrimination. In D.T. Gilbert, S.T. Fiske, & G. Lindzey (Eds.), *The handbook of social psychology* (4th ed., Vol. 2, pp. 357–411). New York: McGraw-Hill.

Ford, R.T. (2008). *The race card: How bluffing about bias makes race relations worse*. New York: Farrar, Straus, & Giroux.

Kinder, D., & Sanders, L. (1996). *Divided by color: Racial politics and democratic ideals*. Chicago, IL: University of Chicago Press.

Kitano, H., & Nakaoka, S. (2001). Asian Americans in the twentieth century. In N. Choi (Ed.), *Psychological aspects of the Asian-American experience* (pp. 7–18). New York: Hawthorn Press.

Marger, M.N. (2003). *Race and ethnic relations: American and global perspectives* (6th ed.). Belmont, CA: Thompson Wadsworth.

Marx, A. (1998). *Making race and nation: A comparison of the United States, South Africa and Brazil*. Cambridge: Cambridge University Press.

Sears. D., Sidanius, J., & Bobo, L (Eds.). (2000). *Racialized politics: The debate about racism in America*. Chicago, IL: University of Chicago Press.

Shipler, D. (1997). *A country of strangers: Blacks and Whites in America.* New York: Knopf.

Sniderman, P., & Carmines, E. (1997). *Reaching beyond race.* Cambridge, MA: Harvard University Press.

Notes

1. It should be noted that social identity theory is simplified in this critique, in that it maintains that comparisons that result in out-group derogation are only made with relevant groups, not all groups. A university student, for example, would simply not compare his group's socioeconomic status with that of his professor's group, because that is not a relevant comparison group. On the other hand, if a student found students in a neighboring university to be generally more wealthy than his own group of students, that would be a relevant comparison group and it may be stereotyped as "a bunch of lazy rich kids who go to school to please their wealthy parents and who don't study." Moreover, social identity theory does maintain that people do not select social competition—that is, behaviors that seek to alter the social status relationship of their group—with those who have greater advantages unless they identify a clear alternative future.

2. There are many important methodological issues associated with getting and measuring an accurate picture of racial attitudes. Question wording; the nature of survey research, from which most of the data is drawn; race of the interviewer; and the use of telephone or person-to-person interviews, are all important in affecting the data. See Chapter 3 of Shuman et al. (1997) for a review.

3. Koreans and Filipinos immigrated in the early 20th century as well, many to provide cheap labor in plantations in Hawaii.

Chapter 9

FROM ETHNIC CONFLICT TO GENOCIDE

What does it mean to be Italian American, or Swiss German, or Yoruba, or Azeri? These labels, which are used to delineate groups of people from each other all over the world, are actually ethnic identities. Ethnic groups have cultural, religious, and linguistic commonalities, as well as a shared view that the group has a common origin or a unique heritage or birthright (Smith, 1981; Young, 1976). As Rothschild (1981) explained, ethnic groups are "collective groups whose membership is largely defined by real or putative ancestral inherited ties, and who perceive these ties as systematically affecting their place and fate in the political and socioeconomic structures of their state and society" (p. 9). Ethnic groups are considered exclusive rather than inclusive: outsiders cannot join an ethnic group with which they do not share a common heritage. For example, a person from Zimbabwe could move to India, work, vote in national elections, and speak Hindi, becoming part of the Indian nation, but could not ever be accepted as an ethnic Indian, because that person does not possess a common ancestral heritage with other ethnic Indians.

Ethnicity has become a particular focus of attention in political psychology because of the explosion of ethnic conflicts in various states within the past decade. However, interest in **ethnocentrism** can be traced back to William Graham Sumner's introduction of the term in 1906. He described it as "the view of things in which one's own group is the center of everything . . . and looks with contempt on outsiders" (p. 12). Ethnocentrism is singled out as the cause of ethnic conflict, political instability, and war (Hammond & Axelrod, 2006). Although ethnic conflict always existed, with the end of the Cold War, the focus and attention of the international community shifted from conflict between the superpowers to ethnic conflicts within countries. In countries where internal conflict has erupted, the state is no longer able to function as an authority over the groups. The conflicts are perplexing and surprising in many cases, because members of one ethnic group are now willing to kill members of another group who were formerly seen as neighbors, coworkers, people they went to school with, and perhaps even friends.

Ethnicity has an enormous impact upon group relations within countries and unfortunately has resulted in many atrocities being committed by one group against another. Rwanda, Bosnia, Chechnya, Democratic Republic of the Congo, Liberia, Sierra Leone, Kosovo, and East Timor are only a few of the countries or regions that have experienced severe ethnic conflict and violence, much of which is ongoing. Even when an area seems to achieve peace, frequently no real political solution has been found. As a result, conflict can resume at any time.

MULTIETHNIC OR MULTISECTARIAN STATES

Before looking at cases of ethnic conflict, it is important to describe some of the political characteristics of the countries most likely to experience ethnic conflict. In multiethnic or multisectarian states, there are at least two ethnic groups, neither of which is capable of assimilating or absorbing the other or of seceding and maintaining independence. This is an important definitional point. Multinational countries, which are discussed in the next chapter, do have national identity groups capable of existing as independent countries. But, by definition, multiethnic and multisectarian states are composed of ethnic groups that cannot realistically establish independent countries. People in multiethnic or multisectarian countries give primary loyalty to their ethnic or sectarian group, rather than to the broader community living in the country (see Figure 9.1). The ethnic groups frequently realize that they do not have the resources to form their own state, but they may strive for the maximum autonomy possible and/or a large share of political and economic power in the state they share with other ethnic groups.[1] Often, members of the groups in multiethnic states maintain separate, geographically concentrated communities, but there are many instances in which ethnic group members are dispersed across the country. As is seen in the Bosnia case, ethnic groups sometimes have ethnic kin living close by in an independent country. In Bosnia, Bosnian Serbs and Croatians wanted to join Serbia and Croatia, respectively. To do that, however, required ethnic cleansing of one another, and of the Muslims living in Bosnia. This case is discussed in detail later. The disintegration of Yugoslavia, of which Bosnia was a part, is discussed more fully in the chapter on nationalism, because, with the exception of its republic of Bosnia-Herzegovina, Yugoslavia was a multinational state. Many of the multiethnic states found today are former colonies. As a result of colonialism, the ethnic groups found themselves part of a state structure created by and imposed upon them by the colonial power. These are artificial states in the sense that they were literally drawn on a map by an external power. In many cases, dominant ethnic groups within these colonial states took on the role as local elite, by serving the interests of the colonial power. Their political behaviors are a reflection of their concern with matters such as the security, autonomy, and welfare of their ethnic group, rather than those of the country as a whole.

In order to accommodate different ethnic groups' concerns, several structural options are employed by many multiethnic states, including consociationalism and federalism. These devices permit some degree of autonomy by offering some local political control, but they also allow for national governmental control to exist. Both consociationalism and federalism are particularly appealing to those states

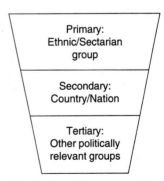

Figure 9.1 Political Identity and Loyalty in Multiethnic and Multisectarian States

that have geographically concentrated communities. Consociationalism, or power sharing, as it is also referred to, has several features. Political parties representing the ethnic groups first form a coalition government and each group is represented in this coalition government through proportional representation. Rules are then implemented that are used to govern the public sector. Each group is also afforded a degree of autonomy over matters deemed important to them. Finally, there are constitutional vetoes for minority groups. Switzerland, with its strong German, French, and Italian ethnic groups, each with their own cantons, or governing regions, is a classic example of consociationalism.

In federal structures, there is a separation between a central government and provincial governments, each having different spheres of influence. This type of government has a governing constitution and bicameral legislature. In constitutional matters, both levels of government must give their approval. As a general rule, in the legislatures, smaller parties are overrepresented.

Even if either of these structures is put in place, there is no guarantee that they will completely solve the conflict between groups within multiethnic states. In former colonies in particular, groups that engaged in conflict do not have short memories of the acts perpetrated against them. For this reason, it is very difficult to foster a sense of community between the groups. An examination of some cases of ethnic conflict will demonstrate how quickly they can become inflamed, how violent they can be, and how difficult they are to stop. Many multiethnic states employ federalist institutional structures. Russia is one, and Nigeria, a case described shortly, is another.

EXPLANATIONS OF CONFLICT

The same psychological explanations of racial conflicts can be used to explain ethnic conflict. There is some basis for realistic conflict and competition among these ethnic groups for power, influence, and autonomy in a political system. In good times, cooperation in pursuit of common goals are possible. In bad times, competition for resources and power can be fierce. But these conflicts are not simply contingent upon good or bad times. The roots are psychological and so deep that conflicts easily erupt when an opportunity or threat is perceived by one ethnic group vis-à-vis another and when at least one group is mobilized, often by political leaders, to challenge the perceived threat or seize the opportunity. From social identity theory, we know that groups engage in social comparison. When the outcome of that comparison is negative, groups are motivated to change their status. An insecure social comparison results in a conclusion that an out-group has an unfair advantage and that the relationship among the groups is conceived of as unfair, among other perceived inequities. One strategy for changing a group's status is social competition, which takes place when a subordinate group engages in direct competition with the dominant group. The group in the dominant position will feel threatened by the challenge to its status by a subordinate group. When this occurs, competition can lead to conflict. Even without conscious social comparisons, social identity theory suggests that the mere presence of different groups is sufficient to cause conflict and competition.

Many of the ethnic conflicts that occurred in the post–Cold War era have been shockingly brutal and can devolve into genocide. The discussions of group behavior in Chapters 3 and 4 provide some insights into how violence can become so severe. These are situations in which the group perceives an intense threat, which, in turn, increases cohesion; dehumanization of other groups; deindividuation, so people see the group as responsible for events, not their own actions as individuals; and strong pressures for conformity and unanimity in the face of threat. Strong emotions associated with out-groups, discussed in Chapter 4, erupt and add to the violence. The emotions emanating from ethnic out-group stereotypes are often extremely powerful. They can change from simmering bitterness and resentment to rage and hatred toward other ethnic groups when underlying conflicts increase in intensity. At the same time, people experience increased love and attachment to their own ethnic group. In addition, in ethnic conflicts, one is unlikely to find the reticence evident in American racial politics, in which political elites resort to implicit code word references to race in race-related issues. In ethnic conflicts, such as those discussed in the next section, political leaders actively manipulate the stereotypes and emotions, in order to mobilize their ethnic brethren against other ethnic groups. They use stereotypes and emotions to arouse intense feelings of hatred and anger toward other ethnic groups. As Kaufman (2001) notes, "If emotional appeals to ethnic themes are simultaneously appeals to ideas that lead one to blame another group, those appeals are apt simultaneously to arouse the feelings of anger and aggression most likely to motivate people to want to fight" (p. 9). Leaders play an important role in defining a threat or an opportunity, in sharpening perceptions of ethnic identity, and in furthering conflict by obstructing diplomatic solutions. In the process, committing acts of violence against others, for the sake of the in-group, becomes more likely, even if the victims once were friends.

In recent years, another psychological explanation, **evolutionary psychology**, has been offered for ethnic conflict and ethnocentrism, an explanation that seeks to contribute to our understanding of the degree of violence that can erupt (Hammond & Axelrod, 2006; Shaw & Wong, 1989; Tooby & Cosmides, 1990; Waller, 2002). The evolutionary psychology perspective on human behavior is that it is "driven by a set of *universal reasoning circuits* that were *designed by natural selection* to solve *adaptive problems* faced by our *hunter-gatherer ancestors*" (Waller, 2002, p. 145). Universal reasoning circuits refer to the information processing and problem solving functions of the brain. These work to enable people to adapt to changes in their environments over time, including changes in communication, warfare capabilities, and economic production. Throughout this evolution, there is competition among groups for resources and other essentials of survival. Some groups win and others lose, and in the long run, as Waller argued, "all of us today owe our existence to having 'winners' as ancestors, and each of us today is designed, at least in some circumstances, to compete" (2002, p. 150). The legacy of the evolutionary process is in-group favoritism, and a predisposition to compete with out-groups. To not compete was, and is, according to this perspective, a recipe for extinction of the group. Hence, ethnocentrism is universal (Shaw & Wong, 1989; Waller, 2002).

At the same time, the evolutionary psychology perspective has attempted to explain in-group solidarity, cooperation, and altruism as a result of an evolutionary need for adaptation. Why, they ask, do individuals in a group cooperate with each other, work together to achieve a common goal, and even sacrifice their lives for one another, when a self-interested individual would never do something so seemingly irrational? It is done for the survival and benefit of the group. Hunting together, cooperating in group-benefit related tasks, all increase the resources, including safety, available for the group, and thus for its individual members (Shaw & Wong, 1989).

THE PERPETRATORS OF VIOLENCE: POLITICAL EXTREMISTS

In many of the cases to be considered below and in the following chapters, horrific violence occurs. It is worth looking at some general arguments about people who commit these acts. These people can be considered political extremists.

One of the central themes of this chapter is that political psychological studies of such people demonstrate that under the right circumstances the most ordinary people can be the perpetrators of extremist actions, or they can be passive bystanders who watch while such acts are carried out and do nothing to stop them. What is an extremist and what makes a person an extremist? An **extremist** is a person who is:

> [e]xcessive and inappropriately enthusiastic and/or inappropriately concerned with significant life purposes, implying a focused and highly personalized interpretation of the world. Politically, it is behavior that is strongly controlled by ideology, where the influence of ideology is such that it excludes or attenuates other social, political or personal forces that might be expected to control and influence behavior.
>
> (Taylor, 1991, p. 33)

Extremists then, are concerned only with the logic of their own behavior and their ideological construction of the world. Extremists tend to disregard the lives of others, and disregard alternatives. It follows that extremists are very resistant to change.

Political psychologists have some thoughts on why people are extremists. There are several explanations ranging from personality attributes to the need for group conformity. Let's examine these insights more closely. People who commit extremist actions are typically lacking in empathy for others and tend to dehumanize their victims. However,

> "You can have people who have a well-developed capacity for empathy, relating, who are very close to their friends, but who have been raised in an ideology that teaches them that people of another religion, color, or ethnic group are bad," says psychologist Bruce Perry . . . "They will act in a way that is essentially evil based upon cognition rather than emotion." But the heart and the head interact.

People who grew up amid violence and cruelty are more susceptible to ideologies that dehumanize the other in favor of the self (Begley, 2001, p. 33).

There is disagreement in political psychology as to whether there are particular personality traits commonly found among political extremists. Studies of torturers in Greece and Latin America do not find any particular personality syndrome that differentiates them from people who do not torture. For example, Mika Haritos-Fatouros (1988) did not find evidence of sadism or extreme authoritarianism in Greek torturers before they entered the armed forces. Rosenberg's (1992) studies of torturers in Argentina, although journalistic rather than scientific, described quite normal, career-minded officers who were in charge of the Argentine torture unit. Claudia Reyes-Quilodran (2001) argued that there appear to be two types of torturers, those motivated by ideology, training, and loyalty to the military and those who are simple criminals, but she also found no particular personality type.

Although there does not appear to be a particular personality associated with political extremists, personality is not unimportant. One characteristic that is arguably quite important in explaining the actions of extremists is their response to authority. As we explained in Chapter 2, in his work on the authoritarian personality, Altemeyer discussed the attributes of submission to authority, aggression against nonconformist groups, and conventionalism, which are strongly linked to right wing authoritarianism. Other studies have demonstrated that it is not only people who are high in authoritarianism who can respond very strongly to instructions from authority. People with more education tend to at least *say* that they would resist authority. The **locus of control** personality trait influences susceptibility to authority. **Internals**, that is, people who believe they have considerable control over their fate, are more likely to resist authority than **externals**, people who believe the external environment determines strongly what happens to them (Blass, 1991; Kressel, 1996). Also, people who do not care much about the impression they make on others (low self-monitors) are less susceptible to authority's demands (Kressel, 1996). The series of experiments by Stanley Milgram (1974) are among the most often-cited studies that demonstrate the power of authority.

In the Milgram experiments, subjects were told that they were going to participate in an experiment on learning. They were instructed by an experimenter in a laboratory setting to deliver shocks to a "learner" when he made a mistake. (The learner was in fact a confederate in the experiment.) With each mistake, the subjects were told to increase the electrical voltage. When the learner started to moan and claim a bad heart, the subjects were told to keep delivering the shocks, with instructions such as "the experiment requires you to go on," and "you have no other choice." More than 62% of the subjects delivered the highest level of voltage, ignoring the printed warnings of danger and the screams and protestations of the learner. Most of the subjects who persisted in delivering the shocks did so with great reluctance and asked for permission to discontinue the shocks or called the experimenter's attention to their learner's suffering, demonstrating that the subjects didn't hate the learners, nor did they even dislike them.

Examining the results of his study, Milgram argued that the subjects were not sadistic because the context of the action had to be considered; that is, there is an important person-situation interaction effect. The experimenter appeared to have the legitimate authority to know what could be done, that is, how much electrical voltage the subject could endure. The subjects became integrated into a situation that carried its own momentum. The problem for individuals is how to become disengaged from a situation that has moved in an apparently terrible direction. In subsequent experiments, Milgram found that obedience diminishes rapidly if one person in a group refuses to obey. In addition, distance from the experimenter reduced compliance. If the experimenter sat next to the subject, compliance was high. The farther away he was physically, the more likely people were to refuse to continue administering the shocks. Personality plays a role as well. Elms and Milgram (1966) found that people higher in authoritarianism were more like to be obedient to authority.

Examining extremists from a group perspective also yielded some interesting insights into their behavior. As Baumeister noted (1997), extremist acts of violence are

> nearly always fostered by groups, as opposed to individuals. When someone kills for the sake of promoting a higher good, he may find support and encouragement if he is acting as part of a group of people who share that belief. If he acts as a lone individual, the same act is likely to brand him as a dangerous nut.
>
> (p. 190)

In earlier chapters, we discussed the importance of belonging to groups and seeing those groups positively in comparison to others. When this is not possible, people look for some out-group to blame. Under normal conditions, conflicts among groups can occur over scarce resources, territory, values, ideology, status, security, power, and many other things (Fisher, 1990; Stroebe & Insko, 1989). In conditions of severe socioeconomic and political despair and depression, the environment is often conducive to the identification of one group as a **scapegoat**, a group that is blamed for all of society's illnesses. During hard times, the groups that people are particularly attracted to are those that "provide an ideological blueprint for a better world and an enemy who must be destroyed to fulfill the ideology" (Staub, 1989, p. 17). This is called **social causality** (Hogg & Abrams, 1988). Typically, a negative stereotype of that group is promulgated on a society-wide scale. Next, **social justification** occurs, wherein that group's poor treatment is justified. The most extreme version of this is **dehumanization** of the scapegoat, wherein the group members are regularly described as less than human and therefore deserving of treatment one would not administer to a human being. In Germany during the Hitler era, Jews were regularly vilified and called rats. In Rwanda, before that genocide, the Tutsis were called insects and cockroaches by the Hutu extremists. Under these conditions, hating the enemy becomes a noble and righteous cause in the minds of group members.

The identification of an out-group to place blame upon is important for groups and their members in order to provide an explanation for their own circumstances. But as was noted in Chapter 4, the group also offers individual members important psychological benefits. While there are certainly many reasons a person may join a group, such as ideology and a sense of social support, among others, once they become members, uniform views tend to reinforce the conformity of individuals. In addition, members face so-called psychological traps and the group experiences the escalation of commitment pattern discussed in Chapter 4 (Taylor, 1991). People find themselves in circumstances that require a great amount time and effort toward the accomplishment of the group's goals. It follows that the more investment a person makes in a goal, the harder it becomes to abandon the group, regardless of actual accomplishment of that goal. Commitment to a group, especially one that requires the use of violent behavior, is very psychologically demanding. The more acts of violence one commits, the more psychologically entrapped a person becomes.

At this point, we can pull together some of the patterns we have reviewed in individual and group behavior with the obedience to authority patterns present in the Milgram experiment. People are obedient not only to individual authority figures, but to groups and their authority structure as well. Why? In Chapter 4 we presented several reasons for conformity in groups, including informational social influence, wherein people conform to group norms because they wish to be correct, and conforming enables people to gather information. Normative social influence was also mentioned, wherein people conform in order to be liked. Situational factors such as group size and unanimity also affect conformity. Commitment to the group is also an important situational factor. Consider what will happen if you are not loyal and obedient to a group. If you do not conform to group norms and goals, the most likely outcome is that everyone in the group will dislike you. In fact, you may even be expelled from the group, which can be very threatening, particularly when the group is cohesive, when members are isolated from other groups, and when the group is an important component of a personal identity. Yet, there is a caveat because how you conduct your deviance from a group makes a significant difference. For example, *heretics*, who do not disavow their membership but deviate from the group, fare better than *renegades*, who denounce their membership in a group. This is because a renegade is questioning the core values of a group as opposed to questioning group tactics.

An individual can be obedient to a group even when the group acts in a way that is contrary to an individual's values. However, when an individual is obedient depends on the social context in which the authority is being used, the character of the authority holders, and the nature of the demands that they make. They are more likely to obey when the action is authorized by authority, when the action is routinized, making it mechanical and possible to do with little thought, and when the victim is dehumanized. Obedience is also more likely when individuals want to comply, not because they necessarily agree with the activity, but because of the positive impression gained from compliance (Kelman & Hamilton, 1989; Staub, 1989; Sabini & Silver, 1993). Often the most fanatical members become group leaders, and they act strongly to prevent dissension within the group.

Groups and their members interact in a symbiotic fashion, and being obedient to group norms and the demands of authority are not simply the product of fear or rejection. Groups often indoctrinate members through initiation rites, training, and providing a feeling of being part of a family. These are the forming and norming stages of group development discussed in Chapter 4. The process can be extremely dramatic. Group members who undergo severe initiations or who endure harsh pain and suffering to become a member tend to be more committed to the group than group members who do not have to suffer to join the group (Aronson & Mills, 1959; Wicklund, Cooper, & Linder, 1967). Indoctrination and initiation rites can be brutal, giving the member who survives and becomes a member of the group a strong sense of belonging, having passed the test of strength and will. Indoctrination presents the member with a world view. Torturers in Northern Ireland and Guatemala, for example, were often given horrifically brutal training and indoctrination in anti-communist ideology and the idea that they were saving the country by torturing deviants (Conroy, 2000; Reyes-Quilodran, 2001).

People do not want to let the group down. Staub (1989, 1999, 2000) and Kelman (1990), among others, argue that the factor of human needs must also be introduced to fully understand this type of phenomenon. Generally, the point is that people are not just cogs in these groups' machinery. The perception of hard times is deeply threatening to the extremists, and this activates basic survival needs. They join groups they think will satisfy those fundamental survival needs. The groups are more than social. Obedience and compliance with group norms that demand extremism and violence is done out of more than fear of rejection or punishment. It is done willingly. The group makes it easier, true enough. The group makes it possible for people to distance themselves from the violence by distributing and diffusing responsibility for it. The group provides the moral authority for the actions the individual takes. Groups with this type of cohesion and dedication to a cause are more likely to experience groupthink, introduced in Chapter 4, particularly if their leaders are charismatic and/or narcissistic and unwilling to hear disagreement or critical information.

Finally, research on how perpetrators of acts that are condemnatory perceive their own actions provides important insights on why people do things causing great suffering and harm. Baumeister's (1997) research found that perpetrators see their actions as much less wrong than the victims do. They minimize the harm done, and often explain their actions as justified by the evil nature of the victim. This is an example of patterns of perception described by attribution theory.

The following illustrations of ethnic conflict and genocide will enable us to flesh out some of these political psychological patterns.

CASE ILLUSTRATIONS OF ETHNIC CONFLICT

Ethnic Clashes in Nigeria

Nigeria is a multiethnic state that was a product of colonialism. Nigeria was colonized by the British. Three main ethnic groups make up two thirds of the population: the Hausa/Fulani (who are Muslim), the Yoruba (who are

Christian and Muslims), and the Ibo (who are Christian). Within these three groups, there are many subdivisions, so that, as a whole, Nigeria has more than 248 distinct ethnic groups (Diamond, 1988). The Hausa/Fulani are found in the north, the Yoruba in the west, and the Ibo in the east. However, each region does contain other ethnic groups.

Social stereotypes, group conflict, and social comparison processes are important factors in understanding ethnic conflict in Nigeria. Under British colonialism, Nigeria was partitioned into three regions, each dominated by an ethnic group. The Hausa were chosen by the British to be their administrative representatives. Although the Hausa were permitted to keep their traditional class hierarchy, social structure, and educational system based upon the Koran, the British imposed their own education system and made the common language English in the areas dominated by Yoruba and Ibo. This set forth the basis for ethnic competition after independence: an outside power, the British colonizers, had already established the basis for Hausa superiority, in terms of political power; the other groups' self-comparison with the Hausa would be negative, at least from the standpoint of political power.

Nigeria achieved its independence from Britain in 1960, and the colonial regional structuring based on ethnicity was initially left in place in a federated political system. Ethnic competition preceded independence and quickly became a central factor in Nigerian politics after independence. The Ibos, in the southeast, were tired of the domination by the north. In the early colonial era, the British had considered the Ibo to be the most backward and inferior of Nigeria's ethnic groups. But during the 1930s, the social and economic position of the Ibo had improved. The perception by the British of the Ibo as backward had shifted to view them as "dynamic, aggressive, upwardly mobile" (Young, 1983, p. 206).

During the 1950s, the Ibo became strongly nationalistic, desiring a role in the existing national institutions. The Ibos also tended to be very entrepreneurial, and moved into Hausa and Yoruba regions. Their economic success, as well as their desire for greater participation and political power, was perceived as threatening to other groups. Increasingly, the Ibo were seen, through an anti-Semitic type of stereotype, as insular, elitist, devious, and power- and wealth-acquisitive. Thus, stereotyping and social identity patterns appear in this case. The Ibos were downtrodden, and sought to alter their social, economic, and political roles in Nigeria. This was threatening to the other groups, who had a strong stereotype of Ibos as bad in a variety of ways, and they were not about to let change occur.

In January 1966, Ibo military officers led a successful coup, overthrowing the government. They, in turn, were ousted later that same year by northerners, bringing Lieutenant Colonel Yakubu Gowon to power. Ethnic clashes followed, and many Ibos were killed, particularly in the north. Continued persecution prompted the Ibos to declare independence in the region of the country where they were the numerical majority, which they called Biafra. The federal government refused to let them secede, and, in 1967, a civil war broke out between the Ibos, seeking to establish an independent Biafra, and the federal government of Nigeria. The war, which lasted for three years, ended in a loss for the Ibos and claimed the lives of over one million people, mostly Ibos. After the war, the federal government developed a very important approach to the defeated Ibo: reincorporation into the country, opportunities in education, and reconstruction. This type of policy is crucial to the future of any multiethnic state that contains a defeated breakaway group. And it worked in Nigeria. Despite the one million Biafran deaths, the war is not a topic of discussion and continued resentment in Iboland today.

After the war, ethnic divisiveness continued to plague Nigerian politics. General Gowon was overthrown in a coup in 1975 (Ihonvbere, 1994). General Olusegun Obasanjo, a Yoruba, took power and adopted measures to pave the way for democratic reform and a return to civilian rule. Those reforms included the creation of a new constitution, with provisions that would accommodate ethnic diversity. A new federal state structure was introduced, with 19 states. In order to win the presidency, a candidate would have to receive at least one third of the popular vote and at least one fourth of the vote in two thirds of the 19 states (Shively, 1993).

Since the end of the first 13 years of military rule in 1979, Nigeria only had a few years of intermittent civilian rule, and ethnic conflict and competition have been instrumental in inhibiting the establishment of stable democracy. For example, elections were finally held in 1979, as promised by Obasanjo, bringing the northerner, Shehu Shagari, to power. However, he was overthrown in 1983, amid accusations of corruption, a failing economy, and his inability to deal with ethnic divisions (Shively, 1993). In 1993, Chief Moshood Abiola, a Yoruba, won the election. However, General Ibrahim Babangida, a northerner who had been in power since 1985, nullified the results. Babangida finally stepped down, naming Ernest Shonekan, a civilian, as interim leader for a few months, until the defense minister, General Sani Abacha, took control. In June 1994, Abacha arrested Abiola, and charged him with treason. When Abacha suddenly died in June 1998, an interim leader, General Abdulsalami Abubakar, succeeded him. After years of promises, elections were finally held, and Olusegun Obasanjo took office once again on May 29, 1999. However, Obasanjo took office amid election irregularities such as inflated turnout, the stuffing of ballot boxes, intimidation and bribery of election officials and voters, and alteration of results (Human Rights Watch, 2000). Obasanjo won reelection in 2003, again amid accusations of irregularities in the electoral process. Vice president Goodluck Johnathan came to power in 2010 after death of the president Umaru Yar'Adua, and was elected in 2011. His support lies mainly in the Christian south.

In each case of regime change, the ethnicity of the old and new power holders is centrally important to the people of Nigeria. Each group continually compares itself with the others, and the propensity to identify some basis for a negative social comparison is strong. The power and economic pie in Nigeria is small. Nigeria is a poor country despite its oil, and each group fears the others will get more than their fair share.

The Nigerian case shows how ethnicity and national identification can become mutually exclusive. In Nigeria, control of the state was associated with ethnicity, so extensively that each of the three dominant ethnic groups was susceptible to ethnicity-based political parties and issues. They were constantly fearful that the essence of being Nigerian would be captured by one of the other ethnic groups, and their own group would lose out on power and security. In fact, the Biafran war served as a catalyst for a struggling Nigerian identity to gain momentum. According to Oyovbaire (1984):

> The quantum or quality of national consciousness generated by [federal efforts during the war] is impossible to assess, but there is no doubt that a new public consciousness of the role of the centre previously unknown in the politics, economics and management of the federation had been generated by the civil war. . . . If before the Biafran occupation, Nigeria was just a name—lacking meaning, attachment and symbolism to the literate and nonliterate, the urban unemployed and rural dwellers—after that experience Nigeria became a fact of existence, the federal government being regarded as protector and benefactor.
>
> (pp. 132–133)

Nevertheless, ethnicity continues to be a dominant factor in Nigerian politics, and it continues to cause frequent outbreaks of violence, resulting in hundreds of deaths, on a regular basis. For example, a state of emergency was declared in central Nigeria in 2004 due to attacks on Muslims by Christian militias. The Muslim Boko Haram movement perpetrates attacks and has killed thousands in its drive to establish control in Nigeria. To satisfy ethnic demands, the country has been divided repeatedly into more and more states, currently standing at 36. In the process, the three largest and dominant ethnic groups are distributed among several states. Thus, Nigerian identity remains secondary to ethnic identities and is unlikely to be enhanced by the ongoing corruption, political instability, poverty, and repression of ethnic discontent, such as the execution in 1995 of nine ethnic Ogoni leaders who protested government policies in Ogoniland. This leaves the glaring question of how Nigeria as a state survives, and the answer must be that no group sees an alternative.

Ethnic Cleansing in Bosnia

Yugoslavia was a multinational and multiethnic country. For many years, the people from different ethnic groups lived together harmoniously. After World War II, Yugoslavia's government was headed by a very charismatic leader, Josip Broz Tito, who encouraged a common Yugoslav political identity. In 1980, Tito died, and during the next decade the unity and brotherhood encouraged by Tito gradually unraveled. The final disintegration of Yugoslavia began on June 25, 1991, with the declaration of independence of Croatia and Slovenia. The Yugoslav republic of Bosnia-Herzegovina was declared an independent country on April 5, 1992, and was subsequently recognized as such by the international community. This left a rump Yugoslavia composed of what was left—Serbia and Montenegro.

The powerful pull of in-groups, as well as the impact of negative threatening images, is useful in explaining the conflict that erupted in Bosnia. Bosnia has three main ethnic groups: the Serbs (who are Eastern Orthodox), the Muslims, and the Croatians (who are Roman Catholic). The Serbs and Croatians in Bosnia were part of larger ethnic groups in the Croatian and Serbian republics of Yugoslavia. As Thomas (1996) explained, during the days of Yugoslavian unity

> in Bosnia-Herzegovina, whether Muslim, Orthodox Christian or Roman Catholic Serbs, Croats and Muslims were all comfortable being labeled "Bosnian" even if they believed themselves to be Bosnian Serb, Croat or Muslim. This was because Bosnia was a smaller and narrower representation of the larger concept of multi-ethnic Yugoslavia, a country voluntarily created in 1918 for the South Slav peoples. . . . Bosnia-Herzegovina, like Yugoslavia, denoted territorial space and not ethnic identity.
>
> (p. 30)

The 1991 census demonstrated the importance of ethnic identity, however: 44% self-identified as Muslim, 31.5% Serb, 17% Croat, and only 5.5% Yugoslav. As a republic in Yugoslavia before it disintegrated, Bosnia-Herzegovina could and did provide these groups with opportunities for social mobilization and social creativity. The Yugoslav state prevented one group from being dominant and provided opportunities for all ethnic groups. In fact, the state created the concept of Bosnian Muslims as a distinct ethnic identity in the 1960s, which was more preferable to the Muslims than their previous identities as Croat or Serb Muslims (Thomas, 1996). Intergroup competition was held in check by the Yugoslav government while efforts were made to forge a common identity.

As Yugoslavia fell apart, the three ethnic communities in Bosnia faced a real dilemma. Should they remain part of Yugoslavia or attempt independence? None of the three had the power to dominate an independent Bosnia. The ethnic populations were territorially dispersed, and there was significant intermarriage among the groups. Therefore, the groups could not simply be divided up geographically, providing each its own state in a multi-ethnic country. Nor, given the distribution of ethnic populations and the complexity of their intermixture, could Bosnia simply be divided up, with its Croatian and Serbian ethnics annexed to their respective national states, Croatia and Serbia. The dilemma, by 1991, therefore, became whether to stay with Yugoslavia, which now consisted primarily of Serbs, or attempt independence. Staying in Yugoslavia was threatening to the Muslim and Croat populations. Bosnian Serbs, on the other hand, had every reason to want to remain in what was left of Yugoslavia, where Serbs would be the dominant group. It was in this context that a referendum was held to decide upon independence. The Serbs boycotted the referendum, and the Muslims and Croats voted for independence from Yugoslavia. Bosnian leaders quickly developed a power-sharing arrangement among the parties representing all three ethnic groups in an autonomous Bosnia. That arrangement was doomed to failure, however. The Croatian and Serb communities in

Bosnia each saw an opportunity to join their ethnic brethren in Croatia and Serbia. The strong pull of group identity made this option very attractive for the Bosnian Croats and Bosnian Serbs. This destroyed any basis for power sharing. The Bosnian Serbs declared themselves part of the Serb nation. The Bosnian Croats insisted that they would not remain in Bosnia, if Bosnia remained in Yugoslavia (Woodward, 1995). Eventually, Bosnian Croats marked for themselves a Croat state in western Bosnia-Herzegovina. The Muslim community, recognizing its inability to maintain sovereign independence for long in this setting, was faced with the options of emigration or accepting minority status in Croatia or Serbia.

In Their Own Words: Radovan Karadžić on the Situation of the Bosnian Serbs

Below are some excerpts from a speech given by Radovan Karadžić to the Parliament of Bosnian Serbia, (Republika Srpska) in 1996. Karadžić was the President of Republika Srpska at the time.

Five years have passed since the first multiparty elections in the former Bosnia-Herzegovina, four years and three months since the founding of the Republic and four years since the beginning of the war. There are few nations in the world who were exposed to such trials and suffering in such a short period as our people have been. Centuries and decades which our enemies had spent working on the denationalization of the Serbs west from the Drina and on their separation from the mother Serbia. Regardless of whether those guilty for this war will be tried, we shall always hold them responsible and will never forget what they did to us. . . . Three weeks after the recognition of our state we were forced to defend it with arms. Our armed struggle and the defense of the state and the people are among the brightest examples of knightly self-sacrifice. . . . We fought against huge powers. Against a more numerous and better equipped enemy . . . The people was on our side, and the God was on our side. . . . Our goal was, and remains, the united state of all Serbs. . . . We saved our people from a genocide and secured a significant proportion of its historic territories. Some precious territories we didn't include in our state, and we will never accept that that loss is definitive. (Karadžić, 1996, pp. 1–2)

Threat perceptions in all three communities were very high. Croatians traditionally saw Serbs as barbarians, that is, through the barbarian image (see Chapter 3); Serbs were horrified at the prospect of being separated from the Serb population that had dominated the old Yugoslavia, at least in size and presence in the military. Moreover, the Serbs recalled the slaughter of Serbs by Croatians during World War II. The Muslims feared both Croatians and Serbs, with good reason. They too had received brutal treatment from the Croatians during World War II, and the Serbs maintained an historical animosity toward the Muslims that went back hundreds of years.

Ethnic Hatreds

Journalist Anthony Loyd's (1999) report from the battlegrounds of Bosnia provides a first-hand illustration of ethnic stereotyping and hatred:

> I had left Citluk at dawn and after walking a few miles had been picked up by a heavily built middle-aged Bosnian Croat woman. . . . Naively I had imagined having to listen to tales of grandchildren or cats for the next leg of my journey. Instead she had launched into a tirade against Islam that gathered momentum with each dragging mile. There were thousands of Arab mujahidin swarming through the hills, she told me. They had radicalized the minds of the Bosnian Muslims who were now waging a jihad, a holy war, upon the beleaguered Croat people who for so long had been persecuted by the filth of the Ottoman Empire. Bosnia was now Europe's frontier against the fundamentalist legions of Allah, the Croatian people the brave hajduk vanguard in the battle for Christianity. As for the Serbs, not one of them would find salvation. . . . Spittle began to fly like sparks from the edge of her mouth.

Describing his next lift, Loyd writes:

> Within five minutes I was hearing the same story: mujahidin, fundamentalism, the Ottoman empire, jihad, Turks, Christ. . . . It was the key to so much of what was happening in Bosnia. If I, a relatively impartial foreigner . . . could be frightened by local scaremongering and propaganda, imagine what it was doing to the minds of isolated rural communities with no access to outside news, no experience of media impartiality . . . You could pop common sense from the minds of villagers in Bosnia like a pea from a pod. Make them afraid by resurrecting real or imagined threats, catalyse it with a bit of bloodletting, and you were only two steps from massacre and mayhem. (pp. 70–71)

The war that ensued was a brutal one. All three ethnic communities had been mobilized and galvanized by leaders (Serbian President Slobodan Milošović, Croatian President Franjo Tudjman, and Bosnian Muslim leader Alija Izetbegovic) in the years preceding Bosnia's war, while Yugoslavia as a whole disintegrated (Kaufman, 2001). Local Bosnian Serb, Croatian, and Muslim leaders also contributed to the slandering and dehumanization of the other ethnic groups. The means selected by all three groups for solving the question of the future of Bosnia-Herzegovina was ethnic cleansing. If living with the other groups is too threatening, they each thought, they would just get rid of the others. In the spring of 1992, Serb-dominated Yugoslav forces, together with Bosnian Serbs, began a campaign to ethnically cleanse the other groups from the country. In addition to forcing Muslims and Croats to flee the country, the list of atrocities committed by the Serbs against the other groups included mass killings, rape, and the creation of concentration camps. The other groups also committed atrocities, but not on the same scale as the Serbs.

In November 1995, the United States brokered talks, which resulted in the Dayton Peace Accord. Bosnian Serbs did not negotiate for themselves, but were represented by Slobodan Milošević. Under the agreement, a Bosnian Serb Republic and Muslim–Croat federation were established. A federal government, with a presidency that rotates among the groups, was also created. NATO peacekeeping troops were also brought in to ensure a peaceful transition.

This war claimed the lives of an estimated 200,000 people (Power, 2002). Hatred in this conflict erupted quickly, in part because of the efforts of leaders to provoke it. It cannot be expected to disappear overnight, particularly after so many died. Ethnic cleansing in Bosnia is a classic example of the group patterns leading to violence that were discussed earlier. Without the Yugoslav state to manage ethnic group competition, concerns began to arise about the domination by one ethnic group. Wrongs done by each group to the others in the past were recalled, threat perceptions increased, stereotyping increased, the salience of group attachments increased, and eventually war erupted. Once the fighting started, it was increasingly possible to dehumanize the others and to divest oneself of personal responsibility for violence; ethnic cleaning, ethnic rape, and thousands of deaths occurred.

The Maya of Guatemala

This case of ethnic conflict we consider also involves various aspects of social identity theory and group competition. In this case, the indigenous Maya of Guatemala were a downtrodden people who were kept in an inferior socioeconomic situation and who lacked political power. The dominant group, the ladino (nonindigenous) population in general, and the military in particular, looked at them with contempt. During the worst years of the conflict there, they were dehumanized by the military, who slaughtered thousands of Maya. In Guatemala, 60% of the 12.5 million citizens are Maya; the rest are ladinos. The two differ in language and custom, but not in appearance, because most ladinos have Mayan ancestry. Ladinos speak Spanish, wear western clothing, and engage in capitalist enterprise. The Maya of Guatemala, however, are composed of 23 subgroups and languages, some of which are mutually unintelligible. Many Maya do not speak Spanish, and many are bilingual (Warren, 1993). They often wear traditional colorful clothing and maintain a traditional communal lifestyle.

Since the Spanish conquest of the Maya in the sixteenth century, the central direction of change has been toward the assimilation of the Maya into Spanish culture. One was ladino or one was Maya. The two identities were not complementary. Being ladino meant one was Guatemalan, whereas being Maya meant one was not. The indigenous Maya were stereotyped as racially and culturally inferior. Their socioeconomic characteristics and political powerlessness reflected this perception of them by the ladino society.

Over the centuries since conquest by Spain, the Maya remained at the bottom of the social and economic ladder in Guatemala. The first stage of the mobilization of the Maya to change this situation began in 1944, with the establishment of a reform-minded government, and ended with the 1954 overthrow of that government and the brutal repression that followed. But, by the late 1970s, the indigenous people were politically and socially mobilized again. This is an illustration of the efforts people make, when they perceive a realistic opportunity, to change their group's status. At that point, they were participating in political party activities, running for office, and had established a Mayan-led labor organization, the Committee of Peasant Unity. This took place in the context of broader social and political discontent in Guatemala, which included sectors of the ladino population. The period also witnessed the emergence of left-wing guerrilla groups intent on overthrowing the government. The guerrilla military offensive reached its height in 1980–1981, with 6–8,000 armed fighters and 250,000–500,000 active collaborators and supporters, operating in most parts of the country (Schirmer, 1998).

This movement was seen as threatening to the dominance of the ladinos in general, and of the wealthy landowner ladinos in particular. The military government's response was a scorched-earth assault on all opposition, including the Mayan communities in rural areas, which were suspected of supporting the guerrillas. The violence was horrific, and the intention was to eliminate as many guerrillas and their supporters as possible and to terrorize the Mayan communities into submission. The tactics used were very brutal. Witness accounts, such as the following, were common:

> A North American priest described how this process took place in an isolated northern province where he worked during the early years of the violence:
> "Between 1975 and 1997, 47 project leaders were assassinated or disappeared. One returned. He suffered torture and witnessed the murder of some 30 members of his community. . . . In March, 1981, 15 members of our co-op were dragged from their homes and murdered by the military. In December 1981, assassins in army uniforms and with government trucks entered a remote village and assassinated several co-op leaders. Five others were found later, crucified with sharp sticks to the ground and tortured to death."
> Another respondent . . . a Peace Corps volunteer, described the following situation in the Indian town where she worked:
> "I was working in one town which was trying to organize a bread-baking and shirt-making co-op to raise funds for community projects such as a pharmacy. Several of the members were murdered in an attack by uniformed government soldiers. I did not witness this, but I saw the effects on the project and the source was truthful beyond any doubt. I later read an account in a U.S. publication that said that these 'terrorists' (bread makers) had been roasted alive in the schoolyard in front of their friends and families."
> (Davies, 1992, pp. 22–23)

Moreover, the military was unabashed about their conduct. They admitted to the tactics they used and felt quite justified in using them. The press secretary for General Ríos Montt, who took control of the dictatorship after a coup in 1983, stated:

> The guerrillas won over many Indian collaborators. Therefore, the Indians were subversives. And how do you fight subversion? Clearly you had to kill Indians because they were collaborating with subversion. And then it would be said that you were killing innocent people. But they weren't innocent; they had sold out to subversion.
>
> (quoted in Carmack, 1992, p. 57)

Villages were routinely attacked, many suspected subversives were killed, women were gang raped, victims were tortured, and the soldiers even engaged in ritual cannibalism, in order to terrorize the civilians (Stoll, 1992).

For the Maya, the consequences of this "dirty war" were disastrous, approaching a "demographic, social and cultural 'holocaust'" (Davies, 1992, p. 21). More than 150,000 people were killed, depending on when one starts the count; 150,000 went into exile in Mexico; and half a million people became internal refugees. Guatemala ended up with more than 40,000 disappearances. Eighty-three percent of the victims of the scorched-earth policy were Maya. Ninety-three percent of human rights violations were attributed to the military or paramilitaries. If the Maya fled the army's assaults by going into the mountainous highlands or Mexico, they faced hunger and misery. When they tried to return, they were imprisoned in "poles of development" (*pollos de desarrollo*)—internment camps for Mayan returnees where they were to be indoctrinated in anti-communism, and where their way of life was to be systematically destroyed. The campaign was not simply directed at the Maya, but was an ideologically based internal security campaign, which combined with ongoing ethnocentrism to devastate the indigenous population.

The military turned the reins of government back to civilians in 1985, but this was only a cosmetic democracy. The military was free to continue to run its counterinsurgency program, and the Mayan people continued to suffer. Although the guerrillas had a resurgence in the late 1980s, they by then recognized that the war could not be won by either side. They suggested peace talks, but it was not until December 1996 that the final peace agreement was reached. The UN brokered the talks and the subsequent reforms of the political system.

Now that the war is over, the Mayan communities have again mobilized, this time to ensure their participation in the establishment of a new Guatemala. Of central importance is that their mobilization appears to be toward achieving a new definition of the national community and what it means to be Guatemalan. During the early 1990s, many ladinos began to accept and prize aspects of Maya culture, the teaching of Mayan languages in schools, and the participation of Maya political organizations in the political system (LaBaron, 1993). That in and of itself did not mean that the ladino community was interested in the creation of a new common third identity incorporating elements of Maya culture. But, by 1996, there were signs that this too might be changing: The Accord on the Identity and Rights of Indigenous Peoples, and constitutional changes agreed to by the government, will, if put into effect, turn Guatemala into a multiethnic, multicultural, and multilinguistic society. It appears, then, that Guatemala has a chance to reconcile competing indigenous versus ladino identities, so that they may still be different, but both will be Guatemalan. We return to this process in our discussion of conflict resolution.

Ethnicity and Sectarianism in Iraq

Ethnic and sectarian differences are a cause of the instability and civil violence that has rocked Iraq since the overthrow of the Baathist regime of Saddam Hussein in 2003. The identity profile of Iraqis is quite complex. The Iraqi population is 75–80% Arab in ethnicity and 15–20% Kurd; the remaining population includes Turkomen, Assyrian, and "other." (CIA World Factbook, 2008). In terms of religious sectarian identity, 97% of Iraqis are Muslims. But that percentage does not reflect the important division within Islam between the Sunni and Shi'a sects, a division that is the cause of serious hostility, stereotyping and, in Iraq, violence. In Iraq the majority are Shi'a, about 60–65%, with 32–37% Sunni, and 3% Christian. Although the Sunnis are the overwhelming majority in the Arab world, Iraq is unique in having a Shi'a majority. Moreover, Iraq's neighbor, Iran, is majority Shi'a as well, but Iranians are not Arabs, and there is a great deal of stereotyping and animosity between Iranians and Arabs.

Added to this complex identity is tribal identity. It is estimated that 75% of Iraq's people belong to one of the 150 tribes in Iraq (Hassan, 2008). The tribes, in turn, are composed of smaller clans, possibly as many as 2,000, with extended families being central elements. The tribes form confederations, called *qabila*. Tribal sheiks have traditionally had extensive political and economic power. Tribal identity was and is powerful and has served to diminish identification with both the Arab community and the Iraqi state (Hassan, 2008). While Saddam Hussein was in power, tribal identity was initially suppressed, but then used and rewarded during the Iran-Iraq war of the 1980s. After the Gulf War of 1991, Saddam Hussein gave tribal leaders more power and authority because he had lost control of the country. He exchanged greater autonomy for their willingness to secure parts of the country (Hassan, 2008).

Much of the post–Saddam Hussein violence in Iraq, as well as questions about Iraq's future viability as a country, can be understood by looking into the Sunni-Shi'a-Kurdish identities. First, consider the fate of the Sunnis. Britain took control of what is now Iraq after World War I with the defeat of the Ottoman Empire, which had previously controlled this land. As they did in many places, British authorities chose one ethnic/sectarian group, the Sunnis, to be the politically dominant group in Iraq. Remember, the Sunnis were and are the numerical minority as a sectarian group, yet they emerged as the institutionalized power holders when Iraq became independent. This continued when the Baathists took over in 1968. Saddam Hussein was a Sunni and their political dominance was maintained under his regime. This, along with the brutality of the regime, fueled deep resentment by Shi'a and Kurds towards the Sunnis.

After Saddam Hussein was overthrown in 2003, the Coalition Provisional Authority (CPA) was established. Ambassador Paul Bremer III became the civilian adviser in Iraq. Bremer would also become head of the CPA. Under CPA tutelage the "de-Baathification" process commenced (Diamond, 2005). Given that the Sunnis dominated positions of power in Saddam's government, and that a position of authority by definition required membership in the Baath Party, the reasoning behind this was that the immediate destruction of the Sunni power base was necessary. The CPA also dismantled the Iraqi armed forces and police and Sunni strongholds.

The Sunnis, who had dominated Iraq for decades, now found themselves out of power and unemployed, and many hand plentiful arms caches. It seemed to the Sunnis that the Coalition was ensuring their marginalization in post–Saddam Iraq. An insurgency was born, and much of it revolves around identity and humiliation of that identity. As Hashim (2006) articulated:

> [P]eople fight to gain more . . . resources. It is equally true that people also fight not only to maintain or advance things they value materially, but also for a set of *nonmaterial* values that are subsumed under the rubric of identity . . . For the Sunni Arabs the downfall of the regime in April 2003 was not only or even primarily the collapse of power and privileges—indeed, many of them had little power and few, if any, privileges—but the entire nationalist edifice that has been in existence for more than eight decades and that had *identified* Iraq with them.
>
> (pp. 67–68)

The Sunni were humiliated, and we saw in Chapter 3 the power of humiliation as an emotion. As one Sunni told Hashim (2006) "We were on top of the system. We had dreams. Now we are the losers. We lost our positions, our status, the security of our families, stability. Curse the Americans. Curse them" (p. 69). Moreover, the Sunni have a very negative stereotype of the Shi'a, which has only exacerbated their sense of humiliation. Their stereotype depicts the Shi'a as dirty, inferior aliens who secretly act as puppets of Iran and the Persians there. Hashim, (2006) quotes one Iraqi Sunni who expresses this stereotype: "They [Shi'a] cannot rule Iraq properly. They cannot take charge of Iraq in the same manner as the Sunni. The Shiites are backwards. They are barbarian savages, they do not know true religion, theirs is twisted, it is not the true religion of Muhammad" (pp. 71–72). As suggested by this quotation, we can reasonably argue that the image the Sunni hold of the Shi'a is that of the barbarian. The barbarian image is a very threatening one, and holds the prospect of the annihilation of the perceivers' group.

Given this loss of power and the crushing humiliation the Sunnis perceive as the majority Shi'a took power, particularly in light of the image they have of the Shi'a, it is not surprising that the Sunni joined insurgent groups trying to oust the Coalition and return the Sunni to their previous position. Moreover, the Sunni do not have effective political leaders who can represent them effectively in the political arena. Insurgency may seem their only hope to return to power. The New Baath Party, the 1920 Revolutionary Brigade, and Jaysh Muhammad became the most prominent Sunni insurgent groups. The insurgency also opened opportunities for al-Qaida to acquire a presence in Iraq. Al-Qaida in Iraq (AQI) was established and was led by Abu Musab al-Zarqawi. Certainly, Iraqis were part of the group, but many foreign fighters filled the ranks for a chance to defend their fellow Muslims against what they believed to be an infidel invader. Alliances were made between the various groups that had a common goal of fighting the Americans, but these relationships were strained. For example, members of the 1920 Revolution Brigades, Army of the Mujahedeen and Ansar al-Sunna were killed by AQI. The killing of Sunnis, in turn, "warranted retaliation under the prevailing tribal code" (Simon, 2008, p. 63). Some tribal leaders soon decided to work against al-Qaida and formed the new Sunni Awakening groups. While the United States welcomed and rewarded this development, it posed the danger of increasing tribal identity, which works contrary to the establishment of a new Iraq with a superordinate common Iraqi identity (Simon, 2008).

The other two major sectarian/ethnic groups in Iraq, the Shi'a and the Kurds, have little sympathy for the Sunnis. The Kurds as a people were originally nomadic and are distributed across Turkey, Iraq, Syria, Iran, and Armenia. They have never had their own nation, despite their size (23–28 million) and the fact that they speak their own language. When the Ottoman Empire dissolved after World War I, the Kurds were not given an independent state. Stirrings of nationalism began in the early twentieth century, but efforts to forge an independent state have been crushed. The Iraqi Kurds were treated brutally by the Saddam Hussein regime. The regime initiated an "Arabization" effort to increase the Arab population in Kurdistan, effectively a policy of ethnic cleansing. During the Iran-Iraq war of the 1980s, the Kurds were severely repressed by the regime, and civil disturbance on the level of civil war broke out. In March 1988, the regime attacked the Kurdish town of Halabja with chemical weapons, killing thousands. Years later the Kurds are still affected by the use of the chemical weapons. In 1992, for example, BBC News ran a story on Halabja.

> The chemical after-effects of the attack are still affecting people. "Traces of the chemical agents are still residing in the water, air and food" said one surgeon. Since the chemical attacks, the number of various forms of cancer, birth deformities, still-born babies and miscarriages is reported to have dramatically increased.
>
> (BBC News, 2002)

In 1989, 180,000 Kurds were killed during the Anfal campaign, and a Kurdish uprising in 1991 was also crushed. After the 1991 Gulf War, the Kurds were protected by the international community. Their region in Iraq was designated a no-fly zone and they had de facto autonomy. They began to develop institutions and military forces, the *peshmerga*.

Needless to say, this autonomy is not something they are willing to give up. The real question for the Kurds is whether they will ultimately remain in the post–Saddam Iraq. For most Kurds, their identity is Kurdish, not Iraqi. Fewer young Kurds speak Arabic today than during the Saddam years and there is a strong negative stereotype of Iraqis. Hashim argued the stereotype verges on racist and depicts Iraqi Arabs as vastly inferior people (2006, p. 216). There are reports that the Kurds are reversing the Arabization campaign and driving Arabs and Turkmen out of towns where they dominated (*Arab News*, 2008; Hashim, 2006). At the moment, Kurdish authorities are not moving toward independence, despite the temptation, largely because the United States does not want to see that develop. The reasons are numerous, ranging from the issue of how to distribute the wealth generated from the oil that lies under Kurdish soil and Turkish fears that an independent Kurdistan would motivate further efforts by Turkish Kurds for independence. Indeed, Turkey bombed Iraqi Kurdistan several times in 2008 in an effort to attack members of the Turkish Kurd independence insurgency, the PKK.

Finally, the Shi'a community in Iraq is the majority community historically kept from having a proportionate share of political power. They were influenced by the revolution in Iran and called for the elimination of the secular Baathist government. As Hashim noted, "the politicization of the Shi'a via the vehicle of religion constituted a national security threat, a threat to the construction of a seemingly progressive and modernizing Arab power—whose despicable acts and corruption were well-hidden as were its victims—and to the national identity of the country as defined by the Ba'th" (2006, p. 239). The retaliation was predictably brutal, and many Shi'a were killed or went into exile in Iran. They naturally welcomed the demise of Saddam Hussein's regime.

In post–Saddam Iraq, the Shi'a are divided on a number of issues, including the role of Islam in the state as well as the issue of power sharing with the Sunnis. Some, like Muqtada al-Sadr, are nationalistic, and do not want to share power with the Sunnis. Others, like Ayatollah Ali al-Sistani, are less amenable to the idea of subordination of the Sunni to the Shi'a majority (Simon, 2008). Supporters of al-Sadr tend to be the poorest residents of the giant Sadr City slum in Baghdad. Shi'a divisions reflect differences of opinion on national unity, the role of religion in politics, the presence of the United States, and class-based issues.

There are many different political and paramilitary Shi'a organizations. Among the most important are the Islamic Dawa Party (the party of Prime Minister Nouri al-Maliki), the Supreme Council of the Islamic Revolution in Iraq (SCIRI), and Jamat al-Sadr al-Thani. The SCIRI is associated with the Badr militia and Jamat al-Sadr al-Thani, led by Muqtada al-Sadr, is associated with the Mahdi militia. There have been very serious disputes between these organizations and their followers regarding constitutional issues and the presence of the United States in Iraq, among other things. In 2005, there were violent clashes between the Badr Brigade and the Mahdi army over constitutional issues. Sadr objected to the SCIRI objective of giving the Kurdish north and Shiite south semi-autonomy (*Christian Science Monitor*, August 26, 2005). In 2008, fighting broke out again, this time between Sadr's supporters and the Iraqi security forces in the southern port city of Basra. Al-Maliki had asked all political parties to disband their militias before provincial elections were held, and Sadr and his supporters viewed this as an effort to weaken his movement before those elections (Raghavan, 2008, p. A01).

The United States withdrew troops in 2011, and instability in Iraq continues. The Islamic State in Iraq, renamed Islamic State in Iraq and Levant (ISIL), remains a destabilizing force and has expanded the scope of its activities into Syria. This prompted U.S.-led airstrikes against the group in 2014. On the political front, al-Maliki was ousted amidst allegations of perpetuating sectarianism, and a government that includes Sunnis and Kurds was formed by Haider al-Abad in September 2014. Iraq demonstrates some of the most complex identity-based problems in the world. The resolution of identity-group conflicts is essential if Iraq is not going to divide into two or three countries.

THE PERPETRATORS OF GENOCIDE

The cases of ethnic conflict described in this chapter have ranged from somewhat to very violent, including the pursuit of ethnic cleansing. But in a few cases, the violence perpetrated against an ethnic group has gone to the extreme of genocide, and we will look at three cases of genocide below. In some cases, such as Rwanda, genocide is planned by an organized group of political extremists. But in other cases, such as the Holocaust in Europe during World War II, it is the product not only of a group (the SS), but also of a large, complex bureaucratic system. In addition, the discussion in this chapter should not mislead readers into thinking that genocide is only the product of extremist groups. In theory, the conditions that produce genocide can occur anywhere, and genocide can be committed by very ordinary people.

What is genocide? The United Nations defines **genocide** as "acts committed with the intent to destroy in part or in whole a national, ethnic, racial, or religious group as such," which Staub (2000) has objected to on several grounds. First, it does not include political groups as specific possible targets of genocide. Second, it groups killing the group in whole or in part as constituting genocide, whereas Staub argues that killing in part is mass killing. Mass killing may kill many people, as does genocide, but genocide as an act is designed to eliminate the group from the face of the earth.

Genocide is a result of an intense feeling of frustration and threat, produced by a combination of many of the psychological patterns discussed in Chapters 3 and 4—social identity factors, stereotyping, and group loyalties—usually operating in the context of extremely difficult social economic and political circumstances. As Staub (1989) explained, "powerful self-protective motives then arise: the motive to defend the physical self (one's life and safety) and the motive to defend the psychological self (one's self-concept, values, and ways of life). There is a need to both protect self-esteem and to protect values and traditions. There is also a need to elevate a diminished self" (p.15), which some argue can be the result of a harsh childhood upbringing (Miller, 1983; Milburn & Conrad, 1996). If an enemy is not readily identified as the cause of the condition, one is created: a scapegoat. Similarly, Monroe (2008) found in interviews with Nazi perpetrators a strong sense of victimization. They felt they were victims, and needed to get rid of the threat before it could intensify. The perception of victimization gives rise to intense emotions, including shame, anger, humiliation, and hatred for the victimizer (Chirot & McCauley, 2006).

Why Not Kill Them All?

In their 2006 book with this title, Daniel Chirot and Clark McCauley address this important question. They argue that one simple explanation is that mass killing is very costly, and it is very dangerous in that threatened groups will react with violence to protect themselves. Killing others may mean getting killed yourself. They also note that many societies throughout history have had codes of conduct that limit the scope of killing during conflict. A third factor they identify is the practice of marrying outside of one's group, exogamy. This has many origins and is common across cultures and time. It enhances the potential to build alliances, and this leads to an incentive to limit violence. Modern manifestations of these practices include arms control agreements, the establishment of strong states that can prevent violence within societies, and assimilation in ethnically and racially mixed countries. Chirot and McCauley also note that "those who have studied modern genocides have noted that the major ones in the twentieth century took place after periods of great social and economic instability. The old rules no longer seemed to apply" (2006, p. 111).

Although some argue that certain cultures are more disposed to this than others (e.g., Staub, 1989), the potential for violence of this magnitude exists in most cultures. The more cohesive a group is, the more likely the potential, particularly when it is accompanied by a sense of superiority. This is especially evident when nationalism is strong in a country. Other predisposing characteristics for mass killing and genocide include strong respect for authority and strong inclination for obedience. Those characteristics make it more likely that personal responsibility will be relinquished and leaders will be followed without question. In addition, people are susceptible to the foot-in-the-door technique, wherein they respond positively to a small request and then become much more likely to respond positively to subsequent requests. Freedman and Fraser (1966) maintained that in the process of complying to first one, and then another, request, people change their attitudes about what they are doing, and they may also change their attitudes about themselves (from, for example, "I'm not the kind of person who hits others" to "I am the kind of person who hits others, and hitting is not a bad thing to do").

Genocides are also facilitated by organizations. Organizations overseeing and promoting genocide enable the perpetrators to divest themselves of responsibility for their actions. Organizations also impose norms and group loyalties so that those individuals who do not like the tasks there are supposed to fulfill will be made to feel guilty for not adhering to the groups' norms, and for not carrying out their fair share of the work (Chirot & McCauley, 2006; Waller, 2002).

In the twentieth century there were a number of horrific cases of genocidal violence. Genocide occurred in Turkey, where approximately one and a half million Armenians lost their lives from 1915 to 1917, and in Cambodia, where two million died from 1975 to 1979. The greatest loss of life in a genocide case took place in the Holocaust during World War II, but the genocide in Rwanda, which took the lives of around one million, occurred in the space of a mere three months, from April through June of 1994, a kill ratio five times greater per day than during the Holocaust. Today there is another genocide taking place in the Darfur region of Sudan. The three cases of genocide we consider offer evidence of all of the political psychological patterns discussed above.

THE HOLOCAUST

As we have seen in the previous chapter, Germans were strongly nationalistic, devoted to the nation as a group. Germany had suffered terribly from the demands of the Treaty of Versailles and the great depression of the 1930s. The Weimar Republic was seen as a government imposed by the victors of World War I and there was considerable political instability on top of the social and economic problems. In 1933, Adolf Hitler achieved his goal of being appointed Chancellor of the German Reichstag, or parliament, and was able to capture the mantle of German nationalism. His regime, the Third Reich, once established, instituted a repressive political system that made dissent increasingly dangerous. The SS (*Schutzstaffeln*, i.e., security echelon), which began in 1922 as Hitler's personal security force, later became the organization responsible for most of the genocide. When Hitler came to power, he established control over the entire police system in Germany, and used it to repress dissent. The concentration camps were set up in 1933, but initially they were used to detain political enemies from leftist political parties, the clergy, liberals, and "undesirables" such as homosexuals (Dicks, 1972).

Thus, the German nation held the in-group quality discussed above, the political and economic situation contained the ingredients that motivate the search for a scapegoat in order to bolster positive group esteem, and Jews were an easy target for vilification and dehumanization by the Nazis. Political repression made resistance difficult and passive acquiescence easy. For those who complied, resistance was far more difficult than under the conditions of the Milgram experiment, and we saw how many complied under those weak conditions. Finally, the Holocaust did not occur overnight. It was a gradual process beginning in 1933 with relatively mild (compared with what was to come) forms of discrimination against Jews in areas like employment and rights. Later they were prohibited from owning businesses and were forced to wear a yellow six-pointed star to identify themselves as Jews. The deportation of Jews to concentration camps began in 1938, but mass extermination in the concentration camps did not come until the order was given by Hitler in 1941, by which time the maltreatment of, and discrimination against, Jews had become "normal." These characteristics of German politics and political psychology help us understand both the willingness to identify with the nation, to vilify a scapegoat, and, for those who did not agree with the government, to become passive bystanders.

Still, there are other important ingredients in this case that help us understand how Germany went from a condition of intolerance, repression, and scapegoating to the establishment of a giant death machine that sought ultimately to annihilate the Jewish population of Europe. A look at the characteristics of the Nazi leadership as well as the followers who carried out the genocide is important, as well. Many Nazi leaders claimed they did what they did because they were following orders, behaving like good citizens and soldiers. But this is far too simple an explanation of their deeds. They did not just follow orders, but willingly carried out and developed enormous acts of cruelty designed not only to kill but to also make victims suffer terribly before they died. Studies have been done of leaders in the SS and report both significant elements of authoritarian personality in many and also fanatic loyalty to the SS, which then lead to a refusal to disobey orders or to admit to qualms about carrying out genocide (Dicks, 1972; Staub, 1989). SS training techniques were similar to those described in other extremist groups—harsh discipline, ideological indoctrination, glorification of the group, and fanaticism. In addition, belonging to the SS provided career opportunities, which was reportedly important for many. The people who participated in the killings of Jews did so under the auspices of authorities that they viewed as legitimate. By obeying these legitimate governmental authorities, perpetrators' judgment was subordinated to them. Thus, they were able to participate in the murdering of Jews, despite personal misgivings, and feelings of guilt in some cases. Norman Dicks (1972), a psychiatrist who interviewed SS officers imprisoned for their crimes against humanity, provided an interesting assessment of these men. He noted their ordinariness, but also the fact that they

> at some point crossed the line between their previous "law abiding" lives and their subsequent killer careers. And—their SS roles ended or interrupted—these same "fiends incarnate" in various ways disappeared quietly into civilian life, in some instances resumed orderly and normal careers, and are in prison "the easiest convicts to handle."
> (p. 234)

Dicks (1972) and Lifton (1986) both believe that they were able to oversee, and participate in the extermination of millions of people, because they could split or compartmentalize those actions from the rest of their lives. Hence, they could be loving fathers at home, murderers at work. They varied in personality, of course, some coming to the extermination of Jews reluctantly, others with enthusiasm. But, they were not "Mad Nazis" (Waller, 2002). After years of controversy regarding the interpretation of personality tests called Rorschachs, a definitive reexamination in the 1980s found that the Nazi leaders who stood trial at Nuremberg were essentially normal people, albeit above average in intelligence (Waller, 2002).

Additional personality characteristics were noted by Monroe (2008). She found Nazi sympathizers had strong values that were integral to their self-identity. These values included "a passionate commitment to the Nazi cause, racial purity, [and] cultural separatism" (p. 723). In terms of their categorization of the world around them, they saw a strong distinction between themselves and Jews, and this distinction included a sense of racial difference and superiority. One generalization that can be made is that these perpetrators were not insane, but were for personal reasons susceptible to the SS indoctrination, and thereafter group dynamics and fanaticism took over.

In addition to the group dynamics, the Nazi political system had some important elements that facilitated the size of the genocide. Much of this was done in concentration camps, but the political police and *Einsatzgruppen* (special mission groups) in the SS units followed the German army as it swept eastward through eastern Europe, and executed thousands of "undesirables"—Jews, Gypsies, communists, homosexuals, etc. Typically they were rounded up, a big ditch was dug, and they were shot and thrown into the ditch, dead or alive. The task was extremely difficult, even for the most dedicated Nazis. Personal contact with those who were to be executed proved to be a major problem. The *Einsatzgruppen* men were actually told they did not have to participate in the executions, because the officers understood that compelling them to do so could backfire and break the units (Browning, 1992). They were also given plenty of alcohol, and were required to work only for short periods of time.

Depersonalization was also important in facilitating the genocide. The camps were organized in such a way that personal identification with the victims did not need to occur. Gas chambers were constructed to kill on a massive scale, and to eliminate personal responsibility for the killing. Some Jews were spared so that they, not the SS, could remove gold from the mouths of victims, collect their clothing, and so on. Then there was the massive bureaucracy that divided the entire process, provided bureaucratic rules guiding the process, and permitted people who participated in the process of exterminating the Jews to deny personal responsibility (Sabini & Silver, 1993). The engineer who drove the cattle cars filled with people destined for the gas chambers could avoid responsibility because he just drove the train, he did not kill anyone. Different ministries handled different portions of the destruction of the Jewish population, one taking their property, another firing them from their jobs, another rounding them up, and another sending them off to die.

This situation parallels the Milgram obedience experiments described earlier. In those experiments, the "learner" (the person who was supposedly receiving electrical shocks) was out of view of the teacher (the person administering the shock). In some ways, this situation allowed the learners to be depersonalized, making it easier for the teacher to administer such high levels of shock. This situation also parallels the Milgram experiment in that the teacher did not feel responsibility for shocking the learner. This **diffusion of responsibility** occurs when there is more than one person present in the situation to take all or some of the responsibility for the outcomes. In the Milgram experiment, many of the participants asked the experimenter if he was going to take responsibility for whatever happened to the learner. When the experimenter responded that he would, this gave the participants a green light to continue shocking the learner. In most cases, however, the diffusion of responsibility is perceived rather than actually distributed among actors in the situation.

RWANDA

For roughly three months in the spring of 1994, the international community witnessed, and did nothing to stop, the genocide of Tutsis and moderate

Hutus by more extremist Hutus in Rwanda. In public view, Tutsis were systematically rounded up and shot, stabbed, beaten, or hacked to death with machetes. The *New York Times* reported on April 10, 1994, just four days after the violence started, "that 'tens of thousands' were dead, 8000 in Kigali [the capital city] alone, and that corpses were in the houses, in the streets, everywhere" (quoted in Power, 2002, p. 256). How could this have happened?

Rwanda, like many African countries, was colonized by Europeans, first Germany and then Belgium. Before colonialism, the Hutus and Tutsis lived in relative harmony. They spoke the same language, practiced the same religion and were economically interdependent. Tutsis were herders and Hutus usually were farmers. As Peterson (2000b) noted, the "caste system was largely apolitical: Tutsi came to mean 'rich,' someone with many long-horned cows; Hutu, or 'servant' came to mean someone with fewer than ten cows" (p. 258). Under certain circumstances, a Hutu could become a Tutsi. Over time, the Tutsi, along with a few Hutu, became the economic and political elite.

When the Belgians arrived in Rwanda after World War I, they sought to impose their own colonial administration. Even though Hutus were the majority, the Belgians chose to put Tutsis in positions of power. The Belgians selected the Tutsis because they had aquiline features, and thus, looked more similar to the Belgians than did than Hutus; therefore, the Belgians reasoned, the Tutsis must be the superior group (Human Rights Watch, March 1999). The Belgians created a system of colonial administration in which the Tutsis were favored in jobs and education. Ethnic identity cards were issued. Tutsis became the administrative elite for Belgian colonial rule. Because they were able to benefit from the colonial system, Hutus considered Tutsis an elitist class and an arm of the colonial state. Ethnicity was thereby politicized by colonialism, and would return to haunt Rwanda many times. Rwanda gained its independence from Belgium in 1959 when the Hutus overthrew the colonizers. During this drive for independence, many Tutsis were driven into exile.

By the late 1980s, the Tutsis in exile desired a permanent home, and wanted to return to Rwanda. However, in 1986, the Hutu government, led by General Juvenal Habyarimana, argued that Rwanda was overpopulated, and could not accommodate the refugees. By July 1990, the government seemed to be making progress toward their accommodation. But, according to the Rwandan Patriotic Front (RPF), a Tutsi-led rebel army operating from neighboring Uganda, Habyarimana not only needed to facilitate the return of the Tutsi refugees, but also establish a democratic government that replaced a one-party state dominated by him (Human Rights Watch, March 1999). On October 1, 1990, hoping to overthrow Habyarimana, the RPF left Uganda and attacked a small detachment of the Rwandan military. From there they made their way to Kigali, the capital. In response, Habyarimana falsely claimed that the RPF had actually attacked the capital, hoping to mobilize Hutus against the RPF and to gain the support of the international community. The government cracked down and 13,000 people were arrested and detained (Human Rights Watch, March 1999). Habyarimana's strategy was to divide those Hutus who supported him from those Tutsis and Hutus who collaborated with the enemy. This resulted in the deaths of many Tutsis and moderate Hutus who were attacked and killed.

By 1991, support for Habyarimana was waning as opposition parties demanding change began to emerge. Habyarimana and his supporters created a militia known as the *Interahamwe* whose members were allowed to attack Tutsis without any repercussions. Civilian defense groups were also created. But the RPF continued to make advancements and forced the Habyarimana government to enter into negotiations. The RPF and the government finally signed a cease-fire in Arusha, Tanzania, in July 1992 and a series of agreements that became known as the Arusha Accords were finally signed in August 1993. This was a power sharing agreement wherein military commanders would be 50/50 Tutsi/Hutu and troops would be 40 percent Tutsi and 60 percent Hutu. This clearly did not reflect the distribution of Tutsi and Hutu population in Rwanda, which was 14 and 85 percent respectively. In an attempt to monitor the implementation of the accords, on October 5, 1993, under the name of the UN Assistance Mission in Rwanda (UNAMIR), the United Nations finally allocated 2,548 peacekeeping troops. Despite the accords, the killing of Tutsis continued, but Hutu extremists were planning much worse to come.

On April 6, 1994, Habyarimana was returning from Tanzania when his plane was hit by two surface-to-air missiles. Even though the identity of those responsible is not certain, after the news of his death broke, the Hutus mobilized. A well-organized and systematic campaign to rid Rwanda of Tutsis and Hutus who were suspected of not supporting the government-backed campaign to eradicate the Tutsis was begun by the armed forces, including the police, and the paramilitaries, the *Interahamwe* and the *Impuzamugambi*. This campaign lasted roughly three months, and over one million people were estimated killed. By April 21, after the murder and mutilation of ten Belgian peacekeepers, the United Nations withdrew the rest of its forces from the country. The slaughter of Tutsis continued unabated for three months. When it ended, as one Hutu told a journalist, "It's not out of kindness . . . but because there are so few Tutsis left alive" (Peterson, 2000b, p. 288).

In July 1994, the RPF defeated the Hutu government. Paul Kagame, the leader of the RPF, installed Pasteur Bizimungu as President. A Hutu, Bizimungu was chosen to reflect the diversity of the new administration although it is widely believed that Kagame was running the government from behind the scenes (Simpson, 2000b). In March 2000, Bizimungu resigned and Kagame was chosen by Parliament to officially become the President of Rwanda.

For the first time since independence, the Tutsis were the governing ethnic group. Yet, the conflict does not seem to be over because the *Interahamwe* militia has regrouped and is now waging a war against the government from the Congo. This has prompted Rwandan and Ugandan troops, together with the Congolese rebel group the Congolese Rally for Democracy (RCD), to wage a war against the Congolese President Laurent Kabila's (Kabila was assassinated on January 17, 2000, and his son Joseph became president) government troops and the Rwandan and Burundian militia fighters (Talbot, 2000). Because ethnicity is the primary basis for group loyalty, and served as a basis to the conflict, the question remains, how long will Tutsis remain in power?

The Rwanda genocide shares many of the characteristics of the Holocaust, but there are some important differences as well. Social and economic conditions in Rwanda before the massacre were difficult, as was the case in Germany when Hitler came to power. Rwanda was overpopulated and one of the poorest countries in Africa. All but five percent of its land was under cultivation, the average woman had nine children, and hunger was rampant (Peterson, 2000b). The majority Hutus had suffered significant strategic losses to the Tutsi rebel forces and faced the prospect of having to share power with them. Germany too had experienced the loss of World War I, a factor in setting the stage for that genocide. In addition, as in Germany, there was a legacy of Hutu-Tutsi stereotyping, mutated by the influence of the colonial powers. By the time this holocaust took place, Tutsis were dehumanized by the Hutu, who called the Tutsis *inyenzi* (cockroaches). The Hutu extremists were organized in a political party, the *Mouvement Révolutionnaire National pour le Développement* (National Revolutionary Movement for Development, MRND), which, in turn, had the paramilitary organization, the *Interahamwe*. The *Impuzamugambi* were associated with the hard-line Hutu organization the *Coalition pour la Défense de la République* (Coalition for the Defense of the Republic, CDR). The party and its leaders promoted an ideology of "Hutu Power" complete with a document of anti-Tutsi "principles" such as "every Hutu should know that every Tutsi is dishonest in business. His only aim is the supremacy of this ethnic group . . . All strategic positions . . . should be entrusted to Hutus . . . The Hutu should stop having mercy on the Tutsi" (quoted in Power, 2002, p. 339). Any Hutu who did not agree was considered a traitor. Again, this resembles Germany's Nazi party and Nazi ideology.

As in Germany, this genocide was planned in advance by the Hutu political and military leaders. The Rwandan army began to train the *Interahamwe* in 1990, which resembled the Nazi SS in that it offered members strong psychological and material rewards. Prominent Hutu leaders began publicly to call for the elimination of the Tutsis as early as 1992. For example, Leoin Mugeser, a member of the MNDR, stated in 1992 "The fatal mistake we made in 1959 was to let [the Tutsi] get out . . . They belong in Ethiopia and we are going to find them a shortcut to get there by throwing them into the Nyabarongo River. I must insist on this point. We have to act. Wipe them all out!" (quoted in Power, 2002). And finally, as in the case of the German commanders of the Holocaust who claimed to be only following orders, the perpetrators of this violence demonstrated little remorse.

But there are differences in these genocides. Rwanda's was not as technical, depersonalized, and hidden as Germany's. There was no complex bureaucracy that carried out the genocide in bits and pieces. Here every Hutu was either involved the killing, or in hiding. Although this permitted diffusion of responsibility, as was the case in Germany, the average citizen took a hand in the direct killing in Rwanda; that is, publicly hacking Tutsis with machetes and clubs, stabbing them, or, if merciful, shooting them. As a Frontline documentary states,

> the main agents of the genocide were the ordinary peasants themselves . . . [E]ven in the cases where people did not move spontaneously but were forced to take part in the killings, they were helped along into violence by the mental and emotional lubricant of ideology. We can see it for example in the testimony of this seventy-four

year-old "killer" captured by the RPF: "I regret what I did. [. . .] I am ashamed, but what would you have done if you had been in my place? Either you took part in the massacre or else you were massacred yourself. So I took weapons and *I defended the members of my tribe against the Tutsi.*"

(Frontline, 1998, p. 4; italics added)

THE NEWEST GENOCIDE

Darfur

Darfur is a region in western Sudan that abuts Chad. Fighting started there in February 2003. In September 2004, Colin Powell, who was then United States Secretary of State, called the situation in Darfur genocide. Nevertheless, the United Nations did not formally deem Darfur genocide and was heavily criticized. It is estimated that close to half a million people were killed in the conflict and three million became refugees (Cotler, 2008). The conflict in Darfur was described as a conflict between Arabs and Africans, but as discussed below, this is a gross oversimplification.

There are numerous groups or tribes in Darfur, the estimate ranging from 40 to 90 (Flint & de Waal, 2005). Darfur was an independent Sultanate from 1600 to 1916, with the exception of a period from 1874 to 1898. The Darfur Sultanate was quite powerful, trading within the Mediterranean. In 1917, it was taken over by the British.

Darfur's population and ethnic mixture is a result of centuries of migration. If there is an indigenous ethnic group, it is the Fur, but as Prunier (2005) noted, it is difficult to know for certain about the population in Darfur before the fourteenth century because of the lack of a written history. Other ethnic groups include the Zaghawa; the Berti; the Bidayat, who came from the northwest; the Birgid; and Meidob, who came from the northeast (Prunier, 2005). Arab ethnic groups began to migrate into the region in the fourteenth century and include the Ziyadiyya, Ta'aisha, Beni Halba, Habbaniya, and Rizzeqat (Prunier, 2005, p. 6). There are also many other ethnic groups.

The Sultanate was a Fur Sultanate, and it was Muslim. As the Sultanate expanded southward, they spread Islam (people had to convert or leave), the Fur language, and over time, people became Fur themselves (Flint & de Waal, 2005; Prunier, 2005). But the nature of the Sultanate evolved as time passed. As Prunier explained:

> The Fur has produced the Sultanate (and the other way around) but it soon stopped being exclusively or even mainly theirs. Since the kingdom's population was largely multi-ethnic (even after the Fur "assimilation" of the first years), it was held together by a complex system of Arabo-Islamic legitimacy and Sudanic sacred ritual.

(2005, p. 11)

The Sultanate had a land ownership system called the *hakura*. Hakura holders collected dues from people living in their hakura, and over time gathered family members in the hakura. These would then form a "tribe" (Flint & de Waal, 2005). The land-holding rights and patterns are important because they influence the crises in Darfur in later years.

Arab migration into Darfur took place largely between the fourteenth and eighteenth centuries. They included individuals and the Juhayna Bedouins. These ethnic groups raised cattle and became sedentary. They were known as the *Baggara*. The four main Baggara groups, Ta'aisha, Beni Halba, Habbaniya, and Rizeigat, were given large hakuras by the Sultan. The other Arabs, the *Abbala* Arabs, did not get land and remained nomads in the northern provinces (Flint & de Waal, 2005).

In typical British colonial habit, they selected local authorities to administer the area. They chose the Arab tribes. The Darfur region of Sudan was largely ignored under British colonialism. In 1935, they had "one elementary school, one 'tribal' elementary school, and two sub-grade schools" (Flint & de Waal, 2005, p. 15). Only the sons of chiefs were allowed to be educated in order to protect their power and privilege. There was no investment or development in Darfur.

Darfur won independence on January 1, 1956. This was followed by a military dictatorship from 1958–65 led by Brigadier-General Ibrahim Abboud. Darfur continued to be neglected. The first post-dictatorship elections were held in May 1965, but there was another coup in 1969 that put Colonel Jaafor al-Nimiery in power. He relied on the backing of the Communist Party, and other political parties were marginalized. Throughout, the country was dominated by the so-called Blue Nile Arabs, the people who lived along the Nile. The people of Darfur remained powerless.

During the 1960s, Darfur was also affected by events in Chad. In 1965, Chad embarked on a civil war between the north and the south. Darfur borders Chad, and because the border is an artificial one, there are many members of the same ethnic group on both sides of the border. Complicating this was the interest of Colonel Gaddafi of Libya in the Chad conflict. Gaddafi supported the revolutionaries (northern and Muslim). Gaddafi was an Arab nationalist and overt racist. In 1976, a Libyan-trained militia of Sudanese attacked the Sudan capital of Khartoum in an effort to over throw Nimieri. As a result, Nimieri gave his support to the Chad faction most hostile to Libya. The impact of these machinations on Darfur, particularly on the inter-ethnic group relationships, was strong. As Prunier (2005) described below, stereotypes and inter-group hostilities were imported into Darfur:

> This rough handling of Darfur by Libyans, the Chadians, and the Khartoum forces decisively worsened the regional ethno-political landscape. Tribes which had seen themselves primarily in local terms were suddenly catapulted into a broader artificial world where they were summoned to declare themselves as either Arab or *zurqa*. The Arabs were "progressive" or "revolutionary" while the Africans were "anti-Arab" and "reactionary."
>
> (p. 46)

Meanwhile, Darfur had years of drought that produced severe hardships and, by 1984, famine. Lack of rainfall forced the semi-nomadic tribes to become completely nomadic, moving their herds farther and farther in search of food. This led them to encroach on the land of farming peasants. The farmers naturally did not like this because it interfered with their traditional way of life, and they blocked nomadic passage. To make things worse, the government of Sudan did not want to admit that a famine was occurring.

The identities politicized by Darfur's role in the Chad civil war, and the resentments produced by the drought and famine, combined to cause negative stereotypes among "Arabs" and "Africans" in Darfur. According to Prunier,

> The "Arabs" did not care about the famine which the "African" governor had tried to prevent. Now that it was over, the "Africans" were trying to make the "Arab" victims pay and to cut them off from available pastureland. The "Arabs" were thieves who were trying to steal the livestock which remained in "African" hands. The selfish "Africans" shot at the "Arabs" who were then just recuperating from the famine. The "Arabs" were killers who got weapons from Libyan troops and the Chadian insurgents to steal what they could from the "Africans."
>
> (2005, p. 58)

The next important development on the path to genocide was the Sudanese civil war between the North and the South. In 1983, Nimieri introduced Islamic Sharia Law to Sudan, which caused the Christian south to revolt. Many of the northern soldiers came from Darfur. In April 1985, Nimieri was overthrown. There was a civilian government, which struggled for a time. A military coup led by General Omar al-Bashir overthrew that government in 1989, and brought the Islamic National Front, whose leader was Hassan al-Turabi, to a position of political power. Bashir declared himself the head of the Revolutionary Command Council. He then became the President when the Revolutionary Command Council dissolved itself in 1993. The Blue Nile people, however, continued to dominate.

The civil war between north and south ended in a negotiated peace in 2002 amidst a new bonanza of oil, which is in the southern part of the country. Things seemed to be going well for Sudan, but the situation in Darfur was deteriorating quickly. There was a great deal of resentment about the lack of resources coming into Darfur, particularly in light of the contribution the region had made to the north during the civil war. In 1996, three Fur activists established a clandestine organization. They then began to try to organize the scattered resistance activities that were merging all over Darfur. Eventually the Fur and Masalit ethnic groups formed an alliance with one of the Zaghawa clans, and established the Sudan Liberation Army. A second rebel organization also formed, called the Justice and Equality Movement (JEM) The rebellion began in February 2003. Their demands were not for independence, but for better treatment, a bigger share of the country's resources, decentralization, and more self-determination (Flint & de Waal, 2005; Prunier, 2005). They launched attacks against villages and government offices.

The response of the Bashir government was to attack the "African" villages of Darfur. They bombed and launched ground attacks. The government forces and the *Janjaweed* militias who supported the government have been accused of mass slaughter, rape, the destruction of entire villages, and other human rights violations. Of particular importance is the Janjaweed. The word means "devil on horseback" and these militias are literally that. They were initially formed during the north-south war and it is alleged that the government has encouraged their actions. The Janjaweed recruits from demobilized soldiers from the army; young members of Arab tribes having land conflicts with neighboring African tribes; common criminals who were pardoned and released from jail on condition they join the militia; members of the Tajammu al-Arabi (Union of Arabs, a militant racist organization); young, unemployed "Arab" men; and bandits (Prunier, 2005, p. 97).

The Darfur Peace Agreement (Doha Agreement) was signed by the government and Sudan Liberation Movement in 2006, but not by the Justice and Equality Movement, and the conflict continued. At the beginning of March 2009, Bashir was indicted by the International Criminal Court for the atrocities committed in Darfur. The Liberation and Justice Movement emerged to represent several rebel groups. In 2010, JEM agreed to the Doha Agreement. In July 2011, Sudan split into two countries, to form Sudan in the north, and South Sudan.

BYSTANDERS AND ALTRUISTS

In New York City one night in 1963, a woman named Kitty Genovese was stabbed to death. Her assailant beat and stabbed her for close to an hour while dozens of people heard her screams and saw her being attacked, but did nothing. This tragic story is often used to illustrate the bystander phenomenon—when people do nothing to help others. Why does this happen? There is a tendency to blame the bystanders as being apathetic or uncaring. But researchers Latane and Darley (1970) argued that situational factors can explain the lack of help given to Kitty Genovese. When people are bystanders in an emergency situation, they sometimes experience *pluralistic ignorance*. They do not know how to respond, so they look to others to see how to respond (as in informational social influence, described in Chapter 4). The problem is, everyone is looking at everyone else to figure out how to respond. Unfortunately, the result is that bystanders become paralyzed and do not respond at all. A second situational determinant that can explain the lack of help often given to those in emergency situations is diffusion of responsibility. If you were the only person available to help, then you would have 100% of the responsibility to give help. But if just one other person is present, then your sense of responsibility drops to 50%. The more people who are present in a situation, the more diffused is the responsibility. It is partly due to group characteristics. When people are part of a group, there is a diffusion of responsibility, and people feel less compelled to intervene and help. Many analysts believe that the **bystander phenomenon** is a crucial component in genocide.

Bystanders know, at least implicitly, that something wrong is happening, and they do nothing about it. A bystander can be a person, a group, an organization, or a country. Indeed, the entire international community knew about the genocide unfolding in Europe and, fifty years later, in Rwanda, and we did nothing. We engaged in **denial**. Stanley Cohen maintained that denial "includes *cognition* (not acknowledging the facts); *emotion* (not feeling, not being disturbed); *morality* (not recognizing wrongness or responsibility) and *action* (not taking steps in response to knowledge)" (2001, p. 9). Milburn and Conrad (1996) argued that at the individual and social level, denial is a product of an unwillingness to face a reality that is horrifically painful. This, they contended, stems from childhood denial of punitive parental treatment. Denial is also often a subtle social pressure. Everyone knows and no one admits what is happening. Those who do are condemned or ostracized by the group. To admit that something bad is happening is often threatening to the group's self-image, so avoiding or ignoring information is necessary to maintain the positive self-image and to be complicit in the general denial. Hence many Germans could ignore the evidence that Jews and others were being exterminated in death camps because Germans, by definition, are good people, and good people do not do such things. It is often extremely difficult for individuals *not* to be bystanders in the face of political violence. They are often threatened with severe punishment if not death, they do not know what to do or how to act, and they know that as individuals they have little power to do anything. Yet still, some individuals do act, hiding a Jew or a Tutsi, managing to save lives, one at a time.

Denial comes in many forms. People deny that they inflicted pain (it was an accident); that an injury occurred (no one was really hurt); that the victim is a victim (he deserved it); and that they had no knowledge about atrocities. Denial also comes in degrees, from knowing about, but refusing to believe information, to knowing, but maintaining only a vague awareness of the facts, to knowing, being aware, and choosing to do nothing (Cohen, 2001; Monroe, 2008). For example, arguments abound to this day as to how much ordinary Germans knew about the Holocaust, and those arguments will inevitably continue because many Germans did not then, and cannot now, recognize the extent to which they knew, but did not attend to information about the extermination of Jews and others. As Walter Laqueur wrote, "It is, in fact, quite likely that while many Germans thought that the Jews were no longer alive, they did not necessarily believe that they were dead" (1980, p. 201).

The likelihood that people will engage in denial and refuse to help victims of violence is augmented when there are many people involved (as in a crowd surrounding an accident victim), when the situation is ambiguous, and when people are fearful of the reaction of others. People are also influenced by the belief in a just world. They believe that the world is benevolent, and that bad things only happen to bad people. Therefore, if the SS hauls someone off, that person must have done something wrong. This belief comforts people by letting them think that the world is stable, certain, and predictable (Cohen, 2001; Staub, 1989). These patterns can be seen in Germany and in Argentina, where bystanders abounded. In both cases the information was, for many, very ambiguous. In both cases there was no free press that provided concrete and undeniable information that atrocities were occurring. To speak out against regime policies was dangerous and deadly, and certainly discouraged by others who did not want to rock the boat. And, as in so many cases of genocide and state terror, there was pride in a civilization that led people to believe that nothing so horrible could happen.

In cases of state terror and genocide, there are always some who help others and speak out. In Europe during the Holocaust, 90% of the Jewish population in Latvia, Lithuania, Poland, and Hungary died. But 90% survived in Denmark, and in Belgium, where there was resistance to German dictates for rounding up Jews, 53% survived (Staub, 1989). Studies of **rescuers** or **altruists**, as these brave people are called, found that one central characteristic is an ability to empathize with others, to imagine themselves suffering in the same way (Beck, 1999; Cohen, 2001; Monroe, 2008). **Empathy** is defined as "an 'other centered' emotion which is produced by observing another individual in need and taking that individual's perspective" (Rumble, 2003, p. 8; Batson, 1991). Rumble (2003) cited numerous studies of empathy and noted that the evidence indicates that people will be empathetic when they see another person in need *and* when they can adopt that person's perspective. In addition, rescuers tend to have an ability to identify with humanity at large, rather than only with their families, local community, or country (Monroe, 2008). Oliner and Oliner (1988) determined in a study of 406 people who attempted to rescue Jews during the Holocaust that they also had a strong sense of personal responsibility. Finally, Cohen noted that "these people reacted instinctively: they did not look for accounts or neutralizations for why *not* to help" (2001, p. 263).

CONCLUSION

In this chapter, a number of theories are used to look at different aspects of ethnic conflict. We examined ethnic conflicts with various levels of violence, including the phenomenon of genocide. In addition, we explored the political psychology of bystanders and altruists. Ethnic conflicts are often bubbling under the surface of multiethnic societies. We examined cases that have involved considerable amounts of mass violence and killing. Governments of many multiethnic/multisectarian states, particularly those that are poor and where resources are the object of tough competition, are constantly forced to fight against upsurges of ethnic conflict.

Topics, Theories/Explanations, and Cases Covered in Chapter 9

Topics	Theories/Explanations	Cases
Ethnic Conflict	Realistic conflict theory	Nigeria
	Social identity theory	Bosnia
	Group conflict	Guatemala
	Evolutionary psychology	Iraq
Genocide		The Holocaust
		Rwanda
		Darfur

Key Terms

denial and bystanders
ethnocentrism
evolutionary psychology
genocide
group loyalty
obedience
prejudice

realistic conflict theory
scapegoat
shared sovereignty strategies
social dominance theory
social learning theory
stereotyping

Suggestions for Further Reading

Chirot, D., & McCauley, C. (2006). *Why not kill them all? The logic and prevention of mass political murder*. Princeton, NJ: Princeton University Press.

Duckitt, J. (1994). *The social psychology of prejudice*. New York: Praeger.

Fiske, S. (1998). Stereotyping, prejudice, and discrimination. In D.T. Gilbert, S.T. Fiske, & G. Lindzey (Eds.), *The handbook of social psychology* (4th ed., Vol. 2, pp. 357–411). New York: McGraw-Hill.

Gourevitch, P. (1998). *We wish to inform you that tomorrow we will be killed with our families*. New York: Picador.

Hashim, A.S. (2006). *Insurgency and counter-insurgency in Iraq*. Ithaca, NY: Cornell University Press.

Horowitz, D. (1985). *Ethnic groups in conflict*. Berkeley: University of California Press.

Ihonvbere, J.O. (1994). *Nigeria: The politics of adjustment and democracy*. New Brunswick, NJ: Transaction Books.

Loyd, A. (1999). *My war gone by, I miss it so*. New York: Penguin.

McGarry, J., & O'Leary, B. (Eds.). (1993). *The politics of ethnic conflict*. New York: Routledge.

Power, S. (2002). *A problem from Hell: America and the age of genocide*. New York: Basic Books.

Prunier, G. (2005). *Darfur: The ambiguous genocide*. Ithaca, NY: Cornell University Press.

Waller, J. (2002). *Becoming evil: How ordinary people commit genocide and mass killing*. Oxford: Oxford University Press.

Note

1. When a multiethnic state has one or more ethnic communities desirous of independence that have the capability to achieve independence, conflict can best be avoided when those communities are territorially homogeneous, by granting them the right of national self-determination. As long as such communities perceive a real option for independence, they are unlikely to respond to efforts to attract a primary attachment to the territorial community.

Chapter 10

THE POLITICAL PSYCHOLOGY OF NATIONALISM

For the past 200 years or so, nationalism has been an important driving force in political behavior. Nationalism is not universal and not everyone is a nationalist, but it lies dormant until the populace perceives a threat or opportunity to the nation. Following the French Revolution, nationalism first emerged in Europe with the development of the modern state. Nationalism is considered one of the most dangerous sources of political behavior in the twentieth century. For example, German nationalism is blamed for World War II, and it certainly played a major role in causing that conflict. The nationalisms of various communities in Yugoslavia tore that country apart in the 1990s. Conflict between the United States and its Latin American neighbors often rests upon nationalistic indignation of one at the behavior of the other. The causes of nationalism, and the impact of nationalism on political behavior, are the topics of this chapter. They are illustrated with many examples from different regions of the world. Various conflict resolution strategies, which can be used to ameliorate these conflicts, are then addressed in Chapter 14.

We begin with a general discussion of nationalism, its definition, the patterns of nationalistic behavior, the psychological roots of nationalism, and a description of different kinds of states with varying arrays of nationalists and nationalism. This is followed by a discussion of the political psychological causes of nationalist passions and behavior. From there, we present case illustrations of patterns of behavior. We begin with a look at nationalists' responses to perceived threats to national values and the case of Western European responses to immigrants. Next, we look at nationalism and the strong desire nationalists have for unity and independence for their people. This is illustrated in the cases of Northern Ireland, Yugoslavia's breakup, the Albanian revolt in Kosovo, the conflict in Cyprus, German unification, the Ukraine, the revolt in Chechnya, and the Kurds' drive for independence from Turkey. Then we turn to the impact of nationalism on foreign policy behavior, and look at World War II and the contemporary war on drugs in U.S.–Mexico relations.

AN OVERVIEW OF NATIONALISM

Definition and Patterns of Behavior

Before beginning any discussion of nationalistic behavior, a definition of the concept is necessary. In this chapter, Emerson's (1960) definition of nationalism is used:

> The nation is a community of people who feel they belong together in the double sense that they share deeply significant elements of a common heritage and that they have a common destiny for the future. . . . The nation is today the largest community which, when the chips are down, effectively commands . . . loyalty, overriding the claims both of the lesser communities within it and those which cut across it or potentially enfold it within a still greater society. . . . In this sense the nation can be called a terminal community with the implication that it is for present purposes the effective end of the road for man as a social animal.
>
> (pp. 95–96)

As Emerson explained, nationalists give their primary loyalty to their perceived nation, which can be considered a political identity in-group—a concept introduced in Chapter 3. For example, people can call themselves Irish, and see themselves as part of that nation of people. A **nation-state** exists when the average citizen of a country is a nationalist. Those who see themselves as part of the Mexican nation would consider the territorial boundaries of Mexico the nation-state. Alternatively, those in Ireland who see themselves as part of the Irish nation would consider the territorial state of Ireland the nation-state. Countries in which people are generally not nationalistic are countries in which primary political loyalty is directed elsewhere, such as to an ethnic group, rather than to the community living within the territorial boundaries of the state. Nationalist identity patterns are in Figure 10.1.

Being strongly attached to their nation, nationalists are committed to the unity, independence, dignity, and well-being of the national community and the nation-state. Even when they dislike their government, they love the nation itself. The concept of nationalism is similar to that of social identity, which was discussed in detail in Chapter 3. Recall that social identity refers to the identification that people perceive with groups and organizations. People strive to maintain a positive sense of self-esteem from their memberships in social groups (Tajfel & Turner, 1986). People are motivated to feel good about their groups. Nationalists are group members who are motivated to have a strong, positive attachment to their nation.

Several patterns of behavior occur in nation-states and by nationalists that are not so evident in states where people are not nationalistic, that is, in nonnation-states. First, nationalists tend to be more sensitive than nonnationalists to threats to the nation-state, and the image through which they view the threatener is extreme. Research (see Dietz-Uhler, 1999) suggests that people who identify strongly with a group react strongly when their sense of positive social identity is threatened. Similarly, nationalists, particularly nationalistic leaders, are very sensitive to opportunities to advance their country's influence and are more likely than nonnationalists to seriously consider the option to expand state influence at the expense of others. Third, there will be a greater tendency among the public of nation-states to be deeply concerned with the objective of gathering together communities existing outside the borders of the state whom they regard as a part of their national community. Generally, nationalists desire a territorial state for their people, and they want all of the community to live in that state. This is referred to as **irredentism**—the desire to join together all parts of a national community within a single territorial state. Those members of the nation who live outside the territory of the country are called a diaspora. Irredentism was an important factor in Bismarck's wars for German national unification in the late nineteenth century, and at the beginning of World War II in the German conquest of Poland and Czechoslovakia, where millions of ethnic Germans lived. Fourth, nationalists are more concerned with their country's prestige and dignity than are nonnationalists, and nationalists are more willing to take action to rectify perceived affronts. Fifth, there is more likelihood that the public of a nation-state will be susceptible to grandeur interests, and will therefore want to see national prestige and status enhanced and recognized globally. Sixth, leaders of nation-states, compared to nonnation-states, are better able to make effective appeals to the citizens to make great sacrifices to enhance the power of the state. Seventh, the public is more willing to serve in the military, and have a more intense commitment to the defense of that state. Finally, the citizens of a nation-state are more likely to grant leaders considerable freedom to take risks in defending the country's interests. However, leaders who fail will be punished by nationalistic people. They will not grant those leaders the freedom to accept defeats or the loss of face.

Given these patterns of behavior, we can begin to generalize about governance in nation-states. All governments have certain tools available to them to keep their populations stable and supportive. They can and must satisfy the utilitarian needs of the population through a functioning economy and political system. They also have at their disposal coercive instruments such as the police and the military, which can be used to keep order, prevent instability, and, if necessary, force the society to comply with the government's decisions. Many governments combine these tools, and have a public accustomed to compliance and political stability. The habit of the public is to obey the laws of the government and accept governmental authority.

However, the governments and leaders of nation-states have an added instrument that helps them govern and, when necessary, mobilize the population to make great sacrifices for the country: they can use nationalistic symbols to arouse passionate feelings of devotion to the nation—symbols such as the flag; historic events, such as success in a great battle; or the idea of the motherland or fatherland. Because nationalists deeply value the independence, unity, dignity, and well-being of their national community, they respond readily to the use of symbols to mobilize them to achieve national goals. Experimental research in social psychology examined the effectiveness of group symbols in arousing and making salient one's group (or national) identity. For example, Wilder and Shapiro (1984) found that the mere presence of an out-group symbol was sufficient to make salient

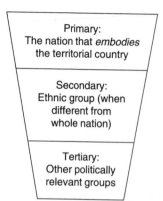

Figure 10.1 Political Identities and Loyalty in Nation-States

one's in-group identity. Specifically, participants were exposed to a pennant of either their own university (in-group condition) or a rival university (out-group condition). Participants were asked to review a list of words, and were later given a word recognition test. The words in the recognition test included words related to either the in-group or the out-group. The results showed that participants were more likely to falsely recognize in-group-related words when an out-group symbol was present. More important, the presence of an out-group was sufficient to increase group members' adherence to their own group's norms. Thus, nationalistic symbols can be powerful motivators of pro-nation behavior.

Nationalism in Non-nation States

There are some countries that are **multinational states**, in which several groups of people, who think of themselves as separate nations and are actually capable of establishing viable independent states, live together in a single country. They do not see the populations of the country as their primary identity group. Instead, their primary identity group is the nationality they belong to (see Figure 10.2). Examples include the Russians and Ukrainians who lived in the Soviet Union. Their primary identity was with the Russian or Ukrainian national community, not the Soviet Union. In these cases, no nation completely controls its own destiny, and no nation has its own independent state. The dynamics of nationalism are likely to be directed toward striving for independence. Thus, multinational states have chronic disintegrative forces that they must try to prevent from exploding. Northern Ireland is a case in point, as we see later. Finally, a third type of state—which is not a nation-state, strictly speaking, but whose leaders often behave like nationalists—is called a **core community nonnation-state**. These are countries with a dominant ethnic or sectarian community that believes that it is the primary nation embodied in the country and that identifies with that nation in the strongest terms. In addition, that community tends to be politically dominant and controls the political system. However, also present within the territorial state are other communities, which give primary loyalty to their ethnic groups. These secondary groups desire autonomy or independent statehood, but they do not have sufficient resources to sustain it. A good example of a core community non-nation-state is Russia. Russians are clearly the dominant group, and Russians tend to be quite nationalistic. Yet, there are many other ethnic groups living in Russia who speak Russian and are part of the country's political system, but who have a different ethnic identity.

In many of these cases, the core community advocates the integration and assimilation of the other groups, encouraging the minorities to speak the dominant group's language, abandon their customs, identify with the country as a whole, and perhaps intermarry. Under these circumstances, minority groups can use social mobility as an option and assimilate into the core community. Social mobility is one of the strategies suggested by social identity theory to cope with a threatened or negative social identity. When a group member's (especially a low-status group member) social identity is at risk, one option is to leave the group, and join a group that is positively valued. Of course, this option is only available when group membership is achieved, rather than ascribed. However, the option of assimilation or social mobility is not always welcome, if assimilation requires the complete abandonment of group identity, and, if the existence of the group is threatened, political conflict may occur. Resistance to assimilation may also come from members of the core community who view these other groups as undesirable. Under some circumstances, such as the events leading up to the Albanian revolt in Kosovo, and the Chechnyan revolt in Russia, those small communities may identify a chance to break free and go for independence, despite the prospect of tremendous loss of life.

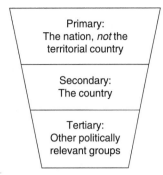

Figure 10.2 Political Identities and Loyalty in Multinational States

CAUSES OF NATIONALISTIC BEHAVIOR

Already mentioned was the importance of social identity theory as an explanation for the power of nationalism. To review, social identity theory notes that people need to belong to groups, and, ideally, they see their groups (in-groups) as better than other groups (out-groups). Nations are groups and, for nationalists, they are a deeply important in-group. Central to in-group–out-group relations is the concept of social categorization. Members of a group see themselves as similar, sharing common attributes, and this group identification inspires behavior that is consistent with the norms of the group. Members of a group also tend to accentuate their positive attributes when they compare their in-groups to relevant out-groups, which they do regularly. When engaging in social comparison, the self-esteem of group members is enhanced when that comparison is positive for the in-group. Sometimes, conflict is a result of engaging in social comparison.

As noted in Chapter 3, the social comparison process is a complicated one. When the comparison is unsatisfactory, people can switch to a new group; they can engage in social creativity strategies, which change the comparison process itself, so that people can find a positive basis for comparison to replace a negative one; or they can engage in competition. The important thing to remember about nationalists is that the first option is out: they are committed to their nation as a group. The second and third options are acceptable, but the potential to engage in the third option (competition with other countries or nationalities within a single country) is high when they perceive a threat to the nation or an opportunity to achieve some important goal. Nationalists reach this point quicker and with greater intensity than nonnationalists. Members of a nation or nation-state—an in-group—will perceive themselves as better than their social comparison groups. They are highly cohesive and very willing to sacrifice for the nation. They are also more likely to be sensitive to things such as insults, frustrations, and aggressive behavior by out-groups (Cottam & Cottam, 2001; Searle-White, 2001). As Cottam and Cottam (2001) further explain, "The nation as an identity group is highly salient for nationalist citizens, indicating that the intensity of emotional responses to threats or opportunities for the nationalist will be strong and volatile" (p. 95).

Nationalism involves very strong positive emotions associated with the nation, and also a propensity for heightened negative emotions associated with the out-group. If the nation is considered an in-group, which it is for nationalists, we can expect a range of positive emotions to be associated with the nation, such as pride in the achievements of one's group or country or happiness when an opportunity to achieve an important goal occurs. As mentioned in Chapter 3, positive emotions tend to make people more flexible, and more creative in problem solving. They are able to see more nuances, and have more complex evaluations of other people when feeling positive emotions. Clearly, these emotions, such as pride in your country, and joy and happiness when the country does well in things like economic development and growth or in international athletic competitions, are associated with politics. There is a potential downside to this, however. Commonly observed in the behavior of nationalists is an inability to look critically at one's own country's behavior. If pride is strong, then recognition of one's own inadequacies is less likely. When things go wrong, someone else is responsible. One's own policies cannot be to blame. This refusal to look at the country's own role in national difficulties also encourages a search for scapegoats upon whom to blame the poor circumstances. This, in turn, can produce behaviors ranging from violation of civil and human rights to genocide. More generally, Kecmanovic (1996) and Searle-White (2001) argued that, in terms of affective properties, nationalistic behavior resembles crowd behavior, in that there is low tolerance for differing views; oversimplification; diminished personal responsibility; a reluctance to consider alternate views; a readiness to act out; a sense of being endowed with unrivaled power, which makes people less critically minded; intensified emotional reactions; and feelings of persecution.

In addition, group factors, such as group loyalty and obedience (discussed in Chapter 4), come into play, in terms of conformity to the in-group's position toward the out-group. There are tremendous internal and social pressures on people to conform when nationalism is aroused. One either faces ostracism and condemnation by friends, neighbors, the community, and even family, or one participates in the flag waving or becomes a passive bystander. This has certainly been evident in the United States after 9/11.

Exactly how nationalists will respond to other countries depends upon the image (see Chapter 3) of other countries or nationalities within a single multinational country. They will confront an enemy with different tactics than a barbarian or an imperialist, for example. The emotions attached to the image will be supercharged among nationalists, because they are so intensely attached to the nation. To refresh the reader's memory, Table 10.1 outlines the images and their attributes.

Let us turn to some case studies. Given the previous description of patterns of nationalistic behavior and the use of social identity theory to explain the underlying psychological causes of nationalism, we use nationalism as the political psychological concept in explaining the cases, rather than repeat the elements of social identity theory over and over again. We also point out the operative images that accompany nationalism and that affect the exact nature of behaviors in the cases that follow.

Table 10.1 Images and Their Attributes From Image Theory

Image	Capability	Culture	Intentions	Decision Makers	Threat or Opportunity
Enemy	Equal	Equal	Harmful	Small Elite	Threat
Barbarian	Superior	Inferior	Harmful	Small Elite	Threat
Imperialist	Superior	Superior	Exploitive	A Few Groups	Threat
Colonial	Inferior	Inferior	Benign	Small Elite	Opportunity
Degenerate	Superior Or Equal	Weak Willed	Harmful	Confused, Differentiated	Opportunity
Rogue	Inferior	Inferior	Harmful	Small Elite	Threat
Ally	Equal	Equal	Good	Many Groups	Threat/opportunity

CASE ILLUSTRATIONS OF NATIONALISM

Nationalism and Perceived Threats to National Values: Western Europe and Immigrants

We mentioned above that, as a group, nationalists see themselves as distinct, and better than others. They are strongly devoted to the identity of the group as it stands and view any perceived contamination of the group, through the imposition of alien values, as extremely threatening. During the 1990s and into the new century, much attention has been devoted to the growth in hostility toward non-European immigrants in Western European countries. This is an illustration of what happens when nationalists perceive a threat to their group identity (Brader & Valentino, 2007). The hostility has been particularly intense toward immigrants from third world countries whose cultures (as well as racial makeup) are distinctly different from European cultures.

This pattern is manifested in the acceptance of falsehoods about the impact of immigrants on European societies and in fear of cultural contamination and change. Many Europeans, for example, believe myths such as the idea that immigrants take jobs from citizens. In fact, countries such as Germany, Italy, and Denmark need immigrant laborers, because their own birthrates are falling (Fijalkawski, 1996). Immigrants are also believed to be responsible for increased levels of crime, and surveys show that Europeans fear that immigrants will change their European culture. Many Europeans explicitly reject multicultural practices that allow immigrants to keep aspects of their culture. Hence, they do not believe that immigrants can enrich the culture of their nation, and they reject instruction of immigrants in native languages.

Surveys demonstrate this pattern. For example, in 1992, two thirds of Italians surveyed explicitly rejected the possibility that their culture could benefit from the influence of immigrants, and two thirds of Danes objected to educating immigrants in their native languages. In 1990, 45% of Austrians agreed that foreigners were a threat to Austrian identity and way of life (Fijalkawski, 1996). Indeed, by 1999, hostility toward immigrants was so strong in Austria that the anti-immigrant Freedom Party, led by Joerg Haider, had enough political power to be part of the governing coalition in Austria. Although the controversial Haider stepped down as party leader, the party held the vice chancellor's office and the ministries of justice and defense. Moreover, in coalition with the right-wing People's party, the governing coalition held 104 of the 183 seats in Parliament. Other European countries, as well as the United States, reacted strongly and negatively, to these events. Although most Europeans condemn violence committed against foreigners, this is an example of the rise of antiforeigner nationalism in Europe, resulting from perceived threats to the nation as a group and the values associated with that group. There has been a resurgence of nationalist parties in Europe since the 2010s.

Nationalism and the Desire for Unity and Independence

Following are a number of case studies illustrating the importance that nationalists attach to independence and unity. Given a perceived opportunity, a perceived realistic chance of achieving independence and unity, or a sense that the deprivation of independence and unity is unacceptably unjust, nationalists will make great sacrifices to achieve those goals. The cases covered are Northern Ireland, the breakup of Yugoslavia, the Albanian revolt in Kosovo, the conflict in Cyprus, the revolt in Chechnya, the Kurds' drive for independence from Turkey, German unification, and the Ukraine.

Northern Ireland

Historical background. Northern Ireland is a region within the United Kingdom, which, since its creation in 1920, has been immersed in nationalism and national identity-based conflict. The Northern Ireland conflict is over national identity, involving several groups, notably British Protestant Unionists and British Protestant Loyalists (the majority) and Irish Catholic Nationalists and Irish Catholic Republicans (the minority). Until 1972, Northern Ireland enjoyed devolved status, meaning that the regional parliament enjoyed a great deal of autonomy, except in fiscal and foreign affairs. The regional Parliament was dominated by the Unionist majority, and allegations soon surfaced of discrimination in areas such as elections, housing, and employment. As a result of the perceived discrimination against Irish Catholic Nationalists, the Northern Ireland Civil Rights Association (NICRA) formed in 1967. The association intended to protest discrimination using nonviolent means such as marches, meetings, and sit-ins. NICRA held its first march on August 24, 1968, but the Orange Order, a Protestant organization formed during the late 1700s, had also planned a march for the same day. To avoid clashes, the Royal Ulster Constabulary (RUC) police force attempted to reroute the Catholic marchers. When some Catholics resisted, the march was broken up by the police and the B Specials—a unit established in 1920 to augment the Ulster police (disbanded in 1969)—resulting in rioting by Catholic Nationalists. The treatment of the marchers by the police sparked allegations of brutality. By 1969, the violence between Protestant Unionists and Catholic Nationalists had escalated, which prompted the British government to send 6,000 troops to quell the disturbances. The British Army assumed responsibility for restoring public order and directing internal security, and the RUC was reserved the authority to investigate criminal activity.

At first, the Nationalist population welcomed the troops, but soon they resented their presence, because the army was viewed as biased in favor of the Protestants. On July 3, 1970, the army raided a Catholic area of Belfast in search of illegal arms. When the army encountered resistance from the Republican paramilitary group known as the Irish Republican Army (IRA), they imposed a curfew. After subsequent clashes between members of the IRA, other Nationalist Catholic civilians, and the army, internment was introduced on August 9, 1971. Internment is a practice of detaining people without formal arrest and is often associated with brutal treatment or torture, including forcing people to stand for long hours with their hands against a wall, putting a hood over their heads for sensory deprivation, continuous noise, deprivation of food and sleep, beatings, and terror, produced by making prisoners believe they will be tossed out of helicopters alive (Conroy, 2000). Of the 342 men interned that same day, only two were Protestants.

Perhaps the most significant incident that enraged the Nationalist community occurred in Derry in January 1972. The army had decided to block the exit from the Catholic area to contain the marchers, some of whom rioted in response. The army then fired upon the marchers, killing 13 people. That day became known as Bloody Sunday. The army claimed that they were provoked, although the allegation was never substantiated.

After the Bloody Sunday incident, the British government proposed assuming total responsibility for the maintenance of order in the North. The RUC was then permanently reserved the authority to investigate criminal activity. When the Unionist government rejected the proposal, the British government dissolved the Northern Irish parliament and imposed direct rule on the region. The six counties were then represented in the British Parliament at Westminster by 12 members elected within the North. Thus, legislation involving Northern Ireland was to be debated in London. However, there were fundamental disagreements over the British solution. There were many attempts at political solutions over the years, culminating in a 1998 peace agreement.

The political psychology of the conflict. There are many ways to characterize the Northern Ireland conflict, but social identity factors and the images the players hold of one another are crucial. In terms of social identity, one way is to delineate and define the groups in the conflict by religion, notably as Catholics and Protestants. However, this characterization simplifies the conflict as one over religious preference. In doing so, it does not indicate that Catholics and Protestants were part of two distinct national groups—British and Irish—with differing national identities and aspirations. Distinct groups within these national groups had their own political parties and paramilitary groups. The Protestant factions identified with Great Britain and considered themselves to be British. The Catholic factions identified with Ireland, and considered themselves to be Irish. The terms Unionist and Loyalist describe British national groups who are pitted against their Irish counterparts, known as Nationalists and Republicans. Unionists and Loyalists also had different perceptions of the appropriate tactics to use in the conflict (specifically, differences about the utility of force and paramilitaries vs. working in the political system), but they were both British in national identity. Nationalists and Republicans also had different tactical preferences regarding how the conflict is to be fought and won, but they are both Irish in national identity. The underlying conflict over national identity has not changed since the inception of the state, even though, over the years, political parties and paramilitary groups under Unionist/Loyalist and Nationalist/Republican auspices emerged, changed names, or reconstituted.

Unionists and Loyalists believe that they are British and that Northern Ireland is rightfully part of the United Kingdom and should remain that way. They perceive their Nationalist and Republican counterparts as threatening. Any discussion of the **images** that they hold of Nationalists and Republicans must also include their perceptions of the Irish government, because the Republic was perceived as a looming enemy with threatening intentions. This enemy had designs on Northern Ireland, and Nationalists and Republicans were merely the dependent arms (colonial image) of the enemy. Together, they made up a pannationalist front, whose intent was to break apart the United Kingdom. Unionists and Loyalists both proclaimed their "Britishness," but they were not a united front because they were divided over the use of violence to ensure their union with Britain. Unionists work through the political process; Loyalists, although participating in the political process, also had corresponding paramilitary groups, such as the Ulster Volunteer Force and the Ulster Defence Association. Thus, their images of each other further complicated the group relationships in Northern Ireland. Loyalists, for example, were seen by Unionists as their dependent children—a **colonial image**—who needed guidance from the Unionists. Loyalists, however, saw the Unionists as weak allies because, in their view, Loyalist parties and paramilitary groups had to form to represent the working-class Protestants, a group that Unionists overlooked and never represented.

The Right to March: Demonstrations of Nationalism

Marching season in Northern Ireland begins in the early summer. Marching parades are a way for both British Protestant Unionists, who see themselves as British subjects, and Irish Catholic Nationalists, who see themselves as Irish subjects, to commemorate their heritage. Thousands of marches take place throughout the summer (the majority of which are Unionist), but at times the marches result in violent clashes between the police and the marchers, as well as between the two communities. In July 2000, several areas of the region were again paralyzed by 10 days of rioting, the catalyst of which was the decision by the police, fearing a confrontation between the two communities, to refuse to allow the Unionists to march through a Nationalist section of Portadown, located outside of Belfast.

Nationalists and Republicans believe they are Irish and that Great Britain should relinquish its illegal rule over the region. Their goal is to see both parts of Ireland reunited. Nationalists and Republicans see the British government as an imperialist power that is holding the North hostage. The British were responsible for partitioning Ireland and creating an artificial majority of Unionists and Loyalists, who were essentially the colonial elite. Like their British counterparts, Nationalists have been divided over the acceptable use of tactics. Nationalists, like the Unionists, worked through the political process; Republicans, like the Loyalists, had both political parties and corresponding paramilitary groups, most notably, on the Republican side, the Provisional Irish Republican Army. However, Nationalists and Republicans have essentially seen each other using an **ally image**—as allies who have represented the same communities, are the same people culturally, and have shared the same problems of discrimination.

Yugoslavia

Historical background. One of the most often mentioned cases, in which nationalists of different nationalities took great risks and committed great acts of violence in pursuit of national independence, is found in what used to be Yugoslavia. There were six nationalities in Yugoslavia before it fell apart: Serbians, Croatians, Macedonians, Slovenians, Montenegrans, and Bosnian Muslims, who were recognized as a national identity group in the 1970s. Except for Slovenians and Bosnian Muslims, each of these peoples had once existed as a medieval state. Some of the nationalities had also been conquered by, and incorporated into, great empires: first the Ottoman Empire and then the Austro-Hungarian Empire. The people of each nation identified with a defined territory, and they differed in language, alphabet, culture, and, most important, religion. However, the majority were ethnically South Slav.

After centuries of conquest by different empires, Yugoslavia was formed as a single South Slav state in 1918. The government was a compromise among the strongest nations, particularly Serbia and Croatia, and reflected their national symbols, religions, and the Cyrillic and Latin alphabets used in Serbia and Croatia, respectively. Their union was motivated primarily by political and security concerns (Crnobrnja, 1994).

Yugoslavia was decimated during the Second World War, and horrible atrocities were committed during that time by the nationalities against one another. Germany invaded Yugoslavia and found allies in the Croatian fascists, whose military forces, the Ustashe, slaughtered Serbs by the thousands. Serbian royalists formed a military force, the Chetniks, who fought against the German Nazi forces, as well as against the Ustashe, and the partisans. The partisan forces, led by Josip Broz Tito, were the only military forces whose members considered themselves Yugoslavs, and who fought for the federation (Crnobrnja, 1994). Tito was also the head of the Yugoslavian Communist Party. The war cost an estimated one million lives in Yugoslavia, half of them Serbs.

After the war, Tito's partisan forces quickly took control of the country, and Tito became head of state. He developed a program for governing Yugoslavia that directly addressed the nationalities problem. His strategy included a brotherhood and unity campaign that promoted a common Yugoslav identity among all nationalities in the country, but not at the complete expense of the national identities. The brotherhood and unity campaign attempted to transform national identities, such as Serbian or Croatian, into ethnic identities, leaving Yugoslav identity as the national identity of all. He hoped to make Yugoslavia the nation to which all gave primary loyalty and with which people identified most strongly. Instead of being a multinational country, he intended to have Yugoslavia become a multiethnic federation. Yugoslavia was divided into six republics, or federal units, which were nationally based in terms of territory (with the exception of Serbs, many of whom lived outside of the Serb Republic): Serbia, Croatia, Bosnia-Herzegovina, Slovenia, Macedonia, and Montenegro. In addition, there were two autonomous provinces in Serbia: Kosovo and Vojvodina. For a communist country, the Yugoslavian state was unusually decentralized. Tito carefully avoided using the largest nation, Serbia, as a foundation for a common Yugoslav identity. In fact, Serbian power, which was in part a result of the fact that the Serb population was the largest of the nationalities in Yugoslavia, was purposefully reduced by Tito. The 1974 constitution is an example of this reduction of power. In that constitution, Tito gave Kosovo and Vojvodina more power and autonomy (their own assembly, representation in the Serbian assembly, and a turn in the rotating presidency), Serbian power was reduced, and the other republics were reassured that Serbia would not be able to control the federal government.

In addition, the Communist party and ideology were used to counter-act periodic upsurges of nationalist sentiment, as well as too-liberal reform movements. Tito believed that the communist ideology would bring the country together as Yugoslavia and ultimately reduce nationalism to a cul-tural artifact, rather than remain a political element in Yugoslavia (Schöpflin, 1993). Nationalism was a crime, and those found guilty were punished with long prison terms. In particular, the nationalists in Croatia were severely punished in the 1970s. Tito himself became a unifying symbol. He was char-ismatic, and very popular among the citizens of Yugoslavia. While he was alive, the international behavior of Yugoslavia appeared to be quite nation-alistic. This was enhanced by the existence of an external threat to Yugoslav independence. Shortly after World War II, Yugoslavia was pressured by the Soviet Union to follow the Soviet model, which they strongly resisted. In later years, Tito became one of the founders of the nonaligned movement, which was an organization of countries that rejected being pulled into either the U.S. or Soviet camp in the Cold War. Yugoslavs enjoyed the grandeur acquired by having this leadership role in an international movement. Yugo-slavia also achieved considerable economic success.

Ironically, the successes of Tito's strategy produced forces that ultimately caused the country to fall apart. With economic success came further eco-nomic liberalization in the 1960s, which, in turn, made the republics more autonomous and weakened the central state. Constitutional changes in 1974 gave each republic and the two provinces a central bank, police, and edu-cational and judicial systems. By the time Tito died in 1980, the economy was on a downward spiral, and no political leader emerged who could fill Tito's role as national unifier. Tito's importance in keeping Yugoslavia whole was evident in the failure of the federal presidency after his death. He did not promote a successor, but instead developed the peculiar idea of a rotat-ing federal presidency, which would rotate among the republics annually. This made it virtually impossible for any single political figure to emerge as a national leader, and it fueled the rise of nationalism among the separate nationalities in Yugoslavia. The presidency was used as a bargaining tool by the different republics. In 1986, for example, Slovenia gave its turn in the presidency to Bosnia in exchange for concessions on economic reforms (Woodward, 1995).

Leader Manipulation of Nationalism

In the post-Tito era, Serbian nationalism was inflamed by a memoran-dum produced by the Serbian Academy of Sciences and Arts in 1986. It focused on Kosovo, where the situation was described as the "physical,

(Continued)

(*Continued*)

political, legal and cultural genocide of the Serbian people" (quoted in Doder & Branson, 1999, p. 37). The document was crafted by Dobrica Cosic, an important author and a leader of intellectual nationalists in Serbia. Slobodan Milošević early on recognized the potential opportunity for his own political ambitions embedded in the arousal of nationalism by the intellectual nationalist camp. In 1987, Milošević, by then leader of the Communist party, was sent by the president of the Serb Republic to Kosovo to address concerns of the Serb minority there about mistreatment by the Albanian majority. In response to protesters' assertion that they were being beaten by Albanians, Milošević stated: "No one will ever dare beat you again . . . You must stay here. Your land is here. . . . You are not going to leave them, are you, because life is hard and because you are subject to injustice and humiliation? It was never in the spirit of the Serb . . . people to succumb before obstacles, to quit when one has to fight, to be demoralized in the face of hardship" (quoted in Doder & Branson, 1999, pp. 43–44). With this statement, and others that followed, Milošević manipulated Serb nationalist symbols, mobilized Serb nationalists, and won the mantle of the defender of Serb nationalism.

The political psychology of the conflict. Within Yugoslavia, the Serbs were the most numerous and were dominant in the military officer corps (Silber & Little, 1996). After Tito's death, Serbia's role and position in the federation became increasingly galling to Serbian nationalists. They believed that they were unfairly deprived of their just desserts. First, unlike the other nationalities, Serbs were not unified in a single republic. Second, they believed that Serbs should control Kosovo and Vojvodina, but particularly Kosovo, a central symbol of Serbian nationalism and the cradle of Serbian civilization. The symbolic importance of Kosovo made irrelevant the fact that only 10% of its residents were ethnic Serbs and the rest were Albanian. Meanwhile, as Serbian nationalism surged, Slobodan Milošević maneuvered his way to the top of the Communist party in Serbia by defeating party rivals less inclined toward radical nationalism (Silber & Little, 1996). He then managed to gain de facto control of the votes of Kosovo, Vojvodina, and Montenegro in the federal government.

The upsurge of Serbian nationalism follows the patterns described earlier that occur when nationalists believe they have the capability for autonomous statehood and, when comparing themselves to other out-groups, believe that they have been mistreated and deprived of natural rights. The case also demonstrates the important role leaders play in manipulating nationalism to mobilize people to fight against other national groups in defense of their own nation (see box). As Kaufman (2001) noted, "Yugoslav politics makes sense only in the context of the nationalist myths and symbols that the peoples of Yugoslavia found so moving. The power of Milosevic had everything to do with his ability to appropriate and manipulate [those symbols]" (p. 199).

Meanwhile, nationalist passions were on the rise in the other republics, particularly Slovenia and Croatia. The Slovenes considered themselves to be culturally superior to their fellow Yugoslavs, particularly the Serbs (they were Roman Catholic; the Serbs were Eastern Orthodox). The Slovenes saw themselves as more like Western Europeans, and their economy was more advanced than those of the other nationalities in Yugoslavia. This also enhanced their self-image. The Slovene nationalists wanted greater autonomy from the rest of the republics and more decentralization in the country. Although Serb nationalists wanted more centralization, not decentralization, they tended not to have severe conflicts with the Slovenes in this regard, because they were far apart geographically, and there were very few Serbs living in the Slovene republic. Eventually, Slovenia pushed for greater and greater autonomy, rejected the legitimacy of federal control, and appeared to be heading toward secession, which the Serbs would not agree to. Conflict between the two republics was then inflamed in 1988, when the Slovenian government supported a strike by ethnic Albanian miners in Kosovo and condemned Serbian efforts to revoke Kosovo's status as an autonomous province and simply make it part of the Serb republic. Slovenian Communist party leader Milan Kucan "portrayed Serbia as the enemy of Slovene democracy, as witnessed by its repression of Albanian rights" in Kosovo (Woodward, 1995, p. 98; Remington, 1996). Serb nationalists were infuriated that the Slovenes would side with the Albanians in Kosovo, who, they believed, prevented Serbians from having their own national territory.

The growth of Serbian power in Yugoslavia, as well as the upsurge in Serb nationalism, contributed to the rise of nationalism in Croatia. Croatians, like the Slovenians, viewed themselves as culturally superior to the Serbs (Silber & Little, 1996). In other words, the Serbs were peasants, the Croatians were sophisticated; Serbs were Orthodox, Croatians were Roman Catholic. Because the Serbs were also powerful, having a strong presence in the military, the Croatian leadership quickly developed a **barbarian image** of Serbia. Recall in Chapter 3 that this image is described as one of people who are perceived to be superior to the perceiver in capability, inferior in culture, and aggressive in intentions. This image was reinforced by statements such as this one, regarding the breakup of Yugoslavia: "If we have to, we'll fight. I hope they won't be so crazy as to fight against us. Because if we don't know how to work and do business, at least we know how to fight" (quoted in Silber & Little, 1996, p. 129).

Croatia had pockets of Serbs in Krajina, who revolted from the newly forming Croatian state. Given the legacy of World War II, they naturally would not want to live in an independent Croatia. Additionally, the Serbs of Serbia would not want this. The rebellion spread to other Serbian-dominant communities in Croatia in the first half of 1991. The Yugoslav army was dominated by Serbs, but was still the army of the federation, and intervened when the Croatian police tried to crush the Krajina Serb revolt. Although the Yugoslav army did not support the rebels, both Slovenia and Croatia interpreted the intervention as an ominous sign that the Yugoslav army was a tool of the Serbs. This was the final straw in their decisions to secede from Yugoslavia. Milošović's official position was that both Croatia and Slovenia had the right to secede from Yugoslavia, but that Serbs living in either one, meaning Croatia, had the right to live in Serbia. Therefore, borders would have to be redrawn, and portions of Croatia where Serbs lived would have to stay in Yugoslavia, but this was unacceptable to Croatian nationalists.

The impact of the Croatian barbarian image of Serbia, on both the mobilization of Croatian nationalism and its movement toward secession, can be seen in late 1990 and early 1991. We noted in Chapter 3 that when this image is dominant, people will look for alliances rather than take on the barbarian directly. Croatia, under President Franjo Tudjman, initially advocated a confederation with the rest of Yugoslavia, rather than complete independence, indicating that they did not want a direct confrontation with Serbia or the Yugoslav army. Croatia did look for allies—which is what one would expect when the barbarian image is operative—and found one in Slovenia. As Slovenia moved toward a bid for independence, Croatia was faced with two options: isolation in the federation, along with a rebellious Serb population in the eastern regions, or declaring independence, as Slovenia had done, and searching for international support as an independent sovereign state. Slovenia had a referendum on independence in December 1990, and Croatia did so in May 1991. Both declared independence on June 25, 1991. Violence escalated in the regions of Croatia where Serbs were in rebellion.

The difference in Serbia's response to Slovenian and Croatian independence is evident in the differences in the wars that followed. The Yugoslav army tried to prevent Slovenia from leaving the federation in a two-week-long conflict with few dead, which ended with a cease-fire agreement, and Slovenia seceded from the Yugoslav federation. This heralded the end of Yugoslavia as a multinational federation, and it became merely another name for Serbia. The Yugoslav army was no longer the military force of the federation, but was Serbia's army, which would be used in a much more destructive war to prevent Croatia from seceding. The difference in these wars is attributable to a number of perceptual factors. Slovenians and Serbians did not have the history of ethnic genocide that Croatians and Serbs did. The Serbian nationalists believed that their own national kindred must be protected from a repeat of the slaughter of World War II and that they should be incorporated into the territory the nation deserved and had been denied for so long. This was not an issue with Slovenia.

Kosovo and Albanian Independence

Historical background. Kosovo was a province within the Serb Republic of Yugoslavia. Of the two million people who inhabit Kosovo, 90% are Albanian and 10% are Serbian. In 1974, when Yugoslavia changed its constitution, the province was granted autonomous status within the Serb Republic of Yugoslavia, angering many Serb nationalists. During the next 15 years, the Albanian majority engaged in ethnic discrimination against the minority Serb population. Kosovo's autonomy was taken away in 1989 by Yugoslav President Slobodan Milošević. In doing this, he abrogated provisions in the constitution that allowed for such things as the Albanian language to be used in schools, as well as for the observance of Islamic holy days. Milošević also sent troops and police to the region. In the view of Milošević and other Serb nationalists, Kosovo is an integral part of Serbian history and a cradle of their civilization. Serbs trace this history to 1389, when they fought and lost the province to Ottoman rule under the Turks.

The Albanians did not want to abide by their loss of autonomy, and in effect, created a shadow government in 1992, led by Ibrahim Rugova. By 1996, the Kosovo Liberation Army (KLA) formed in order to gain independence for the region. They began with attacks on Serb forces. Over the next few years, clashes between the Serbian forces and the KLA increased. Albanians were divided in loyalties, with some supporting the KLA and others, such as Rugova, who was not an advocate of armed resistance to the Serbs, and who preferred a negotiated settlement to the conflict. While the fighting escalated, the Serbs were strongly resistant to outside interference. In a referendum held in April 1998, 95% of Serb voters rejected foreign mediation of the conflict (Judah, 2000). Sanctions were imposed on Serbia in late April, and, in May, Milošević and Rugova agreed to talk. However, Rugova had no influence over the KLA, and lacked the authority to end the fighting.

Concerned about the fighting and the number of refugees fleeing the fighting, in September 1998, the UN Security Council voted in favor of a resolution that called for a cease-fire in Kosovo. The council also warned the Yugoslav government that it would take additional action if they did not comply. In addition to the cease-fire, the UN demanded the withdrawal of Serbian troops from the region, peace talks, a return of the refugees, full access by aid agencies, and cooperation with the International War Crimes Tribunal at The Hague. In October, Richard Holbrooke, the U.S. nominee for ambassador to the UN, met with Milošević. After a series of talks, an agreement was settled on. In that agreement, Serb forces were to be withdrawn, a force of 2,000 troops from the Organization for Security and Cooperation in Europe (OSCE) would verify compliance with the agreement tasks on the ground, and NATO would be permitted to perform air verifications. Finally, elections were to be held in nine months' time.

By mid-October, Milošević was not complying with the guidelines negotiated with Holbrooke. For example, he did move the largest army battalion out of Kosovo, but only just over the Kosovo border. NATO warned again that, if Milošević did not comply, air strikes would ensue. On October 25, the UN Security Council passed another resolution, implicit in which was that military action would take place, again, if Milošević did not abide by the negotiated agreement. Russia and China, however, opposed any unilateral action against Serbia.

By January 1999, it was apparent that, despite negotiations, the fighting had not ceased. Among the incidents were the capture of eight Serbian soldiers by the KLA and the murder of 45 Albanians in the village of Racak. In addition, OSCE observers, who were unarmed, encountered resistance from the Serb forces. Serbia, represented by Minister of Foreign Affairs Milan Milutinovic, once again began to participate in negotiations in Rambouillet, France, on February 6. In that meeting, Milutinovic agreed to autonomy for Kosovo, as well as a cease-fire. However, also proposed in the so-called Rambouillet Agreement was not only that NATO forces be placed in the region, but also that they "shall enjoy . . . unrestricted passage and unimpeded access throughout the FRY [Federal Republic of Yugoslavia] including airspace and territorial waters" (p. 47). This proposal was unacceptable to the Serbian government, which is not surprising, considering that Serbs are very nationalistic and that this was a direct threat to the unity and independence of Serbia. As we have seen, unity and independence are core nationalistic values. Essentially, what was proposed was an occupation force in all of Serbia. At this point, Holbrooke reemerged, but was not successful in trying to convince the Serbs to accept this aspect of the accord. NATO responded by beginning a bombing campaign on March 24, 1999, which lasted 78 days. On June 12, UN forces (Unmik) and NATO forces (K-for) entered the region, at which point Kosovo was considered an international protectorate.

The political psychology of the conflict. The strength of Serbian nationalism enables us to understand why they were so determined to keep Kosovo part of Serbia. This is an outcome of their attachment to the symbols of the country and the people and the desire for unity. Kosovo Albanians, on the other hand, saw an opportunity for independence and for their own unity and took advantage of that opportunity. They knew the history of international (UN and NATO) involvement in Bosnia as Yugoslavia broke up, and they had reason to believe that, if the international community intervened to support the Bosnian Muslims' effort to split from Yugoslavia and Serb domination—which it did—then the international community would help them, too.

The question remains, why would Slobodan Milošević take on the greatest military powers on earth? Here, images play an important role in helping us understand his behavior. Evidence indicates that Milošević held a **degenerate image** of NATO countries, and he simply did not believe that they would carry out their threats to attack Serbia. His previous experiences in negotiating with Holbrooke; the fact that threats were made before and not carried out; his belief that, even if NATO did attack, Serbs were strong enough to resist; his knowledge of disagreements on the use of force within NATO; and many other factors—all supported a degenerate image of NATO countries (Cottam, Mahdasian, & Sarac, 2000). With that image, he could have concluded that risking resistance to NATO demands was worth the gamble to achieve goals driven by nationalism.

A related question is, why would the Albanians rise up and fight for independence from Serbia? **Social identity theory** and its implications for nationalism also provide a plausible answer to that question. People will try to change their group's status and position—in this case a change toward independence—when they identify a realistic cognitive alternative. In the case of the Albanians, there can be no doubt that they too watched as the UN and NATO came to the aid of the Muslims in Bosnia, and they figured that the same could realistically happen for them. Hence, the chances of actually achieving independence would have seemed better in the late 1990s than at any time in history.

Although the bombing succeeded in forcing Milošević to withdraw Serb forces from the region and restored the autonomy of the region, it did not mend the hatred between the still-segregated Serbs and Albanians. The desire for independence by Albanians and the Serbian view that Kosovo is part of Serbia both remain unchanged. Furthermore, it was not until the October 2000 elections that Milošević was ousted from power, and succeeded by Vojislav Kostunica. At first, it did not seem that Milošević would accept the outcome of the election, but widespread protests helped convince him to step down. Milošević remained a face in Serbian politics. Another blow, however, was dealt to his party when Kostunica's alliance, the

Democratic Opposition of Serbia, won two thirds of the seats in the December 24 parliamentary elections. Milošević, who was considered an international war criminal, went on trial in the International Court of Justice, but died in prison before the trial was finished.

Kosovo was under UN supervision after 1999 and security was provided by NATO forces. In February 2008 the parliament voted for independence. Serbs strongly protested this, but the United States and many other European countries supported it. Unrest between the two groups continues, however.

Cyprus

Historical background. Like Northern Ireland, the Cypriot conflict involves two countries, Greece and Turkey, whose people believe that they are rightful owners of Cyprus. However, unlike Northern Ireland, ethnic Greek and Turkish Cypriots coexist on the island as part of two separate nation-states: the Turkish Republic of Northern Cyprus and the Republic of Cyprus. Cyprus was a colony of the British by 1925. In 1955, the Greek majority (about 80%) decided that they did not want to be under British rule and started a campaign known as Enosis, which means union. Greek Cypriots wanted to be unified with Greece. In 1959, the British reluctantly granted unification, and the following year the Republic of Cyprus was established. The Greeks, Turks, and British settled on a Greek president and a Turkish vice president, as well as on proportional power-sharing within the legislature. The British also were given two sovereign military bases. The three powers also left themselves as guarantors, meaning that, if there was any constitutional disruption, they would have the right to intervene.

It was not long before communal violence between the two national groups had broken out. In 1964, the UN sent in peacekeeping troops to deal with the island because of the violence. By this point, the Turks and the Greeks had established their own enclaves. The situation was further exacerbated by the toppling of the Greek Cypriot president by what Turks argued was a pro-Enosis Greek government. As a result, in 1974, the Turkish government invaded the island, arguing they had the right under the Treaty of Guarantee. The Turks established a partition line, known as the Attila Line, resulting in the creation of two countries on the island.

The political psychology of the conflict. The Cyprus conflict is problematic, because it involves two warring national groups—the Greek and Turkish Cypriots—but is further compounded by the involvement of their respective mother countries, Greece and Turkey. Greece and Turkey are highly nationalistic countries and have a long and historical animosity for each other. They are essentially enemies whose perception of each other is highly threatening. The island of Cyprus represents a battleground for these enemies, much like many developing countries were for the United States and the Soviet Union during the Cold War. The Greek and Turkish governments desire to protect and ultimately bolster the power of their own people. And, because of their long-standing historical animosity, both Turkey and Greece have a strategic interest in the island, ultimately not wanting the other to control the island. The national groups on the island, the Greek and

Turkish Cypriots, are simply Greek and Turk **diasporas**. They do not see themselves as Cypriots with common heritages and goals. In essence, there is no conception of a common Cypriot nation (Fisher, 2001). Their view of each other is highly threatening, each perceiving the other to be an arm of the Greek or Turkish government. This is especially problematic for nation building, which would require that they overcome their perceptions of each other and begin to see themselves as one nation whose aim it is to build a country beneficial to both groups.

Chechnya

Historical background. The nationalist uprising in Chechnya has been an ongoing problem for the Russian government. Chechnya is one of six republics in Russia. Chechens are an indigenous group, descendants of herdsmen and farmers, who speak their own distinct language (Kline, 1998). Chechens have a long history of nationalist resistance to Russian rule. As Payin and Popov (1996) explain regarding the early nineteenth century:

> Russian imperialism in the Caucasus lasted several centuries and met its most determined and well-organized resistance on [in] the territory of Chechnya and the bordering regions of Dagestan. There, for a quarter of a century, Shamil's Islamic proto-state fought the Russian army until 1864. The Republic of the North Caucasus, that included Chechnya, declared independence soon after the Bolshevik revolution in May 1918 . . . and fought a brutal war against the Tsarist army, commanded by General Denikin. . . . After Denikin's defeat, the Red Army entered Chechnya in early 1920, and a new rebellion erupted, this time against the Bolsheviks. This revolt was not suppressed until fall 1921. . . . Over the ensuing three years, Chechnya, Ingushetia, and a number of other autonomous oblasts of the Northern Caucuses became independent. A brief period of relative tranquility was cut short by the mass political repression of the collectivization campaign during the late 1920s and early 1930s. This sparked a new wave of anti-Soviet uprisings in Chechnya that continued for the next ten years, gradually taking on the character of guerilla warfare.
>
> (p. 2)

In 1944, Soviet leader Joseph Stalin banished the Chechens to Kazakhstan, after he accused them of collaborating with the Germans. Chechens were permitted to return to their homeland by Nikita Khrushchev in 1957.

The most recent conflict with Russia began in October 1991, when Chechen General Dzhokhar Dadaev declared independence for Chechnya. As in the case of Kosovo's Albanians, it is very likely that the Chechen rebels saw the disintegration of the Soviet Union, and the subsequent independence of neighboring countries, as an indication that a realistic opportunity existed for them to make a successful break from Russia. As we noted in the case of Kosovo, this is something social identity theory would lead us to expect. Similarly, nationalism explains the Russian response: Nyet! Russia had already experienced numerous humiliations, such as loss of territory, severe economic problems, and loss of international status as a superpower. There was no way a nationalistic people would tolerate the further humiliation of losing Chechnya. Consequently, the Russians, who claimed that the republic was rightfully part of the Russian Federation, did not recognize an independent Chechnya. In 1994, Russia sent 40,000 troops to the republic. Even though the Russians were able to occupy the urban centers, they were unable to defeat the guerrillas in the south. The guerrillas were able to retake Grozny, the capital (Grozny was later renamed Djohar by Chechens). Although the Russians anticipated a quick victory, this was not to be. In July 1996, after more than 80,000 people had died, 40,000 homes were destroyed, and an estimated 300,000–400,000 people were displaced, the war-torn Russian army was forced to withdraw its forces (Kline, 1998).

Within the peace agreement signed, in August 1996, by Russian General Alexander Lebed and Chechen Chief of Staff Aslan Maskhadov (who was elected president of Chechnya in January 1997), there was a provision that independence would be addressed in five years, in 2001. In August 1999, the Chechens invaded neighboring Dagestan, in order to help Islamic forces there gain independence. Russia once again invaded Chechnya with 100,000 troops, and, since then, they have been accused of human rights abuses, from torture, summary executions, kidnappings and disappearances, to looting and extortion (Peterson, 2000a). Russian President Vladimir Putin initially saw the solution as direct rule from the Kremlin, which is obviously a different outcome of national liberation than envisioned by the rebels (Weir, 2000). Russia continued to claim that victory over the rebels was imminent. In March 2003, a referendum was called for by the Russian government, which would provide Chechnya with a new constitution and limited autonomy, although it was clearly to remain a part of Russia. In the meantime, the region remains devastated by war and in dire need of a rebuilding of its infrastructure.

The political psychology of the conflict. The position taken by the Russian government, and its actions, shed light on the image it holds of the Chechens. The nationalistic Chechens represent a threat to the Russians, but they are also perceived by them to be inferior in terms of capability and culture, which explains the Russian view that this rogue group needs to be taught a lesson and must be defeated by force. The Russians are also highly nationalistic, and granting the demands of the Chechens would compromise the territorial integrity of a greater Russia. On the other hand, the Chechens clearly view the Russians as imperialists, and this **imperialist image** includes believing they have superior capability. However, the relationship between them is seen by the Chechens as unjust, explaining why they have repeatedly challenged Russian rule, despite the country's perceived strength. Negotiating an end to the conflict would certainly require the perceptions of one group to change: either the Russians would have to accept that the Chechens are a unique national/ethnic group, relinquishing control over the region, or the Chechens would have to see themselves as part of a greater Russia, thus not perceiving themselves as distinct within the country.

Turkey and the Kurdish Revolt

Historical background. Since 1984, over 30,000 people have died as a result of the conflict between the Kurds and the Turkish government. The Kurds, a minority group of 12 million people concentrated in southeastern Turkey, are predominantly Sunni Muslims, who speak two distinct dialects: Kurmanji and Zara. This minority expressed demands ranging from complete independence to autonomy. The Turkish government, however, believes the Kurds should assimilate into Turkish society, and has banned the Kurdish language, television, and the arts.

The conflict between the Kurds and the Turks did not begin with the Kurdish offensive of 1984, nor is it a problem situated solely in Turkey. The Kurds are a nation of around 25 million people without a state. Their traditional homeland is in the area where Turkey, Iraq, and Iran share borders. The majority of the Kurds live in those three countries, with smaller Kurd populations in Syria and Azerbaijan. They have revolted against the governments of Iran and Iraq in recent years, and their aspirations for nation statehood were repressed, often brutally. The conflict in Turkey can be traced to the creation of the post–Ottoman Empire Turkish state in 1923. At the end of the First World War, the Ottoman Empire was defeated, and the Treaty of Lausanne in 1923 divided the multinational holdings of the empire. The Republic of Turkey was established, but the Kurds were left without a homeland. There were three major revolts against the Turkish government between 1925 and 1939, in the southeastern part of the country where the Kurds resided, and the Turkish government responded with brutal repression, attempting to assimilate the minority group. Martial law remained in effect until 1946.

The Kurdistan Workers Party (PKK) formed in 1978. Defining their struggle as one of anticolonialism, the group demanded independence. With the military coup of 1980, and a campaign of repression against the Kurds by that regime, many members of the PKK fled to Iran, Iraq, and Syria. In Syria, members of the PKK were supplied with money, weapons, and training. In 1987, the Syrians agreed to no longer support the PKK and claimed that their bases were closed. However, in reality, the PKK simply moved their bases to an area in Lebanon controlled by Syria and continued their campaign (Graham-Brown & Suckur, 1995).

Beginning in 1984, the campaign was responded to with a declaration of a state of emergency in 10 of Turkey's southeastern provinces. The following year, Prime Minister Turgut Ozal created a system of village guards, whereby local citizens were recruited to help the armed forces fight the PKK (Graham-Brown & Suckur, 1995). In recent years, with the weakening of the movement, the leader of the PKK, Abdullah Ocalan, claimed that he was willing to discuss a political settlement, possibly including autonomy rather than independence (O'Toole, 2000). Ocalan was arrested in Kenya in February 1999, and was given a death sentence. After his arrest, he called for a cease-fire with the Turks. Most of the guerillas have retreated to Northern Iraq and Iran. The PKK claims that they are no longer at war with the Turks (BBC News, 2000). However, in the spring of 2000, Turkish troops crossed into Northern Iraq in an offensive against them, signaling that the Turkish government did not believe the conflict was over. The Turkish government was still threatened by Kurdish nationalist sentiments and was still driven by the perception that this rogue group was not to be negotiated with, but defeated.

The political psychology of the conflict. This conflict can be explained in terms of conflicts about the meaning of national identity, as well as images. The Kurds had a nationalist awakening fairly late in the game, after their nation had already been divided among other countries (Gunter, 1990). During the time when nationalism was sweeping through Turkey and Iran, the Kurds were still divided into parochial communities, that is, communities where the strongest identities were with the clan or tribe, rather than with the Kurdish nation. Indeed, those identities remain very strong in the Kurdish population, and there are significant animosities among the Kurds. As Gunter (1990) notes, in "all of the Kurdish revolts of the twentieth century . . . —whether in Turkey, Iraq, or Iran—significant numbers of Kurds have supported the government because of their tribal antipathies for those rebelling" (p. 6). Kurds also have linguistic divisions. The language has two major dialects (Kurdi and Kurmanji), as well as subdialects, and some are mutually incomprehensible. As national identity grew, however, they came to see the Turks as oppressive imperialists. Kurds in other countries saw their governing regimes in the same manner. By the late 1900s, they reached the conclusion that a favorable international environment would improve their chances of attaining an independent Kurdistan. Their hopes were reinforced by the autonomy of the Iraqi Kurds. We return to this point later.

The Power of National Identity

Bruni (2003) wrote the following story about a 15-year-old Kurdish boy, Bayram, which illustrates the extent to which Turkey is determined to force the assimilation of the Kurds:

> On a school day last November, his teachers in this remote, poor, densely Kurdish area of southeastern Turkey asked him to lead his classmates in the customary Turkish pledge of allegiance, which includes the line "Happy is one who calls himself a Turk." Bayram . . . balked . . . [The teachers] insisted that he press ahead. So he did, and what they heard him say was this: "Happy is one who calls himself a Kurd." The teachers not only sent him home from school for the day, but also summoned the police. Bayram now stands accused of "inciting hatred and enmity on the basis of religion, race, language or regional differences." . . . Bayram's case provides a glimpse into the extreme vigilance of Turkish government officials against any possible flicker of Kurdish separatism, a watchfulness that continues to shape the country's response to the war in Iraq. (p. A3)

Bayram faced up to 5 years in prison if convicted.

Turkish nationalists, on the other hand, do not want the Kurds to have either independence or autonomy within Turkey. They have attempted to force assimilation of the Kurds through repressing their language and culture. But this is not just the determination of one group to suppress another. When modern Turkey emerged from the ashes of the Ottoman Empire, whose heart was in Istanbul, it was not precisely clear who was a Turk. Islam provided a common link between the Turks and Kurds, but the new Turkey was to be a secular state. In the process of repressing the revolts between 1925 and 1939, Turks increasingly denied the existence of an ethnic or national group of Kurds. Instead, they began to refer to them as "mountain Turks" and attempted to force them to assimilate into Turkish society. Speaking the Kurdish language was illegal until 1991. As recently as 1999, after the capture of Ocalan and 15 years of war against the PKK, one member of Parliament refused to acknowledge that there is a "Kurdish" problem in Turkey. He was quoted as saying, "We call it the southeast problem. We don't separate any ethnicity in Turkey in our hearts and minds" (Freeman, 1999). With Turkey pushing to be considered a member of the European Union, they are coming under increasing pressure by the members to grant rights to the Kurdish minority. Turkey argues that granting rights, such as allowing education in the Kurdish language and lifting the ban on broadcasting, could foster separatism (Bruni, 2003). However, the most significant opportunity for the Kurds of Turkey may come from the Kurds in Iraq. With the Gulf War of the first President Bush, they rebelled against the Iraqi Republican Guard, and the United States decided to protect them from retaliation by creating a safety zone in northern Iraq. This in essence established a rump Kurdish state. Then came the second Gulf War, the product of decisions made by the second President Bush, which presented a spectacular opportunity for the Iraqi Kurds to establish a larger and fully independent state. They moved quickly against the Iraqi military.

As mentioned in the chapter on ethnicity, Kurdish military forces took over Mosul and Kirkuk and the rich oil wells there. Their status as an autonomous entity is secure. The whole prospect of instability (i.e., war) in Iraq is deeply worrying to the Turkish government, because they understand full well the impact for the Kurdish community in Turkey of an independent Kurdistan in portions of what used to be Iraq—particularly portions with oil wealth. It would present them with a clear-cut opportunity to try to revolt and unite with the Iraqi Kurds. The United States insisted that the Kurds in Iraq will be asked to pull back, but the future remains very unclear. In 2008, Turkish planes bombed camps of the PKK inside Iraqi Kurdistan, so the problem clearly remains an extremely serious one. The next case demonstrates full well the power of nationalism when the opportunity for unity of a national identity group appears.

German Unification

Our last example of the power of the desire that nationalists have to live together in a unified, independent country is a more positive one—German unification in 1990. Germans are commonly considered to be very nationalistic, and German nationalism is considered a primary cause of World War II. German political behavior is historically replete with examples of popular sacrifice for the sake of the country and the German people. This is a pattern of behavior that derives from strong attachment to the nation as an in-group. After World War II, however, Germany was divided into the Federal Republic of Germany (commonly referred to as West Germany), and the German Democratic Republic (commonly referred to as East Germany). The East became a Soviet ally, and the West became an American and Western European ally. During the Cold War, the option of unification did not exist, despite Soviet statements to the contrary. This led to uncertainty as to the composition of the German national community. Was it the territorial community of both Germanies, or were there two German national communities: the West and East? If the latter, then both West and East Germany could be considered distinctive nation-states. If not, then the desire for national unification would still exist, even if only in a dormant state, because of the constraints imposed on the possibility of unification by the Cold War. The answer to the question of how many German nations there were was dramatically apparent as the Soviet Union relinquished its control in East Europe. The German people moved quickly to take up the new option of reunification.

One of the most interesting aspects of German unification is that it was so attractive to Germans who had in the preceding years demonstrated less and less interest in reunification. West Germany had become prosperous and was closely identified with the NATO alliance. In 1969, the West German government began a process of neutralizing conflict with Eastern Europe, which in effect signaled acceptance of the status quo (Grosser, 1992; Mahncke, 1992). Public opinion polls conducted in West Germany also demonstrated the diminution of hope for unification and the low expectation that it would ever materialize. A 1986 survey found that one third of the West Germans polled believed that East Germany was a foreign land. This was particularly the case among those aged 14–29: 51% of this age group regarded the East as foreign (Plock, 1993). Only 9% of respondents believed Germany would be united in their lifetimes, but Germans still approved of the idea of reunification, as shown in a 1987 poll, in which 70–80% of respondents were advocates of reunification (Plock, 1993). When the opportunity finally came, it took only one year from the disintegration of the East German government, in October 1989, to formal unification, on October 3, 1990, even though the German government had to convince the United States, Britain, France, and the Soviet Union that a newly unified Germany would not be aggressive, and would commit to undertaking the enormous financial commitment and sacrifice that unification would require.

Ukrainian or Russian? Who Are We?

The Cold War ended in 1989, so it was something of a surprise when bloody conflict erupted in eastern Ukraine in November, 2013. Looking at the political psychology of Ukraine, however, it probably should not have been a surprise. Ukraine is a country without much history as an independent country. Nevertheless, Ukrainian identity and nationalism can be very strong. It was part of the Russian empire until the Russian revolution in 1917, after which it became independent, but independence was followed by a civil war among rival factions that wanted to govern the new country. By 1921, the Russian Red Army conquered two thirds of Ukraine, and the western third became part of Poland. Government by Stalin's Soviet Union was extremely brutal in Ukraine as approximately seven million peasants died during the campaign to collectivize agriculture (BBC News, Ukraine Profile, 2015). Stalin also purged political dissidents. Then, in 1941, the Third Reich invaded and occupied Ukraine until 1944. Nazi rule was also extraordinarily brutal. Nevertheless, Ukrainian nationalists did collaborate with the Nazis in 1941; when they tried to get their anticipated reward, independence, the Nazis arrested or killed the Ukrainian nationalist leadership (Snyder, 2014). As the war progressed, Ukrainian nationalists formed the Ukrainian Insurgent Army (UIA), which they hoped would defeat the Soviets once the Soviets drove the Germans out, thus establishing an independent Ukraine. The UIA was vicious, ethnically cleansing Poles in 1943, and fighting a brutal conflict with the Soviets, which the Soviets won (Snyder, 2014). However, many more Ukrainians fought against Germany than collaborated with it, and most who did were part of the Soviet Red Army (Snyder, 2014).

After World War II, the Soviet Union brought Ukraine back into the USSR. Russian was the common language taught in schools, and the Ukrainian language remained in the home. In 1954, Soviet Premier Nikita Krushchev gave the Crimean peninsula to Ukraine. The Crimea was Russian speaking and Russian in identity, except for the 200,000 Tartars who the Soviets deported to Siberia as punishment for collaboration with the Nazis in 1944. After the collapse of the Soviet Union in 1991, Ukraine declared independence, and 250,000 Tartars returned to Crimea (BBC News, Ukraine Profile, 2015).

Ukraine's politics after independence were tumultuous, with major developments occurring in 2004. By that time, the European Union (EU) and NATO were both stretching east, and including more members of the former Soviet Union's political block. Divisions between those who favored a closer association with the EU and the west, and those who favored a closer association with Russia, began to crystalize in Ukraine. In 2004, it was time to elect a new president, and the candidates were Viktor Yanukovich, the prime minister at the time, who was supported by the outgoing president and Russia, and Viktor Yushchenko, who favored a closer association with the west and eventual membership in the EU. Yanukovich narrowly won the election, but there were massive protests against the results, with allegations of vote rigging. These demonstrations were part of a political movement called the Orange Revolution, which demanded greater transparency and democracy in Ukrainian politics. Eventually the election results were thrown out by the Supreme Court, and new elections resulted in Viktor Yushchenko's election to the presidency. Yanukovich resigned as prime minister. In 2010 Viktor Yanukovich won the presidential election and returned to the office. In 2012, parliamentary elections were held, and Yanukovich's Regions and Community Party, as well as the far right Freedom party, did well.

Throughout these years, Ukrainian economic problems, corruption, and continuing political turmoil, including the arrest and imprisonment of political figures, has prompted criticism from western European countries and the European Court of Human Rights. Meanwhile, Russia launched its own Eurasia campaign, which sought to form an economic and political alliance among former Soviet Republics, including Ukraine. Russia applied economic pressure to Ukraine, encouraging it to move closer to Russia, while Europe and the United States applied pressure to Ukraine to move closer to the EU. By November 2013, pressures to lean east or west reached a climax when Yanukovich decided not to pursue the option of an association agreement with the EU, and accepted a Russian offer of $15 billion (Mearsheimer, 2014). Massive protests erupted in Kiev and other cities in Ukraine, with thousands of demonstrators protesting that decision as well as corruption (BBC News, Ukraine Profile, 2015). These protests grew and continued until February 20, 2014, when 88 protesters were killed by government snipers. President Yanukovich then signed a ceasefire with the opposition, according to which he would stay in office until elections could be held. The agreement broke down, and he fled to Russia (Mearsheimer, 2014). The opposition put Olexander Turchynov in office as acting president. Russia refused to recognize the new government, calling the demise of Yanukovich's presidency a coup. Elections were held in May 2014, resulting in Petro Poroshenko's election to the presidency. The new government was "pro-Western and anti-Russian to the core, and it contained four high-ranking members who could legitimately be labeled neofascists" (Mearsheimer, 2014, p. 80).

Protests continued to spread, but now they began to take a different direction, as protesters in the eastern part of Ukraine, particularly Crimea, where most people spoke Russian and identified with Russia, demanded to join Russia. In late February 2014, pro-Russian separatists seized the Crimean parliament and raised the Russian flag. In March, with Russian help, they seized power in Crimea, and Russia annexed the peninsula. Pro-Russian separatists then moved into other sections of eastern Ukraine, including Donetsk and Luhansk areas. Russians were involved as leaders of separatist forces and paramilitaries, and Russian troops entered Ukraine in August 2014. As of this writing, fighting peppered with occasional cease-fires continue between Ukrainian government forces and pro-Russian separatists.

The political psychology of the conflict. This is a very complicated case because it has been aggravated by international political competition. Yet, at its heart it is a case of nationalism and conflicting political identities. Despite the fact that Ukraine is a new country, Ukrainian nationalism and nationalists are not new, and sought their own independent Ukraine for generations. For most of the twentieth century, that meant being free of Russian (or Soviet) domination. Consequently, the desire to affiliate with the EU and Europe is a natural outgrowth of Ukrainian nationalism.

As noted above, images tend to be strongly held in nationalism-based conflicts. The Ukrainian President, Petro Poroshenko, tends to be pragmatic and understands that some sort of tolerable relationship will ultimately have to be developed with Russia. Even so, he describes Russian motivation and behavior as that of a barbarian. For example, in a speech before the United States Congress on September 18, 2014, he stated that Russian aggression will have to be stopped: "If they are not stopped now, they will cross European border(s) and they will absolutely spread throughout the world . . . The choice is simple: it is between civilization and barbarism" (quoted in Shinkman, 2014). His actions also reflect that particular image. In a search for allies he told the European Union leadership that Ukraine must be part of the EU, and that that would "collapse" the idea that Ukraine belongs in the Russian sphere of influence (Harding, 2014). He also asked the United States for aid and support in Ukraine's resistance to Russian actions in eastern Ukraine.

The desire of the "pro-Russian separatists" to join Russia is also a natural outcome of their nationalism. As Ukraine territory moves east, an increasing portion of the population speaks Russian as the first language, and identifies with Russia. This is part of the legacy of Stalin's movement of people across the Soviet Union. Many Russians moved into the Ukrainian Republic of the Soviet Union. When the Soviet Union disintegrated, they suddenly found themselves citizens of a new country, Ukraine. The relationship between Ukraine and Russia was uncertain for several years after Ukraine's independence. There was still significant economic interaction, and many of Ukraine's political leaders were pro-Russian. The question of how strong that relationship would be came to a head in November 2013. At that point people decided that they wanted to be either Ukrainian or Russian, and the country began to split.

The pro-Russian nationalists in Ukraine are not the only Russian nationalists involved in this crisis. Putin is a Russian nationalist, and nationalism is strong throughout Russia (Hale, 2014). Russian nationalists have experienced many losses in the past twenty-plus years, including a dramatic decline in territory, prestige, and influence. Moreover, while Russia has declined, its former Cold War adversaries have expanded both the EU and NATO into countries that used to be part of the Soviet Union's sphere of influence. Putin has tried to restore some of the former grandeur and influence, and supporting a Russian diaspora in the Ukraine and annexing Crimea is part of restoring Russian nationalism. At the same time, it increases security, which has been threatened by the expansion of the EU and NATO.

Russian stereotyping of the pro-Europe Ukrainian leaders, and the protesters who put them in power, is also related to Russian nationalism. Russians derogate them as "fascists" and "Nazis," a reference back to the days of World War II when some Ukrainian nationalists hoped that collaboration with Hitler's regime would win them freedom. While it is true that the anti-Russian Ukrainian opposition included some radical right nationalists, it also included center and left-leaning nationalists. As was noted earlier, nationalism is not an ideology, and it can associate with any ideology of the left, right, or center.

Nationalism and Foreign Policy[1]

Nationalism also has an impact on foreign policy behavior. The heightened propensity to identify threats and opportunities, the importance of national grandeur, and the tendency to be quicker and more extreme in using stereotypical images of others, all influence foreign policy predispositions among nationalists. In addition, nationalists are more easily mobilized by their governments, through the manipulation of symbols important to them, to make sacrifices for foreign policies designed to respond to threats or take advantage of opportunities. Here, we examine a few cases of nationalism and foreign policy.

World War II

World War II is considered possibly the most horrendous illustration of the impact of nationalism on the foreign policy behavior of nation-states.

But, if we look at the policies of two of the major nation-states in the conflict—Germany and the United States—we can see that, although nationalism drove Germans to embark on a policy of expansion that ultimately cost 50 million lives, it also enabled the United States to mobilize the American population in order to prevent Hitler from achieving his goals.

Germany in the 1920s was in terrible condition. The country had been defeated in World War I, and the settlement ending the war, the Versailles Treaty, imposed onerous war reparations and peace conditions upon the country. There was severe inflation in the early 1920s, which wiped out much of the savings of the middle class. The government of the post-war state, known as the Weimar Republic, could not meet the basic needs of the public. Moreover, the Weimar Republic had been imposed by the victors of World War I and was politically alien to Germans, who had never previously lived under democratic rule. The institution of the monarchy was overturned when Germany was defeated in World War I, and there was an uncertain attachment to the new republican institutions. In short, Germany was not politically stable. The Weimar government could not guarantee that Germans would obey its decisions or support it out of principle or habit, and it did not have the ability to provide conditions of economic prosperity for the people. Because of its lack of legitimacy, the government could not mobilize the nationalistic German people by manipulating national symbols to encourage them to make the sacrifices necessary to rebuild and get through the hard times. Any serious effort to manipulate German national symbols would most likely have led the public to insist on the rectification of German national humiliation and to a questioning of the nationalist legitimacy of the Weimar Republic, which had submitted to this humiliation. The Weimar Republic was a consequence of military defeat; thus, it was a symbol of national humiliation (Cassels, 1975; James, 1989).

Under the circumstances, it is not surprising that a right-wing nationalist leader such as Adolf Hitler would appear on the scene to challenge the Weimar Republic, and would be attractive to the German people. Hitler's ability to manipulate national symbols was a major factor in his rise to power in Germany. His defiant nationalism both silenced his opposition and increased his support base (James, 1989). Nevertheless, when he actually came to power, he not only lacked majority support, but also was viewed by large sections of the public with a mixture of fear and loathing (Steinert, 1977). Thus, he developed a system of coercive control that would ensure his authority by intimidating his opposition through violence. It started with street violence during electoral campaigns, even before he came to power, and continued with the development of institutionalized coercion and terror after he came to power. Opponents of the regime were threatened simultaneously with brutal coercion and with appearing unpatriotic by opposing a government that wrapped itself in the flag, declaring itself the savior of the German nation.

By using nationalistic symbols, condemning the humiliations and territorial losses Germany had experienced after World War I, and instituting a strong coercive control system, Hitler was able to mobilize the German people to make the sacrifices necessary to construct a military machine so strong that the Nazi leadership could embark on a plan that not only recovered land lost after World War I, but that also included a goal of vast expansion. He saw an opportunity to achieve nationalist goals, the rectification of the punishment of Versailles, the expansion of Germany into much-needed territory (lebensraum), and the reunification of Germans living in Poland, Czechoslovakia, and Hungary with the broader German nation. German nationalists supported these goals, and the threat of coercive retribution prevented opponents from objecting to those policies. As World War II progressed, the same tactics produced an acceptance of a terrible loss of life and devastating destruction, even as it became clearer and clearer that the goal could not be achieved. The German people became resigned to war (Steinert, 1977). Meanwhile, Germany's opponents were demonized, and Jews were identified as the scapegoats upon whom the blame for Germany's problems was placed.

We often think of the United States' involvement in World War II as simply the fight of good against evil and a normal response to the attack by the Japanese, Hitler's ally, on Pearl Harbor. But American behavior is also attributable to American nationalism. By the 1920s, the United States was a country whose populace was nationalistic. This explains in part why the country made it through the Great Depression without serious instability. The economic crisis of the depression years was a shock to the stability of the system, but the government did not have to respond to instability with coercion. Instead, President Franklin Roosevelt was able to call upon American nationalism to generate a willingness to accept the sacrifices necessary to deal with the economic crisis.

Roosevelt recognized the dangers to the United States emanating from the crisis developing in Europe in the 1930s, but the American public did not yet see events in the same way that Roosevelt did (Dallek, 1983). Instead, the public was concerned with the threat to the nation caused by the economic crisis. Many Americans were isolationists during these years, and believed that the national interest lay in avoiding another involvement in European squabbles. Roosevelt was clearly aware of the public's preference and acquiesced to it, despite his concerns as early as 1935 about the possibility of German aggression in Europe (Dallek, 1979). The Japanese attack on Pearl Harbor on December 7, 1941, erased American isolationism. After the attack, Roosevelt found it easy to mobilize the country. He announced a program to use America's industrial base, resources, and people to create an overwhelmingly powerful military force. He asked for and received enormous material sacrifices, personal sacrifices, and a willingness to risk lives to deal with this threat to the security of the nation. His request was received with approval and even enthusiasm and with little dissent. Americans did not have to be forced to fight for the nation; they were willing to die for it.

This case illustrates one of the most important features of nationalistic behavior: the willingness of a national community to make enormous sacrifices in order to construct the instruments—military, diplomatic, intelligence, and economic—necessary for dealing with an external threat. This ability to generate a willingness to make sacrifices is the most important impact of nationalism on a country's foreign policy. Nationalism makes a state more powerful because people are willing to make great sacrifices for it. These cases show that nationalists can be mobilized by the identification of opportunities to achieve a desired goal, as in Germany, as well as by threats to the nation, as in the United States.

The War on Drugs

U.S. domestic and international counternarcotics policy, known as the "war on drugs," and the responses of other countries to that policy, is another arena that bears the marks of nationalism. Both the United States and Mexico are nation-states, and Mexican and American nationalism has influenced the war on drugs (Cottam & Cottam, 2001; Cottam & Marenin, 1999). Typical of nationalists, American policymakers have had difficulty believing that Americans are responsible for their own drug use. Instead, U.S. policymakers have viewed the drug war predominantly in supply-side terms. In other words, drugs are a problem because they are produced in other countries and sold to Americans, and, although demand for drugs is also seen as a problem, the central solution to drug abuse has been identified as cutting off the supply. To deal with the supply of drugs coming into the country, U.S. policymakers adopted an interdiction campaign on U.S. borders, at ports of entry, on the high seas, and on major foreign transshipment routes and production sites. Other methods include crop eradication in source countries, as well as money for training and supplies for source countries.

The first conflict between Mexico and the United States regarding drugs occurred in the early 1970s, with Operation Intercept. The idea behind Operation Intercept, initiated by the United States, was in effect to close the borders by slowly searching border traffic for illicit drugs, snarling traffic, and dissuading millions of American and Mexicans from trying to cross the borders on regular business and tourist activities. The Mexicans did comply with U.S. demands that it improve its drug interdiction efforts, resulting in increased U.S. aid to the Mexico, the establishment of Mexico's Northern Boarder Response Force, and increased collaboration between the Mexican military and police with U.S. military counternarcotics officials and civilian law enforcement agencies (Dunn, 1996). However, because the United States unilaterally launched Operation Intercept, it placed a great strain on U.S.–Mexican relations. Later, the United States adopted a more bilateral approach, through Operation Cooperation, but that operation was still a result of U.S. demands for improvement in drug interdiction.

U.S. policy toward Mexico concerning drug interdiction continually strained relations between the two countries through the 1980s and 1990s, evoking nationalist resentment in Mexico. International narcotics matters offer plenty of opportunities for threat to nationalist sensitivities, because cooperation requires, at a minimum, an overlap of law enforcement activities. Mexicans were very cautious about that interaction. From their perspective, if you give the United States an inch, they may take a mile. If concessions are made on Mexican sovereignty, the United States will soon be making similar demands in other areas such as immigration. Mexicans were highly suspicious about the intentions of the United States and strongly resisted any effort to give American law enforcement officials free reign on Mexican soil. The United States added credence to that perspective by demanding a certain amount of freedom to operate as law enforcement agents on Mexican soil. In the late 1980s, for example, in response to the murder of a DEA agent in Mexico, U.S. agents participated in the kidnapping of a Mexican national, who was then taken to the United States to stand trial for his role in the murder. The U.S. Supreme Court upheld this action, which infuriated

Mexican nationalists. Mexico argued that the United States could not send agents to Mexico and kidnap Mexican nationals to stand trial for a crime committed in Mexico.

Another U.S. policy that inflamed nationalist sentiments was the decertification process, whereby U.S. monetary funds (as well as international funds, because of U.S. pressure) are to be withheld if a country is not seen as cooperating with the United States in narcotics control. Every year, the executive branch must "certify" other countries before the U.S. Congress. Any country that is not evaluated as cooperating with the United States in its drug war policy is denied assistance from the United States in matters unrelated to drugs. In addition, the United States will recommend against the granting of funds from international aid sources. This is deeply insulting to nationalistic Mexicans, who refused to recognize certification, arguing that it is a violation of international law and a certain illustration of American ignorance and imperialism. Who is the United States to grade other countries, they ask? Moreover, Mexican nationalism is inflamed when the United States argues that Mexico should control the flow of drugs into the United States. Americans view drugs as a supply problem, but when Mexican authorities complain that illegal firearms flood into Mexican criminals' hands from the United States, American officials say it is Mexico's demand that is at fault. They maintain that this too is an illustration of American imperialism and hypocrisy.

By the late 1990s, American policy makers at the executive level finally realized that the battling nationalisms between the United States and Mexico were counter-productive. The executive level could do nothing about Congress' power to require certification hearings, but they did change the tone from decertification to certification hearings. The Clinton Administration started executive level High Level Contact Group meetings in which officials of equal rank from both countries would meet to plan strategies for dealing with the drug problem.

Meanwhile, political change came to Mexico in 2000 when competition among political parties became real. The nationalistic Institutional Revolutionary Party (PRI) lost power at the presidential level for the first time in 71 years in 2000 to the conservative National Action Party (PAN). Cooperation between the United States and Mexico in the war on drugs improved. Both PAN Presidents (Vicente Fox, 2000–2005, and Felipe Calderón, 2006–2012) were less nationalistic than politicians in the PRI typically had been. These administrations coincided with the American President George W. Bush's two terms, also conservative. Bush initiated an aid program called the Mérida Initiative in 2008, which provided $1.9 billion for military training and equipment (Archibald, Cave, & Thompson, 2013). However, the situation in Mexico became dire, with competition between the drug cartels resulting in ever-increasing levels of violence. Between 2006 and 2013, an estimated 60,000 people were killed as a consequence of this violence (Seelke & Finklea, 2014). By the time Calderón became president in late 2006, the situation was so bad that Calderón asked for assistance from the United States, which resulted in the Mérida Initiative. When President Obama took office, the emphasis of the initiative changed from supplying training and equipment to disrupting the operational capabilities of the cartels and building stronger institutions, particularly in justice and criminal justice in Mexico (Seekle & Finklea, 2014). The Calderón administration also took the unusual step of using the Mexican military to combat the drug cartels. This was not very successful.

In late 2012, the PRI returned to power when Enrique Peña Nieto was elected President of Mexico. Initially, it appeared that the level of cooperation achieved in the previous six years would come to an end (Archibald, Cave, & Thompson, 2013) due to a return of intense nationalism that protected Mexican sovereignty. Peña Nieto did plan to make changes to the Calderón approach, and some, such as creating five regional intelligence fusion centers, which Americans will not be allowed into, should give Mexico greater control of its anti-cartel program. Nevertheless, Presidents Obama and Peña Nieto reaffirmed the commitment to the Mérida Initiative in May 2013. Does this mean that nationalism is no longer a source of conflict between the two countries? Not necessarily. Two developments have had an impact on the willingness to cooperate. First, for the last decade Mexico has paid an ever-increasing cost for drug consumption by Americans. The cartels have killed thousands of people, corrupted the Mexican security system, and threatens to turn Mexico into a failed state. This is much more dangerous for Mexico than the drug trade of the 1970s, 1980s, and 1990s. Survival of the country will always come first for nationalists, and Mexican political leaders' willingness to let the United States have more a direct role in Mexico's war on drugs is a reflection of this concern.

Second, American political leaders, particularly at the executive level, have finally become more sensitive to Mexican nationalism and make an effort to treat Mexican leaders with respect and equality. As Seelke and Finklea put it:

> U.S. and Mexican officials have describe the Mérida Initiative as a "new paradigm" for bilateral security cooperation. As part of Mérida, the Calderón government put sovereignty concerns aside to allow extensive U.S. involvement in Mexico's domestic security efforts. The two governments increased cooperation through the establishment of a multi-level working group structure to design and implement bilateral security efforts that included annual cabinet-level meetings.
>
> (2014, p. 6)

While past conflicts have been inflamed by an American tendency to tell Mexicans what to do as though they were children, meetings among equally high ranked officials with a mind to mutual planning helps reduce that potential for conflict.

CONCLUSION

This chapter examined the role of nationalism as a political psychological factor affecting a variety of political conflicts. We looked at nationalistic desires for unity and independence in a number of civil conflicts, from Europe (Northern Ireland, Yugoslavia, Kosovo) to Russia, Ukraine, and the Middle East (Turkey and the Kurds, Cyprus). We also examined the power of nationalism to promote the peace and unity required for substantial sacrifices, in the case of German unification. Fear of contamination of national unity and values was discussed in the case of Western European concerns about immigrants from the third world. Finally, the impact of nationalism on foreign policy was discussed.

Nationalism has been popularly condemned as a force for great violence, and it has indeed been the cause of millions of deaths and tremendous suffering. However, it can also inspire people to make great sacrifices for others. From the standpoint of political psychology, we can see nationalism is normal in-group behavior. It is therefore going to be a factor in politics as long as nations exist; understanding that it is neither good nor bad—it is simply a reality that produces particular patterns of behavior—is much more constructive than condemning it.

Topics, Theories/Explanations, and Cases in Chapter 10

Topics	Theories/Explanations	Cases
Nationalism defined		
Nationalistic behavior described		
Nationalism explained	Social identity theory Image theory	
Nationalism and the drive for unity and independence		Northern Ireland Yugoslavia Kosovo Cyprus Chechnya Turkey German unification Ukraine
Nationalism and foreign policy		World War II Drug war

Key Terms

ally image
barbarian image
colonial image
core community non-nation
    states
degenerate image
deterrence
enemy image
imperialist image
irredentism

multinational states
nationalism
nation-state
rogue image
scapegoat
security dilemma
social identity theory

Suggestions for Further Reading

Carnegie Commission on Preventing Deadly Conflict. (1997). *Preventing deadly conflict: Final report*. New York: Carnegie Corporation of New York.

Cottam, M., & Cottam, R. (2001). *Nationalism and politics: The political behavior of nation states*. Boulder, CO: Lynne Rienner.

Farnen, R. (Ed.). (1994). *Nationalism, ethnicity, and identity*. New Brunswick, NJ: Transaction Books.

Fijalkowski, J. (1996). Aggressive nationalism and immigration in Germany. In R. Caplan & J. Feffer (Eds.), *Europe's new nationalism: States and minorities in conflict*. Oxford: Oxford University Press.

Kecmanovic, D. (1996). *The mass psychology of ethnonationalism*. New York: Plenum.

Searle-White, J. (2001). *The psychology of nationalism*. New York: Palgrave.

Silber, L., & Little, A. (1996). *Yugoslavia: Death of a nation*. New York: Penguin.

Note

1. Many of the cases that follow are developed in greater detail in Cottam & Cottam, 2001.

Chapter 11

THE POLITICAL PSYCHOLOGY OF SOCIAL MOVEMENTS

In the 1950s and 1960s, the United States experienced a massive social movement, the Civil Rights Movement, which changed the American political, legal, and social systems. In 2008, the Tea Party made a major splash in American politics and, in 2011, the Occupy Wall Street movement began. However, social movements have not been seen only in America. In recent years, Europe has experienced the rise of the radical right, and in the Middle East, the "Arab Spring" has resulted in the overthrow of dictatorial regimes in Tunisia, Egypt, and Libya.

What are **social movements**, and why do some people join enthusiastically while others sit the movement out? We can understand a lot about social movements by studying the political psychology underlying them. First, a definition:

> Social movements are collective challenges by people with common purposes and solidarity in sustained interaction with elites and authorities.
>
> (Klandermans, 1997, p. 2)

Klandermans and van Stekelenburg (2013) note that social movements have three essential characteristics. First, they are collective endeavors that challenge existing authority structures, elites, and/or cultural norms. Second, they have a "common purpose and solidarity," which means that they have a shared message and claims and a common identity. Finally, they engage in "sustained collective action" (p. 775).

One question researchers on social movements ask is about why social movements arise. What conditions are necessary for social movements to organize? Klandermans and van Stekelenburg (2013) call this the **dynamics of demand**. The dynamics of demand include grievances, social comparisons, and a lot of emotion. It also involves the development of collective identity that becomes politicized.

A second important question the authors ask is why do some people join social movements and participate actively while others do not? Logically, if a group is a beneficiary of a social movement it can easily sit back and be a free-rider. If the movement succeeds, the group benefits, and if it does not, there is no invested time and/or resources in a failed movement. Moreover, since social movements are outside of the normal political, economic, and social systems, they have no power other than their message. They can expel group members, who may then establish competing groups, and they cannot force people to join the movement. So, why do people join? Individuals join due to the **dynamics of supply or mobilization** (Klandermans & van Stekelenburg, 2013; Walgrave, 2013). This involves variables at the individual level but also at the organizational level.

In this chapter, we will examine these questions, and related subquestions. There are many variables involved in answering these questions and they lie at the individual, group, organizational, and political levels. After reviewing the research on these levels, we will turn to some case studies of social movements. The first case study addressed is a classic: the American Civil Rights Movement. Others are more recent and illustrate the impact of current social media capabilities on social movements. They include the Arab Spring, the Tea Party, and Occupy Wall Street.

BACKGROUND: CHARACTERISTICS OF SOCIAL MOVEMENTS

Social movements have been around for a long time. For example, the movement to eliminate slavery, the movement for women's rights, and the temperance movement all started in the nineteenth century. Social movements are not simple protests. They require some form of minimal organization, including identifiable leaders. Some social movements have **social movement organizations (SMOs)**, which are institutions designed to further the goals of the social movement. The social movement itself tends to be broader than the SMO, and sometimes quite factionalized in terms of goals, strategies, and tactics. Examples of SMOs include the National Organization of Women (NOW), the Ku Klux Klan (KKK), and the National Association for the Advancement of Colored People (NAACP). Often social movements have several SMOs that may be competitive, thus representing competing visions of social movement goals (e.g., the NAACP vs. the Student Nonviolent Coordinating Committee, or SNCC, the latter being more radical). These SMOs are usually not institutionalized, although some are, such as the American Federation of Labor and the United Auto Workers, which started as SMOs in the labor movement and have become legal representatives of organized labor over time (Stewart, Smith & Denton 2012). Social movements, and the SMOs that become part of them, are not part of the political, economic, or social establishment.

Social movements are organized in very different ways. Some are hierarchical; some are loose gatherings. The **structure** of the movement affects recruitment and the preferred form of collective action. Dieter Rucht (2013) developed the following typology of the components of social movements and their environments (see Table 11.1):

Size is also important in determining whether a social movement is effective in achieving goals. The larger a social movement is, the less likely it is to be dismissed as unimportant or irrelevant. Stewart and colleagues (2012) argued that social movements are "large in terms of geographical area, life span, events, organizations, leaders, participants, goals, strategies,

Table 11.1 Structural Components of Social Movements and Their Immediate Environments

Component	Main Characteristic	Examples
Basic action groups	Small, local; informal, face-to-face interaction	Local antinuclear groups, feminist consciousness-raising groups, citizen initiatives
Movement organizations	Greatly varying in size, from local to international levels; importance of formal rules	Robin Wood, National Organization for Women, Campaign for Nuclear Disarmament, Greenpeace
Networks • campaign network • enduring network	Nonhierarchical relationship; components can be basic action groups, organizations, task forces, service structures	Climate Alliance, Preparatory Assembly of the European Social Forum, Global People's Movement
Service structures • material • nonmaterial	Run by volunteers and/or employees, usually offering political instead of market prices for their goods and services in support of social movements	Halfway houses, Ruckus training center for civil disobedience, press houses, informal advisory groups for social movements
Social relations	Open access, not oriented toward movement activity but populated to some extent by activists	Parental group running a kindergarten, educational center for adults, factories, universities
Social milieus	Marked by similar lifestyles and cultural and political tastes	Left-alternative milieu of the 1970s, politicized urban Black communities, rural communes, rural farmer communities, worker communities

Source: Rucht, D. (2013). Social movement structures in action: Conceptual propositions and empirical illustration. In J. van Stekelenburg, C. Roggebans, & B. Klandermans (Eds), *The future of social movement research: Dynamics, mechanisms, and processes* (pp. 37–57). Minneapolis: University of Minnesota Press.

and adaptations. Scope distinguishes them from pressure groups, lobbies, PACs, campaigns, and protest acts" (p. 10). Further, social movements can promote or resist change, and any social movement may have participants who differ in the nature of that change. For example, some members of the environmentalist social movement may encourage the development of wind farms to reduce reliance on carbon-generated power, while others oppose wind farms because they result in the deaths of many birds.

Some researchers differentiate between old social movements and new social movements (Kriesci, Koopmans, Duyvendak, & Guigni, 1997). They maintain that new social movements appeared after World War II and that they are "more spontaneous, informal, and loosely organized network of supporters around a single issue" (Stewart et al., 2012, p. 4). Social movements are also influenced by globalization, the Internet, and social media, all of which made it easier for social movements to have a global scope. These developments made participation in social movements easier and less time consuming, and they dramatically increased the dissemination of information available to social movement members. Their impact on recruitment and mobilization will be discussed later in the chapter. Another distinction made among social movements concerns the types of disadvantages they address. Some groups in social movements face structural disadvantages such as racism, sexism, or ethnocentrism, while others face incidental disadvantages such as an industrial plant polluting the air, or tuition hikes for college students. According to van Zomeren, Postmes, and Spears, "*structural* disadvantage includes structural low group status or discrimination based on membership in a social group or category . . . In contrast, *incidental* disadvantage revolves around issue-based or situation-based disadvantages" (2008, p. 509).

Collective action is another crucial part of social movements. Collective action is defined in the literature as "any action that aims to improve the status, power, or influence of an entire group, rather than that of one or a few individuals" (van Zomeren & Iyer, 2009, p. 646). Collective action can also be designed to stop or prevent harmful actions against a group. The civil disobedience of the civil rights era activism is an example of nonviolent collective action. Many of the violent protests against the regimes in Tunisia, Libya, and Egypt in 2011 and 2012 were examples of violent collective action. Collective action can be ad hoc, occurring suddenly and stopping quickly, or it can be long term and continuous. It can also be costly in terms of time and commitment or it can be easy to do (Klandermans & van Stekelenburg, 2013). For example, being a member of the humane treatment of animals social movement can involve participating in People for the Ethical Treatment of Animals (PETA) and demonstrating at every fashion show where furs are worn, or sitting at the computer and clicking on the link to send money to the American Humane Society.

THE POLITICAL PSYCHOLOGY OF SOCIAL MOVEMENTS

Why do people create and/or join social movements? Clearly, they join because they perceive a wrong that needs to be righted. However, while many people have real and imagined grievances, not all do something about it. Thus, the issue is more complex than simply having grievances. One of the earliest arguments regarding why people join was the rational actor approach, which claims people join after completing a cost/benefit analysis of the likelihood they will gain something through participation. Many reject this argument for a variety of reasons, including findings that people are actually not very good at calculating costs and benefits or probabilities (see van Zomeren, 2013, for a discussion). Thus, participation in social movements is more complex than depicted by the rational actor model.

Another school of thought, **relative deprivation theory**, suggests more complex answers and variables to flesh out an explanation for why people participate in collective action and join social movements (Crosby, 1976; Davies, 1962; Folger, 1986; Gurr, 1970). Relative deprivation is a situation in which people look at their group's condition compared to a socially accepted standard of comparison, and find that their group is not faring as well as it should (Klandermans & van Stekelenburg, 2013). People then feel that they are not getting what they deserve and feel deprived in comparison to others. Although not put in terms of social identity theory initially, later research showed that group-based inequality is more likely to promote action than individual inequality. In other words, people are more likely to take action when a group they identify strongly with suffers inequality or injustice than when they as individuals suffer the insult (van Zomeren, Postmes, & Spears, 2008). In addition, further research demonstrated that the **emotional component** perceiving relative deprivation is more powerful as a motivator for action than the **cognitive component** (van Zomeren, Postmes, & Spear, 2008). As was discussed in Chapter 3, specific emotions lead to specific action-tendencies. When people get angry because they feel that their group is experiencing some form of deprivation, they are motivated to confront those responsible for the grievance. Anger is an approach emotion.

These arguments from the standpoint of relative deprivation theory did not satisfy some critics, who continued to argue that relative deprivation occurs everywhere and often, but social movements do not. Theorists such as Klandermans (1984) argued that people's willingness to engage in collective action in a social movement must have some subjective expectation that by doing so, they will achieve some important goals. This, in turn, grew into the argument that in order to expect that participation in social movements will achieve some goals, people have to feel a **sense of efficacy** (Corcoran, Pettinicchio, & Young, 2011; Mummendey et al., 1999; van Zomeren, Postmes, & Spear, 2008). They need to believe that they are capable of resolving their grievances through collective action. This also relates back to social identity theory as discussed in Chapter 3. In the discussion of social comparisons, we noted that when people make social comparisons, and they are negative for the in-group, one strategy to change this is social competition, which can produce major political and social change. However, people only do this when they see a "cognitive alternative," that is to say, an achievable better future. This is a sense of efficacy.

A final component in peoples' decision to form or join a social movement is the development of a **politicized collective identity** (Drury & Riecher, 2009; van Zomeren, Postmes, & Spear, 2008; Taylor, 2013; van Doorn, Prins, & Welschen, 2013). In Chapter 3, we discussed social identity in general. Some identities are naturally political, such as nationalism or ethnic identity. These identities may or may not be politicized. They can be activated and produce the types of political behaviors discussed in other chapters in this book when threat or opportunity is posed to the identity group. Identity in social movement groups is politicized in terms of the grievances that the group has, but also in terms of a call to collective action. As van Zomeren, Postmes, and Spears (2008) put it: "politicized identity focuses on the political struggle for power with the authorities in the public domain . . . which allows the political to become a (personal) identity project . . . that transforms individuals' identity from one defined by social circumstance [as in ethnic or national identity] into a more agentic one" (p. 507). The identities associated with collective action and social movements take work, and activists endeavor to persuade followers to adopt the identity and join the movement (Taylor, 2013). The work is different for structural and incidental disadvantages. Identities are created and sustained when the disadvantage is incidental, but structural identities are already in existence (van Zomeren, Postmes, & Spears, 2008).

Researchers on the politicization of identities have found that it occurs through several stages. The first is the creation of boundaries that clearly delineate the dominant groups from the subordinate groups with grievances (van Doorn, Prins, & Welschen, 2013). The second is the process of the development of political consciousness or awareness. Groups are not automatically able to see their issue as a political one and their position in the social order as unjust. Being accustomed to poor treatment does not automatically produce an effort to change that treatment, as we saw in our discussion of the belief in a just world. People come to the realization that they are being treated unfairly. In addition, some issues actually have to be defined as political issues for the identity to form and expand. Domestic violence was once considered a private matter between couples, whereas today it is considered a crime. The legalization of same-sex marriage was once not an issue, whereas now it is a widely recognized social movement. The creation of a politicized identity also has an emotional side. Groups with grievances often are socially and politically stigmatized and discriminated against. Their primary feelings about this reality can be shame and fear, particularly if they are strongly repressed. Part of the politicized identity process includes replacing those emotions with pride and anger (Taylor, 2013), thereby making people more inclined to engage in collective action. This can be done through consciousness raising campaigns, as occurred in the civil rights and the feminist movements (Taylor, 2013). The third element in the politicization of identity is called negotiation (van Doorn, Prins, & Welschen, 2013). Negotiation involves redefining the symbolic meaning of the subordinate group's position in society, and the relationship between the dominant and subordinate group. This is an example of social creativity, a social identity strategy discussed in Chapter 3. In part, this can involve name changing. The Civil Rights Movement changed the common name of Black people from *Negro* to *African American*. Social creativity also involves convincing the group and its members to change their defensive posture to a more combative one vis-à-vis the dominant portions of society (Stewart, Smith, & Denton, 2012).

Finally, the formation of social movements and collective action is not a linear process. The act of participation in collective action empowers people, even if the outcome is not a success. It increases the strength of the identity and the willingness to engage in further action (Drury & Riecher, 2009).

Mobilization

The mobilization of people to support a social movement is another crucial element. Mobilization brings the demand for action and the supply of participants together. Social movements are dependent upon social networks to develop group-based collective action. Klandermans and van Stekelenberg (2013) argued that **social capital** plays an extremely important role in the quality of those social networks. Social capital is an old concept, with varying definitions, but it is generally a set of relationships and resources in a community that can be mobilized for the common good. Klandermans and van Stekelenberg (2013) note that it is structural, relational, and cognitive. Social capital provides a basis for social embeddedness through structural elements such as social networks. The richer the social networks, the more people are reached and able to interact. The relationship component refers to relationships in the group—the friendships, trust, and confidence members hold in one another. Finally, according to Klandermans and van Stekelenberg (2013), the cognitive component "is defined as those resources providing shared representations, interpretations, and systems of meaning" (p. 790). This is essentially raised consciousness. The nature of these three components of social embeddedness strongly affect the ability of social movements, and the organizations they build, to mobilize followers. In order to be mobilized to take collective action, people need to be sympathetic to the cause, identify with it, know about upcoming events, and be willing and able to participate (Klandermans & van Stekelenberg, 2013). Social movements provide people with a sense of connectivity to a community, even if that community is at a distance.

The structural aspect of social embeddedness certainly changed with the advent of the Internet. The Internet easily widens the number of people who can be instantly communicated. Social movements no longer depend on standard media to cover their issues. Social movement activists also use the Internet to hack into the websites of organizations they oppose, overwhelm them, and cause them to collapse. For example, this was done in 1999 during the World Trade Organization meetings in Seattle, Washington, when protesters shut down the server for the conference (Stewart et al., 2012). The ease of Internet communication also means that social movements attract followers who are less able and willing to participate in collective action than in pre-Internet days. It makes mobilization with minimal organization more feasible (Klandermans & van Stekelenberg, 2013, p. 793). Finally, the Internet improves the prospects of mobilizing people for collective action in repressive political systems where collective protest is most dangerous.

Social movements have strategies to mobilize members for collective action. Among their tactics are campaigns to encourage collective action and donate to the organization. One progressive political social movement called MoveOn makes extensive use of the Internet to inform people of upcoming political actions, events, votes, and so on. They use persuasive tactics to shore up the identification of adherents with the movement, emphasizing commonalities among members and using phrases and themes that promote the idea that they constitute "a people" and "unity"

(Stewart, Smith, & Denton, 2012). Movements make use of symbols such as suffering animals (American Society for the Prevention of Cruelty to Animals [ASPCA]) or a cup painted with red, white, and blue stripes with a tea bag hanging out of it (Tea Party). Along with symbols are slogans (e.g., "We are the 99%" from Occupy Wall Street) and songs (e.g., "We Shall Overcome" from the Civil Rights Movement). Social movements also make heavy use of **framing**, a concept addressed in other chapters. They develop "collective action frames" that give meaning to facts, defining who has committed an injustice to whom (Klandermans & van Stekelenburg, 2013). Snow, Rochford, Worden, and Benford (1986) argued that the development of an "injustice frame," wherein the actions of authority are seen as unjust and resistance to those actions are seen as legitimate, is necessary for social movements to acquire support and mobilize adherents. Frames often link independent beliefs by "bridging . . . Ideologically congruent but structurally unconnected" frames in SMOs or individuals (Snow et al., 1986, p. 467).

Leaders

Researchers on social movements do not focus much on leaders. Leaders of social movements are in a relatively weak position because these organizations are voluntary, so they have little direct authority (Wilson, 1973). Leaders who form fledgling social movements establish networks and relationships with potential members and effectively communicate a common identity. A leader expresses the injustice of the commonly felt grievance, but in a way that inspires potential members to believe they have the efficacy to change their circumstances through collective action (Ganz, 2010). The leader or leaders are responsible for establishing the symbols and framing the problem to increase solidarity among members. Leaders also strategize to mobilize resources and people, gain attention from potential followers and authorities, and deal with inevitable dissent over beliefs, strategies and tactics, and the use of resources.

Stewart, Smith, and Denton (2012) argue that successful leaders of social movements have at least two of three **personality traits: charisma**, **prophesy**, and **pragmatism**. Charisma comes from an ability to articulate action to achieve an imagined future. It "enables persons to lead fellow activists in direct actions that stir things up, supply vigor to social movements, and make people believe in the impossible" (Stewart et al., 2012, p. 123). Prophets are the purveyors of the movement's beliefs, doctrines, and morality. Pragmatic leaders have organizational skills, are good negotiators and resource mobilisers, and they are inclusive, expanding group membership (Stewart et al., 2012). These traits are useful in different contexts and enable leaders to handle the various roles and conflicts they face across the activities of the social movement. Charisma attracts new members, prophecy creates a politicized identity with meaning, and pragmatism achieves goals.

THE CIVIL RIGHTS MOVEMENT IN AMERICA

One of the most remarkable social movements was the American Civil Rights Movement. Below we will look at some of the most important events of the Civil Rights Movement from 1954 to 1968, and then turn to an analysis of it using the concepts developed regarding social movements. The Civil Rights Movement is commonly thought to have started in the 1950s. However, African Americans struggled for equality continually after the end of slavery in 1865, with boycotts, protests, and the formation of the National Association for the Advancement of Colored People (NAACP) in 1909–1910. This was the first national organization in the struggle against Jim Crow laws and regulations (Morris, 1999). In World War II, 900,000 African Americans enlisted in the armed forces to fight fascism, yet they were denied the opportunity to fight alongside their White countrymen. After the war, African Americans were even more determined that they would not be denied participation in a democracy that they had risked their lives for during the war (Takaki, 2008). Many of the first victories in the post–WWII Civil Rights Movement came through the courts. In 1954, the Supreme Court struck down the "separate but equal" doctrine from the 1896 *Plessy v. Ferguson* ruling in the famous *Brown v. Board of Education* decision. This made segregation in public education illegal, which in principle mandated school integration. The ruling did not result in desegregation because many southern states simply refused to implement the decision. In 1957, three years after the Supreme Court decision and two years of planning, nine Black students attempted to enter the all-White Central High School in Little Rock, Arkansas. Arkansas Governor Orval Faubus deployed the Arkansas National Guard to prevent the school's integration. The Eisenhower Administration responded by sending federal troops to Little Rock to implement the integration and protect the students.

Another important event that stimulated mobilization in the Civil Rights Movement was the lynching of Emmett Till. In August 1955, the 14-year-old Chicago boy went to visit relatives in Money, Mississippi, and made the mistake of whistling at a White woman. Four days later, he was kidnapped and murdered. His murderers were acquitted of the crime, which they later admitted to doing. His murder caused national outrage and his funeral received widespread attention. This galvanized the African American community for further action.

By the end of 1955, the African American community turned to mobilization. On December 1, 1955, in Montgomery, Alabama, Rosa Parks, a Black woman, refused to give up her seat on a bus to a White person and was arrested for violating city law. Her actions were not those of a tired seamstress, but an activist member of the National Association for the Advancement of Colored People (NAACP). Her arrest was followed by a massive protest and a 381-day-long boycott of the bus system in Montgomery. This too was planned, and it started on the day Parks went on trial. Black school children were sent home with flyers informing their parents of the boycott. By the end of the boycott, the Reverend Dr. Martin Luther King, Jr., a member of the NAACP with great oratorical skills, rose to prominence in the Civil Rights Movement.

The boycott ended when the Supreme Court ruled that segregation on buses was illegal on November 13, 1955. During the boycott, King's house and the house of E. D. Nixon (president of the Montgomery chapter of the NAACP) were bombed. Martin Luther King, Jr., was an advocate of nonviolence and civil disobedience, and as he emerged as a leader of the Civil

Rights Movement, these were the tactics adopted by the movement. King also became the president of a new civil rights organization in 1957: the Southern Christian Leadership Conference (SCLC), which was regional in focus and clergy-led (Foner & Garraty, 1991).

Following the events in Montgomery, a group of four students from the North Carolina Agricultural and Technical College staged a sit-in at a segregated lunch counter in Greensboro, North Carolina on February 1, 1960. This ignited sit-ins elsewhere in the south at segregated eateries, and spawned the Student Nonviolent Coordinating Committee (SNCC). As its name implies, this was a student-led group and although it was also nonviolent, it was more aggressive and had a different strategic approach to protest than the SCLC. It advocated autonomous local activity rather than a coordinated local-to-national approach (Foner & Garraty, 1991).

The next major activity of the Civil Rights Movement were the "freedom rides," which began a year after the Greensboro sit-in. The freedom rides were "acts of civil disobedience to integrate interstate buses and bus terminals of the South" (Takaki, 2008, p. 391). The freedom rides were led by the Congress of Racial Equality, a largely White organization, but they involved Black and White people riding buses together. The buses were attacked by White racists and the riders beaten (Takaki, 2008). In 1963, nonviolent protests were held in Birmingham, Alabama, led by the SCLC (the NAACP and SNCC were not very active in Birmingham). Birmingham was a logical choice for protest because its police chief, "Bull" Connor, was an avowed racist, the Ku Klux Klan was very strong there, and many of the freedom rider beatings took place there. Connor behaved in character, and the protesters, many of whom were children, were bitten by police dogs, beat by policemen, and blasted with water from fire hoses. Martin Luther King, Jr. was arrested and not permitted to see his lawyer. The events made national news and drew a lot of sympathy for the protesters.

The years 1963, 1964, and 1965 were years of triumph and tragedy for the Civil Rights Movement. In June, 1963 Mississippi NAACP field secretary Medgar Evers was murdered. August saw the March on Washington wherein two hundred thousand people gathered at the Lincoln Memorial and heard Dr. Martin Luther King, Jr.'s famous "I Have a Dream" speech during a massive interracial support for equality. In September, four little girls were killed when the Sixteenth Street Baptist Church, a church where many civil rights meetings were held, was bombed in Birmingham, Alabama.

"I Have a Dream": An Excerpt From Dr. Martin Luther King, Jr.'s Speech on August 28, 1963

Let us not wallow in the valley of despair, I say to you today, my friends—so even though we face the difficulties of today and tomorrow, I still have a dream. It is a dream deeply rooted in the American dream.

(Continued)

(*Continued*)

I have a dream that one day this nation will rise up and live out the true meaning of its creed: "We hold these truths to be self-evident, that all men are created equal."

I have a dream that one day on the red hills of Georgia, the sons of former slaves and the sons of former slave owners will be able to sit down together at the table of brotherhood.

I have a dream that one day even the state of Mississippi, a state sweltering with the heat of injustice, sweltering with the heat of oppression, will be transformed into an oasis of freedom and justice.

I have a dream that my four little children will one day live in a nation where they will not be judged by the color of their skin but by the content of their character.

I have a dream today.

I have a dream that one day down in Alabama, with its vicious racists, with its governor having his lips dripping with the words of *interposition* and *nullification*—one day right there in Alabama little Black boys and Black girls will be able to join hands with little White boys and White girls as sisters and brothers.

I have a dream today.

I have a dream that one day every valley shall be exalted, and every hill and mountain shall be made low, the rough places will be made plain, and the crooked places will be made straight, and the glory of the Lord shall be revealed and all flesh shall see it together.

This is our hope. This is the faith that I go back to the South with. With this faith, we will be able to hew out of the mountain of despair a stone of hope. With this faith, we will be able to transform the jangling discords of our nation into a beautiful symphony of brotherhood. With this faith, we will be able to work together, to pray together, to struggle together, to go to jail together, to stand up for freedom together, knowing that we will be free one day.

This will be the day, this will be the day when all of God's children will be able to sing with new meaning, "My country 'tis of thee, sweet land of liberty, of thee I sing. Land where my fathers died, land of the Pilgrim's pride, from every mountainside, let freedom ring!"

And if America is to be a great nation, this must become true. And so let freedom ring from the prodigious hilltops of New Hampshire. Let freedom ring from the mighty mountains of New York. Let freedom ring from the heightening Alleghenies of Pennsylvania.

Let freedom ring from the snow-capped Rockies of Colorado. Let freedom ring from the curvaceous slopes of California. But not only that; let freedom ring from Stone Mountain of Georgia. Let freedom ring from Lookout Mountain of Tennessee. Let freedom ring from every hill and molehill of Mississippi. From every mountainside, let freedom ring.

And when this happens, and when we allow freedom ring— when we let it ring from every village and every hamlet, from every state and every city, we will be able to speed up that day when

(*Continued*)

(*Continued*)

all of God's children—Black men and White men, Jews and Gentiles, Protestants and Catholics—will be able to join hands and sing in the words of the old Negro spiritual: "Free at last! Free at last! Thank God Almighty, we are free at last!"

The summer of 1964 came to be known as the Freedom Summer. SNCC activists had confronted the barriers to voting that Blacks faced in Mississippi during their work there. SNCC leaders formed the Council of Federated Organizations (COFO), which brought the other major civil rights SMOs and organized a huge drive to help Blacks in Mississippi register to vote. SNCC had networks of college-age volunteers that they mobilized to go to Mississippi to register Black voters, to teach prospective African Americans the literacy level required to register to vote, and other fundamental subjects that the segregated Mississippi schools failed to teach. Most of the 1,000 volunteers were White (McAdam, 1988). Shortly after the first volunteers arrived in Mississippi, three civil rights workers, Andrew Goodman, Michael Schwerner, and James Chaney disappeared. Six weeks later, their bodies were discovered. They had been murdered, beaten to death by segregationists, including law enforcement officers, because of their civil rights work (McAdam, 1988). Many of the other volunteers experienced violence and arrests, as well. Finally, in July 1964, President Johnson signed the Civil Rights Act, which gave the federal government powerful capabilities to punish segregation and discrimination in schools, housing, hiring, public facilities, and elsewhere.

The next year, 1965, began with the assassination of Malcolm X on February 21. Malcolm X was a Black nationalist who converted to Islam while in prison in the late 1940s. He was part of a more radical portion of the Civil Rights Movement. He was associated with the Nation of Islam, led by Elijah Mohammad. Malcolm X was responsible for a huge upsurge in membership in the Nation of Islam, but he eventually split with Elijah Mohammad and founded Muslim Mosque, Inc. During his activism he faced several attempts on his life, but he was assassinated by members of the Nation of Islam.

A second major event in 1965 was a series of marches for voting rights between Selma and Montgomery, Alabama. There were three marches, and the first was on March 7, 1965. The march was 600 strong and was led by John Lewis and Hosea Williams (CNN Library, 2015). The marchers were attacked by law enforcement officers with tear gas and billy clubs, and they never made it out of Selma. The day was dubbed "Bloody Sunday" because of the violence. Two days later, another march was led by Martin Luther King, Jr., up to the Edmund Pettus Bridge where the earlier march had been halted. Demonstrations in support of the marches occurred in many other cities. After legal maneuvers and other efforts by Alabama Governor George Wallace to stop the marches, President Johnson authorized federal troops to protect the marchers. On March 21, 1965, 3,200 people started to march from Selma to Montgomery. By the time they arrived there were 25,000 people in the march (CNN Library, 2015). The final major events in 1965 came on August 6 and September 24, when President Johnson signed the Voting

Rights Act of 1965 and issued an executive order establishing affirmative action. This required government contractors to make proactive measures to hire minorities.

By 1966, serious divisions over strategies and ideologies began to affect the Civil Rights Movement. Dissatisfaction with the results of the Civil Rights Movement's accomplishments motivated Stokely Carmichael to leave the SNCC and form the Black Power movement; Huey Newton and Bobby Seale formed the Black Panther Party. They advocated separatism rather than integration and rejected nonviolence in favor of self-defense, a reaction to the violence against civil rights activists and Blacks in general. The reality was, it was easier to eliminate the legal segregation of Jim Crow in the south than it was to eliminate the poverty and inequality African Americans everywhere in the United States experienced as a long-term result of discrimination. Additional pieces of legislation and court rulings strengthened the government's enforcement powers in civil rights over time, but that did not change the conditions in which African Americans lived. Indeed, Martin Luther King, Jr., shifted his attention to the issue of African American poverty after the passage of the Civil Rights and Voting Rights Acts. On April 4, 1968, Martin Luther King, Jr., was assassinated, and the Civil Rights Movement lost its greatest leader.

The Civil Rights Movement is remarkable for many reasons, not least of which is the willingness of African Americans to confront the violent oppression of the Jim Crow system. However, the movement has all of the elements discussed above that make social movements possible. First, there was a strong politicized collective identity in the African American population, with all three criteria mentioned above as important to the establishment of a politicized collective identity. Second, there were clear boundaries, particularly in the Jim Crow south, of group membership. A person was White or Black. Further, African Americans had worked for equality long before the big movement of the 1950s and 1960s. The historically Black churches were important in politicizing and mobilizing the people, and they provided relatively safe gathering places. In addition, the segregationists were more likely to overlook these activities given their image of Blacks as inferior and unable to mount an effective opposition to their subordination (Morris, 1999). Finally, there was a concerted effort to redefine the symbolic meaning of the group's position. Black was no longer inferior, but beautiful.

The pre-1950s protests and other efforts to get segregation eliminated achieved many successes. Additionally, the formation of the NAACP early in the twentieth century provided a sense of efficacy, despite continued repression. Participation in the movement increased that sense of efficacy. Takaki (2008) quotes several participants who expressed their sense of pride and efficacy. For instance, after participating in the Woolworth sit-in, Franklin McCain said, "I probably felt better that day than I've ever felt in my life. I felt as though I had gained my manhood, so to speak, and not only gained it, but had developed quite a lot of respect for it." Another said, "I myself desegregated a lunch counter, not somebody else, not some big man, some powerful man, but me, little me." Martin Luther King, Jr., generalized about the sense of efficacy: "a generation of young people . . . has come out of decades of shadows to face naked state power; it has lost its fears, and experienced the majestic dignity of a direct struggle for its own liberation" (all quotes from Takaki, 2008, p. 391).

The Civil Rights Movement certainly had the social embeddedness necessary for mobilization. There were local and national networks of volunteers and supporters. The movement had several major SMOs, including the NAACP, SLCL, SNCC, and CORE, with national and local chapters, as well as very local organizations and churches. Moreover, as Morris (1999) noted, the migration of Blacks from the south to the north in the first half of the twentieth century affected the structural component of embeddedness. It "led to institution building especially within the Black Church and community organizations. These were the kinds of institutions through which protest could be organized and supported. The urban setting also provided the Black community with dense social networks through which social protest could be organized rapidly" (p. 523). In addition, there was the impressive development of television during the Civil Rights Movement era. By 1958, more than 83% of American homes had TVs which, along with communication satellites, "were capable of providing a window through which millions could watch Black protest and become familiar with the issues it raised" (Morris, 1999, p. 522). Finally, the Civil Rights Movement was extremely capable of creating an injustice frame, and it was not limited to African Americans. Inequality and discrimination were at the heart of the frame, bridging the many divides among minorities and women.

The Civil Rights Movement had a variety of leaders, with combinations of the leader characteristics discussed above—charisma, prophecy, and pragmatism. Certainly, King had all three, but there were also many other leaders at the national, church, and local levels with these characteristics as well. For example, at the national and church levels were Rosa Parks, Ralph Abernathy, James Meredith, Bernard Lee, Andrew Young, Malcolm X, Daisy Bates, Charles Evers, James Lawson, and so forth. Student leaders included John Lewis, Julian Bond, Hosea Williams, Stokely Carmichael, Diane Nash, Bob Moses and many others. There was competition and disagreement among the leaders of the movement about goals, ideology, and strategy, but they were effective.

THE TEA PARTY

The Tea Party appeared in the American political scene in 2009 after a commentary by CNBC reporter Rick Santelli. Criticizing the President's stimulus package response to the Great Recession of 2008, Santelli said "The government is promoting bad behavior . . . This is America. How many of you people want to pay for your neighbor's mortgage . . . we're thinking of having a Chicago Tea Party in July. All you capitalists that want to show up to Lake Michigan . . ." (quoted in Williamson, Skocpol, & Coggin, 2011, p. 37). The Tea Party is a reference to the Boston Tea Party of December 16, 1773, when Bostonians, dressed like Native Americans, tossed tea into the harbor in protest of a British colonial Tea Act which forced them to buy tea from the British East India Company. On April 15, 2009, hundreds of Tea Party protests were held across the United States, and some had thousands of participants. One of the Tea Party's earliest concerns was the health reform proposals of newly elected President Obama. This concern expanded to focus on the size of government and the Tea Party supporters' perceived need to follow an interpretation of the Constitution that they believed should replace the current, and in their view, distorted interpretation. Four years later, the Tea Party penetrated the House of Representatives, and used its power to advance its view of the proper role of government.

The Tea Party is often described as a grassroots or populist social movement composed of people fed up with politics as usual. Some disagree, and believe the Tea Party is not a social movement. Early on, the Tea Party phenomenon was considered nonpartisan and antiestablishment (Street & DiMaggio, 2011). When it first emerged after the 2008 election of Barack Obama and the Republican defeats in the House and Senate, the Tea Party was described as helpful for the Republican Party, but equally problematic. Because Tea Party ideology demands small government, a reduction in the deficit, and lower taxes even if it means fewer jobs, its positions were clearly in opposition to the Democratic Party's position. However, because members rejected many of the compromises traditional Republicans were willing to make, they were also seen as a challenge to the Republican old guard and as a force moving the Republican Party to the right or kicking traditional Republicans out of office, replacing them with Tea Party supporters (DiMaggio, 2011). Tea Parties are locally organized and there is no national Tea Party formal organization, although a number of local organizations joined a federation called the Tea Party Patriots in 2009 (McCarthy, Rafail, & Gromis, 2013). The Republican National Committee and state Republican organizations do not control the Tea Parties (Williamson et al., 2011). Local organizations make use of the Internet to organize meetings and activities. Local Tea Parties also differ in their agendas and issues. The idea that government is too big and intrusive is widely shared, but some take positions on social issues such as abortion and gay marriage, while others do not. They have opposed the stimulus, the Affordable Care Act (Obamacare), and amnesty for illegal immigrants. This appears to be a description of a social movement, but is it?

Looking at some of the qualities of the Tea Party several years after it emerged on the scene, many observers are coming to the conclusion that it is not a social movement. In determining the answer, the first consideration is whether there is a mobilized political identity with a clear grievance. Montopoli (2012) argues that Tea Party members are not those who suffer from relative deprivation, although they are angry. Tea Party supporters tend to be rural or suburban dwellers, better educated than the average American, and wealthier than the average American. They are male (59%), middle aged (75% are 45 or older), and White (89%) (Street & DiMaggio, 2011, p. 48). It is also unclear whether they have a distinct collective identity. Most Tea Partiers are Republicans. In a CBS News/*New York Times* survey done in 2010, a majority of Tea Party supporters described themselves as conservative Republicans (Williamson et al., 2011). Fifty-four percent had a favorable view of the Republican Party, and 92% had an unfavorable view of the Democratic Party (Street & DiMaggio, 2011). Moreover, "[f]ewer than 1 in 5 TPS [Tea Party Supporters] thought there was 'a lot

of difference between the Republican Party and the Tea Party Movement'"
(Street & DiMaggio, 2011, p. 63). In a 2012 CBS News poll, 54% identified as
Republican, 41% as Independent, and only 5% as Democrats. Seventy-five
percent called themselves conservative, and 39% very conservative. Sixty
percent said they usually or always vote Republican, and only 40% agreed
that the United States needs a third party, while 52% of Tea Party supporters did not agree with that idea (Montopoli, 2012). Only Tea Party activists
wanted greater independence from the Republican Party, and there are not
a lot of Tea Party activists. For example, the same poll found that only 20%
of those who considered themselves Tea Party supporters ever sent in a
donation or attended a Tea Party activity (Williamson et al., 2011). In a
different poll in 2010, 80% of Tea Party supporters who intended to vote in
the November 2010 election said that they would vote for Republicans, and
this included Independents who leaned Republican (Street & DiMaggio,
2011). Consequently, it cannot be argued that they have a distinct and separate political identity. They are overwhelmingly Republicans. They are a
faction within the Republican voting community with a Tea Party identity.
Does this constitute the kind of politicized identity associated with social
movements?

Another question is whether they are challenging authority and seeking to
change the political system. This is a difficult question to answer definitively.
On one hand, the Tea Party is a vocal movement of protesters who engage
in grassroots lobbying, creating opportunities for people with grievances to
protest (McCarthy, Rafail, & Gromis, 2013). They are effective in challenging
long-term politicians. Tea Party candidates defeated mainstream Republicans such as Lisa Murkowski and Richard Lugar, long-serving Republican
Senators from Alaska and Indiana, respectively, in primary contests in 2010,
and House Majority Leader Eric Cantor in the 2014 Republican primary.
Tea Party Republicans in Congress tried to use the 2013 debt ceiling crisis
to force the repeal of Obamacare. They effectively shut down government
for fifteen days by refusing to vote for a solution to the debt ceiling problem.
In the end, they were defeated, but they demonstrated political muscle by
stalemating the establishment.

On the other hand, the Tea Party has benefited from the political establishment, and most social movements are not associated with institutional support structures. Fox News has consistently placed the Tea Party
front and center in reporting on its activities. Several of its most prominent reporters, Glenn Beck, Sean Hannity, Greta Van Susteren, and Neil
Cavuto, broadcast from Tea party actions (Williamson et al., 2011). Tea
Party had early support from several grassroots organizations, such as
Freedomworks, an organization associated with the activities of former
Congressman Dick Armey; the American Family Association (AFA); and
Americans for Prosperity (AFP), an organization established by the bil-
lionaire Koch brothers in 2003. The Tea Party also benefitted from having
sympathetic current or former elected officials at the national level when
it was formed, including Sarah Palin, Michelle Bachmann, Ron Paul, and
other prominent members of the Republican Party. These characteristics
led some scholars to argue that the Tea Party is not a social movement,
but a "fundamentally top-down, elite-directed affair" (Street & DiMaggio,
2011, p. 127).

OCCUPY WALL STREET

The winter and spring of 2011 were politically dramatic. The Arab Spring began, ending in the demise of dictatorships in Tunisia, Libya, and Egypt. There were protests across Europe against economic cuts by recession-drained European governments. Inspired by these events, the Occupy Wall Street social movement began in the United States. A predecessor of Occupy Wall Street in the United States was an extended protest by the group New Yorkers Against Budget Cuts, who settled in on the sidewalk near New York City Hall to protest Mayor Bloomberg's plan to lay off 4,000 teachers and shut down 20 firehouses. They brought their sleeping bags and dubbed their camp Bloombergville (Sledge, 2011). They started in the middle of June, and by the end of June Bloombergville was gone. However, it helped give birth to the Occupy Wall Street idea. On July 13, 2011, a magazine called AdBusters called for an occupation of Wall Street in New York City. Despite initial difficulties, the idea began to grow, and around 200 veteran activists and organizers from protests such as the Seattle WTO protests in 1999 began to work toward the development of ground rules that would get people mobilized (Sledge, 2011). On September 17, 2011, protesters occupied Zuccotti Park in New York City, and Occupy Wall Street began. By early October, demonstrations spread to other cities across the United States and many other countries. Camps were set up and people settled in with their tents and sleeping bags. Word spread through Facebook, Twitter, media coverage, and electronic communication.

The central grievance of the movement was the economic inequalities and injustices perceived in the capitalist economic system. They noted that 1% of American households owned between 30 and 40% of the nation's wealth, and therefore deemed themselves the 99% who are the have-nots (Gautney, 2011). Initially, other than protesting the growing income inequality in the United States, the Occupy movement did not have specific demands. This served the movement at the time, because their desire was to be inclusive and democratic. Specific demands early on would have had to come from someone, and Occupiers did not believe in top-down directives from authorities. Their identity was that of the outsiders, the "un-mainstream." They were "deeply committed to a radical departure from political norms" (Gitlin, 2012, p. 105). They perceived themselves as practitioners of direct democracy. All viewpoints deserved a hearing, and decisions would be made by consensus. Because of these views, they eschewed support for any candidate in the upcoming 2012 elections, were ambivalent about support from labor unions and celebrities, and were disappointed in Barack Obama. As Todd Gitlin noted:

> It ought to have been obvious what the movement stood for. Anyone with an ear could have figured out the essentials. The loudest, most frequently chanted slogans on the largest marches were "We are the 99 percent" and "Banks got bailed out, we got sold out." The first meant: The Plutocracy that controls the commanding heights of the economy and politics needs to be curbed. The second meant: The federal government under both George W. Bush and Barack Obama

caved into the big banks while failing to relieve householder debt or stop foreclosures.

(2012, p. 82)

In accordance with the principle of direct democracy, the Occupy Wall Street movements were local, not national, organizations, and they were only loosely organized. Encampments were horizontally organized and had no hierarchies (Gitlin, 2012). They each had General Assemblies (GA) where all issues were discussed, but there were no institutions, because none were perceived as necessary. The General Assemblies had "people's mics" so everyone could take the microphone and speak. Minutes were taken and shared. While this was democratic, it also meant that decision making was glacial in pace. The Occupiers also formed "Working Groups" to carry out specific tasks such as food, outreach, security, etc.

Another important characteristic of the Occupy movement concerned leaders: there were none. The GA, for example, would have the daily meetings led by rotating facilitators and anyone could be trained as a facilitator (Gautney, 2011). The Working Groups were also open to anyone, and they reported to the GA. To build a consensus on decision making, proposals were discussed, questions posed and answered, and votes would be cast through hand signals; proposals were recast until 90% agreed with the proposal (Gautney, 2011). The GA had the only legitimate voice for the Occupiers. This manner of governance had its problems. It was very difficult to deal with concrete issues such as how to spend donated money. A solution was developed through setting up "Spokes Councils" (as in the spoke of a wheel). Spokes Councils began to be organized in October 2011. They were made up of members of Working Groups who would meet three times weekly to deal with technical issues like how to use donations. The representatives of the Working Groups were to be backed up by other members of the Working Group, and they would be rotated on the Spokes Councils weekly (Gitlin, 2012, p. 73). After considerable discussion, the Spokes Councils began meeting on November 7, but they did not work well and the meetings became chaotic and hostile (Gitlin, 2012).

The Occupy Wall Street camps lasted until early 2012 when police began to force the camps to disperse (McCarthy, Rafail, & Gromis, 2013). Three months after it started, the Occupy movement had about the same number of supporters as the Tea Party movement, which had started three years earlier (Gitlin, 2012). The two movements were both polarizing and very different. Occupy Wall Street was clearly a grassroots movement, while the Tea Party was not. The Occupy movement lacked leaders, and the Tea Party started with leaders and created more as time went on. The Tea Party has clear electoral goals, and the Occupy Movement did not. Unlike the Tea Party, which became a movement within the Republican Party, the Occupy movement rejected the political parties as part of the problem and refused to become part of the Democratic mainstream. The Tea Party has affected the functioning of the American political system. The effect of the Occupy movement is more likely to be on culture and values, as it has called attention to economic injustice, rather than to policy (McCarthy, Rafail, & Gromis, 2013).

THE ARAB SPRING

The phrase "Arab Spring" is a western term used to describe the dynamic political social movements that began in early 2011 and spread across Tunisia, Egypt, Libya, Yemen, Bahrain, Algeria, and Syria. The outcomes varied, and some are still undetermined, but the movement reflected widespread desires for economic and political change in the Arab countries in North Africa and the Middle East. Protests occurred in several different countries during the decade preceding the events of 2011. These protests expressed grievances about the rising prices of basic food needs, corruption, unemployment, and political repression. Nevertheless, the protests that started in 2011 had a great deal of traction, and spread across the region. These social movements were calls for revolutionary change. In this section, the overall causes of the movement will be discussed, and then attention will turn to three cases, with very different outcomes: Tunisia, Egypt, and Libya.

What caused the social movement called the Arab Spring? There were many causes, and the Arab Spring was not a sudden and unprecedented series of events. The countries in the Arab world are diverse. The oil-producing countries have a great deal of wealth and have been able to provide their citizens with enough benefits to prevent economic discontent. Those without oil resources have high levels of poverty. Some have relatively well educated populaces; others do not. Many have high unemployment, particularly among the legions of young people under the age of 30. Some, like Saudi Arabia, Jordan, the United Arab Emirates, and Morocco, are monarchies, while others have had repressive dictators from various walks of life. Some countries are homogenous in terms of religion, ethnicity, and tribal loyalties; others are heterogeneous. Thus, the factors causing the Arab Spring were different in each country, but some generalizations can be made about conditions that were important in many countries.

The grievances driving the Arab Spring movement were economic and political in nature. Economic growth in the region had not been robust despite the implementation of some neoliberal reforms. Gross Domestic Product (GDP) was only 3% on average for the region during the preceding three decades; oil and gas were the only exports that grew; and nearly 60% of the region's exports went to Europe, meaning there was little penetration of the huge new market potential in China and India (Gelvin, 2012). Moreover, the high oil prices of the 1970s, which had benefited oil producers and nonproducers alike, began to fall in the 1980s. States could no longer provide the benefits they had been able to provide in the past. Unemployment remained high in many countries, and with 60% of the region's population under the age of 30, this could only get worse (Gelvin, 2012). One important sector suffering from unemployment and dashed expectations was the large number of university graduates trying to enter the job market. They ended up being un- or under-employed.

The neoliberal reforms of the 1970s and 1980s so strongly supported by the International Monetary Fund also had an effect on the economies of the region. States in the region began to privatize industry, liberalize economically, and invite foreign investors. This improved the economies for the economic elite and some jobs and resources trickled down to the rest of society, but some of the reforms increased hardship for the poor, as subsidies for important items like wheat (bread) and heating fuel were cut. Moreover, the economic benefits from increased foreign investments "were diluted by crony capitalist systems that ensured the benefits of foreign investment went to a small clique of businesses owned or controlled by key regime figures" (Noueihed & Warren, 2013, p. 27). The corruption was no secret in any of these countries. In addition to corruption, the average citizen faced constant demands for graft. Salaries paid to public servants were low and the states employed large portions of the working population, so people were forced to pay bribes for most transactions. Meanwhile, people who could not get work in oil-poor countries could find work in oil-rich countries, and they sent money home. This caused an increase in housing prices in the home countries, making it difficult or impossible for people with relatively high paying jobs to find affordable housing (Noueihed & Warren, 2013).

Another important characteristic of the region was the persistence of aging dictatorships and traditional monarchies. For example, Egypt's Hosni Mubarak was in office for 31 years, Tunisia's Ben Ali was in office for 24 years, and Libya's Muammar al-Qaddafi had ruled for 42 years when the movements began. The dictatorships were repressive, and by 2010 it looked as though they were going to turn into corrupt dynasties. Hosni Mubarak's son Gamal was widely believed to be his father's designated successor, and Ben Ali in Tunisia was grooming his son-in-law for the role. In Syria, Hafez al Assad's son Bashar took over after his death in 2000. The dictatorships cemented their rule with state of emergency laws, which suspended constitutional rights, empowered security agencies to detain people, and censored news coverage in the name of security. In addition, these dictatorships used formal and informal intelligence agencies that arrested people, kept them in secret prisons, and tortured them, all to prevent political dissent. Spies were everywhere, and people would engage in self-censorship in order not to violate known or unknown rules. The most repressed political groups were Islamists, but anyone could come under the scrutiny of the intelligence forces.

All of this produced an "Arab malaise," particularly among the young, well-educated portions of the populations. A new **politicized collective identity** emerged that included concern for justice, the ability to participate in a transparent political system, and human rights as central themes. As mentioned, protests occurred during the decade before the Arab Spring, but by 2010 there began a "battle for the identity of the region . . . a battle for satisfying jobs, decent housing, and the right of young people to grow up and build families and futures of their own" (Noueihed & Warren, 2013, p. 7). Added to this was the growth of social media, which made a huge difference in awareness of conditions in and among the countries in the region, despite regime efforts to quash information and knowledge. Al Jazeera, which started broadcasting in 1996, was the first news-oriented channel in Arabic, and it offered not only news but debate about the news (Noueihed & Warren, 2013). Viewers were able to call in and express their own opinions, as well. The Internet and mobile phones also had a big impact on the activists of the Arab Spring. They could communicate and organize for action through the Internet and cell phones. Cell phones were available in remote areas where landlines had never existed, which broadened the politically aware community.

Given these circumstances, it is not surprising that the Arab Spring was largely leaderless. The movement was not an ideological one, but represented general concerns for justice and human rights. It was not a movement based upon political organizations, although political organizations like labor and Islamist organizations supported it on a case-by-case basis. As Noueihed and Warren put it:

> Lacking the hierarchical structures of traditional organizations, the loose and leaderless networks flummoxed police, who could not identify the ringleaders and did not see the young Internet-savvy activists as a serious threat. Focusing on a single demand with general appeal, protesters would build coalitions that brought together the Islamist and secular, the trade unionist and the businessman, the young and the old. Those coalitions would be broad, but they would necessarily be loose and easily divided. The online networks that were formed were able to grow very large, very quickly, but they lacked the cohesion of smaller, tight-knit networks based on face-to-face interactions over a long period, and they could vanish as quickly as they appeared.
>
> (2013, p. 59)

Tunisia

Tunisia was ground zero of the Arab Spring. On December 17, 2010, a street vendor named Muhammad Bouazizi set himself on fire in front of municipal buildings in the rural Tunisian town Sidi Bouzid. He had operated his fruit stand without a legal permit and it was confiscated by police, who also humiliated him. Bouazizi was the sole provider for his widowed mother and siblings. This act sparked protests, which quickly spread to Tunis, the capital of Tunisia.

Tunisia was not the obvious first candidate for the Arab Spring. It had a relatively small population of 10 million, 98% of whom were Sunni Arabs. It had a large middle class, the best educational system in the Arab world, and organized labor through the Tunisian General Union of Labor (UGTT), although it was not particularly strong or effective in representing labor interests. Tunisia had a robust tourist business as well and was a popular destination. President Zine el-Abidine Ben Ali cultivated an international reputation as a technocratic ruler (Anderson, 2011). Nevertheless, once one left the developed and relatively prosperous coastal area, poverty and despair were evident.

Ben Ali had been in office since 1987, when he deposed Habib Bouguiba, who took power after independence in 1956. Tunisia had many of the characteristics of the countries affected by the Arab Spring. When Ben Ali took over, his predecessor, who had declared himself president for life, had become mentally incompetent. Ben Ali initially looked as though he would not follow Bouguiba's footsteps, limiting presidential terms to three, and eligibility to serve up to age 75. However, he soon reversed these restrictions and ran for office five times, each time winning 89–98% of the vote (Gelvin, 2012). He allowed his family and extended relatives access to the economy and was notoriously corrupt. More than half of the country's commercial elites were related to them (Anderson, 2011). Islamists were considered the biggest threat to the regime, and the Tunisian Islamist movement, called Ennahda (Renaissance) was severely repressed (Noueihed & Warren, 2013). Ben Ali also established a security force separate from the army and the police over which he had personal control. By the time of Bouazizi's self-immolation, Ben Ali had alienated the business community through corruption, undermined his ruling political party, and displeased the armed forces and police, who resented the power of his separate security force (Noueihed & Warren, 2013). In short, he was vulnerable.

The protests that started after Bouazizi's death started in Sidi Bouzid, and included vendors like Bouazizi as well as his friends and family, young activists, lawyers, teachers, labor activists, and even some politicians (Gelvin, 2012; Noueihed & Warren, 2013). They set up a Popular Resistance Committee to keep the demonstrations going. The protests were encouraged by labor strikes. As Anderson (2011) noted, "the protests also revealed a sharp generational divide among the opposition. The quick-fire demonstrations filled with angry youth made the generation of regime dissidents from the 1980s, primarily union activists and Islamist militants . . . appear elderly and outmoded" (p. 4). Because this was the first Arab Spring event, it was less organized than those that followed. As the demonstrations spread, clashes with police in the town of Thala resulted in five protesters being shot.

Ben Ali attempted to placate the protesters by offering to create fifty thousand new jobs, hold parliamentary elections, end censorship, and step down when he turned 75 (Gelvin, 2012). In order to prevent young people from gathering, he closed down the schools, which, of course, left them free to gather elsewhere. Although the army refused to fire on protesters, 21 people were killed by government snipers in a town near the capital. News of the uprisings spread through social media and al Jazeera. By January 13, the armed forces chief of staff told the army to stand down, and the next day Ben Ali fled for Saudi Arabia (Gelvin, 2012). His departure was not enough, and people demanded an end to the old regime in its entirety. "The regime must go" became their slogan. In October 2011, the country held elections to form a constituent assembly that would create a new constitution. In November 2014, the country held its first election in which people could vote directly for their next president. Tunisia appears to be heading toward a stable democratic political system, despite ongoing economic problems.

Egypt

Egyptian activists watched the unfolding events in Tunisia with great interest. They planned their first protests for January 25, 2011, shortly after Ben Ali left Tunisia. They got their nonviolent tactics, their "the regime must go" slogan, and their determination to bring down the regime of Hosni Mubarak from the Tunisian movement (Gelvin, 2012). They also relied heavily on social media to mobilize people from across the political, economic, and social spectrum. The Egyptian movement, like the Tunisian movement, was also leaderless.

This does not mean that the Egyptian uprising would not have occurred without Tunisia's example. Egypt was similar to Tunisia in terms of factors leading to susceptibility to the Arab Spring movement, and there were many events leading up to the January 25 beginning of the end for the Mubarak regime in Egypt. Between 2006 and 2011, there were 3,000 strikes in Egypt Noueihed & Warren, 2013). A movement called Kefaya had formed in 2004 and called for the end of Mubarak's rule; activists from Kefaya formed another resistance organization called the April 6th Movement and arose in solidarity with textile strikers in Mahalla in 2008 and was very adept at using the Internet to spread its goals of justice and human rights (Iskander, 2013). Egypt had its equivalent to Muhammad Bouazizi as well, Khaled Said, a 28-year-old political activist who was beaten to death by police in June 2010, with many witnesses. His death led to a Facebook-based group calling itself "We are all Khaled Said" (Iskandar, 2013). It attracted more than a million followers (Shehata, 2011). Thus, the potential for much larger mobilization was clearly there before Tunisia bloomed.

Egypt's structural and political characteristics also reveal many of the factors discussed above as important in causing the Arab Spring. In the 1990s, Egypt implemented neoliberal reforms in an agreement with the World Bank, necessitated by unsustainable debt. The reforms involved reduced spending on social services, liberalized trade, privatization of state-owned enterprises, and the end of guaranteed employment for university graduates (Shehata, 2011). Privatization dramatically increased the gap between rich and poor, creating enormous wealth for some, while 44% of Egyptians were poor or extremely poor (Gelvin, 2012, p. 35). By 2010, the only development indicators in Egypt that were not falling were education and access to cell phones, television, and the Internet (Iskandar, 2013). Unemployment was also a problem, and, as in Tunisia, it was particularly severe for the most educated young people. Corruption, always present in Egypt, was galvanized by privatization, and the people who gained the most were those closest to the Mubarak regime, particularly the associates of his son Gamal. The "governing" party, the National Democratic Party (NDP), was basically an association whose elite members used the state and their positions to amass fortunes. It was "an unholy alliance between the ruling elite and the business elite" (Shehata, 2011, p. 27).

Egypt had had three Presidents since the 1952 coup that put Gamal Nasser in office. Nasser and each of his successors came from the military. The governments varied in terms of ideology, but all were dictatorships. Mubarak, who was in office since 1981, had an extensive system of formal and informal security agencies that gathered information on potential troublemakers. Like Ben Ali, Mubarak had a personal security detail, called the Central Security Services. A state of emergency law had been in effect in Egypt since 1981, when Mubarak's predecessor Anwar al-Sadat was assassinated. Political repression had increased in recent years as well. One of the most brutally repressed groups in Egypt was the Muslim Brotherhood. Under Sadat, there was a period of political reform that allowed contested elections as long as the NDP held a majority in the nation's parliament. Mubarak followed this formula until 2006, when he started to impose constraints on opposition parties (Shehata, 2011). The 2010 parliamentary elections were fraudulently manipulated to ensure victory by the NDP, causing the Muslim Brotherhood and the New Wafd Party, in particular, to doubt the utility of continuing to participate in electoral contests (Shehata, 2011). The purpose of these maneuvers was to ensure that Mubarak's son Gamal could take the reins of power in the future (Shehata, 2011).

Young activists called protests for January 25, 2011. They trained in nonviolent tactics before the protests and employed tactics such as having marchers start from twenty different places rather than converging as one large group on Tahrir Square in Cairo (Noueihed & Warren, 2013). Many of the activist groups joined in the demonstrations on January 25; others, such as the Muslim Brotherhood, waited until January 28 to formally join in the protests (some of the younger members were already participating in the protests). The groups participating in the uprising were secular, Islamist, and from all over the political spectrum. As the three weeks of protest went on, more and more sectors of the polity joined. By uniting behind the goal of ousting the regime, their differences did not splinter the movement. The protests spread to Alexandria and other areas across Egypt.

Thousands of people entered into Tahrir Square and, not surprisingly, the police responded with tear gas and rubber bullets. The police disappeared after a day of battling with the protesters, and the protesters took the square. Mubarak ordered the military to restore order, but the protesters welcomed them. The military in Egypt had a much better reputation than the police, and were respected as an institution of the state. They were also economically and politically powerful and had avoided any involvement in political repression over the years. Over the next two weeks, protesters were attacked by hired thugs, some riding on horses and camels.

Mubarak refused to make concessions, although he did remove his son and his son's associates from power, thus addressing the fear that Gamal would be his successor. As violence against the protesters from irregular forces continued, and Mubarak indicated he would stay in office until September, the military became increasing concerned. According to Shehata, "it took new groups joining the protests and the rising prospect of confrontation between the protesters and the presidential guard for the military to finally break with Mubarak" (2011, p. 31). Mubarak left office on February 18, 2011, and the military took control of the country, suspended the constitution, and dissolved parliament.

Egypt's story is unfinished. A new constitution was approved on March 19, 2011, and elections for a new parliament were held at the end of November, giving a majority of seats to Islamists. Muhammad Mursi from the Muslim Brotherhood won the presidential election on June 24, 2011. He lasted little more than a year before being overthrown by the military. Egypt suffered considerable inter-communal conflict among Christians and Muslims, Islamists, and secularists during this time. Egypt held another presidential election in 2014, with a very popular former military general, Abdul Fatah al-Sisi, winning the election.

Libya

Muammar al-Qaddafi came to power in Libya in 1969 as a result of a military coup that overthrew the Libyan monarchy. Although when he came into office Qaddafi was part of the Nasser-era Arab nationalist and socialist camp, his rule was based on a cult of personality, rather than on building a state with strong institutions and a clear set of political principles.

After the coup, he became the chairman of the Revolutionary Command Council, which was the new governing body. As time progressed, he did not take a normal title such as President of Libya, but preferred dramatic titles such as "King of Kings of Africa" and "Brotherly Leader and Guide of the Revolution" (Gelvin, 2012, p. 71). In 1977, he announced his "Third Universal Theory" of governance, which was a theory of direct democracy. Instead of a representative democracy, which Qaddafi thought led to rule by the elite, he called for "people's congresses" which were supposed to operate at the local and national level. There was no private ownership of business as the economy was nationalized, no free press or dissent permitted, no labor unions, no public sector bureaucracies, and no political parties. The military and security apparatus were vicious, and human right abuses were pervasive. Qaddafi's notion that Libya could be ruled by the masses (*jamajiriya*) was a functional impossibility, so people retreated to kinship networks for access to goods and services and for security (Anderson, 2011). Meanwhile Qaddafi's own kinship network of family, friends, and associates benefited from oil profits in an extremely corrupt system.

In addition to internal repression, Qaddafi's security apparatus went after dissident Libyans abroad, intimidating and sometimes assassinating them. Qaddafi's regime was responsible for international acts of terrorism, including the bombing of a club in West Berlin in 1986 and the downing of Pan Am flight 103 over Scotland in 1988, killing all aboard and 11 people on the ground. His regime also involved itself in a brutal civil war in neighboring Chad. Nevertheless, by the 1990s Qaddafi embarked on various steps to improve his relationship with the U.S. and Europe. By the 2000s, foreign investment began to flow into Libya, resulting in new rules on private investment. Nevertheless, within a decade, investors were very disappointed by the constant unpredictability of the government's policy and the pervasive corruption (Noueihed & Warren, 2013).

Qaddafi's son Said al-Islam Qaddafi emerged at this time as both a potential heir (which he repeatedly declined to consider) and as an advocate for reform. He advocated a more open society and engaged in some human rights work as well as international diplomacy. He also faced strong opposition from the old guard, who wanted the political system and distribution of spoils to stay as they were (Noueihed & Warren, 2013). When the Arab Spring came to Libya, he stood by his father.

The Arab Spring came to Libya on February 15, 2011, when protests broke out in Benghazi, a city in eastern Libya. The capital, Tripoli, was in western Libya, where the regime had greater control. Protests spread around the country, and a National Transition Council was established as the political arm of the revolt and temporary interim government. The regime responded with the most violence seen thus far in the Arab Spring. Live ammunition was used against the protesters, and helicopter gunships sought to quash the demonstrations. Qaddafi's forces remained loyal:

> Elite units under the command of four of Qaddafi's seven sons remained loyal, of course, as did the twenty-five-hundred Islamic

Pan-African Brigade, made up of mercenaries from Chad, Sudan, and Niger. Most of the air force, whose leaders were affiliated with Qaddafi's tribe, and the security forces, which consisted of members of Qaddafi's family and tribe and members of allied tribes, also remained loyal. Qaddafi had lavished his special units with military hardware while starving the regular army of resources to prevent a coup.

(Gelvin, 2012, p. 82)

As time went on, the protests became a civil war, with armed rebel combatants facing Qaddafi's forces. The battleground shifted back and forth during February and March 2011, with the rebels taking land to the west, followed by Qaddafi's forces pushing them back to the east. On March 17, 2011, the United Nations Security Council passed Resolution 1973, which authorized the establishment of a no-fly zone over Libya and the use of any means necessary other than a land invasion to protect civilians. The operation was eventually taken over by NATO.

The rebels, of course, eventually won. Muammar Qaddafi was found in Sirte and killed on October 20, 2011. The National Transitional Council became the de facto government for the next 10 months until elections were held. A new General National Congress was elected in July and took over in August 2012. After some maneuvering, Ali Zeidan became Prime Minister, only to be replaced. The government did not have a single dominant political actor or ideology, and its hold on the country was weak, as demonstrated by the 2012 attack on the U.S. consulate in Benghazi. Libya's future remains very uncertain.

CONCLUSION

While the authors were wrapping up this chapter, a new social movement appeared in the news: the democracy movement in Hong Kong, whose protesters were demanding great political choice. It is being called the Umbrella Revolution because the protesters have used umbrellas to protect themselves from tear gas, rain, and sunshine.

Social movements will undoubtedly continue to arise. In this chapter, we have reviewed the political psychology of the social movement phenomenon and examined several different cases. As the cases demonstrate, social movements have many similarities—grievances, a politicized identity, mobilization strategies, and collective action. They differ extensively in leadership, with the American Civil Rights Movement having the most identifiable leaders, and the Arab Spring and Occupy Wall Street movements being largely leaderless. Perhaps future research will reveal the extent to which the Internet has made these movements possible without leaders. The movements examined here have also differed in outcomes. The American Civil Rights Movement had many successes, but inequalities and discrimination persist. The Tea Party has had many electoral victories, but as a relatively new phenomenon, its future electoral power is unknown. Occupy Wall Street has faded as a movement but has made an impact in other ways. The outcome of the Arab Spring is an ongoing development.

Topics/Theories and Case Studies in Chapter 11		
Topics	*Theories*	*Cases*
Social Movements	Relative deprivation	Civil Rights Movement
	Dynamics of supply	Tea Party
	Dynamics of demand	Occupy Wall Street
	Sense of efficacy	Arab Spring
	Politicized collective identity	– Tunisia
	Social capital	– Egypt
	Leaders	– Libya

Key Terms

Arab Spring

charismatic leaders

Civil Rights Movement

cognitive component

collective action

dynamics of demand

dynamics of supply

emotional component

framing

Occupy Wall Street

politicized collective identity

pragmatic leaders

prophetic leaders

sense of efficacy

social capital

social movements

Tea Party

Suggestions for Further Reading

DiMaggio, A. (2011). *The rise of the tea party*. New York: Monthly Review Press.

Gelvin, J. L. (2012). *The Arab uprisings: What everyone needs to know*. Oxford: Oxford University Press.

Gitlin, T. (2012). *Occupy nation: The roots, the spirit, and the promise of Occupy Wall Street*. New York: HarperCollins.

Gurr, T. (1970). *Why men rebel*. Princeton, NJ: Princeton University Press.

Klandermans, B. (1997). *The social psychology of protest*. Oxford: Blackwell.

McAdam, D. (1988). *Freedom summer*. Oxford: Oxford University Press.

Noueihed, L., & Warren, A. (2013). *The battle for the Arab Spring: Revolution, counter-revolution and the making of a new era*. New Haven, CT: Yale University Press.

Street, P., & DiMaggio, P. (2011). *Crashing the tea party: Mass media and the campaign to remake American politics*. Boulder, CO: Paradigm.

Chapter 12

THE POLITICAL PSYCHOLOGY OF TERRORISM

A WORLD OF TERRORISM

Terrorism is not a new subject by any stretch of the imagination. "Each year, terrorist groups commit hundreds of acts of violence." This is the sentence with which the authors started the section in terrorism in the first edition of this book six months before the attack on the World Trade Center in New York City and on Washington, DC, on September 11, 2001. That day was the single most brutal and coordinated attack by a foreign terrorist group on U.S. soil, far worse than the first strike on the World Trade Center in 1993, led by Ramzi Yousef. The 9/11 attack was, for many, unimaginable. After this date, Americans were bombarded with information and images of al-Qaeda, the group that perpetrated the attack. September 11, 2001 changed the way Americans psychologically dealt with terrorism. Americans had a steep learning curve and a higher threat perception of al-Qaeda, and the U.S. government stepped up its counterterrorism initiatives and policies. Terrorism, no matter where it is perpetrated, can have a profound effect on the mind-set of a targeted population.

Before the 9/11 attack, volumes of research and case studies on terrorist groups had already been produced. The media and academics tended to focus particularly on groups found in Europe and Latin America. There were, however, limited books and articles on al-Qaeda, even though it had long been active before September 11, 2001. In fact, the United States was the target of several al-Qaeda attacks, such as the bombings of the U.S. embassies in Tanzania and Kenya in 1998, and the bombing of the USS Cole in Yemen in 2000, amongst others. This threat was not perceived by the U.S. government as important enough to gain our full attention. The importance of such attacks and the existence of intelligence information, coupled with Osama bin Laden's explicit promise of future threats to come, now seem obvious enough to have predicted 9/11. However, these events and information were overlooked, ignored, and discounted.

This chapter covers a lot of different topics on the political psychology of terrorism. It draws on many psychological concepts and theories already covered in the book to discuss terrorism at the individual and group levels. Thus, there are both group-level and individual-level concepts that are relevant to the discussion of terrorism. At the individual level, we examine issues such as personality; that is, we talk about whether there is a **terrorist personality**. We also address specific personality attributes, such as individual traits, and motivations for joining terrorist groups. At the group level, we highlight intra-group level factors such as recruitment, indoctrination, conformity, obedience, group conflict, role, and social control. Throughout the chapter, we use many studies and examples to illustrate both individual- and group-level factors.

Before delving into these aspects of terrorism, it is necessary to first define terrorism and note which groups are proscribed by the United States. We then generally look at why groups turn to terrorism.

DEFINING TERRORISM

There are many different definitions of terrorism in the academic and policy communities. In fact, many different government agencies choose to rely on their own definitions to suit their goals and objectives. Essentially, what we are left with are different perceptions of what it takes to be a terrorist group. Crenshaw (2000) captures the essence of this debate:

> The problem of defining terrorism has hindered analysis since the inception of studies of terrorism in the early 1970s. One set of problems is due to the fact that the concept of terrorism is deeply contested. The use of the term is often polemical and rhetorical. It can be a pejorative label, meant to condemn an opponent's cause as illegitimate rather than describe behavior. Moreover, even if the term is used objectively as an analytical tool, it is still difficult to arrive at a satisfactory definition that distinguishes terrorism from other violent phenomena. In principle, terrorism is a deliberate and systematic violence performed by small numbers of people, whereas communal violence is spontaneous, sporadic, and requires mass participation. The purpose of terrorism is to intimidate a watching popular audience by harming only a few, whereas genocide is the elimination of entire communities. Terrorism is meant to hurt, not to destroy. Terrorism is preeminently political and symbolic, whereas guerilla warfare is a military activity. Repressive "terror" from above is the action of those in power, whereas terrorism is a clandestine resistance to authority. Yet in practice, events cannot always be precisely categorized.
>
> (p. 406)

Crenshaw goes on to argue that the wide-ranging tactics used by terrorists further complicate the problem. For example, some use methods such as kidnapping and hostage taking, others bomb, some use assassination, some may use all of these, and some mix and match. When independent nonstate terrorist organizations are supported by states, terrorism is state-sponsored. They are also organized differently, ranging from hierarchical and centralized to anarchical and decentralized. Finally, classification of terrorist groups is complicated because terrorist groups have many different identities, which includes their definition of the enemy, group norms, and leadership. We cannot settle the definitional debate here. Suffice to say that for the purposes of this chapter, we have taken elements from existing definitions and include groups that are composed of small numbers of people who use, or threaten to use, systematic violence in order to accomplish a political goal. Acts of terrorism are symbolic; that is, the targets of terrorists are symbols of the state or of social norms and structure.

TERRORIST GROUPS

There are numerous terrorist groups in the world. There are also many terrorist groups that are proscribed by the United States government (see Table 12.1). If we examine the number of different groups on the proscribed list, we get an idea of about how many groups the United States perceives through the **rogue image**. Recall that rogues are considered bad children—those one does not negotiate with and those who must be punished. These groups are not seen as formidable, but they threaten U.S. national security and interests. This chapter provides some select examples of terrorist groups to illustrate the general differences among them.

Before doing this, however, of note is that some of these groups we mention are no longer found on the U.S. proscribed list. This is interesting in itself because realistically some of these groups still have threatening intentions, but they are no longer viewed by those in the policy community that compiles the list as having such intentions. The psychology behind the decisions to proscribe is interesting. If the threat is no longer perceived, or if we agree with the goals of the groups, they are not put on the list, even if they remain active participants in terrorist activities. In Chapter 3, we introduced the concept of selective interpretation of information; that is, inconsistent information is ignored or distorted to appear consistent with attitudes or cognitive categories. Remember, ignoring some very threatening information is why 9/11 happened in the first place.

Let's take a look at some specific groups to underscore the general similarities and differences between them. Groups such as the Kurdish Kongra-Gel and the Basque Fatherland and Liberty (ETA) oppose the national identity of the existing state and strive for independent rule (Byman, 1998). Palestinian groups such as Hamas, al-Aqsa Martyrs' Brigade, the Popular Front for the Liberation of Palestine (PFLF), and others dispute the existence of Israel. In the long run, they seek to reclaim the land that Israel occupies, but at this time they cannot defeat Israel. In the short term, they have opted for independence from Israeli rule and in response, the Israeli government has granted limited autonomy in the Palestinian territories of the West Bank and the Gaza Strip. Hamas, which is actually part of an elected government in the Gaza Strip, fights against Fatah, a dominant group in Palestine in an effort to keep control of the territory. The United States has thrown its support behind Fatah (Palestinian Liberation Organization), the group that holds the Presidency of the Palestinian National Authority. President Mahmoud Abbas has stated that there will be no negotiations with Hamas unless they give up control in Gaza (Assadi, 2007). The United States does not recognize the Hamas's right to rule, and the group is proscribed despite its participation in elections. Hezbollah, a Shia group in Lebanon, has explicitly stated it wants to destroy Israel and often confronts the country in

Table 12.1 State Department List of Designated Groups, 2012

Date Designated	Name
10/8/1997	Abu Nidal Organization (ANO)
10/8/1997	Abu Sayyaf Group (ASG)
10/8/1997	Aum Shinrikyo (AUM)
10/8/1997	Basque Fatherland and Liberty (ETA)
10/8/1997	Gama'a al-Islamiyya (Islamic Group) (IG)
10/8/1997	HAMAS
10/8/1997	Harakat ul-Mujahidin (HUM)
10/8/1997	Hizballah
10/8/1997	Kahane Chai (Kach)
10/8/1997	Kurdistan Workers Party (PKK) (Kongra-Gel)
10/8/1997	Liberation Tigers of Tamil Eelam (LTTE)
10/8/1997	National Liberation Army (ELN)
10/8/1997	Palestine Liberation Front (PLF)
10/8/1997	Palestinian Islamic Jihad (PIJ)
10/8/1997	Popular Front for the Liberation of Palestine (PFLF)
10/8/1997	PFLP-General Command (PFLP-GC)
10/8/1997	Revolutionary Armed Forces of Colombia (FARC)
10/8/1997	Revolutionary Organization 17 November (17N)
10/8/1997	Revolutionary People's Liberation Party/Front (DHKP/C)
10/8/1997	Shining Path (SL)
10/8/1999	al-Qa'ida (AQ)
9/25/2000	Islamic Movement of Uzbekistan (IMU)
5/16/2001	Real Irish Republican Army (RIRA)
9/10/2001	United Self Defense Forces of Colombia (AUC)
12/26/2001	Jaish-e-Mohammed (JEM)
12/26/2001	Lashkar-e Tayyiba (LeT)
3/27/2002	Al-Aqsa Martyrs Brigade (AAMB)
3/27/2002	Asbat al-Ansar (AAA)
3/27/2002	al-Qaida in the Islamic Maghreb (AQIM)
8/9/2002	Communist Party of the Philippines/New People's Army (CPP/NPA)
10/23/2002	Jemaah Islamiya (JI)
1/30/2003	Lashkar i Jhangvi (LJ)
3/22/2004	Ansar al-Islam (AAI)
7/13/2004	Continuity Irish Republican Army (CIRA)
12/17/2004	Libyan Islamic Fighting Group (LIFG)
12/17/2004	al-Qaida in Iraq (AQI)
6/17/2005	Islamic Jihad Union (IJU)
3/5/2008	Harakat ul-Jihad-i-Islami/Bangladesh (HUJI-B)
3/18/2008	al-Shabaab
5/18/2009	Revolutionary Struggle (RS)
7/2/2009	Kata'ib Hizballah (KH)
1/19/2010	al-Qa'ida in the Arabian Peninsula (AQAP)
8/6/2010	Harakat ul-Jihad-i-Islami (HUJI)
9/1/2010	Tehrik-e Taliban Pakistan (TTP)
11/4/2010	Jundallah

Date Designated	Name
5/23/2011	Army of Islam (AOI)
9/19/2011	Indian Mujahedeen (IM)
3/13/2012	Jemaah Anshorut Tauhid (JAT)
5/30/2012	Abdallah Azzam Brigades (AAB)
9/19/2012	Haqqani Network (HQN)
3/22/2013	Ansar al-Dine (AAD)
11/14/2013	Boko Haram
11/14/2013	Ansaru
12/18/2013	al-Mulathamun Battalion

Source: United States Department of State. (n.d.) Foreign terrorist organizations. Retrieved from http://www.state.gov/j/ct/rls/other/des/123085.htm

a variety of ways. Hezbollah, the brainchild of the Iranian government, also wants to gain control of Lebanon using elections and has been very successful at doing so. In the view of U.S. policy makers, Hezbollah is a terrorist group, despite the participation in Lebanese politics. Therefore, like Hamas, it is proscribed.

The Red Brigades

The Red Brigades, a left wing group, was formed in 1970 by sociology students in Italy. "A group with its roots in the sociology department in the University of Treto in northern Italy evolved into the Red Brigades. Highly secretive, they counted 5,000 members, many with training in explosives, firearms and forging documents" (Crane, 2007, p. 18). The Red Brigades have committed many acts since their formation. "Their attacks were brazen, including bank heists and prison breaks, and hit factory owners, politicians, journalists, police and military officers" (Crane, 2007, p. 18). By 1988, security forces were successful at debilitating the group. However, in March 1999, a group claiming to be the "new" Red Brigades killed Massimo D'Antona, a professor and government adviser. In February 2007, Italian authorities arrested 15 people who were accused of being part of a terrorist cell.

Other proscribed groups such as the Real Irish Republican Army (Real IRA) and Continuity Irish Republican Army (Continuity IRA) are fighting against British control of Northern Ireland and these groups want to become part of another country, the Republic of Ireland. Historically, Loyalist (Protestant) groups—the Ulster Defense Association/Ulster Freedom Fighters (UDA/UFF) and the Ulster Volunteer Force/Red Hand Commandos (UVF/RHC) also operated in Northern Ireland. They formed because of the activities of the Provisional Irish Republican Army (PIRA), which fought to liberate the territory of Northern Ireland from British rule and the reintegration of Ireland. With a peace process in Northern Ireland that was jump-started in 1998, the British government maintained that all groups should decommission, including the Protestant paramilitary groups. After many years, the Provisional IRA did decommission its weapons and in May 2007, the UVF announced it put its arms beyond reach. While the relationship between Protestant paramilitaries and the state and its security forces was at times seen as collusion, the perception on the part of these groups was that they were doing their duty as part of the defenders of Britain and thus the state.

Many proscribed Pakistani groups are fighting for regional control of the disputed region of Kashmir on behalf of the state of Pakistan and against the Indian government. However, many of these groups also cooperate with al-Qaeda and, in this way, are also a threat to the state of Pakistan.

Gush Emunim Underground

Gush Emunim Underground was formed in 1979 by members of Gush Emunin (Block of the Faithful), a group of Jewish settlers that used squatter tactics in the West Bank. The group conducted attacks in the early and mid-1980s, including car bombings of five Arab mayors in the West Bank and a machine gun and grenade attack on Hebron Islamic College in which three Arab students were killed and 33 wounded.

Finally, Al-Qaeda, "the Base," was originally formed in 1988. Its leader, Osama bin Laden, drew his support base from those that had fought in the Afghan war against the Soviets. Fighters from all over the world participated in this war. Ayman al-Zawahiri, a member of the Egyptian Islamic Jihad (IJ) formed an alliance with Bin Laden in 1998. Until Bin Laden's death in 2011, al-Zawahiri was a key influencer of Bin Laden. Al-Zawahiri took control of the organization several months after Bin Laden's death. The al-Qaeda of today is a transnational network composed of many groups that operate in countries throughout the world. Thus, as the original group of 1988 expanded, it drew in more groups and new ones were created on its behalf. For example, al-Qaeda in Iraq (AQI) only formed after the U.S. invasion in 2003. The group still operates in Iraq and reportedly changed its name in 2013 to the Islamic State of Iraq and the Levant to reflect its broader goals in the region, in particular in Syria. Others, such as the Algerian Salafist Group for Call and Combat (GSPC), is a long-standing group, but one that only recently merged with the al-Qaeda network. The group subsequently changed its name to al-Qaeda Organization in the Lands of the Maghreb (AQIM). As Lav (2007) explained,

> On January 24, 2007, with the blessing of Osama bin Laden, the Algerian Salafist Group for Preaching and Combat (GSPC) changed its name to The Al-Qaeda Organization in the Islamic Maghreb. Thus was cemented a union that had been announced several months previously; this union is the fruit of longstanding relations between the GSPC and Al-Qaeda and represents a further stage in the globalization of the jihad movement. Shortly after joining al-Qaeda, the GSPC, whose operations had for the most part been limited to Algeria and the Sahara, began to attack foreign interests and threaten attacks in Europe.

(p. 1)

AQIM is no longer just a national group committed to overthrowing the Algerian regime. AQIM works to envelop other North African–affiliated al-Qaeda groups into a larger consortium and has expanded its influence in many African countries. In addition to these, there are many other groups operating in different countries that claim membership or some sort of affiliation with the network. These groups have their own leadership structure, norms, and goals—they have distinct identities.

Osama bin Laden and Ayman al-Zawahiri were heralded as the true leaders of al-Qaeda. However, while they may have commented, given advice, and submitted operational guidance, the original group blossomed far beyond their personal reach and total control. That being said, there is still a core al-Qaeda group, led by Ayman al-Zawahiri.

State-Sponsored Terrorism

State-sponsored terrorism occurs when a state supports a terrorist group either directly or indirectly. In its report on state-sponsored terrorism, the U.S. government has identified Cuba, Iran, Iraq, Libya, North Korea, Sudan, and Syria as governments that support or engage in terrorism.

Libya, led by Colonel Muammar Qaddafi, is an example of a country that not only engaged in terrorist activity, but also backed terrorist groups. Libyan agents were accused of the 1988 bombing of Pan Am flight 103, which exploded over Lockerbie, Scotland. United Nations sanctions were imposed on Libya until 1999, when Qaddafi surrendered two men. They were tried in a Scottish court, and, in January 2001, one was found guilty and the other acquitted. In the past, Qaddafi was also accused of supplying many terrorist groups with weapons and training, including the Provisional Irish Republican Army and various Palestinian groups.

Like Libya, the North Korean government was accused of engaging in and backing terrorist activity. For example, in 1983, a bomb exploded, killing 17 South Korean officials visiting Myanmar. Two North Korean officers were caught and confessed to their role in the act. In another incident in 1987, Korean Airlines flight 858 was the target of the North Korean regime. All 115 people on board were killed in that midair bombing. North Korea has also provided a safe haven for members of the Japanese Communist League-Red Army Faction that hijacked a Japanese Airlines flight to North Korea in 1970.

Perhaps the most publicized state supporter of terrorism is Iran; this does, without a doubt, demonstrate the ongoing identity conflict that exists between the United States and Iran. Iran is at the forefront of U.S. policy concerns, especially because Iran is seeking to build a nuclear program and supports groups that are in contravention to U.S. stated values. Hezbollah is at the core of conflict between the two countries, and the creation of the group can be traced to Iran. In fact, Iranians have seats on Hezbollah's governing council. Hasan Nasrallah, the leader of Hezbollah, has a very close relationship with Iran's Supreme Leader Khamenei. The Iranians provide arms, equipment, and training to Hezbollah. Additionally, the group is awash with money, compliments of Iran. This was

(Continued)

(Continued)

evident in the aftermath of the Israeli campaign in Lebanon in which Hezbollah took the opportunity to use their money to rebuild the community (Bejjani, 2006). Syria is a transshipment point for the movement of Iranian equipment to Hezbollah. Therefore, both the Syrians and Iranians are state-supporters of terrorism with regard to this group. The elite Iranian Revolutionary Guard Corp (IRGC) is also heavily involved in Iraq and works squarely against the U.S. goal of stabilizing the country (Simon & Takeyh, 2006). Finally, the Iranians also provide financial support and weapons training to members of militant Palestinian groups.

WHY DO GROUPS TURN TO TERRORISM?

Recall that in Chapter 3, we introduced **social identity theory**. We classify ourselves as part of groups; groups that we belong to are characterized as in-groups and other groups are considered out-groups. Social identity theory rests on the principle of intergroup comparison. When a group compares itself to another relevant out-group and is faced with a threatened identity, group members have three options. They can leave the group and join the higher status group (social mobility), they can change the basis for comparison (social creativity), or they can seek to compete with the higher status group (competition). This competition can lead to conflict. It is at this point where we find an explanation for why groups turn to terrorism. Groups that turn to terrorism find themselves threatened by the status of a superior group, usually the state apparatus of a country. One way to equalize the status between groups is to engage in activities that harm the high-status group. Explanations are also found in other theories. In Chapter 3, we introduced **image theory**. While an individual can hold many different images of an out-group, one image, the **imperialist image**, involves a perception that another group is superior in capability and culture. At times, the subordinate group perceives that this relationship is not legitimate and may seek to change the relationship. Of course, the flip side to this is that the superior status group views this as threatening to their survival. They likely will view the group through the **rogue image**. Rogues are inferior in capability, but are threatening in their intentions. Rogues are not negotiated with; they are taught a lesson. Thus, numerous counterterrorism strategies are put in place to deal with rogue terrorist groups.

PSYCHOPATHOLOGICAL VIEWS

Terrorists suffer from deep psychological problems; they are psychopaths or cold-blooded killers. They are not only crazy—they are evil. This line of thinking is still very widespread, particularly in the media and among some academics. In the academic community, this perspective was dominant in earlier research when terrorism researchers were few and far between. In fact, the literature was dominated by the case study approach and those that broadened the scope of the research to include the study of personality can be considered pioneers of the field of terrorism research (see Corrado, 1981; Crenshaw, 2004; Post, 1984, for reviews).

Some focused on psychopathological causes such as sociopathy/psychopathy. This personality disorder was outlined in the ***American Psychiatric Association's Diagnostic and Statistical Manual of Mental Disorders III (DSM-III)***. In the next versions, DSM-IV and DSM-V, sociopathy/psychopathy fall under antisocial personality disorders, although there is refinement in thinking in DSM-V. Individuals with these disorders tend to disregard and violate the rights of others and fail to feel empathy for their victims. Using the DSM-III classification (relevant at the time), Cooper (1977) and Pearce (1977) argued that terrorists are sociopaths. Lasch (1979) examined individuals in the Weathermen and the Symbionese Liberation Army and found evidence of the narcissistic personality disorder. In his work, Kaplan (1981) traced terrorist behavior to psychopathology—namely a defective personality that stems from childhood experience of humiliation by an aggressor. Pearlstein (1991) also identified narcissistic personality disorders amongst terrorists as central. Post (2004) maintained that although there is no body of evidence that there exists amongst terrorists a specific terrorist personality type or constellation or major psychopathologies, "individuals with particular personality traits and personality tendencies are drawn disproportionately to terrorist careers" (p. 128). Post notes the psychological mechanisms of externalization and splitting, a defense mechanism of individuals with a damaged self-concept, are found amongst those with narcissistic and borderline personality disorders. These are prevalent in terrorists. He argued that terrorists have a special psycho-logic that they construct "to rationalize acts they are psychologically compelled to commit" (p. 128). Thus, "individuals are drawn to the path of terrorism in order to commit acts of violence; their special logic, which is grounded in their psychology and reflected in their rhetoric, becomes the justification for their violent acts." According to him,

> It is not the intent . . . to imply that all terrorists suffer from borderline or narcissistic personality disorders, or that the psychological mechanisms of externalization or splitting are utilized by every terrorist. It is my distinct impression, however, that these mechanisms are found with extremely high frequency in the population of terrorists, particularly among the leadership, and contribute significantly to the uniformity of terrorists' rhetorical style and their special psycho-logic
> (2004, p. 129)

Whether or not there are personality disorders prevalent amongst terrorist is still a debate. As Post (2004) points out, access to terrorists is difficult and therefore they are not particularly well studied. To really understand them, access is key and then we may shed light on their "psycho-logic." However, research on terrorists has grown and other perspectives reflect a different line of thinking on the terrorist personality. Many now argue that there is no such thing as a terrorist personality, especially one that is considered deviant. Those academics familiar with the psychopathological literature can attest that it has certainly sparked a lot of discussion over the validity of such claims. In their work, for example, Mastors and Deffenbaugh (2007) noted that "in dealing with this perspective, many academics tend to offer it as an explanation, and then use it as a jumping off point to make clear why this perspective is at best flawed and should be discounted. According to many academics and practitioners alike, there is simply not enough evidence to support this particular viewpoint and many studies have indicated quite the opposite—that terrorists are not all suffering from pathologies" (p. 20). For example, Silke (2004) argued, "research on the mental state of terrorists has found that they are rarely mad or crazy; very few suffer from personality disorders. But the body of research confirming this state of affairs has not prevented a steady and continuing stream of 'experts,' security personnel, and politicians from freely espousing and endorsing views to the contrary" (p. 177). In addition, McCauley (2002) maintained that "thirty years of research has found psychopathology and personality disorder no more likely among terrorists than non-terrorists from the same background" (p. 1). More specifically, Mastors and Deffenbaugh (2007) argued in their work on al-Qaeda that "there is no compelling evidence found in the research for this book that Osama bin Laden is a psychopath. Granted, he may be a product of his own power designs, like many leaders, but that is a very different matter, and one that does not lend credence to him being a psychopath" (p. 20).

Why is this still a popular view? We suspect that in dismissing terrorists as crazy, we don't have to think much further for an explanation for why they take human life, often in mass numbers. We do not suggest that people with severe psychological problems are not part of the terrorist mix. Any group can recruit them, even unknowingly. These individuals often go on some very brutal killing sprees because they are fulfilling their own need to kill and not a group need to adhere to the beliefs, values, goals, tactics and so forth of the group. Often, groups deal with these individuals, as we shall see later in our discussion of conformity. As a general rule, terrorist groups are, in fact, careful not to recruit those with pathologies (Crenshaw, 2004).

PERSONALITY TRAITS AND MOTIVATION

What about personality traits? Are there specific traits found in the terrorist population? Earlier we discussed the work of Adorno and his colleagues on the **authoritarian personality**. Later criticisms of the work included the notion that those high in this personality trait were assumed to have syndromes. Thus, in light of this criticism, further work was carried out and refined by other scholars, and it did not rely on the psychoanalytical school. Recall that Altemeyer (1996) discussed the attributes of submission to authority, aggression against nonconformist groups, and conventionalism, all strongly linked to right wing authoritarianism. Altemeyer saw right wing authoritarianism as a product of personality predispositions and life events.

Other trait-based approaches include looking at certain constellations of traits seen as important to understand leadership (Hermann, 1980b). Specifically, they include cognitive complexity, self-confidence, ethnocentrism, distrust of others, and motivation (task, power, affiliation). Mastors (2000) applied this trait-based approach to Gerry Adams, leader of Sinn Fein in

Northern Ireland. However, personal interviews were also conducted to supplement analysis to understand certain behaviors not explained by trait analysis.

Recall that in Chapter 4, we discussed motivations in the context of joining a group. Joining a group can satisfy the **need for affiliation** or **need for power**. Additionally, the **Fundamental Interpersonal Relations Orientation (FIRO)** claimed that joining a group can satisfy three basic needs: inclusion, control, and affection. Festinger (1950, 1954) argued that individuals join groups in order to provide standards with which to compare their own beliefs, opinions, and attitudes. Rubenstein and Shaver (1980) suggested that groups can also satisfy interpersonal needs. Looking for more explanatory power, Mastors and Norwitz (2008) examined motivation in the case of Ayman al-Zawahiri and found that he was motivated by power. In another line of research, Taylor and Louis (2004) noted that individuals are looking for individual meaning and join terrorist groups to engage in meaningful behavior. In his discussion of self-esteem, Baumeister (1999) argued that having high self-esteem can lead to violence and aggression. Threats to self-esteem will be met with violence and aggression. Other authors suggest motivations such as frustration, economic misery (Victoroff, 2005), moral disengagement (Bandura, 2004), moral reasoning (Ginges, Atran, Sachdeva, & Medin, 2011), excitement, ultimate meaning, and glory (Cottee & Hayward, 2011), humiliation-revenge (Jurgensmeyer, 2000), need for belonging (Borum, 2004), a personal crisis (Wiktorowicz, 2005; Silber & Bhatt, 2007), quest for personal significance (Kruglanski, Chen, Dechesne, Fishman, & Orehek, 2009) moral outrage (Sageman, 2008), and perceived injustice (Moghaddam, 2007).

Motivations for why individuals join a terrorist group are often very complex. Psychologists provide some understanding, but it is important to note that there is not one approach that can explain the motivation of all individuals. For example, in their study of al-Qaeda recruits and motivation, Mastors and Deffenbaugh (2007) argue that motivations are complex and varied. By examining the personal stories of many al-Qaeda recruits, they discerned many specific motivations for recruitment. They found that individuals join the network for a variety of social, political, economic, and personal reasons. In particular, the authors found personal motivations, such as absent fathers, boredom, camaraderie, desire to fit in, disputes with parents, fame, family influence, lack of purpose, marital problems, parental divorce, peer pressure, poor academic performance, poor job performance, adventure seeking, status/recognition, traumatic event, and vengeance. Social motivations were also evident. Here elements such as alcohol abuse, cultural alienation, drug abuse/addiction, societal alienation, and wanting a cause were evident. Economic motivations include criminal activity, financial problems, lack of motivation to seek employment/work, underemployment, and unemployment. Finally, political motivations can be traced to acts by another country, cultural imperialism, a country's support for a defined enemy, objectionable government policies, and oppression of identity group. As the authors further explain, in many cases, these motivations are not mutually exclusive. Individuals can have one or more than one motivating factor. "Likewise, individuals can have more than one indicator across categories" and "certain indicators within the categories can actually influence each other" (pp. 71–72).

In her research, Stern (2004) conducted interviews with Muslim, Jewish, Christian, Sikh, and Hindu "radicals." According to her, individuals are humiliated and angry and then act:

> My interviews suggest that people join religious terrorist groups partly to transform themselves and to simplify life. They start out feeling humiliated, enraged that they are viewed by some "other" as second class. They take on new identities as martyrs on behalf of a purported spiritual cause. The spiritually perplexed learn to focus on action. The weak become strong. The selfish become altruists, ready to make the ultimate sacrifice of their lives in the belief that their death will serve a supposed public good. Rage turns to conviction. They seem to enter a kind of trance, where the world is divided neatly between good and evil, victim and oppressor. Uncertainty and ambivalence, always painful to experience, are banished. There is no room for the other side's point of view. Because they believe their cause is just and that God is on their side, they persuade themselves that any action—no matter how heinous—is justified. They know they are right, not just politically, but morally.
>
> (2004, p. 1)

There is also body of literature that examines the attractiveness of violence and the role of aggression. However, here the findings are mixed. Some studies on the attraction to violence demonstrated that there is an attraction to violence amongst some (e.g., Merkl, 1980); however, other studies could not provide definitive conclusions (Knutson 1981). In her examination of children in Northern Ireland, Fields (1979) argued that exposure to violence can drive children to become terrorists later. Fields received criticism for this approach. Taylor (1988) noted that Fields looked at only children and not actual terrorists and, therefore, the work suffers from lack of validation.

The role of frustration is another area of investigation. Generally, this literature promotes the idea that when individuals are frustrated from achieving a goal, the result is aggression (Dollard, Doob, Miller, Mowrer, & Sears 1939). According to Borum (2004), the basic premise of the frustration-aggression (FA) hypothesis is twofold: (1) Aggression is always produced by frustration, and (2) Frustration always produces aggression (p. 12). This is a controversial area of study that has been heavily criticized. According to Kruglanski and Fishman (2006):

> But in scientific psychology the simple frustration-aggression has long been questioned. Just because one is frustrated does not necessarily mean that one would aggress against others. Frustration could lead to withdrawal, depression, escape, or aggression against the self rather than against others. Frustration could also motivate the search for alternative means to one's objectives, not necessarily violent means. Indeed, studies have shown that terrorism does not appear to constitute a strategy of last resort, used when all other means have been exhausted.
>
> (p. 196)

This body of literature did evolve over time. Those such as Berkowitz (1989), for example, refined the basic notion. Berkowitz contended that frustration alone does not cause aggression, but also depends on environmental cues. According to Borum (2004), "in an important reformulation of the FA hypothesis, Berkowitz (1989) claimed that it was only 'aversive' frustration that would lead to aggression. The newly proposed progression was that frustration would lead to anger, and that anger—*in the presence of aggressive cues*—would lead to aggression" (p. 12). In some cases, terrorists recognize the consequences of their angry behavior. For example, McCauley (2004) and Wagner (2006) posited that terrorists sometimes commit an act so that the enemy responds with extreme anger. Of course, this is the reaction that the terrorists hoped for in the first place. In addition to anger, frustration can be further inflated by engaging in social comparison. When they compare themselves to others (e.g., salary, number of possessions), the result may not be favorable. If that is the case, then they might experience *relative deprivation*, which refers to the belief that one is less well off than others. Research (Hagerty, 2000) showed that happiness is lower and crime rates higher in nations with large disparities in income. Relatedly, Kampf (1990) argued that intellectuals and affluent youth are frustrated with the conditions of the social climate and therefore want to change their societies. However, Silke (2003) noted, "although the explanation appears attractive (certainly at least in the context of revolutionary notions), the level of integration is weak, not only from being rather too context specific, but also because the ideological control is not considered within a developmental process of involvement" (p. 11).

SUICIDE BOMBERS

Since 9/11, and in light of the violence in Palestine, **suicide bombers** have received considerable attention, especially in the media. Yet suicide terrorists are not new and unique to al-Qaida and Palestinian groups. Indeed, this tactic has been used by the Tamil Tigers in Sri Lanka for a few decades and is a noted tactic of the Turkish PKK, Chechens and other groups. Suicide bombers were and are still only a small part of many groups. Unfortunately, suicide terrorism is a growing tactic and remains a noted weapon of choice for many groups. According to Zedalis (2004),

> Suicide bombers are today's weapon of choice. An action that was once so surprising, horrific, and terrifying has now become the daily fare of the nightly news. From Jerusalem to Jakarta and from Bali to Baghdad, the suicide bomber is clearly the weapon of choice for international terrorists. The raw number of suicide attacks is climbing; suicide bombs are now used by 17 terror organizations in 14 countries. In terms of casualties, suicide attacks are the most efficient form of terrorism. From 1980 to 2001, suicide attacks accounted for 3 percent of terrorist incidents but caused half of the total deaths due to terrorism even if one excludes the unusually large number of fatalities of 9/11.
>
> (p. 1)

Groups that use terrorism vary in the extent to which suicide attacks are institutionalized as a strategy. Some use this form of attack regularly, while others use it only occasionally and as a temporary tactic. According to Sprinzak (2000), neither Hamas nor Hezbollah have permanent suicide units, but recruit bombers on an ad-hoc basis.

As with much of the literature, there are different perspectives on the personality of suicide bombers, what motivates them to join a terrorist group with the goal of killing themselves, and whether these individuals suffer from pathologies.

Ariel Merari, a psychologist, looked at groups such as Hezbollah, Amal, Hamas, the Palestinian Islamic Jihad, and secular groups in Syria, but could not identify a psychological nor demographic profile of suicide terrorists (Sprinzak, 2000). Another study on Hamas argued that suicide bombers deeply value the identity of the group and want to join and do their part for the cause.

> The recruits do not fit the usual psychological profile of suicidal people, who are often desperate or clinically depressed. Hamas bombers often hold paying jobs, even in poverty-stricken Gaza. What they have in common, studies say, is an intense hatred of Israel. After a bombing, Hamas gives the family of the suicide bomber between three thousand dollars and five thousand dollars and assures them their son died a martyr in holy jihad.
>
> (Council on Foreign Relations, 2007)

Fields, Elbedour, & Hein (2002) argue that the motivations of Palestinian suicide bombers are varied.

> Eight of the nine bombers were described by family and friends as very religious. Five expressed the desire at one time or another to meet God and defend their land through martyrdom. Eight bombers were described as very likable guys, devoted to their communities, or noted for helping friends and other community members and, in one case, defending and helping the community's weaker members.
>
> Three bombers were described as peaceful, nonaggressive and/or calm, and were clearly not pathological. Neither did they suffer from psychological or educational problems. Three were especially described as average, normal guys, one of whom loved life, another of whom was generally happy, and two of whom loved to work.
>
> Five bombers were described as being frustrated and depressed at times. One was described as usually serious. And one was described as especially depressed because his family had no money for him to pursue graduate studies and because the Israeli army did not permit him to leave Gaza to pursue his education in the West Bank. None of the bombers drank, took drugs, or engaged in antisocial behavior against the community.
>
> (p. 214)

The authors noted that depression is part of the equation for some. The role of depression has also been brought up by others. Mahmud Sehwait, a psychiatrist in Ramallah, noted the prevalence of post-traumatic stress disorder amongst those who can potentially or eventually become suicide bombers (Perina, 2002). A special issue of *Political Psychology* in 2009 addressed suicide terrorism. The first article was presented by Kruglanski, Chen, Dechesne, Fishman, and Orehek (2009). They advanced the notion of the quest for personal significance involving a collective crisis situation that includes a perceived threat to the in-group, the presence of an ideology supporting terrorism, and attachment to hero status of martyrdom. There were a range of responses from scholars in the field, reflecting different perspectives on the study of the same phenomena. Some will be reviewed here. In response, Bloom (2009) maintained:

> There are significant problems with the case they construct as well as how as [sic] they construct it. The arguments and evidence used to support the authors' claims betray a limited understanding and narrow interpretation of terrorist psychology, a failure to acknowledge the severe limitations with the evidence identified to support their premise, and a failure to acknowledge that complexity of how motivation is conceptualized in contemporary psychology.
>
> (p. 387)

Further, as in any body of research, Mintz and Brule (2009) cautioned there are methodological issues in the study of suicide terrorism, including selection bias, selection effects, contradictory anecdotal evidence, small sample size, and lack of measurement validity. Further, while Kruglanski and co-authors advanced a promising theory, it lacked data and evidence. Others such as Crenshaw (2009) suggested that there is a complex social process involved.

There are others who join the group for the various reasons that we highlighted above, but are later convinced through group pressures that suicide for the group is something that demonstrates ultimate commitment. Here the recruiters use propaganda tactics and **conformity** pressures to gain the ultimate sacrifice from an individual. Either way, when individuals join such a group, they become part of a "special" subgroup of suicide bombers. They are treated separately from the rest of the group and pressure focuses exclusively on reinforcing the person's willingness to die for the group.

Not only men, but also women participate in suicide terrorism. According to Zedalis (2004), "female suicide bombers were used in the past; however, the recent spate of them in different venues, in different countries, and for different terrorist organizations forces us to study this terrorist method" (p. 1). More specifically, research on various groups indicated,

> About 15 percent of suicide bombers have been women. Most of them belonged to the Tamil LTTE or the Turkish PKK; almost two thirds of the PKK's suicide bombers were female. In both of these groups, their charismatic leaders assured the female volunteers that by participating in the suicide campaign, they would support the group cause while proving that they were as brave as their male peers. Until recently, female suicide bombers were unique to the LTTE, PKK, and other non-religious terror organizations, but this trend has changed

recently; some religious leaders have sanctified women's participation in such acts under their "loose" interpretation of Islamic tradition. (Ironically, the same men claim "strict" readings of the Koran to justify terrorism.) Thus, the Palestinian Hamas and PIJ as well as Chechen separatists have started utilizing female bombers. Importantly, those organizations have been operating in very conservative and traditional societies where women have not enjoyed equal rights with men.
(Schweitzer, 2004, p. 1)

In another study looking at support for suicide terrorism, Victoroff, Adelman and Matthews (2012) examined psychological factors relevant to support for suicide bombings in the Muslim diaspora. Looking at Pew Attitude Surveys of Muslims in Great Britain, France, Germany, Spain, and the United States, the authors concluded that perceived discrimination and younger ages were correlated with support for suicide bombings within the diaspora.

DEMOGRAPHIC PROFILING

Another line of research looks for demographic profiles of terrorists. The idea behind this research is that it can lead to identification of notable commonalities among terrorists. When discussing demographics, there are a number of factors that need to be taken into consideration—for example, economic, gender, age, religion, occupation, and education (Mastors & Deffenbaugh, 2007).

However, it is very difficult to generalize about the backgrounds of terrorists. Terrorists come from socioeconomic classes, age groups, gender groups, occupations, educational backgrounds, and, in the case of transnational networks such as al-Qaeda, countries of origin/citizenship/residency (Mastors & Deffenbaugh, 2007). In many terrorist groups, the initial leadership tends to be held by middle and upper middle class people. But as the group evolves over time, new leaders obviously emerge. These are usually drawn from the ranks and are not necessarily from the social classes of the old cadre. The masses tend to be drawn from those with lower or working class backgrounds, but even so, not all the time. For example, Silber and Bhatt (2007) examined five cases and found that individuals were young, often educated, middle class males operating in male-dominated societies. Some were immigrants, but not first generation and not radical or even devout Muslims. Furthermore, the demographics of a recruit may not be indicative of motivation. There is a line of research in both academia and the government that has attempted to look at demographic attributes and then likened these attributes to motivation (Ehrlich & Liu, 2006). Often times, these claims about demographics rely on stereotypes, rather than research. For example, a blanket statement people often make is that recruits are economically disenfranchised. As such, we just need to fix the economic problems of the country and individuals will not be attracted to terrorism. However, for some, economics is not even an important motivating factor. Furthermore, even if a person is economically disadvantaged, there may be another motivating factor that is really the determinant of why that person sought to join a terrorist group in the first place (Mastors & Deffenbaugh, 2007). As more and more data is gathered on the backgrounds of such individuals, it may be possible to make more definitive judgments about where certain characteristics may be coalescing. At the same time, a demographic profile alone does not provide us full picture of why people join. We really need to look at motivation, not simply demographic attributes of recruits (Mastors & Deffenbaugh, 2007).

INDIVIDUALS AND GROUPS

The relationship between individuals and groups is something that isn't totally agreed upon amongst social psychologists and those from other disciplines conducting terrorism research by relying upon these constructs (Brown, 2000). Is there such a thing as group behavior that can influence individual behavior or is group behavior really just a reflection of individuals acting in groups? Allport (1962) argued that it is the psychology of individuals that matter. There is no such thing as a "group mind" (Brown, 2000, p. 5). On the other hand, Sherif (1936), Asch (1952) and others maintained that group processes influence individuals (Brown, 2000). Others such as Tajfel (1978) claimed that we need to distinguish between interpersonal behavior and group behavior. "Group behavior is typically homogenous or uniform, while interpersonal behavior shows the normal range of individual differences" (Brown, 2000, p. 6). Tajfel saw all social behavior as lying on a continuum where at one end the interaction is seen as being determined by the membership of various groups and relations between them, while at the other it is more decided by personal characteristics and interpersonal relationships (Brown, 2000, p. 7). Along the same lines, Turner (1982) explained that individuals have both personal and social identities. Personal identities are self-descriptions that are more personalistic and idiosyncratic (Brown, 2000). Social identity, however, is defined in terms of category memberships (Brown, 2000). When individuals define themselves as part of a group, they identify with norms and attributes that are part of the group.

As was highlighted earlier, personality attributes are also important. Groups are made up of individuals with different personalities even though they subscribe to the same group identity. The group can influence the individual and the individual can influence the group.

RECRUITMENT

Recruitment plays a central role in any terrorist group. Without a flow of new members the existence of the group comes under threat. Within secretive terrorist groups, significant measures are taken to vet recruits. Letting through one person into the group who is a foreign government agent or source can be potentially devastating to a terrorist group. Vetting is a continual process that seems to take place throughout the recruit's and then the member's tenure. Once a member is trusted, some suspicion is alleviated, but groups tend to continually watch their members for potential betrayers. Thus, terrorist groups tend to create their own counterintelligence wings to not only stop penetration from the outside, but to find betrayers. For example, the Provisional Irish Republican Army (PIRA) investigated any potential breaches or events that could have happened because of potential penetration (O'Callaghan, 1998). Diamond and Locy (2002) noted the vigorous vetting tactics used by al-Qaeda. They argued that "Becoming a member of al-Qaida is just as tough, in its own way, as getting into the CIA, an elite American university or even the Mafia. There are no SATs or lie-detector tests, but talent hunters for the group that carried out the Sept. 11 attacks use rigorous vetting techniques that include background checks, interviews with relatives and friends and one-on-one meetings to test a recruit's commitment" (p. 1).

Those who join terrorist groups do so gradually, through a series of steps that remove them from their old lives and lead them to new ones. As we highlighted earlier, some social identity theorists argue that social identity is "intimately bound up with our group memberships." Therefore, joining a group requires a form of self-redefinition (Brown, 2000, p. 28). Other social psychologists argue that when individuals join groups, processes of depluralization and deindividuation take place. Depluralization is when previous group identities are stripped away. Deindividuation refers to a loss of self-awareness and evaluation apprehension that can occur when individuals join groups and become anonymous (Zimbardo, 1971, 2007). Personal accountability and responsibility is shifted away from the individual to the group. Zimbardo (1971, 2007) argued that it is at this point where individuals on behalf of groups commit heinous acts against others. Individuals, as part of groups, can commit acts that they wouldn't have done as individuals. Some subsequent research challenged Zimbardo's perspective. For example, Diener (1976, 1979) and Johnson and Downing (1979) maintained that individuals do not automatically engage in such destructive ways just because they are part of a group. Instead, behavior depends on "which norms are salient in each particular situation" (Brown, 2000, p. 16). Bandura (2004) suggested that individuals who participate in harmful activities toward others go through a process of **moral disengagement**. Thus, they will not participate in such behaviors unless there is a moral justification to do so.

Moving from the theoretical into the realm of examples of recruitment collected about terrorist groups demonstrates that how individuals join these groups can be a difficult problem to unravel. Stories from recruits from different terrorist groups paint a complicated picture of how they come to join a terrorist group. There is not one path to recruitment, and groups employ different recruitment strategies. It is also important to keep in mind that a group can employ many different recruitment strategies at one time, too. Groups are not necessarily beholden to one type of recruitment strategy. Individual motivation, as we already addressed, has some role to play.

Taking this into account, we can only talk generally about what occurs during initial recruitment, and we also use specific examples to illustrate these recruitment strategies. First, terrorist groups have "spotters"—that is, potential recruits are spotted and assessed and the recruiter makes an effort to bring this individual into the group. The places that individuals are spotted are plentiful. For example, an individual can be attending a lecture, in a library, at school, prison, an Internet café, and so forth. In their discussion of recruitment by Islamic terrorist groups in the United States, Silber & Bhatt (2007) describe recruitment venues as "radicalizing incubators"

(p. 20). As they further noted, "generally these locations, which together comprise the radical subculture of the community, are rife with extremist rhetoric. Though the locations can be mosques, more likely incubators include cafes, cab driver hangouts, flophouses, prisons, student associations, non-governmental organizations, hookah (water pipe bars), butcher shops and book stores" (p. 20).

The Internet boom has given spotters an additional opportunity to recruit (and mobilize existing members). As Weimann (2004) illustrated,

> The Internet can be used to recruit and mobilize supporters to play a more active role in support of terrorist activities or causes. In addition to seeking converts by using the full range of website technologies (audio, digital video, etc.) to enhance the presentation of their message, terrorist organizations capture information about the users who browse their websites. Users who seem most interested in the organization's cause or well suited to carrying out its work are then contacted. Sophisticated methods are used by terrorists to refine or customize recruiting techniques on the Net: "Using some of the same marketing techniques employed by commercial enterprises, terrorist servers could capture information about the users who browse their websites, and then later contact those who seem most interested. Recruiters may also use more interactive Internet technology to roam online chat rooms and cyber cafes, looking for receptive members of the public—particularly young people. Electronic bulletin boards and Usenet discussion forums can also serve as vehicles for reaching out to potential recruits. Interested computer users around the world can be engaged in long term 'cyber relationships' that could lead to friendship and eventual membership."
>
> (p. 60)

Some individuals are brought in by existing members through a personal or social connection (Sageman, 2004). Other times an individual finds the message (propaganda) of the group appealing and seeks out members of the group or a way in which to join such as through venues on the Internet, and a variety of other places where groups and individuals are known to operate. Here personal and social ties are also important because these individuals can facilitate introductions to the terrorist groups (Mastors & Deffenbaugh, 2007; Sageman, 2004). We cannot forget that some members of terrorist groups are also forcibly conscripted. The Tamil Tigers in Sri Lanka, for example, use forced conscription of children in their recruitment (UTHR, 2003). This is also true of the Maoists in Nepal who carry out forced recruitment of children (Human Rights Watch, 2007).

Those that do the recruiting focus in on the mind-set of the potential recruit. Therefore, pitches are tailored to the demographic characteristics of the individual. Emotional appeals are especially important. The threat portrayed is imminent and action is necessary. Appealing to an individual's emotions helps to not only draw in new members, but to also sustain old ones (Mastors & Deffenbaugh, 2007). Recruiters are also looking for individuals that they can indoctrinate, and those that will conform to the rules of the group. We discuss conformity in more detail below.

INDOCTRINATION

Recruits also go through a significant indoctrination process and propaganda is central to this process. Propaganda is defined by Jowett and O'Donnell (1999) as "the deliberate attempt to shape perceptions, manipulate cognitions, and direct behavior to achieve a response that furthers the desired intent of the propagandist" (p. 6). Propaganda can shape beliefs or bolster a belief system. Earlier we noted that individuals are motivated to join groups for various reasons. However, not all individuals will join a group simply because of an existing motivation unless there is also a willingness to seek alternative views. It is here where propaganda is an important tool for recruitment because those that do the recruiting focus on the message of the group as much as they do the mind-set of the recruit. Once recruits are assessed (where propaganda is used to draw the member in), they are then further indoctrinated with illustrations of group propaganda. The group central messages are constantly reinforced. When recruits (and members) are faced with conflicting information or question the group's stance, alternatives views are conveniently explained away. If a recruit who is being indoctrinated or a member of the group questions the messages and explanations given to them, they are offered rationalizations that explain away doubt. Here the recruiters can draw upon the aforementioned sources of information that bolster the group's views. Gartenstein-Ross (2007) provided an excellent depiction of this in his autobiographical account of his work with a Saudi charity that had many radical members working within the group. The author takes the reader on his journey of working with those who subscribed to the Salafi view of Islam. He described how at first he would question the explanations provided to him on a variety of issues, but these questions were always answered with a view that would direct him toward the Salafi way of thinking. For example, he would be given an "authoritative" book on the subject at hand. Eventually, Gartenstein-Ross internalized those views, did not seek out alternative information, and became more radicalized over the course of a year.

Propaganda serves several purposes for the group. As already mentioned, it can be used as a recruitment tool. Propaganda can also be used as a conformity measure and to popularize a group's message. Thus, the use of propaganda can serve to entice recruits, exemplify group norms and goals, reinforce these for existing members, and keep existing supporters such as financial donors and the diaspora informed.

PROPAGANDA MESSAGES

Terrorist groups disseminate their propaganda message through a variety of media. There are many different examples, including video and audio tapes, leaflets, pamphlets, books, lectures/sermons, poetry, video games, music videos, songs, CDs, cassettes, among others. The Internet boom has given terrorist groups new ways to disseminate their messages and gain potential recruits. Through websites and chat rooms, blogs and other tools, they are able to reach a wider audience. Terrorist groups can and do learn from each other and often adopt successful strategies of other groups. We now turn to specific examples of propaganda efforts by terrorist groups.

Through media outlets such as al-Manar Television, a website, and al-Nour radio station, Hezbollah has been able to sustain an effective campaign that promotes its message. For example, Hezbollah captured two Israeli soldiers in the summer of 2006, and the Israelis responded with a limited, but very destructive campaign in Lebanon that began in July of 2006. Even though the Israeli campaign was prompted by Hezbollah's actions and, to an extent, the perception was that Hezbollah was responsible for provoking the Israelis, through a concerted propaganda effort, Hezbollah managed to win the war of perceptions and come out on top. Dickey and Norland (2006) pointed out that the Israeli operation had a positive impact on Hezbollah's recruitment efforts.

> No one denies that Hezbollah started the fight, with its unprovoked incursion into Israel, and no one doubts that Israel can win it, at least in conventional terms. But that's not what matters as much as public perceptions, and the impact those perceptions have from Tehran to Cairo. These conflagrations in Gaza, Lebanon and Iraq risk converging, if not on the ground, then in that virtual reality—on satellite television and the Web—where Al Qaeda and Hezbollah find recruits for their global networks. Israel can bomb Lebanon's infrastructure all it wants, but Hezbollah, which operates beyond the limits of a state, ultimately has no infrastructure. Hezbollah's own rockets and missiles can miss nearly all their targets, with comparatively little loss of life, but so long as they keep firing, they shatter the myth of Israeli invincibility and win friends and admirers in a radicalized Muslim world. "The Zionist enemy has not been able to reach military victory," said Hezbollah leader Hassan Nasrallah in a speech Friday on his organization's Al-Manar TV, still broadcasting despite Israeli Air Force strikes that obliterated its studios and transmission towers.
>
> (p. 1)

Like Hezbollah, al-Qaeda also has a very sophistical propaganda effort. Propaganda is one area where al-Qaeda draws on the successes of other groups. In particular, Mastors and Deffenbaugh (2007) explain, "the al-Qaeda network uses propaganda to educate individuals about their perception of the proper codes of behavior, political events, social policy, religion, among other issues and subjects, including letting the followers know about the exploits of the network" (p. 90). As the authors further elaborated,

> A spectrum of themes is associated with these methods. Generally, some of the more consistent themes are anti-American, anti-Western, anti-Christian, anti-Israeli, and anti-Jewish in character. Notably, the United States is depicted as an imperial power, while the Israelis are the enemy supported by them. Both are accused of committing atrocities against Muslims. Other Western governments are added into the mix, especially because of the Iraq war. Many of these themes take aim at what are deemed to be corrupt Arab and Muslim governments, and which the United States stands accused of supporting. In

addition, jihad is often referred to as an honorable duty. Some of the methods openly call for jihad against the United States and Americans, as well as their allies, such as other western countries or corrupt Arab and Muslim regimes, and the network makes Muslims aware of how they can participate in jihad. Other information simply broadcasts events impacting Muslims, such as United States involvement in Iraq. Finally, a dedicated propaganda effort informs the public of the network's nature and pursuits.

The network also clearly informs individuals that it is responding to the ills perpetrated on Muslims throughout the world. Thus, activities are not so much offensive as they are defensive in nature. The imperial West, as well as corrupt Arab regimes, Israel, and many other enemies, started the fight. By these methods, al-Qaida can provide their spin on, or interpretation of, behavior, events, policies, and so forth, while offering violence as the principal solution. Thus, these sources of information are influential in shaping the views of others, and can cause those on the receiving end of the message to act in support of such views. It is in this way that al-Qaida can provide an outlet for pursuing this solution of violence.

(p. 90)

Another interesting example of how the network gets it message out is through music videos. The use of music videos demonstrates the adaptability of the network, especially with regard to recruitment. In other words, they have realized that they need to expand propaganda efforts to draw in more segments of society. For example, "Dirty Kuffar," aimed at Pakistani Muslims, is a rap music video performed by Shaykh Terra and the Soul Salah Crew.

While members of the al-Qaeda network buy into the overall thrust of al-Qaeda's core argument, they do have their own distinct propaganda efforts that are tailored to their own regional concentrations. When Americans were present in Iraq, Iraqi insurgent groups in particular had a notable propaganda machine. For example, they often filmed and then disseminated videos of their attacks on U.S. soldiers. According to Kimmage and Ridolfo (2007),

At the heart of each video clip is the filed record of an actual insurgent operation. The most commonly recorded operation is an IED attack on U.S. forces, usually in a Humvee or Bradley fighting vehicle. In these video clips, a stationary camera films a stretch of road and captures the moment when an IED destroys a passing vehicle. Other frequently recorded operations include sniper and mortar attacks. The most prized videos, judging by download statistics, are the downing of U.S. helicopters and sniper attacks in which a U.S. soldier is seen falling to the ground.

(p. 27)

Filming operations have been used successfully by Chechen groups for many years. Again, groups learn from each other about what works in propaganda.

DEHUMANIZATION AND SCAPEGOATING

Dehumanization of the enemy is an extremely effective tool in getting potential recruits to understand the importance of the defined enemy. Dehumanization also serves to reinforce the beliefs of existing members (Staub, 1989, Zimbardo, 2007). In group propaganda and in the language of members, the enemy is demonized and defined as subhuman and threatening. Violence against this enemy is acceptable. As Zimbardo (2007) explained,

> Dehumanization is the central construct in our understanding of "man's inhumanity to man." Dehumanization occurs whenever some human beings consider other human beings to be excluded from the moral order of being a human person. The objects of this psychological process lose their human status in the eyes of their dehumanizers. By identifying certain individuals or groups as being outside the sphere of humanity, dehumanizing agents suspend the morality that might typically govern reasoned actions toward their fellows . . . Dehumanization stigmatizes others, attributing to them a "spoiled identity." Under such conditions, it becomes possible for normal, morally upright, and even usually idealistic people to perform acts of destructive cruelty.
>
> (p. 307)

We already highlighted Bandura's (2004) discussion of **moral disengagement**. To reiterate, individuals have moral standards that are a product of socialization. Individuals sanction themselves to prevent their inhumanity toward others. However, these self-regulatory mechanisms are not fixed and static, and individuals and groups can disengage this sense of morality in order to commit inhumane acts. Zimbardo (2007) argued that anyone can morally disengage from destructive conduct. For example, an individual disengages by redefining harmful behavior as honorable, thus creating moral justifications for violence. Another option is to "minimize our sense of a direct link between our actions and harmful outcomes by diffusing or displacing personal responsibility." Individuals can also "ignore, distort, minimize or disbelieve any negative consequences of our conduct." Finally, individuals can reconstruct perceptions of the enemy by blaming them for the consequences and by dehumanizing them (pp. 310–11).

There are numerous examples of dehumanization and moral disengagement. For example, amongst many radical Muslim groups, Israel is portrayed as the enemy. Jews are demonized and have even been described as descendants of pigs. Deeds against the evil enemy are portrayed as necessary and justifiable. In his book, O'Callaghan (1998) described this type of thinking by members of the IRA about the British and its Protestant supporters in Northern Ireland.

The enemy is the also **scapegoat** for the problems of the members of the terrorist group. As Staub wrote, "finding a scapegoat makes people believe their problems can be predicted and controlled; and it eliminates one's own responsibility, thereby diminishing guilt and enhancing self-esteem" (1989, p. 48). In al-Qaeda, for example, the United States and Israel are the enemies, responsible for the suffering of Muslims worldwide, and they are vilified.

Many of the problems that Muslims face throughout the world, recruits are told, are because of the actions of the Israeli and American tyrants.

CONFORMITY

Groups often have rituals for newcomers, whether a ceremony or some other form of initiation (Moreland & Levine, 1982). For example, some al-Qaeda members were asked to take a *bayat* (oath of allegiance) to Osama bin Laden. In his court testimony, Zacarias Moussaoui admitted to being a member of al-Qaeda and noted that he took a bayat to Osama bin Laden (Shenon, 2002).

New recruits are put through a variety of measures to ensure their conformity. They are taught the way of the group and pressured to buy into the group norms. Once in a group, a recruit is expected to conform to the norms of the group. Individuals do incorporate these norms into their own behavior (Brown, 2000). Group norms must be constantly reinforced. Even with committed recruits, there are a number of measures that groups have to employ to keep them in line. Usually this task falls on the more experienced members of the group.

As discussed in Chapter 4, individuals conform for two reasons; to be liked (normative social influence) and to be right (informational social influence). Individuals tend to change their beliefs or behaviors so that they are consistent with the standards set by the group. Recall the moving light experiments of Mazur Sherif (1936) discussed Chapter 4: Sherif found a great deal of convergence when it came to the judgments within the group of participants. Because the situation was so ambiguous, group members actually used the judgments of others to modify their own judgments about what they saw. Those individuals who want to be seen as distinct from other members are less likely to conform. Those highly committed to a group are more likely to conform. Finally, conformity in a group drops even if there is just one dissenter in the group.

Another line of research focuses on obedience to authority in groups. Recall the series of electrical shock experiments done by Stanley Milgram (1963) and discussed in Chapter 9. The results indicated that when people are told to do something by someone they view as an authority, most will obey, even if it violates their values. Zimbardo (2007) argued that there are several lessons to be learned from the Milgram experiments about gaining compliance from others. We note a few of them here: prearranging a form of contractual obligation, giving participants meaningful roles, presenting basic rules to follow, offering an ideology to justify use of any means to achieve a goal, and creating opportunities for the diffusion of responsibility or abdication of responsibility for negative outcomes (pp. 273–4).

Deviant group members are problematic because when they don't conform, they threaten the cohesiveness of the group and the conformity of other members. Additionally, they often bring negative and unwelcomed attention to the group. Deviants are dealt with by the group through conformity measures. They can also be expelled or killed, usually after other conformity measures have been tried. For example, the UVF, a group we highlighted earlier, had to contend with a several group members who become known as the "Shankill Butchers." These members went on a sadistic killing spree in the 1970s. Eventually, the PIRA killed Lenny Murphy, the Butchers' notorious leader. His behavior was no longer containable (Dillon, 1989). When faced with problematic members within their group, the UDA in Northern Ireland made moves to contain the behavior and at times decided to have these members expelled. Others were killed (Mastors, 2008; Wood, 2006). Taylor and Quale (1994) illustrate in interviews with Irish Republican Army (IRA) activists that those who betray the organization are killed.

Another example of pressure to conform is found in the al-Qaeda network. In 2005, Ayman al-Zawahiri, a core leader of al-Qaeda, wrote a letter to Abu Musab al-Zarqawi, the now deceased leader of al-Qaeda in Iraq. In the letter, Ayman al-Zawahiri wanted to gain conformity from al-Zarqawi, who ultimately brought negative attention to the network. Al-Zarqawi, however, ignored al-Zawahiri's directive and continued on his own path. But groups have strategies for this problem, as well.

GROUP CONFLICT

As we noted in Chapter 4, there are conflicts that occur in groups and there are reasons why conflict erupts between group members. Scholars have argued that problems such as attributions, harsh criticism, to include nay-saying, and the aggression hypothesis can provoke conflict. Typically, the disaffected in one group take on the leadership role of another group. For example, the Armed Islamic Group (GIA) in Algeria formed in 1991, and arose from the more militant side of Islamic Salvation Front (FIS). From there, even the GIA split, and the Salafist Group for Call and Combat (GSPC) emerged as a new group in 1992.

> The GSPC splintered from a rival Algerian organization, the Armed Islamic Group (GIA) over a disagreement on whether civilians constitute legitimate targets. Since its inception in 1992, the GIA has killed thousands of Algerian civilians, including women and children in targeted massacres.
>
> (Daly, 2005, p. 1)

Again, even after this, the GSPC merged with al-Qaeda to form yet another group, AQIM. Not all members supported this merger. The case of American-born jihadi Omar al-Hammami illustrates inability to conform. While he joined the Somali group al-Shabaab, he fell out with the leadership over the fact that they did not follow true Islamic doctrine. He left the group but was eventually killed by al-Shabaab.

Related to group conflict is the work on disengagement. Horgan (2009) suggested some exploratory propositions about disengagement. Psychological disengagement can take on many forms, such as burnout, conflicting personal priorities, internal disagreements, disagreements over strategy, tactics, politics or ideology, and a "mismatch between the fantasy and the reality" (p. 31). There are also physical disengagement factors related to exiting the movement voluntarily or involuntarily, and involuntary or voluntary movement to a new role. Psychological disengagement can also precede physical engagement.

ROLES

Recruiters tend to be sophisticated and assess recruits for specific roles in the group. Some people are seen as valued for key roles, while others are not. Thus, some recruits are more coveted than others.

Let's consider the case of José Padilla. Padilla was seen as ultimately expendable and therefore not a valued long-term member of al-Qaeda. First, Padilla was pliable and he was easily taught to conform. But, he was not an Arab, a very important ethnic trait in the group. As such, he would never move into the trusted circle. Al-Qaeda wanted him because he followed directions and also held American citizenship, which allowed him to move freely throughout the United States. The haphazard nature of his plan to carry out terrorist operations on U.S. soil was further evidence that Padilla's operation was not thoroughly vetted or seen as of high importance. To put it plainly, the operational planners sent him off to just do something against the United States.

The same can be said for Richard Colvin Reid, the notorious "shoe bomber." Reid is a British citizen and son of an English mother and Jamaican father, and he converted to Islam while in prison in Great Britain for robbery. After his release, he attended London mosques, notably a key recruitment center, the Finsbury Park Mosque. Eventually, he traveled to Afghanistan to participate in al-Qaeda's training camps. Reid's plan to blow up an airliner by lighting his explosive laden-shoes on fire during the flight wasn't particularly well thought out or tested. But Reid, down and out on his luck, was expendable to the organization. He may or may not have succeeded, but he was sent out to cause chaos as Americans were reeling in the aftermath of 9/11. In another case, because al-Hammami was American, al-Shabaab put him in charge of American recruitment.

SOCIAL CONTROL

One of the tactics used by groups is social control of the communities in which they operate. Thus, their view of proper behavior is extended to the wider populace and the communities are often held hostage by fear of the terrorist groups. In a sense, the group wants the wider community to conform. Often these measures are coercive in nature and terrorist groups can and do operate unfettered in their communities. Not everyone in these communities supports the groups, but they are still subject to the domination of these groups and their rules. A good example comes from Northern Ireland and the PIRA. In 2005,

> The IRA offered to shoot the men involved in the murder of Robert McCartney, but his family refused the use of violence, republicans said Tuesday night. In a five-page statement, the Irish Republican Army gave its most detailed account yet of McCartney's brutal murder,

saying four men were behind the killing, two of whom were its members . . . That the IRA felt forced to make such a macabre offer shows the pressure it feels within its own communities, which it effectively polices, and where there has sometimes been tacit support of punishment beatings of local criminals.

McCartney was stabbed and beaten to death outside a Belfast bar on Jan. 30 after a row broke out over an allegedly rude gesture made at a woman. His family, who has launched an international campaign for justice, has blamed IRA members and said there were up to 70 witnesses in the bar but many were too frightened of republicans to give evidence.

The IRA Tuesday night stated that after "voluntary admissions by those involved," it knew four men were involved—two were IRA volunteers and two were not—and "the IRA knows the identity of all these men." The statement described how after a "melee" in the bar, a crowd spilled out onto the street and Robert McCartney and his friend Brendan Devine and two other men were chased. One attacker fetched a knife from the pub's kitchen. A second man used the knife to stab McCartney and his friend. A third man kicked and beat McCartney after he was stabbed. A fourth hit Devine and another of McCartney's friends across the face with a steel bar. The IRA said: "The man who provided the knife also retrieved it from the scene and destroyed it."

The IRA said it had had two meetings with the McCartney family in the presence of an independent observer. In the first five-and-a-half-hour meeting last month, an IRA representative had "stated in clear terms that the IRA was prepared to shoot people directly involved in the killing of Robert McCartney." But the statement added: "The family made it clear that they did not want physical action taken against those involved. They stated that they wanted those individuals to give full account of their actions in court."

The IRA stopped short of declaring whether its offer to shoot those involved in the murder meant they were to be killed, or punished with a kneecapping or "six pack," where victims are shot in the ankles, knees and elbows. The IRA has already expelled three volunteers, and Sinn Fein has suspended seven members over the murder.

(Chrisafis, 2005, p. 1)

The following story illustrates social control on a number of levels. Terrorist group members are feared and operate "above the law." However, they also have measures in place to punish those that bring them bad press or violate acceptable behavior. Here it is important to realize that despite decommissioning, the PIRA and the other Protestant paramilitary groups still commit acts of violence, are engaged in criminal activity, and exercise social control.

Social control measures are adopted by groups to keep the hold of the diaspora as well. Here the tactics of the Tamil Tigers are noteworthy. Individuals in the diaspora are monitored for cooperation and compliance. According to a Human Rights Report in 2006,

Since the ceasefire between the Sri Lankan government and the LTTE in February 2002, increasing numbers of Tamil expatriates have taken advantage of the relative peace to visit family and friends who remained in the North and East of Sri Lanka, areas that are largely under the control of the LTTE. Increasingly, these visits have become a source of revenue for the LTTE as the LTTE has begun to systematically identify visiting expatriates and pressure them to contribute to the "cause."

Visitors to the North of Sri Lanka may travel by one of two routes: fly to Jaffna from Colombo, or travel north by bus or car on the main A9 highway that stretches from Kandy in the south to Jaffna at the northern tip of Sri Lanka. North of Vavuniya, travelers reach the Omanthai and Muhamalai crossing points that separate government- and LTTE-held territory. Leaving government-held territory, they must exit their vehicles and show documentation at a government checkpoint before crossing several kilometers of no-man's land that is monitored by the International Committee of the Red Cross (ICRC). On the other side, visitors stop again at an LTTE checkpoint where they must show documentation before proceeding into LTTE-held territory. At the checkpoint, travelers are directed by signs into separate queues depending on whether they are Sri Lankan nationals, or whether they carry foreign passports.

Recent expatriate visitors to the North report that foreign Tamil visitors are given a pass at the checkpoint, for which they must pay 1,000 rupees (approximately U.S.$10). They are told that within three days of reaching their destination, they must take the pass to the local LTTE office in Jaffna or Kilinochchi.

At the LTTE office, visitors must give detailed personal information, such as their name, home phone and address, employer, salary information, whether or not they own their home, and how long they have lived there. They are also asked for information about their past contributions to the LTTE. If visitors cannot verify a history of regular contributions, they then may be told an amount of money that they "owe" to the LTTE. The amount varies but is often calculated on the basis of $1, £1, or €1 per day, for each day that they have lived in the West. For expatriates who have lived in the West for long periods of time, the amount can be substantial. For example, a Tamil who has lived in Toronto for twenty years might be expected to pay Cdn$7,300. Alternatively, they may be pressured to sign a pledge to pay a monthly amount once they return home.

Thus, the Tamil Tigers not only expected support from the diaspora, they demanded it.

RADICALIZATION

Many scholars attempt to flesh out the radicalization process, depicting it in a series of stages. For example, in his analysis of pathways to radicalization Borum (2003) suggested four stages that result in legitimizing violence against another group. These are based on social psychology and the notion of group comparison. First, individuals reflect on their circumstances and determine "it's not right," compared to other groups. They then use comparative judgments regarding the conditions of others who are in more favorable positions. Borum described this stage as "it's not fair." Next is, "it's your fault," in which blame is assigned to the out-group and vilification and dehumanization occur. Finally, negative stereotyping takes place, leading to the legitimized violence directed at the out-group. In his work, Moghaddam (2005) described his framework as having five staircases of the radicalization process. On the ground floor, deprivation drives group comparison and then the societal factors of social mobility and procedural justice come into play. If the situation is not rectified, individuals progress to the second floor, where the out-group is blamed for deprivation; those with aggressive behavior pass onto the third floor where they interact with like-minded people and consider options. The fourth floor is where individuals join the group and ideas are solidified. On the fifth floor, individuals are ready to commit a terrorist act and are fully committed to the group.

In their examination of radicalization, Silber and Bhatt (2007) looked at five cases and then suggested four stages of radicalization. They talk about preradicalization. As already noted, they found that in their cases, individuals were young, often educated, middle-class males operating in male-dominated societies. Some were immigrants, but not first generation and not radical or even devout Muslims. Individuals engage in self-identification: there is a personal crisis causing them to turn to Islam to deal with that crisis. They are also exposed to radical literature and seek out like-minded individuals. During indoctrination, the radicalized Salafi-worldview is accepted. It is here where the individual goals are supplanted by larger considerations for Muslims and interaction with like-minded people occurs. Finally, jihadization occurs when individuals commit to violent jihad, train, and plan attacks. In his study, Wiktorowicz (2005) focused on individuals joining a group and, in particular, the case of al-Muhajiroun. He contended there was not enough focus on individuals' role in the literature—that is, why they are attracted to the group and the role of socialization. In response to the other social psychology-based approaches, he argued that there is a "cognitive opening" that requires a willingness on the part of individuals to expose themselves to the message. While many would outright reject the claims, the experience of a personal crisis can cause individuals to question their beliefs and open themselves up to alternative views. This crisis can be economic, social, cultural, political, or personal.

Further, the cognitive opening is facilitated by outreach. Outreach occurs as activists in the current social network or new contacts generate discussions, appealing to Muslims and educating them on crises around the world. A common tactic, Wiktorowicz argues, is "moral shock" to generate a cognitive opening. This leads to religious seeking, where individuals explore religious world views "to interpret and resolve his discontent." During this time, individuals seek out religious institutions to provide solutions to the issues they are facing. This generally does not occur in a vacuum; individuals typically look to friends and family for direction and sources. Individuals are also led to events and activities so they can shop around for what appeals to them. Personal ties can also be made with strangers and bonds developed. Activists have at their disposal many social organizations, including charities, professional organizations, cultural societies, mosques, political parties, religious lessons, and study circles, as well as informal institutions.

Determining the validity of religious arguments, Wiktorowicz maintains, is a difficult task, especially in the face of competing perspectives. To determine the validity of arguments, individuals seek out religious authorities (community leaders, mosque imams, self-taught charismatic leaders, trained Muslim scholars). Finally, there is a progression to high-risk activism. "Socialization *redefines* self-interest, and helping produce the collective good is a means, not an end, toward fulfilling individual spiritual goals" (p. 28). There can also be material incentives as well. In the world of radical Islam, individuals are inculcated with views that violence is God's will and the failure to act will impact salvation. Part and parcel to this is the work on the part of the activists to educate individuals about responsibilities and proper behavior. All of it must be accepted to be a good Muslim.

The frameworks proposed above were developed seemingly in isolation from each other (King & Taylor 2011). They are not in total agreement on how radicalization happens, or at what level of analysis, but there is a general understanding that motivation is relevant and some type of indoctrination occurs, leading to an individual joining the group. However, none are supported with significant empirical case studies. Wiktorowicz focused on one case study of al-Muhajiroun; Silber and Bhatt looked at five cases of homegrown terrorism. Thus, their frameworks are born of these limited cases. The other frameworks were general proposals and not based on empirical case studies at all. This suggests the need for cross-talk among academics, more empirical studies to test the assumptions of the frameworks, and cooperation in the future development of theory.

STATE TERROR AND CULTURES OF FEAR

Another form of terror consists of systematic efforts by a government to terrorize the population of the country through torture, political murder, genocide, and other atrocities (Rummel, 1994; Sluka, 2000). The goal is to terrorize the population into political submission and obedience while opponents of the government are being violently repressed or killed. This occurs frequently and across the globe. Amnesty International reported in 1996 that out of 150 countries examined, 55% used torture and 41% had politically motivated murders of opponents of the governing regimes (Sluka, 2000). In Latin America during the 1970s and 1980s, this occurred in Brazil, Chile, Argentina, and Uruguay, among other countries. They came to be known as "dirty wars," and a new term was coined for victims of repression: *desaparecidos*, or the "disappeared." Although the exact number of deaths is not known, and probably never will be known, approximately 30,000 people were killed or disappeared in Argentina, and between 9,000 and 30,000 people suffered similar fates in Chile. Torture was a common instrument used to extract information out of "subversives," anyone expressing opposition to the government or associated with those expressing opposition to the government (relatives, friends, neighbors, students, etc.). Anyone was a potential target.

The populations of these countries were terrorized into submission through the gradual establishment of a **culture of terror**. As Sluka described:

> A culture of terror . . . is an institutionalized system of permanent intimidation of the masses or subordinated communities by the elite, characterized by the use of torture and disappearances and other forms of extrajudicial death squad killings as standard practice. A culture of terror establishes "collective fear" as a brutal means of social control. In these systems there is a constant threat of repression, torture, and death for anyone who is actively critical of the political status quo.
>
> (2000, pp. 22–23)

In these situations, people have little access to substantiated information. Rumors abound, but, not surprisingly, there is little concrete information about what is happening, to whom, and how. Lack of concrete information does two things: it increases fear of the unknown, and it makes it easy for the average person to ignore what is going on, to not even try to find out, for if one knows, one may be the next victim. Knowledge is dangerous in these situations, so people hunker down, attend to their own personal situations, and try not to make waves. This facilitates the state's control of the population by making the political killings possible and the population passively accepting. In these cases, the entire population becomes a massive bystander.

THE DIRTY WAR IN ARGENTINA

In 1976, the Argentine military overthrew President Isabela Perón after a period of economic and political turmoil. During the preceding years, the military had begun a campaign against a leftist guerrilla organization, the Montoneros. The Montoneros engaged in various acts of political violence, such as blowing up banks and kidnapping wealthy people in the late 1960s and early 1970s. In response, right-wing death squads were formed, which then proceeded to kill even more people than the Montoneros killed. By the time the military took power in 1976, it had already suppressed the Montoneros. It then turned to any other apparent dissidents. Those not executed immediately were taken to various locations for the extraction of information. Among the most notorious was the Navy Mechanics School, ESMA, where people were tortured and killed. Not all prisoners were killed. Some were turned into informants, and some survived by performing important functions for the unit, similar to how some prisoners worked in the concentration camps in Nazi Germany. Others, after being tortured, were drugged, stripped naked, placed upon an airplane, and thrown, alive, into the Atlantic Ocean. These were some of the many who simply disappeared. In response, Argentine society became silent. The major exception was the mothers of some of the disappeared. These brave women assembled every Thursday at the Plaza de Mayo wearing white scarves bearing the names of their missing children. Known as the Madres de la Plaza de Mayo, they still assemble every Thursday, still seeking to know what became of their children.

The behavior of the torturers was reflective of the patterns discussed above. They were a tight unit composed of carefully selected men committed to the idea that they were saving Argentina from its own worst enemies, political activists. The torturers were isolated, living in the ESMA building and permitted to see their families only three times per month (Rosenberg, 1992). They were well rewarded with money and other perks, such as the personal belongings of those they disappeared. They dehumanized their victims and joked about them, referring to two French nuns who were tossed into the ocean as "the flying nuns," for example. The torturers used euphemisms for their actions. When prisoners were thrown out of planes into the ocean, they were "transferred" or "sent up." Torturers referred to the administration of electric shocks as "giving the machine" (Rosenberg, 1992, p. 90). Many of the torturers believe to this day that they were only doing their duty and that the victims were to blame for their treatment. In the words of one torturer:

> At first, I'll be honest, it was hard to accustom ourselves to put up with torture. We're like everyone else. The person who likes war is crazy. We all would have preferred to fight in uniforms, a gentlemen's fight where you all go out to have dinner afterward. The last thing we wanted to do was interrogate . . .
>
> In the first phase of the war everyone who was captured was executed . . . We knew if we put them into the courts they would ask for all the guarantees of the system they were attacking. They'd have been freed . . . Let's say that ten thousand guerrillas disappeared. If we hadn't done it, how many more people would have died at the hands of the guerrillas? How many more young people would have joined them? It's a barbarity, but that's what war is.
>
> (quoted in Rosenberg, 1992, pp. 129–130)

This particular torturer simply saw this as another justifiable battle, not something to be ashamed of.

In addition, the silence of Argentinian society, as in so many other cases, encouraged the implementers of state repression to continue on with it. They did, indeed, have support for their actions. The same individual quoted above also stated "we had the backing of the church . . . Not that priests would say 'go ahead and torture,' but that the church said there were two groups here and we were the ones who were right. I really feel that any armed forces with a decent level of culture and human feeling would do the same as we did" (quoted in Rosenberg, p. 130). This form of terror was extremely effective in silencing Argentinian society. Indeed, when the military left power, it did so because it lost a war with Great Britain over the Falklands/Malvinas islands, not because of popular protest of the brutality of the regime.

PARAMILITARIES/DEATH SQUADS

Violence can also be committed by organized groups, paramilitaries, or death squads on behalf of a state, whether sanctioned by that state or not. The state will either turn a blind eye to the actions of these groups or drag its feet when it comes to apprehending them. Paramilitaries and death squads are difficult to define distinctly. Sluka defines **death squads** as "progovernment groups who engage in extrajudicial killings of people they define as enemies of the state" (2000, p. 141). Cubides defines **paramilitaries** as "organizations that resort to the physical elimination of presumed auxiliaries of rebel groups and of individuals seen as subversive of the moral order . . . They mostly operate through death squads" (2001, p. 129). They often act as a close-knit clandestine organization, which many know about but whose members try to hide their association with the group—although the leader of the largest paramilitary in Colombia is well known and the paramilitary has a web site. They kidnap, torture, and kill victims identified as belonging to a political group they believe is undermining them and their country. Thus, the element of intensely perceived threat to the group operates in these cases, as in the others discussed in this chapter.

Death squads and paramilitaries are effective in that they not only destroy the opposition, but terrorize those who object to their activities into silence. Death squads and paramilitaries appear in many countries experiencing severe political instability, and they are not confined to the Third World. The Protestant-loyalist paramilitaries in Northern Ireland, the Ulster Defense Association (UDA) and Ulster Volunteer Force (UVF) and the loyalist death squads, the Ulster Freedom Fighters, Red Hand Commandos, Protestant Action Force and others, have killed around 700 Catholic civilians (Sluka, 2000). There were many paramilitaries and death squads operating in Latin America during the era of repressive military regimes in the 1960s and 1970s, as well as in the civil wars in Central America during the 1970s and 1980s. In El Salvador, for example, the government fought a civil war with leftist rebels called the Farabundo Martí Liberation Front (FMLN) who wanted to gain control of the government. The ARENA Party was the most militant of the right-wing parties in El Salvador and became associated with death squads. Many people from political parties, labor organizations, peasant organizations, universities, and the clergy died at the hands of these squads if they were even thought to have been colluding with the enemy.

The Colombian government has been battling the leftist Revolutionary Armed Forces of Colombia (FARC) and the National Liberation Army (ELN) for over 30 years. Baltodano (2008) developed a typology of membership in the FARC. He argued there were three levels, the *Liderazgo*, or top leadership level, composed of men and women who made a life-time commitment; the *Guerrilla*, armed insurgent members who were full-time fighters; and the *Milicias*, members who supported and fought with the organization, but who left for months at a time to make a living and support their families. While the army is deeply engaged in this war, some Colombians have taken it upon themselves to defend their country from the FARC and the ELN. On December 22, 2000, the paramilitary group called United Self-Defense Forces of Colombia (AUC) declared war on these groups and their supporters (Wilson, 2001a). All three of these groups were designated as terrorist organizations by the U.S. government. The AUC has become infamous for brutal acts of violence used in their counterinsurgency campaign. For example, in April 2001 in the village of Naya, at least 40 civilians were killed with machine guns, machetes, and chain saws (Wilson, 2001b).

Allegations of army collusion lead to questions of whether or not they really want to put an end to their activity. Sixty-two members of the AUC were finally apprehended in April, and the Colombian President at that time, Andres Pastrana, argued that despite international and domestic criticism, this signaled that the government was not tolerating their activities. Since 2012, President Juan Manuel Santos has engaged in negotiations with the FARC. One of the topics includes their participation in government.

CONCLUSION

In this chapter, we have briefly covered a wide variety of topics on terrorism. We noted differences amongst terrorist groups and provided an overview of the basis for intergroup conflict, traits, motivation, recruitment, demographics, propaganda, conformity and obedience to authority, group conflict, role, and social control. The chapter also examined state terror. There is currently a lot of research on terrorism. However, given the plethora of topics and groups, there is definitely more work to be done. It is here where psychology can provide additional interesting insights.

Topics, Theories/Explanations, and Cases in Chapter 12

Topics	Theories/Explanations	Cases
Terrorism	Personality	Al-Qaida
Suicide bombers	Social identity theory	Hamas
Recruitment	Image theory	Hezbollah
	Psychopathology	Al Qaida in Iraq
	Authoritarian	IRA
	personality	UDA
	FIRO	PIRO
	Interpersonal needs	LTTE
	Dehumanization	
	Scapegoating	
State terror	Culture of terror	
Paramilitaries/death		Argentina
squads		Colombia

Key Terms

aggression hypothesis
American Psychiatric
   Association's Diagnostic
   and Statistical Manual of
   Mental Disorders
authoritarian personality
conformity
dehumanization

image theory
imperialist image
moral disengagement
motivation
need for affiliation
need for power
obedience to authority
propaganda

deindividuation

demographic profiles

depluralization

deviants

emotions

frustration-aggression
    hypothesis

Fundamental Interpersonal Relations
    Orientation (FIRO)

group identity

recruitment

rogue image

role

scapegoat

social control

social identity theory

state-sponsored terrorism

state terror

suicide bomber

terrorist personality

Suggestions for Further Reading

Bloom, M. (2009). Chasing butterflies and rainbows: A critique of Kruglanski et al.'s "Fully committed: Suicide bombers' motivation and the quest for personal significance." *Political Psychology, 30*, 387–395.

Borum, R. (2003). Understanding the terrorist mindset. *FBI Law Enforcement Bulletin*, 7–10.

Crenshaw, M. (2009). Intimations of mortality or production lines? The puzzle of "suicide terrorism." *Political Psychology, 30*, 359–364.

King, M., & Taylor, D.M. (2011). The radicalization of homegrown jihadists: A review of the theoretical models and social psychological evidence. *Terrorism and Political Violence, 23*(4), 602–622.

Kruglanski, A.W., Chen, X., Dechesne, M., Fishman, S., & Orehek, E. (2009). Fully committed: Suicide bombers' motivation and quest for personal significance. *Political Psychology, 30*, 331–357.

Mintz, A., & Brule, D. (2009). Methodological issues in studying suicide terrorism. *Political Psychology, 30*, 365–380.

Moghaddam, F.M. (2007). The staircase to terrorism. In B. Bonger, L.M. Brown, L.E. Beutler, J. Breckenridge, & P. Zimbardo (Eds.), *Psychology of terrorism* (pp. 69–80). Oxford: Oxford University Press.

Silber, M.D., & Bhatt, A. (2007). *Radicalization in the west: The homegrown threat*. New York: NYPD Intelligence Division.

Victoroff, J., Adelman, J.R., & Matthews, M. (2012). Psychological factors associated with support for suicide bombing in the Muslim diaspora. *Political Psychology, 33*, 791–809.

Wiktorowicz, Q. (2005). *Radical Islam rising*. Lanham, MD: Rowman & Littlefield.

Winter, D.G. (1980). An exploratory study of Southern African leaders measured at a distance. *Political Psychology, 2*(2), 75–85.

Chapter 13

THE POLITICAL PSYCHOLOGY OF INTERNATIONAL SECURITY AND CONFLICT

Throughout history, people have seemingly been embroiled almost constantly in violence, conflict, and war. And for an equally long period of time, writers from numerous disciplines have sought to understand the causes of such strife (Nieburg, 1969; Brown, 1987). And while a discussion of this subject could reasonably be seen to require a review of the voluminous research into violence and aggression that has been conducted in psychology and sociology, this is really beyond the limited scope of this chapter. In fact, much of this literature is already discussed in our other chapters dealing with ethnic nationalism, violence, and genocide. Instead, this chapter seeks to use international security and conflict as an example in order to illustrate how political scientists have applied political psychological approaches to better understand such problems as the causes of war, the security dilemma, and deterrence. In doing so, it is hoped that students will better appreciate how psychological concepts can be usefully applied to real-world political problems. The portions of the Political Being focused upon in this chapter are cognition, emotion, and perceptions of *them*.

WHY VIOLENCE AND WAR?

There have been many competing explanations for violence and war proposed by scholars across numerous disciplines (Brown, 1987). Some, for example, have looked to biology to suggest that mankind is genetically predisposed to be innately violent (Freud, 1932, 1950, 1962; Lorenz, 1966; Scott, 1969; Wilson, 1978; Shaw & Wong, 1989). Others suggested that human aggression was more of a socially learned response (Skinner, 1971, 1974; Bandura, 1973, 1977, 1986). Over time, a general consensus has emerged in which, as Brown (1987) notes, "most serious students of human violence recognize some mixture of innate predisposition (which may vary with individuals) and situational conditions" (pp. 8–9). Often, explanations of conflict in political science have suggested psychological factors as a key component. For example, the role of perception and misperception between the leaders of states in causing or avoiding international conflict has been described at length across historical crisis cases (Jervis, 1976; Lebow, 1981). Similarly, problems of successful crisis management given leader psychology or organizational limitations as a factor in avoidance of war have been discussed by a number of scholars (George, 1991; Allison & Zelikow, 1999). The dynamics and composition of policymaking groups themselves have been suggested to play a major role in averting or causing conflict (Janis, 1972; Janis & Mann, 1977; Boin & 't Hart, 2003). Finally, the personalities and characteristics of leaders have also been suggested to play a role in causing or preventing conflicts (Stoessinger, 1985; Post, 1991; Birt, 1993; Preston, 2011) Indeed, there is a growing literature focused on how leaders' own individual, unique risk propensities influence their willingness to use force or accept high degrees of risk when pursuing their policy objectives (Kowert & Hermann, 1997; Vertzberger, 1998; Boettcher, 2005; Keller & Foster, 2012).

One of the earliest expositions of the causes of political violence is found in Thucydides' *History of the Peloponnesian War*, which chronicles the events surrounding the bloody conflict between the neighboring Greek city-states of Sparta and Athens over three thousand years ago. Though an ancient Greek historian, Thucydides has often been described as the first "realist" due to his attention to the anarchic, self-help nature of the ancient Greek international system; his emphasis upon how the Spartans and Athenians competed with one another in their pursuit of power, alliances, and influence ("power politics"); and in his clear depiction (captured in the Melian Debate) of the lack of morality in the affairs of states ("might makes right"). Hence, the famous statement by the Athenians to their weaker Melian neighbors, "the strong do what they will and the weak suffer what they must" (see Hans Morgenthau, 1948, for an overview of basic realist, power politics arguments). Yet, while much of Thucydides' history clearly expresses realist, power politics notions of state behavior, including the notion that competition between states for power often leads to conflict, one could also say that Thucydides could be considered one of the first political psychologists as well.

Thucydides, far from using only state characteristics or power motivations to explain the war, suggested (much as a modern day political psychologist might) that the *main spark* igniting this bloody conflict between Sparta and Athens was *fear* on the part of both sides of one another. Fear by the Spartans of what they *perceived* to be the growing power of Athens and its increasingly expansionistic policies. Fear by the Athenians of what they *perceived* to be a ruthless, militaristic power that was bent on competing with them for hegemony over all of Greece. During the councils of war that followed on both sides, speeches by the leaders of Sparta and Athens were replete with immensely negative stereotypes and caricatures of one another, as well as strong **enemy images** (Cottam, 1994). Driven by these perceptions (and misperceptions) of each other, war became inevitable. Yet, the end result of this 23-year struggle was not supremacy over Greece, but the weakening of both combatants to such an extent that they were easily conquered by the Persians almost immediately afterwards! Objectively, if we were to speak the language of realists, the balance of power in that region of the world *never* would have made it in the broader interests of either Sparta nor Athens to go to war with one another. They needed to be allies and pool their military power to offset the might of Persia, as they had in earlier conflicts. But as Thucydides demonstrates, neither side was making such coolly rational calculations of the regional power balance. Instead, *the psychology of fear and misperception* were at work, leading both nations to a disastrous blood-bath. Indeed, as Thucydides makes plain, to ignore the psychological factors at work between Sparta and Athens would be to miss a crucial underlying cause of the war.

Similarly, the events leading up to the First World War (1914–18) provide another powerful illustration of the importance of psychological variables in explaining conflict. While many factors contributed to the speed with which war engulfed Europe in the summer of 1914 (e.g., military alliances, great power competition over colonies and naval forces, etc.), it is also clear that misperception by leaders played a major role as well (Farrar, 1988). Indeed, the Great War was one that was desired by none of the political leaders of the time. Certainly, the Austrians did not envision their dispute with Serbia igniting a World War, nor did the German Kaiser when he (unwisely) gave support to his Austrian ally. Once again, *fear* played a major role among both political and military leaders of the time. It was accepted by all that techno-logical advancements in warfare and the rapid mobilization capabilities pro-vided by modern railway systems had fundamentally altered the nature of warfare. Not only would a major war be so immensely destructive as to last at best three months (a widely held belief prior to 1914), but more impor-tantly, the state that succeeded in mobilizing (getting its armies organized and transported to the front lines) first would automatically be the victor (see Tuchman, 1962; Keegan, 1998). In crisis management terms, this was a highly unstable security environment analogous to a country during the Cold War having the capability of launching a completely disarming nuclear first-strike upon an opponent (Jervis, 1976; Levy, 1991). It gave policy mak-ers precious little time to manage a crisis, and it did not allow for defensive moves (since these would be automatically perceived to be offensive by their opponents). In 1914, you needed a mobilized army at the front line to either *defend yourself from attack OR invade your neighbor.* Offensive and defen-sive capabilities were indistinguishable from one another. As a result, even though statesmen on all sides tried to reassure one another that their mobi-lizations were purely for *defensive* purposes only, each fell into what Robert Jervis (1976) later described as the **security dilemma**, a situation in which the actions taken by each state to increase its own security had the effect of simultaneously decreasing the security of its neighbors. Since the true motivations of their neighbors could not be determined with certainty, each state was left to make decisions based solely upon their beliefs about their neighbors' motivations and capabilities. By the end of August, Europe was in flames in a conflict that would eventually claim over fifteen million lives.

The Security Dilemma

The basic notion of the security dilemma is a simple one. Faced with what is *perceived* to be (either correctly or incorrectly) as a threatening interna-tional security environment, national leaders take actions they *perceive* to be defensive ones (such as arms buildups, increased defense spending, fortifi-cation of borders, development of national missile defenses, etc.) to protect themselves from these external threats. Knowing that their own motivations are peaceful, these leaders tend to make the assumption that their true (peaceful) intentions are equally clear to all of their neighbors (Jervis, 1976). However, unlike the relatively unthreatening steps (at least to law-abiding neighbors) that a homeowner might take to enhance the security of his or her own house from burglars (such as installing alarms or better locks, putting bars on windows, or buying a guard dog), equivalent actions taken by states to enhance their security vis-à-vis other states require the building of more imposing militaries or defenses, actions which inevitably undermine the security of their neighbors.

The reason for this is that what distinguishes offensive and defensive weapons from one another are the *motivations* of their owners, not the basic characteristics of the arms themselves. Hence the long-standing joke among security specialists that the true difference between an offensive and defensive weapon is which end of the barrel you are looking down! Indeed, the problem for policy makers struggling to understand the psychology of their potential opponents (and their real policy intentions) is that they become trapped in a cycle of *trying to divine intentions based solely upon visible indicators of behavior* (i.e., size of militaries, where they are located, what political disputes arise between them, etc.). Unfortunately, as Jervis ably points out with the notion of the "security dilemma," in the real world of security you cannot judge an opponent's true military intentions based solely upon their capabilities. Any military weapon—whether it be guns, tanks, planes, nuclear weapons—can be employed either offensively or defensively (to attack a neighbor or to defend the homeland). It is the military strategy adopted that determines how the characteristics of the weapons will be used, not vice versa. Weapons themselves are agnostic. Further, almost any action taken by a state for defensive purposes could also support offensive military strategies.

For example, national missile defense (NMD) programs that seek to provide states with the ability to intercept and destroy an opponent's incoming missiles (thereby shielding their countries from attack) are often described as purely defensive by their advocates. And clearly, some uses of NMD would be purely defensive (say by a nonnuclear country without an offensive military that sought only to prevent another country from attacking it with nuclear weapons in war). However, as other countries facing proposed NMD defenses have vehemently argued (as Russia and China have against U.S. missile defense plans), a shield can also be offensive in nature. A country that suddenly became invulnerable to nuclear retaliation by other states could use that invulnerability to its own military advantage. It could launch a nuclear first strike of its own with impunity, or invade the other country militarily and fear no retaliation. In this sense, an effective NMD would provide its owner with actual military superiority over all other states and vastly increase its options across the board for using both nuclear and conventional forces (since no retaliation would need to be considered). Thus, NMD can be both offensive AND defensive. It is how it is used, not its characteristics, that make it one or the other. Regardless of the *true motivations* of a country's policy makers (of which other states can never be absolutely certain), the basic security reality is that by strengthening their military postures, states obtain more offensive options should they ever *choose* to become aggressors. In an international system characterized by anarchy, neighboring states must consider all of the possibilities behind their opponent's actions and assume the worst (see Jervis, 1976; Richardson, 1960).

As a result, policy makers pursuing what they believed to be purely defensive military buildups often failed to understand how their actions were likely to be perceived (or misperceived) by neighboring states. Since defensively motivated policy makers know that their own motivations for their military buildups are peaceful, they sometimes assume (incorrectly) that these peaceful intentions are obvious and self-evident to all interested observers. Unfortunately, this is often not the case. For example, during the Cold War, both sides (the United States and the Soviet Union) saw the actions of the other in a threatening light. The formation of the great military alliances of the period—the North Atlantic Treaty Organization (NATO) in the West and the Warsaw Pact in the East—were seen by their creators as defensive in nature, but viewed as evidence of hostile intent and a desire to possibly launch an armed invasion by their opponents. Similarly, Soviet military doctrine of the time held that to defend against Western attack, one needed massive, numerically superior conventional forces that could offset issues of quality with sheer quantity—a strategy that had been employed effectively against the Germans in the Second World War (Legvold, 1988). However, for the West, the massive size of the Red Army, its forward deployment in Eastern Europe, and the buildup of such large numbers of tanks, artillery, combat aircraft, etc. were seen as clearly having offensive potential. The Cold War became a classic example of the security dilemma in action. Though we now know that neither side seriously contemplated invading the other during the Cold War, these motivations or intentions were not accurately perceived or understood by their opponents (see Gaddis, 1992, 1997).

Contributing to these problems of perception are issues of attribution, or how we tend to psychologically assign cause-and-effect relationships in our environment. For example, the fundamental attribution error, which, as we have seen in previous chapters, involves our tendency to explain (or attribute) another person's behavior or actions to their dispositional qualities (their personalities, motivations, etc.) rather than to situational factors in the environment that may have caused the behavior (Heider, 1958). In the security dilemma example above, U.S. policy makers during the Cold War tended to explain the Soviet Union's military buildup and forward deployment of forces in Eastern Europe by the dispositional qualities of Soviet leaders (i.e., Stalin or Khrushchev's aggressive, expansionistic intentions towards Western Europe), and not due to situational factors (such as the formation of NATO, concerns about another invasion from the West, etc.) that actually motivated the behavior. A similar dynamic can be seen today in how Russian President Vladimir Putin's actions in Crimea and Ukraine are often portrayed by policy makers and media in the West as being driven by his authoritarian personality or ambitions for expansionism, instead of the many situational factors that could also be at work (i.e., the threat posed by NATO/EU expansion eastward, the active Western support of an opposition coup in Kiev against a democratically elected, pro-Russian leader, perceptions that Russia's legitimate security interests have been ignored by the West post–Cold War, etc.).

A somewhat similar process of misattribution during the Cold War is described by Ole Holsti's (1967, 1969) work describing the ways in which American policy makers perceived the behavior and motivations of their Soviet counterparts. For example, in describing the belief system of John Foster Dulles, who served as Dwight Eisenhower's secretary of state during the 1950s, Holsti observed that his world view was characterized by an **inherent bad-faith** perspective of the Soviets. Simply stated, if Soviet behavior in the world was *good* (i.e., not threatening to U.S. interests), it was not because Soviet intentions *were* benign, but rather, their good behavior was only due to overwhelming U.S. military strength. On the other hand, when Soviet behavior in the world was bad (i.e., threatening U.S. interests in Berlin or Cuba), this was a true reflection of their real policy intentions. In other words, when the Soviets were good, it was only because the U.S. made them be good, and when they were bad, it's because they really were bad. American policy makers throughout the Cold War routinely shared this perspective on the Soviets (as did many Soviet policy makers of the U.S.). Further illustrations of this belief system include Paul Nitze's formulation of Soviet intentions in NSC-68 (perhaps the most important U.S. foreign policy document of the Cold War) and Ronald Reagan's depiction of the Soviet Union as "the evil empire" and his "peace through strength" arguments of the 1980s to justify the largest peace-time military buildup in American history. Obviously, this belief system made it very difficult for either side to show good faith towards the other, since this would often be interpreted as further evidence supporting the effectiveness of pursuing a tough policy line towards them. It also allowed policy makers to effectively preserve their existing enemy images or negative stereotypes of one another, since the selective perception involved allowed them to discount any cooperative behavior by their opponents as coerced and focus upon the examples of negative behavior that better reflected their existing views of the other side.

The Cold War relationship between the U.S. and Soviet Union has also been described as being characterized by a malignant (spiral) process of hostile interaction (Deutsch, 1986). According to Deutsch (1986), the key elements contributing to the development and perpetuation of a protracted, malignant interaction process include:

> (1) an anarchic social situation, (2) a win-lose or competitive orientation, (3) inner conflicts (within each of the parties) that express themselves through external conflict, (4) cognitive rigidity, (5) misjudgments and misperceptions, (6) unwitting commitments, (7) self-fulfilling prophecies, (8) vicious escalating spirals, and (9) a gamesmanship orientation which turns the conflict away from issues of what in real life is being won or lost to an abstract conflict over images of power.
>
> (p. 131)

The malignant process escalates as these elements interact with one another to gradually worsen ongoing conflicts, causing them to spiral towards more hostile interactions over time. Thus, according to Deutsch, the basic security dilemma problem for the superpowers and their fear of becoming militarily inferior created an anarchic social situation characterized by extreme competitiveness (a win-lose orientation) on their parts. As a result, gains in military capability by one side were viewed as threatening losses to the security of the other. Adding to this problem was the use of the external enemy to serve as justification for internal conflicts in both superpower societies (i.e., the need for Stalin's harsh rule at home or the need for internationalist policies in the U.S.). Cognitive rigidity by policy makers in how they viewed the other side, inherent bad-faith belief systems, etc., led to misjudgments and misperceptions of opponents, unwitting commitments to rigid policy positions, and escalating spirals of conflict. The hostility and suspicion expressed towards the other side became a self-fulfilling prophecy when that hostility was returned in kind (Deutsch, 1986).

The Psychology of Deterrence

During the Cold War, the superpowers sought to deter extreme threats to their national interests (e.g., invasions of their homelands or attacks upon vital allies) through nuclear deterrence—or the threat to retaliate for such aggression by using nuclear weapons. A simple definition of **deterrence** is the threat by one political actor to take actions in response to another actor's potential actions that would make the costs (or losses) incurred far outweigh any possible benefits (or gains) obtained by the aggressor. Of course, definitions of deterrence vary across the literature. Schelling (1960/1980, p. 195), for example, defines deterrence as the use of threats to prevent someone from doing something (or starting something). Stein (1992, p. 147), on the other hand, defines it as threatening punishment or denial to prevent an adversary from taking unwanted action. A classic Cold War example of deterrence is that even if the Soviets could successfully invade and occupy Western Europe and obliterate the United States in a nuclear first strike, the U.S. would still have enough surviving forces to respond with a retaliatory nuclear attack that would utterly destroy the Soviet Union. Thus, no matter how great the potential gains were, the consequences (utter destruction of the home nation in retaliation) would far exceed any gains from the original aggression. As a result, once both superpowers possessed comparable abilities to attack and destroy the other with nuclear weapons by the late 1960s, the famous Mutual Assured Destruction (MAD) nuclear doctrine was established, recognizing this deterrent relationship.

But, the most fundamental element to this deterrence formula has always been *perceptual*. Both sides during the Cold War recognized that the *credibility* of their nuclear retaliatory threats were only effective if the other side truly *believed* that they would really carry them out if suitably provoked. In the final analysis, whether deterrence would fail or succeed depended not upon how many weapons each side possessed, but upon the perceptions each side possessed regarding the willingness of their opponents to really "push the button." Thus, deterrence (whether nuclear or conventional) is, at its heart, a psychological relationship between the deterrer and the deterred. In order for deterrence to function successfully (e.g., prevent any aggression from taking place to begin with), the actor seeking to deter an opponent must be able to effectively communicate to the opponent (and the opponent must accurately perceive) that the deterrer has both: 1) the physical capability to carry out a threat (nuclear weapons, survivable delivery systems, etc.) and that 2) the threat has credibility (that the deterrer truly has the resolve (or willingness) to carry out their promised retaliation, no matter how horrific the consequences). If an opponent does not believe in the credibility of your threat, regardless of your real intentions, then you will not be able to effectively deter them. This is part of the inherent peril of deterrence—that it can unravel due to an opponent's misperception of *either* your substantive military capabilities *or* the credibility of your threats to use these capabilities.

Consider the example of Saddam Hussein's calculations prior to the invasion of Kuwait. Although truly one of history's worst generals, even Hussein understood that the United States enjoyed vast, overwhelming military superiority over Iraq in terms of numbers and quality of equipment. That much was no mystery to him. What he fundamentally misunderstood was the extent to which an immense technological gap had opened up between the U.S. armed forces and those of less advanced states. Indeed, this revolution in military affairs was not fully appreciated, even by U.S. analysts, until after the war was over (Freedman & Karsh, 1993; Cohen, 1996; Biddle, 1998; O'Hanlon, 2000). Yet, for Saddam, the calculation was never one of pure military capabilities. Rather, his calculations were governed by his *perception* (as it turned out, an incorrect perception) of the credibility of the U.S. threat to intervene in the region and reverse his invasion. Indeed, he told both U.S. officials and reporters prior to the Gulf War that after Vietnam, Iraq only needed to have the ability to cause lots of American casualties to deter the U.S. from becoming militarily involved in a conflict. Saddam believed that the U.S. had no willingness to accept casualties and could never sustain substantial losses of troops politically at home. This perception is indicative of the **degenerate image** discussed in Chapters 3 and 10. Recall that that is an image wherein a country of equal or greater power is seen as confused and lacking the will to respond to the actions of another country. The image was supported by previous actions by the United States, particularly communication from the American ambassador that the U.S. would not oppose his position on the dispute with Kuwait on the oil fields. In order to use that perceived lack of will on the part of the U.S. to his advantage, Hussein and his spokesmen spent much time making pronouncements to the world's press regarding the tens of thousands of body bags that would be required to send the Americans back home if they attacked him. Once inside Kuwait, the Iraqi forces dug in and attempted to create for Coalition forces the choice of accepting his invasion or fighting a long, bloody *war of attrition* like the one he had recently waged with Iran (Freedman & Karsh, 1993).[1] This degenerate image-based perception by Saddam—both of actual U.S. credibility (our willingness to accept casualties or use force to reverse the Kuwaiti invasion) and actual U.S. military capabilities *vis-à-vis* the Iraqi forces in Kuwait (the technological gap)—made the Iraqi leader unwisely accept the risk (which he viewed as slight) that the U.S. would intervene in the Gulf and be willing to pay the price in blood to reverse his invasion (Woodward, 1991; Stein, 1992; Freedman & Karsh, 1993). His perceptions of the situation mattered more than calculations of U.S. military capabilities (which he didn't believe Washington would be able to fully exploit).

There exists tremendous debate and disagreement within the political science literature over how to test deterrence theory, with the center of the debate usually revolving around how differing camps of scholars have chosen to operationalize the concept or interpret historical events (cf. Huth & Russett, 1984, 1988, 1990; Lebow & Stein, 1987, 1989, 1990). As Eric Herring (1995, p. 33) observes regarding this debate, "virtually all aspects of how to test deterrence and compellence theory are disputed." The use of historical cases purporting to represent successes or failures of deterrence by these authors has been problematic to say the least, since there are seldom universally accepted, objective interpretations of historical events or records of exactly what was on the minds of the policy makers during the crises (rather important when motivation matters as much as it does for deterrence questions). Although it is beyond the scope of this chapter to delve into these debates at length, there exist a number of excellent overviews and critical analyses of these methodological debates (Herring, 1995; Harvey, 1997a, 1997b, 1997c, 1998). As Harvey (1997b) briefly explains:

> Case selection and coding immediate deterrence encounters remains a key area of difficulty for researchers who test deterrence theory using the dominant success-failure strategy. The approach recommends identifying cases of immediate deterrence, coding these cases as instances of success or failure, isolating conditions that were present or absent during failures, and, based on these differences, drawing conclusions about why and how deterrence works. The problem, as Huth and Russett acknowledge, is that a single crisis frequently encompasses several different types of interactions and outcomes . . . carefully separating the threat/counter-threat sequence that would allow the researcher to pinpoint those aspects of behavior that conform to a direct or extended, immediate deterrence or compellence military encounter is often difficult, if not impossible, to accomplish with any degree of empirical precision, especially if the entire crisis is the unit of analysis.
>
> (p. 13)

Harvey (1997b) seeks to avoid some of the pitfalls of seeking to judge historical cases as a whole as deterrence successes or failures based on a single dominant exchange (as do Huth & Russett, 1984, 1988, 1990; Lebow & Stein, 1985) by employing the **protracted crisis approach**. Explicitly rejecting the assumption that crises should be counted as a "single, dominant encounter," Harvey argues that much like the frames of a motion picture film, crises should be viewed as a long series of "separate and distinct deterrence and compellence exchanges" running throughout the crisis from the beginning until the end of any episode (1997b, p. 13). As Harvey notes,

> Dissecting each crisis to reveal different encounters allows for multiple interpretations of any one foreign policy crisis and, therefore, can help to account for discrepancies across existing case lists; it forces the researcher to specify the precise time frame and exact sequence within which the appropriately designated threats, counter-threats and responses are made.
>
> (p. 13)

In adopting this approach, Harvey follows in the tradition of George and Smoke (1974), who also argued for viewing deterrence cases as involving multiple exchanges in a protracted crisis. As a result, an individual case, such as Bosnia-Herzegovina (1993–94), moves from being a single case of one primary exchange between the parties to one with fourteen total exchanges between the parties (Harvey, 1997c). Indeed, much of the disagreement between Huth/Russett and Lebow/Stein centers upon what stage of a historical crisis they have focused upon for their analysis of deterrence failure or success, a problem that is eliminated through adoption of Harvey's more nuanced approach.

Of course, in order to determine whether or not an actor has been deterred from taking a specified action (or compelled to change course from an already adopted course of action) due to credible threats (military, economic, or political), one has to know the motivations of that actor. In other words, did they actually intend to take the course of action that is the subject of the deterrent or compellent action? You cannot deter an action that was not being considered by your opponent in the first place, nor can you judge an effort at deterrence or compellence as a success or failure in the absence of information about your opponent's intentions. As many scholars have noted, it is the target actor's motivations, their calculations of costs-benefits, their ability to accurately perceive their environments (whether that be military or political ones), and their own particular judgments regarding the correlation of these elements that must drive any discussion of deterrence or compellence success or failure (see Schelling, 1960/1980; George & Smoke, 1974; Jervis, Lebow, & Stein, 1985; George, 1991; Stein, 1992).

A good illustration of this point is found in Stein's (1992) analysis of U.S. deterrence and compellence attempts upon Iraq prior to the Gulf War of 1990–91. While the historical record provides a great deal of data to support any number of hypotheses regarding why deterrence or compellence efforts failed in this case, in the end, it is the motivations and calculations of Saddam Hussein that drive Stein's analysis of these efforts. Stein suggests three possibilities for the failure of U.S. deterrence and compellence efforts against Iraq: 1) that the U.S. failed to mount an effective strategy of deterrence in the period preceding the Kuwaiti invasion; 2) that Saddam Hussein systematically miscalculated the capabilities and resolve of the United States; or finally, 3) that Saddam could not be deterred regardless of the strategy employed (Stein, 1992, p. 148). At the heart of the question, however, is the issue of Saddam Hussein's motives and intentions—was he an "opportunity-driven aggressor" or a "vulnerable leader motivated by need" (Stein, 1992, p. 155)? Stein also points out that many of Saddam's strategic calculations prior to the Gulf War that may have led him to discount the credibility of U.S. threats to use force—i.e., the likelihood of a major U.S. intervention, American willingness to take heavy casualties, the difficulties facing Arab leaders in maintaining public support for a war against another Arab state—were not necessarily irrational. Although traditional realists, like Morgenthau (1948), would argue that imbalances of power between states are often a cause of war, Stein notes that "overwhelming local military superiority does not, however, necessarily lead to crisis and war unless the motive and the intention to use force are also present" (1992, p. 156). In the case of the Gulf War, Stein makes a strong case that it is the psychology of

Saddam Hussein, his motives, calculations, and perceptions of his environment, that in the final analysis determined the outcomes of all of the U.S. influence attempts.

Another important issue to consider when testing deterrence theory is how the analyst will view limited uses of force by one or both parties in a deterrence relationship. This touches upon the distinction between general and immediate deterrence. As Herring (1995, p. 18) explains, "general deterrence is the use of a standing threat in order to prevent someone from seriously considering doing something, while immediate deterrence is the use of specific threats to prevent someone from doing something which is being seriously considered." Although any use of force could be argued to represent a failure of general deterrence, George and Smoke (1974) argue that limited force can be used to probe a general deterrence commitment without compromising deterrence itself. For example, in Kashmir, India and Pakistan have had numerous crises and military clashes that have threatened to escalate into major wars, perhaps even nuclear ones, over the past twelve years. Yet, to argue that these brief, though intense, military incursions, or the periodic shelling that goes on along the borders, represents a failure of general deterrence misses the point that it is likely the fear of nuclear escalation that prevented these skirmishes from growing (Hagerty, 1995/1996, 1998). At the most, such probes should be seen only as "a partial failure of immediate deterrence," and not failures of general deterrence (Herring, 1995, p. 26).

Of course, the strongest critiques of deterrence theory have always had a psychological basis. In particular, critics have noted that the retaliatory threats required by deterrence often demand a state to make arguably irrational decisions (i.e., commit national suicide by launching a retaliatory nuclear strike upon an opponent that would invite an equally devastating retaliation in return by the victim). While one can easily make the argument that an opponent might be deterred by a state if it promised nuclear retaliation in response to aggression (since the costs would outweigh the benefits), it is equally the case that for the state actually carrying out this threat, *the costs would also outweigh the benefits*! The need to make such a fundamentally irrational decision into a rational one for states has led security analysts to rely upon "meta-rational" solutions to game-theory approaches in their search for a logic to support the credibility of some of the more extreme deterrent threats required of nuclear states.

For example, the game of **chicken** (see Figure 13.1) has often been used by scholars to represent the nature of the deterrence problem facing the superpowers during the Cold War (Jervis, 1976; Freedman, 1981; Brams, 1985). In that game, one imagines a long, deserted stretch of highway with two cars facing each other at opposite ends of the road. The object of chicken, predictably, is to get the other driver to chicken out first (i.e., swerve out of the way of your oncoming vehicle) while you continue to drive straight-down the highway. Thus, both drivers (assuming they were not suicidal maniacs) would need to not only demonstrate their capability of causing a horrific, fatal accident by driving straight-down the road as fast as possible, but would also need to somehow communicate the credibility of their threat to continue to do so (regardless of the consequences) to the opposing driver in the hopes of making him swerve out of the way first! Obviously, for both

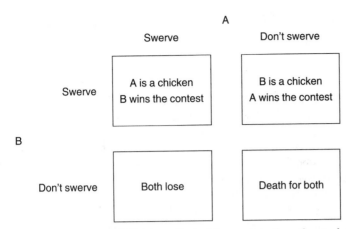

Figure 13.1 The Game of Chicken. Each driver wants the other to believe that they will not swerve, thereby forcing the other to chicken out and swerve first. Whoever swerves first is a chicken. But the dilemma for both drivers is just that: Will the other really swerve first? If neither do, both die.

drivers, the rational solution is to swerve out of the way of the other car every time, since to actually carry out the threat would carry a cost greater than any conceivable benefit a victory might bring to the driver. However, if the drivers insist upon playing chicken (or states to rely upon MAD nuclear doctrines for their security) and, for some reason must play the game to win, then it becomes imperative for them to be able to make an irrational threat credible. For if the threat is not credible, neither driver will swerve and both will die (Brams, 1985).

Making such a threat credible could be accomplished in a number of different ways. For instance, one driver might put the car on cruise-control, throw the steering wheel out of the window, and crawl into the backseat to read a good (hopefully short) book. Seeing such behavior and recognizing it for what it was, an **irrevocable commitment**, the other driver would have no further cause to doubt the credibility of his opponent's threat and would recognize that *only he now had control* over whether the cars crash or not. At this point, the rational decision would be to swerve in the face of this irrevocable commitment by his opponent to this inherently irrational action (Powell, 1990). Similarly, countries have relied upon what Schelling (1966) described as "the threat that leaves something to chance" to make irrational threats credible (Freedman, 1981; Powell, 1990). In other words, even if you really don't believe your opponent would actually go through with a retaliatory strike that would result in their own self-destruction, these threats retain some credibility if your opponent could becoming a "contingently unsafe actor" in the context of a crisis (Rhodes, 1989). Simply put, the country's leaders might not be able to control all of their military forces in the event of a war, especially if nuclear weapons began going off and interrupting command-and-control functions between the nation's leaders and its armed forces. As a result, the leaders would lose positive control over their forces and lack the ability to prevent retaliation from occurring (Feaver, 1992/93; Sagan, 1994).

During the Cold War, both superpowers adopted strategic postures that were roughly the equivalent to climbing into the backseat of the speeding vehicle in Chicken. Subordinates (like submarine commanders) were given preauthorization to launch their weapons in the event of permanently losing contact with the nation's leadership during a crisis. Similarly, both sides adopted "launch-on-warning" or "launch-on-impact" doctrines regarding nuclear weapons, in which subordinates would have authorization to retaliate upon evidence of imminent or current nuclear attack by an opponent. There was even consideration (although this was never adopted except in the Hollywood film *WarGames*) of leaving the actual decision (and ability) to retaliate to computers, thereby removing humans from the decision loop entirely (see, Freedman, 1981; Smoke, 1987). And while this last option would have come closest to the logic of throwing the steering wheel out of the window and curling up to read in the backseat, the earlier options also held with them (and increased) the possibility that an objectively irrational response could still occur. That even if the other country's leaders lacked the resolve to really push the button, they still might not be able to prevent their armed forces from retaliating anyway during an attack. And, the greater the disruption of command-and-control as the result of an attack, or the greater the stress of an ongoing crisis between two nuclear-armed states, the greater the likelihood (or possibility) that the state could become *contingently unsafe* and respond irrationally to a provocation.

In addition, critics of reliance on deterrence for maintaining peace between nuclear states also note the many psychological or information-processing challenges which deterrence must master to function properly (Dunn, 1982; Lebow & Stein, 1989, 1990; Feaver, 1992/1993; Sagan, 1994; Feaver & Niou, 1996). For example, they observe that history is replete with cases in which decision makers have *misperceived* either the nature of their security environments (i.e., the Peloponnesian War; the First World War) or the intentions and motivations of their opponents (i.e., Chamberlain of Hitler at Munich; the superpowers of each other during the Cold War). Given the potential consequences of a breakdown in deterrence (nuclear war), these critics have argued that it was dangerous, given the enormous difficulties facing policy makers in seeking to rely on deterrence, to depend upon it to maintain the peace. Not only did deterrence require policy makers to rationally take irrational actions to support the strategy, it also required them to accurately perceive both their own (and their opponent's) capabilities and intentions, and be able to maintain positive control over their subordinates and arsenals during extremely challenging crisis contexts! Further, by focusing principally on the use of threats, deterrence theory tended to ignore the role that rewards and concessions might play in defusing or preventing conflicts (Jervis, 1976). One possible consequence of relying upon threats rather than more positive inducements is that it reinforces the perception of policy makers of the opposing state as being hostile or aggressive. As a result, **cognitive rigidity** among policy makers can exacerbate the tensions between states as neutral or friendly behavior is ignored or reinterpreted to better fit a preexisting negative stereotype (Holsti, 1967; Jervis, 1976). Because foreign policy beliefs are highly resistant to change (George, 1980), once a particular image or stereotype of a neighboring state is adopted (e.g., as aggressive and likely to attack; or as weak and unlikely to attack), **belief**

perseverance will serve as a barrier to the successful transmission of either warnings of credible threats or the gathering of information that diverges from the accepted belief systems of policy makers (Tetlock et al., 1991).

In contrast to deterrence theory, Jervis (1976) lays out a spiral model that incorporates many of the concerns that critics have about the assumptions of deterrence. Indeed, spiral theorists focus upon many of the same dynamics previously described by Deutsch's (1986) *malignant spiral process of hostile interaction*. As Jervis (1976, p. 67) observes:

> If much of deterrence theory can be seen in terms of the game of Chicken, the spiral theorists are more impressed with the relevance of the Prisoner's Dilemma . . . if each state pursues its narrow self-interest with a narrow conception of rationality, all states will be worse off than they would be if they cooperated . . . A second point highlighted by the Prisoner's Dilemma is that cooperative arrangements are not likely to be reached through coercion. Threats and an adversary posture are likely to lead to counteractions with the ultimate result that both sides will be worse off than they were before.
>
> (p. 67; see Figure 13.2)

Thus, the emphasis of spiral theorists is upon reducing the degree to which rival states overestimate the hostility of each other, countering the dynamics of the security dilemma through confidence building measures, and using concessions to both reduce tensions and induce a less hostile, aggressive perception of the state's intentions by neighbors. Jervis (1976) notes that the two theories contradict each other at every point:

> Policies that flow from deterrence theory (e.g. development of potent and flexible armed forces; a willingness to fight for issues of low intrinsic value; avoidance of any appearance of weakness) are just those that, according to the spiral model, are most apt to heighten tensions and create illusory incompatibility. And the behavior advocated by the spiral theorists (attempts to reassure the other side of one's non-aggressiveness, the avoidance of provocations, the undertaking of unilateral initiatives) would, according to deterrence theory, be likely to lead an aggressor to doubt the state's willingness to resist.
>
> (p. 84)

Further, neither deterrence nor spiral theories have proven adequate to explain all historical cases of conflict or avoidance of conflict (Jervis, 1976). While the outbreak of World War I in 1914 is often used to illustrate spiral dynamics (e.g., misperception and distrust, enemy images, security dilemmas), the experiences of Chamberlain with Hitler at Munich in 1938 (e.g., use of concessions and diplomacy, avoidance of threats) runs contrary to its predictions. Similarly, deterrence theorists are much happier using the example of Munich's appeasement and the aggressive states of the 1930s to illustrate the importance of not appearing weak to opponents through concessions and maintaining credible threat postures than they are using the 1914 example, which illustrates the dangers of this approach. As Jervis (1976, p. 95) observes, "given the histories of these two conflicts, it is not

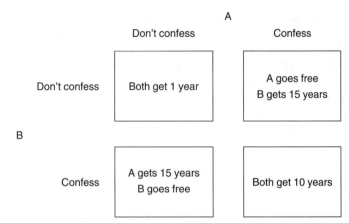

Figure 13.2 The Prisoner's Dilemma. In this classic game, two prisoners, A and B, accused of a crime, have the options of confessing or not confessing. If they maintain their alliance and neither confesses, both get short sentences. If each of them confesses, they each get a heavy sentence. But if one confesses and the other does not, the prisoner who confessed is rewarded with freedom, and the one who did not confess gets a severe sentence. The dilemma for each prisoner is that, if he trusts the other not to confess, his best option is to rat out his partner in crime.

surprising that deterrence theories have little to say about World War I and that the spiral theorists rarely discuss the 1930s."

As the ongoing debates over deterrence effectiveness between Huth and Russett (1984, 1988, 1990) and Lebow and Stein (1987, 1989, 1990) have illustrated, proving that deterrence works empirically through examining past historical cases of deterrence successes and failures is exceedingly difficult. Indeed, since successful deterrence would often be invisible due to the fact that it prevented a state from ever taking an action in the first place that it believed would provoke retaliation, what would be visible in the historical record would generally be only deterrence *failures* that led to war—not successful examples of deterrence that maintained the peace. And, despite decades of research and debate on the subject of deterrence, scholars still greatly dispute whether deterrence is generally successful or not, or what historical cases legitimately represent one or the other outcome. Indeed, the "long peace" of the Cold War and the absence of a World War III between 1947–1991 is still hotly debated among scholars who see it as either: 1) a powerful example of how deterrence can maintain international peace and stability; or 2) a case of extraordinary good luck in which war was avoided for other reasons (see an excellent overview of this debate in Gjelstad and Njolstad, 1996).

The Effects of Problem Representation or "Framing" Upon Perception and Decision Making in the Security Context

How policy makers "frame" or "represent" (structure or assign meaning to) a given policy problem, option, or situation—in other words, how they perceive it, or see it as similar or dissimilar to previous events—can be critically important in determining how they will behave when making decisions in a security setting (see Sylvan & Voss, 1998; Tetlock & Belkin, 1996). At the simplest level, limitations on the ability of decision makers to *accurately perceive* the entirety of their policy environments (or the true range of options available to them in dealing with a given policy problem) may result in decisions being taken that are based upon either a distorted or incomplete understanding of the situation (Jervis, 1976; Vertzberger, 1990; Preston, 2011). In security studies, for example, when assessing military balances of power, it is important to recognize that while there is an *objective reality* regarding a nation's military capabilities (i.e., an actual number of tanks, aircraft, soldiers; specific qualitative characteristics of weapons systems that govern their performance on the battlefield; explicit military doctrines or strategies that will govern the use of a nation's armed forces in battle, etc.), it is *how policy makers perceive their opponent's military forces and capabilities* that will govern how they view them and the decisions they will make vis-à-vis that country.

Recall the earlier example of Saddam Hussein's calculations prior to the Gulf War, in which his misperceptions regarding his own military's abilities to create a war of attrition dilemma for American policy makers were coupled with his mistaken belief that the U.S. was unwilling to absorb large numbers of combat casualties, leading him to discount the credibility of American military threats over Kuwait (Stein, 1992). Indeed, during the 2003 U.S. invasion of Iraq, former Foreign Minister Tariq Aziz later noted that Saddam was so convinced that the Americans would simply bomb him heavily for a period of time and then go away (as had happened before) that he ordered his front-line units to take no action as the Coalition columns crossed into Iraq (Preston, 2011). His prior experiences with the First Gulf War, where G. H. W. Bush was unwilling to assume the costs to occupy Iraq, Operation Desert Fox during the Clinton administration (consisting solely of a cruise missile campaign), and the no-fly zone policy without ground troops, all framed his view of the environment as being one in which the Americans would not want to conquer and occupy Iraq—a view completely divorced from the new reality of how George W. Bush and his advisers viewed the world.

Similarly, while there was an *objective military reality* in 1914 (at that point unknown to Europe's military leaders) regarding how military strategies emphasizing the "cult of the offensive" and infantry assaults would fare against the advent of the heavy machine-gun, more precise and powerful artillery, and their use to defend fortified positions (Tuchman, 1962; Keegan, 1998), decisions were made based upon policy makers' mistaken perceptions of reality (Snyder, 1984; Van Evera, 1984). How policy makers frame their strategic environments can shape what they believe to be their options. For example, it was universally accepted military doctrine prior to 1914 that technological advances (quantified in terms of machine guns, numbers of divisions, ability to mobilize and transport these forces to the fronts using railroads, etc.) made modern war so destructive that it could only last a matter of months. Further, the first nation to fully deploy its forces, given this revolution in military technology, would automatically win (Tuchman, 1962; Keegan, 1998). This representation of the problem by decision makers contributed to their sense of a security dilemma and failure to recognize a new military reality in which weapons technology had rendered the offensive strategy inferior to the defensive one.

To illustrate this point about how our subjective perceptions of the situation are not necessarily driven by objective reality, imagine your professor advises your class that there is a giant pit in the floor in the middle of your classroom, filled to brimming at its great depths with sharp iron spikes. With the room's lights on, and the warnings about its existence given, it is highly unlikely that students would inadvertently stumble into it. Thus, the objective reality was observable (students could see the pit), the credibility of the threat (that falling into the pit would cause serious, if not fatal, injury) was believable, and students' behavior was impacted (no one attempted short-cuts across the center of the room after class). However, if the lights were off and no warnings were given, then many students would likely fall into the pit. In neither case were the students' behaviors irrational, and whether the light was on or off, the pit continued to exist. Simply put, individuals respond to the reality they perceive and their behavior is unaffected by what they either don't believe to be true or do not observe directly. This illustrates the nature of the problem for policy makers in effectively communicating deterrent threats to their opponents (who subjectively perceive reality) and how powerful framing effects might be once policy makers have accepted as truth a particular formulation of reality.

For example, a growing literature has focused upon how policy makers use **analogical reasoning** to frame (or understand) policy problems, and the kinds of policy options that might be appropriate to address their problem (May, 1973; Neustadt & May, 1986; Khong, 1992; Dyson & Preston 2006). An **analogy** is essentially a decision-making heuristic, or short-hand, in which policy makers see a current event or situation as similar to (or sharing many of the same characteristics as) a previous historical event. When U.S. policy makers, for instance, consider intervening militarily in almost any situation—whether it be sending the military to the Persian Gulf to liberate Kuwait after the Iraqi invasion, sending peacekeepers to Bosnia to keep the warring factions apart and maintain regional stability, or even to engage in humanitarian relief efforts to prevent starvation in Somalia—the **Vietnam analogy** is frequently heard (Preston, 2001, 2011). This analogy suggests that any U.S. military intervention will likely result in the same outcome as did American intervention in Vietnam during the 1960s–70s, an open-ended commitment to a losing cause that will result in tremendous bloodshed for our troops and political unrest at home. To say that something will be another Vietnam is to essentially say, "we should not become involved because of how bad our experience in Vietnam was" and that we will be inviting a political disaster.

Of course, while the Vietnam analogy works against policy makers intervening militarily abroad, other analogies encourage such intervention. The **Munich analogy**, for example, argues that if you do not stand up to an aggressor, and instead seek to appease them or make concessions to them in the hopes of keeping the peace, the end result will be to only encourage them to be even more aggressive and likely bring on the very war you sought to avoid (May, 1973; Neustadt & May, 1986; Khong, 1992; Preston 2001). Obviously, this analogy grew out of an earlier historical experience, that of British Prime Minister Neville Chamberlain's efforts at Munich in 1938 to appease Adolf Hitler's territorial demands and achieve "peace in our time" through these concessions. The result of Chamberlain's appeasement has been argued by many to have only emboldened Hitler more and encouraged further actions on his part (such as the invasion of the rest of Czechoslovakia in 1938 and Poland in 1939) that subsequently led to World War II. Clearly, how policy makers perceive the situation, and what kind of analogies they use to understand the problems they face, have a tremendous impact upon the ultimate policy decisions for war or peace. As Khong (1992) illustrates in *Analogies at War*, President Lyndon Johnson and his advisers were influenced the most by the Munich analogy in their decision making on whether or not to intervene militarily in Vietnam in 1965. Seeing the North Vietnamese as aggressive expansionists in the Hitler mold, perhaps as mere surrogates for a general pattern of Soviet-led communist aggression worldwide (the dominant U.S. policy view, given Containment Policy), the choice was clear for Johnson. Intervening in Vietnam, they thought, was the only thing standing between maintaining regional stability and a row of falling dominoes throughout Southeast Asia, as country after country eventually fell to continuing communist aggression after South Vietnam was conquered. Johnson chose to send more and more U.S. troops to Vietnam (Preston, 2001). Similarly, during the lead-up to the Gulf War, President George Bush frequently invoked the Munich analogy in explaining the need to send U.S. forces to oppose Saddam Hussein and liberate Kuwait. In this case, the analogy suggested that Hussein would continue his aggression into Saudi Arabia and beyond if left unchecked in Kuwait (Preston, 2001). In contrast, John F. Kennedy's use of the **Guns of August analogy** during the Cuban Missile Crisis of 1962—an analogy based upon the experience of the events leading up to the outbreak of the First World War, a war which none of the policy makers desired or intended to occur—led him to be far more cautious and mindful of his actions during the tense days of that crisis (Schlesinger, 1965; Sorensen, 1965; Preston, 2001). In this case, one could argue that analogy served a war-avoidance function for Kennedy and sensitized him to how easily the crisis could spin out-of-control and into war.

That analogies are always gross simplifications of reality, and that seldom are two historical situations identical, is beside the point. Policy makers use analogies in their decision making, sometimes well and sometimes poorly, and their use can (as illustrated above) often have significant consequences in terms of the ultimate decisions for war or peace (Neustadt & May 1986).

Another growing body of framing literature in political science seeks to apply **prospect theory** to foreign policy decision-making and security issues (Lebow & Stein, 1987; Levy, 1997; McDermott, 1998; Kahneman & Tversky 2000; Haas, 2001; Mintz, 2004, 2005; Goertz, 2004; Berejikian & Early 2013). Building upon a psychological model developed by Kahneman and Tversky (1979), prospect theory predicts that individuals will tend to be risk averse in the domain of gains and risk seeking in the domain of losses (Tetlock et al., 1991). Further, what determines whether something is considered to be a gain or a loss is determined relative to the original starting, or reference point. In other words, "change is evaluated relative to that position, but value itself derives from the difference between that starting, or reference, point and the amount of any positive or negative shift away from it" (McDermott, 1998, p. 28). As McDermott (1998) observes:

> In theoretical terms . . . people tend to be risk averse in the domain of gains and risk seeking in the domain of losses; this is the crux of prospect theory. In short, prospect theory predicts that domain affects risk propensity . . . losing hurts more than a comparable gain pleases . . . Loss aversion is exemplified by the endowment effect, whereby people value what they possess to a greater degree than they value an equally attractive alternative. This endowment bias makes equal trade unattractive. It also presents a bias toward the status quo in almost any negotiating context.
>
> (p. 29)

This determination of domain is inherently a subjective one, since individual policy makers may value certain outcomes (e.g., policy success, popularity, poll numbers) differently from one another—but prospect theory only needs to have knowledge of how policy makers perceive the domain (gains or losses) in order to predict their risk propensity (McDermott, 1998). In addition, prospect theory takes into account the fact that people assign different weights to the likelihood of certain probability outcomes. As McDermott (1998) observes, highly vivid, yet low probability events (e.g., being in a plane crash) tend to be over-weighted by people, while high or medium probability events (e.g., being in a car wreck) are subjectively under-weighted:

> The classic examples of this are lotteries and insurance. In lotteries, people are willing to take a sure loss, however small, for the essentially nonexistent chance of a huge gain. In this way, people can be risk seeking in gains when the probability of gain is low. In insurance, people are willing to take a sure loss in the present to prevent the small likelihood of a larger loss in the future. In this situation, people can be risk averse in losses when the probability of loss is small. In both these situations, expected utility models might not consider such behavior to be normative. However, prospect theory accounts for these discrepancies by noting the extreme (over)weight and attention that individuals give to small probabilities that potentially involve either huge gains (winning the lottery) or huge losses (losing your house in a fire). This phenomenon helps account for worst-case scenario planning.
>
> (pp. 31–32)

Translated to questions of international conflict and war, one would expect policy makers in nations to take far greater chances (and risk war far more often) to protect their current resources (e.g., national territory, economic relationships, etc.) than they would be in order to gain additional resources beyond what they currently control. In other words, they would be expected to be risk averse in the domain of gains and risk acceptant in the domain of losses. For deterrence, this suggests that the credibility of a threat made by a nation faced with losing its national sovereignty, territory, or very existence is far higher (and more believable) than threats made by states just seeking aggrandizement (more territory). Further, in crisis management terms, this suggests that the danger of war is greatest, and the risks likely to be taken by states more extreme, when a crisis threatens the current resources of the state (the status quo). At the same time, prospect theory poses a serious challenge to traditional realist, power politics formulations of international politics (Morgenthau, 1948), since it questions its main assumptions about power maximizing as the primary goal of states in their interactions with one another (McDermott, 1998). Instead, while states may seek to increase their own power resources when risks are low, they will focus first and foremost upon maintaining what they currently have (the status quo). Further, they will be less likely to go to war to obtain gains from other states when potential risks are high (be risk averse in the domain of gains), and be far more likely to go to war with other states when their own resources are threatened (be more risk acceptant in the domain of losses).

Accountability

Another interesting psychological concept that has implications for understanding international conflict is **accountability** (Tetlock, 1985). Specifically, accountability argues that political leaders will take greater risks and be more likely to engage in conflict the more they lack accountability to a higher power (i.e., a ruling coalition, a voting public, a military junta). Saddam Hussein, for example, answered (and was accountable) to no one domestically and could essentially do as he liked in terms of foreign or domestic policy. Since there was no accountability internally, one would expect him to engage in much riskier, more conflictual behavior towards other nations (such as Kuwait) than we would expect of leaders of more democratic nations who are more accountable to others (such as a voting public, a parliament or Congress, etc.). This basic notion of accountability underpins much of the current "democratic peace" argument—that democracies are inherently more peaceful (and less warlike) than autocracies—and is clearly useful in terms of understanding the psychology of international conflict (Hermann & Kegley, 1995).

Group Dynamics and Malfunctions of Process

Finally, malfunctions of group process or decision-making under stress have often been suggested to increase the likelihood of bad decisions or conflict (Janis 1972; Janis & Mann, 1977; Hermann, 1979; 't Hart 1994). Perhaps the most familiar argument regarding such group malfunctions under stress has been that of Irving Janis (1972) and his **groupthink** concept, presented in Chapter 4. As noted there, Janis argues that governmental policy groups, particularly at high levels, tend to be smaller groups that over time develop a pattern of interactions between group members that emphasize the maintenance of group cohesion, solidarity, and loyalty. While not necessarily a bad thing, this emphasis upon group cohesion can lead to faulty group decision processes, or **group malfunctions**. These faulty processes, which become far more pronounced and prevalent during the high stress conditions of crises, can lead groups to become even more insular and fall into patterns of decision making that increase the chances of conflict. As mentioned in Chapter 4, among the eight symptoms of groupthink listed by Janis are:

1. **The Illusion of Invulnerability**—where group members find a comfort zone within the group because of the psychological belief that there is safety in numbers. Ultimate responsibility for group decisions or actions is dispersed among the entire group, making no one individual ultimately *accountable* for the outcomes. Janis notes that this leads to a tendency towards the **risky shift**, or pattern in which groups tend to take riskier decisions (and more chances) than do individuals.

2. **Rationalization**—where group members rationalize (or explain away) information or opinions that do not support the dominant preexisting beliefs held by the group members.

3. **Belief in the Inherent Morality of the Group**—where group members share with one another the belief that they are making the best decisions possible, that they are trying to do the right thing, that they have a solid moral compass.

4. **Active Use of Stereotypes**—group members simplify reality and their information-processing through reliance upon use of stereotypes and other simplifying heuristics.

5. **Use of Direct Pressure on Dissenters**—where group members pressure individual group members who may disagree with the dominant view of the group not to rock the boat and go along with the group.

6. **Self-Censorship**—where dissenting group members, over time, cease to challenge or question the dominant group views due to the application of direct pressure upon them and a concern for group cohesion.

7. **Use of Mind-Guards**—self-appointed individuals within the group who seek to maintain the group's cohesion and morale by applying direct pressure to dissenters and preventing access of information or views to the group that might challenge its existing beliefs.

8. **The Illusion of Unanimity**—where group members come to believe that everyone in the group agrees with the dominant group view and supports their policy decisions because no one vocally objects. It is an illusion because of the use of direct pressure and the self-censorship of group members, who may well disagree with the group, but lack the will to object.

Janis (1972) argues that these group malfunctions, leading to groupthink by senior decision making groups, led to a number of historical **policy fiascoes** (or failures of policy). Examples of such fiascoes include: U.S. naval leaders' decision making prior to Pearl Harbor, the Kennedy administration's decision making surrounding the Bay of Pigs, the decision by General Douglas MacArthur to approach the Yalu River during the Korean War (thereby provoking Chinese intervention), and the decision by the Johnson administration to intervene in Vietnam in 1965. That Janis identifies only cases of war, or resort to force, as "policy fiascoes" in his book illustrates his strong normative bias against war ('t Hart, Stern, & Sundelius, 1997). However, regardless of the subjectivity of his overall analyses, Janis does make a useful point in observing that the interactional and decision dynamics within groups can sometimes lead policy makers to war. A more detailed discussion of group dynamics is presented in Chapter 4.

Applications of Political Psychology to Modern Security Studies—Deterrence as a Psychological Relationship and the Credibility of Threats

With the continuing proliferation of nuclear capabilities to states in the international system (i.e., Iran's increasingly advanced nuclear program and fissile material producing infrastructure, North Korea's continued nuclear testing, Pakistan and India's expanding arsenals), discussions about the resulting security environment inevitably turn towards whether nuclear deterrence increases or decreases interstate security and stability (Preston 2007/2009). What insights does political psychology have to offer regarding how we think about such modern security problems?

One example of the application of political psychology to security involves looking at a critical dimension of deterrence—the credibility of nuclear threats to opposing decision makers. Moreover, it involves the need to understand deterrence as a psychological relationship between individual policy makers. It requires us to recognize the *constraints* placed upon psychological variables by the *simplicity of the strategic situations* created by nuclear weapons across various contexts. It is an area that has often received only cursory attention within the security studies literature, and one previously utilized only by deterrence skeptics to criticize the concept. However, a more nuanced application of political psychology to the issue of deterrence can be equally useful in fleshing out the possible interactional dynamics within nuclear security relationships between states—especially since policy maker perceptions (regarding the nature of the situation, the type of interests (central or peripheral) at stake, their view of how opponents perceives their threats, etc.) are likely to be key to whether deterrence relationships will be effective or not.

As suggested earlier, the debate between deterrence advocates and skeptics often centered on epistemological disagreements between scholars over their rival's chosen theories or methodological approaches for studying deterrence. Critics pointed to the less than satisfactory treatment of psychological factors relating to deterrence within the security literature (Jervis, 1976; Lebow & Stein, 1989, 1990), which was primarily due to the dominance of rational-choice and game theory approaches in this scholarship (e.g., Zagare & Kilgour, 1993). Others note the dependence of much of the rational deterrence theory literature upon neo-realist, system-level arguments that tend to leave out subsystem or psychological factors—leading critics to note that a more useful theory would incorporate both systemic and subsystemic factors.[2]

In fact, real-life behavior by decision makers varies greatly from the rational model, and is neither as consistent nor predictable as implied by game theory approaches. Indeed, a typical definition of *perception of threat* as "the product of the estimated capability of the opponent's forces multiplied by the estimated probability that he will use them" fits nicely into rational-choice or game theory models, but is a poor approach to understanding or defining policy maker perceptions (cf. Singer, 1958; Legault & Lindsey, 1974). In order to understand the behavior of policy makers, one must develop an understanding of the psychological factors affecting the ways in which individuals perceive the world, process information, respond to stress, and make decisions (e.g., Wohlstetter, 1962; Jervis 1976; Hermann 1980b; Vertzberger 1990; Burke & Greenstein 1991; Khong 1992; 't Hart, Stern, & Sundelius 1997; Preston 2001, 2011; Helfstein 2012). Research by O'Reilly (2012), for example, has shown the importance of understanding policy maker perceptions about their surrounding environments (and perceived strategic context) in explaining decisions to pursue development of nuclear weapons. Similarly, Hymans (2006) has focused upon the role of identity and emotions in influencing nuclear proliferation decisions taken by policy makers. Only through understanding the subjective perceptions of decision makers does it become possible to determine both the effectiveness of deterrent threats and ascertain the nature of security relationships between states. As Johnson et al. (2002) observe:

> Deterrence, like all coercion, occurs in the mind of the adversary. Reality matters in deterrence only insofar as it affects the perceptions of those who will choose whether or not to be deterred . . . [Thus] assessments of the adversary's capabilities are of only limited predictive value unless accompanied by sound understanding of what the enemy values, how it perceives the conflict, and how it makes decisions—to name but a few of the critical variables.
>
> (p. 12)

But, since this involves exploring the complex realm of decision maker perceptions, characterized by substantial interplay between objective and subjective reality, much of the security studies literature has been content to avoid the issue, assume rationality, and emphasize bean-counting approaches instead. As a result, the primary focus has been mistakenly placed on the objective characteristics of the situation (i.e., size of forces, actual military balance, political situation, etc.) as seen by observers, rather than upon the subjective characteristics of the situation as perceived by the decision makers themselves—which actually governs their behavior. These subjective perceptions of reality held by leaders provide the basis for strategic decisions and shape their beliefs regarding the credibility of opponents' nuclear threats or forces. And, despite Lebow and Stein's (1989, p. 224) contention that rational deterrence theories are theories "about nonexistent decision makers operating in nonexistent environments," and other epistemological critiques made by political psychologists regarding rational choice, neo-realist, or game theory approaches, *it is important to note that one can make very strong psychological arguments IN FAVOR OF deterrence and why it should work as well.*

For example, Tetlock et al. (1991) provide a useful overview of many of the psychological factors bearing on the issue of nuclear deterrence and find that their impact upon deterrence effectiveness or success is variable, and not predictably negative in all contexts. Moreover, one does not need to adopt the same conception of rationality employed in rational choice models for deterrence to remain a valid concept. As Johnson et al. (2002) note:

> Because coercion depends on the adversary weighing the expected results of several courses of action and then choosing the more

attractive one, it presumes that policy decisions are made with some degree of rationality. However, the adversary need not behave with perfect rationality for coercion to be applicable, its behavior simply must not be totally irrational . . . In practice, no state acts perfectly rational, stemming from such factors as incomplete information, limited time to make decisions, bureaucratic politics and organizational processes, and leaders' personalities. Yet states (and significant non-state political entities) rarely act in ways that appear truly unreasoning on close analysis. It is far more common for states' actions to be branded as irrational when they are actually being driven by logical and consistent sets of preferences, but these are not well understood by others.

(pp. 17–18)

In fact, deterrence is best understood as a *psychological relationship* (between deterrer and deterree), in which notions like the "credibility of the threat," "attentiveness to signaling," "resolve," "willingness to take risks," "degree to which central or peripheral interests are challenged," or even the basic "awareness of the overall security environment (or military situation) in a given situational context" *are almost completely dependent upon the individual psychologies of the rival policy makers.* As such, deterrence becomes a contingent variable, whose effectiveness is dependent upon both the psychological characteristics of the policy makers involved *AND the structural clarity of the situation created by the absolute nature of the destructiveness of nuclear weapons.* This latter element serves as a constraint upon the impact of individual psychologies upon decision making and serves to clearly distinguish nuclear from conventional deterrence contexts.

Thus, while nuclear deterrence relationships, if properly structured, can be expected to be highly robust and reliable in preventing conflicts—because it is a *psychological* relationship between human beings, it can never be expected to function perfectly across all situational contexts. But, rather than use this argument, as many political psychologists have done, to suggest deterrence to be an unsound or ineffectual policy approach, we need to place this concept into its proper perspective. Just because something *could* potentially fail doesn't mean that it will, especially with any frequency, and in the case of nuclear deterrence, the empirical evidence to date suggests a highly reliable and robust system. The same psychological problems or malfunctions routinely associated by deterrence critics apply equally to any other policy approach one could imagine (e.g., conventional deterrence, diplomacy, sanctions, etc.), all of which have been linked in the last century alone to recourse to very costly wars.[3] Yet, human beings do *generally* make reasonably sound, reasonably rational decisions—especially when the stakes are high and there is little room for ambiguity regarding situational outcomes. In this regard, *nuclear deterrence relationships represent special cases that are not easily compared to fundamentally different kinds of policy contexts* (such as conventional deterrence). Indeed, extrapolating conventional deterrence processes and outcomes to hypothetical nuclear ones (as many deterrence skeptics have done) is as useful for determining the taste of an orange as eating an apple. Instead of placing unrealistic and unfair performance standards upon deterrence, we should recognize that it is like any other policy or strategy—dependent upon the perceptions of policy makers and the constraints on their actions for its success.

On a practical level, one reason why the importance of the psychological characteristics of *individual* policy makers upon determining the effectiveness of deterrence (or other types of security relationships) has been given short attention by scholars is the fact that one cannot (in the absence of unrealistic assumptions about "rational-choice"-type actors) develop broad, general security frameworks that apply to all possible decision makers across all country and cultural contexts. Though it is laudable to seek grand, general theories on security and simple formulations of deterrence relationships, this is—given the central importance of *individual* policy makers in the process—simply unworkable and inappropriate in this context. We are working with social science, not natural science—and the *psychology of individual decision makers*, within or across nations, and how they perceive their security environments, vary drastically from one another. It would be foolish indeed, for example, to assume that Kim Jong-Un, Bashar al-Assad, George W. Bush, Angela Merkel, Barack Obama, Vladimir Putin, Ayatollah Khameini, or any number of other world leaders perceive the world, process information, possess belief systems, face political constraints, or make decisions in the same manner (Hermann et al., 2001). Who the leaders are and what they are like as individuals makes a tremendous difference in determining what a nation's security policies will be, how they will perceive risk and threat, and what limitations they might believe exist in either their own capabilities or in the environment itself. Indeed, Keller (2005) observed, for example, that strongly nationalistic leaders who were distrustful of others were far more likely to ignore domestic constraints against the use of force than leaders with the opposite characteristics. Mumford (2006; Mumford et al., 2007) found that the more ideological leaders were, in terms of their exercising influence based on the articulation of distinct, powerful

OBJECTIVE THREAT MATRIX
(characteristics of the threat environment)

Central vs. peripheral interests threatened

Extremity of potential responses
(believable or incredible)

Capabilities of WMD arsenal

Survivability of WMD arsenal

Contestability of threatened/potential damage
- NMD/TMD
- Civil defense or prevention options
- Preemptive options

Internal or external constraints on behavior (acceptability of options)
- Legitimate vs. nonlegitimate actor
- Self-defense vs. aggression
- Democratic vs. authoritarian regime
- Accountability vs. nonaccountability

Policy-maker filters

- Perceptions of policy makers issuing threat or contemplating action re: character of threat environment
- Perceptions of targeted policy makers re: character of threat environment
- Political/strategic needs or objectives of sought by individual policy makers

Resulting security relationships

Figure 13.3 Individual Policy Maker Filters

ideologies, the greater their propensity for resorting to extreme violence. From group effects to individual characteristics, many factors influence how policy makers perceive their threat environments and their willingness to take risks or resort to violence. Clearly, political psychology has much to say about international conflict and the resort to war. In Figure 13.3, the importance of these individual policy maker filters are emphasized, along with the notion that *the actual security relationships between states rest in the nexus between the objective capabilities/characteristics of the arsenals and the subjective perceptions of this reality by the policy makers.*

CONCLUSION

Throughout this chapter, numerous examples of how political psychological approaches have been applied to the study of international security and conflict in political science have been provided—ranging from the security dilemma, to deterrence and prospect theories, to the impact of group dynamics. Obviously, this brief review merely scratches the surface of this wide-ranging security literature and is by no means intended to be exhaustive. Our task was not to replicate a national security textbook, but to provide students with a useful insight into how psychological approaches have been employed to study important political questions. Further, it should be noted that many of the literatures discussed elsewhere in this textbook, such as the development of social identity, stereotypes, ethnic conflict, etc., can also usefully be applied to the study of international security and conflict. Indeed, psychological approaches have much to offer as we continue to advance our understanding of this important subject.

Topics, Theories/Explanations, and Cases in Chapter 13

Topics	Theories/Explanations	Cases
Why war?	Psychology of fear and misperception	Peloponnesian War World War I
	Security dilemma	
Security dilemma	Fundamental attribution error	Cold War
	Inherent bad-faith	
	Spiral process	
Psychology of deterrence	Cognitive rigidity	Cold War, Iraq protracted crisis; general and immediate deterrence; game of chicken
	Belief perseverance	
	Spiral model	
Problem representation	Framing	Vietnam analogy
	Analogical reasoning	Munich analogy
	Prospect theory	Guns of August analogy
Accountability Groupthink	Group malfunctions	
	Stress	
	Eight symptoms of groupthink	

Key Terms

accountability

analogy

deterrence

group malfunctions

groupthink

Guns of August analogy

Munich analogy

policy fiascoes

protracted crisis approach

prospect theory

risky shifts

security dilemma

Vietnam analogy

Suggestions for Further Reading

Overviews of the Security Literature

Haftendorn, H. (1991). The security puzzle: Theory-building and discipline-building in international security. *International Studies Quarterly, 35*, 3–17.

Krause, K., & Williams, M. C. (1996). Broadening the agenda of security studies: Politics and methods. *Mershon International Studies Review, 40*, 229–254.

Walt, S. M. (1991). The renaissance of security studies. *International Studies Quarterly, 35*, 211–239.

Rational-Choice or Game Theory Approaches

Bilgin, P. (2003). Individual and societal dimensions of security. *International Studies Review, 5*(2), 203–222.

Brams, S. J. (1985). *Superpower games: Applying game theory to superpower conflict*. New Haven, CT: Yale University Press.

Lantis, J. S. (2002). Strategic culture and national security policy. *International Studies Review, 4*(3), 87–113.

Walt, S. M. (1999). Rigor or rigor mortis? Rational choice and security studies. *International Security, 23*, 5–48.

Other Treatments of Security or Deterrence

Brody, B. (1973). *War & politics*. New York: Macmillan.

Mearsheimer, J. J. (1983). *Conventional deterrence*. Ithaca, NY: Cornell University Press.

Powell, R. (1990). *Nuclear deterrence theory: The search for credibility*. New York: Cambridge University Press.

Preston, T. (2007/2009). *From lambs to lions: Future security relationships in a world of biological and nuclear weapons*. Boulder, CO: Rowman & Littlefield.

Schelling, T. (1960/1980). *The strategy of conflict*. London: Oxford University Press.

Schelling, T. (1966). *Arms and influence*. New Haven: Yale University Press.

Sun Tzu. *The art of war*.

Thucydides. *The history of the Peloponnesian war*.

Von Clausewitz, C. *On war*.

Notes

1. See Mearsheimer (1983) for more on wars of attrition and other military strategies.
2. Feaver, P.D. (1992/1993). Command and control in emerging nuclear nations, *International Security 17*(3), 179.
3. Some of the critics of nuclear deterrence using political psychological arguments at times seem to be using a logic that would equally suggest one shouldn't fly on passenger airplanes (because of the potential for catastrophic failure), but rather drive cars everywhere (since the potential for large loss of life in any one incident is smaller). Yet, as we know, flying is far and away the statistically safer means of travel—despite its technical and organizational complexity and potential for catastrophic failure. Indeed, the fatalities from automobile accidents each year dwarf even the very worst years for aviation crashes. Nuclear deterrence (no wars or use at all over last 50 years) versus conventional deterrence (60–70 million killed over last 50 years) are empirically even more dissimilar.

Chapter 14

CONFLICT RESOLUTION AND RECONCILIATION

In the previous chapters on race, ethnicity, and nationalism, we discussed the psychological underpinnings of conflict and illustrated these with numerous case studies. This chapter focuses on conflict avoidance and resolution strategies. It covers conflict resolution strategies that can be used to reconcile groups that have been engaged in various forms of conflict.

Reconciliation after mass violence and killing is very difficult. **Reconciliation** can be defined as "mutual acceptance by groups of each other. The essence of reconciliation is a changed psychological orientation toward the other" (Staub, 2006, p. 868). Reconciliation and **forgiveness** are interrelated. Forgiveness involves the restoration of a positive relationship between perpetrator and victim wherein negative emotions toward the perpetrator are replaced with positive emotions and prosocial behavior (Staub, 2006; Cehajic, Brown, & Castano, 2008). Unlike reconciliation, forgiveness is regarded as one-sided in that the victim forgives the perpetrator. Staub (2006) argues that forgiveness without regret on the part of the perpetrator can have harmful effects: "Victimization creates wounds, as well as an imbalance in the relationship between victims and perpetrators. It diminishes the status of the former in relation to the latter, and also in relations to other, nonvictimized people" (2006, p. 886). In other words, the perpetrator gets away with what he or she has done. On the other hand, forgiveness may make perpetrators less likely to justify their victimization of others (Cehajic, Brown, & Castano, 2008).

By definition, victims, perpetrators, and bystanders must be involved in the reconciliation process. Each has group has its own difficulty reaching the point where it is amenable to reconciliation. Victims have been traumatized, abandoned by, and often brutalized by, people they considered neighbors, friends, even relatives. Many victims suffer from the chronic effects of trauma. Studies of trauma-induced stress show a number of different patterns of psychological and behavioral reactions. Trauma produces hypervigilance, chronic anxiety, insomnia, nightmares when sleep is possible, and a variety of tension related physical problems (Herman, 1992; Gilligan, 1997). People are both numbed and angered by violence and both reactions, when persistent, can lead to Post Traumatic Stress Disorder (PTSD) (Weingarten, 2004). Life is constricted in the sense that daily survival is the focus of victims of trauma, and their sense of the future is surviving until tomorrow. People who have survived genocide also experience a loss of their past. Isolation and fear make an acknowledgment of their past lives intolerably painful, so they disassociate themselves from them (Herman, 1992). Chronic trauma also disempowers people so that they become incapable of planning actions that would change their circumstances, take advantage of opportunities, make opportunities, and offer an alternative future. The trauma of experiencing violence can distort memory to the extent that the experiences are remembered "without reference to time and place. Thus when they are retrieved, it is as if they are happening in the present. They are experienced as a contemporary terror" (Weingarten, 2004, p. 49). Given these wounds, it is easy to see that victims would be reluctant to enter into reconciliation contexts. Having strong institutional support to make them feel safe is crucial.

Meanwhile, although one would expect perpetrators to feel guilty, they often do not. They often continue to see their victims through the negative, dehumanizing stereotypes that led them to commit the violence in the first place. They often continue to believe that what they did was the right thing to do, and they minimize the victims' suffering (Baumeister, 1997; Cohen, 2001; Staub, 2006). Ironically, perpetrators of violence also can experience trauma, and suffer similar ill effects (MacNair, 2005; Staub, 2006). Bystanders often turn away from victims, refusing to acknowledge what happened, and distancing themselves from those who suffered (Cohen, 2001; Staub, 2006). Some perpetrators and bystanders do feel guilt and remorse. Neither are pleasant emotions, and they often result in a desire to compensate the victims in some manner (Klandermans, Werner, & van Doorn, 2008).

In postconflict situations, punishment for crimes against humanity has always been part of the reconciliation process. The trials of the Nazi leadership, the identification of Bosnian Serbs guilty of mass murder, the trials of Rwanda's killers, and the execution of Timothy McVeigh all illustrate the importance attached to punishment by the international community and by victims of the violence. Punishment also is supposed to act as a deterrent to others who would commit such acts. But, at some point, punishment stops, and conflict resolution and reconciliation require returning to the source of the conflict to begin with.

Many studies of conflicts, such as those discussed in the previous chapters, draw upon social identity and human needs theories to explain the conflicts and to propose methods of prevention, resolution, and reconciliation. From this perspective, conflict arises in societies because basic human needs aren't being met, whether those needs are physical and objective, or psychological and subjective. If one's primary identity groups are threatened, then a basic need for safety, through higher needs such as self-esteem, are not being met. As Staub (2000) argues:

> Economic problems, political conflict, and disorganization, and intense and rapid social change (separately or in combination) not only have material effects, but also profoundly frustrate basic human needs . . . To satisfy needs for identity and connection, people often turn to a group. They elevate the group . . . by psychologically or physically diminishing other groups. They scapegoat another group for life problems, which protects their identity, strengthens connection

within the group, and provides a psychologically useful (even if false) understanding of events

(pp. 369–370)

Every group we have considered in the previous chapters reflects these dynamics. Recognizing that these groups are not always going to be stopped before they commit violent actions, what can be done to promote reconciliation afterward? A crucial first step in conflict resolution in the aftermath of violence is for people to feel safe. Once the fighting has stopped, people still have highly charged emotions about other groups, and they will quite reasonably fear that their own safety is still in jeopardy. Even after the fighting has stopped, individuals and groups do not simply forgive and move on. There is usually distrust of intentions of the other groups involved in the conflict. This makes peace-building—that is, reconstructing a new peaceful society—very difficult. The healing process can be long and tenuous. Leaders who have skills are crucial to this effort, enabling them to build coalitions and calm fears.

WAR TRIBUNALS

Reconciliation is necessary to prevent violence from becoming cyclical, with one group seeking violent revenge against another. In addition to punishment, reconciliation requires recognition of the humanity of one another, forgiveness, and the reestablishment of trust. Victims must have an audience that acknowledges their trauma. Perpetrators must explain their actions, which often results in a description of the perceptions of their reality and their sense of mistreatment, and must express contrition. There is then an outlet for understanding for the victims, however unpalatable that understanding may be. In the process, victims recognize that what happened to them is not a result of their own inhumanity (Staub, 2000).

A number of methods have been used in the aftermath of conflict to promote resolution and reconciliation. No approach is perfect, and as Minow (1998) notes, "at best they can only seek a path between too much memory and too much forgetting" (p. 4). Some, in fact many, societies choose not to confront the past, to try to forget the horrors they experienced and to move on. But for others, this is too much forgetting, and they employ approaches ranging from trials and purges, wherein at least some of the perpetrators are put on trial for crimes against humanity and others are removed from positions of authority. This is what happened in Nuremburg after World War II, when Nazi leaders were tried. It was not until nearly 50 years later that another round of international trials for crimes against humanity was established. In 1993 and 1994, the United Nations established war crimes tribunals for Yugoslavia and Rwanda, respectively. The International Court at the Hague indicted 76 people for human rights abuses during the war in Bosnia. The most famous person was Slobodan Milošević himself, who was indicted in 1999 and finally surrendered in 2004. He died in 2006 before a verdict was delivered. Those accused of committing acts of genocide in Rwanda were tried in Arusha, Tanzania, at the International Crimes Tribunal for Rwanda. Sixty-two people were indicated for the Rwandan genocide.

The United Nations tribunals for Rwanda continue. (Updates can be found at http://69.94.11.53/.) The United Nations also established a permanent International Criminal Court in 2002, which the United States does not support. The International Criminal Court is different from the International Court of Justice, which settles disputes between countries. The court has opened up investigations into the situations in Northern Uganda, Democratic Republic of Congo, the Central African Republic, and Darfur, Sudan. The trials of Saddam Hussein and other members of his regime were handled by the Iraqi government. Saddam Hussein, and many other individuals were put on trial by the Iraqi Higher Tribunal (Iraqi Higher Criminal Court) for crimes committed during his rule. In November 2006, he and two other defendants were sentenced to death by hanging for their role in the 1982 murder, torture, and incarceration of individuals in the Shiite town of Dujail. Hussein was executed in December 2006.

War crimes trials have a number of criticisms. The Nuremberg Trials, conducted by the International Military Tribunal, have been criticized for being little more than vengeance by the victors of World War II. The laws, procedures, and judges were all selected by the allies, and the victorious allies, who had committed some horrifying acts of violence against civilians, including the firebombing of Dresden and the atomic bombing of Hiroshima and Nagasaki, were not held accountable for their actions. The crimes defendants were accused of were retroactive, that is, they were not clearly crimes at the time of their commission. The Nuremberg trials were criticized for going too far and for not going far enough. There were 85,882 cases prosecuted, but only 7,000 convictions. Some argued that these individuals should not be held accountable for actions conducted by a state government; others noted that putting only 185 people on trial could hardly be considered enough.

War crimes trials being held today are less susceptible to criticism that the laws and procedures are arbitrary because, in the years since the establishment of the United Nations, there have been international agreements concerning what constitutes genocide and violations of human rights. The United Nations has built upon the Nuremberg trials and used them as precedents for the codification of international laws. The Hague and Geneva Conventions are also important legal statements. These developments help address the retroactivity issue. Now, certain actions have been deemed crimes, in accordance with international laws agreed to by an international organization and its members. The International Court also establishes procedures for trials. Nevertheless, the complaint remains that participants in violence are not treated equally. For example, many Serbs maintain that Croats and Muslims who committed atrocities against Serbs during the Yugoslavian wars are not pursued as vigorously as Serbs are. In addition, the ongoing war crimes trials only seek to indict and try the commanders who gave orders, not those who actually committed the violence, reasoning that the latter were only following orders and would have been shot had they disobeyed. This gives little satisfaction to victims' families, however.

In addition to international trials, individual governments have held trials to bring to justice people who participate in atrocities and state terror. Trials have been held in Argentina, Chile, Brazil, and in several Eastern European countries after the fall of communist regimes there. However, it is not always easy to carry out effective trials. In both Chile and Argentina, for example, the return to democracy was done under the watchful gaze of the military. Government seeking to punish those who commit politically motivated crimes must be in control of the situation, and, in both of these cases, the military could conceivably act again to overthrow the civilian governments. Therefore, in Argentina, after the return to civilian rule in 1982, the newly elected president, Raul Alfonsin, ordered nine top-level military officers to be tried, five of whom were convicted. Middle and junior ranking officers were not tried. His successor, President Carlos Menem, fearful of the military and wanting officers to close the past, pardoned the officers and forbade future trials, but efforts to bring these officers to accountability did not stop. In 1997, for example, an Argentine lawyer, representing 13 families of victims who were disappeared, used the courts to try to bypass that prohibition, by maintaining that the pardons of officers was illegal, because the kidnapping of the victims is continuing and that they were never found. In March 2001, an Argentine judge struck down the amnesty laws that protected middle-level and junior officers from prosecution. In addition, Spain and France are both trying to use legal means to punish Argentine perpetrators of violence against their citizens, such as the "flying nuns," who were captured and disappeared by the military regime. To carry out trials, governments and societies must have the power and will to punish those responsible. However, the trials will never be sufficient to punish everyone in every case, particularly in situations like Rwanda, where so many people were involved in the slaughter of Tutsis. Moreover, trials do not produce reconciliation. To achieve this, people must admit their wrongdoing, but often during trials people will not admit wrongdoing. For example, both Slobodan Milošević and Saddam Hussein both claimed they were innocent of any crimes.

DIALOGUE AND TRUTH AND RECONCILIATION COMMISSIONS

There are different techniques for recovering from violence. Two of these techniques are **dialogue** and the **truth and reconciliation commission**.

Dialogue is a process by which individuals engage with each other in an open forum in order to speak about their side of the story and to also hear the side of others. Dialogue can be used to promote understanding between racial groups. In 1998 President Clinton released *One America in the 21st Century: The President's Initiative on Race*. This document dialogue is described as "a forum that draws participants from as many parts of the community as possible to exchange information face-to-face, share personal stories and experiences, honestly express perspectives, clarify viewpoints, and develop solutions to community concerns" (p. 1). In a document outlining this approach, there are four phases "that have proven useful in moving participants through a natural process from sharing individual experiences to committing to collective action. Whether meeting for one dialogue session or a series of sessions, participants move through all four phases, exploring and building on shared experiences" (p. 11).

The first phase sets the tone and explores the question *Who Are We?* through the sharing of personal stories. The second phase helps participants understand *Where Are We?* through a deeper exploration of personal and shared racial history in the community. During the third phase, participants develop a vision for the community, in response to the question *Where Do We Want to Be?* In the fourth phase, participants answer the question, *What Will We Do As Individuals and With Others To Make a Difference?* Often, they discover shared interests and start working together on specific projects (p. 11).

Truth and reconciliation commissions are designed to reveal the truths of political violence, to let the revelation of truth allow the victims or their survivors to grieve, and to achieve some measure of reconciliation and forgiveness. Truth commissions gather evidence, determine accountability, and often recommend policies for the treatment of victims and perpetrators. As Rigby (2001) notes:

> Whereas trials and purges are aimed at punishing the perpetrators of crimes against their citizens, the prime concern of the truth commission approach is with the victims. The aim it to identify them, to acknowledge them and the wrongs done to them, and to arrive at appropriate compensation.
>
> (p. 6)

Truth and reconciliation commissions were established in a number of countries following periods of massive violations of human rights. Argentina, Chile, El Salvador, and South Africa have all used truth and reconciliation commissions. Truth commissions are often used in situations in which the government replacing the power holders who committed the acts of violence is not powerful or stable enough to challenge all of those agents. This was the case in Argentina, as noted, where the new civilian government could not prosecute all of the military officers responsible for the repression. The military made it clear that this would not be tolerated. Argentina's truth commission was established in 1983 and was called the National Commission on Disappeared People. Its primary mission was to discover what happened to those who disappeared and where their remains could be found. It ultimately produced a 50,000-page report called *Nunca Mas* (Never Again), as well as a documentary. However, as Rigby (2001) argues,

> To many of the relatives and friends of the victims, who were what can be termed secondary victims of the military junta, the report was a whitewash. They know who the victims were: what they wanted was the names of those who had tortured, raped, and killed them.
>
> (pp. 69–70)

Another reason for the use of truth and reconciliation commissions is that often the number of people involved in one way or another with the commission of violence is so great that the prosecutorial approach would only serve to make impossible reconciliation and the reconstruction of a working political and social system. Guilt and blame are also often difficult to discern.

How does one condemn a person who breaks under torture, turns into an informant, and who, then, in that role, causes someone else to be tortured? Truth and reconciliation commissions are also useful in trading amnesty for information about what happened to whom. In many cases, families of victims have no idea what happened to their loved ones, and, when perpetrators of violence are granted amnesty, they are more likely to produce vital information about the fates of victims. They may also provide details on the conduct of violence, including who had what kind of decision-making authority. Finally, truth and reconciliation commissions do serve the fundamental needs of victims and their families to have an audience willing to listen to their accounts and acknowledge publicly the wrongs done to them.

The South African Truth and Reconciliation Commission (TRC), which lasted from 1996–1998, is perhaps the most famous example. During apartheid, tremendous violations of human rights took place, as Whites attempted to suppress the desires of Black South Africans for equality. As shown in the chapter on race, after years of struggle, the White power structure finally dismantled the apartheid state through a negotiated process, and free elections were held. The last apartheid-era White president, F. W. de Klerk, made it clear during the negotiations that a peaceful transition from apartheid to democracy would not be possible if trials were in conducted to punish members of the apartheid establishment. Nelson Mandela, who was the leader of the ANC resistance movement, and who had been held prisoner by the government for 27 years, was elected to hold the office of the president in the new democratic government. The new government approved a law called the Promotion of National Unity and Reconciliation Act, in 1995, thus establishing the TRC. The TRC was headed by another hero of the anti-apartheid resistance, Archbishop Desmond Tutu. The TRC aspired for transparency in its deliberations and attempted therefore to be very public and open in procedures, gathering of testimony, and decision making. The TRC gathered testimony from thousands of victims, and included testimony from those abused by the resistance, as well as by the regime. It was also empowered to grant amnesty to perpetrators of violence who applied for amnesty and confessed about what they did. In this way, information was obtained about victims and the chain of command, and often perpetrators apologized to victims. Not all victims testified publicly, but those who were willing to do so had their testimonies broadcast on radio and television and are available on TRC's website (http://www.doj.gov.za/trc/). For victims, the experience can be very therapeutic (Minow, 1998).

A centrally important element in the South African TRC was the amnesty condition. Unlike Argentina, there was no blanket amnesty. Instead, perpetrators had to apply for amnesty and admit to their actions. Amnesty was not granted until the admission of guilt was evaluated, to determine that the actions were politically motivated, rather than personal or criminal. They had a limited time in which to do this, and those who refused were susceptible to criminal prosecution. In the end, over 8,000 people asked for amnesty.

In South Africa, the human rights abuses were mostly done by the members of the government's security forces. There were also many bystanders—White people who benefited from the apartheid system, but who had not committed human rights abuses themselves. In order to enable these people to admit guilt and shame for indirect complicity, "and to extend the domain of truth telling beyond the confines of the Commission hearing, a Reconciliation Register was opened, with books kept a various locations where people could go and sign them as a personal symbol of regret for their past culpability and commitment to a new beginning" (Rigby, 2001, p. 130).

Do truth commissions accomplish their goals? In some respects, they do. Victims get an opportunity to express their outrage, and it is heard. Families find out what happened to their lost loved ones, and a country learns about the systems of abuse, that is, who ordered what, when and why. But many victims and their relatives object to amnesty for perpetrators and resent the fact that those individuals are free to go on with life. Then there is the question of what the truth is. It is not always clear cut, nor is it immune to wide variations in perceptions. In fact, the South African TRC's final report discussed four truths: factual, personal, social, and healing. Factual is just that, objective, measurable truth; personal is the victims' stories; social is the discussion of conflicting interpretations of what happened; and healing is reconciliation and compensation (Cohen, 2001; Tepperman, 2002).

There is also the question about what reconciliation really is and whether truth commissions can achieve it. Reconciliation is usually thought to occur when there is a willingness to forgive, to tolerate one another, and to live together in harmony in the future. Yet, in South Africa, public opinion polls taken after the TRC finished found that "two thirds of South Africans felt the commission's revelations had only made them angrier and contributed to a worsening of race relations" (Tepperman, 2002, p. 134). It is also necessary to question who considers whom to be a victim. Normally, we think of those who suffered the abuse as victims, and the perpetrators need to accept responsibility to make amends. But it is quite likely that, although perpetrators apologize, other perpetrators see themselves as victims, persecuted by truth commissions, persecuted for only doing their jobs, or persecuted for having tried to save the country. As Minow (1998) puts it, "perhaps acknowledgement of wrongs is most helpful to the victimized and the entire society when it comes from perpetrators, yet no sincere acknowledgement can be ordered or force" (p. 76).

In Rwanda, a combination of tactics has been used to advance punishment and reconciliation. The United Nations International Criminal Tribunal for Rwanda (the ICTR), based in Arusha, Tanzania, handles the cases of those accused of the most horrific actions, particularly those who planned the genocide. However, there has been much criticism of the ICTR for incompetence, lack of adequate progress and resources, and corruption. Other cases have been brought to trial through the Rwandan national criminal justice system. This too has been problematic. After the genocide it was estimated that there were just 10 lawyers left in the country (Zorbas, 2008). The legal system had to be rebuilt and as a result, many thousands of accused prisoners languished in miserable conditions in prison awaiting trial.

A third strategy used in Rwanda is the revival of a traditional, grassroots court called *Gacaca*. The *Gacaca* system is similar to the South African Truth and Reconciliation system in that victims and perpetrators gather in a public forum, often a village center, and the victims tell their stories and the accused expresses an admission of guilt and an apology. However, there are some provisions in the process that have been criticized. As Zorbas notes, "under these provisions, if someone confesses before being denounced, he or she is liable for a substantial decrease in length of the sentence. However, confessions are only acceptable if they include 1) all information about the crime, 2) an apology, and 3) *the incrimination of one's co-conspirators*. This system of incrimination creates rife conditions for vendetta settling; some estimate that an additional 200,000 people could see themselves accused and imprisoned for genocide-related crimes" (2004, pp. 36–37). Nevertheless, public response to the *Gacaca* courts appears to be positive (Zorbas, 2008). There are approximately 10,000 of these courts in Rwanda, and they will be the sites of reconciliation for most Rwandans. By the end of 2007, these courts had tried over one million cases, beginning with property-related cases, torture, and incitement, and then in 2007 taking on rape, attempted murder, and murder. About 30% of the accused have been acquitted (Global Security, 2008).

The Rwandan government has also established a Unity and Reconciliation Commission and has encouraged the development of an overarching Rwandan identity. Other local level efforts to promote reconciliation are widespread, such as coffee cooperatives that bring Tutsi and Hutu together in collaboration in an economic project that brings financial rewards to all (Tobias, 2008). But the government has also used repressive measures, in particular, forbidding people to call themselves Tutsi or Hutu and making "divisionism," or the discussion of differences between Tutsis and Hutus, a crime. This is contrary to the dialogue goals of talking through identity issues.

INTEGRATION STRATEGIES

Over the long term, whether discussing racial or ethnic/national separation and conflict, integration and the elimination of inequalities and their causes have long been considered essential to conflict resolution and avoidance. Integration without discrimination is really the only practical solution in many cases, because separation is not an option. In the following sections, we discuss two types of integration strategies: shared sovereignty and utilitarian. A central feature of these conflicts is fear—the development of the security dilemma wherein different identity groups (racial, ethnic, national) fear that they will lose out in competition for power and justice, fear the destruction of their group as an identity group, or even fear for their very existence. People mobilize to defend themselves against perceived threats by other groups. A good example of this is in Northern Ireland, the Ulster Defense Association, a Protestant paramilitary organization that refuses to decommission its weapons. In the view of the leaders of the organization, they still face threats from the groups that they formed to fight against after the beginning of the "Troubles" in 1969. While some Republican groups are still active, the UDA's biggest competitor, the Provisional Irish Republican Army, decommissioned its weapons and entered the peace process. In fact, Martin McGuiness, a key leader in the group, is second minister in the Northern Ireland Assembly. This heightens the threat even more because the UDA perceives that the Republican goal of a united Ireland can be orchestrated from within the government. The identity of the UDA is being threatened because they are being asked to disarm from the very state they sought to remain a part of. This creates an identity crisis within the group, and their response has been to dig in their heels and refuse to become a political player in the postconflict process.

Ultimately, the best long-term solution to these conflicts is the development of an overarching common identity among the groups. "Yes, I am White and you are Black, but we are both Americans first and can live together harmoniously" or "I am Ibo and you are Hausa, but we are both Nigerians first and can live together harmoniously." An ideal integration strategy to achieve this end would be a plan for developing a population-wide, first-intensity identification with the territorial community, for example, with America, or Nigeria, or Guatemala. Indeed this is the goal of the peace process in Guatemala: to establish a common and multifaceted Guatemalan identity that incorporates both ladino and Mayan culture, rather than ladino alone. But in some cases, the development of an overarching identity, which receives all groups' primary and most intense loyalty, is neither desirable nor possible. Often, distrust is too high or people do not want to be assimilated into a dominant culture and lose their cultural uniqueness. Nevertheless, integration strategies can be developed to resolve conflict in those cases as well. To be successful, an integration strategy requires eliminating racial or ethnic prejudice and the accompanying structural (legal, social) factors that maintain it.

Successful integration strategies require a number of political and psychological components. Psychologically, integration strategies would have to provide different identity groups in a polity with options for **social mobility** and **social creativity**. This way the different groups can maintain their primary identity and do not need to rely on having a common third identity in order to get along. Integration strategies need to establish an environment in which groups feel secure that their identities are not threatened. The greater the disparity in cultural, religious, and racial characteristics, the more complicated the problem. A multifaceted formula is needed here, in which different group characteristics are looked at positively when comparisons are made. When **social comparisons** are different, but equally positive, conflict can be avoided (van den Heuvel & Meertens, 1989). For example, in the United States, the "Black is beautiful" campaign during the civil rights movement and other more current efforts to promote multiculturalism attempt to recognize cultural and racial differences and to celebrate those differences as equally valuable and equally American.

A second psychological element involves a need to address stereotypes and social distance among groups. Possibly most important in this process is addressing perceptions of group inferiority and superiority. Breaking such stereotypes and images is central to a workable integration strategy. The objective should be the replacement of a highly simplified and negative view of the other group with a far more complex and nonjudgmental view. This requires acceptance of, and respect for, group differences and changed expectations about other group members' behavior (Hewstone, 1989; van den Heuvel & Meertens, 1989). An early idea about how to do this was the **contact hypothesis**, which proposed increasing intergroup contact, and exposing people to the complexity of group members and thereby providing information that breaks down stereotypes. But the contact hypothesis works only in an environment or institutional context that is supportive, where contact can be on-going, and in which groups are equal in status (Allport, 1954; Brewer & Brown, 1998; Fiske, 1998). A number of studies note that increased contact may merely lead people to assume that the member of another group who appears to be different from the stereotypical members is simply atypical of the group, meaning that the stereotype of the group will stand, but a particular known individual will be seen as different, not like the others (Brewer & Miller, 1984; Hewstone & Brown, 1986; Mackie & Hamilton, 1993).

The political or policy aspect of integration strategies would have to meet these psychological requirements. Policies would have to address the particular needs, demands, and alternatives regarding conflicting groups' capability, power, and rewards accrued within the political system. Mechanisms used for this part of an integration strategy include supplying multiple channels for acquiring power, so that no group dominates limited channels; promote intragroup, rather than intergroup conflict; policies that promote intergroup cooperation; policies that encourage cross-group alignments based on interests, rather than on group identity; and policies that reduce various kinds of disparities between groups, thereby reducing dissatisfaction (Horowitz, 1985). Politically, the strategy has to be tuned to the distribution of power among groups. Identity groups often vary greatly in terms of perceived power and influence in their political systems. Those who see themselves as strong enough to possibly achieve independence would only be satisfied with institutional and social conditions offering broad autonomy just short of independence. At the other end of the scale are groups far too weak to achieve independence and, for these groups, integration in the form of assurances of equality with other groups, rather than autonomy, would be satisfactory.

Shared sovereignty and utilitarian strategies are good examples of the importance of blending political structures, institutions, and distribution of power with psychological patterns. The strategies recognize that identities are not negotiable, but that interests are (Burton, 1990; Gurr, 1994; Rothman & Olson, 2001).

SHARED SOVEREIGNTY STRATEGIES

The first type of integration strategy considered here is one in which a group is given some degree of self-rule. It accommodates a group's desire to maintain its integrity as an identity group and the primacy of that identity for group members. People must be confident that the integrity, indeed the very continuity, of their primary identity groups will be secure, for these groups to be resolvable. Shared sovereignty strategies usually provide for some degree of regional autonomy or statewide confederation or federation, that is, some form of shared homeland (Rabie, 1994). Autonomy, confederation, and federation all involve the devolution of power. Which of these arrangements works best depends greatly on the specific characteristics of group interaction and settlement patterns (e.g., whether ethnic and national groups are clearly divided territorially or are dispersed and intermixed). In the cases we review in this chapter, shared sovereignty strategies, incorporating some form of autonomy or self-rule designed to reduce threat perceptions, have been attempted in Nigeria, Bosnia, and Guatemala.

Autonomy may be preferred by a group that understands that it does not have the capability necessary to achieve independence. In this type of situation, the option of autonomy can set into motion a gradually intensi-fying identification with the broader national community. Unfortunately, as the Nigerian case shows, these efforts often fail. As Horowitz (1985) notes,

> Most such agreements are concluded against a background of secessionist warfare or terrorist violence. When central authority is secure . . . the appropriate decisions can be made and implemented by the center. But, where the very questions is how far the authority of the center will run, devolution is a matter of bilateral agreement, and an during agreement is an elusive thing.
>
> (p. 623)

These forms of integration strategy address the important political issues of providing groups increased capability and decision-making power in their region or state and with competitive power in the broader country government.

These institutional arrangements can accommodate identity needs of groups, particularly when a group's identity is threatened. But reducing ste-reotypes and promoting equality in group comparisons is very difficult to realize. Often, policymakers rely upon the contact hypothesis, wherein, as mentioned, it is assumed that if people get to know members of groups that they discriminate against, the interaction will disprove those stereotypical ideas, and tolerance and acceptance will result. But in reality, contact is lim-ited in countries where shared sovereignty strategies are employed, because groups tend to be geographically concentrated. Moreover, failure to iden-tify group variability increases with emotions (Mackie et al., 2000; Park & Banaji, 2000; Stroessner & Mackie, 1993), and shared sovereignty integra-tive strategies often come into play after serious violent clashes groups have occurred. Thus, intense emotion is likely to prevail in these situations, mak-ing the breakdown of preexisting stereotyped images extremely difficult.

Integration strategies should explicitly address intergroup perceptions. Some steps can be taken, through policies that prevent systematic integra-tion against groups even in autonomous regions in which they are minor-ities, or that ensure that national institutions, such as the military, are not dominated by one particular ethnic or racial group. Such control can easily cause resentment, because it often involves the reduction in power of domi-nant groups. However, over time, learning nonstereotyped responses to oth-ers is crucial to a change in image. People change perceptions of others by acting differently, not just thinking differently (Pettigrew & Martin, 1989). In other words, people can be trained not to stereotype (Kawakami, Dovidio, Moll, Hermson, & Russin, 2000). In fact, it may be that change in American racial attitudes is a good example of just this. From a policy standpoint, this requires the explicit promotion of tasks that require intergroup coopera-tion to achieve goals and interdependence at equal status levels. Equal sta-tus in group member interaction is important for disconfirming stereotypes (Allport, 1954; Bizman & Amir, 1984; van Oudenhoven, 1989).

Emotions are involved in changing stereotypes, too. Perceptions that the elite of another group is inferior tend to generate anger among those considered inferior, as well as anger and guilt among those considered superior (Duckitt, 1994; Swim & Miller, 1999). This, as was mentioned, can be counterproductive, because strong emotions tend to inhibit the identification of group variance and, thus, the breaking down of stereotypes. On the other hand, emotions can also be used to reduce stereotyping. **Perspective-taking**, for example, involves empathizing with others, experiencing their perspective and the emotions it generates in them. Galinsky and Moskowitz (2000) argue that perspective-taking "appears to diminish not just the expression of stereotypes but their accessibility. The constructive process of taking and realizing another person's perspective furthers the egalitarian principles themselves" (p. 722). Other studies have found that people do both adopt and change stereotypes, when given information about how other in-group members think about the out-group (Sechrist & Stangor, 2000; Stangor, Sechrist, & Jost, 2001).

UTILITARIAN INTEGRATION STRATEGIES

The institutional options of independence or autonomy are not available when the groups are geographically intermingled across a country or minorities are low in power and capabilities. Social distance factors are very important in these cases, as are the nature of existing stereotypes or images. The contact hypothesis probably will be relied upon by policymakers to naturally reduce group stereotyping images, because contact is more likely to occur in countries where groups intermingle and can be more easily promoted by government agencies as a solution to group stereotyping. Of the cases reviewed here, this type of strategy would be prominent, for example, in conflict resolution in the United States, Brazil, and South Africa.

An essential feature of a utilitarian integration strategy is to satisfy the populations' needs, and this requires removing any obstacles to equality of access to important political positions in the country. This most immediately involves unimpeded access to state educational institutions and the elimination of any state-sponsored social discrimination, but the speed with which integration develops varies with the social distances between groups. The greater the distances, the harder and slower integration will be. Memories of historical relationships, such as slavery, and the depth of institutional discrimination also affect the speed of integration.

One of the greatest difficulties in this type of integration strategy is changing traditional perceptions of groups that have been regarded as inferior. The task is complicated when the self-imagery within the subordinate minority is also negative. This kind of imagery is the imperial-colonial pattern referred to in Chapter 3. As mentioned there, conquered people can, through years of repression, come to accept as just the conditions and position in which they live. In countries with histories of this kind of repression, in which one or more of the identity communities is perceived, and perceives itself, as underachieving, there is likely to be a strong, persisting inclination toward the colonial and imperial images. Our earlier discussion of racism in America illustrated this, as well. Breaking these stereotypes requires making opportunities for those in the minority community and persuading them that they can and should try to take advantage of those opportunities.

A key aspect of the utilitarian strategy, in this case, is attracting qualified individuals in the minority community or communities into positions that exceed their expectations, and the majority's. Affirmative action programs are designed to do this. These achievements should help break stereotypes of inferiority, eventually, as people from minority groups come to be increasingly associated with high achievement. A study by Sinclair and Kunda (1999), for example, shows that American subjects high in prejudice did not activate their racial prejudice when motivated to have high regard for a Black person. In their experiments, when subjects were induced to have high regard for a Black doctor, they invoked the doctor stereotype, not the racist anti-Black stereotype.

The American affirmative action program illustrates both the promise and problems associated with this component of the strategy. Inevitably, those perceiving minority groups through the contemptuous colonial image will make the case that the program is ideologically driven and that the individuals who benefit from affirmative action lack the requisite qualifications. The program, they argue, is damaging both in the placement of inherently unqualified individuals into positions in which they will not perform adequately and in causing serious hardship among those who are qualified in achieving communities. Additionally, Brown, Charnsangavej, Keough, Newman and Rentfrow (2000) offer experimental evidence that affirmative action programs may be self-defeating if they become "reminders of peoples' stigmatized status," which can "have dramatic, detrimental effects on their performance. A phenomenon referred to as 'stereotype threat'" (p. 737). Thus, the stereotype of inferiority can become a self-fulfilling prophesy: people who are considered inferior are given fewer opportunities and are inferior in education, income, social standing, and so on, and they know they are. Meanwhile, the high achieving group minority will see integration as an unattractive prospect.

Clearly, dominant groups that are numerical minorities can be pushed from power, but not all dominant groups are numerical minorities, as in the case of White Americans, and it would be hoped that violence can be avoided. What is also clear is that, for utilitarian strategies to occur and for violence to be avoided, dominant groups, whether numerical majorities or minorities, must choose to accept equality with subordinate groups. As both the United States and South African cases show, perceptual change must accompany internal and external pressures for structural change. Stereotypes are shaken when expectations are consistently disconfirmed. The utilitarian strategy applied to subordinate groups should, if successful, do this. As subordinate groups achieve more, the dominant group's expectations, noted in the colonial image, would not be realized, and the image would be challenged. The impact should be a decline in opposition to further expanding access to opportunities and, gradually, a diminution of the colonial image of the disadvantaged groups. Image disconfirmation in this direction also can occur through the direct efforts of the subject of the colonial image to alter it by disconfirming it. This occurs through group mobilization and organization, demonstrating power and control unexpected of those perceived through the colonial image.

Let us conclude this discussion on a practical note, with a look at one component of conflict resolution in divided societies that illustrates the importance of using political institutions to tackle the political psychology of conflict. It has currently become more and more apparent that one of the central elements in conflict resolution and reconciliation in divided societies that have experienced intense violence is the training of a new, impartial professional police force. Political science is only now learning this lesson, but, from a political psychology standpoint, it is not surprising. One of the most important elements in the governance process in a country is the criminal justice system, particularly the police. They can ameliorate competition and perceptions of inequality, or they can exacerbate those perceptions. They are the representatives of government with whom people interact on a daily basis, and, as such, they are the central source of perceptions of justice, or lack thereof, in the political system. They have to be seen as impartial and unbiased in the treatment of citizens, regardless of ethnicity. They are crucial in conflict resolution, because, although military peacekeepers may disarm combatants, police provide the order necessary for people to feel secure. Without this, political reconstruction cannot occur.

In multiethnic and multinational countries, too often the police force itself becomes a tool of one ethnic or national group. Often, the police in these deeply divided countries are characterized by bias in law enforcement. They are politicized and identified with the repressive regime, the dominant group monopolizes top positions, they are not held accountable by authorities for abuses of power, and they have extraordinary power to control the subordinate populations (Call & Barnett, 2000; Mani, 2000). When this pattern occurs, it erodes state legitimacy, increases resentment against the state by unrepresented groups, and increases the possibility of conflict and the need of the state to employ coercion to quell the conflict.

The importance of impartial policing in conflict resolution has been recognized in the cases discussed earlier. Let us return to the Guatemalan case for illustration. Guatemala's Mayan population suffered violence on the scale of mass killing, if not genocide, although cultural genocide was certainly intended. There were death squads operative and a campaign of state terror. Mass murder took place indiscriminately in Mayan villages committed by the military and the police force. Nevertheless, despite many difficulties, Guatemala is today undergoing political reforms that are attempting to dismantle the counterinsurgency state.

During the war, the military and police committed numerous and appalling human rights violations. One of the most important aspects of reform is the separation of the police and military institutions. Before the peace accords, the police in Guatemala were part of the military. This is the case in most Latin American countries. Now the police are a separate institution and have the authority in internal security matters. The military's domain is left to external security. The enabling legislation and the regulations for the new National Civilian Police were designed primarily by the Spanish police, who also took the lead in training and advising the new Guatemalan policy force. The reform of the police was actually part of the peace accords themselves, and the government—particularly then President Alvaro Arzu—was committed. The accord provided the broad outlines for the police, including the provisions that it would be under the authority of the ministry of the interior, rather than under the military; that there would be established a separate academy for police training; and that the police force would take into account the multiethnic nature of the society and would form specialized agencies in that regard. This was to be done in the context of a reformed and impartial justice system.

Progress has been slow. On the negative side, the policing portion of the peace accords was very general and lacked important details. There were no provisions made regarding the inclusion of police officers from the old order; no provisions for vetting officers, to eliminate those involved in human rights abuses during the dirty war years (imagine having your local police officer be the same person who tortured you during the civil war); and no details about the content of training, organization, or disciplinary measures, including no education level requirements, which is an issue in countries with high levels of illiteracy.

The law that went into effect, implementing the government's agreement with the rebels, had no requirement that the new police include members of the different Mayan groups in Guatemala. Only about one fifth of the new recruits are indigenous. And former military personnel, who are prohibited from joining the police, have managed to get in. Guatemala has had a tremendous increase in crime, and the government has permitted joint military-police patrols to combat it, which is a dangerous practice. Finally,

> the constitutional reforms that would have consolidated the separation of police and military functions . . . was defeated in May 1999 in a nation-wide referendum . . . [so] the . . . military continues to have constitutional authority to be involved in internal security, and the future division of roles remains unclear.
>
> (Byrne, Stanley, & Garst, 2000, p. 5)

On the positive side, the government is clearly committed to this reform. By October 1999, the new police force were 17,339 strong and 36.5% were new recruits. The force is more service-oriented and has been positively received by the public. Complaints about human rights violations and corruption have diminished. Those are signs of a healing society and reasons for optimism that Guatemala may recover from its violent past.

Topics, Theories/Explanations, and Cases in Chapter 14

Topics	Theories/ Explanations	Cases
Reconciliation		Bosnia
Forgiveness		Rwanda
Post-Traumatic Stress Disorder	Long-term mental health issues	
War Tribunals		Rwanda
		Nazi Germany
		Yugoslavia
		Argentina
Truth and Reconciliation Commissions		Northern Ireland
		South Africa
		Chile
		Argentina
Integration strategies	Social identity	Guatemala
	Contact hypothesis	
Shared sovereignty strategies	Perspective-taking	

Key Terms

contact hypothesis
dialogue
perspective-taking
shared sovereignty strategies
social comparison

social creativity
social mobility
truth and reconciliation
utilitarian integration
    strategies

REFERENCES

Abanes, R. (1996). *American militias: Rebellion, racism and religion.* Downers Grove, IL: InterVarsity Press.

Abelson, R. P. (1986). Beliefs are like possessions. *Journal of the Theory of Social Behavior, 16,* 223–250.

Adam, H., & Moodley, K. (1993). South Africa: The opening of the apartheid mind. In J. McGarry & B. O'Leary (Eds.), *The politics of ethnic conflict regulation.* New York: Routledge.

Adorno, T., Frenkel-Brunswick, E., Levinson, D., & Sanford, P. (1950). *The authoritarian personality.* New York: Harper.

Aldag, R. J., & Fuller, S. R. (1993). Beyond fiasco: A reappraisal of the groupthink phenomenon and a new model of group decision processes. *Psychological Bulletin, 113,* 533–552.

Alexander, M. G., Brewer, M. B., & Herrmann, R. K. (1999). Images and affect: A functional analysis of out-group stereotypes. *Journal of Personality and Social Psychology, 77,* 78–93.

Alfonsi, C. (2006). *Circle in the sand: Why we went back to Iraq.* New York: Doubleday.

Allen, M. (2005, September 19). Living too much in the bubble?: A bungled initial response to Katrina exposed the perils of a rigid, insular White House. *Time.*

Allen, V. L., & Wilder, D. A. (1979). Group categorization and attribution of belief similarity. *Small Group Behavior, 10,* 73–80.

Allison, G. (1971). *The essence of decision: Explaining the Cuban missile crisis.* Boston, MA: Little, Brown.

Allison, G., & Zelikow, P. (1999). *The essence of decision: Explaining the Cuban Missile Crisis.* New York: Longman.

Allport, F. H. (1962). A structuronomic conception of behavior: Individual and collective. *Journal of Abnormal and Social Psychology, 64,* 3–30.

Allport, G. (1937). *Personality: A psychological interpretation.* New York: Holt, Rinehart, and Winston.

Allport, G. (1954). *The nature of prejudice.* Cambridge, MA: Addison-Wesley.

Allport, G. (1961). *Pattern and growth in personality.* New York: Holt, Rinehart and Winston.

Allport, G. (1968). *The person in psychology.* Boston, MA: Beacon Press.

Altemeyer, B. (1981). *Right-wing authoritarianism.* Winnipeg, Canada: University of Manitoba Press.

Altemeyer, B. (1988). *Enemies of freedom: Understanding right-wing authoritarianism.* San Francisco, CA: Jossey-Bass.

Altemeyer, B. (1996). *The authoritarian specter.* Cambridge, MA: Harvard University Press.

Altemeyer, B. (1998). The other "authoritarian personality." *Advances in Experimental and Social Psychology, 30,* 47–92.

American Patriot Network. (2002). Retrieved from www.patriotnetwork.info

Anderson, J. (1983). *The architecture of cognition.* Cambridge, MA: Harvard University Press.

Anderson, L. (2011). Demystifying the Arab Spring: Parsing the differences between Tunisia, Egypt, and Libya. *Foreign Affairs, 90,* 2–7.

Ansolabehere, S., Behr, R., & Iyengar, S. (1993). *The media game.* New York: Macmillan.

Anti-defamation League (ADL). (n.d.). William Pierce. Retrieved from www.adl.org/learn/ext_us/Pierce.asp

AOL News. (2008, September 20). Racial views may cost Obama election. Retrieved from http://news.aol.com

Arab News. (2008, September 29). Kurds reverse Saddam's ethnic cleansing. Retrieved from www.arabnews.com

Archibald, R. C., Cave, D., & Thompson, G. (2013). Mexico's curbs on U.S. role in drug fight spark friction. *New York Times.* Retrieved from www.nytimes.com/2013/05/01/world/americas

Aronson, E., & Mills, J. (1959). Effect of severity of initiation on liking for a group. *Journal of Abnormal and Social Psychology, 59,* 177–181.

Asch, S. E. (1952). *Social psychology.* Englewood Cliffs, NJ: Prentice Hall.

Asch, S. E. (1955). Opinions and social pressure. *Scientific American, 19,* 31–35.

Asch, S. E. (1956). Studies of independence and conformity: A minority of one against a unanimous majority. *Psychological Monographs, 70* (Whole No. 416).

Assadi, M. (2007, October 12). Fatah rules out talk with Hamas. *Boston Globe.*

Baker, J. A., & Hamilton, L. (2006). *The Iraq Study Group report: The way forward—A new approach.* New York: Vintage Books.

Baker, P. (2007, July 2). A president besieged and isolated, yet at ease. *Washington Post.*

Bales, R. F. (1951). *Interaction process analysis.* Boston, MA: Addison-Wesley.

Bales, R. F., & Strodtbeck, F. L. (1951). Phases in group problem solving. *Journal of Abnormal Social Psychology, 46,* 485–495.

Baltodano, B. (2008). *Becoming an insurgent in Colombia: Images at war in the Putumayo* (Unpublished master's thesis). Washington State University, Pullman.

Bamford, J. (2005). *A pretext for war: 9/11, Iraq, and the abuse of America's intelligence agencies.* New York: Anchor Books.

Bandura, A. (1973). *Aggression: A social learning analysis.* Englewood Cliffs, NJ: Prentice Hall.

Bandura, A. (1977). *Social learning theory.* Englewood Cliffs, NJ: Prentice Hall.

Bandura, A. (1986). *Social foundations of thought and action: A social cognitive theory.* Englewood Cliffs, NJ: Prentice Hall.

Bandura, A. (2004). The role of selective moral disengagement in terrorism and counterrorism. In F. Moghaddam & A. Marsella (Eds.), *Understanding terrorism*. Washington, DC: APA.

Barber, J. D. (1965). *The lawmakers: Recruitment and adaptation to legislative life*. New Haven, CT: Yale University Press.

Barber, J. D. (1972). *The presidential character: Predicting performance in the White House*. Englewood Cliffs, NJ: Prentice-Hall.

Barkow, J. Cosmides, L, & Tooby, J. (1992) (Eds.), *The adapted mind: Evolutionary psychology and the generation of culture*. New York; Oxford University press.

Barley, S. R., & Bechky, B. A. (1994). In the backrooms of science: The work of technicians in science labs. *Work and Occupations, 21*, 85–126.

Barlow, K. M., Taylor, D. M., & Lambert, W. E. (2000). Ethnicity in America and feeling "American." *Journal of Psychology, 134*, 581–600.

Barnes, R., & Shear, M. (2008). Obama makes history. *WashingtonPost.* Retrieved from www.washingtonpost.com/wp-dyn/content/article/2008/11/05

Baron, R. A. (1989). Applicant strategies during job interviews. In G. R. Ferris and R. W. Eder (Eds.), *The employment interview: Theory, research, and practice* (pp. 204–216). Newbury Park, CA: Sage.

Baron, R. S., Vandello, U. A., & Brunsman, B. (1996). The forgotten variable in conformity research: Impact of task importance on social influence. *Journal of Personality and Social Psychology, 71*, 915–927.

Barrera, M., Jr. (1986). Distinctions between social support concepts, measures, and models. *American Journal of Community Psychology, 14*, 413–422.

Bartels, L. (1996). Uninformed votes: Information effects in presidential elections. *American Journal of Political Science, 40*, 194–230.

Bartels, L. (2000). Partisanship and voting behavior, 1952–1996. *American Journal of Political Science, 44*, 35–50.

Bartle, J. (1998). Left-right position matters but does social class? Causal models of the 1992 British general election. *British Journal of Political Science, 28*, 501–529.

Barton, S. L., Duchon, D., & Dunegan, K. J. (1989). An empirical test of Staw and Ross's prescription for the management of escalation of commitment behavior in organizations. *Decision Science, 20*, 532–544.

Bass, B. M. (1955). Authoritarianism or acquiescence? *Journal of Abnormal and Social Psychology, 51*, 616–623.

Bassili, J. N., & Provencal, A. (1988). Perceiving minorities: A factor-analytic approach. *Personality and Social Psychology Bulletin, 14*, 5–15.

Bastien, D., & Hostager, T. (1998). Jazz as a process of organizational innovation. *Communication Research, 15*, 582–602.

Batson, C. D. (1975). Rational processing or rationalization? The effect of disconfirming information on a stated religious belief. *Journal of Personality and Social Psychology, 32*, 176–184.

Batson, C. D. (1991). Rational processing or rationalization? The effect of disconfirming information on a stated religious belief. *Journal of Personality and Social Psychology, 32*, 176–184.

Baumeister, R. F. (1997). *Evil: Inside human violence and cruelty*. New York: Freeman.

Baumeister, R. (1999). *Evil: Inside human violence and cruelty*. NewYork: Henry Holt.

Baumeister, R. F., Vohs, K. D., & Tice, D. M. (2006). Emotional influences on decision making. In J. P. Forgas (Ed.), *Affect in social thinking and behavior* (pp. 143–159). New York: Psychology Press.

Bayulgen, O., & Arbatli, E. (2013). Cold war redux in US–Russia relations? The effects of U.S. media framing and public opinion of the 2008 Russia-Georgia war. *Communist and Post-Communist Studies, 46*, 513–527.

Bazerman, M. H., Beekun, R. I., & Schoorman, F. D. (1982). Performance evaluation in a dynamic context: A laboratory study of the impact of a prior commitment to the rates. *Journal of Applied Psychology, 67*, 873–876.

Bazerman, M. H., Giuliano, T., & Appelman, A. (1984). Escalation in individual and group decision making. *Organizational Behavior and Human Performance, 33*, 141–152.

BBC News. (2000, April 1). Turkish troops pursue Kurds.

BBC News. (2002, March 17). Iraqi Kurds recall chemical attack. Retrieved from http://news.bbc.co.uk/1/hi/world/middle_east/1877161.stm

BBC News. (2015). Ukraine profile. Retrieved from www.bbc.com/news/world-Europe-1801012

Beck, A. (1999). *Prisoners of hate: The cognitive basis of anger, hostility and violence*. New York: Harper Collins.

Beck, P., Dalton, R., Greene, S., & Huckfeldt, R. (2002). The social calculus of voting: Interpersonal, media, and organizational influences on presidential choices. *American Political Science Review, 96*, 57–74.

Beeler, J. D. (1998). Effects of counter-explanation on escalation of commitment: An experimental assessment of individual and collective decisions. *Advances in Accounting Behavioral Research, 1*, 85–99.

Beeler, J. D., & Hunton, J. E. (1997). The influence of compensation method and disclosure level of information search strategy and escalation of commitment. *Journal of Behavioral Decision Making, 10*, 77–91.

Begley, S. (2001, May 20). The roots of evil. *Newsweek*. Retrieved from www.newsweek.com/roots-evil-152587

Bejjani, E. (2006, August 23). Funding Hezbollah: The Iranian connection. Retrieved from www.frontpagemag.com/Articles/Read.aspx?GUID={4D8A52F8-9B8D-4131-8DA0-1884F7C6C4E2

Bennis, W. G., & Shepard, H. A. (1956). A theory of group development. *Human Relations, 9*, 415–437.

Benoit, W. L., & Benoit-Bryan, J. M. (2013). Debates come to the United Kingdom: A functional analysis of the 2010 British prime minister election debates. *Communication Quarterly, 61*, 463–278.

Bentler, P. M., & Speckart, G. (1981). Attitudes cause behaviors: A structural equation analysis. *Journal of Personality and Social Psychology, 40*, 226–238.

Berejikian, J. D., & Early, B. R. (2013). Loss aversion and foreign policy resolve. *Political Psychology, 34*, 649–671.

Berelson, B., Lazarsfeld, P., & McPhee, W. (1954). *Voting: A study of opinion formation in a presidential campaign*. Chicago, IL: University of Chicago Press.

Berent, M., & Krosnick, J. (1995). The relation between political attitude importance and knowledge structure. In M. Lodge & K. McGraw (Eds.), *Political judgment: Structure and process.* Ann Arbor: University of Michigan Press.

Berger, J., Rosenholtz, S. J., & Zelditch, M. (1980). Status organizing processes. *Annual Review of Sociology, 6,* 479–508.

Berkowitz, L. (1989). Frustration-aggression hypothesis: Examination and reformulation. *Psychological Bulletin, 106,* 59–73.

Berscheid, E. (1987). Emotion and Interpersonal communication. In M. Roloff & G. Miller (Eds.), *Interpersonal processes: New directions in communication research.* Thousand Oaks, CA: Sage.

Bertram, B.C.R. (1978). Living in groups: Predators and prey. In P.G. Bateson & R.A. Hinde (Eds.), *Behavioral ecology: An evolutional approach.* London: Blackwell.

Bettenhausen, K., & Murnighan, J.K. (1991). The development of an intragroup norm and the effects of interpersonal structural challenges. *Administrative Science Quarterly, 36,* 20–35.

Biddle, S. (1998). The past as prologue: Assessing theories of future warfare. *Security Studies, 8,* 1–74.

Bilali, R., & Vollhardt, J.R. (2013). Priming effects of a reconciliation radio drama on historical perspective-taking in the aftermath of mass violence in Rwanda. *Journal of Experimental and Social Psychology, 49,* 144–151.

Billig, M., & Tajfel, H. (1973). Social categorization and similiarity in intergroup behavior. *European Journal of Social Psychology, 3,* 27–52.

Birt, R. (1993). Personality and foreign policy: The case of Stalin. *Political Psychology, 15,* 607–626.

Bizman, A., & Amir, Y. (1984). Integration and attitudes. In Y. Amir and S. Sharan (Eds.), *School desegregation.* Hillsdale, NJ: Lawrence Erlbaum.

Blanton, S.L. (1996). Images in conflict: The case of Ronald Reagan and El Salvador. *International Studies Quarterly, 40,* 23–44.

Blascovich, J., Nash, R.F., & Ginsburg, G.P. (1978). Heart rate and competitive decision making. *Personality and Social Psychology Bulletin, 4,* 115–118.

Blass, T. (1991). Understanding behavior in the Milgram obedience experiment: The role of personality, situations, and their interactions. *Journal of Personality and Social Psychology, 60,* 398–413.

Bloom, M. (2009). Chasing butterflies and rainbows: A critique of Kruglanski et al.'s "Fully committed: Suicide bombers' motivation and the quest for personal significance." *Political Psychology, 30,* 387–395.

Bobo, L. (1983). Whites' opposition to busing: symbolic racism or realistic group conflict? *Journal of Personality and Social Psychology, 45,* 1196–1210.

Bobo, L., & Smith, R. (1994). From Jim Crow racism to laissez-faire racism: An essay on the transformation of racial attitudes in America. In W. Katkin & A. Tyree (Eds.), *Beyond pluralism: Essays on the conceptions of groups and identities in America.* Stanford, CA: Stanford University Press.

Boettcher, W.A. (2005). *Presidential risk behavior in foreign policy: Prudence or peril?* New York: Palgrave.

Boin, A., & 't Hart, P. (2003). Public leadership in times of crisis: Mission impossible? *Public Administration Review, 63*, 55–564.

Boin, A., 't Hart, P., McConnell, A., & Preston, T. (2010). Leadership style, crisis response, and blame management: The case of Hurricane Katrina. *Public Administration, 88*, 706–723.

Bond, C. F., Jr., & Titus, L. J. (1983). Social facilitation: A meta-analysis of 241 studies. *Psychological Bulletin, 94*, 265–292.

Bond, R., & Smith, P. B. (1996). Culture and conformity: A meta-analysis of studies using Asch's line judgment task. *Psychological Bulletin, 119*, 111–137.

Bone, P. (1999). Rwanda: The children's return. Retrieved from http://theage.com.au/news/agenews/pbrwanda.htm

Borkenau, P., Riemann, R., Angleitner, A., & Spinath, F. M. (2001). Genetic and environmental influences on observed personality: Evidence from the German observational study of adult twins. *Journal of Personality and Social Psychology, 80*, 655–668.

Borum, R. (2003). Understanding the terrorist mindset. *FBI Law Enforcement Bulletin*, 7–10.

Borum, R. (2004). *Psychology of terrorism*. Tampa: University of South Florida.

Bowen, M. G. (1987). The escalation phenomenon reconsidered: Decision dilemmas or decision errors? *Academy of Management Review, 12*, 52–66.

Boyd, R., & Richerson, P. J. (1985). *Culture and the evolutionary process*. Chicago, IL: University of Chicago Press.

Brader, T., & Valentino, N. A. (2007). Indentities, interested, and emotions: Symbolic versus material wellsprings of fear, anger, and enthusiasm. In W. R. Neuman, G. E. Marcus, A. N. Crigler, & M. Michael (Eds.), *The affect effect: Dynamics of emotion in political thinking and behavior*. Chicago, IL: University of Chicago Press.

Brams, S. J. (1985). *Superpower games: Applying game theory to superpower conflict*. New Haven, CT: Yale University Press.

Brauer, M., Judd, C. M., & Gliner, M. D. (1995). The effects of repeated expressions on attitude polarization during group discussions. *Journal of Personality and Social Psychology, 68*, 1014–1029.

Brawley, L. R., Carron, A. V., & Widmeyer, W. N. (1988). Exploring the relationship between cohesion and group resistance to disruption. *Journal of Sport and Exercise Psychology, 10*, 199–213.

Brehm, J. W. (1976). Responses to loss of freedom: A theory of psychological reactance. In J. W. Thibaut, J. T. Spence, & R. C. Carson (Eds.), *Contemporary topics in social psychology* (pp. 51–78). Morristown, NJ: General Learning Press.

Brewer, M. B. (1979). Ingroup bias in the minimal intergroup situation: A cognitive–motivational analysis. *Psychological Bulletin, 86*, 307–324.

Brewer, M. B. (1988). A dual process model of impression formation. In T. Srull & R. Wyer (Eds.), *Advances in social cognition* (Vol. 1, pp. 1–36). Hillsdale, NJ: Erlbaum.

Brewer, M. B., & Brown, R. J. (1998). Intergroup relations. In D. T. Gilbert, S. T. Fiske, & G. Lindzey (Eds.), *The handbook of social psychology* (4th ed., Vol. 2, pp. 554–594). New York: McGraw-Hill.

Brewer, M. B., & Kramer, R. M. (1986). Choice behavior in social dilemmas: Effects of social identity, group size, and decision framing. *Journal of Personality and Social Psychology, 50*, 543–547.

Brewer, M. B., & Miller, N. (1984). Beyond the contact hypothesis: Theoretical perspectives on desegregation. In N. Miller & M. Brewer (Eds.), *Groups in contact: The psychology of desegregation*. New York: Academic Press.

Brickner, M. A., Harkins, S. G., & Ostrom, T. M. (1986). Effects of personal involvement: Thought-provoking implications for social loafing. *Journal of Personality and Social Psychology, 51*, 763–770.

Bridgeman, B. (2003). *Psychology and evolution: The origins of mind*. Thousand Oaks, CA: Sage Publications.

British National Party. (2007). Manifesto. Retrieved from www.bnp.org.uk/?page_id+51

Brockner, J. (1992). The escalation of commitment to a failing course of action: Toward theoretical progress. *Academy of Management Review, 17*, 39–61.

Brockner, J., Rubin, J. Z., & Lang, E. (1981). Face-saving and entrapment. *Journal of Experimental Social Psychology, 17*, 68–79.

Brockner, J., Shaw, M. C., & Rubin, J. Z. (1979). Factors affecting withdrawal from an escalating conflict: Quitting before it's too late. *Journal of Experimental Social Psychology, 15*, 492–503.

Brodie, F. M. (1981). *Richard Nixon: The shaping of his character*. New York: W. W. Norton.

Brody, R. A., & Rothenberg, L. S. (1988). The instability of partisanship and analysis of the 1980 presidential election. *British Journal of Political Science, 18*, 445–465.

Bronstein, J. (2013). Like me! Analyzing the 2012 presidential candidates' Facebook pages. *Online Information Review, 37*, 173–192.

Brown, R. (1974). Further comment on the risky shift. *American Psychologist, 29*, 468–470.

Brown, R. (2000). *Group processes: Dynamics within and between groups*. Oxford: Blackwell.

Brown, R. P., Charnsangavej, T., Keough, K. A., Newman, M. L., & Rentfrow, P. (2000). Putting the "affirm" into affirmative action: Preferential selection and academic performance. *Journal of Personality and Social Psychology, 79*, 736–747.

Brown, S. (1987). *The causes and prevention of war*. New York: St. Martin's Press.

Brown, V., & Paulus, P. B. (1996). A simple dynamic model of social factors in group brainstorming. *Small Group Research, 27*, 91–114.

Browning, C. (1992). *Ordinary men: Resen police battalion 101 and the final solution in Poland*. New York: Harper Collins.

Browning, R. P., & Jacob, H. (1964). Power motivation and the political personality. *Public Opinion Quarterly, 28*, 75–90.

Bruni, F. (2002). *Ambling into history: The unlikely odyssey of George W. Bush*. New York: Harper Collins.

Bruni, F. (2003, April 11). What's in a name? For a Turkish youth, maybe jail. *New York Times*, p. A3.

Bullock, A., & Stallybrass, O. (1977). *The Harper dictionary of modern thought.* New York: Harper and Row.

Burke, J. P. (1992). *The institutional presidency.* Baltimore, MD: Johns Hopkins University Press.

Burke, J. P. (2004). *Becoming president: The Bush transition, 2000–2003.* Boulder, CO: Lynne Rienner.

Burke, J. P., & Greenstein, F. I. (1991). *How presidents test reality: Decisions on Vietnam, 1954 and 1965.* New York: Russell Sage Foundation.

Burnett, D. G. (2001). *A trial by jury.* New York: Alfred Knopf.

Burns, J. M. (1978). *Leadership.* New York: Harper and Row.

Burnstein, E., & Vinokur, A. (1977). Persuasive arguments and social comparison as determinants of attitude polarization. *Journal of Experimental Social Psychology, 13,* 315–332.

Burton, J. (1990). *Conflict: Its resolution and prevention.* London: Macmillan.

Bushart, H. L., Craig, J., & Barnes, M. (1998). *Soldiers of God: White supremacists and their holy war for America.* New York: Pinnacle.

Butler, D. E., & Stokes, D. (1974). *Political change in Britain* (2nd ed.). New York: Macmillan.

Buzbee, S. (2001, September 18). Bush's use of word "crusade" a red flag. *Seattle Post-Intelligencer,* p. A1.

Byars, R. S. (1972). The task/affect quotient. *Comparative Political Studies, 5,* 109–120.

Byars, R. S. (1973). Small group theory and shifting styles of political leadership. *Comparative Political Studies, 5,* 443–469.

Byman, D. (1998). The logic of ethnic terrorism. *Studies in Conflict and Terrorism, 21,* 149–169.

Byrne, H., Stanley, W., & Garst, R. (2000). *Rescuing police reform: A challenge for the new Guatemalan government.* Washington, DC: Washington Office on Latin America.

Caldwell, D. F., & O'Reilly, C. A. (1982). Response to failure: The effects of choice and responsibility on impression management. *Academy of Management Journal, 25,* 121–136.

Call, C., & Barnett, M. (2000). Looking for a few good cops: Peacekeeping, peacebuilding, and CIVPOL. In T. T. Holm & E. B. Eide (Eds.), *Peacebuilding and police reform* (pp. 43–68). Portland, OR: Frank Cass.

Camacho, L. M., & Paulus, P. B. (1995). The role of social anxiousness in group brainstorming. *Journal of Personality and Social Psychology, 68,* 1071–1080.

Campbell, A. Converse, P., Miller, W., & Stokes, D. (1960/1964). *The American voter.* New York: John Wiley and Sons.

Campbell, C. S. (1986). *Managing the presidency: Carter, Reagan, and the search for executive harmony.* Pittsburgh, PA: University of Pittsburgh Press.

Campbell, D. T. (1958). Common fate, similarity, and other indices of the status of aggregates of persons as social entities. *Behavioral Science, 3,* 14–25.

Carmack, R. (1992). The story of Santa Cruz Quiché. In R. Carmack (Ed.), *Harvest of violence: The Maya Indian and the Guatemalan crisis.* Norman: University of Oklahoma Press.

Carmines, E., & Merriman, R. (1993). The changing American dilemma: Liberal values and racial policies. In P. Sniderman, P. Tetlock, & E. Carmines

(Eds.), *Prejudice, politics and the American dilemma* (pp. 237–255). Stanford, CA: Stanford University Press, 1993.

Carnegie Commission on Preventing Deadly Conflict. (1997). *Preventing deadly conflict: Final report.* New York: Carnegie Corporation of New York.

Carraro, L., & Castelli, L. (2010). The implicit and explicit effects of negative political campaigns: Is the source really blamed? *Political Psychology, 31,* 617–645.

Carson, R. C. (1969). *Interaction concepts of personality.* Chicago, IL: Aldine.

Cassels, A. (1975). *Fascism.* New York: Thomas Crowell.

Cassino, D., & Lodge, M. (2007). The primacy of affect in political evaluations. In W. R. Neuman, G. E. Marcus, A. N. Crigler, & M. MacKuen (Eds.), *The affect effect: Dynamics of emotion in political thinking and behavior* (pp. 101–123). Chicago, IL: University of Chicago Press.

Cattell, R. B. (1964). *Personality and social psychology.* San Diego, CA: Knapp.

Cattell, R. B. (1965). *The scientific analysis of personality.* Baltimore, MD: Penguin.

Cattell, R. B., & Child, D. (1975). *Motivation and dynamic structure.* New York: Wiley.

Cehajic, S., Brown, R. J., & Castano, E. (2008). Forgive and forget: Antecedents and consequences of intergroup forgiveness in Bosnia and Herzegovina. *Political Psychology, 29,* 351–367.

Central Intelligence Agency. (2008). Iraq. Retrieved from www.cia.gov/library/publications/the-world-factbook/geos/iz.html

Chaiken, S. (1980). Heuristic versus systematic information processing in the use of source versus message cues in persuasion. *Journal of Personality and Social Psychology, 39,* 752–766.

Chaiken, S. (1987). The heuristic model of persuasion. In M. P. Zanna, J. M. Olson, & C. P. Herman (Eds.), *Social influence: The Ontario symposium* (Vol. 5, pp. 3–39). Hillsdale, NJ: Erlbaum.

Chen, S., & Chaiken, S. (1999). The heuristic-systematic model in its broader context. In S. Chaiken & Y. Trope (Eds.), *Dual-process theories in social psychology* (pp. 73–96). New York: Guilford Press.

Chirot, S., & McCauley, C. (2006). *Why not kill them all? The logic and prevention of mass political murder.* Princeton, NJ: Princeton University Press.

Chrisafis, A. (2005, March 9). Ready to shoot. *Salon.* Retrieved from www.dir.salon.com/story/news/feature/2005/03/09/irish/index.html

Christian Science Monitor. (2005). Moqtata al-Sadr's militia clashed with Badr fighters, revealing a Shiite divide over the new draft charter. Retrieved from www.csmonitor.com

Cialdini, R. B., & Trost, M. R. (1998). Social influence: Social norms, conformity, and compliance. In D. T. Gilbert, S. T. Fiske, & G. Lindzey (Eds.), *Handbook of social psychology* (Vol. 2, pp. 151–192). Boston, MA: McGraw-Hill.

Clark, R. D. (1990). Minority influence: The role of argument refutation of the majority position and social support for the minority position. *European Journal of Social Psychology, 20,* 489–497.

Clarke, R. (2004). *Against all enemies: Inside America's war on terror.* New York: Free Press.

Clinton, W. (1998). *One America in the 21st century: The president's initiative on race*. Washington, DC: The White House.

CNN Library. (2015, March 2). 1965 Selma to Montgomery March fast facts. Retrieved from www.cnn.com/2013/09/15/us/1965-selma-to-montgomery-march-fast-facts

Coe, K. (2013). Television news, public opinion and the Iraq war: Do wartime rationales matter? *Communication Research, 40*, 486–505.

Cohen, B. (1963). *The press and foreign policy*. Princeton, NJ: Princeton University Press.

Cohen, E. (1996). A revolution in warfare. *Foreign Affairs, 75*, 37–54.

Cohen, S. (2001). *States of denial: Knowing about atrocities and suffering*. Oxford: Blackwell.

Conlon, E. J., & Parks, J. M. (1987). Information requests in the context of escalation. *Journal of Applied Psychology, 72*, 344–350.

Conover, P., & Feldman, S. (1991). Where is the schema? Critiques. *American Political Science Review, 85*, 1364–1369.

Conroy, J. (2000). *Unspeakable acts, ordinary people*. New York: Knopf.

Converse, P. E. (1964). The nature of belief systems in mass publics. In D. Apter (Ed.), *Ideology and its discontents*. New York: Free Press.

Converse, P. E. (1966). The concept of a normal vote. In A. Campbell, P. E. Converse, W. E. Miller, & D. Stokes (Eds.), *Elections and the political order*. New York: Wiley.

Cook, M. (1977). The social skill model and interpersonal attraction. In S. Duck (Ed.), *Theory and practice in interpersonal attraction*. New York: Academic Press.

Cook, T. D., & Insko, C. (1968). Persistence of induced attitude change as a function of conclusion reexposure: A laboratory-field experiment. *Journal of Personality and Social Psychology, 9*, 322–328.

Cooper, H. H. A. (1977). What is a terrorist: A psychological perspective. *Legal Medical Quarterly, 1*, 16–32.

Cooper, M. (2005, September 12). Dipping his toe into disaster. *Time*.

Corcoran, K. E., Pettinicchio, D., & Young, J.T.N. (2011). The context of control: A cross-national investigation of the link between political institutions, efficacy, and collective action. *British Journal of Social Psychology, 50*, 575–605.

Corneille, O., Yzerbyt, V. Y., Rogier, A., & Buidin, G. (2001). Threat and the group attribution error: When threat illicits judgments of extremity and homogeneity. *Personality and Social Psychology Bulletin, 27*, 427–446.

Corrado, R. R. (1981). A critique of the mental disorder perspective of political terrorism. *International Journal of Law and Psychiatry*. 4, 293–310

Coser, L. A. (1956). *The functions of social conflict*. Glencoe, IL: Free Press.

Costa, P. T., & McCrae, R. (1992). *Revised NEO Personality Inventory (NEO PI-R) and NEO Five-Factor Inventory (NEO-FFI): Professional manual*. Odessa, FL: Psychological Assessment Resources.

Costa, P. T., Jr., Terracciano, A., & McCrae, R. R. (2001). Gender differences in personality traits across cultures: Robust and surprising findings. *Journal of Personality and Social Psychology, 81*, 322–331.

Cotler, I. (2008, September 30). Forgetting Darfur. *Montreal Gazette*. Retrieved from www.canada.com/montrealgazette

Cottam, M. (1986). *Foreign policy decision making: The influence of cognition*. Boulder, CO: Westview.

Cottam, M. (1994). *Images and intervention*. Pittsburgh, PA: University of Pittsburgh Press.

Cottam, M., & Cottam, R. (2001). *Nationalism and politics: The political behavior of nation states*. Boulder, CO: Lynne Rienner.

Cottam, M., Mahdasian, S., & Sarac, M. (2000, March). *The degenerate and the rogue: War in Kosovo*. Unpublished paper presented at the International Studies Association, Los Angeles, CA.

Cottam, M., & Marenin, O. (1999). International cooperation in the war on drugs: Mexico and the United States. *Policing and Society, 9*, 209–240.

Cottam, M., & Preston, T. (2007, February 28–March 3). *Building stronger images of leadership: A framework for integrating Image Theory and Leadership Trait Analysis (LTA) into a more powerful tool for analyzing leaders-at-a-distance*. Paper presented at the 48th Annual Meeting of the International Studies Association, Chicago, IL.

Cottam, R. (1977). *Foreign policy motivation*. Pittsburgh, PA: University of Pittsburgh Press.

Cottee, S., & Hayward, K. (2011). Terrorist (E)motives: The existential attractions of terrorism. *Studies in Conflict & Terrorism, 34*, 963–986.

Cottrell, N. B. (1972). Social facilitation. In C. G. McClintock (Ed.), *Experimental social psychology* (pp. 185–236). New York: Holt, Rinehart, and Winston.

Cottrell, N. B., Wack, D. L., Sekerak, G. J., & Rittle, R. H. (1968). Social facilitation of dominant responses by the presence of an audience and the mere presence of others. *Journal of Personality and Social Psychology, 9*, 245–250.

Council on Foreign Relations. (2007). Hamas. Washington, DC: Author. Retrieved from www.cfr.org/publication/8968/#10

Crabb, C. B., Jr., & Mulcahy, K. V. (1986). *Presidents and foreign policy making: From FDR to Reagan*. Baton Rouge: Louisiana State University Press.

Crane, S. (2007, December 13). In Europe, some still cling to dreams. *Wall Street Journal*. Retrieved from www.online.wsj.com/article/SB11975114786325567.html?mod=googlenews_wsj

Crenshaw, M. (2000). The psychology of terrorism: An agenda for the 21st century. *Political Psychology, 21*, 405–420.

Crenshaw, M. (2004). The political psychology of terrorism. In J. Jost & J. Sidanius (Eds.), Political psychology: Key readings (pp. 379-413). New York: Taylor & Francis.

Crenshaw, M. (2009). Intimations of mortality or production lines? The puzzle of "suicide terrorism." *Political Psychology, 30*, 359–364.

Crnobrnja, M. (1994). *The Yugoslav drama*. Montreal: McGill-Queens University Press.

Cronin, T. E. (1980). *The state of the presidency* (2nd ed.). Boston, MA: Little, Brown.

Cropanzano, R. (Ed.) (1993). *Justice in the workplace* (pp. 79–103). Hillsdale, NJ: Erlbaum.

Crosby, F. J. (1976). A model of egotistical relative deprivation. *Psychological Review, 83*, 85–113.

Cubides, F. C. (2001). From private to public violence: The paramilitaries. In C. Berquist, R. Peñaranda, & G. Sánchez G. (Eds.), *Violence in Colombia, 1990–2000*. Wilmington, DE: Scholarly Resources.

Curry, T. (2008, November 7). Young voters not essential to Obama win. *MSNBC*. Retrieved from www.msnbc.com/id/27582147/page 2

Dallek, R. (1979). *Franklin D. Roosevelt and American foreign policy, 1932–1945*. New York: Oxford University Press.

Dallek, R. (1983). *The American style of foreign policy*. New York: Alfred Knopf.

D'Alessio, D., & Allen, M. (2000). Media bias in presidential elections: A meta-analysis. *Journal of Communication, 50*, 133–156.

Daly, S. (2005, March 11). The Algerian Salafist group for call and combat: A dossier. *Jamestown Foundation*. Retrieved from www.jamestown.org/terrorism/news/article.php?articleid=2369399

Dasgupta, N., Banji, M. R., & Abelson, R. P. (1999). Group entiativity and group perception: Association between physical features and psychological judgment. *Journal of Personality and Social Psychology, 75*, 991–1005.

Davies, J. (1962). Toward a theory of revolution. *American Sociological Review, 27*, 5–19.

Davies, S. (1992). Introduction: Sowing the seeds of violence. In Robert Carmack (Ed.), *Harvest of violence: The Maya Indian and the Guatemalan crisis*. Norman: University of Oklahoma Press.

Davis, W. L., & Phares, E. J. (1967). Internal-external control as a determinant of information-seeking in a social influence situation. *Journal of Personality, 35*, 547–561.

Dawes, C. T., & Fowler, J. H. (2009). Partisanship, voting, and the dopamine D2 receptor gene. *Journal of Politics, 71*, 1157–1171.

Dawkins, R. (1976). *The selfish gene*. New York: Oxford University Press.

Dawson, M. (2001). *Black visions: The roots of contemporary African-American political ideologies*. Chicago, IL: University of Chicago Press.

Day, D. V., Schleicher, D. J., Unckless, A. L., & Hiller, N. J. (2002). Self-mentoring personality at work: A meta-analytic investigation of construct validity. *Journal of Applied Psychology, 87*, 390–401.

Deaux, K., Reid, A., Mizrahi, K., & Ethier, K. A. (1995). Parameters of social identity. *Journal of Personality and Social Psychology, 68*, 280–291.

Delli Carpini, M. X., & Keeter, S. (1993). Measuring political knowledge: Putting first things first. *American Journal of Political Science, 37*, 1179–1206.

Delli Carpini, M. X., & Keeter, S. (1996). *What Americans know about politics and why it matters*. New Haven, CT: Yale University Press.

Denton, R. E., & Kuypers, J. A. (2008). *Politics and communication in America: Campaigns, media and governing in the 21st century*. Long Grove, IL: Waveland Press.

Denver, D. (1994). *Elections and voting behaviour in Britain*. London: Harvester Wheatsheaf.

Denver, D. (1998). The government that could do no right. In A. King, D. Denver, I. McLean, P. Norris, P. Norton, D. Sanders, & P. Seyd (Eds.), *The new Labour triumphs: Britain at the polls*. Chatham, NJ: Chatham House.

Desportes, J.P., & Lemaine, J.M. (1988). The sizes of human groups: An analysis of their distributions. In D. Canter, J.C. Jesuino, L. Soczka, & G.M. Stephenson (Eds.), *Environmental social psychology* (pp. 57–65). Dordrecht: Kluwer.

Deutsch, M. (1969). Socially relevant science: Reflections on some studies of interpersonal conflict. *American Psychologist, 24*, 1076–1092.

Deutsch, M. (1973). *The resolution of conflict.* New Haven, CT: Yale University Press.

Deutsch, M. (1986). The malignant (spiral) process of hostile interaction. In R.K. White (Ed.), *Psychology and the prevention of nuclear war* (pp. 131–154). New York: New York University Press.

Deutscher, I. (1973). *What we say/what we do: Sentiments and acts.* Glenview, IL: Scott Foresman.

Devine, P.G., & Elliot, A.J. (1995). Are racial stereotypes really fading? The Princeton trilogy revisited. *Personality and Social Psychology Bulletin, 21*, 1139–1150.

Diamond, J., & Locy, T. (2002, September 22). Al-Qaida recruits undergo rigorous checks, initiation. *USA Today.* Retrieved from www.intellnet.org/news/2002/09/22/11890-1.htm

Diamond, L. (1988). *Class, ethnicity, and democracy in Nigeria: The failure of the first republic.* Syracuse: Syracuse University Press.

Diamond, L. (2005). *Squandered victory.* New York: Henry Holt.

Dickey, C., & Norland, R. (2006, August 7). The wider war. *Newsweek.*

Dicks, H.V. (1972). *Licensed mass murder: A socio-psychological study of some SS killers.* New York: Basic Books.

Diehl, M., & Stroebe, W. (1987). Productivity loss in brainstorming groups: Toward the solution of a riddle. *Journal of Personality and Social Psychology, 53*, 497–509.

Diener, E. (1976). Effects of prior destructive behavior, anonymity, and group presence on deindividuation and aggression. *Journal of Personality and Social Psychology, 33*, 497–507.

Diener, E. (1979). Deindividuation, self-awareness and disinhibition. *Journal of Personality and Social Psychology, 37*, 1160–1171.

Dietrich, B.J., Lasley, S., Mondak, J.J., Remmel, M.L., & Turner, J. (2012). Personality and legislative politics: The big five trait dimensions among U.S. state legislators. *Political Psychology, 33*, 195–210.

Dietz-Uhler, B. (1996). The escalation of commitment in political decision-making groups: A social identity approach. *European Journal of Social Psychology, 26*, 611–629.

Dietz-Uhler, B. (1999). Defensive reactions to group-relevant information. *Group Processes and Intergroup Relations, 2*, 17–29.

Dijksterhuis, A., Aarts, H., & Smith, P.K. (2005). The power of the subliminal: On subliminal persuasion and other potential applications. In R.R. Hassin, J.S. Uleman, & J.A. Bargh (Eds.), *The new unconscious* (pp. 77–106). New York: Oxford University Press.

Dillon, M. (1989). *The Shankill butchers: A case study of mass murder.* London: Arrow Books.

DiMaggio, A. (2011). *The rise of the tea party.* New York: Monthly Review Press.

Dion, K.L. (1979). Intergroup conflict and intragroup cohesion. In W.G. Austin & S. Worchel (Eds.), *The social psychology of intergroup relations* (pp. 211–224). Pacific Grove, CA: Brooks/Cole.

DiRenzo, G.J. (1974). Perspectives on personality and political behavior. In G.I. DiRenzo (Ed.), *Personality and politics* (pp. 3–28). Garden City, N.Y.: Anchor Books.

Doder, D., & Branson, L. (1999). *Milosevic: Portrait of a tyrant*. New York: Free Press.

Doise, W. (1969). Intergroup relations and polarization of individual and collective judgments. *Journal of Personality and Social Psychology, 12,* 136–143.

Dollard, J., Doob, L., Miller, N., Mowrer, O., & Sears, R. (1939). *Frustration and aggression*. New Haven, CT: Yale University Press.

Dowd, M. (2001, July 4). The relaxation response. *New York Times,* p. A1.

Dowd, M., & Friedman, T. (1990, March 6). The fabulous Bush and Baker boys. *New York Times Magazine,* 58–64.

Dragojlovic, N.I. (2011). Priming and the Obama effect on public evaluations of the United States. *Political Psychology, 32,* 989–1006.

Draper, R. (2007). *Dead certain: The presidency of George W. Bush*. New York: Free Press.

Dreben, E., Fiske, S., & Hastie, R. 1979. The dependence of item and evaluative information: Impression and recall order effects in behavior-based impression formation. *Journal of Personality and Social Psychology, 37,* 1758–1768.

Driver, M.J. (1977). Individual differences as determinants of aggression in the inter-nation simulation. In M. G. Hermann (Ed.), *A psychological examination of political leaders* (pp. 337–353). New York: Free Press.

Druckman, J.N. (2004). Priming the vote: Campaign effects in a U.S. senate election. *Political Psychology, 25,* 577–594.

Druckman, J.N., & Chong, D. (2007). A theory of framing and opinion formation in competitive elite environments. *Journal of Communication, 57,* 99–118.

Druckman, J.N., & Holmes, J.W. (2004). Does presidential rhetoric matter? Priming and presidential approval. *Political Science Quarterly, 34,* 755–778.

Druckman, J.N., Jacobs, L., & Ostermeier, E. (2004). Candidate strategies to prime issue and image. *Journal of Politics, 66,* 1180–1202.

Drury, J., & Reicher, S. (2009). Collective psychological empowerment as a model of social change: Researching crowds and power: *Journal of Social Issues, 65,* 707–725.

Duckitt, J. (1994). *The social psychology of prejudice*. Westport, CT: Praeger.

Duckitt J., & Mphuthing, T. (1998). Political power and race relations in South Africa: African attitudes before and after the transition. *Political Psychology, 19,* 809–832.

Duffy, M. (2002, May 6). Trapped by his own instincts. *Time,* pp. 24–29.

Dunn, L.A. (1982). *Controlling the bomb: Nuclear proliferation in the 1980s*. New Haven, CT: Yale University Press.

Dunn, T. (1996). *The militarization of the U.S.-Mexico Border, 1978–1992*. Austin: University of Texas, Center for Mexican American Studies.

Durand, V.M. (1985). Employee absenteeism: A selective review of antecedents and consequences. *Journal of Organizational Behavior Management, 7*, 135–167.

Durkheim, E. (1966). *The rules of sociological method*. New York: Free Press. (Original work published 1938)

Dyer, W.G. (1987). *Team building: Issues and alternatives* (2nd ed.). Reading, MA: Addison-Wesley.

Dyson, S.B. (2001). Drawing policy implications from the "operational code" of a "new" political actor: Russian president Vladimir Putin. *Policy Sciences, 34*, 329–346.

Dyson, S.B., & Preston, T. (2006). Individual characteristics of leaders and the use of analogy in foreign policy decision making. *Political Psychology, 27*, 265–288.

Eades, L. M. (1999). *The end of apartheid in South Africa*. Westport, CT: Greenwood Press.

Eagly, A.H., & Carli, L. (2007). *Through the labyrinth: The truth about how women become leaders*. Boston, MA: Harvard Business School Press.

Eagly, A.H., & Chaiken, S. (1998). Attitude structure and function. In D.T. Gilbert, S.T. Fiske, & G. Lindzey (Eds.), *The handbook of social psychology* (4th ed.). New York: McGraw-Hill.

Easton, D., & Dennis, J. (1973). Governing authorities. In J. Dennis (Ed.), *Socialization to politics*. New York: John Wiley and Sons.

Edgerly, S., Bode, L., Kim, Y.M., & Shah, D. (2013). Campaigns go social: Are Facebook, YouTube, and Twitter changing elections? In T. Ridout (Ed.), *New directions in media and politics*. New York: Routledge.

Eiser, R.J., & Stroebe, W. (1972). *Categorization and social judgment*. New York: Academic Press.

Ehrlich, P., & Liu Jianguo. (2006). Socioeconomic and demographic roots of terrorism. In J. Forest (Ed.), *The making of a terrorist: recruitment, training, and root causes* (pp. 160–171). Westport, CT: Praeger.

El Gazzar, N. (2013). The role of social media in the formation of public opinion towards Islamists: A content analysis. *Journal of Arab & Muslim Media Research, 6*, 35–49.

Elms, A.C., & Milgram, S. (1966). Personality characteristics associated with obedience and defiance toward authoritative command. *Journal of Experimental Research in Personality, 2*, 282–289.

Emerson, R. (1960). *From empire to nation*. Boston, MA: Beacon Press.

Emmons, R. (1997). Motives and goals. In R. Hogan, J. Johnson, & S. Briggs (Eds.), *Handbook of personality psychology*. New York: Academic Press.

Enjolras, B., Kari Steen-Johnsen, K., & Wollebæk, D. (2012). Social media and mobilization to offline demonstrations: Transcending participatory divides? *New Media and Society, 15*, 890–908.

Entman, R. (1993). Framing: Toward clarification of a fractured paradigm. *Journal of Communication, 43*, 293–300.

Epstein, S. (1979). The stability of behavior: I. On predicting most of the people most of the time. *Journal of Personality and Social Psychology, 7*, 1097–1126.

Erikson, E. H. (1950). *Childhood and society.* New York: Norton.

Erikson, E. H. (1958). *Young man Luther.* New York: Norton.

Erikson, E. H. (1969). *Gandhi's truth.* New York: Norton.

Etheredge, L. S. (1978). *A world of men: The private sources of American foreign policy.* Cambridge, MA: MIT Press.

Ewen, R. (1998). *An introduction to theories of personality* (5th ed.). Mahwah, NJ: Lawrence Erlbaum.

Eysenk, H. J. (1975). *The inequality of man.* San Diego, CA: Edits.

Eysenk, H. J. (1979). The conditioning model of neurosis. *Behavior and Brain Sciences, 2,* 155–199.

Ezekiel, R. (1996). *The racist mind: Portraits of American neo-Nazis.* New York: Penguin Books.

Falbo, T. (1977). The multidimensional scaling of power strategies. *Journal of Personality and Social Psychology, 35,* 537–548.

Fallows, J. (2006). *Blind into Baghdad: America's war in Iraq.* New York: Vintage Books.

Farrar, L. L., Jr. (1988). The limits of choice: July 1914 reconsidered. In M. Small & D. Singer (Eds.), *International war: An anthology* (pp. 264–287). Homewood, IL: Dorsey.

Fazio, R. H., & Williams, C. (1986). Attitude accessibility as a moderator of the attitude-perception and attitude-behavior relations: an investigation of the 1984 presidential election. *Journal of Personality and Social Psychology, 51,* 505–514.

Feaver, P. D. (1992/1993). Command and control in emerging nuclear nations. *International Security, 17,* 160–187.

Feaver, P. D., & Niou, E. (1996). Managing nuclear proliferation: Condemn, strike, or assist? *International Studies Quarterly, 40,* 209–234.

Federico, C., & Sidanius, J. (2002). Sophistication and the antecedents of whites' racial policy attitudes. *Public Opinion Quarterly, 66,* 145–176.

Feldman, D. C. (1984). The development and enforcement of group norms. *Academy of Management Review, 9,* 47–53.

Festinger, L. (1950). Informal social communication. *Psychological Review, 57,* 271–282.

Festinger, L. (1954). A theory of social comparison processes. *Human Relations, 7,* 117–140.

Festinger, L. (1957). *A theory of cognitive dissonance.* Evanston, IL: Row, Peterson.

Festinger, L., Schachter, S., & Back, K. (1950). *Social pressures in informal groups.* New York: Harper.

Fields, R. (1979). Child terror victims and adult terrorists. *Journal of Psychohistory, 7,* 71–75.

Fields, R. Elbedour, S., & Abu Hein, F. (2002). The Palestinian suicide bomber. In C. Stout (Ed.), *The psychology of terrorism: Clinical aspects and responses* (pp. 193–223). Westport, CT: Praeger.

Fijalkowski, J. (1996). Aggressive nationalism and immigration in Germany. In R. Caplan & J. Feffer (Eds.), *Europe's new nationalism: States and minorities in conflict.* Oxford: Oxford University Press.

Fiorina, M. P. (1981). *Retrospective voting in American national elections.* New Haven, CT: Yale University Press.

Fishbein, M., & Ajzen, I. (1972). Attitudes and opinions. *Annual Review of Psychology, 23,* 487–544.

Fishbein, M., & Ajzen, I. (1975). *Belief, attitude, intention, and behavior: An introduction to theory and research.* Reading, MA: Addison-Wesley.

Fishbein, M., & Ajzen, I. (1980). Predicting and understanding consumer behavior: Attitude-behavior correspondence. In I. Ajzen & M. Fishbein (Eds.), *Understanding attitudes and predicting social behavior.* Englewood Cliffs, NJ: Prentice Hall.

Fisher, R. J. (1990). Needs theory, social identity and an eclectic model of conflict. In J. Burton (Ed.), *Conflict: Human needs theory.* New York: St. Martin's.

Fisher, R. J. (2001). Cyprus: The failure of mediation and the escalation of an identity-based conflict to an adversarial impasse. *Journal of Peace Research, 38,* 307–326.

Fiske, S. (1998). Stereotyping, prejudice, and discrimination. In D. T. Gilbert, S. T. Fiske, & G. Lindzey (Eds.), *The handbook of social psychology* (4th ed., Vol. 2, pp. 357–411). New York: McGraw-Hill.

Fiske, S., & Pavelchak, M. (1986). Category-based vs. piecemeal-based affective responses: Developments in schema-triggered affect. In R. Sorrentino & E. Higgings (Eds.), *Handbook of motivation and cognition* (pp. 167–203). New York: Guilford Press.

Fiske, S., & Taylor, S. E. (1991). *Social cognition.* New York: McGraw-Hill.

Fleeson, W. (2004). Moving personality beyond the person-situation debate. *Current Directions in Psychological Science, 13,* 83–87.

Flint, J., & de Waal, A. (2005). *Darfur: A short history of a long war.* London: Zed Books.

Fodor, E. M. (1985). The power motive, group conflict, and physiological arousal. *Journal of Personality and Social Psychology, 49,* 1408–1415.

Fodor, E. M., & Farrow, D. L. (1979). The power motive as an influence on the use of power. *Journal of Personality and Social Psychology, 37,* 2091–2097.

Fodor, E. M., & Smith, T. (1982). The power motive as an influence on group decision making. *Journal of Personality and Social Psychology, 42,* 178–185.

Folger, R. (1986). A referent cognitions theory of relative deprivation. In J. M. Olson, C. P. Herman, & M. P. Zanna (Eds.), *Relative deprivation and social comparison: The Ontario Symposium* (Vol. 4, pp. 217–242). Hillsdale, NJ: Erlbaum.

Foner, E., & Garraty, J. A. (1991). *The reader's companion to American history.* Retrieved from www.history.com/topics/black-history

Ford, R. T. (2008). *The race card: How bluffing about bias makes race relations worse.* New York: Farrar, Straus & Giroux.

Forsyth, D. R. (1990). *Group dynamics.* Pacific Grove, CA: Brooks/Cole.

Foschi, M., Warriner, G. K., & Hart, S. D. (1985). Standards, expectations, and interpersonal influence. *Social Psychology Quarterly, 48,* 108–117.

Fowler, J. H., Baker, L. A., & Dawes, C. T. (2008). Genetic variation in political participation. *American Political Science Review, 102,* 233–248.

Fox, F., & Staw, B. M. (1979). The trapped administrator: The effects of job insecurity and policy resistance upon commitment to a course of action. *Administrative Science Quarterly, 24,* 449–471.

Fowler, J., & Dawes, C. (2008). Two genes predict voter turnout. *Journal of Politics, 70,* 579–594.

Franklin, C. H. (1992). Measurement and dynamics of party identification. *Political Behavior, 14,* 297–309.

Franklin, C. H., & Jackson, J. E. (1983). The dynamics of party identification. *American Political Science Review, 77,* 957–973.

Fredrickson, G. (1999). Models of American ethnic relations: A historical perspective. In D. Prentice & D. Miller (Eds.), *Cultural divides: Understanding and overcoming group conflict.* New York: Sage.

Freedman, J., & Fraser, S. (1966). Compliance without pressure: The foot-in-the-door technique. *Journal of Personality and Social Psychology, 4,* 195–202.

Freedman, L. (1981). *The evolution of nuclear strategy.* London: Macmillan.

Freedman, L., & Karsh, E. (1993). *The Gulf conflict, 1990–1991: Diplomacy and war in the new world order.* Princeton, NJ: Princeton University Press.

Freeman, A. (1999, June 11). Turkish Kurds endure conditions "just like Kosovo." *Globe and Mail,* p. A1.

French, J. A., Smith, K. B., Alford, J. R., Guck, A., Birnie, A. K., & Hibbing, J. R. (2014). Cortisol and politics: Variance in voting behavior is predicted by baseline cortisol levels. *Physiology & Behavior, 133,* 61–67.

French, J.R.P., & Raven, B. (1959). The bases of social power. In D. Cartwright (Ed.), *Studies in social power.* Ann Arbor, MI: Institute for Social Research.

Freud, S. (1932). Letter to Albert Einstein, September 1932. (Reprinted in *Great political thinkers: Plato to the present,* pp. 804–810, by W. Ebenstein, Ed., 1951, New York: Rinehart)

Freud, S. (1950). *Beyond the pleasure principle.* New York: Liveright.

Freud, S. (1962). *Civilization and its discontents.* New York: Norton.

Frey, D. (1986). Recent research on selective exposure to information. In L. Berkowitz (Ed.), *Advances in experimental social psychology* (Vol. 19, pp. 41–80). New York: Academic Press.

Freyre, G. (1956). *The masters and the slaves (Casa-Grande and Senzala): A study in the development of Brazilian civilization* (S. Putnam, Trans.). New York: Knopf.

Friedland, N. (1976). Social influence via threats. *Journal of Experimental Social Psychology, 12,* 552–563.

Frijda, N. (1986). *The emotions.* Cambridge: Cambridge University Press.

Fromm, E. (1941). *Escape from freedom.* New York: Holt, Rinehart, and Winston.

Fromm, E. (1955). *The sane society.* New York: Holt, Rinehart, and Winston.

Fromm, E. (1964). *The heart of man.* New York: Holt, Rinehart, and Winston.

Fuller, S. R., & Aldag, R. J. (1997). Challenging the mindguards: Moving small group analysis beyond groupthink. In B. Sundelius, P. 't Hart, & E. Stern (Eds.), *Beyond groupthink: Group decision making in foreign policy.* Ann Arbor: University of Michigan Press.

Funder, D. C. (2010). *The personality puzzle.* New York: W. W. Norton.

Funk, C. (1999). Bringing the candidate into models of candidate evaluation. *Journal of Politics, 61,* 700–720.

Funk, C. (2013). Genetic foundations of political behavior. In L. Huddy, D. O. Sears, & J. S. Levy (Eds.), *The Oxford handbook of political psychology* (2nd ed., pp. 237–261). New York: Oxford University Press.

Funk, C. L., Smith, K. B., Alford, J. R., & Hibbing, J. R. (2010, September 2–5). *Toward a modern view of political man: Genetic and environmental transmission of political orientations from attitude intensity to political participation.* Paper presented at the Annual Meetings of the American Political Science Association, Washington, DC.

Funk, C. L., Smith, K. B., Alford, J. R., Hibbing, M. V., Eaton, N. R., Krueger, R. F., . . . Hibbing, J. R. (2013). Genetic and environmental transmission of political orientations. *Political Psychology, 34*, 805–819. doi:10.1111/j.1467-9221.2012.00915.x

Gaddis, J. L. (1992). *The United States and the end of the Cold War: Implications, reconsiderations, provocations.* New York: Oxford University Press.

Gaddis, J. L. (1997). *We now know: Rethinking Cold War history.* New York: Oxford University Press.

Gaertner, S., & Dovidio, J. (1986). The aversive form of racism. In J. F. Dovidio & S. L. Gaertner (Eds.), *Prejudice, discrimination and racism* (pp. 61–89). Orlando, FL: Academic Press.

Gage, N., Leavitt, G., & Stone, G. (1957). The psychological meaning of acquiescence set for authoritarianism. *Journal of Abnormal and Social Psychology, 55*, 98–103.

Galinsky, A., & Moskowitz, G. (2000). Perspective-taking: Decreasing stereotype expression, stereotype accessibility, and in-group favoritism. *Journal of Personality and Social Psychology, 78*, 708–724.

Gallagher, M. E., & Allen, S. H. (2014). Presidential personality: Not just a nuisance. *Political Psychology, 10*, 1–21.

Gallup Center. (1999). Gay and lesbian rights. Retrieved from www.Gallup.com/poll/1651/gay-lesbian-rights

Gallup Poll. (2000). One in five Americans unaware that either Bush or Gore is a likely presidential nominee. Retrieved from www.gallup.com

Gamson, W. A. (1961). An experimental test of a theory of coalition formation. *American Sociological Review, 26*, 565–573.

Gamson, W. A. (1964). Experimental studies of coalition formation. In L. Berkowitz (Ed.), *Advances in experimental social psychology* (Vol. 1, pp. 82–110). New York: Academic Press.

Gamson, W. A. (1992). The social psychology of collective action. In A. D. Morris & C. M. Mueller (Eds.), *Frontiers in social movement theory* (Vol. 1, pp. 82–110). New York: Academic Press

Gangestad, S. W., & Snyder, M. (2000). Self-monitoring: Appraisal and reappraisal. *Psychological Bulletin, 126*, 530–555.

Ganz, N. (2010). Leading change: Leadership, organization, and social movements. In N. Nohira & R. Kharana (Eds.), *Handbook of leadership: Theory and practice* (pp. 507–526). Cambridge, MA: Harvard Business School.

Gaouette, N. (2008, September 19). Hispanics souring on situation in U.S. *Idaho Spokesman Review*, p. A4.

Gardner, W., & Martinko, M. (1996). Using the Myers-Briggs type indicator to study managers: A literature review and research agenda. *Journal of Management, 22*, 45–83.

Gartenstein-Ross, D. (2007). *My year inside radical islam.* New York: Penguin.

Gautney, H. (2011, October 10). What is Occupy Wall Street? The history of leaderless movements. *Washington Post.* Retrieved from www.washingtonpost.com/national/on-leadershp/what-is-occupy-wall-street

Gazzaniga, M., Ivry, R., & Mangun, G. (Eds.). (2014). *Cognitive neuroscience V.* Cambridge: MIT Press.

Geiger, S. W., Robertson, C. J., & Irwin, J. G. (1998). The impact of cultural values on escalation of commitment. *International Journal of Organizational Analysis, 6,* 165–176.

Gellman, B. (2008). *Angler: The Cheney vice presidency.* New York: Penguin Press.

Gelvin, J. L. (2012). *The Arab uprisings: What everyone needs to know.* Oxford: Oxford University Press.

George, A. L. (1969). The "operational code": A neglected approach to the study of political leaders and decision making. *International Studies Quarterly, 13,* 190–222.

George, A. L. (1979). The causal nexus between cognitive beliefs and decision making behavior: The "operational code" belief system. In L. Falkowski (Ed.), *Psychological models in international politics* (pp. 95–123). Boulder, CO: Westview Press.

George, A. L. (1980). *Presidential decisionmaking in foreign policy: The effective use of information and advice.* Boulder, CO: Westview Press.

George, A. L. (1991). *Forceful persuasion: An alternative to war.* Washington, DC: U.S. Institute of Peace.

George, A. L. & George, J. L. (1964). *Woodrow Wilson and Colonel House: A personality study.* New York: Dover.

George, A. L., & George, J. L. (1998). *Presidential personality and performance.* Boulder, CO: Westview Press.

George, A. L., & Smoke, R. (1974). *Deterrence in American foreign policy.* New York: Columbia University Press.

George, A. L., & Stern, E. (2002). Harnessing conflict in foreign policy making: From devil's advocate to multiple advocacy. *Presidential Studies Quarterly, 32,* 484–508.

George, J., & Wilcox, L. (1996). *American extremists: Militias, supremacists, Klansmen, communists and others.* New York: Prometheus Books.

Gifford, R., & O'Connor, B. (1987). The interpersonal circumplex as a behavior map. *Journal of Personality and Social Psychology, 52,* 1019–1026.

Gilligan, J. (1997). *Violence: Reflections on a national epidemic.* New York: Vintage Books.

Gitlin, T. (2012). *Occupy nation: The roots, the spirit, and the promise of Occupy Wall Street.* New York: HarperCollins.

Ginges, J., Atran, S., Sachdeva, S., & Medin, D. (2011). Psychology out of the laboratory: The challenge of violent extremism. *American Psychologist.* Retrieved from http://artisresearch.com/articles/Ginges_Atran_Sachdeva_Medin_Violent_Extremism.pdf

Gjelstad, J., & Njolstad, O. (Eds.) (1996). *Nuclear rivalry and international order.* London: Sage.

Glad, B. (1980). *Jimmy Carter: In search of the great White House.* New York: W. W. Norton.

Glad, B. (1983). Black-and-white thinking: Ronald Reagan's approach to foreign policy. *Political Psychology, 4,* 33–76.

Glad, B. (1989). Reagan's midlife crisis and the turn to the right. *Political Psychology, 10,* 593–624.

Gliebe, E. (2007, May/June). The people that shall dwell alone: An explanation of Jewish behavior. *National Vanguard*. Retrieved from www.natwan.com

Global Security. (2008). Sustainable peace key to post-genocide reconciliation. Retrieved from www.globalsecurity.org/military/library/news/2008/08/mil-080826-irin01.htm

Glynn, C., Herbst, S., O'Keefe, G., & Shapiro, R. (1999). *Public opinion*. Boulder, CO: Westview Press.

Goertz, G. (2004). Constraints, compromises, and decision-making. *Journal of Conflict Resolution, 48*, 14–38.

Goldberg, J. (2005, October 31). Breaking ranks: What turned Brent Scowcroft against the Bush administration? *New Yorker*, pp. 54–65.

Goltz, S. M. (1992). A sequential learning analysis of decisions in organizations to escalate investments despite continuing costs or losses. *Journal of Applied Behavior Analysis, 25*, 561–574.

Goltz, T. (2012). The successes of the spin doctors: Western media reporting on the Nagorno Karabakh conflict. *Journal of Muslim Minority Affairs, 32*, 186–195.

Graber, D. (1984). *Processing the news: How people tame the information tide*. New York: Longman.

Graham-Brown, S., & Sackur, Z. (1995). The Kurds, a regional issue. Retrieved from www.unhcr.ch/refworld/country/writenet

Grant, A. (2013, September 18). Goodbye to MBTI: The fad that won't die. *Psychology Today*. Retrieved from www.psychologytoday.com/blog/give-and-take/201309/goodbye-mbti-the-fad-won-t-die

Green, D. P., Abelson, R. P., & Garnett, M. (1999). The distinctive political views of hate-crime perpetrators and white supremacists. In D. A. Prentice & D. T. Miller (Eds.), *Cultural divides: Understanding and overcoming group conflict*. New York: Sage.

Greenstein, F. I. (1969). *Personality and politics: Problems of evidence, inference, and conceptualization*. Chicago, IL: Markham.

Greenstein, F. I. (1982). *The hidden-hand presidency: Eisenhower as leader*. New York: Basic Books.

Greenstein, F. I. (2000). *The presidential difference: Leadership style from FDR to Clinton*. New York: Free Press.

Greer, C. R., & Stephens, G. K. (2001). Escalation of commitment: A comparison of differences between Mexican and U.S. decision-makers. *Journal of Management, 27*, 51–78.

Griffith, J., & Greenlees, J. (1993). Group cohesion and unit versus individual deployment of U.S. Army reservists in Operation Desert Storm. *Psychological Reports, 73*, 272–274.

Groeling, T., & Kernell, S. (1998). Is network news coverage of the president biased? *Journal of Politics, 60*, 1063–1087.

Groff, B. D., Baron, R. S., & Moore, D. L. (1983). Distraction, attentional conflict, and drive like behavior. *Journal of Experimental Social Psychology, 19*, 359–380.

Groshek, J., & Ahmed Al-Rawi, A. (2013). Public Sentiment and critical framing in social media content during the 2012 U.S. presidential campaign. *Social Science Computer Review*, 563–576.

Gross, K. (2008). Framing persuasive appeals: Episodic and thematic framing, emotional response, and policy opinion. *Political Psychology, 29,* 169–192.

Gross, K., & D'Ambrosio, L. (2004). Framing emotional responses. *Political Psychology, 25,* 1–29.

Grosser, D. (1992). The dynamics of German reunification. In D. Grosser (Ed.), *German unification: The unexpected challenge* (pp. 1–20). Oxford: Berg.

Gunter, M. (1990). *The Kurds in Turkey.* Boulder, CO: Westview Press.

Gurr, T. R. (1970). *Why men rebel.* Princeton, NJ: Princeton University Press.

Gurr, T. R. (1994). Peoples against states: Ethnopolitical conflict and the changing world system. *International Studies Quarterly, 38,* 347–377.

Haas, M. L. (2001). Prospect theory and the Cuban missile crisis. *International Studies Quarterly, 45,* 241–270.

Hackman, J. R., Brousseau, K. R., & Weiss, J. A. (1976). The interaction of task design and group performance strategies in determining group effectiveness. *Organizational Behavior and Human Performance, 16,* 350–365.

Hackman, J. R., & Lawler, E. (1971). Employee reactions to job characteristics. *Journal of Applied Psychology, 55,* 259–286.

Hackman, J. R., & Morris, C. G. (1975). Group tasks, group interaction process, and group performance effectiveness: A review and proposed integration. In L. Berkowitz (Ed.), *Advances in experimental social psychology* (Vol. 8, pp. 47–99). New York: Academic Press.

Hagan, J. D. (2001). Does decision making matter? *International Studies Review, 3,* 5–46.

Hagerty, D. T. (1995/1996). Nuclear deterrence in South Asia: The 1990 Indo-Pakistani crisis. *International Security, 20,* 79–115.

Hagerty, D. T. (1998). *The consequences of nuclear proliferation: Lessons from South Asia.* Cambridge, MA: MIT Press.

Hagerty, M. R. (2000). Social comparisons of incomes in one's community: Evidence from national surveys of income and happiness. *Journal of Personality and Social Psychology, 78,* 764–771.

Hale, H. (2014, August 29). Russian nationalism and the logic of the Kremlin's actions on Ukraine. *Guardian.* Retrieved from www.theguardian.com/world/2014/aug/29/russian-nationalism-kremlin-actions-ukraine

Hall, C., & Lindzey, G. (1970). *Theories of personality* (2nd ed.). New York: John Wiley and Sons.

Hammond, R. A., & Axelrod, R. (2006). The evolution of ethnocentrism. *Journal of Conflict Resolution, 50,* 1–11.

Hanchard, M. (1993). Movimento negro in Brazil. In Kay Warren (Ed.), *The violence within: Cultural and political opposition in divided nations.* Boulder, CO: Westview.

Handley, I. M., Lassiter, G. D., Nickell, E. F., & Herchenroeder, L. M. (2004). Affect and automatic mood maintenance. *Journal of Experimental Social Psychology, 40,* 106–112.

Haney, P. J. (1997). *Organizing for foreign policy crises: Presidents, advisers, and the management of decision making.* Ann Arbor: University of Michigan Press.

Hantula, D. A. (1992). The basic importance of escalation. *Journal of Applied Behavior Analysis, 25*, 579–583.

Harding, L. (2014, September 12). EU would be safer with Ukrainian president. *Guardian.* Retrieved from www.theguardian.com/world/2014/sep/12

Hardy, C., & Latane, B. (1986). Social loafing on a cheering task. *Social Science, 71*, 165–172.

Hargrove, E. C. (1988). *Jimmy Carter as president: Leadership and the politics of the public good.* Baton Rouge: Louisiana State University Press.

Haritos-Fatouros, M. (1988). The official torturer: A learning model for obedience to the authority of violence. *Journal of Applied Social Psychology, 18*, 1107–1120.

Harkins, S. G. (1987). Social loafing and social facilitation. *Journal of Experimental Social Psychology, 23*, 1–18.

Harkins, S. G., & Petty, R. E. (1982). Effects of task difficulty and task uniqueness on social loafing. *Journal of Personality and Social Psychology, 43*, 1214–1229.

Harper, N. L., & Askling, L. R. (1980). Group communication and quality of task solution in a media production organization. *Communication Monographs, 47*, 77–100.

Harvey, F. P. (1997a). Nuclear deterrence: The record of aggregate testing. New directions for aggregate testing. In F. P. Harvey (Ed.), *The future's back: Nuclear rivalry, deterrence theory, and crisis stability after the Cold War* (pp. 19–46). Montreal: McGill-Queen's University Press.

Harvey, F. P. (1997b). Deterrence and compellence in protracted crises: Methodology and preliminary findings. *International Studies Notes, 22*, 12–23.

Harvey, F. P. (1997c). Deterrence and ethnic conflict: The case of Bosnia-Herzegovina, 1993–1994. *Security Studies, 6*, 181–210.

Harvey, F. P. (1998). Rigor mortis, or rigor, more tests: Necessity, sufficiency, and deterrence logic. *International Studies Quarterly, 42*, 675–707.

Harvey, P. H., & Greene, P. J. (1981). Group composition: An evolutionary perspective. In H. Kellerman (Ed.), *Group cohesion.* New York: Grune and Stratton.

Hashim, A. S. (2006). *Insurgency and counter-insurgency in Iraq.* Ithaca, NY: Cornell University Press.

Haslam, S. A. (2001). *Psychology in organizations: The social identity approach.* London: Sage.

Haslam, S. A., & Platow, M. J. (2001). The link between leadership and followership: How affirming a social identity translates vision into action. *Personality and Social Psychology Bulletin, 27*, 1469–1479.

Haslam, S. A., Reicher, S. D., & Platow, M. J. (2011). *The new psychology of leadership: Identity, influence, and power.* New York: Psychology Press.

Hassan, H. D. (2008). Iraq: Tribal structure, social, and political activities. *CRS Report for Congress.* Washington, DC: Congressional Research Service.

Hastie, R. (1986). Review essay: Experimental evidence on group accuracy. In G. Owen & B. Gofman (Eds.), *Information pooling and group decision making* (pp. 129–157). Westport, CT: JAI Press.

Hastie, R., & Park, B. (1986). The relationship between memory and judgment depends upon whether the task is memory-based or on-line. *Psychological Review, 93,* 258–268.

Hatemi, P. K., Funk, C. L., Medland, S. E., Maes, H. M., Silberg, J. L., Martin, N. G., & Eaves, L. J. (2009). Genetic and environmental transmission of political attitudes over a life time. *Journal of Politics, 71,* 1141–1156. doi:10.1017/S0022381609090938

Hawthorne, J., Houston, J. B., & McKinney, M. S. (2013). Live-tweeting a presidential primary debate: Exploring new political conversations. *Social Science Computer Review, 31,* 552–562.

Heclo, H. (2003). The political ethos of George W. Bush. In F. I. Greenstein (Ed.), *The George W. Bush presidency: An early assessment* (pp. 17–50). Baltimore, MD: Johns Hopkins University Press.

Heider, F. (1946). Attitudes and cognitive organization. *Journal of Psychology, 21,* 107–112.

Heider, F. (1958). *The psychology of interpersonal relations.* New York: Wiley.

Heim, K. (2013). Framing the 2008 Iowa democratic caucuses. Political blogs and second level intermedia agenda setting. *Journalism & Mass Communications Quarterly, 90,* 500–519.

Helfstein, S. (2012). Backfire: Behavioral decision making and the strategic risks of successful surprise. *Foreign Policy Analysis, 8,* 275–292.

Herman, J. (1992). *Trauma and recovery: The aftermath of violence from domestic abuse to political terror.* New York: Basic Books.

Hermann, M. G. (1979). Indicators of stress in policymakers during foreign policy crises. *Political Psychology, 1,* 27–46.

Hermann, M. G. (1980a). Assessing the personalities of Soviet Politburo members. *Personality and Social Psychology Bulletin, 6,* 332–352.

Hermann, M. G. (1980b). Explaining foreign policy behavior using personal characteristics of political leaders. *International Studies Quarterly, 24,* 7–46.

Hermann, M. G. (1983). *Handbook for assessing personal characteristics and foreign policy orientations of political leaders.* Columbus, OH: Mershon Center Occasional Papers.

Hermann, M. G. (1984). Personality and foreign policy decision making: A study of 53 heads of government. In D. A. Sylvan & S. Chan (Eds.), *Foreign policy decision-making: Perceptions, cognition, and artificial intelligence* (pp. 53–80). New York: Praeger.

Hermann, M. G. (1986). Ingredients of leadership. In M. G. Hermann (Ed.), *Political psychology: Contemporary problems and issues* (pp. 167–192). San Francisco, CA: Jossey-Bass.

Hermann, M. G. (1987). Assessing the foreign policy role orientations of sub-Saharan African leaders. In S. Walker (Ed.), *Role theory and foreign policy analysis* (pp. 161–198). Durham, NC: Duke University Press.

Hermann, M. G. (1988). Hafes Al-Assad, President of Syria: A leadership profile. In B. Kellerman & J. Rubins (Eds.), *Leadership in negotiation in the Middle East* (pp. 70–95). New York: Praeger.

Hermann, M. G. (1995). Advice and advisers in the Clinton presidency: The impact of leadership style. In S. Renshon (Ed.), *The Clinton presidency: Campaigning, governing, and the psychology of leadership* (pp. 149–164). Boulder, CO: Westview Press.

Hermann, M. G. (1999a). *Assessing leadership style: A trait analysis.* Columbus, OH: Social Science Automation.

Hermann, M. G. (1999b). *Leadership profile of Bill Clinton.* Columbus, OH: Social Science Automation.

Hermann, M. G. (2000). An appendum: Making empirical inferences about elite decision making politically relevant. *Political Psychologist, 15,* 24–29.

Hermann, M. G. (2001). How decision units shape foreign policy: A theoretical framework. *International Studies Review, 3,* 47–82.

Hermann, M. (2006). *A guide to understanding crisis management through case studies.* Stockholm and Syracuse: CRISMART, Swedish National Defense College and Moynihan Institute of Global Affairs.

Hermann, M. G., & Kegley, C. W., Jr. (1995). Rethinking democracy and international peace: Perspectives from political psychology. *International Studies Quarterly, 39,* 511–533.

Hermann, M. G., & Preston, T. (1994). Presidents, advisers, and foreign policy: The effect of leadership style on executive arrangements. *Political Psychology, 15,* 75–96.

Hermann, M. G., & Preston, T. (1998). Presidents, leadership style, and the advisory process. In E. R. Wittkopf & J. M. McCormick (Eds.), *The domestic sources of American foreign policy: Insights and evidence* (pp. 351–368). Lanham, MD: Rowman & Littlefield.

Hermann, M. G., Preston, T., & Young, M. (1996, April 16–20). *Who leads can matter in foreign policymaking: A framework for leadership analysis.* Paper presented at the annual meeting of the International Studies Association, San Diego.

Hermann, M. G., Preston, T., Korany, B., & Shaw, T. M. (2001). Who leads matters: The effects of powerful individuals. In *Leaders, groups, and coalitions: Understanding the people and processes in foreign* policymaking (pp. 83–131). Boston, MA: Blackwell. Also appears as a Special Issue of the *International Studies Review* (Fall 2001) as part of ISA Millennial Series.

Herr, P. (1986). Consequences of priming: judgment and behavior. *Journal of Personality and Social Psychology, 40,* 843–861.

Herring, E. (1995). *Danger and opportunity: Explaining international crisis outcomes.* Manchester: Manchester University Press.

Herrmann, R. (1985a). *Perceptions and behavior in Soviet foreign policy.* Pittsburgh, PA: University of Pittsburgh Press.

Herrmann, R. (1985b). Analyzing Soviet images of the United States. *Journal of Conflict Resolution, 29,* 665–697.

Herrmann, R. (1988). The empirical challenge of the cognitive revolution: A strategy for drawing inferences about perceptions. *International Studies Quarterly, 32,* 175–203.

Herrmann, R. (1991). The Soviet decision to withdraw from Afghanistan: Changing strategic and regional images. In R. Jervis & J. Snyder (Eds.), *Dominoes and bandwagons* (pp. 220–249). New York: Oxford.

Herrmann, R. K., Voss, J. F., Schooler, T. Y. E., & Ciarrochi, J. (1997). Images in international relations: An experimental test of cognitive schemata. *International Studies Quarterly, 41,* 403–433.

Hess, R., & Torney, J. (1967). *The development of political attitudes in children.* Chicago, IL: Aldine.

Hewstone, M. (1989). Intergroup attribution: Some implications for the study of ethnic prejudice. In J. P. van Oudenhoven & T. Willemsen (Eds.), *Ethnic minorities: Social psychological perspectives*. Berwyn, PA: Swets North America.

Hewstone, M., & Brown, R. (Eds.). (1986). *Contact and conflict in intergroup encounters*. Oxford: Basil Blackwell.

Hill, G. W. (1982). Group versus individual performance: Are $N + 1$ heads better than one? *Psychological Bulletin, 91*, 517–539.

Hill, S., Lo, J., Vavreck, L., & Zaller, J. (2013). How quickly we forget: The duration of persuasion effects from mass communication. *Political Communication, 30*, 521–547.

Hirokawa, R. Y. (1980). A comparative analysis of communication patterns within effective and ineffective decision-making groups. *Communication Monographs, 47*, 312–321.

Hirt, E. R., & Markman, K. D. (1995). Multiple explanation: A consider-an-alternative strategy for debiasing judgments. *Personality and Social Psychology Bulletin, 69*, 1069–1086.

Hobert, R. L., & Tchernev, J. M. (2013). Media influence as persuasion. In J. P. Dillar & L. Shen (Eds.), *The SAGE handbook of persuasion: Developments in theory and practice* (2nd ed., pp. 36–52). Thousand Oaks, CA: Sage.

Hofstede, G., & McCrae, R. R. (2004). Personality and culture revisited: Linking traits and dimensions of culture. *Cross-Cultural Research, 38*, 52–88.

Hoffman, K., & Llagas, C. (2007). *Status and trends in the education of ethnic and racial minorities*. Washington, DC: National Center for Education Statistics.

Hogg, M. A. (2000). Self-categorization and subjective uncertainty resolutions: Cognitive and motivational facets of social identity and group membership. In J. P. Forgas, K. D. Williams, & L. Wheeler (Eds.), *The social mind: Cognitive and motivational aspects of interpersonal behavior* (pp. 323–349). New York: Cambridge University Press.

Hogg, M. A. (2004). Social categorization and group behavior. In M. B. Brewer & M. Hewstone (Eds.), *Self and social identity*. Malden, MA: Blackwell.

Hogg, M. A., & Abrams, D. (1988). *Social identifications: A social psychology of intergroup relations and group processes*. New York: Routledge.

Hogg, M. A., & McGarty, C. (1990). Self-categorization and social identity. In M. A. Hogg & D. Abrams (Eds.), *Social identity theory: Constructive and critical advances*. New York: Springer-Verlag.

Hogg, M. A., Turner, J. C., & Davidson, B. (1990). Polarized norms and social frames of reference: A test of the self-categorization theory of group polarization. *Basic and Applied Social Psychology, 11*, 77–100.

Hollander, E. P. (1985). Leadership and power. In G. Lindzey & E. Aronson (Eds.), *Handbook of social psychology* (3rd ed., Vol. 2, pp. 485–537). New York: Random House.

Holsti, O. (1962). The belief system and national images: A case study. *Journal of Conflict Resolution, 6*, 244–252.

Holsti, O. (1967). Cognitive dynamics and images of the enemy. In R. Fagen (Ed.), *Enemies in politics* (pp. 25–96). Chicago, IL: Rand McNally.

Holsti, O. (1969). The belief system and national images: A case study. In J. Rosenau (Ed.), *International politics and foreign policy* (2nd ed., pp. 543–550). New York: Free Press.

Holsti, O. (1970). The "operational code" approach to the study of political leaders: John Foster Dulles' philosophical and instrumental beliefs. *Canadian Journal of Political Science, 3,* 123–157.

Holsti, O. (1977). *The "operational code" as an approach to analysis of belief systems.* Final Report to the National Science Foundation. Grant No. SOC75-15368.

Holtz, R., & Miller, N. (1985). Assumed similarity and opinion certainty. *Journal of Personality and Social Psychology, 48,* 890–898.

Horowitz, D. (1985). *Ethnic groups in conflict.* Berkeley: University of California Press.

House, R. J. (1990). Power and personality in complex organizations. In B. M. Staw & L. L. Cummings (Eds.), *Personality and organizational influence* (pp. 181–233). Greenwich, CT: JAI Press.

Howard, J. W., & Rothbart, M. (1980). Social categorization and memory for in-group and out-group behavior. *Journal of Personality and Social Psychology, 38,* 301–310.

Hoyt, P., & Garrison, J. (1997). Political manipulation within the small group: Foreign policy advisers in the Carter administration. In P. 't Hart, E. Stern, & B. Sundelius (Eds.), *Beyond groupthink* (pp. 249–274). Ann Arbor: University of Michigan Press.

Hsu, S. (2006, February 12). Katrina report spreads blame: Homeland security, Chertoff singled out. *Washington Post.*

Huckfeldt, R., Levine, J., Morgan, W., & Sprague, J. (1999). Accessibility and the political utility of partisan and ideological orientation. *American Journal of Political Science, 43,* 888–911.

Human Rights Watch. (1999, March). Leave none to tell the story. WSWS. Genocide in Rwanda.

Human Rights Watch. (2000). *Human Rights Watch world report 2000.* New York: Author.

Human Rights Watch. (2006). Funding the final war LTTE intimidation and extortion in the Tamil diaspora. Retrieved from http://hrw.org/reports/2006/ltte0306/index.htm

Human Rights Watch. (2007). Darfur 2007: Chaos by design. Retrieved from http://hrw.org/reports/2007/sudan0907/2.htm#_Toc177544425

Hunter, J. D. (1991). *Culture wars: The struggle to define America.* New York: Basic Books.

Hutchison, E. O. (2007). *The Latino challenge to Black America.* Los Angeles, CA: Middle Passage Press.

Huth, P., & Russett, B. (1984). What makes deterrence work? Cases from 1900–1980. *World Politics, 36,* 496–526.

Huth, P., & Russett, B. (1988). Deterrence failure and crisis escalation. *International Studies Quarterly, 32,* 29–45.

Hymans, J. (2006). *The psychology of nuclear proliferation: Identity, emotions, and foreign policy.* Cambridge: Cambridge University Press.

Ihonvbere, J. O. (1994). *Nigeria: The politics of adjustment and democracy.* New Brunswick, NJ: Transaction.

Insko, C. A., & Schopler, J. (1987). Categorization, competition, and collectivity. In C. Hendrick (Ed.), *Group processes: Review of personality and social psychology* (Vol. 8, pp. 213–251). Newbury Park, CA: Sage.

Isaak, R. A. (1975). *Individuals and world politics.* North Scituate, MA: Duxbury Press.

Isen, A. (1993). Positive affect and decision making. In M. Lewis & I. Haviland (Eds.), *Handbook of emotions* (pp. 261–277). New York: Guilford Press.

Isenberg, D. J. (1986). Group polarization: A critical review and meta-analysis. *Journal of Personality and Social Psychology, 50,* 1141–1151.

Isikoff, M., & Corn, D. (2006). *Hubris: The inside story of spin, scandal, and the selling of the Iraq war.* New York: Crown.

Iskander, A. (2013). *Egypt in flux: Essays on an unfinished revolution.* New York: American University in Cairo Press.

Iyengar, S. (1990). Shortcuts to political knowledge: The role of selective attention and accessibility. In J. Ferejohn & J. Kuklinski (Eds.), *Information and democratic processes* (pp. 160–185). Urbana: University of Illinois Press.

Iyengar, S. (1991). *Is anyone responsible? How television frames political issues.* Chicago, IL: University of Chicago Press.

Iyengar, S., & Kinder, D. (1987). *News that matters.* Chicago, IL: University of Chicago Press.

Iyengar, S., Peters, M., & Kinder, D. (1982). Experimental demonstrations of the not-so-minimal political consequences of mass media. *American Political Science Review, 76,* 848–858.

Iyengar, S., Peters, M., Kinder, D., & Krosnick, J. (1984). The evening news and presidential elections. *Journal of Personality and Social Psychology, 46,* 778–787.

Izard, C. E. (1977). *Human emotions.* New York: Plenum Press.

Jackman, M. (1978). General and applied tolerance: Does education increase commitment to racial integration? *American Journal of Political Science, 22,* 302–324.

Jackson, A. (2001). *Images and police behavior: An analysis of police-community relations* (Unpublished PhD dissertation). Washington State University, Pullman.

Jackson, D., & Messick, S. (1957). A note on ethnocentrism and acquiescent response sets. *Journal of Abnormal and Social Psychology, 54,* 132–134.

Jacobs, L., & Shapiro, R. (1994). Issues, candidate image and priming: The use of private polls in Kennedy's 1960 presidential campaign. *American Political Science Review, 88,* 527–540.

James, H. (1989). *A German identity, 1770–1990.* London: Westfield and Nicolson.

James, J. A. (1951). A preliminary study of the size determinant in small group interaction. *American Sociological Review, 16,* 474–477.

Janes, L., & Olson, J. M. (2000). Jeer pressure: The behavioral effects of observing ridicule of others. *Personality and Social Psychology Bulletin, 26,* 474–485.

Janis, I. L. (1972). *Victims of groupthink.* Boston, MA: Houghton Mifflin.

Janis, I. L. (1982). *Groupthink: Psychological studies of policy decisions and fiascoes* (2nd ed.). Boston, MA: Houghton Mifflin.

Janis, I. L., & Mann, L. (1977). *Decision making: A psychological analysis of conflict, choice, and commitment.* New York: Free Press.

Jennings, M. K. (2004). American political participation as viewed through the political socialization project. In M. G. Hermann (Ed.), *Advances in political psychology.* London: Elsevier.

Jennings, M. K., & Niemi, R. (1974). *Families, schools and political learning.* Princeton, NJ: Princeton University Press.

Jervis, R. (1976). *Perception and misperception in international politics.* Princeton, NJ: Princeton University Press.

Jervis, R. (1995). The drunkard's search. In S. Iyengar & W. McGuire (Eds.), *Explorations in political psychology* (pp. 338–360). Durham, NC: Duke University Press.

Jervis, R., Lebow, R. N., & Stein, J. (1985). *Psychology and deterrence.* Baltimore, MD: Johns Hopkins University Press.

Johnson, A. L., Crawford, M. T., Sherman, S. J., Rutchick, A. M., Hamilton, D. L., Ferreira, M. B., & Petroceli, J. V. (2005). A functional perspective on group memberships: Differential need fulfillment in a group typology. *Journal of Experimental Social Psychology, 42,* 707–719.

Johnson, D. E., Mueller, K. P., & Taft, W. H. (2002). *Conventional coercion across the spectrum of operations: The utility of U.S. military forces in the emerging environment.* Santa Monica, CA: RAND.

Johnson, H. H., & Watkins, T. (1971). The effects of message on immediate and delayed attitude change. *Psychonomic Science, 22,* 101–103.

Johnson, M. P., & Ewens, W. (1971). Power relations and affective style as determinants of confidence in impression formation in a game situation. *Journal of Experimental Social Psychology, 7,* 98–110.

Johnson, R. D., & Downing, L. L. (1979). Deindividuation and valence of cues: Effects on prosocial and antisocial behavior. *Journal of Personality and Social Psychology, 37,* 1532–1538.

Johnson, R. T. (1974). *Managing the White House: An intimate study of the presidency.* New York: Harper and Row.

Joint Center for Political and Economic Studies. (2001). Retrieved from www.jointctr.org/databank/factsht/trendnpov.htm

Jones, B., & Kavanagh, D. (1998). *British politics today* (6th ed.). Washington, DC: CQ Press.

Jones, C. O. (1988). *The trusteeship presidency: Jimmy Carter and the United States Congress.* Baton Rouge: Louisiana State University Press.

Jones, E. E., & Davis, K. E. (1965). From acts to dispositions: The attribution process in person perceptions. In L. Berkowitz (Ed.), *Advances in experimental social psychology* (Vol. 2, pp. 220–266). New York: Academic Press.

Jones, E. E., & Harris, V. A. (1967). The attribution of attitudes. *Journal of Experimental Psychology, 3,* 1–24.

Jowett, G., & O'Donnell, V. (1999). *Propaganda and persuasion* (2nd ed). Thousand Oaks, CA: Sage.

Judah, T. (2000). *Kosovo: War and revenge.* New Haven, CT: Yale University Press.

Judd, C. M., & Krosnick, J. A. (1989). The structural bases of consistency among political attitudes: Effects of political expertise and attitude importance. In A. R. Pratkanis, S. J. Breckler, & A. G. Greenwald

(Eds.), *Attitude structure and function.* Hillsdale, NJ: Lawrence Erlbaum.

Judge, T. A., Bono, J. E., Ilies, R., & Gerhard, M. W. (2002). Personality and leadership: A qualitative and quantitative review. *Journal of Applied Psychology, 87,* 765–780.

Kaarbo, J. (1998). Power politics in foreign policy: The influence of bureaucratic minorities. *European Journal of International Relations, 4,* 67–97.

Kaarbo, J., & Beasley, R. (1998). A political perspective on minority influence and strategic group composition. In M. Neale, E. Mannix, & D. Gruenfeld (Eds.), *Research on groups and teams* (Vol. 1, pp. 125–147). Greenwich, CT: JAI Press.

Kaarbo, J., & Gruenfeld, D. (1998). The social psychology of inter- and intra-group conflict in governmental politics. *Mershon International Studies Review, 42,* 226–233.

Kaarbo, J., & Hermann, M. (1998). Leadership styles of prime ministers: How individual differences affect the foreign policy process. *Leadership Quarterly, 9,* 243–263.

Kahn, J. (2000, December 31). Bush filling cabinet with team of power-seasoned executives. *New York Times,* p. A1.

Kahneman, D., & Tversky, A. (1979). A prospect theory: An analysis of decision under risk. *Econometrica, 47,* 263–291.

Kahneman, D., & Tversky, A. (2000). *Choice, values, and frames.* New York: Cambridge University Press.

Kaid, L., & Chanslor, M. (1995). Changing candidate images: The effects of political advertising. In K. Hacker (Ed.), *Candidate images in presidential elections* (pp. 131–134). Westport, CT: Praeger.

Kampf, H. A. (1990). Terrorism, the left-wing, and the intellectuals. *Terrorism, 13,* 23–51.

Kaplan, A. (1981). The psychodynamics of terrorism. In Y. Alexander & J. Gleason (Eds.), *Behavioral and quantitative perspectives on terrorism.* New York: Pergamon.

Kaplan, J., & Weinberg, L. (1998). *The emergence of a Euro-American radical right.* New Brunswick, NJ: Rutgers University Press.

Karadžić, R. (1996). State of Republic [address]. Retrieved from www.cdsp. neu.edu/info/students/marko/telegraf/telegraf2.html

Karau, S. J., & Williams, K. D. (1993). Social loafing: A meta-analytical review and theoretical integration. *Journal of Personality and Social Psychology, 65,* 681–706.

Katz, D., & Stotland, E. (1959). A preliminary statement of a theory of attitude structure and change. In S. Koch (Ed.), *Psychology: A study of a science* (Vol. 3, pp. 423–275). New York: McGraw-Hill.

Kaufman, S. (2001). *Modern hatreds: The symbolic politics of ethnic war.* Ithaca, NY: Cornell University Press.

Kawakami, J., Dovidio, J. F., Moll, J., Hermson, S., & Russin, A. (2000). Just say no to stereotyping: Effect of training in the negation of stereotypic associations on stereotype activation. *Journal of Personality and Social Psychology, 78,* 871–888.

Kecmanovic, D. (1996). *The mass psychology of ethnonationalism.* New York: Plenum.

Keegan, J. (1998). *The First World War*. New York: Vintage Books.

Keller, J. W. (2005). Constraint respecters, constraint challengers, and crisis decision making in democracies: A case study analysis of Kennedy versus Reagan. *Political Psychology, 26*, 835–867.

Keller, J. W., & Foster, D. M. (2012). Presidential leadership style and the political use of force. *Political Psychology, 33*, 581–598.

Kelley, H. (1967). Attribution theory in social psychology. In D. Levin (Ed.), *Nebraska symposium on motivation* (Vol. 5, pp. 192–240). Lincoln: University of Nebraska Press.

Kelman, H. C. (1958). Compliance, identification, and internalization: Three processes of attitude change. *Journal of Conflict Resolution, 2*, 51–60.

Kelman, H. C. (1961). Processes of opinion change. *Public Opinion Quarterly, 25*, 57–78.

Kelman, H. C. (1965). *International behavior: A social-psychological analysis*. New York: Holt, Rinehart and Winston.

Kelman, H. C. (1990). Applying a human needs perspective to the practice of conflict resolution; The Israeli-Palestinian case. In J. Burton (Ed.), *Conflict: Human needs theory*. New York: St. Martin's.

Kelman, H. C., & Hamilton, V. L. (1989). *Crimes of obedience*. New Haven, CT: Yale University Press.

Kelman, H. C., & Hovland, C. I. (1953). "Reinstatement" of the communicator in delayed measurement of attitude change. *Journal of Abnormal and Social Psychology, 48*, 327–335.

Keltner, D., & Robinson, R. J. (1997). Defending the status quo: Power and bias in social conflict. *Personality and Social Psychology Bulletin, 23*, 1066–1077.

Kernan, M. C., & Lord, R. G. (1989). The effects of explicit goals and specific feedback on escalation processes. *Journal of Applied Social Psychology, 19*, 1125–1143.

Kernis, M. H. (2003). Toward a conceptualization of optimal self-esteem. *Psychological Inquiry, 14*, 1–26.

Kerr, N. L., & Bruun, S. E. (1981). Ringelmann revisited: Alternative explanations for the social loafing effect. *Personality and Social Psychology Bulletin, 7*, 224–231.

Kerr, N. L., & Bruun, S. E. (1983). Dispensibility of member effort and group motivation losses: Free-rider effects. *Journal of Personality and Social Psychology, 44*, 78–94.

Khong, Y. F. (1992). *Analogies at war: Korea, Munich, Dien Bien Phu, and the Vietnam decisions of 1965*. Princeton, NJ: Princeton University Press.

Kiesler, D. J. (1983). The 1982 interpersonal circle: A taxonomy for complementarity in human transactions. *Psychological Review, 90*, 185–214.

Kille, K. J. (2006). *From manager to visionary: The Secretary-General of the United Nations*. New York: Palgrave.

Kim, K., & McCombs, M. (2007). News story descriptions and the public's opinions of political candidates. *Journalism and Mass Communication Quarterly, 84*, 299–314.

Kimmage, D., & Ridolfo, K. (2007, June). Iraqi insurgent media: the war of ideas and images. *Radio Free Europe Special Report*.

Kinder, D. (1986). Presidential character revisited. In R. Lau & D. Sears (Eds.), *Political cognition*. Hillsdale, NJ: Erlbaum.

Kinder, D. R., & Nelson, T. E. (2005) Democratic debate and real opinions. In K. Callaghan & F. Schnell (Eds.), *Framing American politics* (pp. 103–122). Pittsburgh, PA: University of Pittsburgh Press.

Kinder, D. R., & Sanders, L. M. (1990). Mimicking political debate with survey questions: The case of white opinion on affirmative action for blacks. *Social Cognition, 8,* 73–103.

Kinder, D., & Sanders, L. (1996). *Divided by color: Racial politics and democratic ideals.* Chicago, IL: University of Chicago Press.

Kinder, D., & Sears, D. (1981). Prejudice and politics: Symbolic racism versus racial threats to the good life. *Journal of Personality and Social Psychology, 40,* 414–431.

King, A. (1998). Why Labour won—at last. In A. King, D. Denver, I. McLean, P. Norris, P. Norton, D. Sanders, & P. Seyd (Eds.), *New Labour triumphs: Britain at the polls.* Chatham, NJ: Chatham House.

King, M., & Taylor, D. M. (2011). The radicalization of homegrown jihadists: A review of the theoretical models and social psychological evidence. *Terrorism and Political Violence, 23*(4), 602–622.

Kipnis, D. (1984). The use of power in organizations and in interpersonal settings. In *Applied Social Psychology Annual* (Vol. 5, pp. 179–210). Newbury Park, CA: Sage.

Kitano, H., & Nakaoka, S. (2001). Asian Americans in the twentieth century. In N. Choi (Ed.). *Psychological aspects of the Asian-American experience* (pp. 7–18). New York: Hawthorn Press.

Klandermans, B. (1984). Mobilization and participation: Social-psychological expansions of resource mobilization theory. *American Sociological Review, 49,* 583–600.

Klandermans, B. (1997). *The social psychology of protest.* Oxford: Blackwell.

Klandermans, B., & van Stekelenburg, J. (2013). Social movements and the dynamics of collective action. In L. Huddy, D. O. Sears, & J. S. Levy (Eds.), *The Oxford handbook of political psychology* (2nd ed., pp. 774–811). Oxford: Oxford University Press.

Klandermans, B., Werner, M., & van Doorn, M. (2008). Redeeming apartheid's legacy: Collective guilt, political ideology, and compensation. *Political Psychology, 29,* 331–349.

Klang, C. (1998, February 1). Evil, filthy rotten conspiracy. *Idaho Observer.* Retrieved from http://proliberty.com

Klar, S., Robison, J., & Druckman, J. (2013). Political dynamics of framing. In T. Ridout (Ed.), *New directions in media and politics* (pp. 173–192). New York: Routledge.

Kline, E. (1998). ASF Chechnya Brief. Andrei Sakarov Foundation. Retrieved from www.wdn.com/asf

Knutson, J. (1981). Social and psychodynamic pressures toward a negative identity. In Y. Alexander & J. Gleason (Eds.), *Behavioral and quantitative perspectives on terrorism* (pp. 105–152). New York: Pergamon.

Kohut, A. (2012, November 13). Lessons from the 2012 election. Retrieved from www.people-press.org/2012/11/13/lessons

Komorita, S.S., Hamilton, T.P., & Kravitz, D.A. (1984). Effects of alternatives in coalition bargaining. *Journal of Experimental Social Psychology, 20*, 116–136.

Komorita, S.S., & Miller, C.E. (1986). Bargaining strength as a function of coalition alternatives. *Journal of Personality and Social Psychology, 51*, 325–332.

Komorita, S.S., & Nagao, D. (1983). The functions of resources in coalition bargaining. *Journal of Personality and Social Psychology, 44*, 95–106.

Kotter, J.P., & Lawrence, P.R. (1974). *Mayors in action*. New York: Wiley.

Kowert, P.A., & Hermann, M.G. (1997). Who takes risks? Daring and caution in foreign policy making. *Journal of Conflict Resolution, 41*, 611–637.

Kravitz, D.A. (1987). Size of smallest coalition as a source of power in coalition bargaining. *European Journal of Social Psychology, 17*, 1–21.

Kressel, N. (1996). *Mass hate: The global rise of genocide and terror*. New York: Plenum Press.

Kriesci, H., Koopmans, R., Duyvendak, J.W., & Guigni, M. G. (1997). New social movements and political opportunities in Western Europe. In D. McAdam & D.A. Snow (Eds.), *Social movements: Readings on their emergence, mobilization, and dynamics* (pp. 52–65). Los Angeles, CA: Roxbury.

Krosnick, J. (1988). Attitude importance in social evaluation: A study of police preferences, presidential candidate evaluations, and voting behavior. *Journal of Personality and Social Psychology, 55*, 196–210.

Krosnick, J. (1989). Attitude importance and attitude accessibility. *Personality and Social Psychology Bulletin, 15*, 297–308.

Krosnick, J., & Kinder, J. (1990). Altering the foundations of support for the president. *American Political Science Review, 84*, 497–512.

Kruglanski, A., & Fishman, S. (2006). The psychology of terrorism: "Syndrome" versus "tool" perspectives. *Terrorism and Political Violence, 18*, 193–215.

Kruglanski, A. W., Chen, X., Dechesne, M., Fishman, S., & Orehek, E. (2009). Fully committed: Suicide bombers' motivation and quest for personal significance. *Political Psychology, 30*, 331–357.

Krupnikov, Y. (2011). When does negativity demobilize? Tracing the conditional effect of negativity on voter turnout. *American Journal of Political Science, 55*, 797–813.

Krupnikov, Y., & Easter, B. C. (2013). Negative campaigns: Are they good for American democracy? In T. Ridout (Ed.), *New directions in media and politics*. New York: Routledge.

Krznaric, R. (2013, May 15). Have we all been duped by the Myers-Briggs test? *Fortune*. Retrieved from http://fortune.com/2013/05/15/have-we-all-been-duped-by-the-myers-briggs-test/

Kuklinski, J.H., Luskin, R.C., & Bolland, J. (1991). Where is the schema? Going beyond the "s" word in political psychology. *American Political Science Review, 85*, 1341–1355.

Kuklinski, J.H., Riggle, E., Ottati, V., Schwarz, N., & Wyer, R. (1991). The cognitive and affective bases of political tolerance judgments. *American Journal of Political Science, 35*, 1–27.

Kuntner, B., Wilkins, C., & Yarrow, P. R. (1952). Verbal attitudes and overt behavior involving racial prejudice. *Journal of Abnormal and Social Psychology, 47,* 649–652.

LaBaron, A. (1993). The creation of the modern Maya. In C. Young (Ed.), *The rising tide of cultural pluralism: The nation-state at bay?* Madison: University of Wisconsin Press.

La Guardia, J. G., & Ryan, R. M. (2007). Why identities fluctuate: Variability in traits as a function of situational variations in autonomy support. *Journal of Personality, 76,* 1205–1228.

Lake, A. (1994). Confronting backlash states. *Foreign Affairs, 73,* 45–55.

Lambert, A. J., Burroughs, T., & Nguyen, T. (1999). Perceptions of risk and the buffering hypothesis: The role of just world beliefs and right-wing authoritarianism. *Personality and Social Psychology Bulletin, 25,* 643–656.

Lane, R. (1962). *Political ideology: Why the American common man believes what he does.* New York: Free Press.

Lane, R., & Sears, D. (1964). *Public opinion.* Englewood Cliffs, NJ: Prentice-Hall.

Langer, E. (1990, July 16). The American neo-Nazi movement today. *Nation, 215,* 82–105.

La Pierre, R. T. (1934). Attitudes versus actions. *Social Forces, 13,* 230–237.

Lasch, C. (1979). *The culture of narcissism.* New York: W. W. Norton.

Lasswell, H. (1948a). *Power and personality.* New York: Norton.

Lasswell, H. (1948b). The structure and function of communication in society. In L. Bryson (Ed.), *The communication of ideas* (pp. 32–51). New York: Harper.

Lasswell, H. (1960). *Psychopathology and politics.* Chicago, IL: University of Chicago Press. (Original work published 1930)

Latane, B., & Darley, J. M. (1970). *The unresponsive bystander. Why doesn't he help?* New York: Appleton-Century-Crofts.

Latane, B., Williams, K. D., & Harkins, S. (1979). Many hands make light the work: The causes and consequences of social loafing. *Journal of Personality and Social Psychology, 37,* 822–832.

Lau, R. (1986). Political schemata, candidate evaluations and voting behavior. *American Journal of Political Science, 29,* 119–138.

Lau, R. (1995). Information search during an election campaign: Introducing a processing-tracing methodology for political scientists. In M. Lodge & K. McGraw (Eds.), *Political judgment: Structure and processes.* Ann Arbor: University of Michigan Press.

Lau, R., & Redlawsk, D. (1997). Voting correctly. *American Political Science Review, 91,* 585–598.

Lau, R., & Redlawsk, D. (2006). *How voters decide: Information processing during election campaigns.* Cambridge: Cambridge University Press.

Laughlin, P. R. (1988). Collective induction: Group performance, social combination processes, and mutual majority and minority influence. *Journal of Personality and Social Psychology, 54,* 254–267.

Lav, D. (2007, March 7). The Al-Qaeda organization in the Islamic Maghreb: The evolving terrorist presence in North Africa, MEMRI Inquiry and Analysis. Retrieved from http://memri.org/bin/articles.cgi?Page=archives&Area=ia&ID=IA33207

Lavine, H. (2002). On-line versus memory-based process models. In K. Monroe (Ed.), *Political psychology.* Mahwah, NJ: Lawrence Erlbaum.

Lawler, E. J. (1992). Affective attachments to nested groups: A choice-process theory. *American Sociological Review, 57,* 327–339.

Lawler, E. J., & Thompson, M. E. (1978). Impact of a leader's responsibility for inequity on subordinate revolts. *Social Psychology Quarterly, 41,* 264–268.

Lazarsfeld, P., Berelson, B., & Gaudet, H. (1944). *The people's choice.* New York: Duell, Sloan & Pearce.

Lazarus, R. S. (1991). *Emotion and adaptation.* New York: Oxford University Press.

Leary, M. R. (1983). *Understanding social anxiety.* Newbury Park, CA: Sage.

Leary, M. R. (1999). Making sense of self-esteem. *Current Directions in Psychological Science, 8,* 32–35.

Leatherwood, M. L., & Conlon, E. J. (1987). Diffusibility of blame: Effects on persistence in a project. *Academy of Management Review, 30,* 836–847.

LeBon, G. (1960). *The crowd: A study of the popular mind.* New York: Viking. (Original work published 1895)

Lebow, R. N. (1981). *Between peace and war: The Nature of International Crisis.* Baltimore, MD: Johns Hopkins University Press.

Lebow, R. N., & Stein, J. G. (1987). Beyond deterrence. *Journal of Social Issues, 43,* 5–71.

Lebow, R. N., & Stein, J. G. (1989). Rational deterrence theory: I think, therefore I deter. *World Politics, 41,* 208–224.

Lebow, R. N., & Stein, J. G. (1990). Deterrence: The elusive dependent variable. *World Politics, 42,* 336–369.

Lee, M. (1997). *The beast reawakens.* New York: Little, Brown.

Lee, R. (1999). *Orientals: Asian Americans in popular culture.* Philadelphia, PA: Temple University Press.

Leffler, A., Gillespie, D. L., & Conaty, J. C. (1982). The effects of status differentiation on nonverbal behavior. *Social Psychology Quarterly, 45,* 153–161.

Legault, A., & Lindsey, G. The Dynamics of the Nuclear Balance. Ithaca, NY: Cornell University Press, 1974.

Legvold, R. (1988). War, weapons, and Soviet foreign policy. In S. Bialer & M. Mandelbaum (Eds.), *Russia and American foreign policy* (pp. 97–132). Boulder, CO: Westview Press, Inc.

Leites, N. (1951). *The operational code of the Politburo.* New York: McGraw-Hill.

Leites, N. (1953). *A study of Bolshevism.* New York: Free Press.

Leith, K. P., & Baumeister, R. F. (1996). Why do bad moods increase self-defeating behavior? Emotion, risk taking, and self-regulation. *Journal of Personality and Social Psychology, 71,* 1250–1267.

Lerner, M. J., & Miller, D. T. (1978). Just world research and the attribution process: Looking back and ahead. *Psychological Bulletin, 85,* 1030–1051.

Levin, J., & Levin, W. C. (1982). *The functions of prejudice and discrimination.* New York: Harper and Row.

Levin, S., & Sidanius, J. (1999). Social dominance and social identity in the United States and Israel: Ingroup favoritism or outgroup derogation? *Political Psychology, 20,* 99–126.

Levine, J. M., & Moreland, R. L. (1998). Small groups. *The handbook of social psychology* (4th ed., pp. 415–469). New York: McGraw-Hill.

Levine, R. A., & Campbell, D. T. (1972). *Ethnocentrism: Theories of conflict, ethnic attitudes and group behavior.* New York: Wiley.

Levy, J. (1991). The role of crisis management in the outbreak of World War I. In A. George (Ed.), *Avoiding: Problems of crisis management* (pp. 62–102). Boulder, CO: Westview Press.

Levy, J. (1994). Learning and foreign policy: Sweeping a conceptual minefield. *International Organization, 48*, 279–312.

Levy, J. (1997). Prospect theory, rational choice, and international relations. *International Studies Quarterly, 41*, 87–112.

Lewin, K. (1935). *A dynamic theory of personality*. New York: McGraw-Hill.

Lewin, K., Lippitt, R., & White, R. (1939). Patterns of aggressive behavior in experimentally created "social climates." *Journal of Social Psychology, 10*, 271–299.

Lickel, B., Hamilton, D. L., Wieczorkowski, G., Lewis, A., Sherman, S. J., & Uhles, A. N. (2000). Varieties of groups and the perception of group entiativity. *Journal of Personality and Social Psychology, 78*, 223–246.

Lien, P., Conway, M. M., & Wong, J. (2004). *The politics of Asian Americans: Diversity and community*. New York: Routledge.

Lifton, R. J. (1986). *The Nazi doctors: Medical killing and the psychology of genocide*. New York: Basic Books.

Light, P. C. (1982). *The president's agenda: Domestic policy choice from Kennedy to Carter*. Baltimore, MD: Johns Hopkins University Press.

Lindner, E. (2006). *Making enemies: Humiliation and international conflict*. Westport, CT: Praeger.

Link, A. (1996). Woodrow Wilson and the constitutional crisis. In K. Thompson (Ed.). *Papers on presidential disability and the 25th Amendment by medical, historical and political authorities* (pp. 53–80). Lanham, MD: Miller Center, University of Virginia and University Press of America.

Link, M., & Glad, B. (1994). Exploring the psychopolitical dynamics of advisory relations: The Carter administration's "crisis of confidence." *Political Psychology, 15*, 461–480.

Linville, P. (1982). Affective consequences as complexity regarding the self and others. In M. Clarke & S. Fiske (Eds.), *Affect and cognition*. Hillsdale, NJ: Lawrence Erlbaum.

Linville, P., & Jones, E. (1980). Polarized appraisals of outgroup members. *Journal of Personality and Social Psychology, 38*, 698–703.

Lodge, M. (1995). Toward a procedural model of candidate evaluation. In M. Lodge & K. McGraw (Eds.), *Political judgment: Structure and processes* (pp. 111–139). Ann Arbor: University of Michigan Press.

Lodge, M., & Hamill, R. (1986). A partisan schema for political information processing. *American Journal of Political Science, 80*, 505–519.

Lodge, M., McGraw, K. M., & Stroh, P. (1989). An impression driven model of candidate evaluation. *American Political Science Review, 83*, 399–419.

Lodge, M., Steenbergen, M., & Brau, S. (1995). The responsive voter: Campaign information and the dynamics of candidate evaluation. *American Political Science Review, 89*, 309–326.

Lodge, M., & Stroh, P. (1995). Inside the mental voting booth. In S. Iyengar & W. McGuire (Eds.), *Explorations in political psychology* (pp. 225–263). Durham, NC: Duke University Press.

Loftus, E. (1979). *Eyewitness testimony*. Cambridge, MA: Harvard University Press.

Loftus, E. F. (2001). Imagining the past. *Psychologist, 14*, 584–587.

Lorenz, K. (1966). *On aggression*. New York: Harcourt, Brace, and World.

Lott, A. J., & Lott, B. E. (1965). Group cohesiveness as interpersonal attraction: A review of relationships with antecedent and consequent variables. *Psychological Bulletin, 64*, 259–309.

Loyd, A. (1999). *My war gone by, I miss it so*. New York: Penguin Books.

Luce, R. D., & Raiffa, H. (1957). *Games and decisions*. New York: Wiley.

Lyons, M. (1997). Presidential character revisited. *Political Psychology, 18*, 791–811.

Maccoby, E., Matthews, R., & Morton, A. (1954). Youth and political change. *Public Opinion Quarterly, 18*, 23–29.

Mackie, D. M. (1986). Social identification effects in group polarization. *Journal of Personality and Social Psychology, 50*, 720–728.

Mackie, D. M., Devos, T., & Smith, E. R. (2000). Intergroup emotions: Explaining offensive action tendencies in an intergroup context. *Journal of Personality and Social Psychology, 79*, 602–616.

Mackie, D. M., & Goethals, G. R. (1987). Individual and group goals. In C. Hendrick (Ed.), *Review of personality and social psychology* (Vol. 8, pp. 144–166). Newbury Park, CA: Sage.

Mackie, D. M., & Hamilton, D. (Eds.). (1993). *Affect, cognition and stereotyping: Interactive processes in group perception*. New York: Academic Press.

MacKuen, M., Marcus, G. E., Neuman, W. R., & Keele, L. (2007). The third way: The theory of affective intelligence and American democracy. In W. R. Neuman, G. E. Marcus, A. N. Crigler, & M. MacKuen (Eds.), *The affect effect: Dynamics of emotion in political thinking and behavior* (pp. 124–151). Chicago, IL: University of Chicago Press.

MacNair, R. (2005). *Perpetration-induces traumatic stress: The psychological consequences of killing*. New York: Author's Choice Press.

Maddi, S. R. (1996). *Personality theories: A comparative analysis* (6th ed.). Washington: Brooks/Cole.

Madigan, T. (2001). *The burning: Massacre, destruction, and the Tulsa race riot of 1921*. New York: St. Martin's.

Madsen, K.B. (1961). *Theories of motivation: A comparative study of modern theories of motivation* (2nd ed.). Cleveland OH: Howard Allen.

Magnavita, J. (2002). *Theories of personality: Contemporary approaches to the science of personality*. New York: John Wiley and Sons.

Mahncke, D. (1992). Reunification as an issue in German politics, 1949–1990. In D. Grosser (Ed.), *German unification: The unexpected challenge* (pp. 33–54). Oxford: Berg.

Malici, A., & Malici, J. (2005). The operational codes of Fidel Castro and Kim Il Sung: The last cold warriors? *Political Psychology, 26*, 387–412.

Mani, R. (2000). Contextualizing police reform: Security, the rule of law and post-conflict peacebuilding. In T. T. Holm & E. B. Eide (Eds.), *Peacebuilding and police reform* (pp. 9–26). Portland, OR: Frank Cass.

Manis, M., Nelson, T., & Shedler, J. (1988). Stereotypes and social judgment: extremity, assimilation and contrast. *Journal of Personality and Social Psychology, 51*, 493–504.

Marcus, G. (2013). *Political psychology: Neuroscience, genetics, and politics*. Oxford: Oxford University Press.

Marcus, G., & MacKuen, M. (1993). Anxiety, enthusiasm, and the vote: The emotional underpinnings of learning and involvement during presidential campaigns. *American Political Science Review, 87*, 672–685.

Marcus, G., Neuman, W. R., & MacKuen, M. (2000). *Affective intelligence and political judgment.* Chicago, IL: University of Chicago Press.

Marfleet, B. G. (2000). The operational code of John F. Kennedy during the Cuban Missile Crisis: A comparison of public and private rhetoric. *Political Psychology, 21*, 545–558.

Marger, M. N. (2003). *Race and ethnic relations: American and global perspectives* (6th ed). Belmont, CA: Thompson Wadsworth.

Marilla Communications Group. (2001). American attitudes toward Chinese Americans & Asian Americans: A Committee of 100 survey. New York: Committee of 100.

Marks, M. L., Mirvis, P. H., Hackett, E. J., & Grady, J. F. (1986). Employee participation in a Quality Circle program: Impact on quality of work life, productivity, and absenteeism. *Journal of Applied Psychology, 71*, 61–69.

Markus, G. (1982). Political attitudes during an election year: A report on the 1980 NEW panel study. *American Political Science Review, 76*, 538–560.

Markus, G., & Converse, P. (1979). A dynamic simultaneous equation model of electoral choice. *American Political Science Review, 73*, 1055–1070.

Marques, J., Abrams, D., Paez, D., & Hogg, M. (2001). Social categorization, social identification, and rejection of deviant group members. In M. A. Hogg & S. Tindale (Eds.), *Blackwell handbook of social psychology: Group processes* (pp. 406–424). Malden, MA: Blackwell.

Marques, J., Yeerbyt, V. Y., & Leyens, J. P. (1988). The "black sheep effect": Extremity of judgments towards ingroup members as a function of group identification. *European Journal of Social Psychology, 18*, 1–16.

Marsella, A. J., Dubanoski, J., Hamada, W. C., & Morse, H. (2000). The measurement of personality across cultures: Historical, conceptual, and methodological issues and considerations. *American Behavioral Scientist, 44*, 41–62.

Martin, J. L. (2001). *The authoritarian personality*, 50 years later: What lessons are there for political psychology? *Political Psychology, 22*, 1–26.

Marx, A. (1998). *Making race and nation: A comparison of the United States. South Africa, and Brazil.* Cambridge: Cambridge University Press.

Maslach, C., Stapp, J., & Santee, R. T. (1985). Individuation: Conceptual analysis and assessment. *Journal of Personality and Social Psychology, 49*, 729–738.

Maslow, A. (1954). *Motivation and personality.* New York: Harper and Row.

Mastors, E. (2000). Gerry Adams and the Northern Ireland peace process: A research note. *Political Psychology, 21*, 839–846.

Mastors, E. (2008). The UDA and post-conflict transformation. *Journal of Policing, Intelligence and Counterterrorism.*

Mastors, E., & Deffenbaugh, A. (2007). *The lesser jihad: Recruits and the al-Qaida network.* Boulder, CO: Rowman & Littlefield.

Mastors, E., & Norwitz, J. (2008). Influencing and disrupting leaders of armed groups: the case of Ayman al-Zawahiri, in J. Norwitz (Ed.,) *Armed groups: studies in national security, counterterrorism and counterinsurgency* (pp. 323–242). New York: McGraw-Hill.

Mattoso, K. M. de Queiros. (1986). *To be a slave in Brazil, 1550–1888*. New Brunswick, NJ: Rutgers University Press.

May, E. R. (1973). *Lessons of the past: The use and misuse of history in American foreign policy*. New York: Oxford University Press.

Mayer, W. (1996). In defense of negative campaigning. *Political Science Quarterly, 111*, 437–455.

Maznevski, M. L. (1994). Understanding our differences: Performance in decision-making groups with diverse members. *Human Relations, 47*, 531–552.

Mazur, A. (1985). A biosocial model of status in face-to-face groups. *Social Forces, 64*, 377–402.

McAdam, D. (1988). *Freedom summer*. Oxford: Oxford University Press.

McCain, B. E. (1986). Commitment under conditions of persistent failure: Escalation and de-escalation. *Journal of Applied Psychology, 71*, 280–284.

McCarthy, J. D., Rafail, P., & Gromis, A. (2013). Recent trends in public protest in the United States: The social movement society thesis revisited. In J. van Stekelenburg, C. Roggebans, & B. Klandermans (Eds.), *The future of social movement research: Dynamics, mechanisms, and processes* (pp. 369–396). Minneapolis: University of Minnesota Press.

McCauley, C. R. (2002). The psychology of terrorism. *Social Science Research Council*, 1–6.

McCauley, C. R. (2004). Psychological issues in understanding terrorism and the response to terrorism. In C. E. Stout (Ed.), *Psychology of terrorism, condensed edition: coping with the continuing threat* (pp. 33–66). Westport, CT: Praeger/Greenwood.

McClain, P., Carter, N., DeFrancesco Soto, V., Lyle, M. Grynaviski, J., Nunnally, S., . . . Cotton, K. (2006). Racial distancing in a southern city: Latino immigrants' view of black Americans. *Journal of Politics, 68*, 578–584.

McClellan, S. (2008). *What happened: Inside the Bush White House and Washington's culture of deception*. New York: Public Affairs.

McClelland, D. C. (1975). *Power: The inner experience*. New York: Irvington.

McClelland, D. C. (1985). How motives, skills, and values determine what people do. *American Psychologist, 40*, 812–825.

McClelland, D. C., & Boyatzis, R. E. (1982). Leadership, motive pattern and long-term success in management. *Journal of Applied Psychology, 67*, 737–743.

McClosky, H., & Zaller, J. (1984). *The American ethos: Public attitudes toward capitalism and democracy*. Cambridge, MA: Harvard University Press.

McCombs, M., & Shaw, D. (1972). The agenda-setting function of the press. *Public Opinion Quarterly, 36*, 176–187.

McCrae, R. (1993). Moderated analyses of longitudinal personality stability. *Journal of Personality and Social Psychology, 65*, 577–585.

McCrae, R., & Costa, P. T. (1997). Conceptions and correlates of openness to experiences. In R. Hogan, J. Johnson, & S. Briggs (Eds.), *Handbook of personality psychology*. San Diego, CA: Academic Press.

McCrae, R., & Costa, P. T. (2006). Reinterpreting the Myers-Briggs type indicator from the perspective of the five-factor model of personality. *Journal of Personality, 57*, 17–40.

McDermott, R. (1998). *Risk-taking in international politics: Prospect theory in American foreign policy.* Ann Arbor: University of Michigan Press.

McDermott, R. (2008). *Presidential leadership, illness, and decision making.* New York: Cambridge University Press.

McDonald, M. M., Navarrete, C. D., & Sidanius, J. (2011). Developing a theory of gendered prejudice: An evolutionary and social dominance perspective. In R. M. Kramer, G. J. Leonardelli, & R. W. Livingston (Eds.), *Social cognition, social identity, and intergroup relations: A festschrift in honor of Marilynn B. Brewer.* New York: Psychology Press Festschrift Series.

McDonald, M. M., Navarrete, C. D., & Van Vugt, M. (2012). Evolution and the psychology of intergroup conflict: The male warrior hypothesis. *Philosophical Transaction of the Royal Society Biological Sciences, 367,* 670–679. doi: 10.1098/rstb.2011.0301

McGraw, K. (2000). Contributions of the cognitive approach to political psychology. *Political Psychology, 21,* 805–827.

McGraw, K., Lodge, M., & Stroh, P. (1990). On-line processing in candidate evaluation: The effects of issue order, issue importance, and sophistication. *Political Behavior, 12,* 41–58.

McGraw, K., & Steenbergen, M. (1995). Pictures in the head: Memory representations of political actors. In M. Lodge & K. M. McGraw (Eds.), *Political judgment: Structure and process.* Ann Arbor: University of Michigan Press.

McLeod, P. L., & Lobel, S. A. (1992). The effects of ethnic diversity on idea generation in small groups. *Academy of Management Best Paper Proceedings, 22,* 227–231.

McNamara, R. S. (1995). *In retrospect: The tragedy and lessons of Vietnam.* New York: Random House.

McVeigh helped speed militias demise. (2001, June 10). *Idaho Spokesman Review,* p. A10.

Mearsheimer, J. J. (2014). Why the Ukraine crisis is the west's fault. *Foreign Affairs, 93,* 77–89.

Meloen, J. (1994). A critical analysis of forty years of authoritarianism research: Did theory testing suffer from cold war attitudes? In R. F. Farnen (Ed.), *Nationalism, ethnicity, and identity* (pp. 127–165). New Brunswick, NJ: Transaction.

Mendelberg, T. (2001). *The race card: Campaign strategy, implicit messages, and the norm of equality.* Princeton, NJ: Princeton University Press.

Merelman, R. (1969). The development of political ideology: A framework for the analysis of political socialization. *American Political Science Review, 63,* 750–767.

Merelman, R. (1986). Revitalizing political socialization. In M. G. Hermann (Ed.). *Political psychology* (pp. 279–319). San Francisco, CA: Jossey-Bass.

Merkl, P. (1980). *The making of a stormtrooper.* Princeton, NJ: Princeton University Press.

Messe, L. A., Kerr, N. L., & Sattler, D. N. (1992). "But some animals are more equal than others": The supervisor as a privileged status in group contexts. In S. Worchel, W. Wood, & J. A. Simpson (Eds.), *Group process and productivity* (pp. 203–223). Newbury Park, CA: Sage.

Messick, D. M., & Brewer, M. B. (1983). Solving social dilemmas: A review. In L. Wheeler & P. Shaver (Eds.), *Review of personality and social psychology* (Vol. 4, pp. 11–44). Beverly Hills, CA: Sage.

Michaelsen, L. K., Watson, W. E., & Black, R. H. (1989). A realistic test of individual vs. group consensus decision making. *Journal of Applied Psychology, 74*, 834–839.

Michener, H. A., & Burt, M. R. (1975). Use of social influence under varying conditions of legitimacy. *Journal of Personality and Social Psychology, 32*, 398–407.

Michener, H. A., & Lawler, E. J. (1975). The endorsement of formal leaders: An integrative model. *Journal of Personality and Social Psychology, 31*, 216–223.

Milbank, D. (2001). *Smashmouth: Two years in the gutter with Al Gore and George W. Bush: Notes from the 2000 campaign trail.* New York: Basic Books.

Milburn, M. A. (1991). *Persuasion and politics: The social psychology of public opinion.* Pacific Grove, CA: Brooks-Cole/Wadsworth.

Milburn, M. A., & Conrad, S. D. (1996). *The politics of denial.* Cambridge. MA: MIT Press.

Milburn, M. A., Conrad, S. D., Sala, F., & Carberry, S. (1995). Childhood punishment, denial and political attitudes. *Political Psychology, 16*, 447–478.

Milburn, M. A., & McGrail, A. B. (1992). The dramatic presentation of news and its effects on cognitive complexity. *Political Psychology, 13*, 613–632.

Milgram, S. (1963). Behavioral study of obedience. *Journal of Abnormal and Social Psychology, 67*, 371–378.

Milgram, S. (1974). *Obedience to authority.* New York: Harper and Row.

Miller, A. (1983). *For your own good. Hidden cruelty in child rearing and the roots of violence.* Translated by Jildegarde and Hunto Hannum. New York: Farrar, Straus & Giroux.

Miller, A., Wattenberg, M. P., & Malanchuk, O. (1986). Schematic assessments of presidential candidates. *American Political Science Review, 80*, 521–540.

Miller, C. E. (1980). Effects of payoffs on coalition formation: A test of three theories. *Social Psychology Quarterly, 43*, 154–164.

Miller, C. E., & Komorita, S. S. (1986). Changes in outcomes in coalition bargaining. *Journal of Personality and Social Psychology, 51*, 720–729.

Miller, J. (2007). Examining the mediators of agenda setting: A new experimental paradigm reveals the role of emotions. *Political Psychology, 28*, 689–717.

Miller, J., & Krosnick, J. (1996). News media impact on the ingredients of presidential evaluations: A program of research on the priming hypothesis. In D. C. Muntz, P. Sniderman, & R. Brody (Eds.), *Political persuasion and attitude change.* Ann Arbor: University of Michigan Press.

Miller, W., & Shanks, M. (1996). *The new American voter.* Cambridge, MA: Harvard University Press.

Minard, R. (1952). Race relationships in the Pocohontas coal field. *Journal of Social Issues, 8*, 29–44.

Mindiola, T., Nieman, Y. F., & Rodriguez, N. (2002). *Black-Brown: Relations and stereotypes.* Austin: University of Texas Press.

Minow, M. (1998). *Between vengeance and forgiveness: Facing history after genocide and mass violence.* Boston, MA: Beacon Press.

Mintz, A. (2004). How do leaders make decisions? A poliheuristic perspective. *Journal of Conflict Resolution, 48,* 3–13.

Mintz, A. (2005). Applied decision analysis: Utilizing poliheuristic theory to explain and predict foreign policy and national security decisions. *International Studies Perspectives, 6,* 94–98.

Mintz, A., & Brule, D. (2009). Methodological issues in studying suicide terrorism. *Political Psychology, 30,* 365–380.

Mischel, W. (1968). *Personality and assessment.* New York: Wiley.

Mischel, W. (1973). Toward a cognitive social learning reconceptualization of personality. *Psychological Review, 30,* 252–283.

Mitchell, D. (2005). *Making foreign policy: Presidential management of the decision-making process.* Burlington, VT: Ashgate.

Mitchell, D. (2007). Determining Indian foreign policy: An examination of prime ministerial leadership styles. *India Review, 6,* 251–287.

Mitchell, E. (2000). *W: Revenge of the Bush dynasty.* New York: Hyperion.

Moens, A. (2004). *The foreign policy of George W. Bush: Values, strategy, and loyalty.* Burlington, VT: Ashgate.

Moghaddam, F. M. (2005). Staircase to terrorism: A psychological exploration. *American Psychologist, 60*(2), 161–169.

Moghaddam, F. M. (2007). The staircase to terrorism. In B. Bonger, L. M. Brown, L. E. Beutler, J. Breckenridge, & P. G. Zimbardo (Eds.), *Psychology of terrorism* (pp. 69–80). Oxford: Oxford University Press.

Molm, L. D. (1987). Extending power-dependence theory: Power processes and negative outcomes. In E. J. Lawler & B. Markovsky (Eds.), *Advances in group processes* (Vol. 4, pp. 171–198). Greenwich, CT: JAI.

Molm, L. D. (1988). The structure and use of power: A comparison of reward and punishment power. *Social Psychology Quarterly, 51,* 108–122.

Mongar, T. M. (1974). Personality and decision-making: John F. Kennedy in four crisis decisions. In Gordon J. DiRenzo (Ed.), *Personality and politics* (pp. 334–372). Garden City, NY: Doubleday-Anchor.

Monroe, K. R. (2008). Cracking the code of genocide: The moral psychology or rescuers, bystanders, and Nazis during the Holocaust. *Political Psychology, 29,* 699–737.

Montopoli, B. (2012, December 14). Tea party supporters: Who they are and what they believe. *CBS News.* Retrieved from www.cbsnews.com/news/tea-party-supporters-who-they-are-and-what-they-believe/

Moon, H. (2001). The two faces of conscientiousness: Duty and achievement striving in escalation of commitment dilemmas. *Journal of Applied Psychology, 86,* 535–540.

Moreland, R. L. (1987). The formation of small groups. In C. Hendrick (Ed.), *Review of personality and social psychology* (Vol. 8, pp. 80–110). Newbury Park, CA: Sage.

Moreland, R. L., & Levine, J. M. (1982). Socialization in small groups: Temporal changes in individual-group relations. In L. Berkowitz (Ed.), *Advances in experimental social psychology* (Vol. 15, pp. 137–192). New York: Academic Press.

Morgenthau, H. J. (1948). *Politics among nations: The struggle for power and peace.* New York: Alfred A. Knopf.

Morris, A. (1999). A retrospective on the civil rights movement: Political and intellectual landmarks. *Annual Review of Sociology, 25,* 517–539.

Morris, W. N., & Miller, R. S. (1975). The effects of consensus-breaking and consensus-preempting partners on reduction in conformity. *Journal of Experimental Social Psychology, 11,* 215–223.

Moscovici, S. (1985). Social influence and conformity. In G. Lindzey & E. Aronson (Eds.), *Handbook of social psychology* (3rd ed., Vol. 2, pp. 347–412). New York: Random House.

MSNBC.com. (2008). No hidden white bias seen in vote. Retrieved from www.msnbc.msn.com/id/2758972

Mullen, B., Brown, R., & Smith, C. (1992). Ingroup bias as a function of salience, relevance, and status: An integration. *European Journal of Social Psychology, 22,* 103–122.

Mullen, B., & Copper, C. (1994). The relation between group cohesiveness and performance: An integration. *Psychological Bulletin, 115,* 210–227.

Mullen, B., Johnson, C., & Salas, E. (1991). Productivity loss in brainstorming groups: A meta-analytic interpretation. *Basic and Applied Social Psychology, 12,* 3–24.

Mumford, M. D. (2006). *Pathways to outstanding leadership: A comparative analysis of charismatic, ideological, and pragmatic leaders.* Mahwah, NJ: Lawrence Erlbaum Associates.

Mumford, M. D., Espejo, J., Hunter, S. T., Bedell-Avers, K. E., Eubanks, D., & Connelly, S. (2007). The sources of leader violence: A comparison of ideological and non-ideological leaders. *Leadership Quarterly, 18,* 217–235.

Mummendey, A., Kessler, T., Klink, A., & Mielke, R. (1999). Strategies to cope with negative social identity: Predictions by social identity theory and relative deprivation theory. *Journal of Personality and Social Psychology, 76,* 229–245.

Mycock, A., & Hayton, R. (2014). The party politics of Englishness. *British Journal of Politics and International Relations, 16,* 251–272.

Myers, D. G. (1978). Polarizing effects of social comparison. *Journal of Experimental Social Psychology, 14,* 554–563.

Myers, D. G., & Lamm, H. (1976). The group polarization phenomenon. *Psychological Bulletin, 83,* 602–627.

Myrdal, G. (1944). *The American dilemma.* New York: McGraw-Hill.

National Society of Hispanic Professionals. (2008). Hispanic stereotypes: How they affect us at work. Retrieved from www.nshp.org/career_and_jobs/hispanic_Stereotypes_how_they_affect_us_at_work

Navarrete, C. D., Olsson, A., Ho, A., Mendes, W., Thomsen, L., & Sidanius, J. (2009). Fear extinction to an out-group face: The role of target gender. *Psychological Science, 20*(2), 155–158.

Nelson, T., Clawson, R., & Oxley, Z. (1997). Media framing of a civil liberties conflict and its effect on tolerance. *American Political Science Review, 91,* 567–583.

Nelson, T., & Oxley, Z. (1999). Issue framing effects on belief importance and opinion. *Journal of Politics, 61,* 1040–1067.

Nemeth, C. J. (1986). Differential contributions of majority and minority influence. *Psychological Review, 93,* 23–32.

Nemeth, C.J., Connell, J.B., Rogers, J.D., & Brown, K.S. (2001). Improving decision making by means of dissent. *Journal of Applied Social Psychology, 31*, 45–58.

Neuman, W.R. (1986). *The paradox of mass politics*. Cambridge, MA: Harvard University Press.

Neuman, W.R., Marcus, G.E., Crigler, A.N., & MacKuen, M. (2007). Theorizing affect's effects. In W.R. Neuman, G.E. Marcus, A.N. Crigler, & M. MacKuen (Eds.), *The affect effect: Dynamics of emotion in political thinking and behavior* (pp. 1–23). Chicago, IL: University of Chicago Press.

Neustadt, R.E. (1990). *Presidential power and the modern presidents: The politics of leadership from Roosevelt to Reagan*. New York: Free Press. (Original work published 1960)

Neustadt, R.E., & May, E.R. (1986). *Thinking in time: The uses of history for decision makers*. New York: Free Press.

Newcomb, T.M. (1943). *Personality and social change*. New York: Dryden.

Newcomb, T.M. (1960). Varieties of interpersonal attraction. In D. Cartwright & A. Zander (Eds.), *Group dynamics: Research and theory* (2nd ed., pp. 104–119). Evanston, IL: Row, Peterson.

Newcomb, T.M. (1979). Reciprocity of interpersonal attraction: A nonconfirmation of a plausible hypothesis. *Social Psychology Quarterly, 42*, 299–306.

Nicholson, N., Soane, E., Fenton-O'Creevey, M., & William, P. (2005). Personality and domain-specific risk taking. *Journal of Risk Research, 8*, 157–176.

Nie, N., Verba, S., & Petrocik, J. (1976). *The changing American voter*. Cambridge, MA: Harvard University Press.

Nieburg, H.L. (1969). *Political violence: The behavioral process*. New York: St. Martin's Press.

Niemi, R. (1973). Political socialization. In J. Knutson (Ed.), *Handbook of political psychology* (pp. 117–138). San Francisco, CA: Jossey-Bass.

Niemi, R., & Hepburn, M. (1995). The rebirth of political socialization. *Perspectives on Political Science, 24*, 5–16.

Niemi, R., & Weisberg, H. (Eds.). (1993). *Controversies in voting behavior* (3rd ed.). Washington, DC: Congressional Quarterly.

Nolan, P. (2013). *Northern Ireland peace monitoring report Number 2*. Belfast: Community Relations Council.

Norpoth, H., & Bednarczuk, M. (2013). Primary model gets it right and early. *PS: Political Science and Politics, 46*, 37.

Norris, P. (1997). *Electoral change since 1945*. Cambridge: Blackwell.

Northcraft, G.B., & Neale, M.A. (1986). Opportunity costs and the framing of resource allocation decisions. *Organizational Behavior and Human Decision Processes, 37*, 348–356.

Northcraft, G.B., & Wolf, G. (1984). Dollars, sense, and sunk costs: A life-cycle model of resource allocation decisions. *Academy of Management Review, 9*, 225–234.

Noueihed, L., & Warren, A. (2013). *The battle for the Arab Spring: Revolution, counter-revolution and the making of a new era*. New Haven, CT: Yale University Press.

Nunn, C., Crockett, H., & Williams, J.A. (1978). *Tolerance for nonconformity*. San Francisco, CA: Jossey-Bass.

Nydegger, R V. (1975). Information processing complexity and leadership status. *Journal of Experimental Social Psychology, 11,* 317–328.

O'Callaghan, S. (1998). *The informer.* New York: Bantam

O'Dell, J. W. (1968). Group size and emotional interaction. *Journal of Personality and Social Psychology, 8,* 75–78.

O'Hanlon, M. (2000). *Technological change and the future of warfare.* Washington, DC: Brookings Institution Press.

Oliner, S., & Oliner, P. (1988). *The altruistic personality: Rescuers of Jews in Nazi Europe.* New York: Free Press.

Olson, B. D., & Evans, D. L. (1999). The role of the big five personality dimensions in the direction and affective consequences of everyday social comparisons. *Personality and Social Psychology Bulletin, 25,* 1498–1508.

Olson, D. V. A., & Caddell, D. (1994). Generous congregations, generous givers: Congregational contexts that stimulate individual giving. *Review of Religious Research, 36,* 168–180.

O'Reilly, K. P. (2012). Leaders' perceptions and nuclear proliferation: A political psychology approach to proliferation. *Political Psychology, 33,* 767–789.

Ortony, A., Clore, G., & Collins, A. (1988). *The cognitive structure of emotions.* Cambridge: Cambridge University Press.

O'Toole, P. (2000, November 21). Hate-figure and hero. *BBC News.*

Ottati, V., & Wyer, R. (1990). The cognitive mediators of political choice: Toward a comprehensive model of political information processing. In J. Ferejohn & J. Kuklinski (Eds.), *Information and democratic processes* (pp. 186–215). Urbana: University of Illinois Press.

Ottati, V. C., & Wyer, R. S. (1993). Affect and political judgement. In S. Iyengar & W. McGuire (Eds.), *Explorations in political psychology* (pp. 296–315). Durham, NC: Duke University.

Oyovbaire, S. (1984). *Federalism in Nigeria.* New York: St. Martin's.

Padilla, A., Hogan, R., & Kaiser, R. B. (2007). The toxic triangle: Destructive leaders, susceptible followers, and conducive environments. *Leadership Quarterly, 18,* 176–194.

Page, B. I., & Jones, C. C. (1979). Reciprocal effects of policy preferences, party loyalties, and the vote. *American Political Science Review, 73,* 1055–1070.

Papic, M., & Noonan, S. (2011). Social media as a tool for protest. *Stratfor Global Intelligence.* Retrieved from www.stratfor.com/weekly/20110202-social-media-tool-protest

Pardos-Prado, S., Lancee, B., & Sagarzazu, I. (2014). Immigration and electoral change in mainstream political space. *Political Behavior, 36*(4), 847–875.

Park, B. (1993). *Ailing, aging, addicted: Studies of compromised leadership.* Lexington: University Press of Kentucky.

Park, J., & Banaji, M. R. (2000). Mood and heuristics: The influence of happy and sad states on sensitivity and bias in stereotyping. *Journal of Personality and Social Psychology, 78,* 1005–1023.

Parker, C. F., & Stern, E. K. (2005). Bolt from the blue or avoidable failure? Revisiting September 11 and the origins of strategic surprise, *Foreign Policy Analysis, 1,* 301–331.

Patterson, M. L., & Schaeffer, R. E. (1977). Effects of size and sex composition on interaction distance, participation, and satisfaction in small groups. *Small Group Behavior, 8*, 433–442.

Patterson, T. (1993). *Out of order.* New York: Alfred A. Knopf.

Paul, A. M. (2004). *The cult of personality testing: How personality tests are leading us to miseducate our children, mismanage our companies, and misunderstand ourselves.* New York: Free Press.

Payin, E. A., & Popov, A. A. (1996). Chechnya—From past to present. Santa Monica, CA: RAND.

Pearce, K. (1977). Police negotiations. *Canadian Psychiatric Association Journal, 22,* 171–174.

Pearlstein, R. M. (1991). *The mind of the political terrorist.* Wilmington, DE: Scholarly Resources.

Pearson, C.A.L. (1987). Participative goal setting as a strategy for improving performance and job satisfaction: A longitudinal evaluation with railway track maintenance groups. *Human Relations, 40,* 473–488.

Pearson, C.A.L. (1992). Autonomous work groups: An evaluation at an industrial site. *Human Relations, 45,* 905–936.

Peffley, M., & Hurwitz, J. (1998). Whites' stereotypes of blacks: Sources and political consequences. In J. Hurwitz & M. Peffley (Eds.), *Perception and prejudice: Race and politics in the United States.* New Haven, CT: Yale University Press.

Perera, V. (1993). *Unfinished conquest: The Guatemalan tragedy.* Berkeley: University of California Press.

Perina, K. (2002). Suicide terrorism. *Psychology Today, 35*(5), 15.

Perloff, R. M. (1993). *The dynamics of persuasion.* Hillsdale, NJ: Lawrence Erlbaum Associates.

Perreault, S., & Bourhis, R. (1999). Ethnocentrism, social identification, and discrimination. *Personality and Social Psychology Bulletin, 25,* 92–103.

Pervin, L. A., & John, O. (1997). *Personality: Theory and research* (7th ed.). New York: John Wiley and Sons.

Peterson, S. (2000a, December 11). Heavy civilian toll in Chechnya's "unlimited violence." *Christian Science Monitor,* p. A7.

Peterson, S. (2000b). *Me against my brother: At war in Somalia, Sudan, and Rwanda.* New York: Routledge.

Pettigrew, T. (1979). The ultimate attribution error: Extending Allport's cognitive analysis of prejudice. *Personality and Social Psychology Bulletin, 5,* 461–476.

Pettigrew, T., & Martin, J. (1989). Organizational inclusion of minority groups: A social psychological analysis. In J. P. van Oudenhoven & T. Willemsen (Eds.), *Ethnic minorities: Social psychological perspectives* (pp. 169–200). Berwyn, PA: Swets North America.

Pettigrew, T., & Meertens, R. (1995). Subtle and blatant prejudice in western Europe. *European Journal of Social Psychology, 25,* 57–76.

Petty, R. E., & Cacioppo, J. T. (1986). The elaboration likelihood model of persuasion. In L. Berkowitz (Ed.), *Advances in experimental social psychology* (Vol. 19, pp. 123–205). New York: Academic Press.

Petty, R. E., & Wegener, D. T. (1998). Attitude change: Multiple roles for persuasion variables. In D. T. Gilbert, S. T. Fiske, & G. Lindzey (Eds.), *The handbook of social psychology* (pp. 323–390). New York: McGraw-Hill.

Pew Research Center. (2007). *Blacks see growing values gap between poor and middle classes.* Washington, DC: Author.

Pew Research Center. (2008a). Fewer voters identify as Republicans. Retrieved from www.pewresearch.org/pubs/773/fewer-voters-identify-as-republicans

Pew Research Center. (2008b). Inside Obama's sweep. Retrieved from www.pewresearch.org/pubs/1023/exit-poll-analysis-2008

Pew Research Center. (2012). Media bias. Retrieved from www.people-press.org/subjects/media-bias

Pika, J. A. (1988). Management style and the White House. *Administration and Society, 20,* 3–29.

Pittenger, D. J. (1993). Measuring the MBTI . . . And coming up short. *Journal of Career Planning & Placement, 51,* 48–52.

Plock, E. (1993). *East German-West German relations and the fall of the GDR.* Boulder, CO: Westview Press.

Plous, S. (1993). *The psychology of judgment and decisionmaking.* New York: McGraw-Hill.

Popkin, S. (1994). *The reasoning voter: Communication and persuasion in presidential campaigns.* Chicago, IL: University of Chicago Press.

Porter, R. B. (1980). *Presidential decision making: The economic policy board.* Cambridge: Cambridge University Press.

Post, J. (1984). Notes on a psychodynamic theory of terrorist behavior. *Terrorism: An International Journal, 7,* 241–256.

Post, J. (2004). *Leaders and their followers in a dangerous world.* Ithaca, NY: Cornell.

Post, J., & Robins, R. (1993). *When illness strikes the leader: The dilemma of the captive king.* New Haven, CT: Yale University Press.

Post, J. M. (1991). Saddam Hussein of Iraq: A political psychology profile. *Political Psychology, 12,* 279–289.

Post, J. M. (1993a). The defining moment of Saddam's life: A political psychology perspective on the leadership and decision making of Saddam Hussein during the Gulf Crisis. In S. A. Renshon (Ed.), *The political psychology of the Gulf War: Leaders, publics, and the process of conflict* (pp. 49–66). Pittsburgh: University of Pittsburgh Press.

Post, J. M. (1993b). Current concepts of the narcissistic personality: Implications for political psychology. *Political Psychology, 14,* 99–122.

Powell, R. (1990). *Nuclear deterrence theory: The search for credibility.* New York: Cambridge University Press.

Power, S. (2002). *"A problem from hell": America and the age of genocide.* New York: Basic Books.

Pratkanis, A. R. (1989). The cognitive representation of attitudes. In A. R. Pratkanis, S. J. Breckler, & A. G. Greenwald (Eds.), *Attitude structure and function* (pp. 71–98). Hillsdale, NJ: Lawrence Erlbaum Associates.

Pratkanis, A. R., & Greenwald, A. G. (1989). A sociocognitive model of attitude structure and function. *Advances in Experimental Social Psychology* (Vol. 22, pp. 245–285). New York: Academic Press.

Pratto, F., Sidanius, J., Stallworth, L., & Malle, B. (1994). Social dominance orientation: a personality variable predicting social and political attitudes. *Journal of Personality and Social Psychology, 67,* 741–763.

Prentice, D.A., Miller, D.T., & Lightdale, J.R. (1994). Asymmetries in attachments to groups and to their members: Distinguishing between common-identity and common-bond groups. *Personality and Social Psychology Bulletin, 20,* 484–493.

Preston, T. (1997). "Following the leader": The impact of U.S. presidential style upon advisory group dynamics, structure, and decision. In P. 't Hart, E. Stern, & B. Sundelius (Eds.), *Beyond groupthink: Political group dynamics and foreign policymaking* (pp. 191–248). Ann Arbor: University of Michigan Press.

Preston, T. (2001). *The president and his inner circle: Leadership style and the advisory process in foreign policy making.* New York: Columbia University Press.

Preston, T. (2007/2009). *From lambs to lions: Future security relationships in a world of biological and nuclear weapons.* Boulder, CO: Rowman & Littlefield.

Preston, T. (2008). Weathering the politics of responsibility and blame: The Bush administration and its response to Hurricane Katrina. In A. Boin, A. McConnell, & P. 't Hart (Eds.), *Governing after crisis: The politics of investigation, accountability, and learning* (pp. 33–61). Cambridge: Cambridge University Press.

Preston, T. (2011). *Pandora's trap: Presidential decision making and blame avoidance in Vietnam and Iraq.* Boulder, CO: Rowman & Littlefield.

Preston, T. (2012). The role of leaders in sequential decision-making: Lyndon Johnson, advisory dynamics, and Vietnam. In C.F. Hermann (Ed.), *When things go wrong: Foreign policy decision making under adverse feedback* (pp. 53–88). New York: Routledge.

Preston, T., & Hermann. M.G. (2004). Presidential leadership style and the foreign policy advisory process. In E. R. Wittkopf & J. M. McCormick (Eds.), *The domestic sources of American foreign policy: Insights and evidence* (4th ed., pp. 363–380). New York: Rowman & Littlefield.

Preston, T., & 't Hart, P. (1999). Understanding and evaluating bureaucratic politics: The nexus between political leaders and advisory systems. *Political Psychology, 20,* 49–98.

Pritchard, R.D., Jones, S.D., Roth, P.L., Stuebing, K.K., & Ekeberg, S.E. (1988). Effects of group feedback, goal setting, and incentives on organizational productivity. *Journal of Applied Psychology, 73,* 337–358.

Pronin, E., Puccio, C., & Ross, L. (2002). Understanding misunderstanding: Social psychological perspectives. In T. Gilovich, D. Griffin, & D. Kahneman (Eds.) *Heuristics and biases: The psychology of intuitive judgment* (pp. 636–665). Cambridge: Cambridge University Press.

Pruitt, D.G., & Kimmel, M.J. (1977). Twenty years of experimental gaming: Critique, synthesis, and suggestions for the future. *Annual Review of Psychology, 28,* 363–392.

Pruitt, D.G., & Rubin, J.Z. (1986). *Social conflict: Escalation, stalemate, and settlement.* New York: Random House.

Prunier, G. (2005). *Darfur: The ambiguous genocide.* Ithaca, NY: Cornell University Press.

Rabbie, J.M., & Wilkins, G. (1971). Intergroup competition and its effects on intragroup and intergroup relations. *European Journal of Social Psychology, 1,* 215–234.

Rabie, M. (1994). *Conflict resolution and ethnicity*. Westport, CT: Praeger.

Rabinowitz, J. L. (1999). Go with the flow or fight the power? The interactive effect of social dominance orientation and perceived injustice on support for the status quo. *Political Psychology, 20*, 1–24.

Raden, D. (1999). Is anti-Semitism currently part of an authoritarian attitude syndrome? *Political Psychology, 20*, 323–343.

Raghavan, S. (2008, April 7). Between Iraqi Shiites, a deepening animosity. *Washington Post*. Retrieved from www.washingtonpost.com

Rahn, W., Aldrich, J., Borgida, E., & Sullivan, J. (1990). A social cognitive model of candidate appraisal. In J. Ferejohn & J. Kuklinski (Eds.), *Information and democratic process* (pp. 136–159). Chicago, IL: University of Chicago Press.

Rane, H., & Ewart, J. (2012). The Framing of Islam and Muslims in the tenth anniversary coverage of 9/11: Implications for reconciliation and moving on. *Journal of Muslim Minority Affairs, 32*, 310–322.

Raven, B. H. (1965). Social influence and power. In I. D. Steiner & M. Fishbein (Eds.), *Current studies in social psychology* (pp. 371–382). New York: Holt, Rinehart, and Winston.

Redlawsk, D. P., Civettini, A., & Lau, R. R. (2007). Affective intelligence and voting: Information processing and learning in a campaign. In W. R. Neuman, G. E. Marcus, A. N. Crigler, & M. MacKuen (Eds.), *The affect effect: Dynamics of emotion in political thinking and behavior* (pp. 1–23). Chicago, IL: University of Chicago Press.

Remington, R. (1996). The Yugoslav army: Trauma and transition. In C. Danopoulos & D. Zirker (Eds.), *Civil-military relations in the Soviet and Yugoslav successor states* (pp. 153–173). Boulder, CO: Westview Press.

Renshon, S. (2012). *Barack Obama and the politics of redemption*. New York: Routledge.

Renshon, S. A. (1996). *High hopes: The Clinton presidency and the politics of ambition*. New York: New York University Press.

Reyes-Quilodran, C. (2001). *The main factors that could determine the behavior of a torturer* (Unpublished master's thesis). Washington State University, Pullman.

Rhodes, E. (1989). *Power and MADness: The logic of nuclear coercion*. New York: Columbia University Press.

Richards, J. M., & Gross, J. J. (1999). Composure at any cost? The cognitive consequences of emotion suppression. *Personality and Social Psychology Bulletin, 25*, 1033–1044.

Richardson, L. (1960). *Arms and insecurity*. Pittsburgh, PA: Boxwood Press.

Ridgeway, J. (1995). *Blood in the face* (2nd ed.). New York: Thunder's Mouth Press.

Ridout, T. N., & Franz, M. M. (2011). *The persuasive power of campaign advertising*. Philadelphia, PA: Temple University Press.

Rigby, A. (2001). *Justice and reconciliation after the violence*. Boulder, CO: Lynne Rienner Press.

Ringelmann, M. (1913). Research on animate sources of power: The work of man. *Annales de L'Institut National Agronomique* (2e serie), 12, 1–40.

Roberts, B. W., & Donahue, E. M. (1994). One personality, multiple selves: Integrating personality and social roles. *Journal of Personality, 62*, 201–218.

Robinson, R., Keltner, D., Ward, A., & Ross, L. (1995). Actual versus assumed differences in construal: "Naive realism" in intergroup perception and conflict. *Journal of Personality and Social Psychology, 68*, 404–417.

Rogers, R., & Prentice-Dunn, S. (1981). Deindividuation and anger-mediated interracial aggression: Unmasking regressive racism. *Journal of Personality and Social Psychology, 41*, 63–73.

Rogow, A. (1963). *James Forrestal: A study in personality, politics, and policy*. New York: Macmillan.

Rokeach, M. (1973). *The nature of human values*. New York: Free Press.

Romano, L. (2001, May 4). An enigma awaits death. *Washington Post*, pp. A1, A3.

Roper Center. (2012). How groups voted in 2012. Retrieved from www.ropercenter.uconn.edu/polls/us-elections

Rosati, J. A. (1987). *The Carter administration's quest for global community: Beliefs and their impact on behavior*. Columbia: University of South Carolina Press.

Rosati, J. A. (1990). Continuity and change in the foreign policy beliefs of political leaders: Addressing the controversy over the Carter administration. *Political Psychology, 9*, 471–505.

Rosch, E. (1978). Principles of categorization. In E. Rosch & B. Lloyd (Eds.), *Cognition and categorization* (pp. 27–38). Hillsdale, NJ: Lawrence Erlbaum Associates.

Rosenberg, T. (1992). *Children of Cain: Violence and the violent in Latin America*. New York: Penguin Books.

Rosenthal, S. A., & Pittinsky, T. L. (2006). Narcissistic leadership. *Leadership Quarterly, 17*, 617–633.

Ross, J., & Staw, B. M. (1986). Expo 86: An escalation prototype. *Administrative Science Quarterly, 31*, 274–297.

Ross, L. (1977). The intuitive psychologist and his shortcomings: Distortions in the attribution process, In L. Berkowitz (Ed.), *Advances in experimental social psychology* (Vol. 10, pp. 174–221). New York: Academic Press.

Rothbart, M., & Johns, O. (1993). Intergroup relations and stereotype change: A social-cognitive analysis and some longitudinal findings. In P. Sniderman, P. Tetlock, & E. Carmines (Eds.), *Prejudice, politics, and the American dilemma* (pp. 32–59). Stanford, CA: Stanford University Press.

Rothman, J., & Olson, M. L. (2001). From interests to identities: Towards a new emphasis on interactive conflict resolution. *Journal of Peace Research, 38*, 289–305.

Rothschild, J. (1981). *Ethnopolitics: A conceptual framework*. New York: Columbia University Press.

Rotter, J. B. (1966). Generalized expectancies for internal versus external control of reinforcement. *Psychological Monographs: General and Applied, 80*.

Rowe, A. J., & Mason, R. O. (1987). *Managing with style: A guide to understanding, assessing, and improving decision making*. San Francisco, CA: Jossey-Bass.

Rubenstein, C. M., & Shaver, P. (1980). Loneliness in two northeastern cities. In J. Hartog & R. Audy (Eds.), *The anatomy of loneliness*. New York: International Universities Press.

Rubenzer, S. J., & Faschingbauer, T. R. (2004). *Personality, character, and leadership in the White House: Psychologists assess the presidents.* Washington, DC: Bassey's.

Rubin, J. Z., & Brockner, J. (1975). Factors affecting entrapment in waiting situations: The Rosencrantz and Guildenstern effect. *Journal of Personality and Social Psychology, 31,* 1054–1063.

Rucht, D. (2013). Social movement structures in action: Conceptual propositions and empirical illustration. In J. van Stekelenburg, C. Roggebans, & B. Klandermans (Eds.), *The future of social movement research: Dynamics, mechanisms, and processes* (pp. 169–190). Minneapolis: University of Minnesota Press.

Ruder, M. K., & Gill, D. L. (1982). Immediate effects of win-loss on perceptions of cohesion in intramural and intercollegiate volleyball teams, *Journal of Sport Psychology, 4,* 227–234.

Rule, N. O., Freeman, J. B., Moran, J. M., Gabrieli, J. D. E., Adams, R. B., & Ambady, N. (2010). Voting behavior is reflected in amygdala response across cultures. *Social Cognitive and Affective Neuroscience, 5*(2–3), 349–355.

Rumble, A. (2003). *Empathy induced cooperation and social dilemmas: An investigation into the influence of attribution type* (Unpublished doctoral dissertation). Washington State University, Pullman.

Rummel, R. J. (1994). *Death by government.* New Brunswick, NJ: Transaction Books.

Russell, D., Peplau, L. A., & Cutrona, C. E. (1980). The revised UCLA Loneliness Scale: Concurrent and discriminant validity evidence. *Journal of Personality and Social Psychology, 39,* 472–480.

Ryan, N. (2003). *Into a world of hate.* New York: Routledge.

Sabato, L. (1991). *Feeding frenzy: How attack journalism has transformed American politics.* New York: Free Press.

Sabini, J. P., & Silver, M. (1993). Destroying the innocent with a clear conscience: A sociopsychology of the Holocaust. In N. Kressel (Ed.), *Political psychology: Classic and contemporary readings* (pp. 192–217). New York: Paragon House.

Sagan, S. D. (1994). The perils of proliferation: Organization theory, deterrence theory, and the spread of nuclear weapons. *International Security, 18,* 66–107.

Sageman, M. (2004). *Understanding terror networks.* Philadelphia: University of Pennsylvania Press.

Sageman, M. (2008). *Leaderless Jihad: Terrorist networks in the 21st century.* Philadelphia: University of Pennsylvania Press.

Sanchez, G. (2006). The role of group consciousness in Latino public opinion. *Political Research Quarterly, 59,* 435–446.

Sanger, D. E. (2002, April 21). War was easy. The rest of the world is a mess. *New York Times,* sec. 4, pp. 1, 4.

Sanger, D. E. (2005, September 22). Bush compares responses to hurricane and terrorism. *New York Times.*

Schafer, M. (1997). Images and policy preferences. *Political Psychology, 18,* 813–827.

Schafer, M., & Crichlow, S. (2000). Bill Clinton's operational code: Assessing source material bias. *Political Psychology, 21,* 559–571.

Schaffner, B. F. (2011). Racial salience and the Obama vote. *Political Psychology, 32,* 963–988.

Schafer, M., & Walker, S. (2006). *Beliefs and leadership in world politics: Methods and applications of operational code analysis.* New York: Palgrave Macmillan.

Schatz, E., & Levine, R. (2010). Framing, public diplomacy, and anti-Americanism in Central America. *International Studies Quarterly, 54,* 855–869.

Schelling, T. (1966). *Arms and influence.* New Haven, CT: Yale University Press.

Schelling, T. (1980). *The strategy of conflict* (2nd ed.). Cambridge, MA: Harvard University Press. (Original work published 1960)

Schimmack, U., Oishi, S., Diener, E., & Suh, E. (2000). Facets of affective experiences: A framework for investigations of trait affect. *Personality and Social Psychology Bulletin, 26,* 655–668.

Schirmer, J. (1998). *The Guatemalan military project: A violence called democracy.* Philadelphia: University of Pennsylvania Press.

Schlesinger, A. M., Jr. (1965). *A thousand days: John F. Kennedy in the White House.* Boston, MA: Houghton Mifflin.

Schöpflin, G. (1993). The rise and fall of Yugoslavia. In J. McGarry & B. O'Leary (Eds.), *The politics of ethnic conflict* (pp. 172–203). New York: Routledge.

Schopler, J., Gruder, C., Miller, M., & Rousseau, M. (1968). The endurance of persuasion induced by a reward and a coercive power figure. *Human Relations, 20,* 301–308.

Schouten, R., & Silver, J. (2012). *Almost a psychopath: Do I (or does someone I know) have a problem with manipulation and lack of empathy?* Cambridge, MA: Harvard University Press.

Schroder, H., Driver, M., & Streufert, S. (1967). *Human information processing.* New York: Holt, Rinehart, and Winston.

Schultz, D. (1981). *Theories of personality* (2nd ed.). Monterey, CA: Brooks/ Cole.

Schultz, T. (2005). *Handbook of psychobiography.* New York: Oxford University Press.

Schuman, H., Steeh, C., Bobo, L., & Krysan, M. (1997). *Racial attitudes in America: Trends and interpretations.* Cambridge, MA: Harvard University Press.

Schutz, W. C. (1958). *FIRO: A three-dimensional theory of interpersonal behavior.* New York: Rinehart.

Schweitzer, Y. (2004, June 18). Suicide bombers. *PBS.* Retrieved from www. pbs.org/wnet/wideangle/shows/suicide/briefing.html

Scott, J. P. (1969). Biological basis of human warfare: An interdisciplinary problem, In M. Sherif & C. W. Sherif (Eds.), *Interdisciplinary relationships in the social sciences* (pp. 121–136). Chicago, IL: Aldine.

Scott, J. P. (1981). Biological and psychological bases of social attachment. In H. Kellerman (Ed.), *Group cohesion.* New York: Grune and Stratton.

Searle-White, J. (2001). *The psychology of nationalism.* New York: Palgrave.

Sears, D. (1993). Symbolic politics: A socio-psychological theory. In S. Iyengar & W. McGuire (Eds.), *Explorations in political psychology* (pp. 113–149). Durham, NC: Duke University Press.

Sears, D., Henry, P. J., & Kosterman, R. (2000). Egalitarian values and contemporary racial politics. In D. O. Sears, J. Sidanius, & L. Bobo (Eds.), *Racialized politics: The debate about racism in America* (pp. 75–117). Chicago, IL: University of Chicago Press.

Sears, D., Hetts, J., Sidanius, J., & Bobo, L. (2000). Race in American politics. In D. O. Sears, J. Sidanius, & L. Bobo (Eds.), *Racialized politics: The debate about racism in America* (pp. 1–43). Chicago, IL: University of Chicago Press.

Sears, D., & Kinder, D. (1971). Racial tensions and voting in Los Angeles. In W. Hirsch (Ed.), *Los Angeles: Viability and prospects for metropolitan leadership*. New York: Praeger.

Sears, D. O. (1975). Political socialization. In F. Greenstein & N. W. Polsby (Eds.), *Handbook of political science.* (Vol. 4, pp. 93–153). Cambridge, MA: Addison-Wesley.

Sears, D. O., Sidanius, J., & Bobo, L. (Eds.). (2000). *Racialized politics: The debate about racism in America*. Chicago, IL: University of Chicago Press.

Seashore, S. E. (1954). *Group cohesiveness in the industrial work group*. Ann Arbor, MI: Institute for Social Research.

Sechrist, G. B., & Stangor, C. (2001). Perceived consensus influences intergroup behavior and stereotype accessibility. *Journal of Personality and Social Psychology, 80*, 645–654.

Seelke, C. R., & Finklea, K. (2014). *U.S.-Mexican security cooperation: The Mérida initiative*. Washington, DC: Congressional Research Service.

Settle, J. E., Dawes, C. T., & Fowler, J. H. (2009). The heritability of partisan attachment. *Political Research Quarterly, 62*, 601–613.

Seyd, P. (1998). Tony Blair and New Labour. In A. King, D. Denver, I. McLean, P. Norris, D. Sanders, & P. Seyd (Eds.), *New Labour triumphs: Britain at the polls* (pp. 49–73). Chatham, NJ: Chatham House.

Shakur, S. (1993). *Monster: The autobiography of an L.A. gang member*. New York: Penguin.

Shapley, L. S. (1953). A value for *n*-person games. In H. W. Kuhn & A. W. Tucker (Eds.), *Contributions to the theory of games* (Vol. 2, pp. 53–65). Princeton, NJ: Princeton University Press.

Shaw, J. I., & Condelli, L. (1986). Effects of compliance outcome and basis of power on the powerholder-target relationship. *Personality and Social Psychology Bulletin, 12*, 236–246.

Shaw, M. E. (1981). *Group dynamics: The psychology of small group behavior* (3rd ed.). New York: McGraw-Hill.

Shaw, R. P., & Wong, Y. (1989). *Genetic seeds of warfare: Evolution, nationalism and patriotism*. Boston, MA: Unwin Hyman.

Shehata, D. (2011). The fall of the pharaoh: How Hosni Mubarak's reign came to an end. *Foreign Affairs, 90*, 26–32.

Shenon, P. (2002, July 19). Traces of terror: The terror suspect; 9/11 defendant in guilty plea; judge rejects. *New York Times*. Retrieved from www.nytimes.com/2002/07/19/traces-terror-terror-suspect-9-11-defendeant-guilty-plea-judge-rejects-it-html?pagewanted=all

Sherif, C. W., Sherif, M., & Nebergall, R. E. (1965). *Attitude and attitude change: The social judgment-involvement approach*. Philadelphia, PA: Saunders.

Sherif, M. (1936). *The psychology of social norms*. New York: Harper and Row.

Sherif, M., Harvey, D. J., White, B. J., Hood, W. R., & Sherif, C. W. (1961). *The Robbers' cave experiment*. Norman, OK: Institute of Group Relations.

Shils, E. (1954). Authoritarianism: Right and left. In R. Christie & M. Jahoda (Eds.), *Studies in the scope and method of "the authoritarian personality"* (pp. 24–49). Glencoe, IL: Free Press.

Shimko, K. (1991). *Images and arms control*. Ann Arbor: University of Michigan Press.

Shinkman, P. (2014). Ukrainian president: Russian aggression sparking new Cold War. *US News and World Report*. Retrieved from www.usnews.com/news/article/2014/09/18/uk

Shipler, D. (1997). *A country of strangers: Blacks and whites in America*. New York: Knopf.

Shively, W. P. (1993). *Power and choice*. Boston, MA: McGraw-Hill.

Shuman, H., Steeh, C., Bobo, L., & Krysan, M. (1997). *Racial attitudes in America: Trends and interpretations*. Cambridge, MA: Harvard University Press.

Sidanius, J. (1993). The psychology of group conflict and the dynamics of oppression: A social dominance perspective. In S. Iyengar & W. McGuire (Eds.), *Explorations in political psychology*. Durham, NC: Duke University Press.

Sidanius, J., & Kurzba, R. (2013). Toward an evolutionarily informed political psychology. In L. Huddy, D. O. Sears, & J. S. Levy (Eds.), *The Oxford handbook of political psychology* (2nd ed., pp. 205–236). New York: Oxford University Press.

Sidanius, J., & Pratto, F. (1993). The dynamics of social dominance and the inevitability of oppression. In P. Sniderman & P. Tetlock (Eds.), *Prejudice, politics, and race in America today*. Stanford, CA: Stanford University Press.

Sidanius, J., & Pratto, F. (1999). *Social dominance: An intergroup theory of social hierarchy and oppression*. New York: Cambridge University Press.

Sidanius, J., Singh, P., Hetts, J., & Federico, C. (2000). It's not affirmative action, it's the blacks. In D. O. Sears, J. Sidanius, & L. Bobo (Eds.), *Racialized politics: The debate about racism in America*. Chicago, IL: University of Chicago Press.

Sigel, R. (1995). New directions for political socialization research: Thoughts and suggestions. *Perspectives on Political Science, 24*, 17–33.

Silber, L., & Little, A. (1996). *Yugoslavia: Death of a nation*. New York: Penguin.

Silber, M. D., & Bhatt, A. (2007). *Radicalization in the west: The homegrown threat*. New York: NYPD.

Silke, A. (2003). Becoming a terrorist. In A. Silke (Ed.). *Terrorists, victims and society: psychological perspectives on terrorism and its consequences.* (pp. 29–53). London: John Wiley and Sons.

Silke, A. (2004). Courage in dark places: reflections on terrorist psychology. *Social Research, 71*(1), 177–198.

Simon, S. (2008). The price of the surge. *Foreign Affairs, 87*, 57–76.

Simon, S., & Takeyh, R. (2006, May 21). Iran's Iraq strategy. *Washington Post*. Retrieved from www.washingtonpost.com/wp-dyn/content/article/2006/05/19/AR2006051901761.html

Simpson, C. (2000, November 14). Quiet soldier who runs Rwanda. *BBC News*.

Sinclair, L., & Kunda, Z. (1999). Reactions to a black professional: Motivated inhibition and activation of conflicting stereotypes. *Journal of Personality and Social Psychology, 77*, 885–904.

Singer, John D. "Threat Perception and the Armament-Tension Dilemma." *Journal of Conflict Resolution*, 2 (1958): pp. 90–105.

Sipress, A. (2001, April 26). Policy divide thwarts Powell in Mideast effort: Defense Department's influence frustrates State Department. *Washington Post*, p. A10.

Skinner, B. L. (1971). *Beyond freedom and dignity*. New York: Knopf.

Skinner, B. L. (1974). *About behaviorism*. New York: Knopf.

Skovertz, J. (1988). Models of participation in status-differentiated groups. *Social Psychology Quarterly, 51*, 43–57.

Sledge, M. (2011, November 10). Reawakening the radical imagination: The origin of Occupy Wall Street. *Huffington Post*. Retrieved from www.huffingtonpost.com/2011/11/10.occupy-wall-street-origins_n_1083977.html

Slothuus, R. (2008). More than weighting cognitive importance: A dual-process mode of issue framing effects. *Political Psychology, 29*, 1–28.

Sluka, J. A. (2000). Introduction: State terror and anthropology. In J. A. Sluka (Ed.), *Death squad: The anthropology of state terror*. Philadelphia: University of Pennsylvania Press.

Smith, A. (1981). *The ethnic revival*. Cambridge: Cambridge University Press.

Smith, C. P., Atkinson, J. W., McClelland, D. C., & Veroff, J. (Eds.). (1992). *Motivation and personality: Handbook of thematic content analysis*. Cambridge: Cambridge University Press.

Smith, E. (1989). *The unchanging American voter*. Berkeley: University of California Press.

Smith, E. (1993). Social identity and social emotions: Toward new conceptualizations of prejudice. In D. M. Mackie & D. L. Hamilton (Eds.), *Affect, cognition and stereotyping: Interactive processes in group perception* (pp. 297–315). San Diego, CA: Academic Press.

Smith, H. K. (1988). *The power game: How Washington works*. New York: Ballantine Books.

Smith, R. J. (2000a, November 25). West is tiring of struggle to rebuild Bosnia. *Washington Post*, p. A4.

Smith, R. J. (2000b, November 10). Ethnic hatred permeates Bosnia's bitter peace. *Washington Post*, p. A2.

Smoke, R. (1987). *National security and the nuclear dilemma* (2nd ed.). New York: Random House.

Sniderman, P., Brody, R., & Tetlock, P. (1991). *Reasoning and choice: Explorations in political psychology*. Cambridge: Cambridge University Press.

Sniderman, P., & Carmines, E. (1997). *Reaching beyond race*. Cambridge, MA: Harvard University Press.

Sniderman, P., Crosby, G., & Howell, W. (2000). The politics of race. In D. O. Sears, J. Sidanious, & L. Bobo (Eds.), *Racialized politics: The debate about racism in America* (pp. 236–278). Chicago, IL: University of Chicago Press.

Sniderman, P., Glaser, J., & Griffin, R. 1990. Information and electoral choice. In J. Ferejohn & J. Kuklinski (Eds.), *Information and democratic processes* (pp. 117–135). Urbana: University of Illinois Press.

Sniderman, P., & Hagen, M. (1985). *Race and inequality: A study in American values.* Chatham, NJ: Chatham House.

Sniderman, P., & Piazza, T. (1993). *The scar of race.* Cambridge, MA: Harvard University Press.

Sniderman, P., & Piazza, T. (2002). *Black pride and Black prejudice.* Princeton, NJ: Princeton University Press.

Sniderman, P., Piazza, T., & Harvey, H. (1998). Prejudice and politics: An intellectual biography of a research project. In J. Hurwitz & M. Peffley (Eds.), *Perception and prejudice: Race and politics in the United States.* New Haven, CT: Yale University Press.

Sniderman, P., & Tetlock, P. (1986). Reflections on American racism. *Journal of Social Issues, 42,* 173–187.

Sniderman, P. M., & Theriault, S. M. (2004). The structure of political argument and the logic of issue framing. In W. E. Saris & P. M. Sniderman (Eds.), *Studies in public opinion: Attitudes, non-attitudes, measurement error and change* (pp. 133–165). Princeton, NJ: Princeton University Press.

Snow, D., Rochford, E., Jr., Worden, S., & Benford, R. (1986). Frame alignment processes, micro-mobilization, and movement participation. *American Sociological Review, 51,* 464–481.

Snyder, J. L. (1984). *The ideology of the offensive: Military decision making and the disasters of 1914.* Ithaca, NY: Cornell University Press.

Snyder, M. (1987). *Public appearances/private realities: The psychology of self-monitoring.* New York: W. H. Freeman.

Snyder, T. (2014). Europe and Ukraine: Past and future. *Eurozine.* Retrieved from www.eurozine.com/search.html

Sorensen, T. C. (1965). *Kennedy.* New York: Harper and Row.

Spink, K. S., & Carron, A. V. (1992). Group cohesion and adherence in exercise classes. *Journal of Sport and Exercise Psychology, 14,* 78–86.

Sprinzak, E. (2000, September/October). Rational fanatics. *Foreign Policy, 113,* 66–73.

Srull, T., & Ottati, V. (1995). Political information processing. In S. Iyengar & W. McGuire (Eds.). *Explorations in political psychology.* Durham, NC: Duke University Press.

Srull, T., & Wyer, R. (1989). Person memory and judgment. *Psychological Review, 96,* 58–83.

Stangor, C., Sechrist, G. B., & Jost, J. T. (2001). Changing racial beliefs by providing consensus information. *Personality and Social Psychology Bulletin, 27,* 486–495.

Stasser, G., Kerr, N. L., & Davis, J. H. (1989). Influence processes and consensus models in decision-making groups. In P. B. Paulus (Ed.), *Psychology of group influence* (2nd ed., pp. 279–326). Hillsdale, NJ: Lawrence Erlbaum Associates.

Stasser, G., & Titus, W. (1987). Effects of information load and percentage of shared information on the dissemination of unshared information during group discussion. *Journal of Personality and Social Psychology, 53,* 81–93.

Staub, E. (1989). *The roots of evil: The origins of genocide and other group violence.* Cambridge: Cambridge University Press.

Staub, E. (1999). The roots of evil: Social conditions, culture, personality and basic human needs. *Personality and Social Psychology Review, 3,* 179–192.

Staub, E. (2000). Genocide and mass killing: Origins, prevention, healing and reconciliation. *Political Psychology, 21,* 367–382.

Staub, E. (2006). Reconciliation after genocide, mass killing, or intractable conflict: Understanding the roots of violence, psychological recovery, and steps toward a general theory. *Political Psychology, 27,* 867–894.

Staw, B. M. (1976). Knee deep in the Big Muddy: A study of escalating commitment to a chosen course of action. *Organizational Behavior and Human Performance, 16,* 27–44.

Staw, B. M., & Fox, F. V. (1977). Escalation: The determinants of commitment to a chosen course of action. *Human Relations, 30,* 431–450.

Staw, B. M., & Ross, J. (1987). Behavior in escalation situations: Antecedents, prototypes, and solutions. *Research in Organizational Behavior, 9,* 39–78.

Staw, B. M., & Ross, J. (1989). Understanding behavior in escalation situations. *Science, 246,* 216–220.

Steel, R. (1969, March 13). Endgame. *New York Review of Books, 12,* 15–22.

Stein, J. G. (1992). Deterrence and compellence in the Gulf, 1990–91: A failed or impossible task? *International Security, 17,* 147–179.

Stein, N., Trabasso, T., & Liwag, M. (1993). The representation and organization of emotional experience: Unfolding the emotion episode. In M. Lewis & J. Haviland (Eds.), *Handbook of emotions* (pp. 279–300). New York: Guilford.

Steiner, I. D. (1972). *Group process and productivity.* New York: Academic Press.

Steinert, M. (1977). *Hitler's war and the Germans: Public mood and attitude during the Second World War.* Athens: Ohio University Press.

Stephan, W., & Stephan, C. (1993). Cognition and affect in stereotyping: Parallel interactive networks. In D. Mackie & D. Hamilton (Eds.), *Affect, cognition, and stereotyping: Interactive processes in group perception.* New York: Academic Press.

Stern, E. (1997). Probing the plausibility of newgroup syndrome: Kennedy and the Bay of Pigs. In P. 't Hart, E. Stern, & B Sundelius (Eds.), *Beyond groupthink* (pp. 153–189). Ann Arbor: University of Michigan Press.

Stern, E., & Sundelius, B. (1994). The essence of groupthink. *Mershon International Studies Review, 1,* 101–108.

Stern, E., & Sundelius, B. (1997). Understanding small group decisions in foreign policy: Process diagnosis and research procedure. In P. 't Hart, E. Stern, & B. Sundelius (Eds.), *Beyond groupthink* (pp. 123–150). Ann Arbor: University of Michigan Press.

Stern, J. (2004, June 12) Holy avengers. *Financial Times.* Retrieved from www.ksg.harvard.edu/news/opeds/2004/stern_avengers_ft_061204.htm

Stevenson, R. W. (2005, September 3) In first response to crisis, Bush strikes off-key notes. *New York Times.*

Stewart, C. J., Smith, C. A., & Denton, R. E., Jr. (2012). *Persuasion and social movements* (6th ed.). Long Grove, IL: Waveland Press.

Stewart, P.D., Hermann, M.G., & Hermann, C.F. (1989). Modeling the 1973 Soviet decision to support Egypt. *American Political Science Review, 83*, 35–59.

Stimson, J.A. (1975). Belief systems: Constraint, complexity, and the 1972 election. *American Journal of Political Science, 20*, 393–417.

Stoessinger, J.G. (1985). *Why nations go to war.* New York: St. Martin's Press.

Stogdill, R.M., & Bass, B.M. (1981). *Stogdill's handbook of leadership: A survey of theory and research.* New York: Free Press.

Stoll, D. (1992). Evangelicals, guerrillas, and the army: The Ixtil triangle under Ríos Montt. In R.T. Carmack (Ed.), *Harvest of violence: The Maya Indian and the Guatemalan crisis* (pp. 109–116). Norman: University of Oklahoma Press.

Stone, W., & Schaffner, P. (1988). *The psychology of politics.* New York: Springer-Verlag.

Stoner, J.A.F. (1961). *A comparison of individual and group decisions involving risk* (Unpublished master's thesis). Massachusetts Institute of Technology, Cambridge.

Stouffer, S. (1955). *Communism, conformity, and civil liberties.* New York: Doubleday.

Strategic Assessment Group. (2003). *The next generation of world leaders.* Washington, DC: Central Intelligence Agency.

Street, P., & DiMaggio, P. (2011). *Crashing the tea party: Mass media and the campaign to remake American politics.* Boulder, CO: Paradigm.

Stroebe, W., & Insko, C. (1989). Stereotype, prejudice, and discrimination: Changing conceptions in theory and research. In D. Bar-Tal, C. Graumann, A. Kruglanski, & W. Stroebe (Eds.). *Stereotyping and prejudice: Changing conceptions* (pp. 54–68). New York: Springer-Verlag.

Stroessner, S., & Mackie, D. (1993). Affect and perceived group variability: Implications for stereotyping and prejudice. In D. Mackie & D. Hamilton (Eds.), *Affect, cognition and stereotyping: Interactive processes in group perception* (pp. 63–86). New York: Academic Press.

Stroud, N.J., & Muddiman, A. (2013). The American media system today: Is the public fragmenting? In T.N. Ridout (Ed.), *New directions in media and politics* (pp. 6–23). New York: Routledge.

Stuart, D., & Starr, H. (1981). The "inherent bad faith model" reconsidered: Dulles, Kennedy, and Kissinger. *Political Psychology, 3*, 1–33.

Suedfeld, P., & Rank, A.D. (1976). Revolutionary leaders: Long-term success as a function of changes in conceptual complexity. *Journal of Personality and Social Psychology, 34*, 169–178.

Suedfeld, P., & Tetlock, P. (1977). Integrative complexity of communication in international crisis. *Journal of Conflict Resolution, 21*, 169–184.

Sullivan, J., Piereson, J., & Marcus, G. (1979). An alternative conceptualization of political tolerance: Illusory increases, 1950s–1970s. *American Political Science Review, 73*, 781–794.

Sullivan, J., Piereson, H., & Marcus, G. (1982). *Political tolerance and American democracy.* Chicago, IL: University of Chicago Press.

Suskind, R. (2004). *The price of loyalty: George W. Bush, the White House, and the education of Paul O'Neill.* New York: Simon and Schuster.

Swain, C., & Nieli, R. (2003). *Contemporary voices of white nationalism in America.* Cambridge: Cambridge University Press.

Swim, J. K., & Miller, D. (1999). White guilt: Its antecedents and consequences for attitudes toward affirmative action. *Personality and Social Psychology Bulletin, 25*, 500–514.

Tafoya, S. (2004). Report: Shades of belonging. Washington, DC: Pew Hispanic Center. Retrieved from www.pewhispanic.org

Tajfel, H. (1970). Experiments in intergroup discrimination. *Scientific American, 223*, 96–102.

Tajfel, H. (1978). Social categorization, social identity, and social comparison. In H. Tajfel (Ed.), *Differentiation between social groups: Studies in the social psychology of intergroup relations* (pp. 61–76). New York: Academic Press.

Tajfel, H. (1982). *Human groups and social categories.* Cambridge: Cambridge University Press.

Tajfel, H., & Billig, M. (1974). Familiarity and categorization in intergroup behavior. *Journal of Experimental Social Psychology, 10*, 159–170.

Tajfel, H., & Turner, J. C. (1979). An integrative theory of intergroup conflict. In W. G. Austin & S. Worchel (Eds.), *The social psychology of intergroup relations* (pp. 38–48). Monterey, CA: Brooks Cole.

Tajfel, H., & Turner, J. C. (1986). The social identity theory of intergroup behavior. In S. Worchel & W. G. Austin (Eds.), *Psychology of intergroup relations* (pp. 1–24). Chicago, IL: Nelson-Hall.

Takaki, R. (2008). *A different mirror: A history of multicultural America.* New York: Back Bay Books.

Talbot, C. (2000, December 23). Rwanda on the offensive in Congo war. *Washington Post.*

Tam, K.-P., Leung, A., & Chiu, C.-Y. (2008). On being a mindful authoritarian: Is need for cognition always associated with less punitiveness? *Political Psychology, 29*, 77–91.

Tannenbaum, F. (1947). *Slave and citizen: The Negro in the Americas.* New York: Knopf.

Taylor, D. W., Berry, P. C., & Block, C. H. (1958). Does group participation when using brainstorming facilitate or inhibit creative thinking? *Administrative Science Quarterly, 3*, 23–47.

Taylor, M. (1988). *The terrorist.* London: Bassey's.

Taylor, M. (1991). *The fanatics: A behavioral approach to political violence.* London: Bassey's.

Taylor, M., & Louis, W. R. (2004). Terrorism and the quest for identity. In F. Moghaddam & A. J. Marsella (Eds.), *Understanding terrorism: Psychosocial roots, consequences, and interventions* pp. 169–185). Washington, DC: APA Press.

Taylor, M., & Quale, E. (1994). *Terrorist lives.* London: Bassey's.

Taylor, P., & Fry, R. (2007). Hispanics and the 2008 election: A swing vote? Washington, DC: Pew Hispanic Center. Retrieved from www.pewhispanic.org

Taylor, S. E., & Crocker, J. (1981). Schematic bases of social information processing. In T. Higgins, C. P. Herman, & M. P. Zanna (Eds.), *Social cognition: The Ontario symposium.* (Vol. 1, pp. 89–134). Hillsdale, NJ: Lawrence Erlbaum Associates.

Taylor, V. (2013). Social movement participation in the global society: Identity, networks, and emotions. In J. van Stekelenburg, C. Roggebans, &

B. Klandermans (Eds.), *The future of social movement research: Dynamics, mechanisms, and processes* (pp. 37–57). Minneapolis: University of Minnesota Press.

Taysi, T., & Preston, T. (2001). The personality and leadership style of President Khatami: Implications for the future of Iranian political reform. In O. Feldman & L. O. Valenty (Eds.), *Profiling political leaders: Cross-cultural studies of personality and behavior* (pp. 57–77). Westport, CT: Praeger.

Teens sharper on Bart than news. (1998, September 6). *Idaho Spokesman Review*, A6.

Teger, A. (1980). *Too much invested to quit*. New York: Pergamom Press.

Tepperman, J. (2002). Truth and consequences. *Foreign Affairs, 81*, 128–145.

Tetlock, P. (1983). Integrative complexity of American and Soviet foreign policy rhetorics: A time-series analysis. *Journal of Personality and Social Psychology, 49*, 565–585.

Tetlock, P. (1985). Accountability: The neglected social context of judgment and choice. In B. M. Staw & L. Cummings (Eds.), *Research in organizational behavior* (Vol. 7, pp. 297–332). Greenwich, CT: JAI Press.

Tetlock, P., & Belkin, A. (Eds.). (1996). *Counterfactual thought experiments in world politics: Logical, methodological, and psychological perspectives*. Princeton, NJ: Princeton University.

Tetlock, P., McGuire, C., & Mitchell, G. (1991). Psychological perspectives on nuclear deterrence. *Annual Review of Psychology, 42*, 239–276.

Tetlock, P., Peterson, R. S., McGuire, C., Chang, S., & Feld, P. (1992). Assessing political group dynamics: A test of the groupthink model. *Journal of Personality and Social Psychology, 63*, 403–425.

Tetlock, P. E., & Tyler, A. (1996). Churchill's cognitive and rhetorical style: The debates over Nazi intentions and self-government for India. *Political Psychology, 17*, 149–170.

't Hart, P. (1990/1994). *Groupthink in government: A study of small groups dynamics and policy failure*. Baltimore, MD: Johns Hopkins University Press.

't Hart, P. (1997). From analysis to reform of policy-making groups. In P. 't Hart, E. Stern, & B. Sundelius (Eds.), *Beyond groupthink Political group dynamics and foreign policymaking* (pp. 3–33). Ann Arbor: University of Michigan Press.

't Hart, P., Stern, E. K., & Sundelius, B. (1997). *Beyond groupthink: Political group dynamics and foreign policy-making*. Ann Arbor, MI: University of Michigan Press.

Thomas, E. (2005, September 19). How Bush blew it. *Newsweek*.

Thomas, E., & Wolffe, R. (2005, September 19). Bush in the bubble. *Newsweek*, pp. 31–39.

Thomas, R. (1996). History, religion, and national identity. In R. Thomas & H. R. Friman (Eds.), *The south Slav conflict: History, religion, ethnicity, and nationalism*. New York: Garland.

Tobias, J. (2008) *The role of entrepreneurship in conflict reduction in post-genocide Rwandan coffee industry*. Unpublished PhD dissertation, Washington State University, Pullman, WA, defended August 28, 2008.

Tooby, J., & Cosmides, L. (1990). The past explains the present: Adaptations and the structure of ancestral environments. *Ethology and Sociobiology, 11*, 375–424.

Towles-Schwen, T., & Fazio, R. H. (2001). On the origins of racial attitudes: Correlates of childhood experiences. *Personality and Social Psychology Bulletin, 27*, 162–175.

Triplett, N. (1898). The dynamogenic factors in peacemaking and competition. *American Journal of Psychology, 9*, 507–533.

Trost, M. R., Maass, A., & Kendrick, D. T. (1992). Minority influence: Personal relevance biases cognitive processes and reverses private acceptance. *Journal of Experimental Social Psychology, 28*, 234–254.

Tuchman, B. (1962). *The guns of August.* New York: Macmillan.

Tuckman, B. W. (1965). Developmental sequence in small groups. *Psychological Bulletin, 63*, 384–399.

Tuckman, B. W., & Jensen, M.A.C. (1977). Stages of small-group development revisited. *Group and Organization Studies, 2*, 419–427.

Tufekci, Z., & Wilson, C. (2012). Social media and the decision to participate in political protest: Observations from Tahrir square. *Journal of Communication, 62*, 363–379.

Tumulty, K., Thompson, M., & Allen, M. (2005, September 25). How many more Mike Browns are out there? *Time.*

Turner, J. C. (1982). Toward a cognitive redefinition of the social group. In H. Tajfel (Ed.), *Social identity and intergroup behavior* (pp. 15–40). Cambridge: Cambridge University Press.

Turner, J. C. (1985). Social categorization and the self-concept: A social-cognitive theory of group behavior. In E. J. Lawler (Ed.), *Advances in group processes: Theory and research* (Vol. 2, pp. 77–122). Greenwich, CT: JAI Press.

Turner, J. C. (1986). Social categorization and social discrimination in the minimal group paradigm. In H. Tajfel (Ed.), *Differentiation between social groups: Studies in the social psychology of intergroup relations* (pp. 235–250). New York: Academic Press.

Turner, J. C., Hogg, M. A., Oakes, P. J., Reicher, S. D., & Wetherell, M. S. (1987). *Rediscovering the social group: A self-categorization theory.* New York: Basil Blackwell.

Turner, R. (1978). The role and the person. *American Journal of Sociology, 84*, 1–23.

Tversky, A., & Kahneman, D. (1982). Judgment under uncertainty: Heuristics and biases. In D. Kahneman, P. Slovic, & A. Tversky (Eds.), *Judgment under uncertainty heuristics and biases* (pp. 3–20). Cambridge: Cambridge University Press.

United States Department of Commerce. (2005). U.S. Census Bureau News. Retrieved from www.census.gov/Press-Release

United States Department of State. (n.d.). Foreign terrorist organizations. Retrieved from www.state.gov/j/ct/rls/other/des/123085.htm

University Teachers for Human Rights (UTHR). (2003). Child conscriptions and peace: A tragedy of contractions. Retrieved from www.uthr.org/SpecialReports/spreport16.htm

Valentino, N. A., & Nardis, Y. (2013). Political communication: Form and consequence of the information environment. In L. Huddy, D. O. Sears, & J. S. Levy (Eds.), *The Oxford handbook of political psychology* (pp. 559–590). Oxford: Oxford University Press.

Valenzuela, S. (2013). Unpacking the use of social media for protest behavior: The roles of information, opinion expression, and activism. *American Behavioral Scientist, 57*, 920–942.

van den Heuvel, H., & Meertens, R. (1989). The culture assimilator: Is it possible to improve interethnic relations by emphasizing ethnic differences? In J. P. van Oudenhoven & T. Willemsen (Eds.), *Ethnic minorities: Social psychological perspectives* (pp. 221–236). Berwyn, PA: Swets North America.

van Doorn, M., Prins, J., & Welschen, S. (2013). "Protest against whom?": The role of collective meaning making in politicization. In J. van Stekelenburg, C. Roggebans, & B. Klandermans (Eds.), *The future of social movement research: Dynamics, mechanisms, and processes* (pp. 59–78). Minneapolis: University of Minnesota Press.

van Egeren, L. F. (1979). Cardiovascular changes during social competition in a mixed-motive game. *Journal of Personality and Social Psychology, 37*, 858–864.

Van Evera, S. (1984). The cult of the offensive and the origins of the first World War. *International Security, 9*, 58–107.

van Knippenberg, A., & Ellemers, N. (1990). Social identity and intergroup differentiation processes. In W. Stroebe & M. Hewstone (Eds.), *European Review of Social Psychology* (Vol. 1, pp. 137–169). Chichester: Wiley.

van Oudenhoven, J. P. (1989). Improving interethnic relationships: How effective is cooperation? In J. P. van Oudenhoven & T. Willemsen (Eds.), *Ethnic minorities: Social psychological perspectives* (pp. 201–220). Berwyn, PA: Swets North America.

van Zomeren, M. (2013). Discussion: Opening the black box of dynamics in theory and research on the demand side of protest. In J. van Stekelenburg, C. Roggebans, & B. Klandermans (Eds.), *The future of social movement research: Dynamics, mechanisms, and processes* (pp. 79–92). Minneapolis: University of Minnesota Press.

van Zomeren, M., & Iyer, A. (2009). Introduction to the social and psychological dynamics of collective action. *Journal of Social Issues, 65*, 645–660.

van Zomeren, M., Postmes, T., & Spears, R. (2008). Toward an integrative social identity model of collective action: A quantitative research synthesis of three socio-psychological perspectives. *Psychological Bulletin, 134*, 504–535.

Vertzberger, Y. (1990). *The world in their minds: Information processing, cognition, and perception in foreign policy decisionmaking.* Stanford, CA: Stanford University Press.

Vertzberger, Y. (1997). Collective risk-taking: The decision-making group. In P. 't Hart, E. Stern, & B. Sundelius (Eds.), *Beyond groupthink: Political group dynamics and foreign policymaking* (pp. 275–208). Ann Arbor: University of Michigan Press.

Vertzberger, Y. (1998). *Risk taking and decisionmaking: Foreign military intervention decisions.* Stanford, CA: Stanford University Press.

Victoroff, J. (2005). The "mind of the terrorist": A review and critique of psychological approaches. *Journal of Conflict Resolution, 49*, 2–43.

Victoroff, J., Adelman, J. R., & Matthews, M. (2012). Psychological factors associated with support for suicide bombing in the Muslim diaspora. *Political Psychology, 33*, 791–809.

Volkan, V. (1980). Narcissistic personality organization and reparative leadership. *International Journal of Group Psychotherapy, 30*, 131–152.

Volkan, V. D., Itzkowitz, N., & Dod, A. W. (1999). *Richard Nixon: A psychobiography*. New York: Columbia University Press.

Volpato, C., Maass, A., Mucchi-Faina, A., & Vitti, E. (1990). Minority influence and social categorization. *European Journal of Social Psychology, 20*, 119–132.

Wagner, R. V. (2006). Terrorism: A peace of psychological analysis. *Journal of Social Issues, 62*, 155–171.

Walgrave, S. (2013). Changing mobilization of individual activists? In J. van Stekelenburg, C. Roggeband, & B. Klandermans (Eds.), *The future of social movement research: Dynamics, mechanisms, and processes* (pp. 205–215). Minneapolis: University of Minnesota Press.

Walker, S. G. (1977). The interface between beliefs and behavior: Henry Kissinger's operational code and the Vietnam War. *Journal of Conflict Resolution, 21*, 129–167.

Walker, S. G. (1983). The motivational foundations of political belief systems: A re-analysis of the operational code construct. *International Studies Quarterly, 27*, 179–202.

Walker, S. G. (1995). Psychodynamic processes and framing effects in foreign policy decision-making: Woodrow Wilson's operational code. *Political Psychology, 16*, 697–718.

Walker, S. G., & Falkowski, L. (1984). The operational codes of U.S. Presidents and Secretaries of State: Motivational foundations and behavioral consequences. *Political Psychology, 5*, 237–266.

Walker, S. G., & Schafer, M. (2007). Theodore Roosevelt and Woodrow Wilson: Realist and idealist archetypes? *Political Psychology, 28*, 747–776.

Walker, S. G., Schafer, M., & Young, M. (1998). Systematic procedures for operational code analysis: Measuring and modeling Jimmy Carter's operational code. *International Studies Quarterly, 42*, 175–190.

Wallace, M. D., & Suedfeld, P. (1988). Leadership performance in crisis: The longevity-complexity link. *International Studies Quarterly, 32*, 439–452.

Wallach, M. D., Kogan, N., & Bem, D. J. (1962). Group influence on individual risk taking. *Journal of Abnormal and Social Psychology, 65*, 75–86.

Waller, J. (2002). *Becoming evil: How ordinary people commit genocide and mass killing*. Oxford: Oxford University Press.

Warren, K. (1993). Interpreting *La Violencia* in Guatemala: Shapes of Mayan silence and resistance. In K. Warren (Ed.), *The violence within: Cultural and political opposition in divided nations* (pp. 1–23). Boulder, CO: Westview Press.

Watson, W. E., Michaelsen, L. K., & Sharp, W. (1991). Member competence, group interaction, and group decision making: A longitudinal study. *Journal of Applied Psychology, 76*, 803–809.

Webb, P. (2013). Who is willing to participate? Dissatisfied democrats, stealth democrats and populists in the UK. *European Journal of Political Research, 52,* 747–772.

Wegener, D. T., & Petty, R. E. (1994). The hedonic contingency hypothesis. *Journal of Personality and Social Psychology, 66*(6), 1034–1048.

Wegener, D. T., Petty, R. E., & Smith, S. M. (1995). Positive mood can increase or decrease message scrutiny: The hedonic messaging view of mood and message processing. *Journal of Personality and Social Psychology, 69,* 5–15.

Weimann, G. (2004, March). *How modern terrorism uses the Internet.* Washington, DC: United States Institute of Peace. Retrieved from www.usip.org/publications/wwwterrornet-how-modern-terrorism-uses-the-internet

Weinberger, J., & Westen, D. (2008). RATS, we should have used Clinton: Subliminal priming in political campaigns. *Political Psychology, 29,* 631–651.

Weiner, B. (1986). *An attribution theory of motivation and emotion.* New York: Springer-Verlag.

Weingarten, K. (2004). *Common shock: Witnessing violence every day.* New York: New American Library.

Weinstein, E. (1981). *Woodrow Wilson: A medical and psychological biography.* Princeton, NJ: Princeton University Press.

Weintraub, W. (1981). *Verbal behavior: Adaptation and psychopathology.* New York: Springer.

Weintraub, W. (1986). Personality profiles of American presidents as revealed in their public statements: The presidential news conferences of Jimmy Carter and Ronald Reagan. *Political Psychology, 7,* 285–295.

Weintraub, W. (1989). *Verbal behavior in everyday life.* New York: Springer.

Weir, F. (2000, May 24). Taming Chechnya, Russia too. *Christian Science Monitor,* pp. A1, A5.

Westen, D. (1998). The scientific legacy of Sigmund Freud: Toward a psychodynamically informed psychological science. *Psychological Bulletin, 124,* 333–371.

Westen, D. (2007). *The political brain: The role of emotion in deciding the fate of the nation.* New York: Public Affairs.

White, R. K. (1968). *Nobody wanted war: Misperception in Vietnam and other wars.* Garden City, NY: Doubleday.

White, R. K. (1977). Misperception in the Arab-Israeli conflict. *Journal of Social Issues, 33,* 190–221.

Whitley, B. E., Jr. (1999). Right-wing authoritarianism, social dominance orientation, and prejudice. *Journal of Personality and Social Psychology, 77,* 126–134.

Whitney, K., Sagrestano, L. M., & Maslach, C. (1994). Establishing the impact of individuation. *Journal of Personality and Social Psychology, 66,* 1140–1153.

Whyte, G. (1986). Escalating commitment to a course of action: A reinterpretation. *Academy of Management Review, 11,* 311–321.

Whyte, W. F. (1943). *Street corner society.* Chicago, IL: University of Chicago Press.

Wicklund, R. A., Cooper, J., & Linder, D. (1967). Effects of expected effort on attitude change prior to exposure. *Journal of Experimental Social Psychology, 3,* 41–78.

Widmeyer, W. N., Brawley, L. R., & Carron, A. V. (1990). The effects of group size in sport. *Journal of Sport and Exercise Psychology, 12*, 177–190.

Wiktorowicz, Q. (2005). *Radical Islam rising*. Lanham, MD: Rowman & Littlefield.

Wilder, D. A., & Shapiro, P. N. (1984). Role of outgroup cues in determining social identity. *Journal of Personality and Social Psychology, 47*, 342–348.

Williamson, V., Skocpol, T., & Coggin, J. (2011). The tea party and the remaking of Republican conservatism. *Perspectives on Politics, 9*, 25–43.

Wilson, E. O. (1978). *On human nature*. Cambridge, MA: Harvard University Press.

Wilson, J. Q. (1973). *Political organizations*. New York: Basic Books.

Wilson, S. (2001a). Colombian right's "cleaning" campaign. *Washington Post*. April 17.

Wilson, S. (2001b). Colombian massacre large, brutal. *Washington Post*. April 21.

Winter, D. G. (1973). *The power motive*. New York: Free Press.

Winter, D. G. (1980). Measuring the motive patterns of Southern African political leaders at a distance. *Political Psychology, 2*, 75–85.

Winter, D. G. (1987). Leader appeal, leader performance, and the motive profiles of leaders and followers: A study of American presidents and elections. *Journal of Personality and Social Psychology, 52*, 196–202.

Winter, D. G. (2003). Assessing leaders' personalities: A historic survey of academic research studies. In J. D. Post (Ed.), *The psychological assessment of political leaders* (pp. 11–38). Ann Arbor: University of Michigan Press.

Winter, D. G. (2011). Scoring motive imagery in documents from four Middle Eastern opposition groups. *Dynamics of Asymmetric Conflict, 4*, 144–154.

Winter, D. G., & Carlson, L. A. (1988). Using motive scores in the psychobiographical study of an individual: The case of Richard Nixon. *Journal of Personality, 56*, 75–103.

Winter, D. G., Hermann, M. G., Weintraub, W., & Walker, S. G. (1991). The personalities of Bush and Gorbachev measured at a distance: Procedures, portraits, and policy. *Political Psychology, 12*, 215–245.

Winter, D. G., & Stewart, A. J. (1977). Content analysis as a technique for assessing political leaders. In M. G. Hermann (Ed.), *A psychological examination of political leaders* (pp. 21–61). New York: Free Press.

Wittenbaum, G., & Stasser, G. (1996). Management of information in small groups. In J. Nye & A. Bower (Eds.), *What's social about social cognition?* Thousand Oaks, CA: Sage.

Wohlstetter, R. (1962). *Pearl Harbor: Warning and decision*. Stanford, CA: Stanford University Press.

Wolfenstein, E. V. (1971). *The revolutionary personality*. Princeton, NJ: Princeton University Press.

Wood, W., Lundgren, S., Ouellette, J. A., Busceme, S., & Blackstone, T. (1994). Minority influence: A meta-analytic review of social influence processes. *Psychological Bulletin, 115*, 323–345.

Woods, J. (2011). Framing terror: An experimental framing effects study of the perceived threat of terrorism. *Critical Studies on Terrorism, 4*, 199–217.

Woodward, B. (1991). *The commanders*. New York: Simon and Schuster.

Woodward, B. (2002). *Bush at war*. New York: Simon and Schuster.

Woodward, B. (2004). *Plan of attack*. New York: Simon & Schuster.

Woodward, B. (2006). *State of denial: Bush at war, part III*. New York: Simon and Schuster.

Woodward, B. (2008). *The war within: A secret White House history 2006–2008*. New York: Simon and Schuster.

Woodward, S. (1995). *Balkan tragedy: Chaos and dissolution after the cold war*. Washington, DC: Brookings Institute.

Worchel, S., & Brehm, J. W. (1971). Direct and implied social restoration of freedom. *Journal of Personality and Social Psychology, 18*, 294–304.

Young, C. (1976). *The politics of cultural pluralism*. Madison: University of Wisconsin Press.

Young, C. (1983). Comparative claims to political sovereignty: Biafra, Katanga, Eritrea. In D. Rothchild & V. Olorunsola (Eds.), *State versus ethnic claims: African policy dilemmas* (pp. 199–232). Boulder, CO: Westview Press.

Zaccaro, S. J. (1984). Social loafing: The role of attractiveness. *Personality and Social Psychology Bulletin, 10*, 99–106.

Zagare, F. C., & Kilgour, D. M. (1993). Asymmetric deterrence. *International Studies Quarterly, 37*, 1–27.

Zajonc, R. B. (1965). Social facilitation. *Science, 149*, 269–274.

Zajonc, R. B. (1980a). Feeling and thinking: Preferences need no inferences. *American Psychologist, 39*, 139–151.

Zajonc, R. B. (1980b). Compresence. In P. B. Paulus (Ed.), *Psychology of group influence* (pp. 35–60). Hillsdale, NJ: Lawrence Erlbaum Associates.

Zakaria, F. (2002, April 29). Colin Powell's humiliation: Bush should clearly support his secretary of state—otherwise he should get a new one. *Newsweek*, p. 28.

Zaller, J. R. (1992). *The nature and origins of mass opinion*. New York: Cambridge University Press.

Zander, A. (1985). *The purposes of groups and organizations*. San Francisco, CA: Jossey-Bass.

Zedalis, D. (2004, June). Female suicide bombers. *Strategic Studies Institute*. Retrieved from www.strategicstudiesinstitute.army.mil/pdffiles/PUB408.pdf

Zenger, T. R., & Lawrence, B. S. (1989). Organizational demography: The differential effects of age and tenure distributions on technical communication. *Academy of Management Journal, 32*, 353–376.

Ziller, R. C., Stone, W. F., Jackson, R. M., & Terbovic, N. J. (1977). Self-other orientations and political behavior. In M. G. Hermann (Ed.), *A psychological examination of political leaders* (pp. 337–353). New York: Free Press.

Zimbardo, P. (1971). *The Stanford prison experiment*. Stanford, CA: Stanford University Press.

Zimbardo, P. (2007). *The Lucifer effect*. New York: Random House.

Zorbas, E. (2008). Reconciliation in post-genocide Rwanda. *African Journal of Legal Studies, 1*, 29–52.

Zurcher, L. A., Jr. (1969). Stages of development in poverty program neighborhood action committees. *Journal of Applied Behavioral Science, 15*, 223–258.

GLOSSARY

achievement motive. A person's concern with excellence and task accomplishment.

accountability. To have one's actions be transparent and evaluated by authorities with the power to punish wrongdoing. Political leaders will take greater risks, and be more likely to engage in conflict, the more they lack accountability to a higher power.

adjourning. A group's decision to dissolve. It can be planned or spontaneous.

affect. A generic term for a whole range of preferences, evaluations, moods, and *emotions*.

affect referral heuristic. Describes the mental tool used in voting when the voter feels familiar with the candidate and also regards the candidate highly.

affiliation-intimacy motive. Concern with establishing, maintaining, or restoring warm and friendly relationships with other persons or *groups*.

agenda setting. When the media defines which issues need attention and in what form.

agreeableness. A *Big Five* personality trait. It means a person is trusting, positive, and good-natured.

ally image. A country or group perceived to be equal to the perceiver's country in terms of culture and capability, with good intentions, multiple groups in decision-making roles, and associated with threat or opportunity.

altruists. People who help others and who speak out despite risks to their personal safety.

analogical reasoning. Using analogies to help decide what policies will work in a current situation.

analogy. A decision-making heuristic, or shorthand, in which policymakers see a current event or situation as similar to (or sharing many of the same characteristics as) a previous historical event.

anchoring and adjustment. When individuals make estimates by starting from an initial value that is adjusted to yield the final answer.

assimilation effect. When information similar to other information is perceived as even more similar than it objectively is.

associative networks. *Knowledge structures* embedded in long-term memory, consisting of nodes linked to one another, forming a network of associations.

attitude. An enduring system of positive or negative *beliefs*, affective feelings and *emotions*, and action tendencies regarding an attitude object—that is, the entity being evaluated.

attitude object. The entity about which one has an attitude.

attributions. The explanations generated for the causes of our own and others' behavior.

attribution theory. A psychological theory that argues that people process information as if they are naïve scientists; that is, they search for causes in the behavior of others.

authoritarian personality. A personality type. Originally the type was said to contain the traits of conventionalism (rigid adherence to conventional values), submission to authority figures, authoritarian aggression (i.e., aggressive impulses toward those who are not conventional), anti-intraception (i.e., rejection of tenderness, imagination, subjectivity), superstition and *stereotype* (fatalistic belief in mystical determinants of the future and rigid thinking), high value placed on power and toughness, destructiveness and cynicism, projectivity (i.e., the *projection* outward of unacceptable impulses), and an excessive concern with the sexual activity of others. In Altemeyer's (1996) reconceptualization, the type has three traits: authoritarian submission, authoritarian aggression, and conventionalism.

autokinetic effect. A perceptual illusion that occurs when a single point of light in a darkened room appears to be moving.

availability heuristic. When people predict the likelihood of something based on the ease with which they can think of instances or examples of it.

avoidance of value trade-offs. When people mistakenly believe that a policy that contributes to one value also contributes to several other values, even though there is no reason why the world should be constructed in such a neat and helpful manner.

balance. The cognitive harmony that people attempt to achieve and maintain among the situation and their feelings about the situation and its components.

barbarian image. A country or *group* perceived to be superior in capability, inferior in culture, monolithic in decision making, and associated with extreme threat.

bargaining theory. When coalitions form on the basis of considering expected payoffs.

behavioral genetics. Explains how individual traits and patterns of behavior get passed down from parents to children, as well as how those traits are shared between siblings.

beliefs. Associations people create between an object and its attributes.

belief system. A clustering of *beliefs*.

Big Five. Core personality dimensions or traits: *neuroticism, extroversion, agreeableness, openness to experience,* and *conscientiousness*.

black and white model. A model developed by Converse (1964), describing responses to *attitude* questions, which from some people remain very stable; for others, the responses change in an apparently random pattern.

bolstering. When people limit their exposure to information to find multiple reasons for the correctness of a decision and none (or discounted ones) against it.

Bradley effect. A term referring to white voters' reluctance to say they would not vote for a black political candidate, causing polls to inaccurately predict the vote for a black candidate.

bystander phenomenon. When people are part of a *group*, there is a *diffusion of responsibility*, and people feel less compelled to intervene and help.

charisma. A personality characteristic that makes one an attractive leader.

chicken, game of. A hypothetical game in which two drivers race toward one another head on, each assuming that the other will swerve and avoid an accident.

childish games. A bias occurring when people communicate something to another person that is familiar and meaningful to them, but not to the other person.

Christian identity. An unusual reading of the Bible often adhered to by racist groups in America which maintains that White people, but not non-Whites, are descended from Adam and Eve. Non-Whites are deemed "mud people."

coalition. A small collection of group members who cooperate in order to achieve a common goal.

coalition of autonomous actors. A decision unit composed of multiple groups that can act independently.

coercive power. The capacity to punish those who do not comply with requests or demands.

cognition. A collective term for the psychological processes involved in the acquisition, organization, and use of knowledge.

cognitive complexity. Ability to differentiate the environment: Degree of differentiation a person shows in describing or discussing other people, places, policies, ideas, or things.

cognitive neuroscience. A field of study that focuses on how the function and structure of the brain and nervous system explain thoughts, feelings, and actions.

cognitive processes. What happens in the mind while a person moves from observation of a stimulus to a response to that stimulus.

cognitive rigidity. An inability to recognize alternatives caused by high tension situations.

cognitive style. The way a person gathers and processes information from his environment.

cohesion. The factors that cause a *group* member to remain in the group.

collective action. "Any action that aims to improve the status, power, or influence of an entire group, rather than that of one or a few individuals" (van Zomeren & Iyer, 2009, p. 646).

collective fences. When individual members of a group avoid behaviors costly to them as individuals, resulting in harm to the group as a whole.

collective trap. Behaviors that reward an individual *group* member can be harmful to the rest of the group, especially if engaged in by enough group members.

collegial management style. Emphasizes teamwork, shared responsibility, and problem solving within a *group*.

colonial image. A country or *group* perceived as inferior in culture and capability, benign in intentions, monolithic in decision making, and associated with opportunity.

common-bond groups. These groups, such as social groups, are based mostly on the attachments between group members. In common-bond groups, the attachments to the group are based on such things as member similarity, likeability of fellow group members, and familiarity with group members.

common-identity groups. Groups based primarily on attachments to the group identity.

compensatory strategy. A voting selection strategy that involves the careful assignment of positive or negative values to each issue position. The voter then engages in an assessment of the trade-offs involved and resolves the conflict with a choice.

competitive frames. People are often exposed to more than one frame, and those frames may provide different competitive pictures of a candidate or issue.

competitive management style. Relatively unstructured information network, with leader placed in arbiter position among competing advisers with overlapping areas of authority.

compliance. Doing what one is asked to do by a more powerful member of one's group.

confirmation bias. A bias occurring when people favor information that confirms already-existing beliefs.

conformity. The tendency to change one's *beliefs* or behaviors so that they are consistent with the standards set by the *group*.

conscientiousness. A *Big Five* personality trait. It means a person is responsible, dependable, and goal-directed.

contact hypothesis. The argument that increasing intergroup contact, exposing people to the complexity of *group* members, breaks down *stereotypes*.

content analysis. A research method wherein written statements are systematically examined in order to infer psychological characteristics of individuals.

contrast effect. A social category serves as an anchor or central reference point for incoming information. When information is compared to that anchor and when it is different from expectations, the contrast effect makes it seem more so.

coverage bias. A form of media bias referring to how much time or space is devoted to a particular story.

core community nonnation-states. Countries with a dominant ethnic or sectarian community that believes that its members are the primary nation embodied in the country and that identifies with that nation in the strongest terms. In addition, that community tends to have great capability and control of the political system.

critical bases of power. A typology of group-based power.

culture of terror. An institutionalized system of permanent intimidation of the masses or subordinated communities by the elite, characterized by the use of torture, disappearances, and other forms of extrajudicial *death squad* killings as standard practice. A culture of terror establishes collective fear as a brutal means of social control. In these systems, there is a constant threat of *repression*, torture, and death for anyone who is actively critical of the political status quo.

death squads. "Progovernment *groups* who engage in extrajudicial killings of people they define as enemies of the state" (Sluka, 2000, p. 141).

defense mechanisms. *Unconscious* techniques used to distort reality and prevent people from feeling anxiety. They are also used to defend the *ego*.

degenerate image. A country or *group* perceived as superior or equal in culture and capability, but lacking resolve and will. It is associated with perceptions of opportunity.

dehumanization. A process in which a particular social *group* is regularly described as less than human and therefore deserving of treatment one would not administer to a human being.

deindividuation. This occurs when people attribute their behavior to the *group*'s behavior and thereby abandon individual responsibility for their own actions. There is a *diffusion of responsibility*.

denial. A *defense mechanism* wherein people may refuse to acknowledge reality (e.g., denying the country is going to war, despite the mobilization of troops) or deny an impulse (e.g., proclaiming that they are not angry when they are).

deterrence. The threat by one political actor to take actions in response to another actor's potential actions, which would make the costs (or losses) incurred far outweigh any possible benefits (or gains) obtained by the aggressor.

dialogue. A conflict resolution and reconciliation process by which individuals engage with each other in an open forum in order to speak about their sides of the story and to also hear the sides of others.

diasporas. Communities of one nation who live outside of that national territory.

diffusion of responsibility. When individuals feel no responsibility for their actions. It occurs when there is more than one person present in the situation to take all or some of the responsibility for the outcomes.

dissonance. An aversive state that results when behavior is inconsistent with *attitudes*.

drunkard's search. An informational shortcut named after the drunkard who loses his keys in the street and looks for them under the lamppost because the light is better there—not because that is where he lost the keys. This is analogous to the use of information in political decisions when people reduce complicated issues and choices among candidates to simple comparisons because that is easier.

dynamics of demand. The dynamics of demand for a social movement include grievances, social comparisons, and emotion.

dynamics of supply or mobilization. Variables at the individual and organizational level that explain why people are mobilized to support a social movement.

ego. The part of the personality that moderates between *id*, and its desire for pleasure, and the realities of the social world.

egocentric bias. The tendency of individuals to accept more responsibility for joint outcomes than others attribute to them.

Elaboration Likelihood Model (ELM). A model attitude change that focuses on cognition and rests upon the concept of the elaboration likelihood continuum. The continuum delineates how motivated and able people are to assess something by putting in effort to study it and evaluate it. The model proposes two routes to attitude change through persuasion: a central route and peripheral route.

emotion. A complex assortment of *affects*, beyond merely good or bad feelings, to include delight, serenity, anger, sadness, fear, and more.

empathy. An *emotion* produced when observing another person in need and taking the perspective of that person.

endorsement heuristic. A mental shortcut wherein people select a candidate who has been endorsed by people the voter has confidence in.

enemy image. The enemy is perceived as relatively equal in capability and culture. In its most extreme form, the diabolical enemy is seen as irrevocably aggressive in motivation, monolithic in decisional structure, and highly rational in decision making (to the point of being able to generate and orchestrate multiple complex conspiracies).

entiativity. The extent to which a collection of people is perceived as a coherent entity.

escalation of commitment. This occurs in situations in which some course of action has led to losses, but there is a possibility of achieving better outcomes by investing further time, money, or effort.

ethnocentrism. The view of things in which one's own *group* is the center of everything and looks with contempt on outsiders.

evolutionary psychology. A study of the biological origins of human behavior. Understanding how particular traits and behaviors and abilities evolved over time allows for a richer and more comprehensive understanding of human behavior today.

expected payoffs. Expectations based on *norms* of equity and equality and *group* members will appeal to whichever norm provides them with the largest payoff.

expert power. Power derived from having expert knowledge or skills. Physicians, for example, are often afforded a great deal of power because of the knowledge and ability they possess. Of course, expert power can only be exerted if the target of power is aware of the power holder's special knowledge or talent.

externals. People who believe the external environment determines strongly what happens to them. They are more susceptible to authority. Contrast with *internals*.

extremist. A person who is excessive and inappropriately enthusiastic and/or inappropriately concerned with significant life purposes, implying a focused and highly personalized interpretation of the world. Politically, it is behavior that is strongly controlled by *ideology*, in which the influence of ideology is such that it excludes or attenuates other social, political, or personal forces that might be expected to control and influence behavior.

extroversion. A *Big Five* personality trait. It means a person is outgoing, talkative, assertive, and likes to socialize.

familiarity heuristic. A short cut that comes into play when people are familiar with one candidate, but not the others, and they are at a minimum at least neutral toward that candidate.

forgiveness. The restoration of a positive relationship between perpetrator and victim wherein negative emotions toward the perpetrator are replaced with positive emotions.

formalistic management style. Emphasis upon strictly hierarchical, orderly decision structures.

forming. The first stage of *group* formation. This stage is also referred to as the orientation stage, because prospective members are orienting themselves to the group.

framing. The manner in which an issue is presented and the suggestions for how to think about it. People are often exposed to competitive frames about a candidate or issue.

fundamental attribution error. Occurs when people attribute other people's behavior to internal, dispositional causes, rather than to situational causes.

Fundamental Interpersonal Relations Orientation (FIRO). An explanation of how joining a *group* can fulfill psychological needs. According to this perspective, joining a group can satisfy three basic needs: inclusion (the desire to be part of a group), control (the need to organize an aspect of the group), and affection (the desire to establish positive relations with others).

funnel of causality. Distinguishes long-term factors that affect how Americans vote (attachment to a party or *party identification* and *group* interests) from short-term factors (currently important issues and candidates and their qualities).

gatekeeping. A form of media bias wherein the editors or program managers decide which stories will be told and which stories are not reported.

genocide. Actions designed to eliminate a *group* of people from the face of the earth.

Gresham's law of political information. An informational shortcut wherein the use of a small amount of personal information about a candidate dominates a large amount of historical information of that candidate's historical record.

group. A collection of people who are perceived to belong together and who are dependent on one another.

group development. The stages of growth and change that occur in a *group*, from its formation to its dissolution.

group malfunctions. Faulty *group* decision processes.

group polarization. The tendency for individuals' opinions to become more extreme after a *group* discussion than they were before the discussion.

groupthink. Governmental policy *groups*, particularly at high levels, tend to be smaller groups that, in time, develop a pattern of interactions between group members that emphasizes the maintenance of group cohesion, solidarity, and loyalty. This emphasis upon group cohesion can lead to faulty group decision processes, or *group malfunctions*.

Guns of August analogy. An *analogy* based upon the experience of the events leading up to the outbreak of the First World War, a war that none of the policymakers desired or intended to have occur.

habit heuristic. The mental shortcut of voting as the same way as the last time.

Hedonic Contingency Model. Model that posits that mood has an effect on persuasion; for example, when individuals have an expectation of happiness from a message, those in a happy mood pay more careful attention.

heuristic. Mental shortcuts in processing information about others.

Heuristic-Systematic Model (HSM). This model posits the *sufficiency principle*, which holds that people attempt to maintain a balance between their desire to expend as little cognitive effort as possible and their desire to be accurate in their judgments. If a person uses heuristics to evaluate a message, which are low-effort cognitive devices, but is not confident that they have made a judgment that is as correct or accurate as they would like, the person will engage in systematic information processing, which is essentially the same as the ELM's concept of the central route.

hindsight bias. A bias occurring when people recognize information consistent with pre-existing ideas

id. The warehouse for all instincts and drives. The id follows the pleasure principle.

identity. A deeply held sense of who a person is, where he or she fits in the political and social world.

ideologue. A person who knows what liberal and conservative values are, what positions on important political issues are liberal and conservative positions, which party represents liberal and which party represents conservative principles, and which candidates stand for which issues.

ideology. An elaborate, intertwined, and broad-reaching structure of *attitudes* and *beliefs*.

image. A political psychology concept equivalent to a *stereotype* of a political *group* or country. Images contain information about a country's capabilities, culture, intentions, the kinds of decision-making groups (lots of people involved in decision making or only a few), and perceptions of threat or opportunity.

image theory. A political psychological concept equivalent to a stereotype of a political group or country. Images contain information about a country's capabilities, culture, intentions, the kinds of decision-making groups (lots of people vs. a small group), and perceptions of threat or opportunity.

imaginability. The tendency to retrieve information that is plausible without any regard for actual probabilities.

imperialist image. A country or *group* perceived to be superior in capability, dominating in culture, exploitive in intentions, and associated with threat.

impression-based model of information processing. The argument that, as information is acquired, it is used to enhance and update the *beliefs* about a candidate or party and the specific details of the information are forgotten.

individuation. The desire to be distinguishable from others in some aspect.

informational social influence. Conformity that results from the use of other people's actions or opinions to define reality.

in-group. *Groups* we belong to.

inherent bad faith. A belief that another actor is inherently harmful in its intentions toward the perceiver's group or country. This means that actions that appear to be benign are actually caused by external forces, not the actor's intentions.

integrative complexity. A decision maker's focus on both differentiation, the distinct dimensions of a problem, and integration, the connections made among differentiated characteristics.

internals. People who believe they have considerable control over their fate. They are more likely to resist authority. Contrast with *externals*.

irredentism. The desire to join together all parts of a national community within a single territorial state.

issue. A dispute about public policy.

issue frames. Alternative definitions, constructions, or depictions of a policy problem.

knowledge structures. The mental organization of knowledge about political actors and issues.

Leader Trait Assessment (LTA). A content analytic technique for assessing leaders' personality characteristics.

legitimate power. Power to require compliance held by people by virtue of their position. For example, when a military officer orders troops to battle, that officer is exerting legitimate power.

levels of conceptualization. A classification scheme of Americans' political sophistication, ranging from *ideologues*, those who are very sophisticated, to "absence of issue content," those with very little knowledge of politics.

locus of control. View of the world in which an individual does or does not perceive some degree of control over situations in which they are involved and whether government can influence what happens in or to a nation.

Maximalists. Challengers to the *Michigan model*, who argue that people do not necessarily think linearly about politics, that *emotions* play a role as well, and that the average American is more politically sophisticated than the Michigan model maintains.

media bias. A much debated argument that the media is dominated by political liberals, and their reporting leans in a liberal direction.

Michigan model. A pioneering framework examining the political *attitudes* of Americans. The scholars of the Michigan school developed a model of American attitudes, in which it was assumed that Americans should have an integrated mental map of the political system, connecting candidates, parties, issues, and *groups* to ideological principles, in a consistent manner. Their research revealed that this is fairly rare in the American public.

minimal group paradigm. Competition can occur, even when the stakes are only psychological, and among *groups* that are arbitrarily formed by experimenters with no real interaction or conflict.

minimum-power theory. When coalition members expect payoffs that are directly proportional to their ability to turn a losing coalition into a winning one.

minimum-resource theory. When *group* members form coalitions on the basis of equal input–equal output.

moral disengagement. The suspension of moral principles that enables individuals to commit inhumane acts.

motivation. The reason or reasons why individuals look for alternatives to their present life situations.

motives. Those aspects of personality concerned with goals and goal-directed actions.

mujahedin. Holy warriors who fought to get the Soviet Union out of Muslim Afghanistan.

multiethnic or multisectarian state. A country with at least two ethnic *groups*, neither of which is capable of assimilating or absorbing the other nor of seceding and maintaining independence, where primary identity is with the ethnic group.

multinational states. A country in which several *groups* of people, who think of themselves as separate nations and who actually have the capacity to establish viable independent states, live together in a single country.

multiple advocacy. A group decision-making process in which manipulation is avoided by having the deliberation process managed by a neutral person, a custodial manager, while advocates of different positions are allowed to fully develop their proposals and advocate their advantages.

Munich analogy. If you do not stand up to an aggressor, and instead seek to appease them or make concessions to them in the hopes of keeping the peace, the end result will be to only encourage them to be even more aggressive and probably to bring on the very war you sought to avoid.

narcissism. A personality characteristic which causes people to see the world in terms of their own needs and desires rather than objective reality.

nation-state. A state in which the average citizen has a primary identity with the national community, believes that community should be an independent state, and grants that community primary loyalty.

nationalism. The *belief* that a *group* of people, or a community, belong together in an independent country, and a willingness to grant that community primary loyalty.

need for achievement. A personality trait involving concern with excellence and task accomplishment.

need for affiliation-intimacy. A personality trait involving concern for close relations with others.

need for power. A personality trait involving concern for impact and prestige.

negative campaign ads. Ads in which one candidate criticizes another candidate by name.

negativity effect. The tendency to attribute behavior to dispositional rather than situational factors for people we dislike.

neurotic anxiety. A person's fear of being punished for doing something the *id* wants the person to do.

neuroticism. A *Big Five* personality trait. It means that a person is anxious, has maladaptive coping abilities, and is prone to depression.

noncompensatory strategy. A voting selection strategy that essentially avoids conflict among issue positions by not getting complete information.

normal vote. An election in which people voted according to their *party identification* and in which independents split evenly between the two parties.

normative social influence. Conformity that is a result of the desire to be liked by others.

norming. The third stage of *group development*, a phase in which conflict is replaced with cohesion and feelings of unity.

norms. Expectations about how all group members should behave in a *group*.

openness. A *Big Five* personality characteristic. It means a person is proactive, independent, and tolerant of different viewpoints.

operational codes. Constructs representing the overall *belief* systems of leaders about the world (i.e., how it works, what it is like, what kinds of actions are most likely to be successful, etc.).

orientation toward political conflict. Relates to how open a president is to face-to-face disagreements and confrontations among his advisers.

out-group. *Groups* that we do not belong to.

paramilitaries. "Organizations that resort to the physical elimination of presumed auxiliaries of rebel groups and of individuals seen as subversive of the moral order. . . . They mostly operate through *death squads*" (Cubides, 2001, 129).

paranoia. A personality characteristic that causes people to believe they are being persecuted. They often respond to those believed to be persecuting with aggression or narcissism.

party identification. An *attitude* regarding attachment to (identification with) a political party.

performing. The fourth stage of *group development*. Performance usually only occurs when the groups mature and have successfully gone through the previous stages of development. Many groups do not reach the performing stage.

personality. There is no single universally accepted definition of personality. However, it generally refers to relatively stable aspects of an individual's behavior that accounts for patterns of behavior.

perspective-taking. The practice of empathizing with others, experiencing their perspective and the *emotions* that it generates in them.

persuasion. An effort to convince people to adopt a particular attitude or position on an issue or candidate.

phenomenal absolutism error. When a judgment that the observer makes about the *group* is not perceived as a judgment about the group, but as an attribute of the group itself.

pleasure principle. The motivation to satisfy aggressive and sexual drives.

policy fiascoes. Failures of policy.

politicized collective identity. A social identity that has political meaning for groups of people.

politics-is-complicated model (also known as the **principled objection model**). The argument that White Americans vary in the degree to which they blame the inequalities between the races on structural factors (such as the historical legacy of slavery and current system-wide discrimination), as opposed to individual factors (individual acts of *prejudice* and discrimination, rather than system-wide factors).

positivity effect. The tendency to attribute positive behaviors to dispositional factors and negative behaviors to situational factors with individuals we like.

power motive. Concern with establishing, maintaining, or restoring one's power, (i.e., one's impact, control, or influence over others).

pragmatism. Having organizational and managerial skills, the ability to negotiate, and to mobilize resources.

predominant leader. A type of group with a powerful leader who can make decisions without consulting other groups members.

prejudice. A negative evaluative orientation toward an out-group and consequently an aversion to its members; an attribution of negative characteristics toward a group and its members that is incorrect; and, finally, consistency in the negative orientation toward the group and its members.

priming. When the media points out to the public which elements of which issues are important.

prior policy experience or expertise. Policy makers' years in a variety of political positions, and their specializations in particular policy domains. There are different advisory group usages among people with little or a lot of experience and expertise.

prisoner's dilemma. When participants cannot communicate with one another, yet the outcome of the game for each person is contingent on what the other person decides.

projection. A defense mechanism attributing one's own objectionable impulses to another person, projecting them onto another.

prophesy. An ability to act as a purveyor of a movement's values and beliefs.

prospect theory. Predicts that individuals will tend to be risk averse in the domain of gains and risk seeking in the domain of losses.

protracted crisis approach. The perspective that a crisis should be viewed as a long series of separate and distinct *deterrence* and compellence exchanges running throughout the crisis from the beginning until the end of any episode.

psychoanalytic or psychodynamic theories. Psychoanalytic theories assess the role of the *unconscious* in human behavior and the motives and drives that underlie behavior.

rationalization. A defense mechanism wherein people reinterpret their own objectionable behavior to make it seem less objectionable.

reality principle. According to the reality principle, the demands of the *id* will be blocked or channeled in accordance with reality, but also in accordance with the personality.

realistic conflict theory. Proposal that intergroup *stereotyping* and derogation occurs as a result of competition for resources and competitive goals.

rebellion. A term referring to a pattern in group behavior wherein people refuse to do what one is told to do because a group member has abused power.

Receive-Accept-Sample (RAS) model argues that individuals have competing opinions on issues. The view that prevails results from what is on one's mind at the time.

reconciliation. Mutual acceptance of groups formerly engaged in conflict.

referent power. Power a person possesses when others identify with that person because the person is similar to them or because they want to be like that person.

relative deprivation theory. A theory that explains political action as resulting from the comparison of one's group with other groups and finding that one's own group has less than it deserves.

representativeness heuristic. A shortcut using probability expectations to make judgments about others.

repression. A defense mechanism in which a person involuntarily eliminates an unpleasant memory.

rescuers. People who help others and who speak out despite risks to their personal safety.

reward power. The ability to control the distribution of positive and negative reinforcers.

right wing authoritarianism. Submission to perceived authorities, particularly those in the establishment or established system of governance.

risky shift. When *groups* tend to take riskier decisions (and more chances) than do individuals.

rogue image. A country or *group* perceived as inferior in culture and capability, with monolithic decision making, and associated with threat.

roles. Expectations about how a person ought to behave in a *group*.

satisfice. To make a decision that is adequate rather than optimal and based upon consideration of all relevant information.

scapegoating. Blaming a *group* for society's problems.

schema. A cognitive structure that represents knowledge about a concept or type of stimulus, including its attributes and the relations among those attributes.

scientific method. Four cyclical steps that researchers repeatedly execute as they try to understand and predict behavior: making observations, formulating tentative explanations, making further observations and experimenting, and refining and retesting explanations.

security dilemmas. Conflicts in which the efforts made by one state to defend itself are simultaneously seen as threatening by its opponents, even if those actions were not intended to be threatening.

self-serving bias. A tendency individuals have to take responsibility for successes but not for failures.

sense of efficacy. A presidential stylistic variable involving presidents' confidence and interest in particular policy areas. Presidents give high priority to policy areas in which they have a strong sense of efficacy.

shared sovereignty strategies. An integration strategy in which an ethnic or racial *group* is given some degree of self-rule.

single group. A type of group wherein all members collectively make decisions.

social capital. A set of relationships and resources in a community that can be mobilized for the common good.

social causality. During hard times, the *groups* that people are particularly attracted to are those that provide an ideological blueprint for a better world and an enemy who must be destroyed to fulfill the *ideology*.

social comparisons. An inevitable tendency of groups to compare themselves with other relevant groups, hoping that they compare favorably with the others.

social creativity. Changing the basis of comparison between one's group and another group so that one's own group can be considered better than the comparison group.

social-decision schemes. The process by which *groups* combine the preferences of all the members of the group, to arrive at a single group decision.

social dominance theory. Presents a social dominance orientation measure that differentiates those who prefer social *group* relations to be equal or hierarchical, and the extent to which people want their *in-group* to dominate *out-groups*.

social identity. The part of a person's self-concept that is determined by the *groups* to which the person belongs.

social identity theory. Explores the impact on behavior of *group* identity and desire for positive comparisons to other groups.

social justification. When a *group*'s poor treatment is justified.

social learning theory. The argument that children learn negative *attitudes* and discriminatory behavior from their parents, teachers, family, friends, and others when they are rewarded for such behavior.

social loafing. The tendency of *group* members to work less hard when in a group than when working alone.

social mobility. Leaving one's group to join a more successful group.

social movements. "Social movements are collective challenges by people with common purposes and solidarity in sustained interaction with elites and authorities" (Klandermans, 1997, p. 2).

social movement organizations (SMOs). Institutions designed to further the goals of the social movement.

spiral conflicts. Conflicts in which each side matches and one-ups the actions taken by the other side. This can produce arms races and other types of aggression that result from misunderstanding each other's motives.

statement bias. A form of media bias wherein a member of the media inserts his or her own views in the reporting of a story.

status. How power is distributed among members in a *group*.

stereotypes. *Beliefs* about the attributes of people in particular *groups* or social categories.

storming. The second stage of *group development*, often marked by conflict.

structure. Varies greatly among social movements. Some are hierarchical, others loose and informal.

suicide bomber. A person who is willing to commit suicide in order to ensure maximum effectiveness in a terrorist attack.

superego. The moral arm or conscience of the personality.

symbolic racism. The argument that racism in America still exists, but is disguised as traditional American individualist values.

task–interpersonal emphasis. Relative emphasis in interactions with others on getting the task done versus focusing on feelings and needs of others.

terrorism. "In principle, terrorism is deliberate and systematic violence performed by small numbers of people, whereas communal violence is spontaneous, sporadic, and requires mass participation. The purpose of terrorism is to intimidate a watching popular audience by harming only a few, whereas *genocide* is the elimination of entire communities.

Terrorism is meant to hurt, not to destroy. Terrorism is preeminently political and symbolic, whereas guerilla warfare is a military activity. Repressive terror from above is the action of those in power, whereas terrorism is a clandestine resistance to authority." (Crenshaw, 2000, p. 406)

third-party intervention. A party that helps to reduce conflict in a group, by serving various functions.

three-stage model of group decision making. According to Bales and Strodtbeck (1951), *groups* proceed through three stages before eventually arriving at a decision: orientation, discussion, and decision making.

traits. Personality characteristics that are stable over time and in different situations. Traits produce predispositions to think, feel, and act in a particular way toward people, events, and situations.

transactional leadership. When the leader approaches followers with an eye toward exchanging one valued thing for another.

transformational leadership. When leaders engage their followers in such a way that they raise each other to higher levels of motivation and morality.

truth and reconciliation commission. An investigative commission designed to reveal the truths of political violence and to achieve some measure of reconciliation and forgiveness. It gathers evidence, determines *accountability*, and often recommends policies for the treatment of victims and perpetrators.

ultimate attribution error. The use of *prejudices* and preexisting *beliefs* in evaluation of others.

unconscious. A part of the mind that people are unaware of. Freud introduced the idea that the mind is like an iceberg. Only a small part of the iceberg is visible, floating above water. Around 90% is underwater and unobservable. Similarly, people are conscious of only a small part of the mind.

utilitarian integration strategy. A strategy to promote integration by satisfying the populations' needs. It requires removing any obstacles to equality of access to important political positions in the country.

values. Deeply held *beliefs* about what should be true, even if it is not currently true.

variable. Something that is thought to influence, or to be influenced by, something else.

viability heuristic. A short cut involving selecting a candidate based on the likelihood that he or she will win.

Vietnam analogy. This analogy suggests that any U.S. military intervention will likely result in the same outcome as did American intervention in Vietnam during the 1960s and 1970s: an open-ended commitment to a losing cause that will result in tremendous bloodshed for our troops and political unrest at home.

INDEX